Electronic Commerce

From Vision to Fulfillment

SECOND EDITION

Elias M. Awad

McIntire School of Commerce
University of Virginia

PEARSON
Prentice Hall
Pearson Education International

Executive Editor: David Alexander
Project Manager (Editorial): Kyle Hannon
Editorial Assistant: Robyn Goldenberg
Publisher: Natalie E. Anderson
Media Project Manager: Joan Waxman
Senior Marketing Manager: Sharon Koch
Marketing Assistant: Danielle Torio
Managing Editor (Production): John Roberts
Production Editor: Renata Butera
Production Assistant: Joe DeProspero
Permissions Supervisor: Suzanne Grappi
Manufacturing Buyer: Michelle Klein
Cover Design: Jayne Conte
Cover Photo: Ian McKinnell/Getty Images, Inc.
Manager, Print Production: Christy Mahon
Composition/Full-Service Project Management: BookMasters, Inc.
Printer/Binder: Phoenix

Credits and acknowledgments borrowed from other sources and reproduced, with permission, in this textbook appear on appropriate page within the text.

Pearson Education LTD.
Pearson Education Singapore, Pte. Ltd
Pearson Education, Canada, Ltd
Pearson Education—Japan
Pearson Education Australia PTY, Limited
Pearson Education North Asia Ltd
Pearson Educación de Mexico, S.A. de C.V.
Pearson Education Malaysia, Pte. Ltd
Pearson Education, Upper Saddle River, New Jersey

PEARSON
Prentice
Hall

10 9 8 7 6 5 4 3 2 1
ISBN 0-13-122902-8

To Bill Beville, whose professionalism and support
are hallmarks of a first-class publisher

CONTENTS

PREFACE

Welcome to the world of the Internet, the World Wide Web, e-commerce, mobile-commerce, and e-business. The Internet has rapidly become the primary commerce and communications medium for virtually every industry, large or small. Global competition, laws, ethics, security, privacy, and consumer preferences are among the issues being impacted by e-commerce. It is predicted that by the year 2010, one will think about the Internet in the same way one thinks about electricity today. This superhighway continues to improve and expedite e-traffic, e-commerce, and e-business. Today, we enjoy the growing success of business-to-consumer, business-to-business, and business-to-government interfaces. Each interface requires effective Web sites, regular maintenance and upgrades, and bandwidth and ISPs that will accommodate the growing volume of business with minimum delay.

One unique thing about e-commerce is doing business over the Internet around the clock, 365 days a year. An e-business can reach potential customers around the world. As a result, some companies are being bypassed by the Internet revolution as more companies that create goods and services interact directly with the consumer without the help of intermediaries.

The latest explosion in the use of the World Wide Web as a vehicle for e-commerce assumes a direction for continued growth and prosperity. The impact of the Web on business is far-reaching and unique. The process requires redefining business models, changing corporate culture, reinventing business processes, and establishing reliable customer service. The goal of this edition is to inform students of business and practitioners of the concepts, strategies, and techniques used in building e-commerce applications and the changes that have taken place since the first edition came out in 2002.

WHY THIS BOOK?

During the past 18 months, I have been clipping e-commerce reports and articles about events and ongoing technical activities from a number of different sources. I also have been consulting in this field in various industries in the United States and abroad. This edition makes use of practitioner, academic, and field work completed since 2002. The overall conclusion is that e-commerce is a fast-moving target, surpassing even the most optimistic expectations. Forecasters are constantly moving their projections in an upward direction.

Clearly, we are witnessing exciting events. Businesses are fast building Web sites for presence as well as for online business, reaching potential customers and markets in ways that were never before possible. College programs are adding e-commerce as the course to complement required MIS or IT courses at the undergraduate and graduate levels. With today's lack of guidelines in terms of e-commerce content and process, this book sets standards based on the author's four decades of teaching, publishing, and IT consulting experience.

This edition is unique in terms of coverage, approach, lucidity, and overall treatment of the key life cycle phases of e-commerce. It is an exciting opportunity to know how to strategize, design, and evaluate Web sites; how to launch an e-business from scratch; how mobile-commerce is thriving on wireless technology; what technology is needed for doing e-business on the Web; how to market products; what ethical and legal factors to consider in e-commerce; and how to ensure security and integrity of data traffic through encryption, firewalls, and other electronic devices and software. Managerial and organizational implications are cited at the end of each chapter to note the important relationships between a business and the technology that runs a business on the Internet.

The second edition gives a highly readable treatment of the topic. It approaches building an e-business from a systems analysis and design viewpoint, which includes feasibility analysis, design issues, security considerations, implementation procedures, and organizational implications. A career box is included in various chapters to address the human and occupational areas of e-commerce.

Who Should Read This Book?

This edition can be an ideal choice for undergraduate students majoring in MIS, IT, management, finance, marketing, accounting, or e-commerce. Students majoring in computer science or systems engineering also will find the approach, content, and treatment of e-commerce principles and procedures an appropriate addition to their field of specialization. First-year MBA students, especially those with a concentration in information technology, will benefit from the technology and practical orientation presented in the text.

Professionals, general managers, and practitioners can use this text as a reference or as a way to learn e-commerce as a unique way of doing business. Examples of such occupations are Webmasters, ISP managers, CIOs, system designers, project managers and planners, e-commerce sales staff, and e-commerce consultants.

Book Organization

This text is organized into five parts. Each part represents a critical component of the e-commerce process. Terminology and an index are provided at the end of the text.

Each chapter begins with "In a Nutshell," which tells the reader what to expect in the chapter. Chapter content includes boxes, easy-to-read figures, and tables designed to help summarize the essence of the material. Definitions of key terms are available in the margin where first cited. Each chapter ends with a comprehensive summary, terms to learn, review (Test Your Understanding) questions, discussion questions, Web exercises, and a list of references for further research.

I. Foundations of Electronic Commerce

Chapter 1 is an updated overview of e-commerce—justification for starting an e-commerce business; the pros and cons of this unique approach to doing business; the roles of strategy and the value chain in e-commerce; and how e-commerce may integrate within Intranet, business-to-business, business-within-business, business-to-government, and mobile-commerce. Managerial implications are cited at the end of the chapter.

Chapter 2 is a review of the history and uses of the Internet, its limitations, how to search online, the role of URLs and HTTPs in helping you navigate on the Internet, and the language of the Internet. A distinction between the Internet and the World Wide Web also is made throughout the text.

Chapter 3 presents comprehensive coverage of Internet architecture. It begins with a description of a network and how information is transferred via standards and protocols from the browser to the Web server and back. The chapter also talks about video and movie standards. A summary of the necessary network hardware, cable types, and network components (hubs, switches, routers, and gateways) is included toward the end of the chapter. A section on the key steps in designing a network and how to manage the corporate network also is included.

II. The Technology of E-Commerce

The focus of Chapter 4 is on the distinctive features of Intranets and Extranets. Specifically, the chapter covers the technical infrastructure, how to plan for an Intranet installation, and the role of e-mail in data communication. Key considerations in Extranets also are covered.

Chapter 5 is a new chapter, addressing Web management tools and portals. Portals and search engines are explained in detail. Other areas of importance include enterprise portal technologies, market potential of portals, content management, intelligent agents, and Web services via portals.

The focus of Chapter 6 is on the Internet service provider and how to host a Web site. Specifically, it covers the actual work of the ISP, how to start one, how to choose one, and how to choose and register one's domain name.

Chapter 7, also new, is a comprehensive treatment of mobile-commerce. The chapter begins with justification for wireless technology and the critical success factors that favor the use of this emerging technology. The chapter also covers how wireless technology is employed, citing Bluetooth, satellite technology, 2G digital cellular technology, palm pilot, and cellular phones. Wireless LAN design and wireless application protocol (WAP) are covered in detail.

III. E-Strategies and Tactics

Chapter 8 addresses Web site design. Specifically, it begins with the justification for a Web site, the life cycle of site building, how to build Web sites, design criteria, and what to look for in hiring a Web designer. This is a critical chapter that sets the tone for the user-merchant interface.

The focus of Chapter 9 is on how to evaluate Web sites and manage Web traffic. It begins with an anatomy of a Web site, uses and limitations of cookies, and the criteria that make a Web site usable. Web site content and traffic management also are discussed. At the end of the chapter, the role of the Web site administrator is explained in detail.

Chapter 10 is about the skills and techniques that are unique to e-marketing. It begins with the pros and cons of online shopping, followed by Internet marketing techniques. The e-cycle of Internet marketing is covered in detail. The latter part of the chapter focuses on how to market presence, how to attract customers to the site, and how to keep track of customers. The principles of customer service also are included in the chapter.

Chapter 11 is a comprehensive coverage of Web-based business-to-business e-commerce. The focus is on B2B models (buyer- and supplier-oriented B2B, electronic auctions, and intermediary-oriented B2B), B2B building blocks, and tools. A separate section that looks beyond B2B and addresses the role of leadership also is included.

Chapter 12 addresses ethical, legal, and international issues related to e-commerce. In the ethical issues section, we cover major threats to ethics, a code of ethics, the privacy factor, and the role of the professional ethicist. The legal issues section discusses liability, copyrights, trademarks and trade names, warranties, and the taxation issue on the Internet. Web linking, domain name disputes, and encryption laws also are covered.

IV. Security Threats and Payment Systems

Chapter 13 devotes full attention to the concept and serious nature of e-security. The critical components include security in cyberspace, how to design for security, how much risk a company can afford, the privacy factor, how to protect against various types of viruses, and how to recover from security failure.

Following the security chapter is Chapter 14, which addresses the main principles and procedures of encryption. Essentially, it addresses cryptographic algorithm, authentication and trust, digital signatures, major attacks on cryptosystems, digital certificates, key management, Internet security protocols and standards, and government regulations that relate to encryption. The role of biometrics security is a new section in this chapter.

Chapter 15 is about e-payments or how the e-merchant gets the money resulting from the sale of goods and services on the Internet. The chapter explains money properties; Internet-based systems requirements; and electronic payment media such as credit cards, debit cards, smart cards, digital cash, e-cash, and the e-wallet. Electronic funds transfer and Automated Clearinghouse also are covered.

V. Managerial and Customer-Related Issues

Chapter 16 focuses on the procedure and mechanics of launching a new business on the Internet. It begins with strategizing reality (planning), followed by considering the necessary hardware, software, security, and setup phase. The next step is the actual design phase, which focuses on Web site design, the Web storefront, and whether the work should be done in the company's IT department or outsourced to professionals. The last three steps are marketing, fulfillment, and maintenance. Each step is covered in some detail at the end of the chapter.

ACKNOWLEDGMENTS

My heartfelt thanks to the reviewers of both the current and previous editions of the text who helped to shape and mold the final product: David Ambrosini, Cabrillo College; Hilton Barrett, Cumberland University; Dave Croasdell, Washington State University; Sasa Dekleva, DePaul University; Joseph L. Fowler, Florida Community College at Jacksonville; Saiid Ganjalizadeh, The Catholic University of America; Babita Gupta, California State University, Monterey Bay; Faith M. Heikkila, Davenport University; Bunny Howard, St. Johns River Community College–St. Augustine Campus; Paul J. Hu, University of Southern Florida; Jeff Johnson, Utah State University; Marios Koufaris, Baruch College; Laura Lally, Hofstra University; Claudia Loebbecke, University of Cologne; Jane Mackay, Texas Christian University; Michael E. McLeod, East Carolina University; Rick Mull, Fort Lewis College; Graham Peace, Duquesne University; Tom Seymour, Minot State University; James Shaw, San Francisco State University; Joe Teng, Barry University; Linda Volonino, Canisius College; Barbara Warner, Hillsborough Community College–Brandon Campus; and Stephanie Y. Zedler, Keiser College.

About the Author

Dr. Elias M. Awad is the Virginia Bankers Association Professor of Bank Management at the University of Virginia. Dr. Awad has more than 40 years of IT experience in the academic, publishing, and consulting areas. He is one of the world's leading IT instructors and seminar presenters in the banking industry here and abroad. He is also the CEO of International Technology Group, Ltd., an IT consulting group with offices in Chicago, New York, Beirut, and Charlottesville, Virginia. Dr. Awad's consulting work has taken him to 26 countries, including Russia, Korea, Hong Kong, Cambodia, Canada, Mexico, Kazikhstan, Moldova, Uzbekistan, Armenia, Ukraine, Slovak Republic, Saudi Arabia, Lebanon, Jordan, and Egypt.

E-Commerce is one of Dr. Awad's most recent books. He has been writing since the early 1960s and has authored several best-sellers across the IT discipline about such topics as systems analysis and design, database management, knowledge management, management information systems, human resources management, building knowledge automation systems, and building expert systems. His publications have been translated into German, Spanish, Portuguese, Chinese, Arabic, Russian, and Braille. They have earned international recognition for lucidity, logical flow, and presentation of material based on experience in the field.

Dr. Awad may be reached at the University of Virginia, Monroe Hall, Charlottesville, Virginia 22903; e-mail: ema3z@virginia.edu; voice: (434) 924-3423; private: (434) 984-AWAD.

Elias M. Awad, Ph.D.
University of Virginia

Part I: Foundations of Electronic Commerce

Chapter 1

In the Beginning

Contents

In a Nutshell

If you have access to a personal computer (PC) and can connect to the Internet with a browser, you can do business online. No more worries about programming. No more searching for outdated catalogs as a customer or printing catalogs as a merchant. No more looking for phone numbers, paying long-distance fees to connect, or keeping the store open late into the evening. Just get on the Web, open an online store, and watch your business grow.

Welcome to the wired world of business, where technology, human talent, and a new way of doing business make up today's growing worldwide economy. The backbone of this electronic commerce is the Internet. The wired world is not about technology; it is about information, decision making, and communication. The wired world is changing life for everyone, from the single household to the largest corporation. No business can afford to ignore the potential of a connected economy.

If we look closely at the changes that have taken place during the past 2 decades, we find that computers, information technology, and networking have combined to replace labor-intensive business activities across industries and in government. In banking, for example, the change has been seen in the widespread use of Automated Teller Machines (ATMs), credit cards, debit cards, smart cards, and Internet lending. This type of computer-based, bank-to-bank, bank-to-consumer, and consumer-to-consumer transactional and informational exchange is what electronic commerce is all about.

More recently, wireless transmission paved the way for consumers to shop, trade, or access information from anywhere in a matter of seconds, using just a cell phone. Mobile commerce has taken on the "business of time," as we shall see in Chapter 7. It is already providing savings and adding value in business-to-business transactions and other Internet-based areas, as well.

In this chapter, we cover the essence of electronic commerce—what it is, what it is not, where it is used, its benefits and limitations, and its impact on the value-chain concept of doing business.

What Is E-Commerce?

Box 1-1 focuses on one of the legends of e-commerce, Jeff Bezos of Amazon.com. By careful evaluation of buying patterns, promotions, and selling, Bezos fine-tuned Amazon.com to become a highly respected Internet business. It also has become the model success story of e-commerce.

E-commerce brings the universal access of the Internet to the core business processes of buying and selling goods and services. It helps generate demand for products and services and improves order management, payment, and other support functions. The overall goal is to cut expenses by reducing transaction costs and streamlining all kinds of processes. The Internet's worldwide reach helps businesses discover new markets while increasing the speed of access and transactions.

electronic commerce (EC): the marketing, buying, and selling of products and services on the Internet.

E-commerce is used everywhere in everyday life. It is utilized for everything from credit card authorization, travel reservations over a network, wire fund transfers across the globe, point of sale (POS) transactions in retailing, electronic banking, fund-raising, political campaigning, and auctioneering, to online consultation with doctors (see Box 1-2).

BOX 1-1
E-commerce trends: The story of Amazon.com

One way of looking at the total picture of this emerging technology is the success story of a young financial analyst by the name of Jeff Bezos. In 1994, Bezos was full of hope about the potential of doing business on the Internet. He sat down one evening and came up with a list of 20 products he believed would sell well on the Internet. Books were number one. Three years later, he formed Amazon.com.

Bezos had never sold a book in his life, but he figured books are small-ticket items that are easy and inexpensive to ship. They are the type of product customers do not have to inspect before they decide to buy. Bezos figured that more than 5 million book titles probably are published worldwide in a given year, and that no bookstore could conceivably stock more than a fraction of the total. He developed a strategic plan for selling books online.

You know the rest of the story. Bezos improved on the initial plan of selling books by capturing the comments and recommendations of buyers for visitors to the site to read—like the friendly salesperson in a store offering advice on which books to buy. After this initial success, he expanded the online business to include music, videotapes, tools, and home-type hardware. The Web site tracks customer traffic, the number of visitors who access the site, how long they stay, what pages they click on, and so forth. By careful evaluation of buying patterns, promotions, and selling, Bezos fine-tuned Amazon.com to become a highly respected Internet business. It has become the model success story of e-commerce.

If you surf the literature, you will find much confusion between e-commerce and e-business. Most people use the two terms interchangeably, which is not accurate. In this book, e-commerce refers to far more kinds of transactions than just online shopping. Electronic commerce (EC) can be defined in several ways:

1. From a *communications* perspective, e-commerce is the ability to deliver products, services, information, or payments via networks such as the Internet and the World Wide Web.
2. From an *interface* perspective, e-commerce involves various information and transaction exchanges: business-to-business, business-to-consumer, consumer-to-consumer, and business-to-government.
3. From a *business process* perspective, e-commerce includes activities that directly support commerce electronically by means of networked connections. Within business processes (manufacturing, inventorying, operation) and business-to-business processes (supply-chain management) are managed by the same networks as business-to-consumer processes. (Supply-chain management is covered later in the chapter.)
4. From an *online* perspective, e-commerce is an electronic environment that makes it possible to buy and sell products, services, and information on the Internet. The products may be physical such as cars, or services such as news or consulting.
5. From a *structural* perspective, e-commerce involves various media: data, text, Web pages, Internet telephony, and Internet desktop video.
6. As a *market*, e-commerce is a worldwide network. A local store can open a Web storefront and find the world at its doorstep—customers, suppliers, competitors, and payment services.

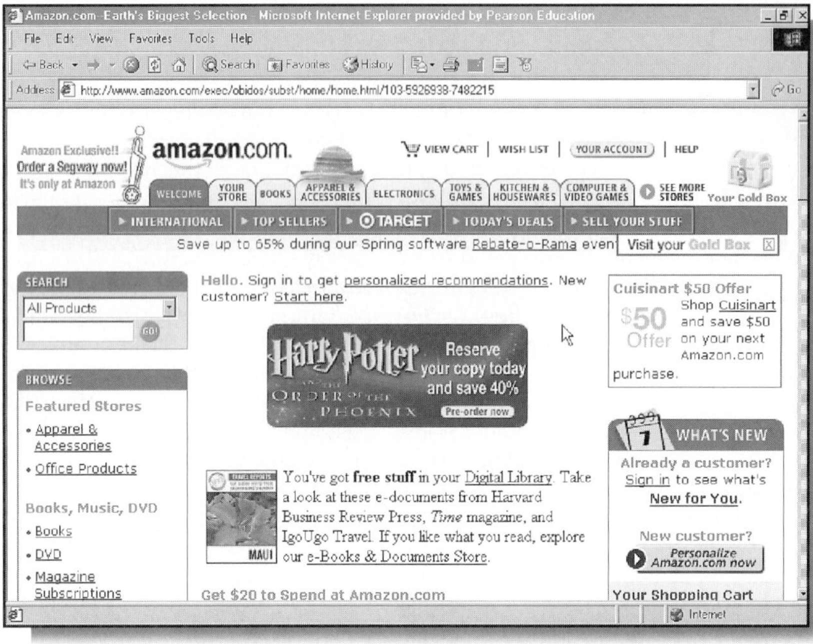

Screen Capture 1-1

Source: Amazon.com ® is the registered trademark of Amazon.com, Inc. All rights reserved.

e-business: connecting critical business systems and constituencies directly via the Internet, Extranets, and Intranets.

In contrast, e-business means connecting critical business systems directly to critical constituencies—customers, vendors, and suppliers—via the Internet, Extranets, and Intranets. It means using electronic information to boost performance and create value by forming new relationships between and among businesses and customers. It goes beyond a Web site on the Internet to affect all aspects of business, from strategy and process to trading partners and the ultimate consumer. It combines the resources of traditional information systems with the global reach of the Web.

E-business enables organizations to accomplish the following goals:

1. Reach new markets.
2. Create new products or services.
3. Build customer loyalty.
4. Enrich human capital.
5. Make the best use of existing and emerging technologies.
6. Achieve market leadership and competitive advantage.

transaction: a block of information exchanged between the merchant and its customers via the corporate Web site.

Electronic commerce means commerce with anyone, anywhere, anytime. It emphasizes new business opportunities that result in greater efficiency and more effective transactions.

Part of the reason why it is difficult to understand electronic commerce is the speed with which it is growing. That growth is happening so quickly and in so many ways that even experts can no longer compare it to anything from the past. Its impact already has exceeded that of radio in the 1920s, television in the 1950s, and personal computers in the 1980s. Every indicator points to a profound, long-term impact on the world economy.

BOX 1-2
E-commerce trends: The checkup is in the e-mail

When John Patrick moved to Pittsburgh earlier this year, the teacher's longtime allergies flared up. He hadn't had the time to find a local allergist, so Mr. Patrick visited his former specialist—in Montgomery, Alabama—via an online service provided by Medem, Inc. He logged on to his allergist's Web site, entered his password, and sent a secure e-mail describing his problem. Within a few hours, for a $20 fee paid with his credit card, he received detailed suggestions for allergy-proofing his new office, such as removing old carpeting, and recommendations for finding a local doctor to update his medications. Two follow-up questions were permitted free of charge.

Patients who have used Medem's service say they like getting medical advice without having to spend the time to go to the doctor's office, or even connect by phone. "I don't have time to play phone tag," says Mr. Patrick. "The Internet is so much easier for routine matters." Physicians like the service because they can be more accessible to patients—and get paid for it, unlike regular e-mail, which does not have a built-in payment system.

Some specialists in relatively short supply may find they are able to charge much higher fees. Washington Bryan, a pain-management specialist in Los Angeles, says he handles about two online consultations a week, charging between $150 and $200 each. Dr. Bryan's experience with the service is also unusual in that he often uses it for new patients from out of state who are seeking advice and referrals in their local area. As for the ethical concerns that have surrounded such contacts without a prior examination, Dr. Bryan says, "Not everyone has access to a pain-management specialist." He also does not prescribe medications to these new patients, though if they already are taking prescription drugs, he will often evaluate their regiments and make suggestions for changes that patients can discuss with their own doctors.

SOURCE: Excerpted from Carrns, Ann, "The Checkup Is in the E-Mail." *Wall Street Journal*, November 11, 2002, R8.

EC is breaking the following traditional rules of commerce.

- Companies do not share information with competitors.
- Suppliers do not share information with buyers, especially information that determines pricing.
- Corporate procurement should be determined solely on price.
- No financial transaction occurs without the involvement of a bank.

Nowhere is EC changing the rules more profoundly and rapidly than in the banking industry. The increase in online banking calls into question the role of banks. Businesses and consumers now have more choices about how and where to pay their bills.

Cost savings, opportunism, and threats drive action and innovation even in the most conservative companies. These factors have influenced how companies reposition themselves to take advantage of opportunities that include establishing new service delivery channels and new markets for existing services. Leveraging the power of the Web means a shift from static pages to dynamic applications. For example, Web services that give merchants real-time access to bankcard payment information rather than waiting for hard-copy bank statements already are available. J. P. Morgan has replaced hardware codes with digital certificates that verify the identity of the sender, place a seal on a message, and provide proof that a transaction has occurred. The service saves the company at least $1 million in the process. Other Web benefits for a changed world are exemplified in Box 1-3.

E-Commerce Drivers

Several drivers promote e-commerce.

1. **Digital convergence.** The digital revolution has made it possible for almost all digital devices to communicate with one another. The Internet's massive growth during the past 10 years, which is completely a creation of market forces, will continue (see Figure 1-1).
2. **Anytime, anywhere, anyone.** Today's e-commerce is available to anyone, anywhere in the world, 24/7 (24 hours a day, 7 days a week). E-commerce ties together the industrial sector, merchants, the service sector, and content providers using text, multimedia, video, and other technologies (see Figure 1-2).
3. **Changes in organizations.** More and more of today's business empowers front-line workers to do the kind of work once performed by junior management. A trend also

BOX 1-3
Web smart for a changed world

As corporate profits fall and companies adapt to a more sober reality in the wake of the September 11, 2001, terrorist attacks, spending on e-business initiatives is getting more focused—with a renewed emphasis on projects that promise a quick return. Here are examples.

- For years, casino operator Harrah's has had a database of customers it woos with cheap hotel rooms. However, getting promotions out meant using snail mail. Harrah's linked the database to its Web site, allowing customers to go online and book rooms at discount prices based on their past spending habits. After September 11, 2001, occupancy at Harrah's flagship Las Vegas hotel fell by 25 percent. The chain sent e-mails with bargain offers, filling 4,000 rooms that otherwise would have stayed empty and bringing the hotel back to near 100% occupancy by September 30.
- Bank of America was spending nearly $100 million annually on human resources paperwork such as enrollment for its retirement programs. Simple changes often required weeks to complete. The company moved those programs to the Web. Now all 140,000 employees can change doctors, monitor retirement accounts, and submit travel expenses online. The bank is saving with the system. Some processes, such as benefits enrollment, now take just minutes to process because they are done online. That is down from months under the old system.
- Mexican steelmaker Hylsa's Bar & Rod Division needed to improve customer satisfaction and lower inventory costs at its two plants. The company spent $800,000 on software, computers, and consulting to automate the process of planning production, managing inventories, and scheduling deliveries. The new system helped improve on-time deliveries from 70 percent to 88 percent, and boosted inventory turns from 2.2 to 2.8 times monthly.

SOURCE: Excerpted from Rocks, David, "The Net as a Lifeline," *BusinessWeek e.biz*, October 29, 2001, 18–19.

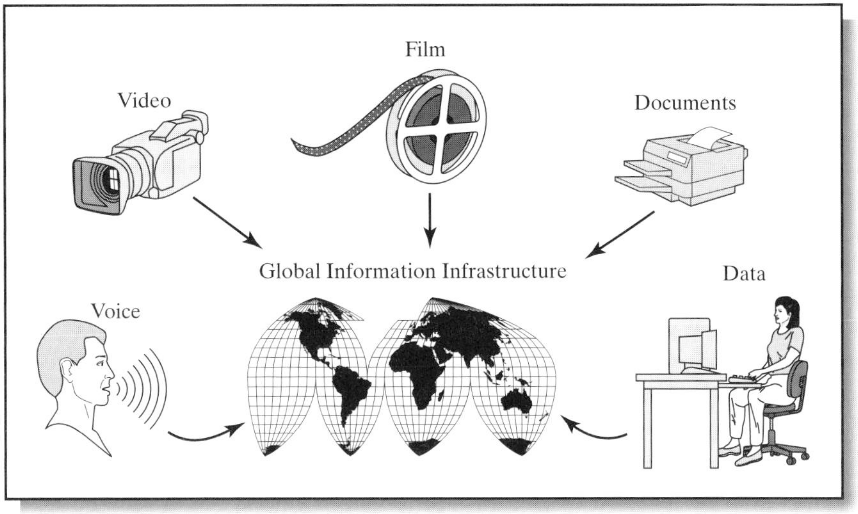

Figure 1-1
Digital convergence

Source: The concept of EC business drivers is courtesy of Dr. Richard Welke, professor of CIS, Georgia State University.

Figure 1-2
Global e-commerce

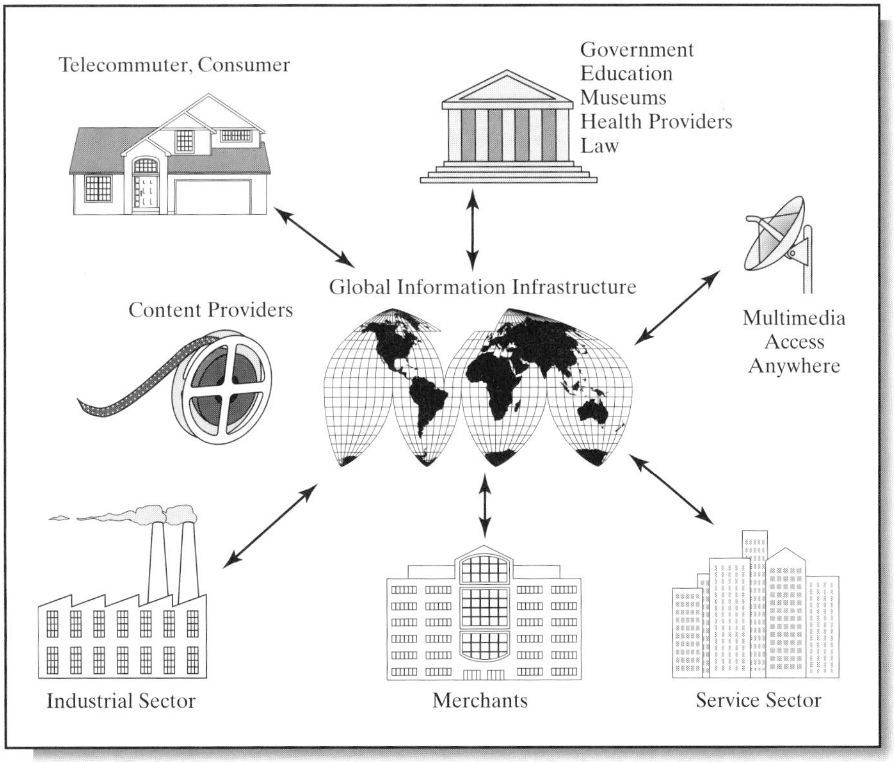

Source: Courtesy of Dr. Richard Welke, professor of CIS, Georgia State University.

is developing toward partnering owners and managers across departments to develop a chain of relationships that adds value to the enterprise. In addition, downsizing of large organizations, outsourcing of specialized tasks, and encouraging cross-functional business processes all require better communication between the departments that perform these functions. E-commerce, which makes communication easy, is an ideal method of making these connections (see Figure 1-3).

4. **Increasing pressure on operating costs and profit margins.** Global competition and the proliferation of products and services worldwide have added unusual pressure to keep a close watch on operating costs and maximize profit margins. E-commerce addresses these concerns quickly, efficiently, and at low cost (see Figure 1-4).
5. **Demand for customized products and services.** Today's customers are collectively demanding higher quality and better performance, including a customized way of producing, delivering, and paying for goods and services. Mass customization puts pressure on firms to handle customized requests on a mass-market scale. The prediction is that firms that don't move with the trend eventually will lose out (see Figure 1-5).

E-Commerce Myths

Confusion still exists regarding what e-commerce can and cannot do. The following are only some of the myths that need to be addressed.

1. **Setting up a Web site is easy.** This is true, except that ensuring performance of the site is not easy. Technology, networking infrastructure, and design criteria must be considered.
2. **E-commerce is cheap when compared to purchasing a mainframe.** It all depends on the size and volume of business and on the level of sophistication of the Web storefront. Larger organizations can spend an average of $750,000 just for the baseline technology. The annual cost of a major licensing deal on a high-traffic portal runs well into eight figures.
3. **E-commerce means the end of mass marketing.** The Web is the first commercial channel that enables cost-effective, one-to-one marketing on a large scale, but the business still has to market its Web presence.
4. **E-commerce means a new economy.** No "new" economy has been created, but something new has occurred in the real economy. It is the Internet that provides a powerful new business environment and a universal information system for handling transactions for buyers and sellers.
5. **Everyone is doing it.** Yes, but a Web presence is not commerce. Many organizations still do not see a compelling business reason to move to e-commerce. Strategic planning is a critical first step.
6. **E-commerce is lucrative.** For many medium-size and smaller organizations, it might still be early to enter the e-commerce game. A company must have deep pockets and be willing to invest in customer support in order to succeed.
7. **E-commerce is revolutionary.** Although Internet technology has created a new way to shop, most rules of retailing still apply. Merchandise is obtained from vendors, warehoused, and shipped to customers. Some of it is returned. Along the way, products are made more desirable by the information presented on the Web sites and by the sales support provided over the telephone or through e-mail. Unfortunately, many Internet retailers spend a disproportionate amount on the "revolutionary"

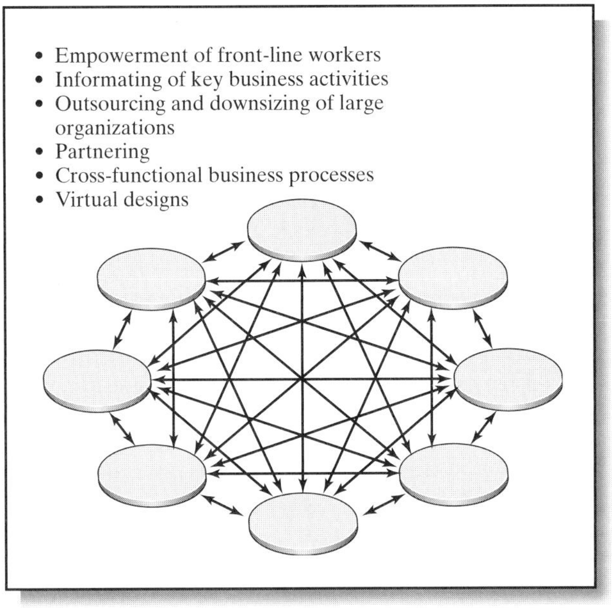

Figure 1-3
Changes in organizational makeup

Source: Courtesy of Dr. Detmar Straub, professor of CIS, Georgia State University.

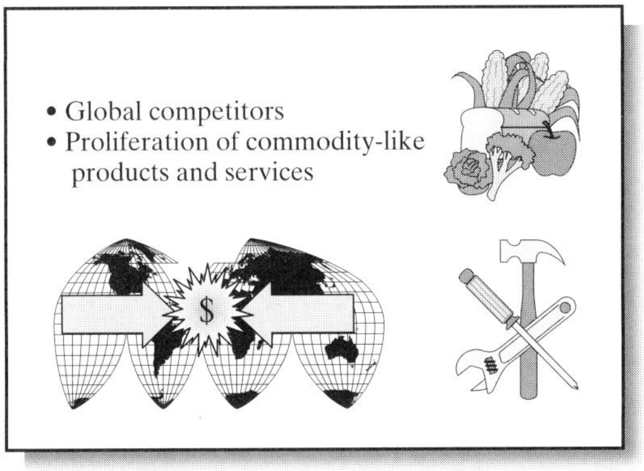

Figure 1-4
Increasing pressure on costs and margins

Source: Courtesy of Dr. Richard Welke, professor of CIS, Georgia State University.

Figure 1-5
Mass customization

Source: Courtesy of Dr. Richard Welke, professor of CIS, Georgia State University.

tasks of Web site construction and marketing and too little on the less glamorous aspects of customer support and fulfillment.

8. **The Internet is a commercial fad that crashed in 2000.** No question, the dot.com mania came to a halt in 2000. But the Internet continues to reshape businesses and the information systems that run them. The Internet is an infrastructure for a new way of doing business.
9. **Business-to-consumer e-commerce is dead.** The one aspect of e-commerce that is dead is the astronomical valuation of Internet stocks in 2000. Most of the business-to-commerce business will be done by established businesses and known brands.
10. **Online retailing is always the low-cost channel.** According to recent figures, Internet retailers spend up to five times what store and catalog retailers spend on customer acquisition. Unless more cost-effective methods are developed, marketing costs alone will bury many companies. The moment customers begin to demand quality customer service and fulfillment, the typical Internet retailer's overhead increases dramatically.
11. **All products can be sold online using identical business models.** Different products require different selling techniques and customer support. For example, what works for book selling does not work for consumer electronics or furniture. Internet sales should follow different business models, depending on the product.
12. **Build it and they will come.** It is a known fact that a Web site has to be advertised and promoted just like any other business. Customers bought with price promotions and giveaways are rarely loyal customers. The moment a competitor lowers the price, they click over to that site. The best customer is a recurring customer who is happy with quality service.
13. **Size is not that important for online firms.** In one respect, to a first-time visitor, the small Web site of a local wine store is no different than that of a major wine seller. Yet size continues to be critical to online firms. Size pays off in brand awareness and allows a firm to take advantage of lower costs and consumer concerns about service. Cyber-consumers prefer to buy from the largest storefronts and from strong content providers that can identify them and their preferences.
14. **The middleman is out.** Intermediaries are the traditional organizations that deliver products to the retailer from the manufacturer or the wholesaler. Despite the interface between consumers and merchants who deliver products directly to the consumer, new intermediaries have surfaced on the Web. In fact, the intermediary is one of the fastest-growing Internet businesses. Web intermediaries are resellers of products, such as Amazon.com, E*Trade, and Egghead.com. Intermediaries will continue to be in demand in situations where consumers expect choice at the point of purchase.

Advantages and Limitations of E-Commerce

The digital age and the digital revolution affect every one of us. Changes in telecommunications are affecting the way we receive and transmit information, product announcements, purchase orders, and so on. As the telephone, the fax machine, PCs, and printers have become essential ingredients in doing business, so have e-mail, Web storefronts, and integrated digital communications. The much-talked-about "digital convergence" will drive all these pieces of hardware into one digital platform, whether it is a computer connected to the Internet or a computer interacting with other computers or devices, because such connectivity will prove to be more efficient and effective. The case of *Amazon.com vs. Barnes & Noble*, where Barnes & Noble sued Amazon for billing itself as the largest bookstore, demonstrates that the very definition of "store" must be reevaluated.

Any way you look at it, e-commerce is everywhere. As soon as you click onto the Net, some attractive banner advertisement invites you to its Web site and tries to sell you products or services. Areas that are growing by leaps and bounds are financial services, entertainment, travel, medicine, and retailing. Even Uncle Sam (U.S. government) wants e-commerce (see Box 1-4). Based on a recent source, the Office of Management and Budget (OMB) projects that the federal government will spend nearly $53 billion on technology and Web service in fiscal 2003. That is a 25 percent increase from just 2 years ago. Most of the federal agencies that will make up the new Homeland Security Department propose technology infrastructure spending increases in fiscal 2003. The federal government has become a click-and-mortar enterprise, from customer interfaces to supply chain (Low and Goldberg 2002).

E-commerce is everywhere. After boom and bust, it is not new or unique anymore. The advantage is that the focus now is on basic business principles such as return on investment, building trust, and telling the customer what is, in fact, available in stock. E-commerce has become just plain commerce. It is just another channel to reach customers, vendors, and suppliers.

Schwab customers trade more than $2 billion per day online. The system allows customers to buy and sell securities, tap into research, and ask questions over the Net. The Web service has generated more than 1 million online accounts totaling $70 billion in assets.

The latest survey conducted by telephone between September 15, 2002, and October 15, 2002, found that three in five make online purchases on a regular basis. That is double the

BOX 1-4
Uncle Sam wants e-commerce

For all the complaints about government being behind the times, the era of e-government is here: Government agencies are optimizing their internal computer operations. As a logical next step, the possibilities of B2G (business-to-government) e-commerce are emerging as governments look at moving procurement online. The initiatives span all levels of government: The Clinton administration pushed to move federal procurement online by 2003, and even local school districts are buying supplies online. The Gartner Group projects rapid growth, with online government procurement increasing by 400 percent, to $6.2 billion, in 5 years. The market for providing these B2G services is wide open, and a clear leader has yet to emerge. However, success in the government arena requires several adjustments for potential market entrants accustomed to fast-moving, market-driven clients.

The government of the state of Washington provides a good example of the cost savings potential. The state shifted its procurement to what it calls its Buysense system, designed by American Management Systems (AMS), a Fairfax, Virginia-based consulting firm with strong ties to the government. Washington is saving money by buying in greater bulk, controlling renegade purchasing, and reducing paperwork; AMS charges a small transaction fee to each side. Although the program started only last June, Washington is already a model for other governments to follow.

SOURCE: Excerpted from Furth, John, "Uncle Sam Wants e-Commerce." www.line56.com, February 2001, 21.

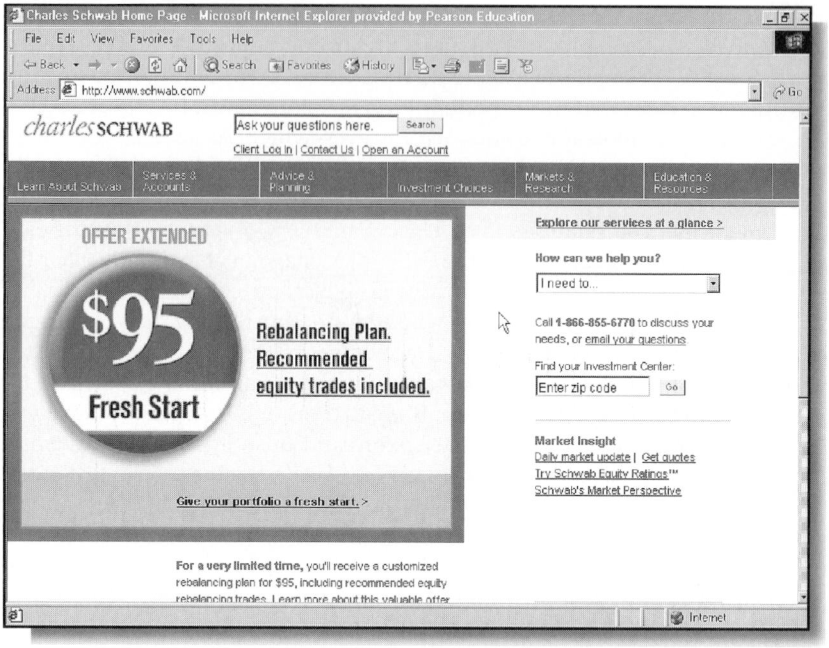

Screen Capture 1-2

number who said so 4 years ago. Among the drivers behind the growth in Web shoppers is convenience. More than three quarters of the survey group said they go online to check prices before they buy. Making travel reservations or purchasing tickets was the most popular activity, and the least popular online activity was downloading books. The bottom three activities in the ranking were arranging home grocery deliveries (4 percent), buying pet food (2 percent), and purchasing stamps online (1 percent) (NY Staff 2002).

Advantages

E-commerce has several advantages.

Lower Cost

Doing e-business on the Internet is cost-effective; it reduces logistical problems and puts a small business on a par with giants like Amazon.com, Sears, General Motors, or Bank of America. In a commercial bank, for example, a basic over-the-counter transaction costs $1.07 to process; over the Internet, the same transaction costs about 1 penny. Every financial transaction eventually turns into an electronic process. The sooner the conversion occurs, the more cost-effective the transaction becomes.

Economy

E-commerce is economical. Unlike the brick-and-mortar environment, in e-commerce no rental of physical store space, insurance, or infrastructure investment are needed. All that is required is an idea, a unique product, and a well-designed Web storefront to reach cyber-customers, plus a partner to do fulfillment.

Higher Margins

E-commerce means higher margins. For example, the cost of processing a conventional airline ticket is $8. According to one travel agency, processing the same ticket (called an e-ticket) over the Web costs $1. Along with higher margins, businesses can gain more control and flexibility and are able to save time when manual transactions are done electronically.

Better Customer Service

E-commerce means better and quicker customer service. Web-based customer service makes customers happier. Instead of calling your company on the phone, holding for 10 minutes, then getting to a clerk who taps into your account, the Web merchant gives customers direct access to their personal accounts over the Web. It saves time and money. It is a win-win proposition. For companies that do business with other companies, adding customer service to the Web is a competitive advantage. The overnight package delivery service, where tracking numbers allow customers to check the whereabouts of a package online, is one good example.

Quick Comparison Shopping

E-commerce helps consumers comparison shop. Automated online shopping assistants called hopbots scour Net stores and find deals on everything from applesauce to printer ribbons. For example, mySimon (www.mysimon.com) *learns* the navigation preferences of its runner (a tool that fills out the request form asking the bot to search Web pages for solutions). It lets the user enter basic keywords such as *ladies dress* to search its database of Web stores for the best buys.

Productivity Gains

E-commerce means productivity gains. Weaving the Web throughout an organization means improved productivity. Take the example of IBM, which incorporated the Web into every corner of the firm—products, marketing, and practices. The company figured it would save $750 million by letting customers find answers to technical questions via its Web site. (See www.IBM.com for recent details).

Teamwork

E-commerce helps people work together. E-mail is one example of how people collaborate to exchange information and work on solutions. It has transformed the way organizations interact with suppliers, vendors, business partners, and customers. More interaction means better overall results.

A study of 40 corporate Intranets by the META Group found that the typical Intranet (within-company network) had an average return on investment (ROI) of 38 percent. Networks that provided collaborative capabilities had a 40 percent ROI, and those that gave people direct access to needed information had a 68 percent ROI. The implication is that the more interactive and the more "collaborative-rich" the Web site is, the higher the payoff is for the business (see www.IBM.com).

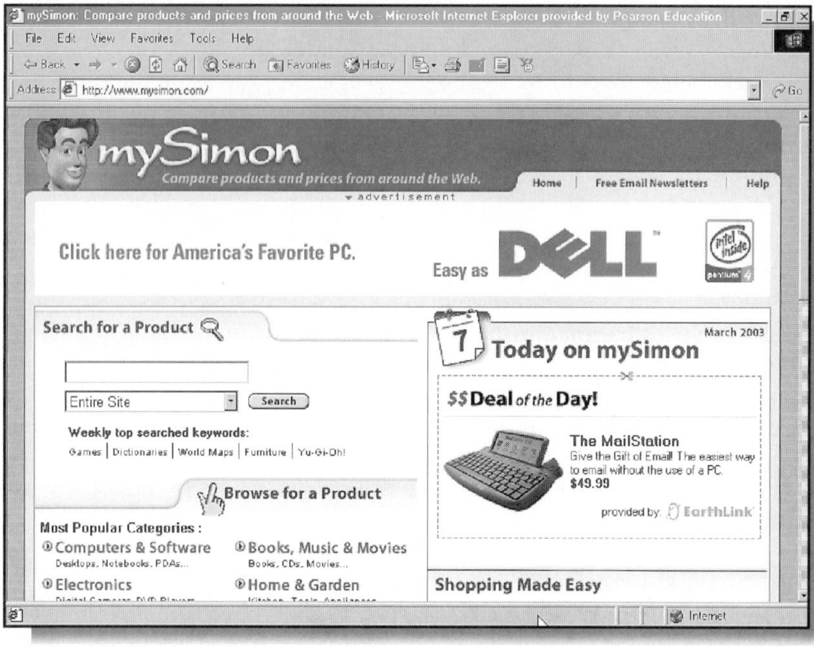

Screen Capture 1-3

Screen Capture 1-4

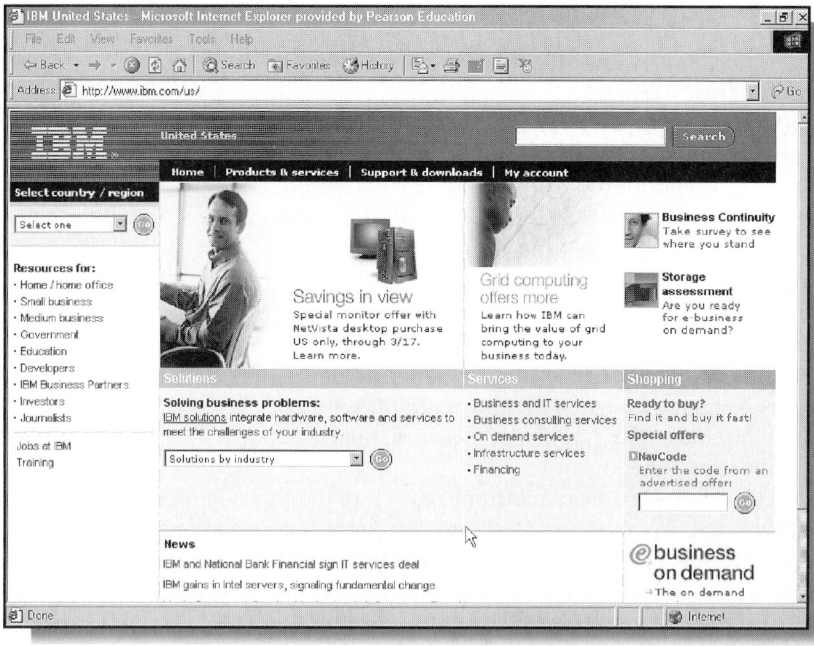

Knowledge Markets

E-commerce helps create knowledge markets. Small groups inside big firms can be funded with seed money to develop new ideas. For example, DaimlerChrysler has created small teams to look for new trends and products. A Silicon Valley team is doing consumer research on electric cars and advising car designers.

Information Sharing, Convenience, and Control

Electronic marketplaces improve information sharing between merchants and customers and promote quick, just-in-time deliveries. Convenience for the consumer is a major driver for changes in various industries: Customers and merchants save money; are online 24 hours a day, 7 days a week; experience no traffic jams and no crowds; and do not have to carry heavy shopping bags.

Control is another major driving factor. For example, instead of banks controlling the relationship with the customer, customers today can have more control of their banking needs via Internet Web sites. Banks like Bank of America and Wells Fargo now give customers access to their accounts via the Web.

Swapping Goods and Services

Swapping is trading something you have for something you want more. Offering goods or services through barter is gaining in popularity through sites like BarterTrust.com and Ubarter. Here is how it works. Sam, a networking consultant, offers his technical services through a barter company. People pay currency into Sam's account in exchange for his

Screen Capture 1-5

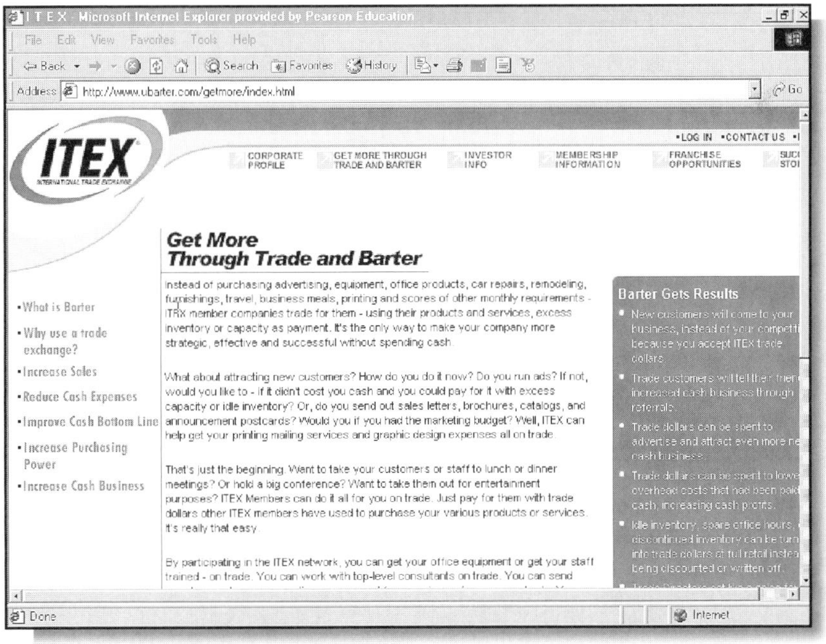

Source: Copyright © 2003–2004~ ITEX is a registered service mark of ITEX Corporation.

services. Instead of accepting the cash, he turns around and buys things (e.g., a PC, carpeting). The barter house keeps a modest commission to expedite the exchange.

Here are examples of hot deals made available on Ubarter.

1. A total of $250,000 worth of denim merchandise, including shirts, vests, jackets, robes, and hats.
2. Commercial radio airtime, in 30- or 60-second spots, on nearly 120 radio stations in 21 U.S. markets (prices start at 15 U.S. Ubarter dollars per ad).
3. Soda vending machines (1,250 U.S. Ubarter dollars each).
4. Five-page e-commerce Web sites (999 Canadian Ubarter dollars each).
5. Gourmet coffee (12 Canadian Ubarter dollars per pound).
6. Beach resort getaways on the southwestern corner of Washington's Olympic peninsula, with ocean views ($2,000 in accommodations available).

Source: www.ubarter.com/getmore/index.html

Customization

Digital products are highly customizable. They are easy to reorganize, revise, or edit. With information about consumer tastes and preferences, products can be differentiated (customized) and matched to individual needs (see Box 1-5).

Limitations

Even though we can generate a long list of advantages and benefits, some problems and drawbacks still need to be considered before plunging into the Web business. Here are just a few of these problems.

Security

Security continues to be a problem for online businesses. In a 2000 *Economist* article, 95 percent of Americans expressed reluctance to give out their credit card numbers via the Internet. For millions of potential cyber-customers, the fear of credit card theft is a real one. Consumers have to feel confident about the integrity of the process before they commit to the purchase.

System and Data Integrity

Data protection and the integrity of the system that handles the data are serious concerns. Computer viruses are rampant, with new viruses discovered every day. Viruses cause unnecessary delays, file backups, storage problems, and the like. The danger of hackers accessing files and corrupting accounts adds more stress to an already complex operation.

System Scalability

scalability: ability of a computer system, database infrastructure, or network to be upgraded to new standards.

A business develops an interactive interface with customers via a Web site. After a while, statistical analysis determines whether visitors to the site are one-time or recurring customers. If the company expects 2 million customers and 6 million show up, Web site performance is bound to experience degradation, slowdown, and eventually loss of customers. To keep this problem from happening, a Web site must be scalable, or upgradable, on a regular basis.

BOX 1-5
E-commerce trends: Buying a car

THE OLD WAY

1. Carmaker decides to build thousands of cars based on forecasts taken from sales trends over the past 3 years. Carmaker sends out bids to secure parts suppliers. Spare parts and supplies are shipped to the carmaker's warehouse. Time frame is several weeks.
2. Carmaker ships vehicles to dealers based on dealers' estimates of their local market. Time frame is 2 to 8 weeks.
3. Vehicles sit on parking lot waiting for buyers. Time frame is 1 to 3 months.
4. Consumer stops by, looking for a two-door sedan with a leather interior. Dealer tries to sell consumer a four-door car with options that the customer does not need. Alternatives are for the customer to order a car (8-week wait), have the dealer look for the car from another dealer (2 days to 2 weeks), or buy what is on the lot.

THE NEW WAY

1. Consumer orders a two-door sedan online, picking options, color, and so on.
2. Order is sent to the closest dealer in a matter of minutes.
3. If car is not available, factory receives order. Suppliers, which have been hired via bidding on Internet exchange in auctions that last a few hours, are notified online to ship customized components (few hours, depending on availability).
4. Car is built by assembling a few dozen preassembled modules to a simplified frame (several hours).
5. Car is shipped directly to the dealer. Vehicle is tracked using a bar-code system similar to how UPS tracks packages (few days).
6. Dealer and consumer are contacted at the same time the car arrives at the dealership.
7. Consumer picks up the car at the dealer, signs proper forms, and drives the car home.

Total time: 10 days

Payoff: Increased brand loyalty and consumer satisfaction. Billions formerly locked up in idle inventory are freed up for massive shareholder dividends or megamergers.

SOURCE: Ansberry, Clare, "Let's Build an Online Supply Network!" *Wall Street Journal*, April 17, 2000, R65.

E-Commerce Is Not Free

So far, success stories in e-commerce have favored large businesses with deep pockets and good funding. According to a recent report, small retailers that go head-to-head with e-commerce giants are fighting a losing battle. As in the brick-and-mortar environment, they simply cannot compete on price or product offering (Blackmon 2000, p. R30).

Brand loyalty is related to this issue, which is supposed to be less important for online firms. Brands are expected to lower search costs, build trust, and communicate quality. According to Blackmon, users have difficulty using online search engines such as Yahoo! to locate product information and rely instead on recognized dot.com brands for purchases. A search engine can come up with the best music deals, for example, yet consumers continue to flock to trusted entities like CD-Now.

Consumer Search Is Not Efficient or Cost-Effective

On the surface, the electronic marketplace appears to be a perfect market, where worldwide sellers and buyers share information and trade without intermediaries. However, a closer look indicates that new types of intermediaries are essential to e-commerce. They include electronic malls that guarantee product quality, mediators for bargaining, and certification authorities to ensure legitimacy of transactions. All of these intermediaries add to transaction costs.

Fulfillment Problems

Tales of shipping delays, merchandise mix-ups, and Web sites crashing under pressure continue to be a problem in e-tailing. Customer confidence in e-commerce's ability to deliver during heavy shopping seasons continues to be a headache. Even happy customers say the experience could be improved.

Customer Relations Problems

The interpersonal part of e-commerce between e-merchants and customers continues to be a major setback. Many Web sites lack a phone contact to discuss order problems with humans on the merchant's end. This is also the case with HELP desks that are designed to help customers wade through technical problems. The lines are either busy or simply do not get answered. This limitation is related to fulfillment problems, where customers have a difficult time returning or exchanging items purchased over a company's Web site. The best approach to date is one taken by a brick-and-mortar firm like Barnes and Noble, where customers who purchase items via the company's Web site can go to the nearest store and settle the complaint in person.

Products People Won't Buy Online

Imagine a Web site called furniture.com or living.com, where venture capitalists have invested millions in selling home furnishings online. Furniture.com's site enabled browsers to design floor plans using existing furniture on the Web site. In the case of a sofa, you'd want to sit on it, feel the texture of the fabric, and so on. In addition to the "sofa road-test" factor, online furniture stores faced costly returns and the kinds of deliveries that could not be expedited via FedEx. Living.com folded in August 2000, and Furniture.com followed a few months later (Totty and Grimes 2002).

Corporate Vulnerability

Web farming: systematically refining information resources on the Web for business intelligence gathering.

The availability of product details, catalogs, and other information about a business through its Web site makes it vulnerable to access by the competition. The idea of extracting business intelligence from the competition's Web pages is called **Web farming**, a term coined by Richard Hackathorn.

Lack of a Blueprint for Handling E-Commerce

The shortage of *e-literate* people in the workplace continues. In a survey published in *Computerworld* (Copeland, p. 54), nearly 9 out of 10 respondents said only a few of their key managers have e-commerce skills, Internet experience, and foresight. Sixty-six percent also said they are having a tough time attracting people wanting to take advantage of online opportunities. Finally, traditional organizational structures and cultures were found to inhibit progress in e-commerce.

High Risk of Internet Start-Up

Many stories unfolded in 1999 and 2000 about successful executives in established firms leaving for Internet start-ups, only to find out that their "get rich" dream with a dot.com was just that—a dream. With the looming recession, many retailers are rethinking their e-strategy anew (see Box 1-6).

THE ROLE OF STRATEGY IN E-COMMERCE

The road map for a successful e-commerce business is identifying the critical success factors (CSFs) and developing a realistic strategy for the business. IBM identified four CSFs that make e-commerce work in any industry:

1. A sound strategy that has the full support of top management.
2. A clear goal of long-term customer relationships and value.

BOX 1-6
Retailers mull pulling plug on e-commerce

Federated Department Stores, Inc. stunned the retail world late last year when it ceased selling merchandise on its Bloomingdales.com site. They said the harsh economy is forcing retailers to take a harder look at their Internet commerce operations, which were expensive to launch and can be costly to maintain. For most retailers, online sales still represent a very small fraction of overall sales.

"It'd be naïve to think there isn't going to be some fallout," said Brian Kilcourse, CIO at Longs Drug Stores, Inc. in Walnut Creek, California. One problem is the high cost of entry for e-commerce. "You need to spend $20 million to get the beginnings of a Web offering—well, in our case, that's four or five stores." In retrospect, today's focus is on Return on Investment (ROI). Retailers are facing tremendous pressure to focus on the bottom line and e-commerce is an obvious area to look at first, because it's the newest and it's taking a lot of money out of the budget. A lot of companies are realizing they spent a lot of money on this channel and haven't necessarily gotten anything out of it.

SOURCE: Excerpted from Sliwa, Carol, "Retailers Mull Pulling Plug on E-Commerce," *Computerworld*, February 18, 2002, 14.

3. Making full use of the Internet and related technologies.
4. A scalable and integrated business process and infrastructure.

We will see in Chapter 12 that the first step to becoming an e-commerce business is adopting a sustainable business strategy based on unique opportunities to provide value for the firm. To do so requires a clear understanding of the company, the industry in which it does business, and available Internet technologies. As a matter of common sense, the strategy should be difficult to duplicate, have high barriers to entry for competitors, and have high switching costs for customers.

To ensure a successful e-commerce business, a realistic strategy is a must. The objectives of the business should be based on the technology in use at the time and a budget. The resulting Web site should reflect the company's current image because e-commerce is an extension of any business. In the final analysis, you need to build a community of loyal customers; keep track of their needs and preferences; and make your site responsive, easy to use, and easy to navigate.

VALUE CHAINS IN E-COMMERCE

In e-commerce, a number of business processes and activities go unnoticed by the consumer and are often taken for granted. Within an online merchant's business, value-added activities work together to make the business-to-consumer interface operational. In this section, we systematically analyze a company's **value chain** and how it makes commerce on the Internet a reality.

value chain: a way of organizing the activities of a business so that each activity adds value (*value-added* activity) or productivity to the total operation of the business.

In 1985, Michael Porter wrote a book called *Competitive Advantage*, in which he introduced the concept of the value chain. Businesses receive raw materials as input, add value to them through various processes, and sell the finished product as output to customers. This means that organizations do not consist of isolated sets of functions, but they are a chain of value-creating activities that assure competitive advantages by the way they deliver value to the customer. A communication process that extends from a firm backwards to suppliers and forward to customers ties all sorts of activities together.

Competitive advantage is achieved when an organization links the activities in its value chain more cheaply and more effectively than its competitors. For example, the purchasing function assists the production activity to ensure that raw materials and other supplies are available on time and meet the requirements of the products to be manufactured. The manufacturing function, in turn, has the responsibility to produce quality products that the sales staff can depend on. The human resource function must hire, retain, and develop the right personnel to ensure continuity in manufacturing, sales, and other areas of the business. Bringing in qualified people contributes to stability, continuity, and integrity of operations throughout the firm.

Figure 1-6 shows the relationships between and among activities in the value chain.

No time sequence or special sequence of activities must occur before a business is considered successful or effective. The idea is to link different activities in such a way that the value-added output of one activity (department, process, etc.) contributes to the input of another activity. The integration of these activities results in an organization that is fine-tuned for profitability and growth.

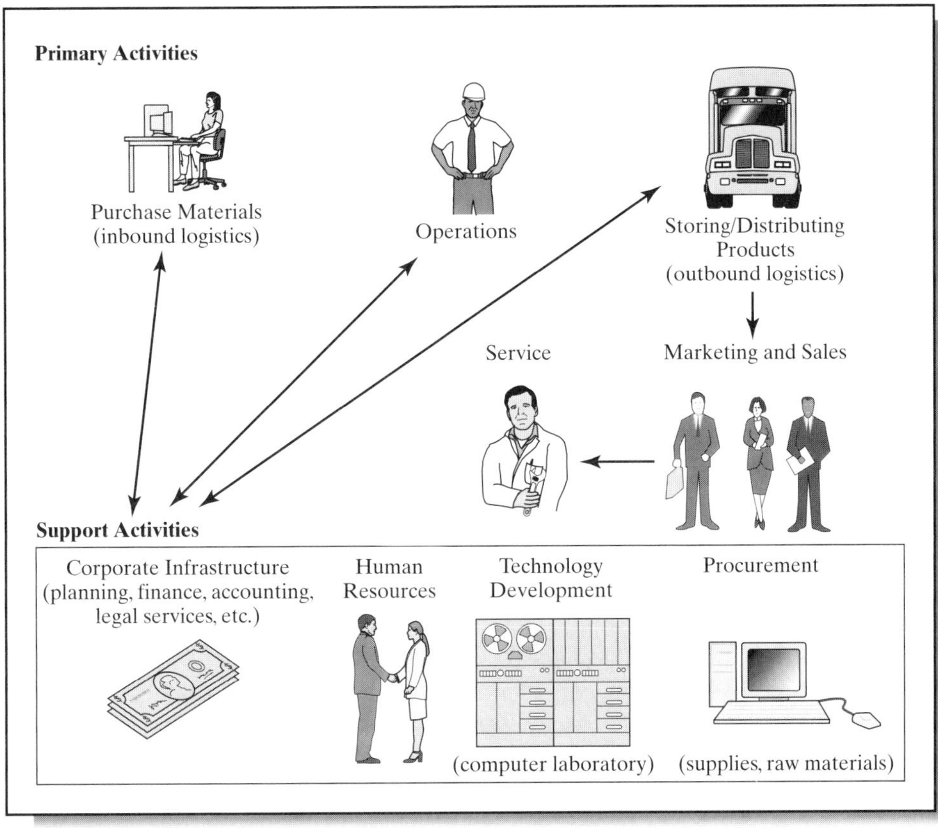

Figure 1-6
The value chain, showing relationships between and among activities

Source: Reprinted by permission of *Harvard Business Review*. From Porter, Michael E. and Millar, Victor E., "How Information Gives You Competitive Advantage," *Harvard Business Review*, July–August 1985, 151. Copyright © 2003–2004 by Harvard Business School Publishing Corporation, all rights reserved.

According to Porter, the primary activities of a business are:

1. **Inbound logistics.** These are procurement activities—vendor selection, comparative shopping, negotiating supply contracts, and just-in-time arrival of goods. They represent the supply side of the business. In e-commerce, the business must be capable of exchanging data with suppliers quickly, regardless of the electronic format.
2. **Operations.** This is the actual conversion of raw materials received into finished products. It includes fabrication, assembly, testing, and packaging the product. This production activity provides added value for the marketing function. Operational activities are the point in the value chain where the value is added. These happen in the back office where the pizza is baked, the PCs are assembled, or the stock trades are executed. Data are shared at maximum network speed among internal and external partners involved in the value-adding processes.
3. **Outbound logistics.** This activity represents the actual storing, distributing, and shipping of the final product. It involves warehousing, materials handling,

shipping, and timely delivery to the ultimate retailer or customer. The output of this activity ties in directly with marketing and sales.

4. **Marketing and sales.** This activity deals with the ultimate customer. It includes advertising, product promotion, sales management, identifying the product's customer base, and distribution channels. The output of this activity could trigger increased production, more advertising, and so on.
5. **Service.** This activity focuses on after-sale service to the customer. It includes testing, maintenance, repairs, warranty work, and replacement parts. The output of this activity means satisfied customers; improved image of the product and the business; and potential for increased production, sales, and so on.

Primary activities are not enough. A business unit needs support activities to make sure the primary activities are carried out. Figure 1-6 shows the relationship between support and primary activities. Imagine, for example, a manufacturing concern with no people or with poorly skilled employees.

The key support activities in the value chain are:

1. **Corporate infrastructure.** This activity is the backbone of the business unit. It includes general management, accounting, finance, planning, and legal services. It is most often pictured in an organization chart showing the relationships among the different positions, the communications network, and the authority structure. Each position holder must add value to those above as well as below.
2. **Human resources.** This is the unique activity of matching the right people to the job. It involves recruitment, retention, career path development, compensation, training and development, and benefits administration. The output of this activity affects virtually every other activity in the company.
3. **Technology development.** This activity adds value in the way it improves the product and the business processes in the primary activities. The output of this activity contributes to the product quality, integrity, and reliability, which make life easier for the sales force and for customer relations.
4. **Procurement.** This activity focuses on the purchasing function and how well it ensures the availability of quality raw materials for production.

Where does e-commerce fit in? The value chain is a useful way of looking at a corporation's activities and how the various activities add value to other activities and to the company in general. E-commerce can play a key role in reducing costs, improving product quality and integrity, promoting a loyal customer base, and creating a quick and efficient way of selling products and services. By examining the elements of the value chain, corporate executives can look at ways of incorporating information technology and telecommunications to improve the overall productivity of the firm. Companies that do their homework early and well ensure themselves a competitive advantage in the marketplace.

INTEGRATING E-COMMERCE

The trend in e-commerce is to integrate the entire transaction life cycle, from the time the consumer purchases the product on the Web site to the time the product is received. This life cycle centers around three major e-commerce applications: **business-to-consumer (B2C)**, done on the Internet; **business-to-business (B2B)**, done on the Internet and Extranets; and business-within-business, done on the Intranet (see Table 1-1).

Table 1-1
Key elements of Internet, Extranet, and Intranet e-commerce

Element	Internet	Extranet	Intranet
E-Commerce type	Business-to-consumer (e.g., mail order via the Web)	Business-to-business (procurement and fulfillment)	Internal procurement and processing
Access	Unrestricted (anyone can access a URL address)	Restricted to company employees, staff, and business partners	Restricted to company customers, employees, and staff
Security	Generally minimal, except for verifying credit cards and financial transaction integrity	Firewalls and restricted access to data and applications	Firewalls to eliminate noncompany employees
Payment method	Credit card or electronic cash	Predefined credit agreement between businesses	Within-business charges

Business-to-Consumer (Internet)

The focus of this e-commerce application is on the consumer's use of a merchant's Web storefront or Web site. Consumers anywhere can browse and order goods or services online anytime. This approach is modeled on the traditional shopping experience found in stores like Safeway, Kroger, and K-mart. For example, a shopping cart is used to hold goods until the customer is ready to check out. Checkout is order and payment processing. B2C is the electronic equivalent of the traditional mail order or telephone-based ordering system.

shopping cart: online order form supported by the appropriate software.

Business-to-Business (Internet and Extranet)

Having a Web storefront is not a big deal anymore. Everyone has one. The real power of e-commerce lies not in the direct sale of products to consumers, but in the integration of relationships among merchants and suppliers for prompt, quality customer service. Business-to-business e-commerce is industrial marketing: Among the processes it handles are fulfillment and procurement. As soon as an online purchase is entered and payment is approved through a credit card clearance procedure, a message generally is displayed saying, "Thank you for your order. The amount of $xxx will be charged to your credit card. The product should reach you within 5 to 7 working days." The moment the message is displayed on the customer's monitor, an electronic order is sent to the vendor to fill the order and ship it directly to the customer. Doing this electronically means reduced inventory and quicker service.

However, B2B is more than fulfillment: There is the potential for the Internet to become like a central computer system for all industries. Companies can check their suppliers' inventories or make instant purchases quickly and conveniently. Overhead should decline as Web-driven systems eliminate many of the traditional workers who do the faxing and handle purchase orders. Competing online also should force prices for materials and supplies to drop dramatically. An **Extranet** is a shared Intranet deploying e-commerce within the larger community of an organization, including its vendors, contractors, suppliers, and key customers.

According to a Forrester report, by 2003 more than 90 percent of businesses that sell goods to other companies will be doing business on the Web. B2B online sales also are predicted to jump to $6.3 trillion in 2005, up almost fifteenfold from the $1.1 billion in 2002. This is far larger than B2C (Greenemeier, October 3, 2000: News4@daily.information.week.com). See Table 1-2.

supply chain management (SCM): integrating the networking and communication infrastructure between businesses and suppliers to ensure having the right product, in the right place, at the right time, at the right price, and in the right condition.

The concept of supply chain management (SCM) means having the right product, in the right place, at the right time, at the right price, and in the right condition. This is an integral part of the business-to-business framework. SCM cuts across application infrastructures and business relationships. It transforms the way companies deal with suppliers, partners, and even customers. The goal is to improve efficiency and profitability, but it also means creating new opportunities for everyone involved.

Supply chain management employs powerful tools that allow companies to exchange information (inventory levels, sales trends, etc.) in an effort to reduce cycle times, to have quicker fulfillment of orders, to minimize excess inventory, and to improve customer service. This communication is done quickly from one database to another. According to an *InformationWeek* research survey of 300 IT executives using supply-chain systems, the majority of respondents said the most important strategic advantages of supply-chain systems are better collaboration with business partners, lower operational costs, and reduced cycle times (Stein, p. 2). See Box 1-7.

In SCM, the name of the game is *collaboration* among business partners, *coordination* of logistics for timely delivery of goods or products, *cooperation* among businesses and

Table 1-2
B2B boom ($ in billions)

Industry	2002	2003	2004
Computing and electronics	$ 427.3	$ 506.2	$ 592.9
Motor vehicles	190.2	311.5	411.5
Petrochemicals	103.2	184.5	299.2
Utilities	101.3	170.1	266.4
Paper and office products	73.9	143.5	235.3
Consumer goods	58.5	116.5	216.5
Food	73.9	128.1	211.1
Construction	34.6	74.2	141.0
Pharmaceutical and medical products	26.2	60.2	124.0
Industrial equipment and supplies	23.8	41.9	70.3
Shipping and warehousing	22.4	42.5	68.1
Aerospace and defense	23.1	29.0	32.9
Heavy industries	8.6	15.3	26.5
TOTAL	$1,166.9	$1,823.4	$2,695.5

Source: Adapted from Forrester Research, Inc., quoted in Blackmon, Douglas A., "Where the Money Is," *Wall Street Journal*, April 17, 2000, R30.

BOX 1-7
E-commerce trends: Killer supply chains

For most retailers, one of the trickiest links in the supply chain is moving goods from the supplier to the warehouse, then on to the store. Home Depot Inc. has found a simple way around that problem: Remove it. The Atlanta-based building supplies retailer now moves 85 percent of its merchandise—nearly all of its domestic goods—directly from the manufacturer to the storefront. Product no longer languishes in warehouses, saving both suppliers and Home Depot money. "We're treating each of our stores as if it were a distribution center," says CIO Ron Griffin. Because of Home Depot's high volume—its stores average $44 million in sales and 5-1/2 full inventory turns a year—the products frequently ship in full truckloads, making the system even more cost-effective.

Associates walk store aisles, watching for goods that need replenishment. As they enter orders directly into mobile computing devices, called the Mobile Ordering Platform, the request can go almost instantly via EDI connections to more than 80 percent of Home Depot's manufacturers, which can respond immediately. Home Depot offers its partners recognition incentives to get them on board.

Short-term forecasting is handled locally, with up to 65 weeks of data at the store level, and store managers are given latitude to adjust for demand based on merchandising programs. Home Depot prepares long-range forecasts of 3 to 5 years on a national level for its suppliers; they contain product-volume data, of course, as well as where growth is expected and where Home Depot plans to build new stores. That helps suppliers decide where to build new plants and distribution centers, and it puts Home Depot in the position of helping determine facility location instead of simply working around it. "Rather than assume fixed capacity, we help shape it," Griffin says.

Home Depot opens up even more data to its biggest partners. Electric-tool manufacturer Black & Decker is Home Depot's largest supplier, and Home Depot is its largest customer. So it benefits both companies to share information. Home Depot passes point-of-sale data to Black & Decker, which helps the Baltimore company analyze sales and determine future manufacturing volume.

SOURCE: Stein, Tom, and Sweat, Jeff, "Killer Supply Chains," *InformationWeek*, January 16, 2000, 1–3.

suppliers to make sure orders and inquiries are filled correctly, and *connectivity* through networking infrastructure to ensure speed and good response time at all times. More and more, companies are extending their focus from internal operations like scheduling and enterprise resource planning to relationships with external customers and suppliers. They are looking for the perfect virtual enterprise that will link their suppliers' suppliers to their customers' customers to operate together under one umbrella with seamless connections among databases, manufacturing, inventory systems, and Web servers.

Now, supply chain management is beginning to address perhaps the most critical link in the value chain—the end customer. The integration between sales-force automation applications and between consumers and business customers means all partners can now configure and order online what they need, when they need it. This means better business value, with tighter collaboration between customers and suppliers, and ultimately with the end user.

What about everyone in the middle—the wholesaler, the jobber, intermediaries in general? Middlemen are probably the most vulnerable to the killer supply chain. Based on various reports, dramatic changes are transforming the business of many intermediaries.

Today's wholesaler is taking a hard look at its current activities and extracting valuable skills it can offer outside the traditional way of doing business. Wholesalers are becoming financiers, logistics specialists, outsourced presales and post-sales support providers, and the like. What all this means is that they are wrapping information around the products they handle and adding significant value in the process.

As you can see, B2B exchanges pave the way for a new business model for the digital economy. It is a distinct network of suppliers, distributors, Internet service providers, and customers that use the Internet for communications and transaction handling. As communication tools get better and cheaper, transaction costs should drop. With the Internet, many transaction costs are approaching zero. People around the world can now quickly and cheaply access the information they need almost instantly. Companies also can add value to a product or service from any location, at any time, day or night.

To illustrate, General Motors (GM), Ford, and DaimlerChrysler announced in early 2000 that they were moving all their business-to-business activity, involving more than $250,000 billion and 60,000 suppliers, to the Internet. The new system will replace a mammoth procurement process built on phone calls and fax processing. For GM, the average processing cost of a purchase order is $125. With the Internet, the cost is expected to drop to $1. Bidding also will drive down the cost of some goods. Parts such as tires and headlights are already purchased through online reverse auctions, where the automaker names the price of the part it needs, leaving it to a supplier to accept the price. It is much like Priceline.com. This approach should capture millions of dollars in savings.

This is all well and good, but installing the necessary SCM software can be a big challenge. The serious task is overhauling the way work gets done in a company, which for large corporations can take years and cost hundreds of millions of dollars. For example, Ford wants to revamp its manufacturing plants to begin building customized cars for consumers in just 2 weeks. This means major changes for employees, dealers, and suppliers worldwide. Early in 2000, General Motors launched an SCM project with similar goals. The work is scheduled for completion by 2003 and will cost well over $100 million. It could mean reengineering almost all of GM's business processes and a big investment in new technology, but the payback also is expected to be in the hundreds of millions. Select e-business leaders and innovators are shown in Table 1-3.

Another problem with business-to-business e-commerce is understanding the technology and making it work. Many companies are relying on in-house talent to do the job rather than bringing in specialists from outside. The upside of this is that insiders know the business, the products, and the customers. The downside is the time-consuming learning curve. It is like building a business from scratch. It is one thing to create an in-house Web site and sell to business customers and buy supplies, but it is quite a different thing to try to link Web sites together, integrate internal inventory and accounting, and manage them in a global e-marketplace.

Business-Within-Business (Intranet)

The **Intranet** plays a role as a corporate and product information center and is strictly a "within company" type of information exchange. This networked environment is restricted to internal employees and customers, with firewalls to keep out nonemployees. E-mail replaces paper for the communication of messages, order acknowledgment and approvals, and other forms of correspondence within the firm. In terms of requisitions and procurement, the Intranet makes it possible to link a company's requisition system to Web-based supplier catalogs or shipment-tracking systems for quick and responsive delivery.

Table 1-3
Select e-business leaders and innovators

Rank	Company	URL Address	E-Business Leader	E-Business Profile
1	Office Depot	www.officedepot.com	Monica Luechtefeld, sr. v.p., "Our success is **measured** not by traffic, but by sales."	Office-supply company integrates e-business technology across all channels of its business, increasing customer self-service and order sizes while reducing transaction costs.
2	eBay	www.ebay.com	Meg Whitman, CEO, "predicts eBay will host $30 billion in gross sales by 2005."	Turned eBay into the largest site for e-commerce, with 30 million registered users. Remarkably, the site has been profitable since it began in 1996.
3	AOL Time Warner, Inc.	www.aol.com	Steve Case, chairman, "His goal is to make sure new rules for the Internet won't inhibit his company, or the growth of the Net."	AOL Time Warner is arguably the most powerful company on the Net since the merger of America Online Inc. and Time Warner. Case is moving beyond the role of company visionary to industry statesman.
4	Dell Computer Corp.	www.dell.com	Michael Dell, chairman, "He must find growth in the midst of shrinking PC demand."	Wrote the book on e-business tapping the Net to do everything from handling customer orders to linking suppliers.
5	General Electric Co.	www.ge.com	Gary Reiner, CIO, "The challenge is to push cultural change among GE's 340,000 employees and getting customers to buy GE stuff online."	Helped make GE the e-business leader among large manufacturers, with savings of $1.6 billion in 2001.
6	Amazon.com, Inc.	www.amazon.com	Jeff Bezos, CEO, "Keeps a relentless focus on customer satisfaction creating a gold standard for other online outfits to meet."	The world's biggest consumer e-commerce company. Bezos has made Amazon more efficient, turning over inventory faster and closing some facilities in an effort to show profit.
7	Microsoft	www.microsoft.com	Rick Belluzzo, COO, "Challenge is building a new Web business by adding subscription services like stock trading alerts through Microsoft's .Net technologies."	Reversed the fortunes of Microsoft's consumer Web business, making MSN the second-most-popular family of Web sites on the Net after 5 years of fits and starts.

Source: BusinessWeek e.biz, May 14, 2001, 24–59.

An Intranet has no true payment process. Transfers of funds or charges against budget accounts are purely an accounting transaction as part of the intracompany billing procedure. In effect, an Intranet becomes a facilitator for the exchange of information and services among the departments or divisions of a large company. For example, using a Web browser, regional managers of a retail chain can inquire about the status of their region's quarterly sales. The query is sent to the company server dedicated to its Intranet. To get such information, the system verifies the authenticity of the request and then transmits the requested information to the manager's monitor via the company Intranet.

Different departments with different PCs or local area networks can interact on an Intranet. For example, the human resources department can use the company's Intranet to post employee handbooks, company policies, job openings, and state and government employment regulations. The company also can post white papers, special announcements to all employees, corporate phone books, and online training courses so employees can do their training anytime, anywhere, at their convenience. The benefits of an Intranet are many and include the following.

1. Low development and maintenance costs.
2. Environmentally friendly because it is company specific.
3. Availability and sharing of information.
4. Timely, current information.
5. Quick and easy dissemination of information.

However, remember, an Intranet is not free. It costs money to install and takes regular maintenance to monitor reliability and integrity. As information becomes more abundant, the Intranet tends to contribute to congestion, especially in e-mail traffic. Employees are always being reminded to purge their e-mail files and work within the space allotted to their e-mail box.

Intranet software is hardware independent and runs well on a PC, a Macintosh, or in a UNIX-based environment. The Intranet infrastructure generally includes a Transmission Control Protocol/Internet Protocol (TCP/IP), Web server hardware and software, and a firewall server. (Intranets are covered in detail in Chapter 3.)

Business-to-Government (B2G)

Federal and state government business is an institution in and of itself. E-commerce has emerged as governments look at moving procurement online. Today, even local school districts are buying supplies online. The government market is strikingly similar to B2B. Most of the software and technology are directly usable. Some said, "If the 20 percent cost savings claimed by B2B proponents can be replicated in B2G, the ramifications for taxpayers as well as market entrants will be enormous in this $1.5 trillion market (state and local government procurement expenditures represent another $1 trillion) (Furth 2001).

Like any new entrant, B2B comes with its own set of difficulties. Changing the status quo in government is not so easy. Process efficiencies could mean job cuts, and powerful unions may not view the change in a positive light. Also, the tax-saving potential of B2G is not easily recognized by the taxpayers or government officials. At the same time, committing to technology means constant need for upgrades and additional costs.

To date, government-to-consumer business has done well. For example, paying for speeding tickets and renewing one's driver's license online have paid dividends to government agencies as well as customers. E-procurement is the latest stage, where government agencies announce "Request for Proposals" on their Web sites, then suppliers bid

Table 1-4
Worldwide mobile commerce revenues, 2002–2005 (in billions)

Region	2002	2003	2004	2005
Asia	$2.6	$5.0	$7.4	$9.4
Latin America	0.0	0.1	0.2	0.5
North America	0.2	0.7	1.8	3.5
Western Europe	0.5	1.7	4.6	7.8
Rest of world	0.1	0.2	0.4	1.0
TOTAL	**$3.4**	**$7.7**	**$14.4**	**$22.2**

Source: Adapted from Raczkowski, Gilda, "Mobile Economics: Focusing on the Future," *Dash* 30, October 2002, 1–3.

on each proposal by e-mail or through the Web site. The potential savings from e-procurement in time and costs could be impressive.

Mobile Commerce (M-Commerce)

With the increasing use of laptop computers and wireless networks and satellites, a trend to support "computing and people on the move" has emerged. It is called mobile commerce or nomadic computing. E-business unplugged the Internet, taking flight on the wireless Web with new opportunities and challenges. Mobile or m-commerce is a technological frontier that makes it possible for anyone from anywhere to do business via cordless phones or cordless devices. In 2003, hundreds of companies will be flocking to the wireless Web, following the trend that gives rise to new applications and new services worldwide. Worldwide mobile commerce revenues are forecast to grow exponentially. See Table 1-4. By another estimate, the global m-commerce market is expected to be worth a staggering $200 billion by 2004 (Singh 2002).

Detailed presentation of m-commerce is covered in Chapter 7. What we need to keep in mind at this early phase is that consumers and business organizations are beginning to shift their views of the mobile device from that of a voice phone to that of a personal e-commerce device that can extend business flexibility and decision making from anywhere. Some legal, political, and technological risks have yet to be cleared. For example, m-commerce risks include data integrity, user authentication, and merchant reliability. Yet, mobile consumers want to be able to make m-commerce payments in the same way they make physical-world payments—quickly, safely, and with confidence.

Managerial Implications

Given the challenges posed by today's e-commerce and its potential, when it comes to success in this emerging field, it is people and managerial talent that matter. It is people with a vision of the future who know how to handle the speed of change. The person who figures out how to harness the collective genius of the organization will blow the competition away.

With change now accepted as a way of life, the human resource department has the option of getting new people or changing the people who are already on staff. A new focus is being placed on building a productive organizational culture, managing change and results, building intellectual capital, creating future leaders, managing organizational learning, and pushing for growth and innovation. As someone said, "If you are not the lead elephant, you'll never charge."

In terms of success in today's digital economy, the real asset is not money; money is just a commodity. The real asset is information and how it is used to create value for the customer. More than half of doing business no longer depends on the brick-and-mortar side of commerce; it depends on the core personnel of the firm and the customer. Having employees be part of the organization and improving their skill sets adds value and contributes to the success of the firm.

Finally, the top challenge in managing an e-business is understanding the consumer. Most successful companies form a 360-degree consumer view by gathering data from every possible source and analyzing it to shed light on the kinds of details that mark the way consumers shop and buy. Companies that better understand their customers' preferences can sell more. They know which customers are most important, most profitable, and most loyal.

SUMMARY

1. Electronic commerce (EC) is the ability to deliver products, services, information, or payments via networks such as the Internet and the World Wide Web. From a structural perspective, EC involves various media—data, text, Web pages, Internet telephony, and Internet desktop video.
2. Electronic business connects critical business systems directly to key constituents—customers, vendors, and suppliers—via the Internet, Intranets, and Extranets.
3. Several drivers promote EC: digital convergence, 24/7 availability, changes in organizational makeup, increasing pressure on operating costs and profit margins, the demand for customization, and the need for speed.
4. The advantages of EC include: low cost; economical; higher margins; better and quicker business service; easy comparison shopping; productivity gains; creation of knowledge markets; information sharing, convenience, and new customer control; ability to swap goods and services; and customization.
5. The limitations of EC include: security issues, concerns about data protection and the integrity of the system that handles the data, system scalability, fulfillment (delivery) problems, customer relations problems, products people won't buy online, Web site access by the competition, and high risk of Internet start-ups.
6. A value chain is a way of organizing the activities of a business so that each activity provides added value or productivity to the total operation of the business.
7. Supply chain management (SCM) means having the right product, in the right place, at the right time, and in the right condition. The goal is to improve efficiency and profitability.
8. The transaction life cycle includes three major e-commerce applications: business-to-consumer (B2C), business-to-business (B2B), and business-within-business.
9. An Intranet wires the company for information exchange. E-mail replaces paper. An Intranet links a company's requisition system to Web-based supplier catalogs or shipment-tracking systems for quick and responsive delivery.

10. Success in the e-commerce field depends on attracting and keeping qualified technical people and managerial talent.

Attracting qualified technical people is a challenge; finding ways to retain them is a full-time job.

Key Terms

- business-to-business (B2B), 22
- business-to-consumer (B2C), 22
- business-to-government (B2G), 28
- electronic business, 4
- electronic commerce (EC), 2
- Extranet, 24
- Intranet, 26
- scalability, 16
- shopping cart, 23
- supply-chain management (SCM), 24
- transaction, 4
- web farming, 18
- value-chain, 20

Test Your Understanding

1. What indicators suggest that e-commerce is here to stay? Explain.
2. What is e-commerce? Give a definition of your own.
3. Contrast e-commerce with e-business.
4. Explain in detail the drivers that promote e-commerce. Why are they called drivers?
5. What is meant by digital convergence? What does it include?
6. List the e-commerce myths and explain briefly why they are myths.
7. What are the advantages and limitations of e-commerce? Do you think the advantages outweigh the limitations? Explain.
8. In what way is security a limitation of e-commerce?
9. Define the following terms:
   a. Scalability
   b. Value chain
10. Distinguish between:
    a. Value chain and supply chain management
    b. Intranet and Extranet
    c. E-commerce and e-business
11. What is a shopping cart? Where does it fit in B2C e-commerce? Explain.
12. Cite the key benefits of an Intranet. Is it beneficial in every type of business? Why or why not?

Discussion Questions

1. "E-banking will have a more profound effect on banking than ATMs (Automated Teller Machines) ever did." Do you agree? Surf the Internet, investigate the topic, and defend your answer.
2. EC means the end of mass marketing. Do you agree? Surf the Internet and try to bring recent opinions to the discussion.
3. It has been said that "in almost all cases, EC does not change some fundamental rules of banking." Contact a local commercial bank and explore the likelihood that this statement is true. Write a one-page report of your findings.

4. Is the Internet different from other media? Discuss.
5. One of the factors for success in doing business on the Internet is to deliver personalized service. How can this be done?
6. Find a company that chose not to use EC in its business. What factors or problems did it consider in staying away from EC?
7. Explore two industries that can greatly benefit from EC in reducing production cycle time.
8. Give an example of how EC can help a firm reach its customers in a very low-cost fashion.

WEB EXERCISES

1. Check the following Web sites to learn more about these practices in EC:
   a. Let customers help themselves: www.edmunds.com
   b. Nurture customer relationships: www.amazon.com
   c. Streamline customer-focused business processes: www.onsale.com
   d. Target markets of one: www.wsi.com
   e. Build a community of interest: www.cnet.com
2. Discuss the value chain by visiting the FedEx Web site at www.fedex.com. Discuss the company's automated package tracking, virtual ordering, and shipping activities.
3. Visit the following sites off the Internet, analyze them, and report your findings. Include the title of each site with your report:
   a. www.sportszone.com for live interviews, play-by-play calls, and other interesting audio and animated information
   b. www.cai.com for animations from engineering automation
   c. www.paris.org/musees/louvre for exhibits at the Louvre
   d. www.virtualproperties.com for video tours of real estate
4. Wireless terminals will use the Internet to access ATMs and other technologies to transact business. Surf the Internet and write a two-page report on this subject.
5. Internet transactions will alter the traditional form of money as security and privacy solutions allow for extensive use of digital cash. Review the literature and report.
6. Look up Amazon.com on the Internet (www.amazon.com) and report the number and types of EC books available for sale.
7. Interview a business or a technical person who is involved with EC. What has been his or her experience in incorporating the technology into the company's day-to-day operations? What performance criteria are used to judge the success (or failure) of EC in the business? Write a short news release for the college or university newspaper to share your findings.
8. Locate a Web site for each of the following items:
   a. Airline tickets
   b. Personal computers
   c. Clothes
   d. Books
   e. Automobile tools
   f. Road maps
   g. Looking up the address and phone number of a friend

Explain how you looked up the Web site (by subject, URL address, etc.). Write the Web address and company name. Would you go back to the site or, if you had more time, would you look up a better one? Explain.

9. You have decided to upgrade to a new laser printer. Let's say you have decided to purchase a Hewlett Packard inkjet color printer via the Web sites of e-merchants such as Office Depot or Staples. Use the Internet to look up three such Web sites and report on the outlet from which you have chosen to buy the printer. Include your reasoning for the final choice.
10. You are an Internet consultant to a company that wants you to do a one-hour presentation to top management about the importance and potential of the Internet in the company's business. What information do you need before you prepare the presentation? Write a three-page report detailing the content of the speech.

Chapter 2

The Internet and the World Wide Web

Contents

In a Nutshell

Since 1960, when the first business computer appeared, information technology has changed the way commerce is conducted around the globe. The personal computer (PC) revolution, local area networks, electronic data interchange, client/server design, and enterprise resource planning have all had a hand in shaping today's business organization. The past few years have been Internet years, as companies worldwide have embraced a change without equal. It is a change that promises to have more impact and be more lasting than anything that has occurred to date. Technology is setting the pace for how a company does business, how it launches new products and enters a new market, how it deals with suppliers, and how it communicates with customers and others in the new marketplace. Any way you look at it, business will never be the same again.

The primary technology for this transformation is the Internet—a universal global data network that moves closer and closer to the ubiquity of the telephone with each day. What makes the Internet so powerful is that it is more about information and communication than it is about technology. It is a medium and a market. As a result of the Internet, transaction and communication costs have been reduced dramatically. It is virtually unstoppable, forcing all kinds of businesses to reexamine their practices and their futures. This chapter covers the Internet—its functions, contributions, and potential.

THE INTERNET TODAY

For all the directions the Internet has taken and all the companies it has spawned, this technology was first developed as a tool for people (originally scientists) to keep in touch with one another. This is the way many people use the Internet today. The greatest strength of the Internet is its ability to bring together individuals, governments, and businesses, and facilitate the exchange of information among them (see Box 2-1). It allows users to entertain children, buy a house, fill prescriptions, make new friends, find new music, learn a foreign language, get driving directions, keep romance alive, or engage in a political discussion (Rout 2002).

On the personal side, the Internet is giving people power they never had before, and they are enjoying it. Sophisticated Web tools let people assess treatments. For example, the Heart Profiler site (www.americanheart.org) is one of the many sophisticated and personalized tools consumers can use to figure out their risk of serious disease such as heart failure or coronary artery disease, and to make life-and-death treatment decisions once they are diagnosed through their specialist (see Box 2-2). The number of such tools is growing.

Extranet: a shared intranet deployed within the larger business community of an organization, including its vendors, contractors, suppliers, and key customers.

On the business side, the rise of the Internet as the enabler of e-commerce is changing how companies manage their business. Closed-enterprise systems are giving way to open-system environments, where customers connect to the company's Web site, and trading partners connect by an **Extranet** and the Internet.

plug-in: specialized programs.

Web site: a representation of a company's products or services on the Internet.

The Internet is the fastest-growing, most user-friendly, and most commercially popular technology to date. Anyone with a PC connected to the Internet, a browser, and few **plug-ins** can surf the Internet and download text, graphics, and even voice. A **Web site** is a unique representation of a company's products or services on the Internet. It consists of pages connected to one another by links. A page from one Web site can be linked to a page on another Web site halfway

BOX 2-1
People connecting online

When members of a Richmond hiking club gather for day hikes, they usually meet early at a West End parking lot before carpooling to the Blue Ridge. Of the new hikers, more are showing up after first learning about the club and its activities through its relatively simple Web site. "You go on almost any outing and half the people there are new people," club president Randy Wendell said.

New research suggests the trail club's experience is indicative of how many Americans use the Internet today. Nearly 85 percent of those who use the Internet do so to connect with online communities that reflect their hobbies, professions, passions, and beliefs. The Internet is a tool for social engagement.

But there is a dark side to the prevalence of online communities. Church groups and hiking clubs connect online, but so do pedophiles and terrorists. There are hate groups that do the same thing. The Internet is just the mechanism by which people find them.

SOURCE: Excerpted from McCance, McGregor, "Internet Has Unifying Effect," *Richmond Times-Dispatch*, November 4, 2001, Section F, 1.

Screen Capture 2-1

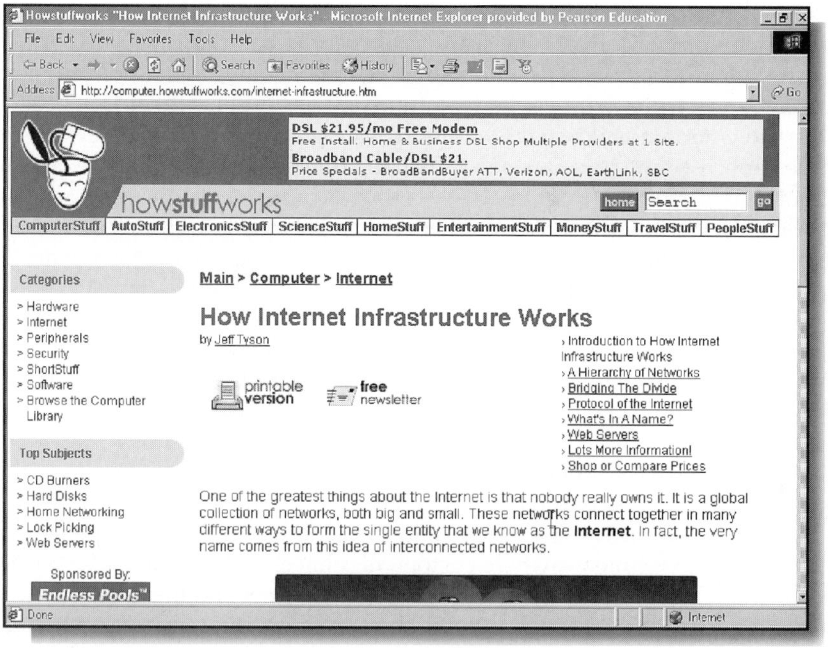

Source: © 2003–2004. How Stuff Works, Inc. All rights reserved.

BOX 2-2
Life-and-death decisions online

Diagnosed with high cholesterol at the age of 25, Arun Menon knew he was a ticking time bomb. His father had died of a heart attack, and his doctor warned a few years ago that he'd probably have one himself by the age of 40 if he didn't start taking medication and watching his health. Mr. Menon, now 37 years old and a Dallas auto-service manager, says he went on the cholesterol-fighting drug Lipitor—but wanted to start taking a more active role in his long-term treatment plan.

Surveying the Web, Mr. Menon came across the American Heart Association's Heart Profiler site, an interactive tool that asked for personal medical data—ranging from age, gender, and race to triglyceride level and blood pressure. After filling out a questionnaire, he got back a personalized list of treatment options, questions to ask his doctor, even clinical trials he might be eligible for.

Mr. Menon says he found "validation" for the treatment plan his doctor recommended but also learned more about other options. Now, he regularly updates his profile on the site so he can monitor his own risks and keep up on the latest research. "It was a real eye opener," he says. "Now when I go see the doctor, I am informed, and really know what he is talking about."

Here are some of the sites for making health decisions online:

Cancer: www.cancerfacts.com. This site provides personalized decisionmaking for 20 kinds of cancer. Licensed to more than 200 health care providers, insurers, and nonprofits. There is also the American Cancer Society (www.cancer.org) and the American Lung Association (www.lungusa.org) that gives information and advice regarding bladder, breast, cervix, kidney, lung, ovarian, pancreas, testicular, and other cancers.

Heart: www.americanheart.org. provides guides on high blood pressure, heart failure, coronary artery disease, and cholesterol. The site includes a professional section for use by doctors.

General: www.mayoclinic.com includes eight useful screens on a wide range of medical areas that include breast cancer, hormone-replacement therapy, and children's middle-ear infections.

SOURCE: Excerpted from Landro, Laura, "Going Online to Make Life-and-Death Decisions," *The Wall Street Journal*, October 10, 2002, D1ff.

around the globe. The whole idea is to make information available anytime, anywhere, to anyone 24 hours a day, 7 days a week (24/7). The sharing and integration of information means improved decision making and efficiency of operations for everyone.

One feature of the Internet is not available on the telephone. The Net allows you to send messages to multiple persons at the same time, much like television or radio broadcasting. It began with message communication, but now it is possible to transmit and receive computer data containing graphics, voice, photos, and even full-motion videos. The part of the Internet that can accomplish these tasks is called the World Wide Web, also known as WWW or the Web.

More than half of American adults now surf the Web. How companies define an "Internet user" is subject to interpretation. Some companies count a 2-year-old as a Net surfer, but others begin at age 16 or 18. The latest reported demographic profile information from Mediamark Research shows that 40 percent of surfers are college graduates, 40 percent have household incomes above $75,000, and 63 percent hold white-collar jobs. The trend, however, is toward a rapid increase in use among lower-income and less-educated demographic groups.

IN THE BEGINNING

Basically, the Internet is the infrastructure that links thousands of networks together. No one knows exactly how many computers are connected to the Internet. It is certain that the number is in the millions and is increasing at a rapid rate. By linking the large computers that manage individual networks, the Internet becomes an information highway that makes the information stored on thousands of computers worldwide available to millions of people everywhere. The Internet transmits messages among servers using satellites, dedicated and fiber-optic cables, microwaves, and other technologies, including the simple phone line used in everyday conversation.

One interesting thing about the Internet is that no one is in charge:No governing body is in control. The Internet backbone through which Internet traffic flows is owned by private organizations. The Internet owes its existence to the Pentagon and the Cold War. The original networked sites were military installations, universities, and business firms with defense department contracts. Fearing that centralizing computer operations under one roof might make systems vulnerable to bomb attack, scientists at the RAND Corporation in 1964 developed the concept of connecting thousands of computers in the same way the human brain is built, so that the loss of a few neurons does not disrupt normal function. The initial goal was to design a network that would maintain the safe transition of data between military computers at select sites through redundant communication routes. The built-in redundancy meant that in case of war, military data transfer would continue uninterrupted. It also meant that no single site would be the vulnerable one. Five years later, two nodes (in this case, computers) were connected to a network on ARPAnet (Advanced Research Projects Agency), which was the sponsor of the research. This was the beginning of what we now call the Internet.

Researchers at Stanford Research Institute, Massachusetts Institute of Technology (MIT), University of California at Los Angeles, and the British National Physical Lab devised a way of bundling information into **packets** that carried the address of the recipient of the packet coming via the network. Such a packet is sent into a so-called "cloud" across the vast array of computers on the network. Each computer checks to see if the information belongs to any of its clients and forwards it to the next computer to which it might belong. Once claimed by the right computer, the packet is opened to reveal the message. This message delivery system is moved by a **protocol.** (This technology is covered in greater detail in Chapter 3.)

packet: a short message, sent through a network.

protocol: a set of rules for ordering and formatting data across a network.

ARPAnet was decommissioned in 1969. In 1984, it split into two interconnected networks: The military part was named MILNET, and the educational part kept the name ARPAnet, which became known as the Internet. Since the mid-1980s, the National Science Foundation (NSF) and other agencies of the U.S. government have controlled access to the Internet. At first, Internet traffic was government related and government subsidized: No ordinary person or company could use the Internet. In fact, the story is told that in 1994, a consultant informed a firm inquiring about the potential uses of the Internet that if it used the Internet for commercial purposes, its officials could be shot by the military. Things changed in April 1995 when the U.S. government relinquished control of the Internet to independent governing bodies, which relaxed entry for almost everyone.

The Internet today offers a variety of services including e-mail, file transfer, interest group membership, multimedia displays, real-time broadcasting, shopping opportunities, access to remote computers, and the quick and easy transmission of information among computers worldwide. Many federal agencies now allow anyone to access timely information. The agencies include the Social Security Administration, Veterans Administration, and the U.S. Postal Service.

The Internet is sustained by interested parties, private and public. It grew of its own accord to meet the expanding needs of its users. The rapid development of the PC and local area networks in the 1980s and the 1990s also contributed to its growth. Part of the Internet is a variety of access protocols, featuring programs that allow users to search for and retrieve information made available by the protocol. More information on protocols is provided in Chapter 3.

Understanding the World Wide Web

In 1990, a programmer by the name of Tim Berners-Lee, who worked in the European Particle Physics Laboratory, wrote a program called a hypertext editor that allowed information highlighted in a document to link to other documents on a computer network with a mouse click. Soon, physicists associated with the lab began to use the hypertext editor and the Internet to send papers to each other. Later, their electronic mail became more elaborate as they built links that crossed the Internet to transmit information and documents. This virtual space became known as the World Wide Web.

hypertext: any text that contains links to other documents.

link: also referred to as hyperlink; connects current document to another location in the same document or to another document on the same host computer.

World Wide Web (WWW, the Web): an organization of files designed around a group of servers on the Internet programmed to handle requests from browser software on users' PCs.

A **hypertext** is a document that contains keywords to connect to other documents. Such keywords, called **links,** are selectable by the designer of the Web site. Hypertext for the Web can be generated with a language called HyperText Markup Language (HTML). With HTML, the designer places tags within the text to do page formatting, italics, bold, font size, and hypertext links. The language is upgraded regularly, and new tags are added with each upgrade. To access a Web page, you do the following.

- Enter an Internet address to retrieve a page.
- Browse through pages and select links to move from one page to another.
- Enter a search statement at a search engine to retrieve pages on the designated topic.

The **World Wide Web**, also known as the **WWW** or the **Web,** is an organization of files designed around a group of Internet servers programmed to handle requests from browser software that resides on users' PCs. The name is based on the fact that the sound, text, animation, pictures, or information that make up a document may come from anywhere in the world. A single document can be perceived to stretch—weblike—throughout the world.

When a document is accessed in Washington or Singapore or Madrid, all of the components are pulled from different computers worldwide and integrated in the document displayed on the user's screen. The request is received by one computer, which interprets its content to see if it has what is requested. If not, the request hops across other computers until the entire document is assembled.

A brief summary of the key events in the creation of the World Wide Web is shown in Table 2-1. Note that when you are on the Web, you are on the Internet, but not the other way around. For example, those sending e-mail are not on the Web unless they are sending e-mail via a Web browser.

Table 2-1
Major events in the creation of the World Wide Web

Date	Event
March 1989	WWW project originated by Timothy Berners-Lee
November 1990	Revised version of the project developed NeXT computer
March 1991	WWW released to a select group for testing
September 1993	The National Center for Supercomputing Applications (NCSA) released first working version of Marc Andreessen's Mosaic for all common platforms
October 1993	More than 500 known HTTP servers in operation
October 1994	More than 10,000 known HTTP servers in operation

architecture: hierarchical physical structure of the Internet.

backbone: the main network of connections that carry Internet traffic.

network access point (NAP): primary connection point for access to the Internet backbone.

TCP/IP: a set of protocols or rules that provide the basis for operating the Internet.

The physical structure, or **architecture,** of the Internet is hierarchical: High-speed **backbones** are at the top, with regional and individual networks at the bottom. The bulk of Internet traffic is fed onto the backbone via **network access points (NAPs),** which are maintained by Sprint and other service providers at strategic locations throughout the United States (see Figure 2-1). This grand network of networks shares a common set of communication protocols called a **TCP/IP** suite, which is covered in Chapter 3.

The Web supports hypertext to access several Internet protocols on a single interface (Cohen 2001). Internet protocols are specific rules that make it possible to conduct "between machine" communications on the Internet. Protocols are covered in greater depth in Chapter 3. The key protocols accessible on the Web are as follow.

- E-mail—The protocol for e-mail is *Simple Mail Transport Protocol,* or SMTP. The major job is to distribute electronic files and messages to one or several e-mail boxes. Also, electronic files can be attached to an e-mail message. Called MIME (Multipurpose Internet Mail Extensions), it enables users, for example, to send a document created in Microsoft Word to another party who retrieves it with the appropriate e-mail program.
- HTTP—HyperText Transfer Protocol makes possible transmission of hypertext over networks. HTTP has been designated as the protocol of the World Wide Web.
- VoIP—Voice over Internet Protocol makes it possible to place a telephone call over the Web.

Webmaster: a person who is skilled in Web design, Web maintenance, and Web upgrade.

The newness of the Web—along with its rapid, phenomenal growth—has been a challenge for corporations that want to create a presence on the Internet. They have found it difficult and too costly to invest employees' time in doing professional Web design work. The demand has created a new industry specializing in Web design and Web mastering. Because of the increasing number of Web sites, **Webmaster** is a lucrative new career.

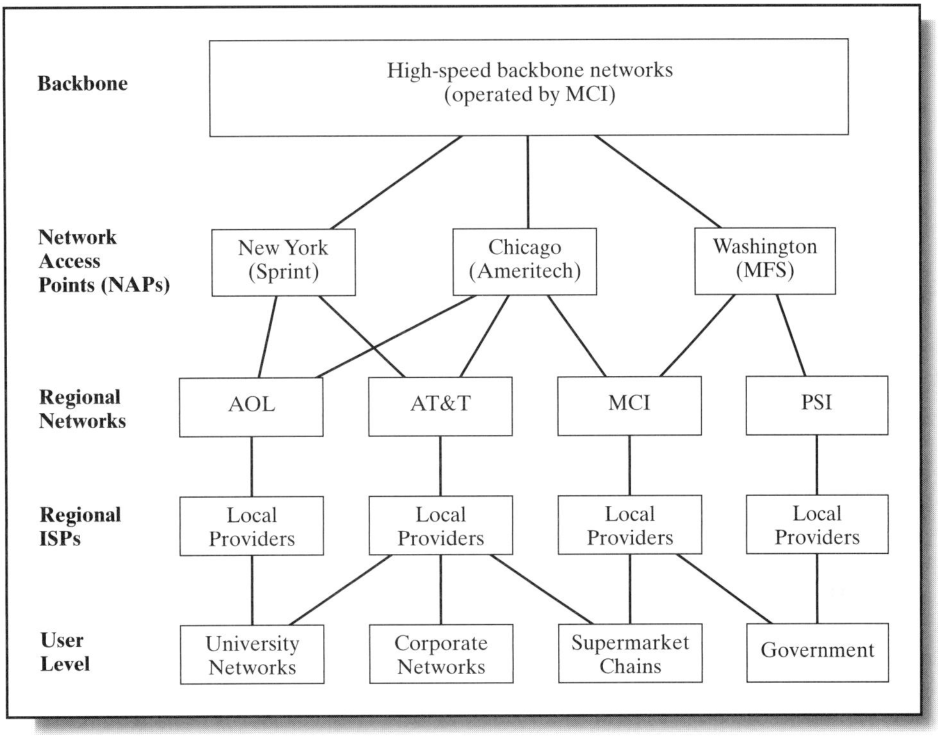

Figure 2-1
General Internet network architecture

How to Search the Web

The Web has been viewed as "the world's largest library—without a librarian" (www.onenw.org/bin/page.cfm?pageid=53). Finding what you need on the Internet is not difficult and can be fun. Searching has become extremely popular. It also can be a problem depending on the traffic to the particular site, the search engine handling the traffic, the bandwidth, and so on.

The Internet contains thousands of Web sites dedicated to tens of thousands of topics. Knowing how to search and what search engines are the most productive can make the difference between searching with profitability or simply wasting time into endless loops and dead ends. The sites are not always accurate. Therefore, it is a good idea to know how to evaluate Web sites.

The Browser

To access the Web, you need a Web browser. A *browser* is a piece of software that allows users to navigate the Web. There are two types of browsers.

- **Text**- only mode such as Lynx. You navigate the Web by highlighting emphasized words on the screen with the arrow up and down keys and pressing the forward arrow (or Enter) key to follow the link. For more information, see "Guide to Using Lynx" (http://library.albany.edu/internet/www.html).

- **Graphic** mode involves a graphical software program that retrieves text, audio, and video. Examples are Netscape Navigator and Internet Explorer. You navigate the Web by pointing and clicking with a mouse on highlighted words and graphics. Navigator is available for downloading on Netscape's Web site, http://home.netscape.com. Microsoft's Internet Explorer is downloaded from Microsoft's Web site, www.microsoft.com.

Plug-Ins

Software programs are configured to a Web browser to improve its capabilities. For example, when a browser senses a sound, an image, or a video file, it passes the data to other programs, called plug-ins, to run or display the file. Working together with plug-ins, browsers today offer seamless multimedia experience. Many plug-ins are available on the Internet free of charge.

A popular plug-in on the Web is the Adobe Acrobat Reader. This program allows the user to view documents created in Adobe's Portable Document Format (PDF). When the Acrobat Reader is configured to your browser, the program will display the requested file when you click on a hyperlinked file name with the suffix .pdf. Once configured to your browser, a plug-in will become active automatically when you choose to access a file type that it uses.

Microsoft developed software, called **Active X,** which makes plug-ins unnecessary. The software makes it possible to embed animated objects and data on Web pages. For example, one can use Active X to view the three-dimensional **Virtual Reality Modeling Language (VRML)** world in a Web browser without a VRML plug-in. Being a Microsoft product, Active X works best with Microsoft's Internet Explorer browser.

Multimedia

Since 1999, the Web has become a broadcast screen. It is now common to use the Web to listen to audio and watch video—prerecorded or live off the Internet. Even the nightly television news can be watched on one's PC monitor. The old problem of slow download time is answered by a multimedia capability, called **streaming media.** With this technology, audio or video can be played as they are downloaded (streaming) into your computer. **Buffering** is used to minimize the wait time between downloading and actual viewing of the material on the monitor. Netscape Communicator includes a Cosmo viewer for experiencing a three-dimensional world.

The **Realplayer** and **Windows Media Player** are alternative options for the broadcast of real-time (live) events. Beyond that, **shockwave** is multimedia software that allows for an entire multimedia display of audio, graphics, animation, and sound. This means that sound files containing music also can be heard on the Web with the appropriate plug-ins.

A unique aspect of the multimedia experience on the Web is **Live Cam.** This software is essentially a video camera that digitizes images

Active X: a Microsoft program that embeds animated objects and data on Web pages.

Virtual Reality Modeling Language (VRML): a Microsoft product that allows three-dimensional view of objects in a Web browser.

streaming media: audio or video that begin to play as it downloads (streaming)—done through buffering.

buffering: a PC features that serves to minimize the wait time between downloading and actual viewing of the material on the monitor.

Realplayer: an alternative option or program for broadcast of real-time (live) events via Microsoft's Windows operating system.

Windows Media Player: an alternative option or program for broadcast of real-time (live) events via Microsoft's Windows operating system.

shockwave: multimedia software that allows for an entire multimedia display of audio, graphics, animation, and sound.

Live Cam: software that is essentially a video camera that digitizes images and transmits them in real time to a Web server.

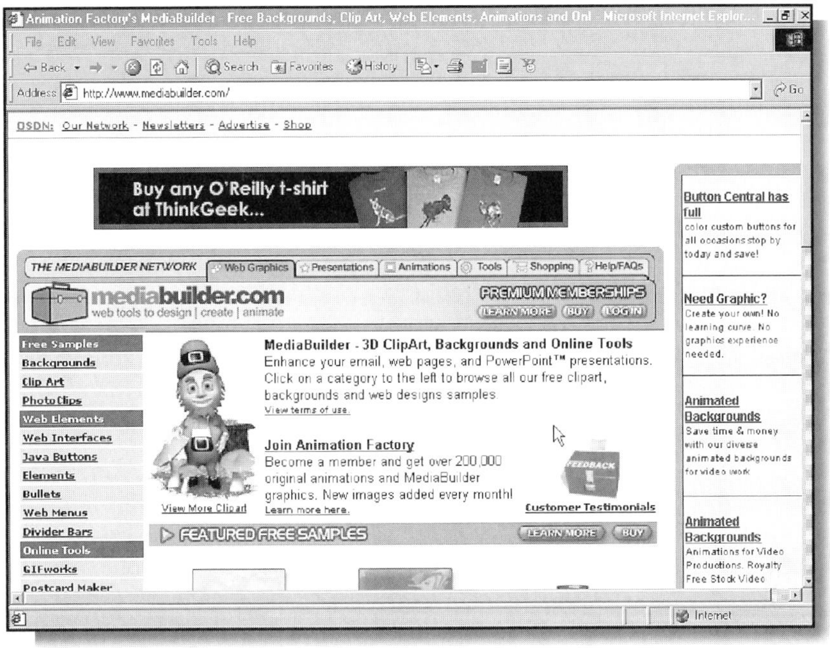

Screen Capture 2-2

Source: Used with permission of the Animation Factory.com.

and transmits them in real time to a Web server. From there, the video can be downloaded off any PC connected to the server.

chat program: a facility that makes it convenient for people to "talk" to each other in real-time by typing messages and receiving a response.

Finally, in terms of real-time collaborative communication, **chat programs** make it convenient for people to "talk" to each other in real time by typing messages and receiving responses. An example of such software is America Online's Instant Messenger.

The Search Process

search engine: a Web site or a database and the tools to search it.

A search process begins with a **search engine.** A search engine is a Web site or a database, along with the tools to generate that database and search its contents for "keywords" that describe what you're looking for. The collection part of a search engine (also known as automated robots like Wanderer, Spider, Harvest, and Pursuit) roams Internet sites; retrieves messages; and sorts, indexes, and creates a database from them. Web robots keep a list of Web pages to index and then downloads them one by one. On a well-connected Web, a robot can index every page it can read.

The two main elements of Web research are indexes and search engines. Both are useful, depending on the goal of the search. Searching by index can help a writer who has a general topic but does not yet have a specific focus within the topic. An **index** can help a searcher acquire general information or gain a feel for the general topic.

index: a database that stores a copy of each Web page gathered by the spider.

Steps to follow, for example, could be:

- Go to Google (an index).
- Think of a topic that is of interest (e.g., "universities").
- Follow it through specific type or level (e.g., "private universities," "private small universities," "private small Virginia universities").

An index could be hierarchical or alphabetical. Search engines have some type of index attached to them. Examples are Yahoo!, Google, and InfoSeek. Hierarchical indexing leads from general to specific topics, and alphabetical indexing contains sources with a focus on a specific topic or area of concern. A search engine sends inquiries to Web sites without evaluating them. The results found by various search engines differ from one another. Because search engines maintain tens of thousands of sites, narrowing your topic is necessary to get the kind of information you need. Otherwise, you could end up with page after page set of sources, which is costly in time and timeliness.

In addition to an index, there are two other components of a Web search engine.

- **Spider** is program that roams the Web from link to link, identifying and scanning pages. The index contains a copy of each Web page gathered by the spider.
- **Software** unique to a search engine allows users to query the index and returns results in relevancy-ranked order (alphabetical).

second-generation search engine: a search engine that organizes search results by peer ranking, concept, domain, or site rather than by relevancy. Also called "off the page" information to determine the order of the search results.

first-generation search engine: a search engine that returns results in a schematic order. It constructs a term relevancy rating of each hit and presents search results in this order. Also called "on the page" ranking.

spider: a software tool that prowls the Internet looking for new sites where information is likely to reside.

portal: a location on the Web that acts as a launching point for searching for and retrieving information.

It is important to remember that spider cannot tell whether a resource is good or bad, current or outdated, inaccurate or incomplete. It is up to you to evaluate each resource and decide how relevant it is to your research. A new, **second-generation search engine** technology orders search results by concept, keyword, links, site, domain, or level of popularity. These search engines are more reliable in the ranking of results. A Web page becomes highly ranked if it is linked to other highly ranked pages. For example, Google derives its results from the behavior and judgment of millions of Web users. In contrast, with **first-generation search engines,** the engine merely searches its index and generates a page with links to resources that contain your terms, and the results are presented in term-ranked order. A checklist of Internet research tips is summarized in Figure 2-2.

Many of the newer search engines differentiate themselves by providing a "best-of-breed" search offering, which adds ease-of-use features to the search process, making it easier for users to surf the Internet. Some search engines use a **spider.** The quality of a search site today, however, depends on the number of sites to which it is linked. Search engines such as Yahoo!, Lycos, Excite, and others have gone beyond simple search capabilities, adding everything from free e-mail to games and chat rooms. Their goal is to become a **portal,** or an all-purpose home base for Web users. How easy it is to surf the Net has a lot to do with the quality and attractiveness of the Web site.

Search engines are about to get smarter yet. Some sites are adding different languages to draw in more users worldwide. Others have enhanced conversational language to make it easier for novice surfers to wade through the ever-growing volume of information online. It is

1. Evaluate everything on the Internet for its appropriateness for research use.
2. Try out a handful of sites when researching a topic on the Internet. Do not rely on only one site or one type of site.
3. When searching for a proper name, capitalize the first letter of each word.
4. When searching for several names that are linked together, use a comma to separate them (e.g., George Bush, President).
5. Use quotation marks when doing a phrase search (e.g., "Congressional E-Mail Addresses"). If you leave out the quotation marks, the engine will search for all documents with the word *congressional,* all documents with the word *e-mail,* and all documents with the word *address*. You will get tens of thousands of hits. With the quotation marks, you will get only documents with those three words exactly as you have placed them.
6. Use hyphens when searching for words that must appear within one word of each other (e.g., cable-networks). The words can otherwise have numerous connotations.
7. Use brackets to find words that appear within 100 words of each other, (e.g., bus safety).
8. Use a plus sign to find two or more words that must be in the documents together (e.g., bus schedule +SEPTA. No space should be placed between the + sign and the second word).
9. If you have a multiple-term search, decide on the logical relationship between them. For example, a search about the relationship between Bush and terrorism would be formulated as: +bush +terrorism on many Web search engines in order for AND logic to apply.
10. If you want images, place a colon between the word *image* and the image topic name (e.g., image:comet).
11. Use an asterisk to find all combinations of a word or word fragment (e.g., edu*). This will yield pages containing *education, educator,* etc.
12. To find URLs, use *url:* and the address fragment (e.g., url:mciu.kl2). This will match pages with the words *mciu* and *kl2* together in the URL.
13. Keep in mind that phrases are strings of words that are adjacent in a document.
14. Take advantage of capitalization if the search engine is case sensitive.
15. Check your spelling. You'd be surprised how important correct spelling is.
16. Work with different search engines, as no two engines work from the same index.
17. If you are unhappy with the results, repeat the search using alternative terms.

Figure 2-2
Checklist of Internet research tips

Source: Excerpted from http://phoenix.liunet.edu/~jberger/websearch.html. Accessed April 2003. See also Cohen, Laura, "Conducting Research on the Internet." http://library.albany.edu/internet/research.html (July 2002, 1–14). Accessed April 2003.

predicted that before too long, search engines literally will converse with the surfers, speak their language, and produce the desired information within seconds. On the drawing board is "thinking in pictures" as an alternative way to search the Web. When you type a search phrase into www.kartoo.com, you face a screen dominated by a flowchart. The chart is filled with words related to the search phrase. You can simply click on the term(s) to add them to your phrase and focus your search. Such an approach is designed to appeal to creative learners and children (Shmukler 2002, R6).

To illustrate the search process, take the author's first-choice search engine—Google. Google is a relative newcomer to the Internet but quickly captured the preference of surfers and researchers alike. One of the unique features of this search engine is its ability to search for all the words you type in. You don't need to customize the entry by + or – or place words in quotes, and so on. For example, to search for Civil Liberty Union, you'd search for "Civil Liberty Union" rather than Civil Liberty Union. Every phrase that matches the quote is listed rather than listing the individual words "Civil" "Liberty" "Union."

In addition, Google allows you to exclude certain terms from web searches by adding a minus sign before the word to be deleted (–). For example, to find pages that present Professor Allen's publications but not Booz-Allen Consulting, try not searching for Booz-Allen Consulting. For more tips on how to search on Google, go to Google's online help pages.

For an online merchant, it is important to know some basic facts.

1. **People look up Web sites with search engines.** A frequently visited Web site is one that appears on several search engines. Other sources include printed media, Web site addresses on business cards, and inserts in customers' monthly statements. Make sure that search engines and other sites bring up your site in the top 10 or so sites. As will be explained later in the text, you need to embed many meta-tags in the home page. A meta-tag is a word that is similar to your company product, service, or mission. For example, a commercial bank's Web site would use meta-tags such as "commercial bank," "financial institution," or "loan" so that Web surfers can access your bank by a number of synonyms—meta-tags. To register a Web site on search engines, look up- www.selfpromotion.com, which is a free registration site. Follow the instructions and, in few weeks, the facility will submit your site to dozens of search engines. Different search engines take their time to load your site, depending on the volume of new sites, staff limitations, and other considerations. After all is done, the site will ask you for a donation.

bookmarking: action taken on a facility of a Web browser that allows you to save URL addresses for future quick access and use.

2. **People usually use bookmarks to visit their favorite Web sites. Bookmarking,** or saving URL addresses for future use, is one of three methods used by surfers to search. The other two are entering the URL address or entering a subject on the search engine homepage. When advertising a Web site, users or customers should be encouraged to bookmark the site. It is easy, quick, and the most convenient way of getting the visitor to make a habit of visiting a Web site.
3. **A Web site must be quick and current.** Study after study has shown that more than two thirds of visitors cite Internet speed as a major problem. Users simply click away if the information they seek is not displayed on the screen within a few seconds. Slow speed, broken links, and difficulty in finding a given site do not promote loyalty. The trick is to keep a Web site simple and easy to maintain. It is also good to know that because Web sites are set up in a single physical location, performance is limited by the speed of that single connection. It is up to the Internet Service Provider to expand its Internet network and hardware to accommodate more data performance and minimize latency (delay).
4. **A Web site should address the privacy and navigation concerns of the user.** Various studies have shown that censorship is the leading concern of Internet users, followed by privacy concerns. Ease of navigation is an added concern for Web traffic. For a commercial Web site to build customer loyalty, it is important to protect user information and ensure ease of use of the Web site at all times, regardless of the amount of traffic.

5. **The "last mile" problem.** Anyone who uses a 56-kbps modem knows the so-called "last mile" bottleneck. A modem tapping into the Internet via a narrowband connection is bound to cause frustratingly slow performance. Connecting to DSL line or high-speed line would help, but as more and more people go that route, congestion is bound to happen.
6. **People are reluctant to pay to surf a Web site.** Given the increasing cost of building and maintaining Web storefronts, the majority of Web surfers say they would not pay to surf a Web site. Very few sites that began to charge have stayed in business. This is similar to the early days of the 1970s, when banks started charging customers for withdrawing through the ATM (automated teller machine). Today, most banks offer this service free of charge with minimum balances in checking or savings accounts. Foreign customers (customers from other banks), however, continue to be charged a fee for using ATMs that are not their bank's machine. On the Web, about the only exceptions to the no-pay rule are specialized services such as online stock market quotations, adult-oriented material, and the like. Charges also are associated with retrieval of full text from many research sites.

In contrast, for a surfer, knowing where to look, how to phrase a search term, and how to make use of sites returned by the search engine are what makes the difference between successful surfing and utter failure. As exemplified in Box 2-3, each factor should be considered.

BOX 2-3
Search know-how is a way of e-life

Knowing where to look in the first place, how to phrase a search term, and how to weed through sites returned by the search engine are techniques that consumers learn over time.

Assignment: Hawaiian Shirt. My friend Alesia Powell, 38, has never surfed waves in her life, and she goes out of her way not to go to stores. So, she seemed the perfect person to assign the task of finding a Hawaiian shirt. It's not something that she has ever done or ever would do. Alesia started at Yahoo!, typing in "Hawaiian shirt." Why there? "Yahoo! was easier and offered a lot more specific choices," she said. "I always think of Excite afterwards, and I can never remember the name of Larcos, or is it Lycos?" Her search returned 10 entries, listed under "Business and Economy. Companies Apparel. Specialty. Hawaiian." She chose the third one on the list: "Big Kahuna Hawaiian Shirts" (www.aloha-bigkahuna.com/bkframe.html).

Why? The name jumped out at me," she said. "I associated it with Hawaiian shirts, although the listing above it was for a company called Aloha, and that's very Hawaiian, I guess. Big Kahuna just looked interesting to me."

The site, however, proved to be not as interesting as its name. Being a high-end fabric kind of person, Alesia clicked on one of five areas offered on the site—a page pertaining to silk shirts. "These don't look like the classic shirt," she said. "But then again, I hate Hawaiian shirts."

Interesting to note: Using "Hawaiian shirts," plural, turned up a different set of shops from "Hawaiian shirt," singular. Though it didn't happen in this case, nuances in keywords often trip up Web surfers. Our search experts added, "The more tenured online users have a better sense of how to construct the right keyword searches."

Lesson learned: Watch your search terms. Try a plural if singular does not yield what you're looking for.

SOURCE: Napoli, Lisa, "Better Ways to Search Than Typing 'Needle + Haystack,'" *The New York Times*, March 28, 2000, 36.

INTERNET SERVICE PROVIDERS

To link the rapidly growing commercial Internet landscape, the Internet Service Provider (ISP) industry was born in the mid-1990s. As we discuss in detail in Chapter 7, the ISP industry offers a variety of services including:

1. Linking consumers and businesses to the Internet (e.g., America Online, Microsoft Network, CompuServe).
2. Monitoring and maintaining customers' Web sites.
3. Network management and system integration.
4. Backbone access services for other ISPs like PSI and UUNET.
5. Payment systems for online purchases.

Internet Service Provider (ISP): a company that links users to the Internet for a fee.

As public demand for access to the Internet surged, ISPs began to add more lines and better access to accommodate the traffic. Initially, the cost for Internet access often exceeded $1,000 per month, but with new ISP arrivals and competition, prices plummeted. Many of today's ISPs offer unlimited access for as low as $5 per month. Many local governments are funding the use of the Internet because of its political, educational, and commercial benefits. Once on the Internet, no additional charges are accrued. You can contact anyone, anywhere, anytime for that monthly fee. The exceptions are Web sites that charge a membership fee or a fee for access to privileged information.

Almost everything one needs on the Internet is free. The following are among the free services.

Hotlists that tell the user what is popular and what is not.
Comics that focus on entertainment events.
Software archives that list the latest free software available.
Weather services that provide free weather forecasts anywhere in the world.
Magazines and broadcasting stations that constantly update the news.
Searchers that help locate items or subjects on the Internet.
Dictionaries that include thesauruses and "fact" books on almost all subjects.
Government services that publicize what is available from them.

The problem for some ISPs is sudden growth without advance planning to accommodate that growth. As a result, response time slows down, triggering customer complaints. The challenge is to maintain profitability and meet or beat the competition, while maintaining customer satisfaction. To do all this well requires professional management, a highly skilled technical staff, and a healthy budget to bring the technology in line with the voracious appetite of today's consumer. The trick is to ensure a balance between creativity and control and between managing growth and a stable technical infrastructure.

Stability and Reliability of the Web

No one single agency or company owns the Internet. Each company on the Internet owns its own network. The links between these companies and the Internet are owned by telephone companies and ISPs. The organization that coordinates Internet functions is the Internet Society. It does not operate any of the thousands of networks that make up the Internet but works with ISPs by providing information to prospective users. This association's Internet Architecture Board consists of work groups that focus on TCP/IP and other protocols. Various committees also handle technical issues and day-to-day operational aspects of the Internet.

The Web itself, because it resides everywhere and nowhere at the same time, simply cannot cease functioning by itself. Also, because it is based on the Internet, its stability is as good as that of the Internet, which is fairly good so far. The Internet is designed to be indefinitely extendable. Reliability depends primarily on the quality of service providers' equipment. Inadequate phone lines, bandwidth, or mediocre computers can affect the reliability of the overall service.

Unique Benefits of the Internet

The Internet is the enabler of e-commerce, just as the highway is the enabler for the automobile. Managers use it to glean intelligence about rivals, monitor sales, and so on. At Cisco Systems, for example, the company's chief executive required executives from various departments to demonstrate how they would use the Web. Cisco and other companies like Dell Computers and Microsoft's Expedia Travel Service use Internet technology in their businesses: Dell, for example, sells more than $6 million worth of computers a day from its Web site, and Expedia's service generates more than $16 million a month from its Web site.

Among the uses and advantages of the Internet today are the following.

Marketing and Selling Products and Services

The "buy and sell" aspect of Internet commerce has attracted more media attention than any other networked activity to date. Thousands of e-corporations have sold more than $1 million each in 2000 (Brahma, p. 31). The highest sales volume was in business-to-business commerce, and it is growing. The next-highest sales were to government agencies, followed by colleges and universities. In terms of revenue, business-to-consumer ranks fourth in Internet revenue.

More than 100,000 companies, large and small, have opened virtual storefronts on the World Wide Web. Unfortunately, more than two thirds continue to lose money due to poor planning, lack of good customer support, inefficient fulfillment of orders, and the like.

When it comes to advertising and reaching customers quickly and cheaply, the Internet is "marketing heaven." You can reach anyone, anywhere without paying extra for distance or duration. The Internet is host to thousands of electronic publications that provide promotional opportunities for any business. Web sites attract millions of readers on a daily basis. Companies use the Internet to send electronic mass mailings to customers and prospects. They also send surveys to selected customers, notices about special sales, and the like. In addition electronic media are much easier to update.

Doing Business Fast

E-selling is conducted in minutes rather than hours or days, compared to waiting on the phone to place an order or filling out a form for mailing. This speed compresses business processes and promotes the growth of a customer base.

Gathering Opinions and Trying Out New Ideas

The Internet is an ideal place for trying out new ideas at low cost. Interactive surveys provide quick feedback. Opinions can be gathered from just about anywhere. Many online opinion polls provide real-time statistics to the user after a computer package analyzes the user's response in real time.

Companies unsure about going all out to do business on the Internet can start small by designing a "who we are" Web site to gain online experience and exposure. The site can be used for sales promotions and to build customer awareness of the company's people, products, and services.

Leveling the Playing Field

When a company advertises its products or services on the Internet, it is on equal footing with larger companies. The nice feature about the Internet is that it allows your business to appear alongside big-name companies. Here is a case in point: Caribbean Tour wanted to put its business on the Internet but did not have much money to spend. It designed a basic Web site, just to have a presence, and spent only $800 per month to gain experience with online commerce. The Web site broke even after 2 years.

Even mere presence is a benign way of expanding a business and creating new selling opportunities to a unique type of customer who otherwise would have gone to the competition. In an interview session with a client, here is what one merchant said about her experience in Web commerce: "The Internet is a great equalizer. It makes me feel as big as the guy next door. I might still be small, but it encourages me to be very good at what we do in the business that we're in" (D'Antoni, April 3, 2000).

Promoting a Paper-Free Environment

In addition to cutting down on the paper used for catalogs and promotional material, company memos, employee handbooks, and reports can be placed on the company's Intranet and retrieved or circulated electronically anytime by authorized personnel. These steps contribute to a paper-free environment.

Providing a Superior Customer Service and Support Resource

Most Web sites generate customer feedback in the way of comments, suggestions, and complaints. The challenge for the online merchant is to have adequate staff to address this feedback in a timely fashion. In late 1999, Amazon.com dismissed a senior customer service representative for not meeting the quota of answering 12 e-mail customer messages per hour. E-businesses are under increasing pressure to provide prompt customer service and support.

A common support resource is the **Frequently Asked Questions (FAQ)** list. An FAQ list eliminates having staff answer the same questions over and over again. If a new question comes up, the answer is added to the list. Using e-mail to handle customer support also frees company personnel from being tied to a telephone.

frequently asked questions (FAQs): answers to repeatedly asked questions that a business places in a simple list on the Web site so users can find solutions anytime.

Efficiency and Unequaled Cost-Effectiveness

Major corporations are known for spending hundreds of millions of dollars on sales promotion. By contrast, the cost of establishing and maintaining even a sophisticated Web site for that purpose is affordable. For many niche products and services, the Web is the only cost-effective sales method available. A commercial Web site also can provide addresses, directions, online order tracking, and the like, reducing phone calls, phone interruptions, and staff time. From a marketing view, the Web site provides user information more quickly, in a more timely fashion, and at the convenience of the user, regardless of location or distance.

Supporting Managerial Functions, Spreading Ideas, Ease of Technical Support

The traditional managerial functions of planning, organizing, directing, and controlling require managers to collect, evaluate, and distribute management information, especially in organizations with branches worldwide. The Internet sends business information through a company's networks and across networks around the globe. E-mail is a convenient tool for managers to reach employees, bosses, customers, and suppliers quickly and at no charge.

The Internet has spawned discussion groups, chat rooms, and online interactive sessions in which technical and managerial staff evaluate products and processes, and arrive at value-added decisions that result in lower costs and increased performance.

Better technical support is one of the key benefits of linking to the Internet. IBM, for example, offers customer and technical support, fixes bugs, and handles software upgrades on the Internet. Thousands of free software programs are available for anyone to download.

Market research firms are a natural for the Web. Credit bureaus, lawyers, private detectives, accountants, baby-sitters, and teachers are all examples of people or agencies that use the Internet for scheduling or advertising their services. The Internet continues to deliver thousands of databases of research data, ranging from topics such as medicine, vehicles, and food preparation, to suggestions for the ideal baby diaper, to hundreds of research and development (R&D) discussion groups. For thousands of research journals, automated searches through current and back issues are available in minutes rather than the days and weeks it once took to find the information in a brick-and-mortar library. White papers that research centers place on their Web sites provide current information about the latest developments in various fields.

Company research is no different. Companies use the Internet to seek information about customer tastes and preferences, to profile a customer base for a new product, or to test a new concept to see if it is worth developing. All of this can be done in a matter of days rather than the months it once took to get the same results.

Triggering New Businesses

Given the worldwide networking of business and commerce, mere presence is bound to trigger one type of business activity or another. This includes business-to-business, business-to-government agencies at all levels, business-to-colleges and universities, as well as business-to-consumers. For example, a tiny commercial filter maker in Lynchburg, Virginia, landed a $6 million contract with the government of Saudi Arabia from the Internet.

Internet Use Today: A Snapshot

The *Wall Street Journal* reported survey results based on key questions Internet users were asked about their preferences, expectations, popular products, and so on. Of the products reported, information products such as books and CDs were highly rated. Technical products such as software and PC peripherals also were highly ranked. Purchases of other products such as travel and hotel reservations appeared to be on the rise. Overall, the Internet is truly moving from novelty to necessity. More and more people are relying on it for shopping, information, logistics, marketing, and entertainment.

Providing Web Services

Web services are essentially business services, composed of standards that allow different platforms, operating systems, and languages to exchange information or carry out a business process together. They also make it easier for people to construct and integrate applications via the Web. Adopting Web services is expected to improve the way a company conducts transactions with trading partners (e.g., shipping, ordering supplies, billing, etc.) electronically and the way information moves through the supply chain (Violino 2003).

Business processes are becoming increasingly complex, global, and intertwined between and among different organizations. Pressure to reduce costs drive the increasing need for better information and higher productivity round the clock. Further, globalization has increased competition, which prompted shorter time-to-market. Web services make it possible for an organization to instantly connect and interoperate with divisions, partners, customers, and suppliers 24/7 year round.

Standing in the way of interoperability are inconsistent platforms and different languages and Internet protocols. Web services overcome these barriers and renders information to business-to-business (B2B), a customer service portal or a logistics provider's wireless device (Dunn 2003). They reduce cycle times and managerial costs by providing procurement/order tracking, invoice/billing, receiving, and payment in the most efficient way possible. They also promise improved collaboration with customers, suppliers, partners, and authorized outsiders.

The Web services framework is a process and a select set of protocols for connecting to software exposed as services over the Web (Coyle 2003, p. 39). The general framework is shown in Figure 2-3. The major aspects to Web services are:

- A service provider who provides an interface for software that can perform specified tasks.

Figure 2-3
Web services framework

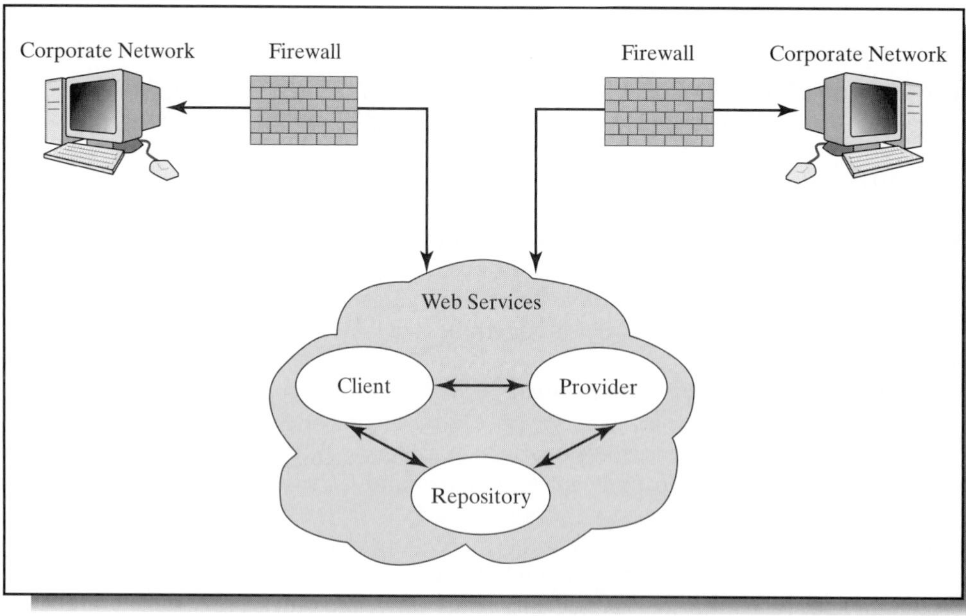

- A client who invokes a software service to provide a business solution or service.
- A repository that manages the service. Service providers place their services with the repository. Clients request the services placed in the repository by the service provider.

It should be noted that Web services is more about successful business strategy than about technology. It is proving to be a great implementer to assure effective strategy. The focus is on collaboration, cooperation, and coordination among people, partners, and their ultimate success (Dunn 2003).

LIMITATIONS

Like any system with unique benefits, the Internet and the World Wide Web also have unique limitations. The following discussion highlights the importance of continuing to work on these limitations in the interest of advancing use of the Internet in general and the Web in particular.

Security and Privacy

Key questions that are brought up continually by online consumers are: "How do I know I am paying for a product on a secure line? How do I know the Web site assures me privacy for the product I am buying?" Various devices have been embedded into Web storefronts to ensure security. (For a full discussion of Internet security, see Chapter 13.) For a discussion about a political hole in Web security, see Box 2-4.

In terms of privacy, according to a study of major Web sites by the Federal Trade Commission (FTC), only 20 percent met FTC standards for protecting consumer privacy, but the study also found a 90 percent compliance rate by Internet companies for posting their privacy policies. (Simpson, May 11, 2000). The major FTC Fair Information principles are shown in Box 2-5.

BOX 2-4
Saddam's mail

I don't know for sure, but I suspect that neither Saddam nor President George W. Bush checks his e-mail as often as you or I do. But it turns out that Saddam's e-mail folder was hacked last month by Brian McWilliams, a journalist who writes about the Internet, privacy, and computer security.

On his first try, McWilliams said, he correctly guessed Saddam's user name and password (www.uruklink.net/iraq/epage1.htm) (no longer active, since the end of the war with Iraq.). As a result, we know a fair amount about the kind of mail that people have been sending to the top guy in Baghdad. McWilliams reported that Saddam's inbox contained several offers from companies, including some in the United States, to sell technology that they claimed would be militarily useful.

Near the top of the first screenful was a message, which appeared to be an offer from a company in California to come to Iraq and meet with Saddam and discuss importing the California company's technology. I went to their Web site, and they make a wireless technology that they claim has some military purposes.

Besides the offers to do business, McWilliams said Saddam's inbox also contained some spam (though none, he said, offering "mortgages or penis enlargement") and political opinions.

SOURCE: Excerpted from Dembart, Lee, "Saddam's Mail," *International Herald Tribune*, November 4, 2002, 1–2.

BOX 2-5
E-commerce trends: FTC finds Web sites fail to guard privacy

While overall the industry showed little improvement in meeting the FTC's privacy principles, much of that is based upon the failure of sites to give consumers access to information that is collected about them. That is one of the few recommended privacy practices that haven't gained acceptance by major e-commerce companies, in part because it is difficult to implement. The other factors on which sites are graded are the posting of privacy policies, the freedom of consumers to limit use of their personal data, and the secure handling of such information.

The major FTC "Fair Information" Principles are:

1. Notice/Awareness. Does the site post a privacy policy?
2. Choice/Consent. Can consumers control how their information is used?
3. Access/Participation. Can consumers view and correct information collected about them?
4. Security/Integrity. Is the information safe from theft or "hacking?"

In addition, the survey this year for the first time judged sites on "qualitative" factors, such as the ease with which a consumer can locate a privacy policy. Those results are considerably more subjective. "The FTC has a real tough call." While widespread industry deficiencies are increasingly difficult to ignore, many struggling e-commerce sites could find it difficult to comply with tough new rules. "Investors are looking for clear and quicker moves toward profitability, and data-privacy rules potentially limit the ability of companies to drive revenues via either personalized services or higher ad rates."

SOURCE: Excerpted from Simpson, Glenn R., "FTC Finds Web Sites Fail to Guard Privacy," *The Wall Street Journal,* May 11, 2000, B12.

Fakes and Forgeries

The availability of the Internet has spawned the online sale of fake passports, Social Security cards, driver's licenses, college diplomas, birth certificates, and even IDs for police officers and FBI agents. Some of them are so authentic looking that it takes a real expert to detect the forgery. This new and growing Internet problem accounts for more than 30 percent of all fake ID documents in the United States (see Associated Press, May 20, 2000).

There are three levels of fake-ID procurement: Some Web sites sell authentic-looking documents in the customer's name. Others sell templates that allow customers to make their own phony documents. The third level is the do-it-yourself counterfeiter. Thomas W. Seitz, who used the phony documents to get car loans, currently is serving a 3-year state prison term for theft by deception and forgery (Associated Press, May 20, 2000).

Cyberterrorism

The September 11, 2001, terrorist attacks struck fear in the heart of America and made us rethink our safety, security, and well-being. The attacks of Al-Qaeda inspired a newfound sense of vulnerability, demonstrating that terrorists of all types may be knocking on our door and threatening us with unforeseen intelligence and zeal.

A new generation of Al-Qaeda members and of other terrorist organizations—foreign and domestic—is growing up with technology. They have identified cyberspace as an invaluable tool for economic growth, promotion of civil liberties, and a tool to improve everyday life. They also have looked at cyberspace as a forum for expressing malcontent against governments, businesses, and people, potentially in devastatingly harmful ways. To protect against attacks, intrusion detection systems, firewalls, and encryption methods may provide adequate shields to stymie terrorist endeavors. These tools are covered in detail later in the text.

Hackers, worms, Trojan horses, viruses, and zombies are weapons of terror to the security and functioning of Web sites. (For definitions of these and other Internet terms, see the section entitled The Language of the Internet, later in the chapter.) Viruses are the best-known malicious software. These programs secretly attach themselves to other programs, then infect and reproduce in a manner similar to biological viruses.

Because hackers (those who access others' computer systems illegally) continue to threaten the integrity of Internet files and transactions, hacking schools that teach students how to hack or break into software to protect their own computer systems and Web sites have begun to appear in various cities. In one typical 4-day seminar, students (usually network administrators) pay $3,500 to learn the tricks of the trade. They are provided with hacking tools that are available over the Internet for free (e.g., an information-gathering tool, Sam Spade, and a port-scanning tool, SuperScan, which sends queries to Internet servers to check their security status). At the completion of the course, they sign an affidavit that they will use their experience appropriately (Nelson, March 27, 2000).

Worse than hackers and viruses are Web sites seen as terrorist aids. Since the tragic events of September 11, 2001, audits have found that many Web sites represent a gold mine for potential attackers. Descriptions of physical locations of backup facilities; the number of people working at specific facilities; the type and number of wired and wireless networks operating in a specific division; and specifications of a company's elevator systems, patterns of traffic, photographs, floor plans, and virtual tour information are all

Screen Capture 2-3

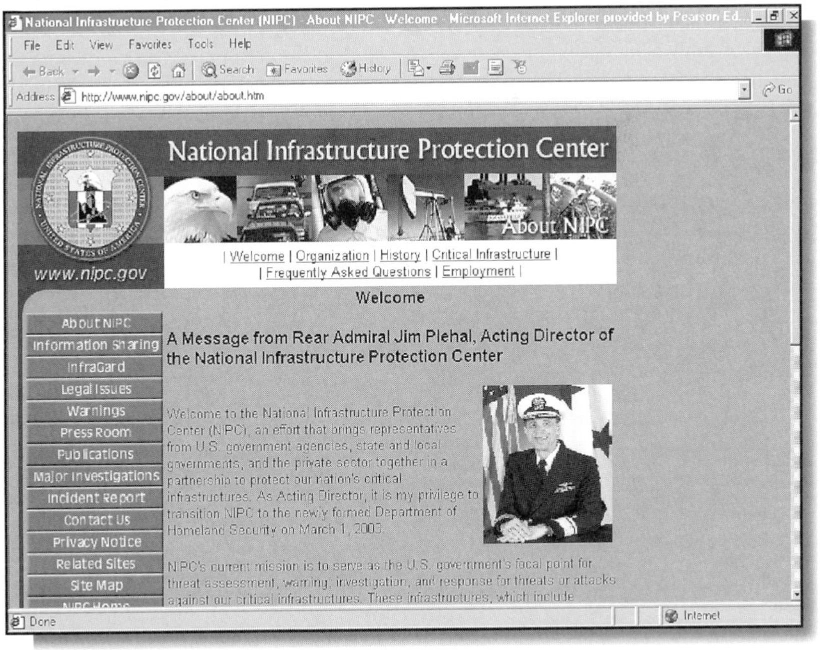

ready information for terrorists. Detailed information about the nation's nuclear power plants and other sensitive energy data are readily available on the Internet (Verton 2002). See Box 2-6 for how Al-Qaeda relies on the Internet to wage terrorism.

The U.S. government has worked hard, creating strategies to resist cyber terror. Since 1998, the federal government has worked with public and private businesses to develop a comprehensive plan to deal with this serious threat. (See www.computeruser.com/newstoday/99/10/10/news6.htm. Accessed February 16, 2003) Only since the September 11, 2001, attacks have these discussions made real progress toward a full strategy. The Bush administration has appointed a special advisor for cyberspace security and created the Homeland Defense Department to protect and handle threats to the United States.

Problems and Stress

Growing e-business has put a constant and increasing demand on existing network infrastructures. Managers have been under pressure to upgrade and maintain more complex networks to ensure site performance, while at the same time keeping costs from skyrocketing. Regardless of what tools are used, there is still the nagging headache of deciding whether to add a second and third shift to address network problems when they occur (Klein, May 8, 2000).

BOX 2-6
Uploading terror

In February 2000, an Egyptian merchant here in the commercial hub of southern China asked a local Internet firm for help in setting up a Web site. After lengthy haggling over the fee, he paid $362 to register a domain name and rent space on a server.

Chen Rongbin, a technician at Guanghou Tianhe Siwei Information Co., and an aide went to the Egyptian's apartment. They couldn't fathom what the client, Sami Ali, was up to. His software and keyboard were all in Arabic. "It just looked like earthworms to us," Mr. Chen says.

All he could make out was the site's address: "Maalemaljihad.com." Mr. Chen had no idea that meant "Milestones of Holy War." Nor that China, one of the world's most heavily policed societies, had just become a launchpad for the dot.com dreams—and disappointments—of Osama bin Laden's terror network.

Since the September 11 attacks, radical Islam's use of technology has stirred both scrutiny and fear. The White House has warned that video footage of Bin Laden could hold encrypted messages. Some experts have wondered if terrorism might even lurk in pornographic Web sites, with instructions embedded in X-rated photos.

Al-Qaeda chiefs communicate mainly by courier, say U.S. officials. But their underlings make wide use of computers: sending e-mail, joining chat rooms, and surfing the Web to scout out targets and keep up with events. Since late last year, U.S. intelligence agencies have gathered about eight terabytes of data on captured computers, a volume that, if printed out, would make a pile of paper over a mile high. The rise and eventual demise of maalemaljihad.com—pieced together from interviews, registration documents, and messages stored on an Al-Qaeda computer provides an inside glimpse of this scattered, sometimes fumbling, but highly versatile fraternity.

SOURCE: Adapted from Higgins, A., Leggett, K., and Cullison, A., "How Al-Qaeda Put Internet in Service of Jihad," *The Wall Street Journal*, November 11, 2002, A1ff.

Many of today's Internet companies continue to have problems processing and fulfilling online customer orders. The main cause is the merchant's link with the vendor and the vendor's responsiveness. For example, the faulty technical infrastructure between a high-visibility online mail-order company and its vendors resulted in shipping duplicates of thousands of customer orders before the error was found months later. The company went bankrupt, with losses in the millions.

For the small retailer, it is a struggle to compete with the giants on the Internet. Many barely break even; others show a profit but at a high cost. Small businesses cannot afford the cost of maintaining and upgrading Web sites and the security and other issues that must be addressed round the clock.

Despite sophisticated FAQs, e-mail, and other technologies, customers still have problems with simple issues like returning unwanted items and securing information (e.g., "No one told me your company gives a discount for items received past the promised delivery date"). The heavy demand for customer service also puts added pressure on customer service personnel.

In addition, people will not buy certain products online. Items like houses, cars, and diamonds have yet to make headway on the Internet. Diamonds are best seen before purchase. People have found that they can't pick a dream house and close on the property with a mouse click. Even if they were to do so, a slew of state and local regulations require physical presence and legal processing in person.

A thicket of state and federal regulations about shipping alcohol over state lines poses a serious constraint to selling wine on the Net (see Weber, May 22, 2000). WineShopper.com, a San Francisco start-up backed by Amazon.com, is tailoring its business model to the interlocking regulatory framework, but so far, the going has not been easy.

Despite this success, or perhaps because of it, the surge of e-commerce and e-business on the Internet has far outgrown the availability of qualified technical people to handle the technology and the traffic.

Abuses in the Workplace

In addition to being a channel for communication and commercial exchange, the Internet provides employees with the world's greatest playground and provides distractions in cubicles and the workplace. One way of looking at nonwork-related surfing (also called *cyberloafing* is that a certain amount of playful use of computer applications can contribute to learning, which could have potential value to the job or to the organization. The deviation from the immediate job might be the break that makes happy and productive workers.

Yet, a conservative organization is likely to look at it differently. Any time spent away from catering to the job requirements is unnecessary waste and should be addressed in a serious way. In fact, some psychologists have suggested that Internet access in the workplace could transform some employees into Internet junkies (Anandarajan 2002).

In either case, Internet abuse has become rampant. This is especially the case when employees are caught using the Internet to download pornography and other illicit or immoral material. The question then is, does the company have the right to regulate, snoop at, or monitor employee Internet traffic? This issue along with work/play ethics will be addressed in Chapter 12 on legal, ethical, and international issues.

- Internet abuse is a worrisome trend for several reasons including the following.
- The rising cost of doing business. Much of such cost is attributable to losses in employee productivity due to employees accessing the Internet on company time for nonwork reasons. One study estimated that as much as $1 billion in costs are incurred each year

(Lim et al. 2002). Another study found that most employees are willing to cyberloaf when they perceive being overworked or underpaid by their employer (Lim et al. 2002).

- Employees regularly violate software licenses by copying company-owned software for their personal use or for friends. This trend puts the employers in jeopardy in terms of the licensing agreement with the software houses involved.
- Downloading unrelated software or applications off the Internet subjects company files and networks to all kinds of viruses and hackers. These are serious threats that make sensitive files and applications vulnerable.

One conclusion is that Internet access must be managed properly and professionally based on policy and standards. If an employer is to monitor employee e-mail traffic, for example, employees should be informed in what ways they are being monitored. Companies also should back up policies with consistent disciplinary action. The IT department that carries out the monitoring should establish an open line with company managers to keep them abreast of developments, violations, and the like (Siau et al. 2002).

Bulletin Board Systems (BBS) and Pay Services

bulletin board system (BBS): a computer-based meeting and announcement system that allows local people to exchange information free of charge.

People often confuse **bulletin board systems (BBS)** and pay services. A BBS generally has a simple interface to the Internet for users to access services like e-mail and NetNews. By calling a BBS via your PC, you can locate all kinds of information. The e-mail part of this system, for example, accepts e-mail during the day, compiles it, and sends it once or twice a day as a batch. It also receives incoming e-mail the same way. This is probably satisfactory service for small-time users or those with no time requirements.

An alternative type of BBS is service by subscription. These systems are so popular that system owners have added better computer hardware, better storage, more phone lines, and so on. The cost of keeping the system current requires users to pay a set fee per month. Pay services like America Online and Prodigy have become household names, offering millions of users access to popular telecommunications offerings that include stock quotes, Internet access, setting up your stock portfolio, and other specialized services.

Many pay services follow a similar procedure. First, you subscribe at a fee, which covers basic access to the service. The fee allows you to do e-mail, interactive real-time communication, watch the news, and the like. Pay services offer other options that are hard to get on the Internet. For example, a live news feed and free online (no delay) stock quotes are available at a membership fee; some are free. Security software also is included to ensure privacy, confidentiality, and integrity of the exchange process.

Some Web Fundamentals

Hypertext Transfer Protocol (HTTP): an Internet protocol designator that allows transfer and display of Web pages.

The World Wide Web is a global network of millions of Web servers and Web browsers connected by the **Hypertext Transfer Protocol (HTTP)** and its many derivatives. The World Wide Web is like a client/server system: Content is held by Web servers and requested by clients or browsers. Clients display the information sent by the

Web server on their monitors. Web servers provide pages of multimedia information in seconds. The most important element of a Web site is its links to other pages within the site or across sites. By clicking on the link, a user can navigate from page to page without having to worry about the location of the information or how it travels across the network.

Web history dates back to the Berlin airlift in June 1948, when U.S. Army Master Sergeant Edward A. Guilbert developed a standard manifest system to track thousands of tons of cargo per day until the main road to Berlin was reopened a year later. In 1965, Holland-America Steamship Line sent shipping manifests as telex messages that automatically converted into computer data. The next major step was in 1982, when General Motors (GM) and Ford mandated Electronic Data Interchange (EDI) for suppliers. EDI became popular in several industries, especially in banking. In 1994, Netscape Navigator 1.0 introduced "cookies" to recognize repeat customers to Web sites. Finally, in 2000, GM, Ford, and DaimlerChrysler formed the Covisin B2B exchange, which created supply-chain management (Hayes 2002, 24).

URLs and HTTPs

Uniform Resource Locator (URL): a name that represents the address of a specific Web site.

Uniform Resource Locators (URLs) are central to the Web in e-commerce.

As we discuss in detail in Chapter 4, a URL such as http://www.virginia.edu/consists of two key parts:

1. http:// The http (Hypertext Transport Protocol) is a protocol designator. It is a special method used in moving files that contain links to other documents related to the material requested across the Internet. It simply tells the browser what protocol to use in connecting to the Web server (in this case, http). Web browsers also can use other protocols, such as FTP (file transfer protocol) for file transfer and SMTP (simple mail transfer protocol) for electronic mail.
2. www.virginia.edu is the server name. The series *www* after the double slash tells the network that the material requested is located on a dedicated Web server somewhere. *Virginia* is the name of the Web site requested, and *edu* is a code indicating that the site is an *edu*cational institution. Other codes like *org* (*org*anization; e.g. www.ACM.org), *gov* (*gov*ernment; e.g., www.Whitehouse.gov), and *mil* (*mil*itary; e.g., www.defenselink.mil) also are used. The most common code is *com* (*com*mercial; e.g., www.dell.com). (Http and networking are covered in detail in Chapter 4.)

To locate a resource on the Internet, the user simply enters an address in the standard format discussed here.

secure sockets layer (SSL): a protocol for transmitting private information in a secure way over the Internet.

Security Protocols

There are two main security protocols. The first is **Secure Sockets Layer (SSL),** developed by Netscape Communications Corporation. To date, it is the most widely used security protocol on the Internet,

secure HTTP (S-HTTP): an extension to HTTP that provides various security features such as client/server authentication and allows Web clients and servers to specify privacy capabilities.

providing security services for messages or streams of data. The second security protocol is **Secure HTTP (S-HTTP).**

THE LANGUAGE OF THE INTERNET

In order to take this course, you need to become Internet-literate. Like many areas of computing, the Internet and the World Wide Web have terms that are unique to the field. Here are some key terms that will make it easier to understand the technology covered in Chapter 3.

Provider

Internet Service Provider (ISP), provider: a company that links users to the Internet for a fee; the entrance ramp to the Internet.

A **provider** (also called an **Internet Service Provider** or **ISP**) is an organization whose specialty is to provide an entrance ramp to the Internet. The ISP purchases expensive, high-speed Internet feed from a major Internet source and a number of telephone lines from a local phone company. By placing computers at the site that interface the phone lines with the Internet, the ISP can begin to sell online commercial access. The faster the Internet feed is, the more data or users it can accommodate simultaneously. More data means more users or more revenues coming from users. The ISP recoups its investment by selling Web services, providing service to many people simultaneously, and selling major Internet hookups to large corporations in their area of operation.

When you purchase Internet access from an ISP, you first receive an account that allows you to store files and do your Internet work. You are connected to a NetNews feed that brings you thousands of interest groups on virtually any topic imaginable. You also receive an e-mail address that links you with the world at large and provides access to the entire Internet.

Browser

browser: a program designed to search for and display Internet resources.

A **browser** is a software program loaded on a PC that allows you to access or read information stored on the Internet. It is the vehicle that enables you to interface with the Internet. The browser takes your instructions and converts them into a language and a format that can be sent to a remote site and executed.

Server

A server is the destination point on the Internet. It is where the information you are seeking is stored. We will see in Chapter 4 that when you send a message to retrieve a piece of information through the Internet, the browser picks up the message, reformats it, and sends it through various layers to the physical layer, where cables and wires transmit the message to the appropriate server. Once there, the server retrieves the information and sends it back to the browser to be viewed by the user. There are all kinds of servers, depending on the information sought by the user. Because most of the focus in this book is on the World Wide Web, we will use the word *server* to refer to Web servers.

Telnet: a protocol that allows users to log on to a computer and access files from a remote location.

Telnet is a basic Internet service that allows you to access remote computers as if they were local. To use Telnet, you must have the

login: entering your user name and password.

Internet address of the remote computer. Once you transmit the computer address, you are asked to **login** before being allowed to access computer files or use the computer. Once logged in, the information you read and actions you take are acted upon by the remote computer.

File Transfer Protocol (FTP)

File transfer protocol is a standard protocol that allows you to copy files from computer to computer. Like Telnet, FTP allows you to access remote computers. When you FTP to a remote computer, you log in as *anonymous,* which means simply entering your e-mail address as the password. The Web makes heavy use of FTP protocol. Most browsers know how to access information from FTP sites. This feature allows you to store Web homepages at low-cost FTP sites anywhere in the world.

Malicious Software

Any software (program) that causes damage by spreading itself to other computers via e-mail or infected floppy disks is malicious software. It comes in many forms and types.

Trojan horse: a program that seems to perform legitimate work but causes damage when executed.

zombie: a launching program residing on an Internet-attached computer, which uses the computer as a base to attack other computers on the Internet and tie up Internet traffic.

virus: malicious software that causes damage to stored files when activated.

macro: facility that stores a series of commands that happen in sequence.

worm: a program that replicates itself on a computer's hard disk and in computer memory, slowing down the computer's performance and servers.

A **Trojan horse** is a program that seems to perform legitimate work but causes damage when executed. Most Trojan horse software is used for stealing passwords from unprotected computers. Trojan horse software is localized and does not replicate itself like a virus does.

A **zombie** is a launching program that resides in an Internet-attached computer. It uses the computer as a base for attacking other computers on the Internet and ties up Internet traffic. Zombies are hard to detect and can be more than a nuisance to cope with. They lie hidden in hundreds of unsuspecting Internet-tied computers of third parties such as universities and banks.

A **virus** is a program that performs unrequested and often destructive acts. Viruses are the biggest computer security problem. In the mid-1990s, viruses were spread by floppy disks and were mostly regional. Thereafter, programs like Microsoft Outlook attracted macro-viruses—a virus that appears in a **macro** that is part of a document like Microsoft Word or an Excel spreadsheet. In 1999, we experienced Melissa through mass e-mail, and later BubbleBoy, which also wreaked havoc through e-mail.

A **worm** is a program that replicates itself on a computer's hard disk and computer memory, slowing down the computer's performance and servers. Unlike a virus, worm programs have one goal and that is to reproduce through e-mail.

Acronyms

In the Internet language, there are several acronyms and symbols worth knowing. These include:

1. **24/7**—A Web site that is available 24 hours a day, 7 days a week, year-round.
2. **NRN**—No response necessary.
3. **RTM**—Read the manual.

MANAGERIAL IMPLICATIONS

The Web has changed the way business and information technology work together. The two are becoming equal partners. The best partnership takes place when the technical staff understands the business, and business users are technology-literate. Today companies seek out techies with business acumen and look for businesspeople who, by background or experience, understand technology. The trend in recruitment is to look for people who have both a technology orientation and business literacy. The fundamental skills that IT people bring to the new corporate world are useful if they get the proper managerial and technical training. Then they become the true problem solvers of e-commerce.

E-commerce is transforming the Internet from a "browse-and-surf" environment into a mammoth information exchange. In just a few years, the Internet has moved from novelty to necessity. It is a dynamic entity with a life of its own. The standards that help make the Internet work mean that a company's business has a good chance of surviving entry and competing on an equal footing with those already in the marketplace.

The important thing to remember is to keep an eye on the technologies as they evolve and to be familiar with the changes before taking a dive into the Internet. If your business does not have internal expertise in developing Web-based systems, hire this expertise after investigating the competence of the Web design agency. In the meantime, try to learn as much as possible about the process so you eventually can bring these activities in-house.

Critics often warn that the Internet has been oversold. Many businesses have entered the Web with fancy sites and injected millions in start-up money, only to learn that they would have been better off to stick to the brick-and-mortar environment. Many have pulled out poorer but wiser. The bottom line is to strategize first, test the waters, and be sure you have a unique product supported by qualified staff to follow up on the Web traffic that it attracts.

The implication behind the IT staff shortage is that less than 10 percent of a company's qualified IT staff is safe from recruiters and headhunters. According to a 2000 study, 40 percent of those interviewed said they plan to be with the company no more than 1 year. The reasons given were "lack of adequate training," "not enough money," "broken promises," "unappreciated and taken for granted," and "management indifference" (see Box 2-7).

In another study reported by *Computerworld* (Watson, May 15, 2000), companies hired IT employees as salaried professionals, planning to work them overtime and on weekends with no bonuses and no overtime pay. When there is little pay and no respect, it is the end of job loyalty and the beginning of a job search.

BOX 2-7

E-careers: End of job loyalty?

Two weeks after Damon Remy joined a hospitality company, his boss quit and almost all of the IT department was outsourced to a consulting firm. "I was misled about the company and my role in it," Remy says. For example, though his title was director of information technology, Remy wasn't involved in making decisions about the firm's technological or strategic directions. "My boss had sent out a quarterly update memo listing 15 projects IT was involved in—and I only knew about three of them," he says.

But the straw that broke Remy's back was when he was ready to spend about $9,000 of his own money to get his Cisco and Microsoft network certifications—and the company wouldn't give him time off for the training. Then he got a raise of just 3 percent after 18 months—even though his boss agreed that it wasn't commensurate with the value of Remy's performance. "I felt like the abused stepchild," Remy says. He left in March to join a communications company where he hopes to work with the latest wireless data technology, be part of a team and see his impact on the bottom line. "I want to feel good about coming to work," he says.

Management is often cited as the wellspring of dissatisfaction. Take the senior project manager at a multinational IT services firm managing the national network of a U.S. financial institution. Of the dozen people in his group, six are job hunting and the rest are polishing their resumes, he says, even though the employer offers excellent training, leading-edge technology, and fine benefits. The problem? "I've been managed to death and I don't see any leadership," says the project manager.

Dissatisfied IT professionals say another thing that leaves a sour taste in their mouths is when their bosses don't share the glory. For example, staff at a firm in Illinois worked New Year's Eve and New Year's Day on Y2k issues. "Our IT director looked great, but we didn't get any recognition," says a network professional there. "They didn't even replace the lost holidays on our vacation schedule."

SOURCE: Excerpted from Watson, Sharon, "End of Job Loyalty?" *Computerworld*, May 15, 2000, 52–53.

SUMMARY

1. The Web is the fastest-growing, most user-friendly, and most commercially popular technology to date. Anyone with a PC connected to the Internet through an Internet Service Provider (ISP), a browser, and a few plug-ins can surf the Internet and download text, graphics, and even voice. The part of the Internet that can accomplish these tasks is called the World Wide Web, WWW, or

the Web. When you are on the Web, you are on the Internet, but not the other way around.

2. The Internet owes its existence to the Pentagon, where it originally was created for military research. It linked military labs, universities, and business firms with defense department contracts. Two nodes were connected to a network on Advanced Research Projects Agency (ARPAnet), which was the sponsor of the research. ARPAnet was decommissioned in 1969. In 1984, it split into MILNET and ARPAnet, which became known as the Internet. In 1995, the U.S. government relinquished control of the Internet to independent governing bodies and relaxed entry to the Internet for anyone.
3. The Internet is physically hierarchical. High-speed backbones are at the top, with regional and individual networks at the bottom. The bulk of Internet traffic is fed onto the backbone via network access points (NAPs).
4. Internet Service Providers link commercial traffic to its destination. This involves paying for transactions, management of networks, and linking consumers and businesses to the Internet. Some of the free services are hotlists, comics, weather services, dictionaries, and government services.
5. As the enabler of e-commerce, the Internet has many uses; it also has many limitations. It can be a tool for marketing and selling products and services; doing business at high speed; gathering opinions and trying out new ideas; providing equal opportunity for all businesses; and as a vehicle for inexpensive, easy mass distribution of information, products, and services, among other advantages. There are limitations as well: securing and privacy issues; fakes and forgeries; hackers, worms, Trojan horses, and viruses; fulfillment and customer relations problems; products that are not candidates for online selling; and a shortage of e-literate people in the marketplace.
6. The World Wide Web is a global hypertext network of millions of Web servers and browsers connected by Hypertext Transfer Protocol (HTTP) and its many derivatives. The most important element of a Web site is its hypertext links to other pages within the site or across sites.
7. It is important to learn the language of the Internet before starting an e-commerce project.
8. The Internet and the Web have changed the way business and technology work together; the two are becoming equal partners. The important thing for managers to remember is that they need to be knowledgeable about the technology before diving into the Internet with their business. They also need to know when to outsource and how to hire the right people.

KEY TERMS

- Active X, 42
- architecture, 40
- backbone, 40
- bookmarking, 46
- browser, 60
- buffering, 42
- Bulletin Board System (BBS), 58
- chat program, 43
- Extranet, 35
- first-generation search engine, 44
- frequently asked questions (FAQs), 50
- hypertext, 39
- Hypertext Transfer Protocol (HTTP), 58
- index, 43
- Internet Service Provider (ISP), provider, 48
- link, 39
- Live Cam, 42
- login, 61
- macro, 61
- network access points (NAPs), 40
- packet, 38

- plug-in, 35
- portal, 44
- protocol, 38
- Realplayer, 42
- search engine, 43
- second-generation search engine, 44
- secure HTTP (S-HTTP), 60
- secure sockets layer (SSL), 59
- shockwave, 42
- spider, 44
- streaming media, 42
- Telnet, 60
- transmission control protocol/internet protocol (TCP/IP), 40
- Trojan horse, 61
- Uniform Resource Locator (URL), 59
- Virtual Reality Modeling Language (VRML), 42
- virus, 61
- Web site, 35
- Webmaster, 40
- Windows Media Player, 42
- World Wide Web, 39
- worm, 61
- zombie, 61

Test Your Understanding

1. The Internet is a medium and a market. Do you agree? Discuss.
2. Review a brief history of the Internet, how it got started, and where it is now.
3. How does the World Wide Web differ from the Internet? Which one implies the other?
4. What were the key events in the building of the Web?
5. What is a Webmaster? Briefly explain his or her functions.
6. How are second-generation search engines different from their first-generation counterparts?
7. Distinguish between the following:
   a. Network access point (NAP) and Network address.
   b. Search engine and Internet Service Provider (ISP).
   c. HTTP and URL.
   d. Web client and Web server.
8. Briefly describe some uses of the Web.
9. In what way does the Web provide equal opportunity for all businesses? Elaborate.
10. Do you see any limitations of the Web? What are they? Explain in detail.
11. What security and privacy issues are limitations of the Web? Discuss.
12. How would one look up a Web site? Explain.
13. Explain the makeup of a URL address.

Discussion Questions

1. How does the Web fit with company strategy? Discuss.
2. What does the Web mean to a company's competitive situation?
3. If you were asked to sell a first-time business on the Web's potential advantage for that business, what would you need to know first? What would you say?
4. How does the Web affect our traditional sales channels, partners, and suppliers? Explain in detail.
5. How would you show a company how it can best prepare to use the Web as a profitable venture?

6. If you were talking with a first-time surfer who is a student in your school, what advice or tips would you give to help the person get started researching the Internet for a term paper?
7. One of the recommendations for success in doing business on the Internet is to deliver personalized service. How can this be done?
8. Find a company that chose not to use e-commerce in its business. What factors or problems did it consider in staying away from e-commerce?
9. Go on the Internet and look up a tutorial on the World Wide Web. Review the tutorial and explain why you think it is easy (or difficult) to use as a learning tool.
10. What implications does the Web have for managing a small e-business?

Web Exercises

1. At the end of an e-commerce course, five business students and a computer science student got together and decided to start a catering business for students, faculty, and administration within the university. This is a "party" school, so every weekend is busy with socials at fraternities, sororities, and other occasions. Catering can be big business. The students formed a partnership, designed a Web site on one of the business school servers, and advertised their presence in the daily student newspaper. They contracted with a local restaurant as the supplier of the food, drink, and other needs customized to the special requirements of the client.

   Questions:
   a. Devise ways that this new student-run business can deliver warm, personalized service.
   b. What information and service should be included in the Web site?
   c. How would the university community be encouraged to place orders and become loyal customers?
2. Look up two car manufacturers' Web sites on the Internet (e.g., www.ford.com/ and www.toyota.com). Configure the car of your choice and report your findings. Make sure to include payment options, shipping charges, financing (if any), and delivery schedule.
3. Evaluate four high-volume items that are sold on the Internet (e.g., www.dell.com for PCs, www.amazon.com for books). What makes these e-merchants so successful? Elaborate.

Chapter 3

Internet Architecture

Contents

In a Nutshell

The building blocks of e-commerce are the technologies of the World Wide Web—protocols, standards, browsers, and servers. Applications like satellite communication, cable television, telecommunication networks, and wireless networks are made possible by the underlying Internet infrastructure. Internet architecture comprises the servers, software, and storage—all enabling the working functions of the Internet: load balancing, firewall security, backup, and content distribution and management. Every time surfers or users order a product, check a stock quote, or transfer funds online, they are relying on the integrity of the architecture to deliver. It is crucial and timely apparatus.

Satellite companies are setting up new broadband networks to reach people where telephone service is not available. Cable television providers have prepared their networks for two-way Internet traffic via set-top boxes that act as converters for inbound and outbound traffic, for data other than video or voice. Telecommunications companies have developed new technologies for higher-bandwidth communication across existing networks. Wireless networks are being converted for Internet use and m-commerce (mobile-commerce). MPEG standards for video and audio compression and multimedia delivery is now commonly available. Providers for each technological area play a major role in the expansion of the Internet. As Figure 3-1 shows, they form the overall building blocks of electronic commerce.

The Internet is a network of networks. A network is any-to-any communication. This communication is made possible by assigning to each station (called a **node**) on the network a unique address. This technical architecture is like the telephone network connecting your phone to any other phone. All you need is the other party's phone number. Intermediary nodes (normally special computers) for-

node: station or component linked as part of a network.

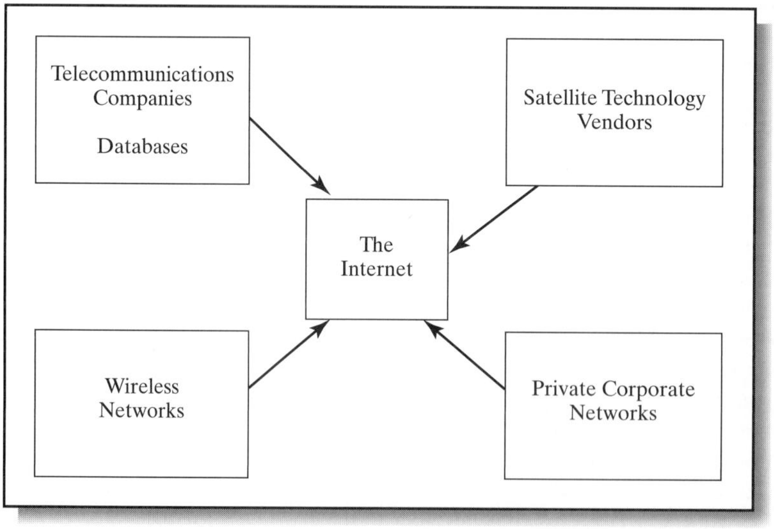

Figure 3-1 Building blocks of electronic commerce

ward traffic between network segments. These nodes include routers, bridges, and switches. Linking the nodes together within a network and among networks is called data communications.

This chapter is about Internet architecture—the technologies of the Internet. Technologies are specified by protocols, meaning rules that govern the way a network operates, how applications access the network, how data travel in packets, and how electrical signals represent data on a network cable. In Internet terminology, any computer of any size attached to the Internet is a host. This includes servers as well as home PCs. Each host has an assigned number to identify it to other hosts, much like a phone number. This is called an IP address. Throughout this chapter, we use the term *host* when we explain the various aspects of the technology and how it works.

To have a general understanding of networking, you need to understand how the Internet works. This chapter begins by reviewing some core networking concepts; how the Internet sends data from one place to another; and the standards used when you dial into the Internet from home, from the office, or on the road. We also will look at the TCP/IP-OSI standards architecture that governs the Internet worldwide.

As a business or a management information systems (MIS) student, you will not need to learn how to build bridges, switches, or hubs, but you will need to understand how they work and the functions they perform. This background will help you work with planners and users to explain how networks can help them do their work better.

local area network (LAN): a cluster of networked computers within a department, a company, or an office building.

wide area network (WAN): communication between networks using a third-party carrier to transmit between networks; connects a company's networks across the globe.

metropolitan area network (MAN): a network in a specific geographic region like a city or a county.

peer-to-peer network: the linking of several PCs (usually fewer than 10) so that each acts as a peer, sharing and exchanging information without the need for a centralized server.

What Is a Network?

Before we get into the technical aspects of the Internet and how computers communicate on the Internet, it is important to have a clear idea of the concept of a network. Put simply, a network is a connection between at least two computers for the purpose of sharing resources. All networks are based on the concept of sharing.

There are three types of networks: **local area networks (LANs)**, **wide area networks (WANs)**, and **metropolitan area networks (MANs).**

LANs, WANs, and MANs can be peer-to-peer or client/server.

Peer-to-Peer Networks

Computers in **peer-to-peer networks** are linked together as equals, with no centralized server or control. Any computer can share its resources with any other computer on the same network in any way and whenever it chooses to do so. Users are network administrators in that they can control access to the resources that reside on their own computer. Because of the flexibility of this arrangement, peer-to-peer networks can result in institutionalized chaos, and security can be a problem (see Figure 3-2).

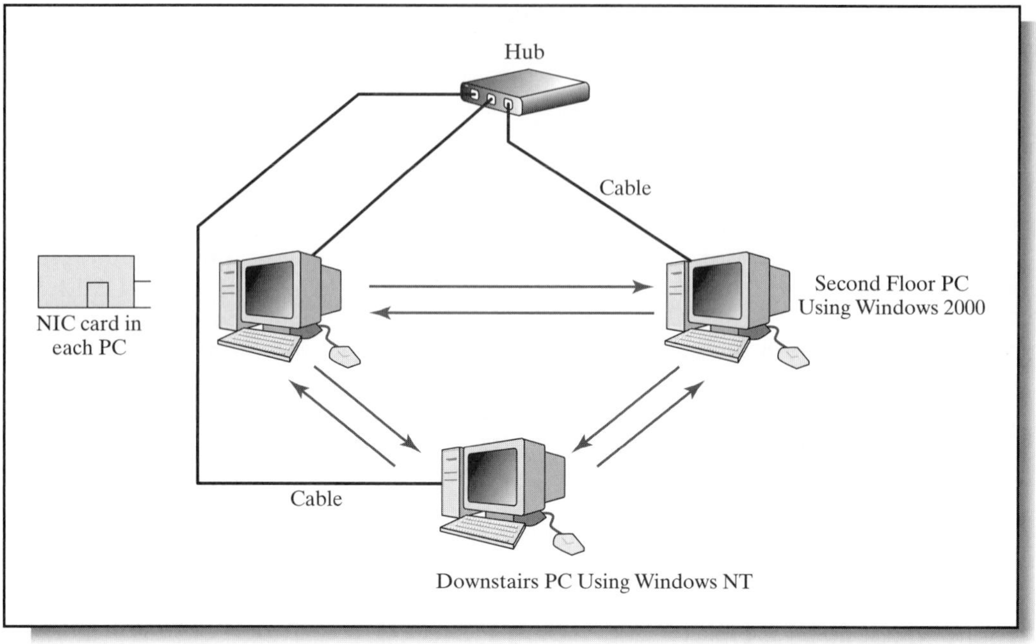

Figure 3-2
A basic peer-to-peer network

A peer-to-peer setup normally connects fewer than 10 computers. It may be appropriate for a dental clinic or a small travel agency. As the number of users increases, the peer-to-peer environment becomes impractical. The more users who try to access resources on any particular computer, the worse the performance is of the user's machine being accessed across the network. For example, if a user's printer is network accessible, it slows down every time another user in the network sends a job to that printer.

Another drawback is the status of information. With each machine behaving like a server, it is difficult for users to know what information is on which computer. Backing up files is difficult. Each network computer has to back up its own data, which makes the whole process inefficient and unwieldy. The flip side of these disadvantages is the distinct benefits of low cost and ease of installation, ability to protect one's own resources, and allowing users to act as their own network administrator. Table 3-1 presents a summary of the benefits and drawbacks of peer-to-peer networks.

server: special-purpose computer or specialized hardware and software designed for one function.

client: any computer or workstation connected to the server within a network.

client/server network: a cluster of computers (called clients) connected to one or more servers to form a network.

Client/Server Networks

A **server** is simply a special-purpose computer or specialized hardware and software designed for one function—to address a client's requests. A **client** is any computer or workstation connected to the server within a network. One of the main advantages of **client/server networks** is centralized control over network resources.

Table 3-1
Pros and cons of peer-to-peer networks

Key Benefits	Key Drawbacks
Users can control their own shared resources.	Network security is applied to one computer at a time.
Easy to install.	Every time a computer in the network is accessed, performance suffers.
Easy to configure the system.	Backup is performed on each machine separately to protect shared resources.
Inexpensive to purchase and operate.	Users have to use a separate password on each computer in the network.
No dependence on a dedicated server.	No centralized setup to locate, manage, or control access to data.
Ideal for small business of 10 users or less.	
All you need to set up this network is an operating system and a few cables.	
No need for a full-time network administrator.	

All programs or applications reside on the server. For example, a client might send a request to the server to use Microsoft Word. The server allows the client to download the executable portion of Word. When the work is finished, the program is uploaded onto the server for storage and future use. A client/server system is a multiuser environment. More than one authorized user can access any program or application that resides on the server (see Figure 3-3).

Other benefits of a client/server design are security and speed of access. Servers are usually fast computers with physical and logical security capable of controlling who accesses what resource. They provide centralized verification of user passwords and established accounts. For network users to access an application on the server, they must provide a name and password to the server's domain controller, which checks the user's credentials. The whole setup is monitored by a network administrator, who is the only person authorized to make changes in passwords or to issue passwords. The pros and cons of client/server design are summarized in Table 3-2.

Compared to peer-to-peer designs, a client/server network costs more, requires more knowledgeable staff to manage it, and causes problems for everyone should it go down. A client/server design is appropriate when more than 10 users must share network resources, when centralized security and control are required, and when users require access to specialized servers on a regular basis.

IP Addresses

IP address: a host number represented by strings of 32 bits.

When you look at a Web site, the address includes the name of the host computer the Web site resides on. The address looks like this: www.wachovia.com. When you are looking for specific information on a specific host computer, each host is identified by a host number (called an **IP address**), which identifies it to other hosts, and by a name that is easier to remember than the number. To transmit a message, a source host (the sender) needs to know only the official IP address of the destination host, regardless of location.

An IP address consists of strings of 32 bits (ones and zeros). Because it is nearly impossible to remember this many bits, the same address is written in dotted decimal notation. Here are the three main steps in creating an IP address in decimal notation.

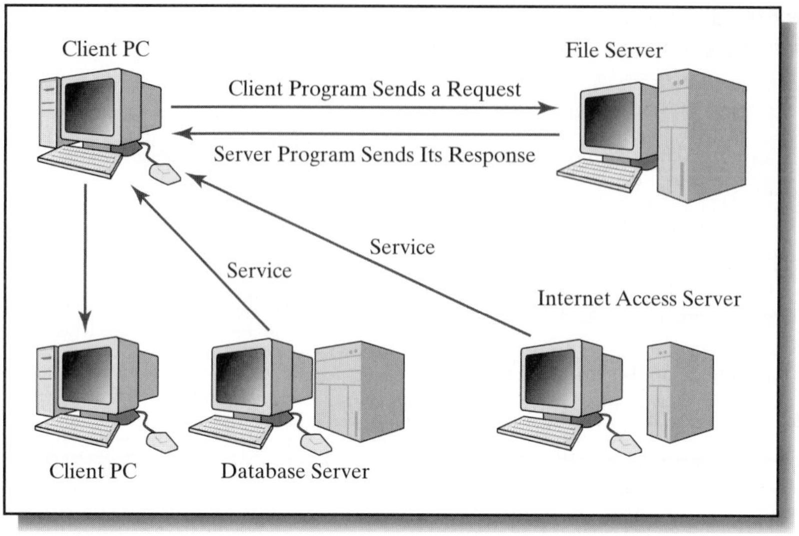

Figure 3-3
Client/server network

1. An IP address in raw form: 10111111010101010010000000001100
2. Divide the 32-bit string into four 8-bit blocks or four octets.
   10111111 010101010 01000000 00001100
   (In computer memory, a collection of 8 bits is called a byte; in data networking, it is called an octet.)
3. Represent each.

host name: Internet address consisting of text labels separated by dots.

The IP address contains four number groups separated by dots. The decimal numbers represent the bits and are easier to remember. These numbers may be computer friendly, but they are not human friendly. For this reason, another type of Internet address, called a **host**

Table 3-2
Pros and cons of client/server network

Key Benefits	Key Drawbacks
Ideal for more than 10 users.	Network failure means clients are almost helpless.
Centralized security access and control.	Specialized staff needed to manage the specialized hardware and software.
Simpler network administration than peer-to-peer networks.	Higher costs than peer-to-peer network because of the specialized hardware and software architecture.
Users remember only one password.	
Ideal when user computers are not in close proximity.	
More scalable (upgradable) than peer-to-peer networks.	

name, was introduced. It consists of several text labels separated by dots. Operationally, it serves the same purpose: It represents a host computer. For example, 191.170.64.12 has the host name *peersbrewer@net.net.*

In the United States, transmission lines and are owned by commercial organizations. To use the Internet, your computer must be connected to an organization called an **Internet Service Provider (ISP).** When you send a message or request information from another host computer, you dial into an ISP, whose router connects you to the router of the other host computer. This might involve intermediary routers that bounce your message across routers to its eventual destination (see Figure 3-4).

Internet Service Provider (ISP): a company whose router connects a user to the Internet, usually for a fee.

Networks and Numbers

Take a look at this phone number: 434-924-3423. What do you see? The first six digits identify the location of the phone exchange. In this example, it is Charlottesville, Virginia. The last four digits are a unique phone number in the exchange. Internet host numbers are organized in a similar way. Our host number 191.170.64.12 is divided into two parts: the network part and the local part. The first two numbers are the network part and represent the organization's unique IP address. The remaining two numbers are two levels of IP addresses assigned by the organization to computers within its area of operation.

To illustrate, the University of Virginia's unique IP address network part is assigned by an IP address registrar as 191.170.0.0. The first two decimal numbers are the network part of the address. Each of that network's host IP addresses must begin with that network sequence. They become the first 16 bits in every host IP address in the university. The university then assigns a unique third decimal number (also called an 8-bit subnet) to each of its colleges, schools, or divisions. For example, the School of Commerce might be

Figure 3-4
Sending messages and the Internet Service Provider (ISP)

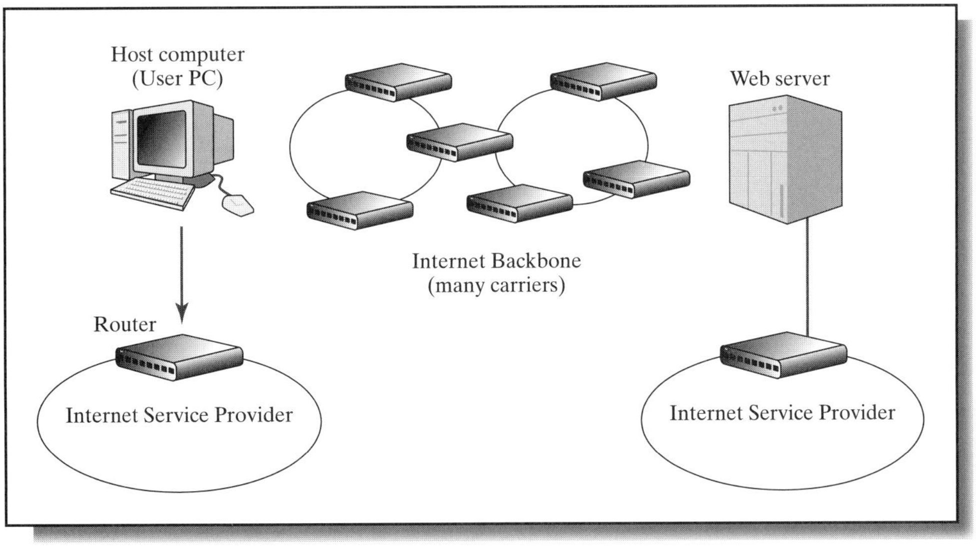

assigned 64 as the third part of the IP address or 191.170.64.0. From the university's view, 64 is a local part of the university's IP address.

The School of Commerce, in turn, assigns a unique IP address (fourth decimal number) to each of the PCs within its operations (faculty, lab PCs, etc.). So, a particular faculty member's PC as a host computer might be 191.170.64.12. Every other faculty member in the commerce school will have an IP address that has a unique fourth decimal number plus the preceding three decimal numbers. This is like a *child-parent relationship*, where the fourth decimal number (e.g., 12) is the *child* of 64 (the commerce school). The commerce school's decimal number 64 is the child of the parent—the University of Virginia—191.171. Reading the IP address from right to left:

191. 171	.64	.12
(network part)	(local part or the subnet)	
University of Virginia	Commerce School	Bob Johnson's PC

Networks and Sizes

A 32-bit IP address by itself does not tell you anything about the size of its network, subnet, or host part. Because some networks have more hosts than others, networks are classified in three sizes: Class A (large), Class B (medium), and Class C (small). There is also a Class D multicast network. As Table 3-3 shows, the initial bits of the IP address tell whether an IP address is for a host on a Class A, Class B, or Class C network, or whether it is a Class D multicast address. In our IP address example, the first 8-bit octet is 10111111. The first 2 bits (10) indicate that the IP address is a Class B address, with 14 remaining bits in the network part, 16 bits (2 octets) in the local part, and a maximum of 65,000 possible hosts in the network.

Class A Networks

You can tell the IP address represents a host in a Class A network if the beginning bit of its first octet is 0. This leaves 7 bits or 216 (2^7) possible Class A networks. Each of these networks could hold up to 16 million hosts.

Class B Networks

An IP address that represents a host in a Class B network begins with 10 in its first octet, leaving 14 bits in the network part to specify more than 16,000 Class B networks. With 16 bits left in the host part, there are more than 65,000 hosts in each of the Class B net-

Table 3-3
IP address classes

Class	Beginning Bit(s)	Bits in Remainder of Network Part	Number of Bits in Local Part	Maximum Number of Networks	Maximum Number of Hosts in Network
A	0	7	24	136	16 million
B	10	14	16	16,000	65,000
C	110	21	8	2 million	254

works. Because of the even distribution of 16 bits for the network part and 16 bits for the local part, this class of network has been popular from its inception. It is now virtually exhausted. More and more IP address assignments are now being made in a new scheme called Classless InterDomain Routing (CIDR). With CIDR, an IP address can be used to designate several IP addresses. A CIDR IP address ends with a slash followed by a number called the IP prefix. For example, the CIDR IP address 147.200.0.0 would be displayed as 147.200.0.0/12. The IP prefix of /12 can address 2^{12} or 4,096 Class C addresses.

Class C Networks

An IP address that represents a host in Class C networks begins with 110 bits. The network part is 24 bits. With 3 bits used to represent the class, there are 21 remaining unoccupied bits, allowing more than 2 million Class C networks. With an enormous number of networks, Class C networks leave only 8-bit (2^8) or 254 hosts in each network. In the 1970s and 1980s, when mainframes were popular, a small number of hosts was reasonable. With the growing use of PCs as hosts, a limited number of hosts per network is almost useless. CIDR was developed to address this problem.

Class D Networks

Class D addresses begin with 1110 and are used for multicasting. Unlike unicasting, where the packet goes to only one host IP address, IP multicasting means the packet is broadcast to all the hosts on that subnet.

Zones and Domain Names

zone name: the last (right-most) part of a domain name preceded by a dot. It specifies the type of domain name.

domain name: a Web address that contains two or more word groups separated by periods.

An Internet name is decoded from right to left. Take, for example, the Internet name www.Virginia.edu. The right-most part, edu, is a **zone name;** it tells us that the site is an educational site. The next part, Virginia, is the name of the University of Virginia. The host naming system is also somewhat egalitarian. In it, virginia.edu, a university of 18,000 students, is right up there with other schools like Harvard, Dartmouth, and Yale. In the eye of the Internet, they are all the same, regardless of size or halo. In contrast to a zone name is a domain name. An address like www.virginia.edu is called a **domain name**. It contains two or more word groups separated by periods. The most specific part of a domain is the left-most part (in this example, Virginia). WWW is a Web address.

Zones are classified in two ways: three-letter zone names and two-letter zone names (see Table 3-4). In the United States, most Internet sites fall into one of the two categories. Two-letter zone names are codes of countries and are the last ones shown in the Internet name. For example, the American University of Beirut (Lebanon) is www.aub.edu.lb. Three-letter zone names are types of organizations. For example, www.Dell.com is the name of a commercial organization.

INFORMATION TRANSFER

Messages, invoicing, and other information transmission on the Internet is made possible by protocols, standards, and other software that transmit information via packets through a cable to its destination. Look at the U.S. Postal Service. When you mail a package to someone, you wrap the goods in a box and supply the recipient's address, and also

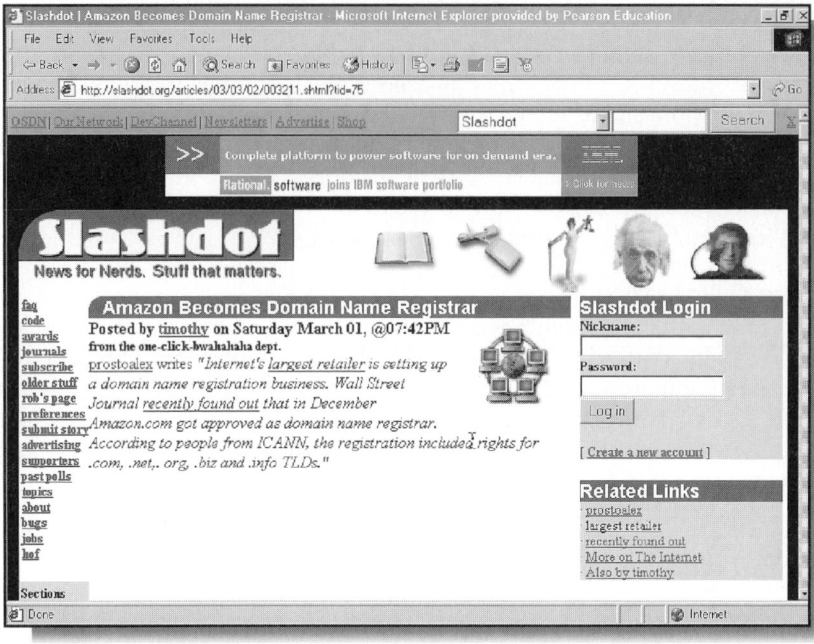

Screen Capture 3-1

Source: Used with permission of Slashdot.org.

Table 3-4

Select list of zone names

	TRADITIONAL THREE-LETTER ZONE NAMES
com	Commercial organizations
edu	Four-year colleges and universities
gov	U.S. government agencies and departments
int	International organizations
mil	Military agencies or sites
net	Network access providers
org	Any other sites or organizations, but primarily professional societies
	SAMPLE COMMON GEOGRAPHICAL TWO-LETTER ZONE NAMES
au	Austria
be	Belgium (Kingdom of)
ca	Canada
dk	Denmark (Kingdom of)
fl	Finland (Republic of)
fr	France
de	Germany (Federal Republic of)
in	India (Republic of)
il	Israel (State of)
it	Italy (Italian Republic)
jp	Japan
ru	Russian Federation
es	Spain (Kingdom of)
ch	Switzerland (Swiss Confederation)
uk	United Kingdom (Official Code is GB)
us	United States (United States of America)

your return address in case it is refused, proves to have the wrong address, or has to be returned. The U.S. Postal Service routes the package from a local post office to a central facility by truck. The package goes from one office to another by plane or by truck until it reaches the local office closest to the recipient's home or office address. From there, it is carried and delivered by hand.

The Internet works much the same way. When you send a message to another host, the message is sandwiched in one or more packets and forwarded via routers that identify its destination and send it from one router to another until it reaches the host computer. Forwarding messages electronically from one part of a net to another is common. To standardize the way Internet traffic is managed, rules have been developed to ensure successful transmission and delivery.

Packets and Protocols

Let's use the U.S. Postal Service analogy again. Suppose you want to send a 5-pound package to a friend in Uzbekistan (never mind where it is). On the last segment of the trip from Frankfurt, the package can be flown only on Uzbek Air, which restricts the weight of any package to 2 pounds. You split the package into three smaller packages, label them in some sequence, and send them off. When they arrive, the recipient reorganizes them based on the way they are labeled.

packet: the grouping of data for transmission on a network.

network: any-to-any communication or connectivity system. Any station (PC) can communicate with any other station on the network.

Internet protocol (IP): a set of rules used to pass packets from one host to another.

protocol: a rule that governs how communication should be conducted between two parties, two computers, or a source and a destination.

In Internet terms, all data sent through the Internet are sent as **packets.** Technically, a packet is a sequence of bits that carries identifying information for transmitting the data as well as the data itself. A single packet contains a header to keep track of the actual data it carries. The general size of a packet is between 100 and 2,000 octets (bytes), with a typical size of 1,536 octets per packet. This happens to be the limit of an Ethernet **network** (Ethernets are discussed later in the chapter). Messages that are larger than the standard packet size are split into a series of packets for transmission. Putting the packets back together at the destination is no problem.

Packets and **Internet protocols** have one thing in common: One cannot function without the other. For example, when A dials B, B answers the phone by saying "Hello." So, the term *Hello* is the protocol for answering the phone. **Protocols** are pieces of software that run on every node or computer, and allow every pair of computers to communicate directly without having to know much about each other, except for the IP address. More specifically, protocols govern communication between peer processes on different systems. The different systems are the user PC and the Web server. The Internet is named as the collection of networks that pass packets to one another using Internet protocols or IP.

Protocols used in connection with the IP include many functions. They are called an Internet protocol suite, or Transmission Control Protocol, or TCP/IP. This is the most widely used protocol suite on the Internet and is explained later in the chapter.

Internet Protocols: The OSI Reference Model

Now that you have an idea of what a protocol is and does, you need to know the various Internet protocols and the standards on which Internet protocols are based. In an effort to standardize how we look at network protocols, in 1978 the International

OSI Reference Model: a seven-layer model that defines the basic network functions.

Standards Organization (ISO) created a seven-layer model that defines the basic network functions. This model is called the **OSI Reference Model;** OSI stands for Open-Systems Interconnection. Each layer of the model handles a different portion of the communications process and has specific network functions. This means that two different networks supporting the functions of a related layer can exchange data at that level. The model was revised in 1984 and became the international standard for networked communication.

The best way to understand the OSI Reference Model is to assume you are requesting access to information on a server via your PC. The message that carries the IP address of the Web server goes through a series of layers from the application layer down to and across the physical layer (where it is carried across electrical cables) and up the same layers to the Web server (see Table 3-5). Once the information is found and verified, it is sent back to your PC in reverse sequence in a matter of seconds. One way to remember the sequence of the layers is to remember the phrase "**P**lease **D**o **N**ot **T**hrow **S**ausage **P**izza **A**way" (PDNTSPA), where the letters represent physical, data link, network, transport, session, presentation, and application layers, respectively (see Table 3-5). The first letter of each word should remind you of each layer in sequence. Now let's examine each layer.

The Application Layer

Hypertext Transfer Protocol (HTTP): technology that allows the browser on the user's PC to look at a standard set of codes called HTML to decide how the text or graphics should be displayed.

Hypertext Markup Language (HTML): a standard set of codes representing text or graphics.

The application layer communicates with the actual application in use. It answers the question "What data do I send to my partner?" It is simply two useful programs talking to each other. For example, an e-mail client browser program talks to the e-mail server program, saying: "Deliver this message to ema@Georgia.com." Remember that each type of program (e-mail) has its own protocol. The application level protocol assumes that the next layer down (presentation layer) will take care of passing the message along to its destination.

Standards at the application layer specify how two application programs should communicate. The main standard on the application layer is the **Hypertext Transfer Protocol (HTTP).** Its function is to govern requests and responses between the browser and the Web server applications program. HTTP allows the browser on the user's PC to look at a standard set of codes called **HyperText Markup Language**

Table 3-5
The OSI reference model

Layer	Information Transacted	TCP/IP Protocols
7. Application Layer	Application messages	HTTP, SNMP, FTP DNS
6. Presentation Layer	Compressed data, encrypted data	
5. Session Layer	Session messages	
4. Transport Layer	Multiple packets	TCP
3. Net (Internet) Layer	Packets	IP
2. Data Link Layer	Frames	Ethernet, PPP
1. Physical Layer	Bits	Wiring, cables

(HTML) to decide how text and graphics should be displayed. HTTP decides how an HTML document transfers from a Web server to a client (see Figure 3-5).

The application layer is where the user begins to do something useful—browse a Web site, send e-mail, or transfer a file between file servers and client computers. This is where File Transfer Protocol (FTP) plays a major role. FTP is another member of the TCP/IP protocol suite. **Simple Network Management Protocol (SNMP)** is a TCP/IP protocol used for controlling network devices at the application layer. **Domain Name Service (DNS)** converts IP addresses into easy-to-remember names for the user. It is easier to enter www.virginia.edu than the IP address 191.172.54.12. DNS takes the name and looks up the equivalent IP address, which it sends along for processing.

Simple Network Management Protocol (SNMP): protocol that controls network devices at the application layer.

Domain Name Service (DNS): software that converts IP addresses into easy-to-remember names for the user.

Although all layers are important to make applications work, it is the application layer that is the most important for conducting business on the Internet.

The Presentation Layer

The presentation layer asks the question "What do the data look like?" Its function is to convert data into a format for network transmission. For incoming messages, it converts the data into a format the receiving application can understand. Called the network's translator, the presentation layer allows two application processes to decide on a common format for representing information such as text or graphics.

The Session Layer

This layer allows two parties to have communications across a network, called sessions. It answers the question "Who is my partner?" Applications on each end of the session are able to exchange data for the duration of the session. This layer keeps track of the status of the exchange and ensures that only designated parties are allowed to participate. It enforces security protocols for controlling access to session information.

The Transport Layer

The function of the transport layer is to manage the transmission or the flow of data between two computers or across a network. It makes sure that the program on one computer connected to another program on another computer receives and sends information accurately. The transport layer answers the question "Where is my partner?"

It also allows two computers to communicate, regardless of being made by different vendors. The way it manages the data flow is by segmenting data into multiple packets (see Table 3-5). If a lot of traffic is flowing, it tells other computers to pause. The transport layer also acknowledges successful transmissions and requests retransmission if packets are damaged or arrive in error. It breaks the connection when transmission ends.

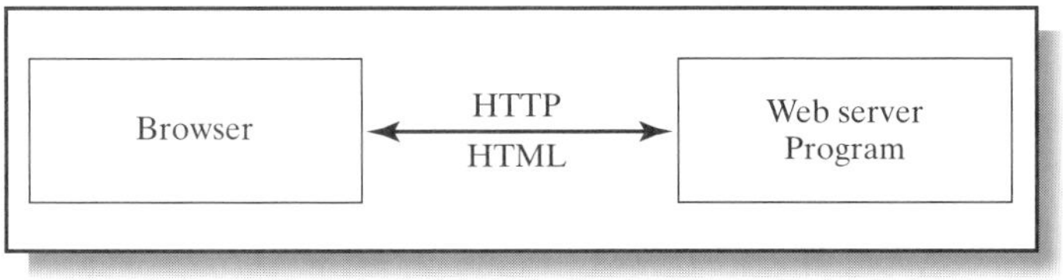

Figure 3-5
Key function of HTTP

Transmission Control Protocol (TCP): protocol that specifies how two host computers will work together.

The standard for the transport layer is the **Transmission Control Protocol (TCP).** TCP assumes that the next level down (the Internet layer) will take care of moving packets of data on to their destination without a problem. TCP is the most popular standard in use on the Internet. When you use a Web server, it does not matter if it is a PC or a mainframe. Your PC can communicate with it using TCP. HTTP also requires the use of the TCP standard at the transport layer.

In addition to ensuring data delivery from one computer to another, TCP performs another important job: flow control. Sometimes a fast computer sends data at a rate that the slower, receiving computer cannot process. TCP moderates data flow to the speed of the slower computer to avoid network congestion and ensure reliability of data transmission.

The Internet Layer

The Internet layer answers the question "Which route do I use to get there?" The function of this layer is to route messages across multiple. It also handles network congestion. A typical message is "Send this packet to computer number 190.172.63.08 via computer number 123.32.12.14, which is on a network one hop away."

The standard at the Internet layer specifies how hosts and routers will route packets from source host to destination host across several subnets or single networks connected by routers. It is at this layer that messages are referred to as packets. The standard for routing packets is the Internet Protocol (IP). You can see now why Internet addresses are called IP addresses.

TCP/IP: a set of protocols that guarantee data delivery.

TCP/IP is the most widely used protocol on the Internet. If packets get lost, they are resent automatically. It is also a communications protocol that connects Internet hosts. It defines how data are subdivided into packets for transmission across a network, and how applications can transfer files and e-mail. TCP/IP provides the basis for high-performance networking.

The Data Link Layer

The data link layer is the basement of the Internet. It takes care of the actual transfer of data between two computers located on the same network. The data link layer answers the question "How do I make it through the route?" A typical message is "Send this packet to computer number 110.42.21.13, which I can see right next door."

point-to-point protocol (PPP): a standard at the data link layer used for framing and error detection.

data frame: basic unit of Internet traffic.

Ethernet: a protocol that makes it possible for personal computers to contend for access to a network.

When we dial in with a telephone line and a modem, the main standard at this layer is the **point-to-point protocol (PPP).** Its main job is framing and error detection. Framing marks the boundary between packets. Messages at the data link layer are called **data frames.** At the receiving end, the data link layer packages bits of data from the physical layer into data frames for delivery to the Internet layer. This data frame is the basic unit of Internet traffic. Data from upper layers are placed for sending, and data are sent from it to the upper layers.

A more effective way to send packets is over an **Ethernet.** Ethernet is a protocol that makes it possible for personal computers to contend for access to a network. Framing and error detection are handled automatically by Ethernet hardware. A typical Ethernet has 100 computers linked to it. There must be a way to tell which of these computers the packet is intended for. A commonsense way to do it is to place the IP address of the destination computer in front of the packet. As each packet whizzes by, only the computer with the correct address receives it. Although the Ethernet broadcasts a message to all the computers linked to it, only the computer with the right address broadcasts an answer. The rest ignore both the question and the answer.

The Physical Layer

The physical layer is the lowest layer in the journey of a message from source to destination. It converts bits into signals for outgoing messages and signals into bits for incoming messages. It answers the question "How do I use the medium (cable, physical wiring) for transmission?"

Summing Up

If you are going through this material for the first time, it probably seems incredibly complicated. It is, but all you need to know is how computers communicate across the Internet. Can you imagine a highway without street signs, speed limits, or police to enforce traffic rules? The Internet is the same. For message traffic to flow smoothly and reliably, we need standards for communication and ways for systems from different vendors to work together. We also need protocols to set the rules of transmission and overall communication at each layer of the communication cycle.

Here is an example: A user sends a request via PC to access a company's Web page (e.g., Dell.com). The PC's browser activates the application layer to communicate between the client program on the user's PC and the Web server application program. At the application layer, for the Web the standard is HTTP. The application layer reviews the message and its destination and *stamps* it or *tags* it with a special identifier to keep track of it before it is sent to the next layer (transport) for processing.

At the transport layer, the goal is to ensure that the user's computer and the host computer (Web server) can work together, regardless of the vendor or make of the two computers. HTTP mandates the use of TCP at the transport layer. Before the message is sent to the Internet layer, the transport layer divides it into chunks (packets) if it is too large, and provides checks to make sure it is error free when delivered. The chunks are resequenced at the destination (see Figure 3-6).

At the Internet layer, the decision is made as to how the packet will be routed to the destination host (Web server), using IP as a standard. It translates the network address and names into their physical equivalents and uses one or more routers connected by single networks to do the job. IP messages are called IP packets because that is the generic name for Internet layer messages. This layer handles packet switching and ensures the best way to route a packet. It also handles network congestion and delivery priorities to minimize any unnecessary delay in packet delivery. Once it leaves the Internet layer, the packet is in the hands of the physical layer.

The physical layer uses modems and telephone network standards to transmit the message as raw data to its destination. It actually converts bits into signals for outgoing messages and signals into bits for incoming messages. Modems are used only to link a user host to the first router. By now the message is halfway to its destination. The physical layer is at the bottom in the data communication model. The data link layer picks up the raw data (incoming message) from the physical layer and converts it into frames for delivery to the Internet layer.

The standard used between the user's PC and the first router is the Point-to-Point Protocol (PPP). It checks to make sure the message is intact before sending it to the Internet layer. At the Internet layer, the frame is encapsulated into an IP packet. This layer decides on the best way to route the message to the destination host computer (Web

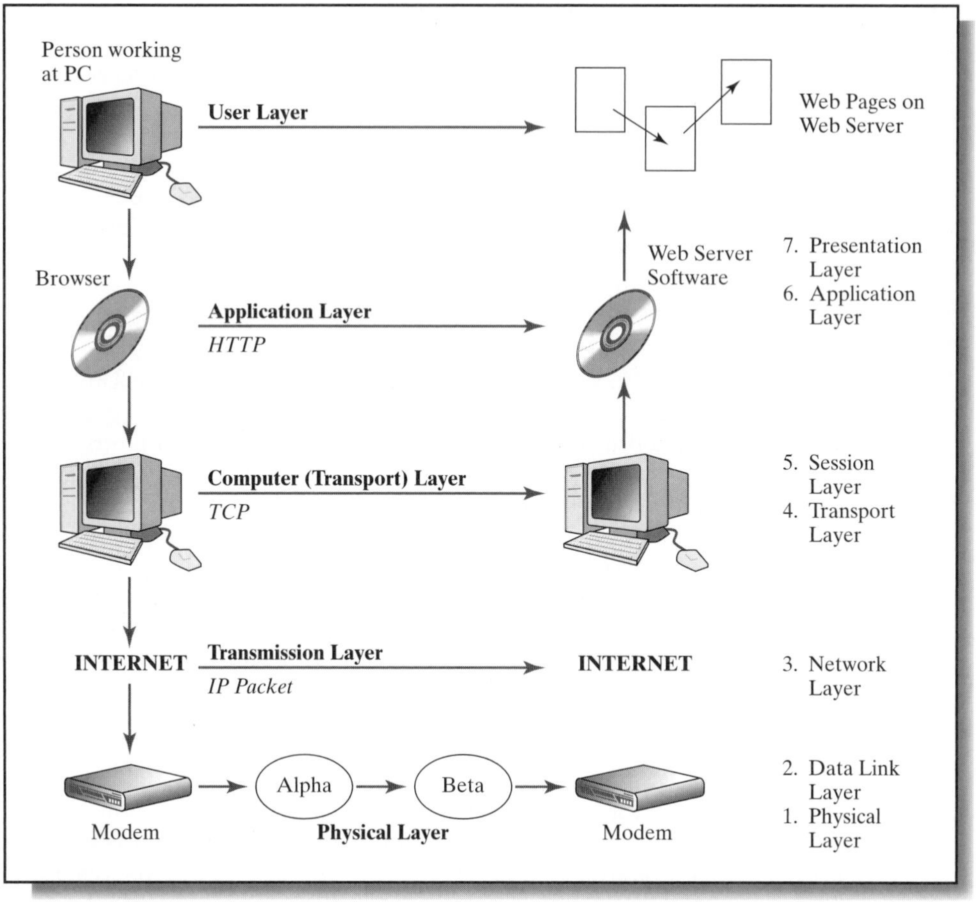

Figure 3-6
The transmission life cycle of a client request

server). At the transport layer, the IP packet is received, de-encapsulated, and checked for errors, and the content is sent to the next-higher level—the session layer.

At the session layer, the message is checked to determine which host computer should get it. The presentation layer merely decides on the format the message should have before it reaches the Web server. When the message reaches the application layer of the Web server, it is acknowledged and responded to, and the home page of the firm (in our example, www.dell.com) is displayed on the user's monitor.

In preparation for the journey, a message is divided into manageable packets. Each network level adds its own header information to keep track of its whereabouts. With the encapsulation of headers, a packet can easily end up with more headers than actual data. This uses extra memory space and eats up more transmission time. Unfortunately, it is the price we pay for the security and integrity of the Internet.

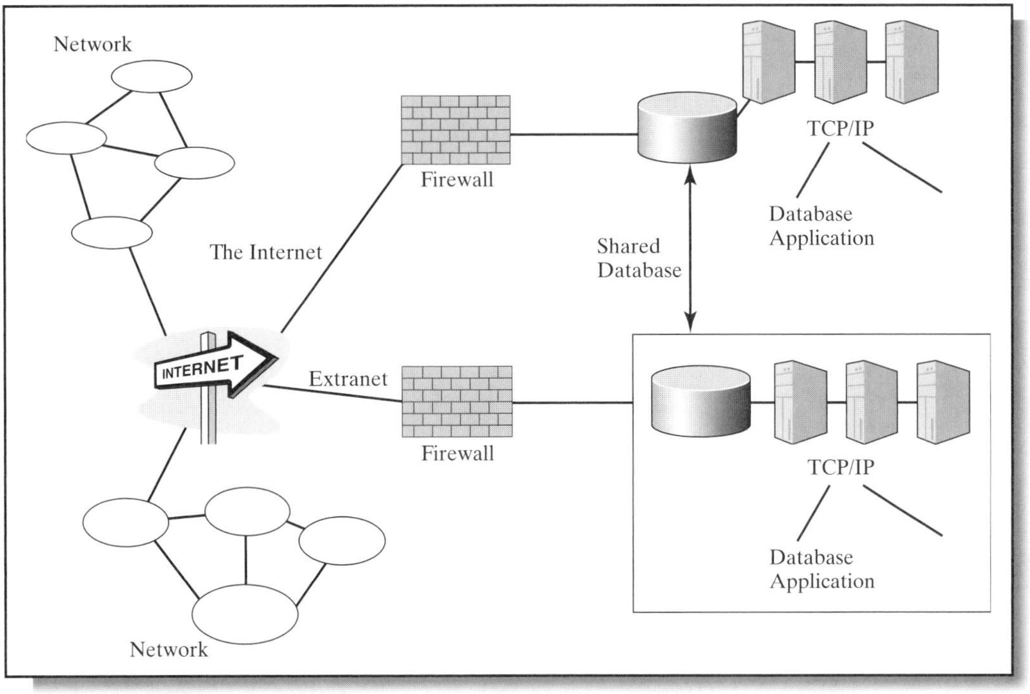

Figure 3-7
Internets, Intranets, and Extranets

Other Networks

Intranet: a network using TCP/IP to share information within an organization.

Extranet: a network that connects separate companies with a shared database.

TCP/IP protocols are not restricted to the Internet. Companies have found them useful in creating **Intranets,** or internal company networks using TCP/IP to share information within an organization. Companies wishing to connect with vendors and suppliers establish shared databases and use TCP/IP to form **Extranets.** This infrastructure is part of business-to-business e-commerce. Figure 3-7 shows the connections among the Internet, an Intranet, and an Extranet. (Intranets and Extranets are covered in detail in separate chapters later in the text.)

Video and Movie Standards

If you watch a video on your monitor or listen to music through the Internet, you probably use a unique standard called Moving Picture Experts Group (MPEG). This is an evolving compression and decompression standard for delivery of video, audio, and multimedia over computer systems and networks. According to Lais (2002), MPEG algorithm compresses data into small bits for easy transmission and then decompresses it quickly on the destination end to allow high-fidelity reconstruction. Box 3-1 summarizes the method used in generating MPEG pictures.

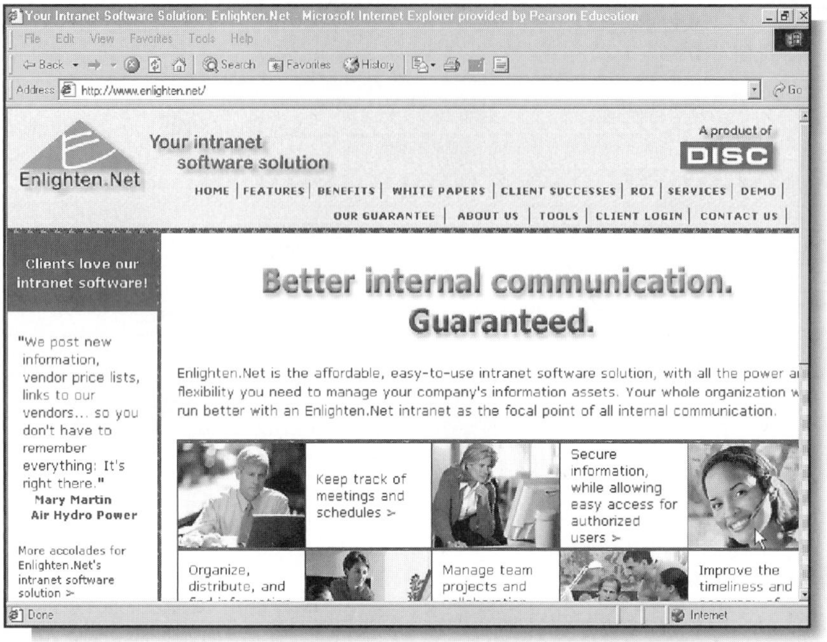

Screen Capture 3-2

Source: DISC 2003–2004. All rights reserved.

BOX 3-1

MPEG standards

In 1988, the Moving Picture Experts Group Licensing Administrator (MPEG LA), which is made up of nine companies and a university, developed MPEG-1 and submitted the standard to the U.S government. Permission to license the standard was received in 1991. MPEG algorithms compress the data to form small bits that can be easily transmitted and then decompressed accurately and quickly to allow high-fidelity reconstruction. MPEG standards aim for a compression ratio of about 52:1, requiring the reduction of, for example, 7.7 MB to less than 150 KB.

For interlaced images, like those on a conventional TV, half of the screen—every other field—is drawn at a rate of 60 times per second. The other half of the fields is drawn in the next second. The two sets alternate continuously, producing an even data stream and images that the human eye perceives as smooth motion.

The ease with which a 90-minute movie can be copied onto a CD using MPEG-4 prompted moviemakers, fearing a Napster-like furor, to petition Congress for copyright protection—now standard—on DVDs to prevent such copying. Built on previous MPEG standards, MPEG-21 is a multimedia framework designed for creating and delivering multimedia. Work on the standard began in June 2000. Key elements are digital item declaration, identification, content handling, use and representation, intellectual property management and protection, terminals and network, and event reporting.

SOURCE: Excerpted from Lais, Sami, "MPEG Standards," *Computerworld*, October 7, 2002, 36.

Network Hardware

So far, we have focused on the software part of the Internet. In trying to understand system design, software is the first consideration. Then we must assess the hardware required to drive the software. Network hardware plays a crucial role in helping information flow through the Internet. In its simplest form, a computer network includes two or more PCs connected to a printer. In some of the largest multinational organizations, it means thousands of PCs, printers, servers, firewalls, routers, switches, hubs, repeaters, and gateways. It's like comparing a two-bedroom apartment to a skyscraper. Each piece of hardware serves a special function, such as connecting a PC to the network, managing and routing traffic, boosting performance, and connecting different parts of a network.

Complex networks require people with specialized skills to manage them effectively. The level of technical skill and the size of the technical staff depend largely on the size of the network, the time requirements of the organization, and the type of information transmitted. Unless a company has a network with fewer than 20 users, companies need at least one full-time network administrator.

Cable Types

Our coverage of network infrastructure is incomplete without a basic understanding of the types of cables used to link network components. The type of cable affects speed of data transfer, network size, cost, and ease of installation. There are three types of cable (twisted pair, optical fiber, coaxial), plus wireless technology.

Twisted-Pair Cable

Twisted pair is probably the most commonly used type of networking cable in the United States. It originally was used to connect a telephone to a wall jack. It consists of two pairs of insulated copper wires twisted around each other, then enclosed in a plastic sheath. Twisting the wires this way protects against cross talk or natural signal overflow and interference from one wire to another.

twisted-pair cable: two pairs of insulated wires twisted around each other, then enclosed in a plastic sheath.

Twisted pair has the advantage of making it easy to add computers to an existing network, and it is the least expensive cable medium. The main disadvantages are susceptibility to noise and distance limitations. It is also the least secure, which means it is the easiest to tap.

Shielded and Unshielded Twisted Pair

The cheapest LAN transmission medium is the copper wire. Ensuring a complete electrical circuit requires only a pair of copper wires. A pair of wires usually is twisted to reduce interference problems but does not have shielding against electrical interference. Therefore, it is called **unshielded twisted-pair** cabling, or UTP.

unshielded twisted pair (UTP): a pair of wires twisted to reduce electrical interference but without the shielding.

UTP cabling is defined in terms of five cable categories, with category 5 used for handling data transfer rates of 100 Mbps. UTP cabling is not without its drawbacks. First, there is vulnerability to electromagnetic interference and cross talk. Second, UTP is subject to attenuation, which means weakening of the signal beyond 100 meters. Attenuation makes signals unreadable after a specified distance unless a repeater (a device that regenerates and retransmits the signal) is used.

shielded twisted pair (STP): cable with an electrically grounded, woven copper mesh or aluminum foil wrapped around each twisted pair.

In contrast to UTP cabling, **shielded twisted pair** (STP) cabling traditionally has been used in networks. STP has an electrically grounded woven copper mesh or aluminum foil wrapped around each twisted pair and another metal mesh wrapped around a multiple bundle of wires. This cable type reduces electromagnetic interference, but the wiring is thick and difficult to lay and maintain.

Fiber-Optic Cable

Fiber-optics communication and data transport use light rather than voltage to transmit data. Fiber optics relies on the principle that light can travel in a glass medium and carry more information than other predecessors of data communication. The fiber enables digitized light signals to be transmitted more than 60 miles without being amplified. This medium has a number of benefits that outperform copper and coaxial media such as fewer transmission losses, lower interference, and higher bandwidth.

fiber-optic cable: transmission system that uses light rather than voltage to transmit data.

With **fiber-optic cable**, when light reaches the central glass core, it hits a layer of glass cladding, resulting in internal reflections at the boundary. Because no light escapes, there is little attenuation and zero interference or eavesdropping.

Fiber-optic speed for data transmission ranges from 100 Mbps to 2 Gbps (gigabits per second). Data are reliably transmitted over a distance of 2 kilometers (1.4 miles) without a repeater. Unlike other cable types, fiber-optic cable supports voice and video, as well as data transmission. These features make fiber-optic cabling a good candidate for networks that must be very secure and require fast transmission over long distances. Its main drawbacks are:

- It is the most expensive of all network media types.
- Each segment that transmits incoming and receiving data must contain an incoming cable and an outgoing cable.
- It requires highly skilled installers and special connectors.

Selection Criteria

According to the International Engineering Consortium for fiber optics, three performance parameters need to be considered.

- **Attenuation—**This is a term that means "delay." It is the reduction of signal strength due to gravitational pull. For fiber optics, reduction of light is measured in decibels per kilometer. Optical fiber is superior to other transmission media, because it provides higher bandwidth with low attenuation that requires fewer amplifiers and allows the signal to be transmitted over longer distances.
- **Dispersion—**Dispersion is the time distortion of an optical signal that results from discrete wavelength components traveling at different rates, causing distortion of wavelengths and limiting data rates as well as capacity of a fiber.
- **Mode-Field Diameter (MFD)** This performance parameter is the functional parameter that determines optical performance when a fiber is coupled to a light source, spliced, or bent. It is essential in deciding on the resistance to bend that might cause loss in strength of the signal.

In summary, fiber optics has proven itself as the networking technology of the future. It is reliable, because the data delivered over this medium are the least susceptible to the propagation effects witnessed in traditional networking media. Advanced fiber-optic technologies are expected to provide for greater network capabilities than ever seen in the past.

Coaxial Cable

coaxial cable: a cable consisting of a copper center shielded by a plastic insulating material, which allows high data transmission rates over long distances.

Coaxial cable is an early version of the way computers were connected to a network, and it worked well. It is the cable in "cable TV." This cable has a copper core that is much thicker than twisted-pair cable, so it allows higher data transmission rates over long distances. The core is shielded by a plastic insulating material surrounded by a second conductor that looks much like woven copper mesh or aluminum foil. The outer shield is used as an electrical ground that simultaneously protects the inner core from interference.

Coaxial cable can transmit up to 10 Mbps for a distance of up to 500 meters. The main drawback of this type of cable is its inflexibility and low security, but it requires little maintenance and is simple to install. It also provides better resistance to electrical noise over long distances, and its electronic support components are affordable.

Wireless Technology

A relatively new addition to physical media like coaxial, twisted-pair, and fiber-optic cable is wireless data transmission. Going wireless is like scuba diving wearing lightweight gear and not being linked by a long umbilical cord to a ship for air. Wireless transmission is data communication without physical attachments. At present, it varies in speed, signal type, transmission distance, and frequency (the higher the frequency is, the higher the transmission rate is).

wireless data transmission technology: data transmission without physical attachments; microwave, radio wave, and infrared.

The three types of **wireless data transmission technology** are microwave, radio wave, and infrared. *Microwave* transmission is used to connect LANs in separate buildings (e.g., two skyscrapers) where physical media are impractical. The main limitation is that the transmitter and receiver must be within the line of sight of each other, usually 30 miles apart. For global transmission, the technology relies on satellites and ground-based satellite dishes to meet the line-of-sight requirements.

Radio technology transmits via radio frequency but has no distance limitations. It is susceptible to atmospheric and electronic interference, and is subject to government regulation. Because of security limitations and the potential for eavesdropping, most radio transmission is encrypted.

Infrared transmission operates at frequencies approaching the speed of light. Because it can experience interference from bright light, this type of technology is limited to line-of-sight or short-distance applications. It is commonly found in department stores or office buildings. A summary of the pros and cons of network cabling is shown in Table 3-6.

Key Components of a Network

A typical network has a number of critical components. In this section, we briefly review the main pieces of hardware, their functions, and how they contribute to a reliable network.

Network Interface Card (NIC): a card installed in a slot in the PC to allow communication between the PC and other PCs in the LAN and beyond.

Network Interface Card (NIC)

At the user's end of the network, the most direct physical connection from the PC is through the **Network Interface Card (NIC).** A NIC card

Table 3-6
Pros and cons of cabling types

CABLING TYPE	ADVANTAGES	DISADVANTAGES
Twisted pair	Protects against cross talk and interference Easy to add computers to network Well-understood technology Less expensive than other cabling media	Susceptibility to noise Least secure Distance limitations Requires more expensive hubs
UTP	Inexpensive Easier to install than STP	Interference from outside electromagnetic sources Cross talk Vulnerable to tapping Subject to attenuation
STP	Reduces EMI High-speed transmission	Difficult to lay and maintain Delicate cable
Optical fiber	Reliable transmission High security Supports voice, video, data Smallest in size Longest in longevity	Most expensive medium in terms terms of installation and maintenance Requires incoming and outgoing cable Requires special connections
Coaxial cable	Can transmit up to 10 Mbps over 500 Meters Low maintenance Simple to install Good resistance-to-noise ratio Inexpensive electric support components	Inflexible, thick cable Low security cable is rigid Limited distance Susceptibility to tapping
Wireless technology	Convenient alternative to network cabling connections	Relatively new
Microwave	Connects two buildings where physical media are impractical	Transmitter and receiver must be within line of sight
Radio wave	No distance limitations	Susceptible to atmospheric and security limitations
Infrared	Operates at speed of light Wireless data transfer	Limited to short distance and line-of-site applications

modem (modulator/demodulator): a device that converts digital signals into analog format for outgoing transmission and converts incoming messages from analog to digital format for computer processing.

is installed in a slot in the PC, with a cable plugged into the back of it (see Figure 3-8). The other end of the cable is plugged into a wall-jack connection or directly into the hub or switch for a small network (see following text). Another cable runs from the hub to the route to complete the connections.

To communicate over a telephone line, the PC needs a **modem,** which has the dual function of converting digital signals into analog form for transmission across the telephone line, and converting

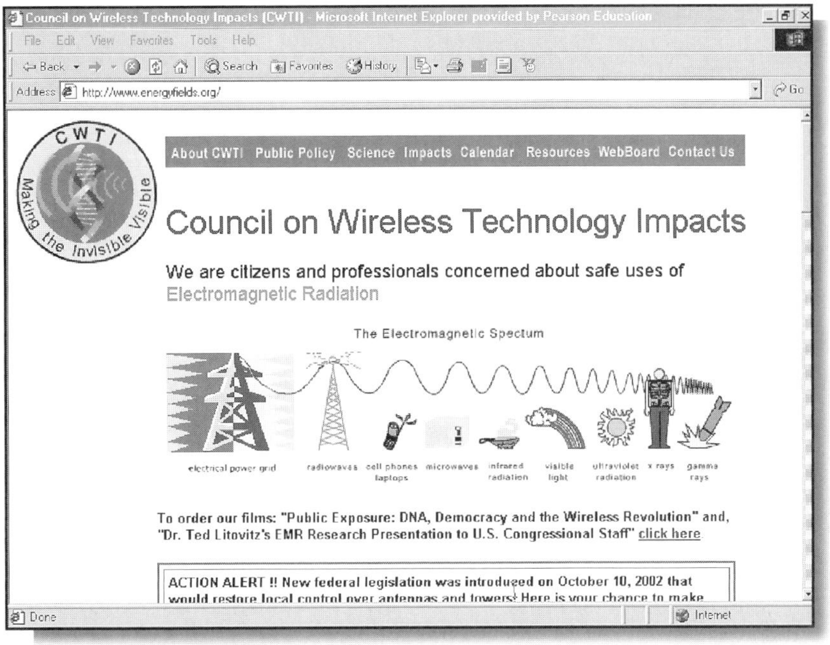

Screen Capture 3-3

Source: Used with permission of the Council on Wireless Technology Impacts © 2003–2004.

Figure 3-8

Network Interface Card and hub or switch in a local area network

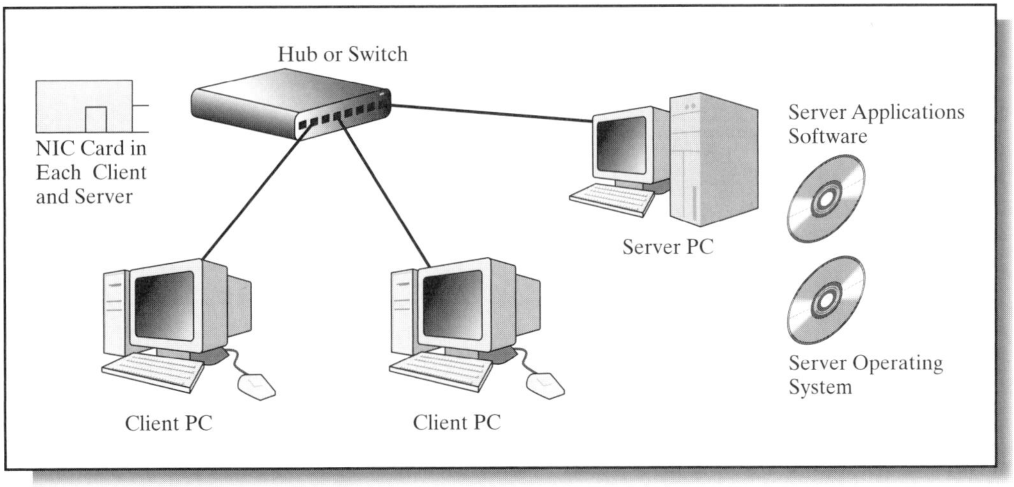

incoming analog signals into digital signals. Computers represent data in bits or digital format; the telephone line is analog (see Figure 3-9).

Hubs and Switches

hub: a piece of hardware that operates as a connecting point for many PCs in a network.

A **hub** is a piece of hardware that operates at the OSI physical layer and acts as a connecting point—like a one-way road where all cars share the same lane. Hubs are a party line where everyone talks at once (see Figure 3-8). There are three types of hubs.

- *Passive* hubs require no power and merely act as a physical connection point for the PCs that are part of the local area network.
- *Active* hubs require power to strengthen signals passing through them for transmission.
- *Intelligent* hubs have built-in programmable features to handle packet switching, routing traffic, and the like.

switch: a piece of hardware that offers a direct connection to a particular PC.

In contrast to hubs, **switches** are like a highway where every car has its own lane. This means no traffic congestion. Unlike a hub, where everyone talks at once, a switch offers direct connection to a particular PC. Hubs are phasing out because they do not offer the same efficiency as switches. The types of switches are summarized in Box 3-2.

Routers

router: network hardware that operates at the OSI Internet layer, linking a network to other networks.

A **router** is a piece of hardware that operates at the OSI Internet layer, linking the network into little chunks, called network segments, so users on different LAN segments can talk to one another. Routers are usually "intelligent": They evaluate the network traffic and can stop local traffic from entering and causing congestion on other local area networks. Routers also can make intelligent path choices. They can filter out packets that need not be received. In this way, they can reduce network congestion and boost data performance. Because routers can select an alternative path for a packet if the default route is down, they make data delivery more reliable.

routing table: software that logs the pattern of traffic coming from neighboring routers.

Routers have certain drawbacks. They are expensive and difficult to operate. At times they are slow, because they must perform additional processing on the data packet. Some advanced routers also can add excessive traffic to the network because of constant messages to one another when updating their routing tables. A **routing table** on a

Figure 3-9
How a modem works

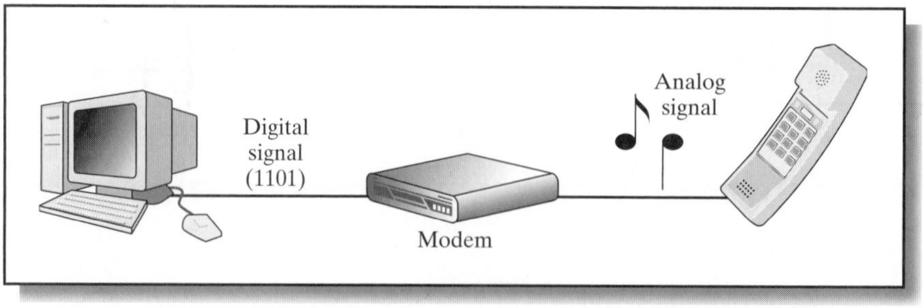

BOX 3-2
E-commerce trends: Which switch is which?

It seems as if companies these days are trying to hawk switches operating at virtually every layer of the OSI protocol stack. When should which switch be deployed? The answer isn't always easy—but here's our take on the market at present.

General Purpose. Starting at the bottom of the stack are the Layer 1 switches. . . . The only people buying these switches are service providers and ISPs with truly massive data needs.

Hopping up one level to the data-link layer are traditional Layer 2 switches. They are . . . used . . . mostly to increase the amount of bandwidth available. In almost every situation, switches are better than hubs.

Layer 3 network switches should be used by any large enterprise that has routing needs going from Ethernet to Ethernet. These switches basically are routers that operate at wire speed.

Specialized Devices. Layer 4 switches work at the transport layer and are quickly becoming passé, but they still do perform a needed function in today's network. . . .

Layer 7 application layer switches or Web switches are quickly becoming a mainstay of the Net economy. These switches forward requests based on the URL in the packets. . . . Layer 7 switches are needed by everyone—from service providers to dot.com companies of every size.

SOURCE: Chowdhry, Pankaj, "Which Switch Is Which?" Sm@rt *Reseller*, May 15, 2000, p. 50.

Screen Capture 3-4

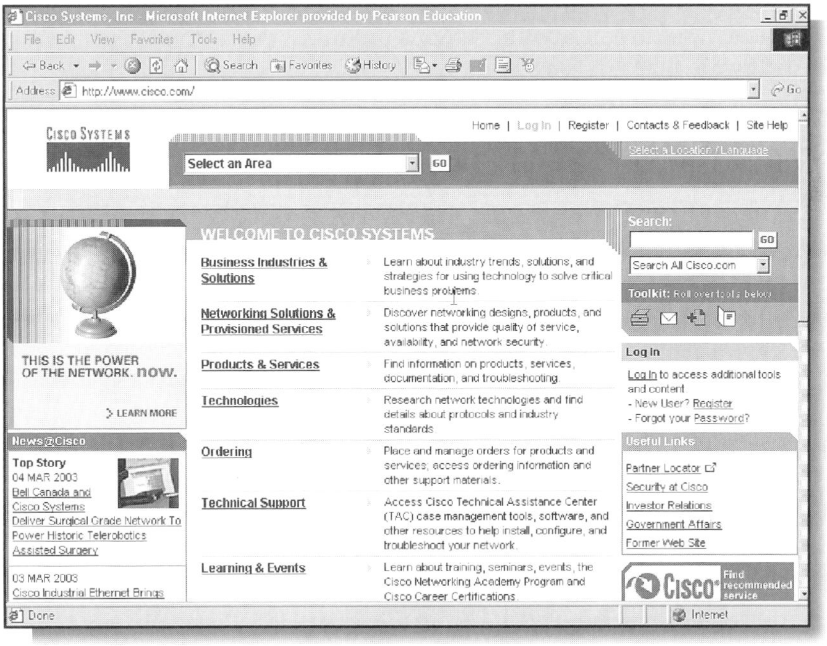

Source: These materials have been reproduced by Prentice Hall Business Publishing with the permission of Cisco Systems, Inc. Copyright © 2003 Cisco Systems, Inc. All rights reserved.

router is a log of the pattern of traffic coming from neighboring routers so that the next time the router sends out or receives packets, it can tell whether to take a certain route based on information stored in its routing table. Every few seconds, each router on the Net consults the router to which it is directly connected (its neighbor). By comparing notes, the router can decide which way to send packets to each of the hundreds of routers on the Internet. The goal for the router is to minimize the number of *hops* a packet must take before it reaches its destination.

Gateways

gateway: a special-purpose computer that allows communication between dissimilar systems on the network.

A **gateway** is a special-purpose computer that runs gateway software. It facilitates communications between dissimilar systems connected to a network, TCP/IP, or IBM's System Network Architecture (SNA). Gateways operate primarily at the application layer of the OSI. They have many advantages, but they are difficult to install and configure. They are also more expensive than other devices. Because of the extra processing time it takes to translate from one protocol to another, gateways can be slower than routers and similar hardware devices.

Designing a Network

It should be clear by now that network communication functions are performed primarily by a combination of hardware and software specifically designed to support the network. The hardware part typically includes the Network Interface Card, the cables, and the hub that connects the workstations to the router and beyond. To implement the network, you need to consider the various protocols and the architecture that will support the hardware.

Step 1: Factors to Consider

When designing a network, you need to consider several factors.

- **Location**—Where will the network be installed? How convenient is the location? How easy is it going to be to install in terms of the cabling, space allocation, and other issues?
- **Capacity**—What is the optimum traffic capacity of the network? How scalable (upgradable) is it? How efficient is its performance at that capacity?
- **Distance limitations**—What is the distance of the farthest PC to the server? How does distance affect network performance during peak hours? How does distance invite security threats?
- **Cost**—What is the estimated cost of the proposed network installation? Is the cost within the client's budget? What are the hidden costs? Given the cost, how would you justify the return on investment?
- **Potential growth**—How easily and how well can the network be expanded to meet the growing demands of the client organization? What is the expected cost of such growth?
- **Security**—How secure is the proposed network? What security measures should be incorporated? Who will be in charge of monitoring security?

Step 2: Selecting Network Architecture

The next step is to consider these factors when selecting network architecture.

Hardware Requirements

These include servers; workstations; and peripherals such as printers, hubs, routers, minicomputers, and backup systems in case the primary hardware fails. Amount of usage is also important. For example, it makes no sense to install a high-powered networked environment for a company with limited usage and low potential for growth. If network utilization is high and the organization expects rapid growth, it makes sense to replace aging terminals and dumb hubs with intelligent workstations and intelligent routers.

Software Requirements

These requirements depend largely on the kind of hardware and applications available. For example, if the company has mission-critical applications with high performance requirements, then the only choice would be to revisit the existing infrastructure and bring in the software that can meet immediate and future needs. The choice of network architecture will depend on the factors cited earlier regarding network design.

Disaster Recovery and Fault-Tolerance Requirements

Recovery from disaster can be important to an organization, depending on the sensitivity of data, size of the files, and reliability of the network that must be available in a secure environment around the clock. The network infrastructure must be protected by an Uninterruptible Power Supply (UPS), which takes over in the event of a blackout or any loss of power. All file servers and CD files should be kept under lock and key. Redundant equipment (hubs, switches, routers, servers) also should be available as backup for the main network. Fault tolerant means the system has built-in features that would allow it to recover from failure. Fault-tolerant hard disks are defined by a set of specifications known as Redundant Array of Inexpensive Disks, or RAID, which mirror resident disk drives.

Corporate Culture and Organizational Factors

The nontechnical aspect of network design is the corporate culture and the human factor. If the network is for a small company that cannot afford a full-time network administrator, it makes sense to install a basic peer-to-peer network that is fault tolerant and requires almost zero maintenance. If considering a network for a police department, where security is mandatory, a dedicated file server with a full complement of security features would be the best choice, even though it would be expensive.

The final choice depends on the type of user, how the network will be used, and whether the vendor or network developer will be allowed to access the network. User-level security (passwords) and system-level security (physical and logical) usually are required.

Successful Installation

Successful installation of a network needs to be planned in advance. Here are some things to do.

- Conduct a survey of current technology. Existing conditions and their constraints form the basis for any network design.

- Clarify and document network requirements including the number and type of computers in use, the required peripherals, whether the proposed local area network would interface with a mainframe or be a stand-alone system, the software in use or to be used, and the level of resource sharing required.
- Decide on the network operating system. This will determine the type of file server hardware and the transport protocols the system will support.
- Decide on the network technology and the file server hardware platform. This
- involves estimating the client traffic volume and how well certain technology will support the load. Any file server chosen should be supported by the network's operating system.
- Plan on the physical environment and client support. User and company requirements dictate where and how file servers, routers, and switches are stored and maintained. Any planned network must win client support, especially during the implementation and training phases.

MANAGING THE NETWORK

The job of finding qualified staff to manage a network has become a prime consideration when planning a corporate system. It is no longer enough to simply wire the user to the Internet. Someone has to maintain an acceptable level of system availability; assure good response time; run the network at optimal capacity; route voice and data traffic around the clock; and enable managers, employees, and customers to communicate effectively regardless of time, distance, or location.

The job of the network manager has become not only more complex, but the tools also have become more specialized. Today, tools help the network administrator ensure network performance by monitoring, analyzing, testing, diagnosing, and fixing the network.

Figure 3-10 shows a typical network management system to support a centralized network. The key components are as follows.

- **The manager**—The network administrator manages the network via software that is loaded on a special workstation. The manager's main function is to monitor various parts of the network, including printers, routers, switches, hubs, and other pieces of software and hardware. In a simple network, the manager uses a management protocol such as Simple Network Management Protocol (SNMP) to govern the way the manager communicates with the agent. It is a way of controlling network devices at the application layer.
- **Managed nodes**—The manager monitors various nodes. These nodes are pieces of software called agents that communicate with the manager on behalf of the node, much the same way a professional athlete's agent negotiates on behalf of the athlete.
  - **Objects**—**Objects** are ports or specific outlets on the managed node that the agent represents to the manager. This way, for example, managers can communicate to the agent that they want information about a specific port or that a port is to be disabled by a switch. Through SNMP, a manager can ask a file server agent about the status of an attachment like a printer and its readiness to print.

agent: node or software that communicates with the manager on behalf of the node.

object: port or specific outlet on a managed node that the agent represents to the manager.

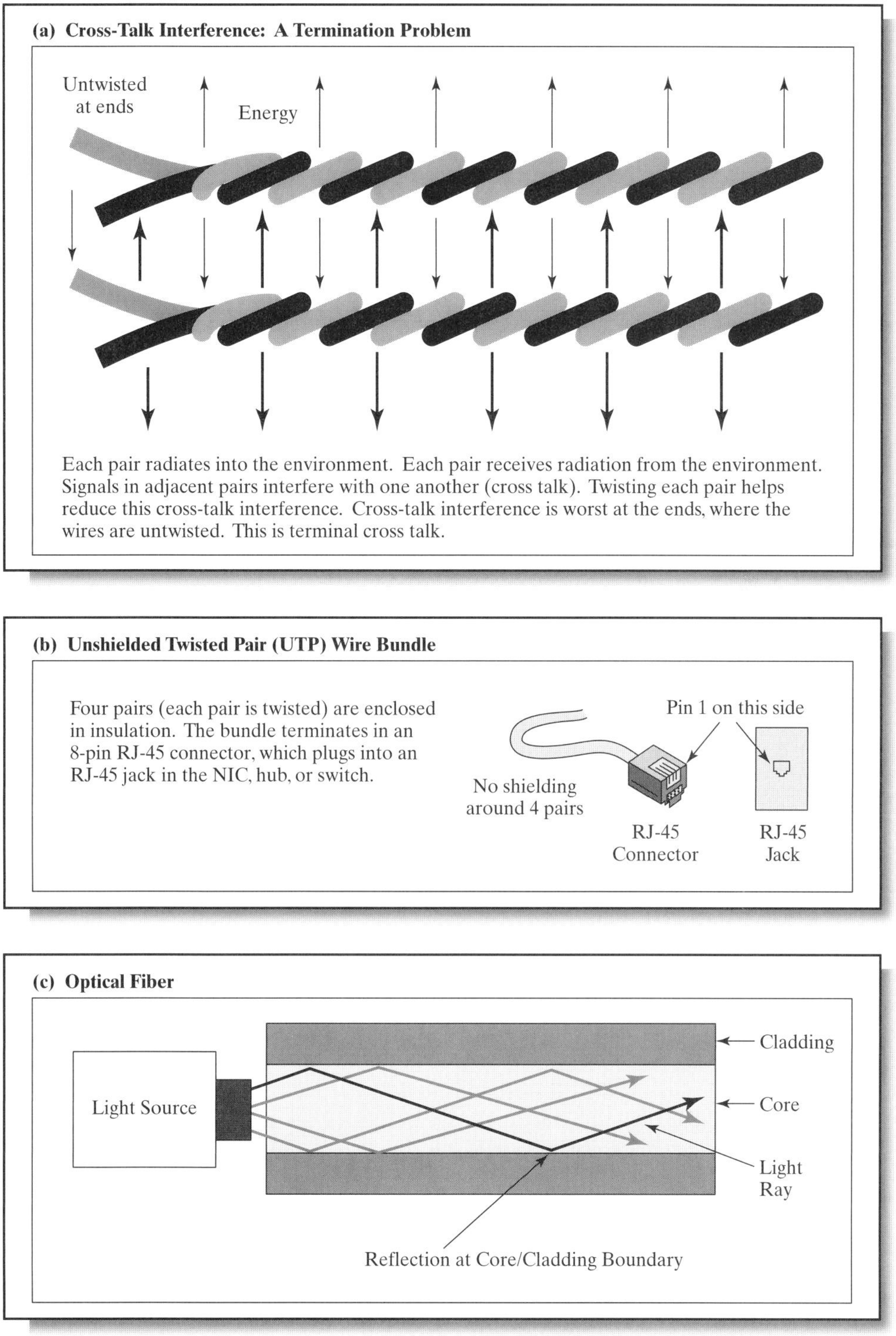

Figure 3-10

Network management system—an example

Source: Adapted from Panko, Raymond, *Business Data Communications and Networks* (3rd Ed.), Upper Saddle River, NJ: Prentice Hall, 2001, p. 278.

Management Information Base (MIB): software that defines the objects that can exist, based on the initial design of the database.

- **Management Information Base (MIB)**—The **management information base (MIB)** is another piece of software that defines the objects that can exist, based on the initial design of the database. An MIB on each managed node contains information about that node's objects. Sound confusing? It is, especially when you have to look at how data are stored, how they are accessed, and so on.
- **Requests and responses**—This aspect of the network management system simply uses SNMP to allow the manager and agents to work through preestablished cycles. A cycle begins when the manager sends a request. The agent sends a response that it has received the request, sends the requested data, or sends an error message. If an agent senses a condition that the manager should know about, it sends a message (called a **trap**) alerting the manager.

trap: message sent to the manager by an agent, alerting the manager to a special condition.

We have been building networks much larger than we can manage. When problems come up, it can take hours just to find the cause. What is needed are skilled technicians and highly trained specialists to monitor, diagnose, and fix the network to ensure reliability at all times. Companies must have policies to control the quality of service and security. We are entering an era of disciplined network management, with an array of intelligent devices and new technology, and a much faster and more reliable Internet.

LARGE-SCALE E-COMMERCE ISSUES

Security management is a continuous and vigilant process in high-volume e-commerce. The key issues deal with firewall security, intrusion detection, and various security breaches in an internetworking environment. Several exposures are worth mentioning:

- **Financial exposure**—This factor can cause irreparable monetary damage to a corporation. For example, the *New York Times* reported a disgruntled IT executive who sabotaged the computer systems of his company after being laid off, causing up to $20 million in damages (Berinato 2002).
- **IP exposure**—The ease in identifying IP addresses significantly increases a networked computer's vulnerability to hacking (google.icq.com/search/sitesearch/?q=ip+security).
- **Legal security**—The wealth of information that is accessible to anyone generated a growing concern and heightened the risks of infringing copyright and defamation laws. Companies are responsible for providing adequate security for the protection of privileged information on the Internet.
- **Packet sniffing**—This occurs when outsiders use programs to steal information traveling through a company network. The unauthorized interception of this proprietary information can result in significant losses for the company.
- **Firewalls**—One approach to ensuring corporate information security is through firewalls. A firewall serves as an intermediary between an internal network and the Internet. It controls which packets can pass into the network. Packet filter firewalls check the fields of the IP packet and screen out entries by invalid source addresses or port numbers. Application firewalls are application specific and also are known as proxy firewalls. Proxy firewalls reduce IP exposure by intercepting outgoing

packets and attaching their own IP address to it to conceal the client PC's IP address.

- **IPSec**—Another approach to network security is IP Security (IPSec), which is a set of standards that allow virtual private networks (VPNs) to improve packet filtering and enable application-layer firewalls to have better means of host verification by using the IPSec authentication header in addition to the actual IP address (Interhack.net).
- **Intrusion Detection Systems (IDS)**—This security tool serves as a watchdog for unauthorized activities by first identifying suspicious activities, notifying the administrator, and then responding to the attack. IDSs often fall into two categories: network based, which inspect packets passing through the network, and host based, which monitor log files and data on individual computers. Each category has unique benefits and potential.

In 2001, a team at the University of Idaho did cost-benefit analysis on intrusion-detection systems. They assigned values to tangible and intangible assets, as well as the cost of different types of hacks based on a taxonomy developed by the Department of Defense. With this, they were able to calculate Annual Loss Expectancy (ALE), which constitutes the cost of the attack multiplied by the frequency. As a result, return on security investment (ROSI) can be determined easily by subtracting security investment from the damage prevented. A positive ROSI means a company's security measures are in good shape, but a negative ROSI indicates either too much or too little investment in security. This is a warning sign to companies that the current security system needs to be changed (Berinato 2002).

Management Implications

The area of Internet and networking continues to attract the best talent, with more job openings than there are qualified people to fill them. Choose any IT job, no matter what its title, and it is likely woven into the Web one way or another. Every firm wants to have faster and better technology than the competition. The demand for technical help makes it a candidate's job market. Most jobs are new, triggered by the continuing surge of e-commerce, especially business-to-consumer and now business-to-business.

Of the skills required in the Internet and e-commerce areas, technology alone is not enough. Most recruiters look for candidates with good project management skills, interpersonal communication skills, and business knowledge. Even college graduates with a liberal arts and business background and good PC experience are attractive candidates

Table 3-7 is a summary of the most wanted Internet, networking, LAN, and client-server skills, based on responses from IT recruiters to the sixth annual skills survey conducted by *Computerworld* in the fall of 1999. Good, experienced network designers and people in TCP/IP are not easy to find. So where do IT recruiters find needed talent? After placement and recruiting firms, the second-best sources are Internet ads and Internet job sites (see Box 3-3).

What types of companies have the highest demand? E-commerce companies and those developing business-to-business applications are in the lead. Many experienced Java programmers working on a contract basis earn at least $100 per hour. Any company in e-commerce with a focus on designing a network and Web site has a high demand for those who have technical skills, with a bachelor's degree in fine arts and knowledge of computer animation (Brandel 2000, p. 91).

Table 3-7
Internet business careers

THE MOST WANTED SKILLS FOR THE YEAR 2000		
SKILL	PERCENTAGE OF COMPANIES WITH SKILL NOW	PERCENTAGE OF COMPANIES HIRING NEXT YEAR
INTERNET SKILLS		
Java	30	24
HTML	54	18
Active X	17	10
Netscape Server	13	03
NETWORKING SKILLS		
TCP/IP	77	24
IPX	29	05
SNA	19	05
INTERNET WORKING SKILLS		
Ethernet switching	42	07
10Base-T switching	40	07
Routing	37	05
LAN SKILLS		
Windows NT server	62	17
Novell NetWare	42	08
Ethernet	50	04
CLIENT/SERVER APPLICATION SKILLS		
Internet App. Development	34	27
E-commerce App. Dev.	20	15
Project Management	41	14

Source: "Business Careers," *Computerworld,* November 15, 1999, p. 66.

When all the necessary technical talent has been hired, a company must find ways to keep its IT employees. Regular training and the chance to work with the latest technology seem to be the best motivators (Watson 2000, p. 56). Good benefit packages are important. Recognition for a job well done, pleasant working conditions, and a good working relationship with IT staff also boost job satisfaction.

Here are some tips for retaining Internet and technical personnel.

- **Constructive and timely feedback**—One of the most important issues in managing and motivating technical people is consistent and constructive feedback on a day-to-day basis. This is especially true for new hires. Feedback is also important in helping personnel develop new skills and advance to more challenging positions.
- **Recognition and appreciation of good, value-added work**—It is human nature that recognition is a reinforcer, especially when it is made in a timely manner. A simple

BOX 3-3
E-careers: The best way to find a job

Forget typesetting resumes, drafting cover letters, and making follow-up calls. Many job seekers these days are taking to the Internet. But with an estimated 2,500 job-search sites, how do you decide what is best?

Most major sites offer job lists that can be searched by keyword and location. They also let you post your skills and experience without divulging your name or current employer. And many have software programs, called agents, that send an e-mail when a job listing matches specific criteria. It is worth checking out several sites for the types of listings they attract. One option is to go through a huge general site, such as Monster.com. The site receives some 2.5 million unduplicated visitors a month. The Internet's second-most frequented job site, CareerPath.com, boasts the highest number of open jobs—some 400,000 jobs.

Some job hunters believe it pays to use more than one site. Take the experience of Dan Reardon, a 33-year-old computer manager who recently relocated to Massachusetts from Texas. He used Monster.com, Boston.com, and CareerPath.com for his search. When calls came tumbling in, he discovered the importance of keeping track of which employers he contacted and which have responded.

Of course, the giant sites may not be the right stop for everyone. Niche sites such as Netshare Inc.'s netshare.com that caters to executives with salaries of $100,000 may have jobs that won't be found on more general-purpose sites. Such niche sites can help round out a job search. Bristol-Myers Squibb uses two of the giants, Career Builder.com and Monster.com, to achieve "comprehensive coverage," but also lists highly technical jobs on science.com.

SOURCE: Excerpted from McWilliams, Gary, "The Best Way to Find a Job," *The Wall Street Journal*, December 6, 1999, R16ff.

thanks from the heart is what it often takes to restart a project that has been going nowhere (Watson 2000, p. 57).

- **Championing staff causes—**A champion in IT is someone who uses every opportunity to promote a project with those on higher organizational levels. Sometimes top management reluctantly approves a project, not knowing how it is going to turn out. An IT manager can keep top managers interested and reinforce the progress made by example, by scenarios, or by online displays of completed work.
- **Support of employee career goals—**Technical employees should not only have opportunities to undergo training and improve their skills, but they should be able to utilize those skills. Technical people often are motivated more by opportunities for creativity than by money alone.
- **Match industry salary standards for in-house personnel—**Regardless of how well IT personnel are treated, it is still important to provide competitive salaries and attractive benefits to discourage defection to the competition. Many corporations now offer sign-up bonuses, stock options, pleasant office surroundings, flextime, and other opportunities to ensure job satisfaction and loyalty to the organization.

In the final analysis, it takes sensitivity, communication skills, timely feedback, and a genuine interest in people and their careers to make a department or a corporation successful.

SUMMARY

1. A network is a connection between at least two computers for the purpose of sharing resources. There are three types of networks: local area networks (LANs), wide area networks (WANs), and metropolitan area networks (MANs). These networks can be peer-to-peer, client/server, or hybrid networks. Each has benefits and drawbacks.
2. Transmission lines and routers in the United States are owned by commercial organizations. To use the Internet, a computer must be connected to an organization called an Internet Service Provider, or ISP. The ISP router connects the computer to the router of the other host computer on the Internet.
3. Internet host numbers are divided into two parts: the network part (first two numbers) and the local part (second two numbers). The four numbers are separated by dots. The initial bits of the IP address tell whether it is on a Class A, Class B, or Class C network, or whether it is a Class D multicast address.
4. Messages, invoicing, and other information transmission on the Internet are made possible by protocols, standards, and other software that transmits information via packets through a cable to its destination.
5. The OSI Reference Model is a seven-layer model that defines the basic network functions: application layer, presentation layer, session layer, transport layer, Internet layer, data link layer, and physical layer.
6. The standard for the transport layer is TCP, which is the most popular standard used on the Internet. It handles flow control, sequence assurance, and reliability and integrity issues.
7. To communicate over a line, you need a modem, which converts digital signals into analog form for transmission, and converts incoming analog signals into digital signals. To complete the transmission infrastructure, a hub is used to connect PCs to routers for transmission. A router is a piece of intelligent hardware that links the network into segments so users on different LAN segments can talk to one another.
8. Several factors need to be considered in designing a network: location, capacity, distance limitations, cost, potential growth, and security.
9. Several factors need to be considered in selecting network architecture: hardware requirements, software requirements, disaster recovery and fault-tolerance requirements, and corporate culture and organizational factors.
10. The main implication of networking for management is that firms need to have a work environment that technical people find conducive for long-term employment and one that promotes a career path for qualified employees.

KEY TERMS

- agent, 94
- client, 70
- client/server network, 70
- coaxial cable, 87
- data frame, 80
- domain name, 75
- Domain Naming Service (DNS), 79
- Ethernet, 80
- Extranet, 83
- fiber-optic cable, 86
- gateway, 92
- host name, 72
- hub, 90
- Hypertext Markup Language (HTML), 78
- Hypertext Transfer Protocol (HTTP), 78
- Internet Protocol (IP), 77
- Internet Service Provider (ISP), 73
- Intranet, 83
- IP address, 71
- Local Area Network (LAN), 69
- Management Information Base (MIB), 96

- Metropolitan Area Network (MAN), 69
- modem, 88
- network, 77
- Network Interface Card (NIC), 87
- node, 68
- object, 94
- OSI Reference Model, 78
- packet, 77
- peer-to-peer network, 69
- point-to-point protocol (PPP), 80
- protocol, 77
- router, 90
- routing table, 90
- server, 70
- shielded twisted pair (STP), 86
- Simple Network Management Protocol (SNMP), 79
- switch, 90
- TCP/IP, 80
- Transmission Control Protocol (TCP), 80
- trap, 96
- twisted-pair cable, 85
- unshielded twisted pair (UTP), 85
- Wide Area Network (WAN), 69
- wireless data transmission technology, 87
- zone name, 75

TEST YOUR UNDERSTANDING

1. What is a network? How does it differ from the Internet? Elaborate.
2. Distinguish between:
   a. Packets and IP addresses
   b. Protocols and TCP/IP
   c. Routers and hubs
3. In what way(s) are LANs, WANs, and MANs similar? Be specific.
4. Explain the function of a NIC card. Why is it needed in a PC or workstation?
5. Summarize the key benefits and drawbacks of peer-to-peer networks.
6. How does a peer-to-peer network differ from a client/server network?
7. Explain the role of the ISP in the Internet.
8. Does a 32-bit IP address tell you anything about the size of its network? Why?
9. In your own words, explain how computers communicate on the Internet.
10. Describe the types of cables used to link the network components.
11. More and more network installations employ fiber optics. Do you think this is the way to go? Explain.
12. What is so unique about wireless transmission? Elaborate.
13. List and briefly explain the key components of a network.
14. What are the factors to consider in designing a network? Discuss.
15. Describe the key components of a typical network management system.
16. Which of the following describes a LAN and why?
    a. Connects networks across the globe.
    b. A collection of computers residing within a small physical region.
    c. Uses WAN to interconnect networks within a geographical region.
17. What layer of the OSI Reference Model converts data into a generic format for networking transmission? Explain.
18. What layer of the OSI Reference Model manages flow control and error detection? Be specific.
19. Which protocol is considered a transport protocol—SNMP, TCP, or HTTP?
20. Of the three cable types, which is the most susceptible to cross talk: coaxial, fiber optic, or Category 5 unshielded twisted pair (UTP)?
21. Cost out an actual network installation and report your findings. Make sure you include labor costs.

Discussion Questions

1. Think about the network concept and the material covered in the chapter. What managerial implications can you draw that relate to a small to medium-size organization like a regional bank?
2. A number of surveys have been conducted to determine the most wanted technical skills in 2000. Table 3-7 gives a summary of one such survey. Review the journals and surf the Internet. Write a three-page report, reflecting new findings for 2001.
3. You are a college graduate with a major in IT from a large university located in a metropolitan area. On your first consulting job, you were assigned to design a network for a small liberal arts college of five departments (science, business, religion, political science, and history) and 800 students in a town of 9,000 people. What aspects of your alma mater's networking applies to your new client? What aspects do not apply? Explain in detail. Sketch out a basic LAN for one department.
4. Is networking in a government agency any different from networking in a traditional business organization? Elaborate.
5. Netscape and Microsoft are battling over leadership in the Web browser market. Search the Internet to learn more about the offerings, strategies, and tactics of the two companies. Write a two-page report explaining why you think the competition will be good (or bad) for the consumer.
6. A company decided to start a networking operation that would allow it to sell various products on the Internet. What do you need to know before you recommend the network infrastructure that it must install? Be specific.

Web Exercises

1. Which of these two statements is true about a server-based network? The server-based network can grow as an organization grows. One can implement centralized security to protect network resources.
2. Contact an Internet Service Provider (ISP) in your area and determine the procedure and cost of linking a company's Intranet to the Internet.

Chapter 4

Intranets and Extranets

Contents

IN A NUTSHELL

Using the Internet and Web technologies together as an enterprise-wide information system is just beginning to gain a foothold in business, industry, and government. Such systems are referred to as Intranets. They are a new approach to internal information management and a powerful tool for client/server computing.

Intranet is a term we use when we apply Internet technologies to serve the internal needs of an organization. More technically, it is a network connecting a set of clients using standard Internet protocols, especially TCP/IP and HTTP. Internet technologies are superior to conventional internal communication systems. The Web browser, for example, is a readily available and familiar access tool. Documents are handled easily, and multiple media can be supported as well. Mid- to large-size organizations are spending thousands of dollars just to keep their documents under control. Managers constantly share documents on an inter- and intradepartmental level. With various operating systems, network protocols, and application suites, trying to ensure homogeneity in managing documents can be a challenge. Intranets handle all these problems with ease.

groupware: programs or software that help people work together when they are located far from one another.

Groupware is software that helps people work together when they are located far from one another. It includes shared databases, e-mail handling, electronic meetings that allow participants to display and see others' information, and shared calendars. Groupware also includes document management, handling in-house form requests, and report filing. It seems logical to invest in an Intranet that can perform locally (within the company) and link globally (via the Internet). Groupware applications on a company's Intranet can help the organization do more for less.

The technology operates with standards, protocols, languages, and tools that are easy to learn and to use. The Intranet can be viewed as a tool that provides Internet-like capabilities at the internal organizational level. The user can simply point and click to access the available information. The drill is easy. Click on an icon, a button, or a link on the screen and go to different pages, and go forward or backward until the information sought is finalized.

The following scenario is typical of what an Intranet is and can do. Flameless Electric, the second-largest manufacturer of electric parts in Virginia, needed to roll out and sell two major products in 2000. Its strategy used the Internet, Intranet, and Extranet. The Internet part was easy. The company's Web site displayed the products for customers to see and order. The company's Intranet was accessible only by its 743 employees. Flameless's priority was to support its 112 sales reps statewide. The Intranet supplied them with marketing and technical information about the products and an automated sales application that minimized paperwork, regardless of location or size of order.

The third part was Flameless's Extranet. An Extranet is an Intranet with extensions that allow clearly identified customers or top suppliers to reach and access company-related technical and educational information. In

Flameless's case, its Extranet was accessible to 950 electricians and small electrical parts dealers via a special company Web page. An electrician, for example, enters an assigned password to access information about new products and special deals that are available to high-volume buyers. After 7 months of use, Flameless's Net-based system was paying dividends. It cut down on phone calls and fax orders, and gave sales reps in the field immediate online support. It even improved shipment schedules and deliveries.

This is all well and good, but what did it cost Flameless to set all this up? The company hired a talented Webmaster on a full-time basis. The same person, along with a part-time IT person, was able to manage the entire operation. All design and implementation work was outsourced to a local consulting firm. The Intranet ran on a Web server using Windows NT Netscape Enterprise Server on an IBM Aptiva PC. For online Extranet security, a firewall was installed in front of an Oracle database. The results were reduced costs, improved efficiency, and increased market penetration by sales reps, as well as direct customer access to the company's internal sales and marketing files.

In this chapter, we address three major issues: the role and contributions of the Intranet in the company's technology-based architecture, the uses of Extranets and how they relate to the Intranet and the Internet, and e-mail uses and abuses. Later in the chapter, we discuss ethical issues related to e-mail and communication traffic.

INTRANETS: THE BASICS

What Is an Intranet?

Major organizations and companies as small as 15 employees are enjoying the benefits of working in an Intranet environment. They have discovered a new way to deliver collaboration and coordination to employees around the clock. An Intranet is simply an organization-wide software and information distribution system that applies Internet technology and standards to a closed network within the organization. It connects the various pieces of information and communications technologies in such a way that all the authorized resources of the organization are readily available to any authorized person who needs them, wherever and whenever they are needed. In the final analysis, it is a way of thinking about how people in a business work together.

Intranet operation is a communication project designed by technical staff. It is a network of people, not of wired machines. The focus is the message, not the media. Concentrating on the technology of the Intranet is like a book author worrying about the presses and typesetting rather than the manuscript. Yet, Intranet projects often are run by technical people. When it comes to planning an Intranet, users should worry about content, and technical staff should concentrate on the media—on how the script is delivered.

An Intranet normally runs in a client/server environment and a local area network configuration. The Internet Protocol (IP) connects the computers. This internal company network is separated from other networks by **firewalls,** which are a means of preventing unauthorized access to the company's internal data or leaks of sensitive company information.

firewall: a means of preventing unauthorized access to the company's internal data or leaks of sensitive company information.

Technically, the Internet and the Intranet are the same, except that only selected people are allowed to connect to the Intranet. An Intranet

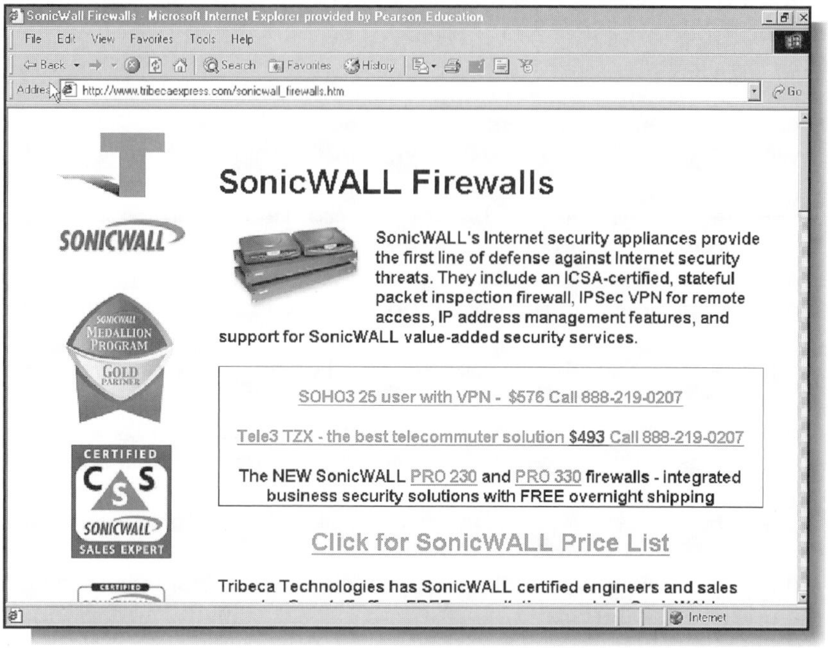

Screen Capture 4-1

uses TCP/IP as an Internet-derived communication protocol and user interface via Web browsers, e-mails, and so on. Intranets have grown by leaps and bounds among corporate users, which demonstrates the strength and potential of Internet networking. The complementary relationship between the Intranet and the Internet is a significant contributor to the digital economy. In B2B e-commerce, for example, producer and seller information is readily accessible to suppliers, making it easy to share and disseminate information to the ultimate consumer.

Benefits

For almost a decade, companies have been looking for cost-effective ways of distributing information throughout their organization. The Intranet provides better information faster. It provides many benefits and has distinctive features. For example, it links employees and managers around the clock and automates a lot of intraorganizational traffic. Today's communication systems are labor intensive, involving a stream of documents that are sent manually or by fax from one floor to another and from one building to another. Personal messages and memos also are carried in person or by fax, which takes time and causes numerous interruptions in a normal work process. This is where an Intranet begins to pay off (see Box 4-1).

A well-designed Intranet makes it possible for a company to gain better access to its primary resource—the knowledge and experience of the decision makers who work within it. It is a creative and empowering tool for a company and the foundation for developing enterprise-wide information systems. It is a model for internal information

BOX 4-1
Re-focusing the Hunter health intranet

Despite all the effort dedicated to the Hunter health intranet, it was not being used, and no one knew why. With the initial start-up activities completed, the challenge was also to define the future direction of the intranet, and to ensure that it became better aligned with corporate strategy. To this end, a brief but intense project was initiated to evaluate the current intranet and Web site.

In consultation with the intranet team, a number of activities were scheduled: expert review, stakeholder interviews, usability testing, and information architecture. The current intranet scored high marks. Yet, the intranet was not being used by most staff. The following key site problems were identified:

- Few users were progressing beyond the front page, because of the difficulty of use.
- The in-house search engine was inadequate for an intranet of 6,000+ pages.
- The homepage did not assist users to find key information or recent updates.

Stakeholder interviews revealed the following problems:

- Lack of time.
- No one seems to want news about social events.
- The corporate phone directory was needed by everyone, but was just not meeting that need.

When it came to usability testing:

- Few users understood the meaning of the "text only" button; none have used it.
- Many users have overlooked the buttons at the top of the page.
- All users extensively used the "back" button.
- Many users navigated the site based entirely on past experience and struggled when in unfamiliar areas.

One conclusion was the high-level structure of the intranet was preventing users from finding information.

SOURCE: Robertson, James, "Case Study: Refocusing the Hunter Health Intranet." *Internet Journal,* December 4, 2002, 1–21.

management and collaborative computing. Technically, Intranets are portable and scalable, which means that a company can expand the system as it grows.

Using the Intranet as part of a company's integrated environment means a wealth of information is available to employees, managers, and the company as a whole. It also means much easier integration of processes. For example, a company with field reps in remote locations has to manage continuous inflows and outflows of data from the field and integrate them into manufacturing, supply management, and delivery services. The cost of such a system based on an Intranet is low. In this case, cost advantages and ease of access are unique benefits of the Intranet. See Box 4-2 for an example.

Applications

An Intranet can provide several applications at low cost. Some of these are described in the following sections.

Human Resources

In human resources, employees can produce or reach information on the Internet. They can access company news, employee benefits, employee phone books, vacation schedules, cafeteria menus—any documents, software, or data that company managers want to

BOX 4-2
E-commerce trends: Dow's intranet is a classroom

The Dow Chemical Co. this year plans to leverage its corporate Intranet to replace up to 1 million hours of training now performed in classrooms. The company has deployed software that takes presentations and integrates them into course material. The material can be disseminated in a virtual classroom setting, enabling Dow to train employees by simply having them logon to its Web-based training system, called Dow University Online. "We are expecting a 17-month return on our investment," said Jon Walker, project manager of Dow University Online. Dow invested $300,000 for the online learning software from WBT Systems and $800,000 for the integration.

About 50,000 employees receive some form of classroom training. On the manufacturing side, 15,000 employees and 5,000 contractors are trained on topics that range from environmental safety to health issues. That accounts for 600,000 hours per year. The other 400,000 hours are directed to managers and knowledge workers in computer training, financial issues, purchasing, and management.

"The biggest challenge we have is to get the organization to want to use this and to move forward with it. Culturally, we are used to going into classrooms. We have to change our mind-sets, not just from a user point of view but from a management point of view. It will be tough to make that transition, especially with the goals that we have set," says Walker.

SOURCE: Schwartz, Jeffrey, "Dow Intranet Becomes Classroom," *InternetWeek*, January 18, 1999, 17.

provide. It is no longer necessary to call human resources or inquire by phone or in person about such information. For human resources, it means streamlining the recruitment process and keeping employees informed about the company. Employees can have immediate access to the latest information. They spend less time searching and are no longer overwhelmed by cumbersome manuals. The main human resources Intranet applications and their benefits are as follows.

- **Employee handbook**—saves the cost of printing and updating the handbook.
- **Benefits information**—human resources staff relieved from answering routine questions and enrolling employees in benefits programs.
- **Employee surveys**—all survey data are captured online, which saves time and paper.
- **Internal/external recruiting**—helps retain current employees and promotes wide dissemination of job information, which means a shortened recruiting cycle.
- **Candidate screening**—the online screening application speeds the processing of candidates and means faster resume handling.
- **Organization charts**—immediate access to and update of the company's organization chart.
- **Newsletters**—keep employees current on company events.
- **Company calendar**—keeps employees apprised of holidays and special events.

Sales and Marketing

In sales and marketing, the sales staff can use the Intranet to keep sales personnel and customers up to date on products, pricing, and sales trends. The Intranet also is used to collect and integrate sales forecasts and monitor sales performance. The marketing staff uses the Intranet to keep the sales department informed of marketing strategies, special promotions, and competitive information. The key sales and marketing applications and their advantages are as follows.

- **Product information**—speeds the distribution of product data; sales representatives can obtain product availability and delivery dates quickly.
- **Market research**—instant access to a wealth of marketing information for product planning and forecasting.
- **Prospecting**—easy way to collect information about future customers quickly.
- **Managing sales contacts**—effective distribution of sales leads to appropriate salespersons in the field; ensures quick follow-up on profitable leads.
- **Sales training**—a ready forum for sales training, regardless of the location of trainees.

Accounting and Finance

In accounting and finance, the Intranet facilitates a secure, central point for gathering financial and accounting data from multiple databases. It also generates consolidated statements to those who need them when they need them. In addition, Intranets allow select business partners limited access to financial data to build an ongoing relationship as part of an Extranet environment. The key accounting and financial applications and their advantages are as follows.

- **Financial reports**—sensitive financial reports can be published on a secure-access Intranet Web site.
- **Expense reports**—employees can e-mail expense reports on secure Web sites, reducing paperwork and delays in reimbursement.
- **Accounts receivable/payable processing**—faster collection of receivables and transmission of payables; allows fast access by customers and vendors to status information.
- **Asset management**—current assets can be placed online for review and update.
- **Policies and procedures**—corporate policies and procedures related to accounting and finance can be centralized for quick access by authorized personnel.
- **Payroll**—online submission of payroll data by managers and employees, including automated deposits and time sheets, promotes a high level of efficiency, regardless of the transaction or location.

Manufacturing and Operations

In manufacturing and operations, the main benefits of the Intranet are maintaining effective inventory control, production scheduling, quality, and low operating cost. The quality assurance staff can update existing databases and maintain accurate quality statistics for management decision making. The Intranet also provides a centralized facility for disseminating manufacturing information. It fosters collaboration between the production team and other functional teams within the firm, identifying product problems, improving inventory control, and the like. The key applications and advantages are as follows.

- **Inventory control**—reduces inventory costs by online tracking of raw material inventory, movements, expiration dates, and so on.
- **Production schedules**—key persons have instant access to products or parts for reordering or making just-in-time adjustments.

- **Quality assurance—**facilitates quality improvement quickly and reliably by allowing production personnel to obtain information that improves manufacturing quality and reduces costs.
- **Part order/requisition system—**allows customers and dealers to order products or parts quickly and in time to be of immediate use. This cuts down on inventory and storage space.

Other Applications

Some other uses of the Intranet include the following.

- Real-time broadcasting of news, including medical information, from the county, the state, nationally, or from abroad.
- Document management to minimize unnecessary paperwork and waste of paper.
- Customized application modules like travel or document library.
- Complete e-mail for interoffice and intraoffice communication.
- Internal company office circulars can be routed electronically.
- Bulletin board service.
- Real-time chat service that electronically logs all data for record keeping.
- Complete company staff, operations, and organizational chart directories.
- Channel for confidential exchange of data for electronic funds transfers (EFTs) and checks.
- Executive information system record consolidations.

Screen Capture 4-2

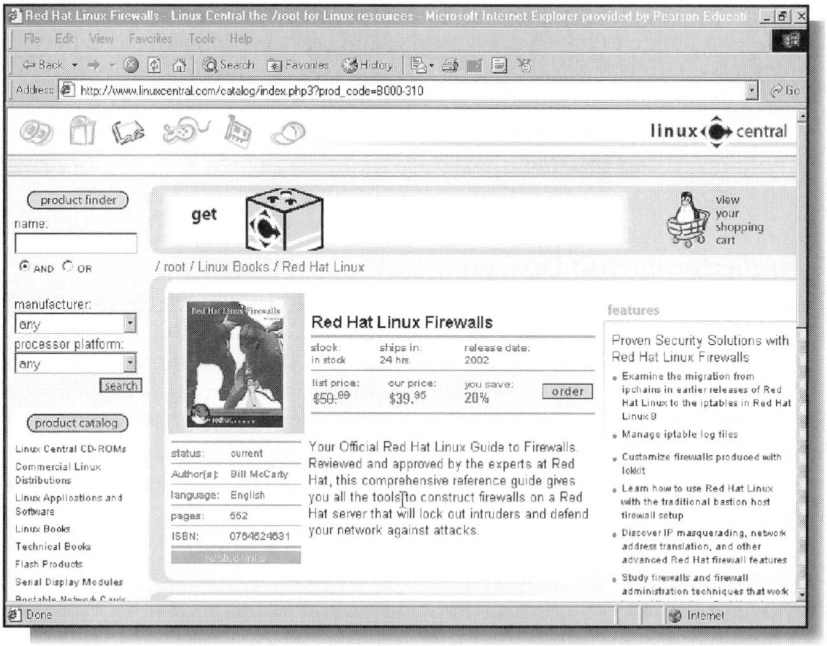

Source: Copyright © 2003–2004 Linux Central Inc. All rights reserved.

- A daily to-do list and assignments from a central desk to all connected desks.
- Foreign news and financial data broadcasting (running ticker) from direct feeds.

Why Does a Company Need an Intranet?

Not every organization needs an Intranet: The dividing line for Intranet payback is 100 or more employees, or more than one branch. An Intranet can reduce phone bills, fax bills, and other charges. If nothing else, it will help branches work more closely together.

Many organizations set up an Intranet because of a demand from human resources managers. Human resources (HR) frequently distributes updated information to everyone in the firm. HR personnel spend a lot of time on the phone with employees, answering variations on the same questions over and over again. Intranets are the best news to hit the human resources profession since help-wanted ads began to surface in newspapers. Major applications for an Intranet are listing employee benefits, vacation schedules, and job openings, and recognizing special employees.

A company needs an Intranet for the following reasons.

1. When it has a large pool of information to share among hundreds of employees. It is an effective way of cutting the cost of producing conventional multiple hard copies. It combats the problem of information overload. Intranets help individuals sort, filter, and store the mountain of information that otherwise comes across their desks.
2. Because company information can be distributed at low cost. Intranets are cheap, robust, and fast. Any employee with access to a TCP/IP can disseminate and publish information. Also, much of the technology in use on the Internet has been robust and reliable. Any information accessed is available in seconds rather than minutes or hours.
3. Because Intranets operate across platforms—Windows, UNIX, Mac. They are the easiest way to get people communicating.
4. Because information is available 24/7 to all employees at the click of a mouse.
5. Because information available on the Intranet can be updated quickly, which keeps employees informed in a timely way.

THE TECHNICAL INFRASTRUCTURE

The trend in Intranet design is to rely on the company's TCP/IP Internet infrastructure to implement an Intranet utilizing Internet protocol suite technologies and newly developed client/server Web technologies. The client/server environment is user oriented and gives clients (users) great flexibility in the way they use data to make timely decisions.

Client/Server Basics

Intranets have a multi-tier application architecture. The terms related to Intranet design and implementation appear in Box 4-3. Anyone interested in understanding the basics of Intranet architecture should be familiar with them. The client/server architecture on which Intranets are based is a versatile, message-based, modular infrastructure intended to improve usability, flexibility, interoperability, and scalability as compared to centralized, mainframe, time-sharing computing. Within mainframe software architectures, all intelligence resides within the central host computer. Mainframes do not easily support

BOX 4-3
Intranet design and implementation terms

1. **Client:** A requester of services (e.g., an employee or a manager).
2. **Server:** A machine or a PC that provides services, files, database information, and so on.
3. **Interoperability:** The ability of two or more systems to exchange information and to use the information that has been exchanged.
4. **Scalability:** The ease with which a system can be modified or expanded.
5. **Graphic User Interface (GUI):** A feature that can be used for developing complex user interfaces because it increases software development speed.
6. **Client/Server Architecture:** A model that introduces a database server to replace the file server. User queries can be answered directly. This architecture reduces network traffic by providing a query response rather than total file transfer. It also improves multiuser updating through a GUI front end to a shared database.
7. **Remote Procedure Call (RPC):** A client/server infrastructure that increases the interoperability, portability, and flexibility of an application by allowing the application to be distributed over multiple and different platforms. It also reduces the complexity of developing applications that span multiple operating systems and network protocols.

graphic user interface (GUI) or access to multiple databases from geographically dispersed sites. As GUIs became popular, mainframes and terminal displays became less so. PCs are now being used in client/server architectures.

Types of Client/Server Architecture

There are two types of client/server architecture for Intranet design: two-tier architectures and three-tier architectures.

Two-Tier Architectures

The two-tier model is a good solution for distributed computing when an organization has between 12 and 100 users interacting on a LAN at the same time. It requires minimal operator intervention and is used frequently in noncomplex, non-time-critical information processing systems. This model has three components.

1. User System Interface (e.g., session, text input, dialog, display management).
2. Processing management (e.g., process development and process resource services).
3. Database management (e.g., data and file services). See Figure 4-1.

The limitations associated with this model are as follows.

1. When the number of users exceeds 100, performance begins to deteriorate. This is because the server maintains a connection with each client, even when no work is being done.
2. Implementation of processing management services using vendor proprietary database procedures restricts flexibility.

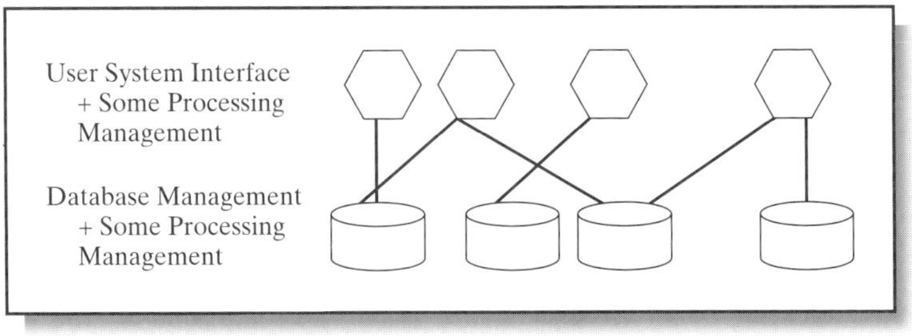

Figure 4-1
Two-tier client/server architecture

3. Current implementations of the two-tier architecture provide limited flexibility in moving (repartitioning) program functionality from one server to another without manually regenerating procedural code.

Three-Tier Architecture

The alternative to two-tier client/server architecture is three-tier client/server architecture. In this model, a *middle tier* is sandwiched between the user system interface client environment and the database management server environment. This middle tier manages distributed database integrity in a two-phase process. It provides access to resources based on names rather than locations and, therefore, improves scalability and flexibility as system components are added or moved. It also can perform queuing, application execution, and database staging. For example, if the middle tier provides queuing, the client can deliver its request to the middle layer and disengage because the middle tier will

Screen Capture 4-3

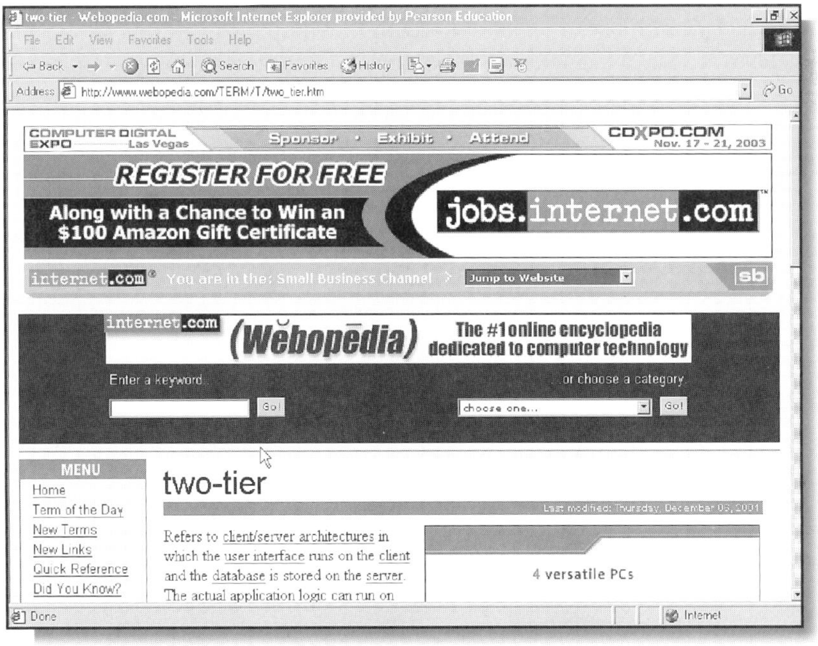

Source: Copyright © 2004 Jupitermedia Corporation. All rights reserved. Reprinted with permission from http://www.internet.com, www.webopedia.com.

access the data and return the answer to the client. In addition to all of this, the middle layer adds scheduling and prioritization for work in progress (see Figure 4-2).

The third tier provides database management and is dedicated to data and file services that can be optimized without using any proprietary database management system languages.

Three-tier architectures are used in commercial distributed client/server environments, where shared resources like different databases and processing rules are required. It supports hundreds of users, making it easier to upgrade than the two-tier architecture. It also facilitates software development because each tier can be built and executed on a separate platform, making it easier to organize the implementation. Three-tier architectures also readily allow different tiers to be developed in different languages.

What is important is the ease of moving data from an old system to a three-tier architecture. It is low risk and cost-effective. Overall, the three-tier model improves performance for groups with a large number of users (in the thousands). It also improves flexibility, maintainability, reusability, and scalability, while hiding the complexity of distributed processing from the user. These features have made three-layer architectures a popular choice for Intranet applications and Net-centric information systems. In the long run, it is better than the two-tier model.

Basic Intranet Enabling Technologies

An Intranet infrastructure allows online communication between divisions and among employees within each division, and it provides an interface between any contact point within the organization and the Internet. This means that specified operating systems, dedicated servers, and communication links must be in place for the environment to be operational.

The technology involves protocols, standards, tools, and languages that are easy to use. As you read about the following technical building blocks, keep in mind that an Intranet has Internet-like capabilities within a company's internal network.

Here are the key enabling technologies—the software cluster that must be acquired.

1. **Server PC**—the PC that stores all applications and Web pages. The user (client) downloads Intranet information from the server PC for decision making.
2. **Client PC**—the employee's or user's PC that accesses the Intranet information available on the server PC.

Figure 4-2
Three-tier server architecture design

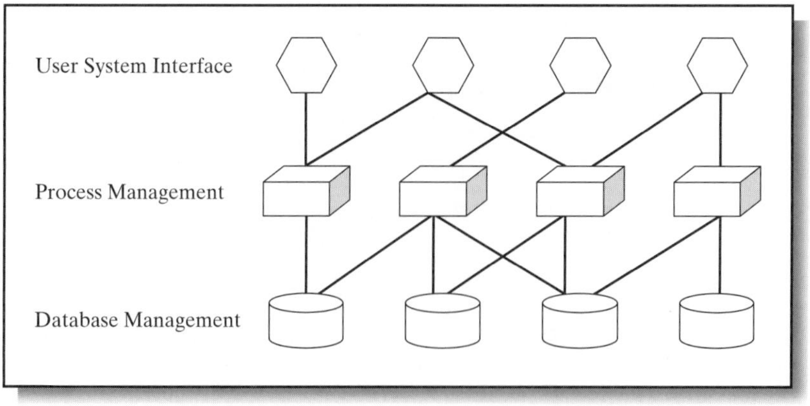

3. **Web server**—the cluster of software that manages and updates HTML files and allows online communication with other programs in the Intranet infrastructure.
4. **Browser**—software installed on the user's PC for accessing and presenting HTML files on Web sites.
5. **TCP/IP electronic mail**—normally available in most organizations.
6. **Graphic and multimedia files**—files containing images and sound, respectively.
7. **Network File System (NFS)**—a distributed file system developed by Sun Microsystems that is also compatible with UNIX-based and DOS systems.
8. **Internet Relay Chat (IRC)**—a UNIX utility that allows multiple users to communicate interactively; allows users on the Internet to chat.
9. **HTML authoring tools**—the software that makes it possible to create pages in HTML.
10. **HyperText Markup Language (HTML)**—the text that has links to other information. It is a programming language that manages and controls the way Intranet information is displayed on the user's screen.
11. **Portable electronic document (PED)**—technology that addresses the shortcomings of HTML, while trying to maintain compatibility with it.

An Intranet consists of a Web server running on an internal corporate network that manages Intranet files and viewing tools, such as a browser running on a client PC; this allows the end user to access Intranet information. The interface to the company's Intranet will be key to success. Browsers greatly simplify access to the company's computing resources and information by operating as the interface to available applications.

Using Firewalls

Intranets can be protected from unauthorized access via firewalls. As discussed in Chapter 3, a *firewall* is a hardware/software security system that can be programmed to prevent unauthorized access to a company's Intranet or the Internet. Firewalls vary in complexity. Some permit all access that is not specifically forbidden (default commit), some forbid all access that is not specifically permitted (default forbid), and others permit only e-mail traffic.

proxy:
a go-between agent that acts on behalf of another.

packet filter:
device that checks each packet at the network level and stops any packet that might be a security risk.

Most firewalls are either proxies or packet filters. A **proxy** is a *go-between* agent that acts on behalf of another. Network proxies act on behalf of a company to transfer information to and from the Internet. Typically, a proxy receives a request from a user to connect to a site on the Internet. It first makes a decision as to whether the user is authorized to use the proxy before it decides on completing the connection. A **packet filter** checks each packet (small chunk of information) at the network level and stops any packets that might be a security risk.

Security, in general, is not easy to sell. It is hard to sell a fire extinguisher to someone who has never seen a fire. Intranet security, properly designed by knowledgeable users and administrators, can ensure that the system is run properly. One person, a security czar, should be responsible for the entire Intranet. In the case of a company with branches or remote sites, each location should be part of the total security umbrella. Like the Webmaster, the security czar should have a combined background in technology, communication skills, and knowledge of the company's practices and processes. Leadership attributes, foresight, and creativity are also important (see Box 4-4).

BOX 4-4
E-careers: Oh, will you behave?

Many IT managers nowadays need ask potential hires only two questions: What do you know? When can you start? At some corporations, hiring is still a complex and extensive process using a variety of techniques to select individuals who will be as right for the culture of the company as for the job itself. Among the complex and interlocking methods used by Capital One Financial Corporation are a series of behavioral interviews that are a key part of the hiring process.

A behavioral job interview is designed to reveal a pattern of behavior. "We actually ask what you did in specific situations," Madigan, IT human resources vice president at the Hartford Financial Services Group Inc., says. "Concrete examples will demonstrate a person's preferred way of dealing with those situations and give you a better idea of that person and how they are likely to act on the job." For a higher-level IT professional's ability to lead a team, he suggests questions along these lines: "Tell me about a time when you were most successful in leading a group or team toward accomplishing an important goal." Then, as follow-up questions, "What was the goal and who defined it? When did this happen? How were the steps leading to the goal defined? What was your role in implementing the process? How close did you come to meeting the goals?"

Behavioral interview questions are good for all types of IT positions because they ask the candidate to describe his accomplishments and the work he has actually done. Behavioral interview questions are very open-ended and deal a lot with, how did you do that? What exactly did you do? Why did you do it that way? We're really looking at how they think.

Technology jobs require logical, sequential thinking. The key to success for an IT team is to have a mix of people with the right instincts for the jobs they have and the right balance in terms of their approaches to problem solving. While people vary, people's instinctive approaches fall within the following general "action modes": (1) Fact finders: precise, data-driven individuals who are able to see patterns and organize systems; (2) Quick starters: people who have the ability to deal with the unknown and innovate; (3) Follow thru: employees who excel at planning, designing, and programming; (4) Implementers: individuals who are skilled in the use of tools and in hands-on, 3-D problem solving. A team with too many people with similar personalities could produce conflict. For example, if a group of programmers all want to hold off putting a system into effect until it's perfect, the project would never get done.

SOURCE: Excerpted from Trosky, Judith, "Oh, Will You Behave?" *Computerworld*, January 8, 2001, 42–43.

Planning an Intranet

With complex technology, differing client demands, and heavy information traffic in a typical firm, a fair amount of planning is needed to design, implement, and maintain a corporate Intranet. Planning is part of a five-step procedure that is explained briefly in the following sections.

Plan Ahead

The first step is to define the goal of an Intranet and plan accordingly. A lot of the failures reported in the journals can be attributed to lack of preparation. "The competition has one, so why shouldn't we?" is not good enough for committing company resources to an

Intranet. It is important to determine who the primary users are, what content should be shared, and how the information will be accessed.

In principle, company information is there to be shared, and the larger the number of users is, the richer the information is. However, the designer should consider the risks of this information falling into the hands of the competition. Typically, the company has a license for only a certain number of users. Assigning passwords is a traditional way to help protect and limit access. In addition, each department should be evaluated to determine the type of information it needs. For example, the research and development department needs to know the pricing of a competitor's new product(s) before developing a new design.

As part of planning, it is sometimes helpful to visit a firm that has been successful in installing an Intranet site. Meeting with designers and users may bring up the problems and possible solutions. Seminars can be another source of information.

Once you have an idea of what an Intranet can and cannot do, the next phase in planning is to outline the scope of the project. This means deciding on, among other things, the size of the Intranet, how long it should take to install, the training involved, and the required financial and technical resources. The key is to map out the site well in advance. The map must account for every detail that contributes to a successful installation. "I forgot about that . . ." after the site is underway can be costly.

Provide Justification and Management Support

In the process of planning an Intranet, some homework should be done to justify the investment and ensure support from top management. The traditional approach to justification that makes sense to management is to do a return on investment analysis, where total costs are compared with benefits. The human factor also must be considered: Planners need to map out strategies to acculturate employees to using the Intranet once it becomes operational. Stories abound about companies that spend millions on Intranet technology, only to learn that employees still feel more comfortable printing out their e-mail messages.

An effective strategy for selling upper management on the change is that an Intranet can be modified to address changing needs. It can be demonstrated that hearing a president's quarterly report on the Intranet is more effective than reading it. With an Intranet, all it takes is one click on a button.

Build an Intranet In-house or Outsource It?

After top management approves the master plan, the next step is to decide whether the technology should be built by the IT department or contracted to an outside firm. In deciding what to do, several factors must be considered.

- In-house resources—how available are they? How qualified are they?
- Cost—which way is cheaper?
- Hardware and software—do existing company networks support an Intranet?
- Budget—are adequate funds available to fully implement the proposed Intranet?

Outsourcing has definite advantages. An outside firm, dedicated to full-time Intranet design, has lots of specialists available. They are likely to be more efficient than in-house staff, who might better be used for other critical projects. Depending on the company's technology infrastructure, an outside firm might end up doing a better job, especially if the Intranet site is to be hosted by the consulting firm.

In contrast to the benefits of outsourcing, limitations need to be considered. An outside firm will need more time to learn your business processes and requirements before beginning to design the site. Some sensitive information or files might be unnecessarily exposed to an outside firm. It is also likely that an outside firm will charge more for the work than it would cost to do it in-house, and additional costs may be incurred later when enhancements or upgrades have to be done.

The main advantage of building the Intranet in-house is that in-house people are familiar with the company's goals, politics, and processes. Maintenance, upgrades, and enhancements will be easier to handle. With the basic infrastructure in place, future development can be done at a lower cost than if an outside contractor were used. Sensitive information also remains protected. On the negative side, lack of expertise in Intranet design could cause all kinds of unexpected problems and delays.

Form an Intranet Team

A company-wide project like an Intranet requires a representative team from various divisions or departments to oversee the process from beginning to end. In addition to a representative from each department, one should be included from the IT department, as well as a consultant and a project coordinator. In the case of outsourcing, a representative from the contracted firm should set up an agenda with the company team and provide progress reports on a regular basis.

A tricky part of forming a team for this type of project is appointing people who have no political strings or hidden agendas that might affect the process adversely. For example, a representative from a large department might want to secure high-priority access for the department. This might mean compromising equal response time for smaller or remote departments.

The team normally consists of a representative from each department or division. When the team size increases beyond seven or eight members, it requires a chairperson with an agenda, predefined procedures, and subcommittees, all of which could make the whole process unwieldy.

Build and Test a Prototype

Before going all out to develop a corporate-wide Intranet, it would be wise to build a piece of the site and allow users to test it. The feedback could be a timely contribution to the final system. One problem with prototypes is that when they work well, many users comment, "This is great. It is all I want." However, prototypes are only a representation of the system, not the system itself.

The champion is important to the prototype phase. A *champion* is a person in the organization (usually a respected manager or a senior person) who supports the project from the beginning, promotes it, and acts as an ambassador to explain to users how the system could do them a lot of good. Unfortunately, with complex projects that affect processes and people, more people will resist change than welcome it. A champion can do wonders to ensure the success of the new installation.

Ensure Effective Maintenance

Keeping corporate information up to date and available around the clock is the most critical part of Intranet operations. Poor maintenance means dated information, which quickly gives the impression that nothing new or different is going on in the company. E-mail will continue, but an Intranet means more than just e-mail. Maintenance means making sure the Intranet continues to operate based on the standards set in the design. An

Intranet can take more effort to update than to create. Included in maintenance is enhancement, which is the daily (sometimes hourly) upgrade of news, reports, and procedures.

Maintenance includes assigning a full-time person to be the site Webmaster. This person's main job is to keep in touch with management at all levels, gather and post news items, monitor the Intranet traffic, and provide technical leadership. Communication skills, technical expertise, and ability to work with people are critical to a Webmaster's job.

E-Mail and the Intranet

Intranet and e-mail is a marriage made in CyberHeaven. E-mail is what a company's Intranet is best known for. It is "the Net's killer app" (Downes and Mui 1998). Almost 90 percent of Net users report e-mail as the most frequently used online contact. It is a major communication platform in business and government. Scott McNealy, chief executive officer of Sun Microsystems, Inc., once commented: "You can take out every one of the 300 to 400 computer applications that we run our company on and we could continue—but if you took out our e-mail system, Sun would grind to an immediate halt."

Over 200 million in boxes are active worldwide. Frequent e-mailers already recognize that their in box is as much a database of documents, appointments, and news as it is a place to store messages. With e-commerce volumes on the rise, this communication tool is becoming part of e-marketing and sales. It is a tool for bill presentation, customer feedback, shipping notices, and the like.

E-mail also is becoming smarter: It now can direct specific messages to defined folders and be a place to check voice, text, and fax messages. This is called content management or unified messaging services. Managing data and documents with e-mail is more efficient than dealing with the flood of paper (letters, faxes, and bills) we handle today. As e-mail becomes the standard for content dissemination of all kinds, it should attract more and more users and become as popular as the cell phone.

Intranets inherit Simple Mail Transport Protocol (SMTP) from the TCP/IP suite to operate e-mail. On top of SMTP, which enables plain text messaging, Intranets rely on Multipurpose Internet Mail Extensions (MIME) to carry diverse content.

Spamming and Appropriate E-Mail Use

spamming: sending unwanted advertisements or literature through e-mail or the Internet.

flaming: an angry response to an e-mail message or phone call.

Spamming is sending unwanted advertisements or literature through e-mail or the Internet. It comes from a Monty Python comedy skit, where every item on a restaurant menu included Spam, regardless of how well it fit into the dish. This type of intrusion is similar to receiving a phone call from a telemarketer right in the middle of dinner. Spamming generates **flaming**—an angry response to a message or a call.

Companies have been overwhelmed by e-mail traffic and spam is out of control. It is the No. 1 complaint of most e-mail users. America Online says as much as 80 percent of incoming e-mail to its system is spam (Mangalindan 2003). E-mail may have become a valuable business tool, but users' in boxes are cluttered with unsolicited and virus-ridden messages, sales pitches, and irritating news that once was the talk around the water cooler. Companies also have been increasingly concerned about what is being sent out in e-mail, such as company secrets.

Many firms have learned that spot checks are no longer adequate. The trend is more toward systematic monitoring of e-mail traffic using content-monitoring software. Most such software scans messages for keywords. Messages that are suspect can be prevented from leaving the firm or forwarded to a company official in charge of reviewing them. The key problem is junk mail and inappropriate attachments that are a waste of employee time, whether they are sending or reading such mail.

Spamming has reached a point where it is nearly impossible to eliminate, but solutions exist. One of the most widely used tools is Eudora.pro, which collects mail from different accounts and consolidates and manages all one's messages. First, the program asks you to pick a message as an example and specify certain rules. For example, you can set a rule to divert to a junk mail folder all messages not clearly marked to you. A filter also can be used to flag priority messages such as those coming from top management. You can even identify such messages by color (e.g., red = top priority, green = memo coming to you, yellow = junk mail, and so on).

A more recent approach to handling spammers is to give spammers a dose of their own medicine. Take the case of Scott Richter, a mass commercial e-mailer, who has become a frequent target of attackers known as anti-spammers. One of them is Mark Jones, a software engineer, who from his home at night, tracks down spammers by tracing their complex routing code hidden in e-mail messages. After his three children go to bed one Saturday night for one session of "spammer-flaming," he programs his personal computer to send a letter to a select number of alleged spammers downloaded from a Web site, slashdot.org. As he finishes the letter, he will have sent the message to each spammer 10,000 times (Mangalindan 2003).

Spammers are not easy to catch, to sue, or to collect damages from. Earthlink, a major Internet service provider, uses lawyers and private investigators to track senders of online junk. In a well-documented case, a so-called "Buffalo Spammer" kept harassing Earthlink customers for over 3 months, using 243 different accounts and dozens of telephones registered in other people's names. He sent 825 million spam e-mails and taunted Earthlink's investigators and other experts. Even when lawyers were trying to serve papers on him, the Buffalo spammer continued to spam (Angwin 2003).

There are dozens of products and services available to help block spam. They have several techniques in common:

- Blacklist the sender; that is, obtain each spammer's address and block any e-mail from those addresses
- Accept e-mail only from a list of approved addresses—called "whitelist" the sender.
- Look for signs of a spam—999, FREE, Get, Money, Lose, $$$, Earn, etc.
- Most anti-spam software analyzes new messages and determines how likely they may be spam. Examples of enterprise-class spam-fighters are IronMail (www.ciphertrust.com), Authority (www.cloudmark.com), SpamKiller (www.networkassociates.com), and MailFrontier (www.mailfrontier.com). The two best ways to avoid spam are:
  - Stop giving away your e-mail address, period. In March 2003, a Washington-based Center for Democracy and Technology reported on research into where spammers get their address. The key source (97%) was public Web sites.
  - Do not "unsubscribe," because it simply confirms that your e-mail address is real and solid. If you did, it is likely that you'll get more, not less spam mail (Kay 2003).

Lawmakers have never been under greater pressure to address the spam problem. So far, 26 states have adopted spam laws that focus on things like placing "ADV for advertising" be placed in the subject line of unsolicited business e-mail. Congress is pressed to act, at least to preempt state laws with one national law.Spamming, if it continues, is bound to drain resources. If public relations agencies and vendors followed commonsense guidelines, it could be controlled. Go to the book's Web site, www.prenhall.com/awad, for examples. One Internet site that provides guidelines on eliminating industry spam is www.ecofuture.org/jmtips.html. Here are sample guidelines.

1. Write to the Direct Marketing Association and credit bureaus.
2. Contact your credit card companies, credit union, and mortgage company and tell them not to release your name, address, and similar data.
3. Contact all organizations you belong to, schools, magazines you subscribe to, airline frequent flyer programs, your long-distance telephone carrier, and just about anyone who sends you a bill.
4. As a last resort, contact your phone company and change your listing in the phone book, or simply list your name with no address (Elbel 2001, 1).

The question of what is inappropriate e-mail brings us to the privacy issue. Companies have been wrestling with the issue of privacy versus liability for employees' e-mail activity. This concern was spurred by several well-known court cases where e-mail was produced as evidence.

In *Smyth vs. Pillsbury* (1996), the U.S. District Court in Philadelphia ruled that the company's interest in preventing inappropriate comments or even illegal activity over its e-mail system outweighs any privacy interest employees might have. From the company's point of view, the employer has the right to monitor and access employee e-mail because the company owns the Intranet and the e-mail is generated during working hours. Employees, however, view such access as an invasion of privacy. Three company concerns relate to

Screen Capture 4-4

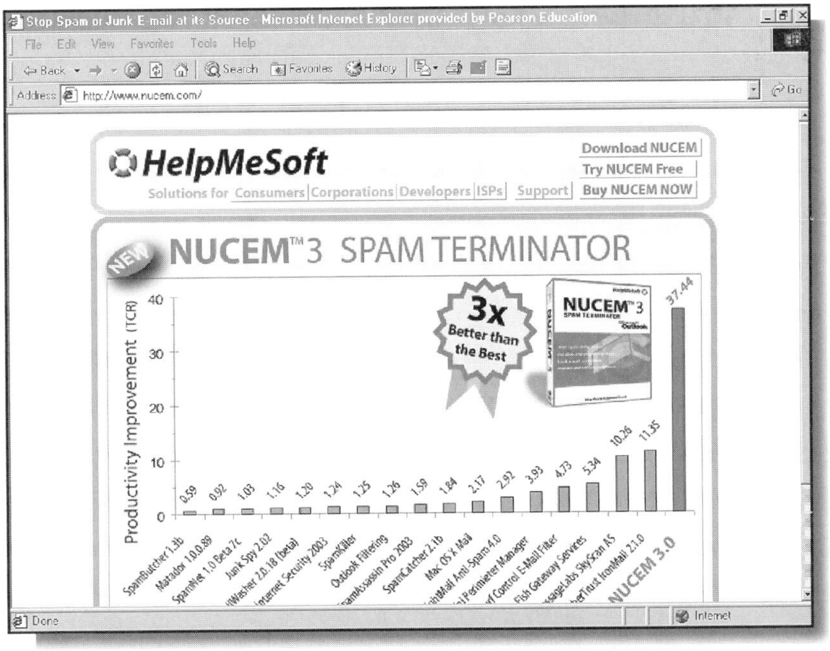

e-mail and privacy: Potential legal liability from e-mail contents, leakage of company secrets or sensitive information, and use of e-mail for sexual harassment. Any of these concerns is a good reason for companies to step in and control their own Intranet traffic.

The upshot of the privacy controversy is that firms must have a company policy that addresses the issue. At a minimum, such a policy should state in writing the following.

1. The company's Intranet and the networks that carry e-mail are company property, to be used for business purposes only. Any violators could be subject to disciplinary action or even dismissal (see Box 4-5).
2. The company clearly defines what is and what is not appropriate use of e-mail. Examples should help.
3. It should be made clear to all employees that e-mail of any kind cannot be private and that all e-mail may be monitored at any time.

E-Mail Etiquette

When the secretary of the loan department of a commercial bank found her lunch taken from the staff refrigerator, she immediately sent an e-mail message to the 165 bank employees: "My lunch has disappeared from the refrigerator. Whoever took it, I hope you have a good lunch. Now, I am left with no lunch. No response necessary. Sandy." Within minutes, there were offers to take Sandy to lunch and a pizza was delivered anonymously to her desk. Early that afternoon, the senior vice president of the bank stopped by

BOX 4-5
E-commerce trends: E-mail probe triggers firings

As part of an ongoing corporate crackdown, employees and contractors at pharmaceutical giant Merck & Co. last week faced discipline, including dismissal, for inappropriate e-mail and Internet usage. While Merck spokeswoman Sharyn Bearse confirmed the most recent disciplinary measures, she wouldn't say how many employees had been terminated or otherwise disciplined. Bearse also declined to say how many employees had been subjected to e-mail and Internet monitoring or what, specifically, employees had communicated or downloaded to provoke the measures.

Shortly before a February announcement of employee terminations related to e-mail and Internet abuse, Merck instituted a companywide standards and values program. Within 2 years, all 65,000 Merck employees around the world will attend a training session on these standards, many of which refer to proper workplace communications.

Companies of all sizes are wrestling with the issue of employee privacy vs. their own liability for employees' online activity. Jeff Uslan, manager of information protection at Hollywood-based Twentieth Century Fox, said he has to deal with thorny intellectual property issues that require close scrutiny of employee communications. In some circumstances, inappropriate language is difficult to monitor, he said.

Dallas attorney B. J. Thomas, who specializes in computer law, said that, as counsel for the city of Cleveland, Texas, her rule of thumb is that e-mail is a tool like any other.

Thomas and Uslan both said red flags on improper e-mail and Internet use don't usually come up unless an employee isn't performing satisfactorily. "People think it's a lot more private than it really is," Thomas said.

SOURCE: Excerpted from DiSabatino, Jennifer, "E-Mail Probe Triggers Firings," *Computerworld*, July 10, 2000, 1.

and gave her the first lesson in e-mail etiquette: "Don't send e-mail when you're angry. Choose your language, and although brevity is OK, don't discard manners."

Here is another episode: A Web designer asked a friend (another designer) to evaluate a client's homepage. The answer by e-mail was "Your choices of purple for logo and triangle for buttons are ugly. I wouldn't mess with it. Your client is probably too dumb to notice it." Somehow, the client got a copy and was furious. It took the designer some explaining to continue on the project. He almost lost his job.

Like the traditional "hello" when answering the phone, e-mail etiquette is important. In terms of e-mail etiquette, here are some mistakes to avoid:

- Do not write when you're in a bad mood or angry. Simmer down and let things settle before you attempt to send
- Read what you write carefully and stop the compulsion of clicking on the "send" button until you are sure of what you're sending.
- Do not use sarcasm in an attempt to be clever. E-mail was never designed to promote gags or ridicule.
- Stay away from using all uppercase. In the e-mail quarters, it is tantamount to yelling at the receiver. Exclamation marks are not welcome either. They are a sign of authoritarianism.
- Place the nature of the message in the subject line. It gives the receiver advance notice of the nature of the e-mail.
- Write short e-mails, normally less than two paragraphs. This author had a 3-page e-mail from one senior, explaining in anger why his grade should be an A rather than an A−.
- Sending e-mail to the wrong person can be annoying and embarrassing. Think before you "send."
- Watch your grammar, spelling, and vernacular. Words like "ain't" and double negatives like "I ain't saying nothin'" certainly show no class.
- Remember to send your attachment when you say you will. When this happens often with a given recipient, he or she might think you're growing senile.

Extranets

If a company Web site links two or more trading partners, it is referred to as an Extranet. It is a B2B Intranet that lets limited, controlled business partners interact with the firm for all kinds of exchanges (see Figure 4-3). Intranets, Extranets, and e-commerce have a lot in common. Intranets are localized within a firm and move data quicker than the more widely distributed Extranets.

The use of Internet (primarily Web) protocols is common to connect business users. On the Intranet, Web administrators prescribe access and policy for a defined group of users. On a B2B Extranet, system designers at each participating company must collaborate to make sure there is a common interface with the company they are dealing with. One participating business partner might be using Microsoft Explorer, and another might use Netscape Navigator 4.7. To collaborate via Extranet, the applications have to perform consistently on all platforms.

Extranets are not a passing trend. They are already the backbone of the e-business future. The obvious benefits are faster time to market, customer loyalty, increased partner interaction, and improved processes. The easiest way to quantify return on investment

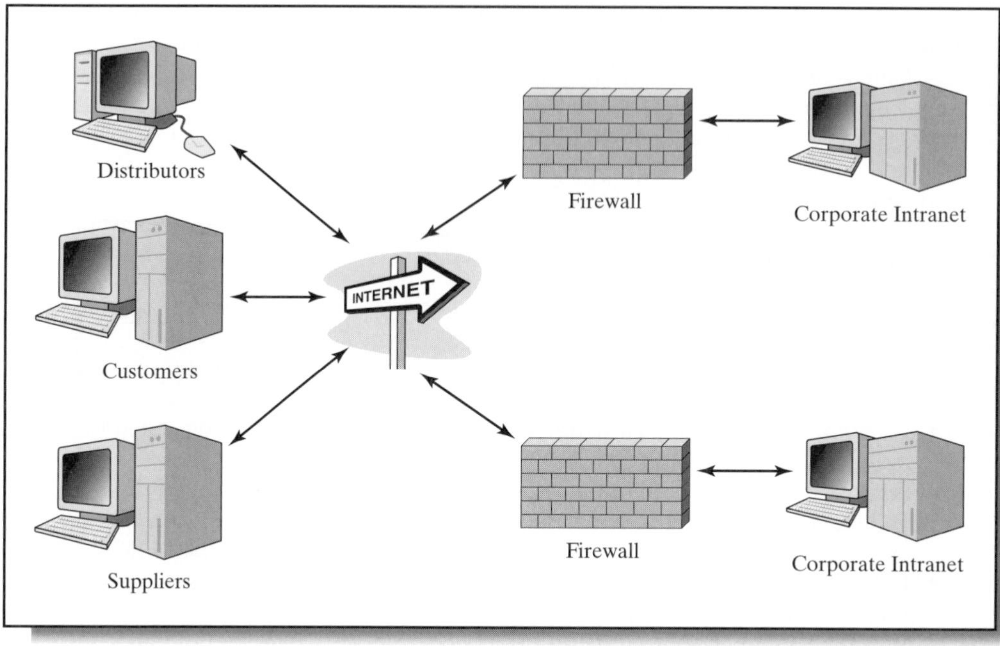

Figure 4-3
Basic extranet layout

for Extranets is to identify a business unit within a company that might benefit from one. This means identifying a business goal (increasing revenue, improving customer base, and so on) before deciding on feasibility, justification, and return on the investment.

Once a business goal has been established, the next step is to get together with the IT department to discuss feasibility. In a vertical industry like manufacturing, the focus is on improving operations through the existing supply chain, whereas in horizontal retail chains, the focus would be on improving revenue. Working with the IT group should bring technical and business information together for a master design of the Extranet.

Understanding corporate business processes is the key to successful deployment of an Extranet. By planning the deployment around a well-defined business plan, it is easier to prove how the technology is helping the bottom line. See Box 4-6 for a case in point.

Key Considerations

When contemplating an Extranet installation, here are some key factors to consider.

1. Identifying the user(s).
2. Listing the technology components.
3. Specifying the security requirements.
4. Discussing the administration of the Extranet.
5. Understanding the functions of the Extranet.

The users of an Extranet are normally nonemployees—customers, suppliers, distributors, outsourcers, consultants, and vendors. They are categorized as an outside group with whom frequent contacts are made, and as business partners who yield high returns. In planning an Extranet, questions should be raised early in the process regarding who

BOX 4-6
E-commerce trends: Kodak's extranet push

Eastman Kodak Co. is rapidly expanding its use of extranets to cut costs and boost sales by sharing critical information with major business partners. Kodak has created extranet links to about 25 organizations, including dealers, contractors, joint-venture partners, and subsidiaries, and is adding new extranets at the rate of two per week. It's considering linking electronically to key suppliers and retail chains as well, says VP and CIO John Chiazza.

The extranets are being used mainly to exchange information. Kodak continues to rely on electronic data interchange for transactions, but the company is talking to some partners about the potential for conducting transactions over the extranets. "We've been involved in B2B e-commerce for many years as a user of classic EDI, but what has been emerging recently is more intimate interactions through the use of extranets, where we or our customers can reach into certain internal applications, so that, for example, we can learn how products are moving through their stores and do a better job planning for future orders from them," says Chiazza.

The extranets let authorized users at other companies "tunnel" under Kodak's firewall to access specific servers and even specific applications, Internet, intranet, extranets and groupware users. Authorized outsiders can get past Kodak firewalls and run applications as they need to. Joint-venture partners have access to even more resources, such as intranets, databases, and mailboxes. Some of the networks give Kodak access to its partners' applications.

To ensure that only authorized users get under the firewall, Kodak uses an extranet management and security system that includes integrated VPN (virtual private network) services, as well as data encryption and authentication for security. Administrators can define privileges based on user identification, the method of authentication and encryption, the information resource being accessed, company affiliation, and day and time.

SOURCE: Excerpted from Violino, Bob, "Kodak's Extranet Push," *InformationWeek Online*, March 29, 1999.

will be included, how they will be prioritized, and what specific benefits (decreased inventory, increased revenue, and so on) will produce the best measurable improvements.

In assessing the technology components, the key point is to make sure that any technology meets open standards and can work with multiple technologies. Planners need to ask questions, such as How will the technology integrate with existing business partners' networks? Will it support all network protocols? Can the technology guarantee interoperability for business partners? Can the technology support all of the encryption and authentication methods for the type of interaction needed? Will the Internet be the only access path?

Security varies with the type of user, the sensitivity of the information transacted, and the communication lines used. Security questions deal with access control, authentication, and encryption. Access control relates to what users can and cannot access, what users can access and from which server(s), which accessible data are for display only, and which accessible data can be restricted to certain times of the day. In terms of authentication, decisions must be made regarding the level of authentication for each user, whether passwords and user names are adequate security, and how well other security measures complement the authentication. Is encryption required? If so, how strong should it be? What type of communication line or data should be encrypted?

The next item to consider is the administration of the Extranet. Here, several questions must be raised: Does the company need to monitor all incoming traffic? Are staff skills adequate for handling the complexity of the Extranet? How will the Extranet fit in with the rest of the company's IT security? Although supporting every technology is not practical, knowing what to expect early in the planning phase undoubtedly will contribute to effective management.

Finally, usability should be discussed. An Extranet must be usable to be attractive to customers and business partners. Like other issues, usability brings up several questions: How will users be authenticated? Will users need special training? Is client software required for allowing users to access the Extranet? How will it be configured? Who will administer it?

In summary, installing an Extranet brings up many issues involving different types of people in the organization. This is where planning becomes critical. Security and effective management make an Extranet viable. Companies that have assessed these issues and weighed the risks and rewards stand to benefit significantly over the long run. As Spence said, "The focus is on the journey, not the short sprint" (Spence 2000, p. 4).

Role of the Champion

Extranets are changing how organizations share internal resources and interact with the outside business world. Built with technology and used by people, they can ensure lasting bonds between business partners and corporate members. The entire commitment should be viewed as a knowledge management asset rather than a mere networking expense to expedite business. This is where a champion becomes a critical part of the installation.

A champion who best promotes an Extranet is someone who knows the organization's processes, goals, and politics, and who has technical experience and leadership qualities. This person is an advocate with the ability to build company-wide support. It is a demanding role, requiring a detail-oriented expert who can sell top management on the potential of the Extranet. The key to making the champion's case heard is to demonstrate how an Extranet can help the company meet its revenue goals. Specifically, a convincing argument should be made for how the Extranet will generate revenue, how the technology will solve the business problems defined in advance, and how the work will get done through the Extranet.

A champion must drive home the key advantages of an Extranet including the following.

- An Extranet helps the organization ensure accountability in the way it does business with partners.
- An Extranet promotes more effective collaboration with business partners, which improves the potential for increased revenue.
- An Extranet is a long-term investment in competitive advantage. Sooner or later, having an early start on the competition is bound to pay off.

Think of a manufacturing organization with an e-business environment that allows its business partners, distributors, contractors, and suppliers to access Extranet resources through a preestablished interface. Two of the applications could be an e-commerce storefront for suppliers or an enterprise resource planning application and a procurement system. The Extranet can be used to manage and tie all these applications into one integrated system for deriving real value from the company's entire range of business relationships. The Extranet is bound to be the technical community that eventually will generate revenue and ensure competitive advantage.

Management Implications

Intranets are tools to manage corporate intelligence. They offer unique leverage and a competitive advantage at all levels of the organization. Among the key success factors are strong leadership, a focus on users, and effective management of the Intranet. From a managerial viewpoint, change should be nurtured with care. This author spent 7 weeks designing and implementing a $700,000 Intranet site for a foreign central bank of 950 employees. After 3 months of training, coaching, selling, and demonstrating the uses of the new Intranet, less than 20 percent of the employees made a habit of using the new system. The rest of the staff continued to deliver memos, documents, reports, and messages the old-fashioned way—in person.

Change is closely related to employee satisfaction, and the effect of the Intranet on the way employees do their jobs is important. Those who are forced to use a new system will find a way to get back at the company. Gripe sites are available on the Internet where employees can state their dissatisfaction with the employer. For example, www.vault.com or www. brandstupid.com are gripe sites that accept such complaints. Competitors, disgruntled employees, whistle-blowers, or activists generally start these sites. Anyone with an ax to grind can smear the employer for the public to read. IT and company recruiters should review such sites and check what is posted about the company.

Another management implication is the strategy for recruiting qualified technical personnel. The trend used to be to offer significantly higher salaries than the industry average for technical personnel, but most organizations today look for applicants with stability, loyalty, and commitment to the work ethic (see Box 4-7). They offer bonuses based on performance rather than raises because they don't have to repeat them in later years.

Extranets are career enhancers for many IT professionals. Those who work on a successful Extranet project usually end up having the biggest impact on their employer. In one case, a designer deployed an Extranet with the goal of driving down costs. The system met the goal by automating processes, improving overall efficiency, and decentralizing functions for faster and better decision making. In addition to knowledge of the company's business processes, her skills included client/server technology, data communication and networking, and HTTP. She saw a way of securely linking customers, suppliers, and vendors to the corporate network. When the Extranet was implemented, the company recognized the change in revenue, which translated into a hefty raise for the 23-year-old newcomer.

BOX 4-7
E-careers: Demise of the skill premium

You've just interviewed a candidate for an open Oracle database administrator position. Now what do you do? (A) immediately offer a salary that's 25% higher than the industry average, (B) offer a competitive salary, supplemented with workplace perks, or (C) structure a compensation package that rewards the candidate with bonuses throughout the year.

Not long ago, you could have picked A, B, or C and considered yourself a savvy hiring manager. Midway into the year 2000, however, option A is increasingly considered more hasty than prudent. Having lived through Y2k fever and a market correction, information technology managers have become slightly more patient and a bit more conservative about the outer limits of salary premiums. "A year ago, it was the open-bank-vault syndrome because

(continued)

BOX 4-7
Continued

people were so desperate, and we had the Y2k thing bearing down," says Ed Grasing, a director at Pencom Systems Inc., a recruiting firm in Atlanta.

Today, Grasing says, companies are more conscious of what they're spending. "People are more patient about finding a person they trust rather than anybody with a pulse who walks in with Java or C++ skills," he says. "Just because you've got Java on your resume, you're not going to get $75 an hour."

Companies have moved to substitute bonuses for raises. Bonuses are the preferred route at the Mahwah, N.J., office of Atlanta-based United Parcel Service of America Inc. "We're very team-oriented, so with regard to compensation, we have to be very conscious of how it affects the existing workforce," says Jim Diancola, a workforce planning manager at UPS.

The conservative approach to salary premiums isn't just a cooling of the market or a refusal on the part of employers to get blackmailed. "These salary scales have to max out at some point and I think they have," he says. "And the companies that have maxed out will have to look at nonmonetary compensation. It is a wake-up call—why don't we treat people like human beings and have some fun?"

SOURCE: Excerpted from Brandel, Mary, "Demise of the Skill Premium," *Computerworld*, July 31, 2000, 62.

SUMMARY

1. An Intranet is a network connecting a set of company clients using standard Internet protocols, especially TCP/IP and HTTP. Intranets can handle all kinds of communication with ease.
2. An Intranet offers several benefits. It links employees and managers around the clock; companies gain access to their primary resources; and it is the foundation for developing an enterprise-wide information system and a model for internal information management and collaborative computing. In addition, there are cost advantages and ease of access, plus portability and scalability.
3. The two types of client/server architecture for Intranet design are two-tier architecture and three-tier architecture.
4. Intranets can be protected from unauthorized access via firewalls. In the case of a company with branches or remote sites, each location should be part of the total security umbrella of the Intranet.
5. Planning an Intranet is a 6-step procedure: Define the goal, provide justification and management support, build an Intranet in-house or outsource it, form an Intranet team to oversee the process, build and test a prototype, and ensure effective maintenance.
6. E-mail is getting smarter: Now it can be used not just to store messages but to direct specific messages to defined folders and to check voice, text, and fax messages. This is called content management.
7. An Extranet or company Web site links two or more trading partners. When contemplating an Extranet installation, five key factors need to be considered: identifying the user, listing the technology components, specifying the security requirements, setting up the administration, and understanding the usability.
8. From the managerial perspective, Intranets are tools to manage corporate intelligence. Among the key success factors are strong leadership, a focus on users, and effective management.

KEY TERMS

- firewall, 105
- flaming, 119
- groupware, 104
- packet filter, 115
- proxy, 115
- spamming, 119

TEST YOUR UNDERSTANDING

1. Is there a relationship between the Intranet and groupware? Be specific.
2. Distinguish between the following:
   a. Intranet and Extranet.
   b. two-tier and three-tier architecture.
   c. server PC and client PC.
   d. spamming and flaming.
3. Explain briefly the function and purposes of a firewall.
4. What main benefits can one expect of an Intranet installation?
5. In what way(s) can an Intranet be useful in human resources? Explain in detail.
6. How is an Intranet useful in manufacturing and operations?
7. In your own words, why does a company need an Intranet?
8. Summarize the essence of client/server architecture.
9. Is there a relationship between RPC and GUI? Explain.
10. What would be some of the limitations of a two-tier architecture? Be specific.
11. "Browsers greatly simplify access to the company's computing resources and information." Do you agree? Explain.
12. In what way(s) do firewalls vary in complexity?
13. Summarize the key steps in planning an Intranet.
14. What would be a deciding factor in building an Intranet in-house or outsourcing it?
15. The chapter mentions that "Intranet and e-mail is a marriage made in CyberHeaven." Do you agree? Justify your answer.
16. List four key items that should be followed under e-mail etiquette.
17. Why is an Extranet viewed as a B2B Intranet? Explain.
18. Several factors should be considered when contemplating an Extranet installation. Elaborate.
19. Within the framework of the chapter material, what is your definition of a champion?

DISCUSSION QUESTIONS

1. "Technically, there is no difference between the Internet and Intranet, except that only select people are allowed to connect to the Intranet." Evaluate this statement in the light of the way Intranets are designed.
2. Do you think an Intranet environment is the best way to communicate within the firm? In answering this question, assess alternative modes of communication and report your findings in class.

3. If Intranets offer so many good benefits, why do you think some companies resist having them? Is it the size of the firm? The nature of the product? The caliber of personnel? Discuss.
4. If you have a choice between two-tier and three-tier server architecture, which one would you consider? Which factors or criteria would you use in making your final decision? Be specific.
5. Within the framework of an Intranet, what do you look for when considering a filter in large business?
6. Would one be correct in thinking that more abuses than uses of e-mail occur in an Intranet environment? Discuss.
7. Of the three applications mentioned in the chapter (human resources, accounting and finance, and manufacturing and operations), which application justifies the most frequent use of an Extranet? Why?

WEB EXERCISES

1. Visit a large firm that has an Intranet site. Identify the technology that operates the site.
2. Identify a large retailer in your area and determine whether it is ready for adopting Intranet and Extranet. If the retailer already has one, interview the head of the IT division and learn about the technology in use. Report your findings to the class.
3. Design an Intranet (on paper) for a small bank of 65 employees. Explain the details of the infrastructure to a local IT specialist. What did he or she find right and wrong with your design? Write a four-page report summarizing your experience.

Chapter 5

Web Management Tools and Web Portals

Contents

IN A NUTSHELL

One of the most important contributions of the Internet is information access via Web portals. Companies are fast learning that certain information or applications can become available more quickly and reliably via portals.

Portals are among the leading success stories of e-business. They are the most powerful tools that help achieve communication goals. An e-commerce solution employs a portal for capturing information wherever it exists (in documents, managers' minds, databases, and historical data). Another important tool is a user interface that makes information available to a larger community of employees and knowledge workers. By providing an integrated framework for linking together people, processes, and information, portals play a central role in simplifying managerial complexity, increasing operational productivity, and adding value to a company's business operations.

content management: also referred to as content management system (CMS); a system used to manage the content of a Web site.

personalization: software system that allows an Internet site to provide the user with a Web page that reflects the interests, needs, and actions of the user.

Portals can be valuable tools for enhancing business processes (Fox 2002). They employ distribution channels such as the Internet, Intranets, and Extranets that allow companies to take advantage of information lying dormant in their databases. Portals evolved from pure information providers to sophisticated interfaces containing knowledge management features such as **content management** for knowledge categorization, collaboration tools for knowledge sharing, and **personalization** capabilities to facilitate the search function. Box 5-1 is a summary of one area where portals have been useful.

THE BASICS

What Are Portals?

portal: a Web page that offers links to other Web sites. Portals can be broad or narrow, specific or general.

vertical portal: electronic exchanges that combine upstream and downstream e-commerce activities of specialized products and/or services.

A **portal** is a Web site featuring common services as a starting point. It can refer to virtually any type of Internet entry point. Examples are corporate Web pages, Yahoo!, and state portals for renewing driver's licenses. A portal is effectively a complex piece of software that delivers functionality and information coming almost exclusively from outside the portal. The portal provides coherent delivery and integration across the content sources (Harris-Jones 2002). It also assures secure and reliable interface to participants in a business process and collaborates with users through the integration of external Web-based applications or internal back-office systems. Such a site is a frequent gateway to the Web (Web portal) or a niche topic (**vertical portal**).

Portals are considered virtual workplaces for the following functions:

- Promoting knowledge sharing among different categories of end users such as customers, partners, and employees.
- Providing access to structured data that are stored in data warehouses, database systems, and transactional systems.

BOX 5-1
Role of portals in the insurance industry

While Web portals have been around for a while, the trend now is toward ones specifically designed to meet the demands of an industry, and insurance is among those adopting this KM strategy. Although insurers face the same basic needs as any organization—customer service, human resources, and accounting—the industry also has some distinctive **work flow** requirements that can be met through a tailored Web portal.

For example, a claim that has come in for processing might take one route if the dollar amount is under a certain figure, and another route if the claim is above a certain figure. An application must be reviewed by a number of people in the organization before it is approved, and the group of people reviewing an application might vary, depending on the type of insurance the applicant is seeking and the level of documentation required.

The need for more effective communication and improved service spurred Humana (http://humana.com) to look for a Web-based KM system. In August, Louisville, Kentucky-based Humana launched a Web-based community "hub" for doctors, patients, employers, and insurance brokers called Emphesys. The insurer deployed technology from InSystems. Electronic certificate delivery provides a dramatic reduction in the time it takes to put benefit plan information in customers' hands, as well as improved efficiency and customer satisfaction.

Certificate revision is also paperless. With InSystems' Calligo, new versions can be generated, delivered, and maintained in the repository without having to reissue everything on paper. If a state mandates a change, for example, the system can generate and deliver the revised document electronically, as well as highlight the differences for customers to see. The potential to do changes and put the documents in the hands of the insured quickly is a tremendous benefit and enhances company relationships with customers.

SOURCE: Excerpted from Zimmermann, Kim A., "Portals Help Insurers and Their Customers," *KMWorld*, September 2002, 23.

- Organizing unstructured data such as electronic documents, paper documents, lessons learned, stories, and the like.
- Offering varieties such as portals on Intranets, customer-facing information portals, supplier-facing information portals, and enterprise portals.

Portals are emerging as the most promising tool for simplifying the access to data stored in various application systems, facilitating collaboration among employees, and assisting the company in reaching its customers. Other benefits include reduced cost, better quality, keeping pace with technology, improved customer satisfaction, and attracting skilled staff.

From a business perspective, portals provide the company's employees with task-relevant information. They also can supply partners and customers with knowledge quickly. The goal of such a portal is the transparent enterprise, reducing the complexity of reaching needed information. In contrast, portal disadvantages include the following.

- Difficulty integrating with other applications.
- Organizational and financial costs.
- Culture shock.
- The need for additional investment in technology.
- The difficulty of retaining skilled staff.
- Uncertainty of benefits. Expense of technology.

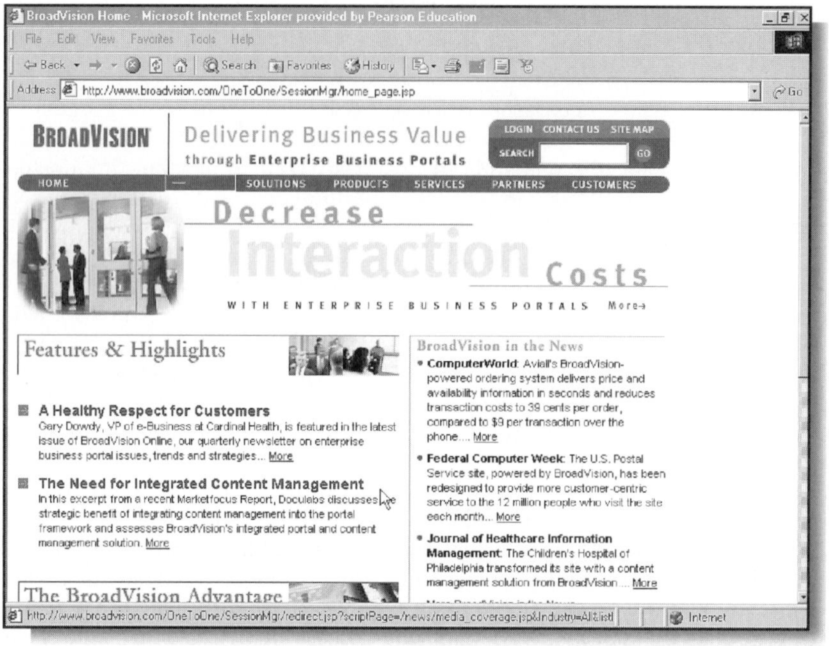

Screen Capture 5-1

Source: Copyright © 2003–2004 Broadvision, Inc.

- Unprepared suppliers.
- Incompatibility with existing IT infrastructure (Pickering 2002).

Evolution of Portals

The original purpose of a portal was to consolidate a company's disparate data and allow ready access to that data. Web portals were mere search engines for news, e-mail, maps, stock quotes, shopping, and the like. They employed simple search technology for locating information on the Web applied to HTML documents. The first Web portals were online services such as AOL. They provided access to the Web and were one-step destinations for advertisers and marketers, offering a variety of choices and options. Advertising formats included banners and buttons, text links, and multiformat sponsorships.

The next phase transformed today's portals to navigation sites; this describes the functions available at sites such as Quicken, MSN, Yahoo!, and Lycos. Such portals categorize personal interests into groups (e.g., news, sports, finance, education, science, and others). An example of the logical hierarchy of groups is shown in Screen Capture 5-1. The groups are referred to as Internet public portals.

horizontal portal: electronic exchange that focuses on many subjects (e.g., Yahoo!).

A portal may focus either on many subjects (**horizontal portal** like Yahoo! or MSN) or a specific subject (vertical portal like WebMD). Portals also can be enterprise or Internet public portals. To facilitate access to a large accumulation of information, portals evolved to include advanced search capabilities and taxonomies. With emphasis on information, they were called information portals. The evolution of the portal concept is shown in Figure 5-1.

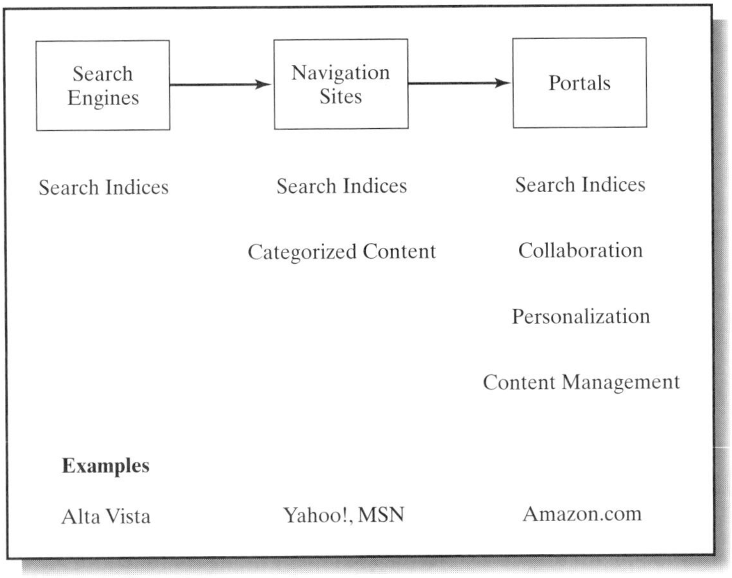

Figure 5-1
Evolution of the portal concept

enterprise information portal: a portal that ties together multiple, heterogeneous internal repositories and applications, as well as external content sources and services, into a single browser-based view that is individualized to a particular user's task or role.

Enterprise information portals provide the next step in the portal technology evolution. In November 1998, Christopher Shilakes and Julie Tylman of Merrill Lynch's Enterprise Software team introduced the concept of the enterprise information portal. The concept was described as "applications that enable companies to unlock internally and externally stored information and provide users a single gateway to personalized information needed to make informed business decisions." They are an amalgamation of software applications that integrate, manage, analyze, and distribute information across and outside an enterprise (including business intelligence, content management, data warehouse and data mart, and data management applications).

Companies are becoming more aware of the potential value of information lying dormant in various repositories. Integration and consolidation are important goals of enterprise portals. Applications are integrated by combining, standardizing, analyzing, and distributing relevant information and knowledge to the end user—customers, employees, or partners (see Box 5-2).

Knowledge Portals

knowledge portal: a Web page or a facility that offers a single, uniform point from which all of an enterprise's data sources can be accessed.

Today's trend is to build applications that combine the search, analysis, and dissemination of information through knowledge portals. In **knowledge portals,** the focus is less on information content and more on improving knowledge worker productivity. Knowledge portal is a key component in the knowledge management architecture and the central piece that allows producers and users of knowledge to interact. It provides a variety of information on various topics and can be customized to meet a user's individual needs online. Two types of interface are provided.

BOX 5-2
The next generation of portals

The second wave is shifting the primary focus of the Enterprise Intelligence Portal (EIP). Whereas EIP did emphasize broadly based and generalized decision processing and mass dissemination of corporate information, it now targets collaboration and highly targeted and personalized distribution of content, bundled with multiple types of specialized, expertise-oriented services. These trends, happening over the past year or so, indicate that the EIP concept is on the verge of an explosion along four key directions:

- **Enterprise Collaborative Processing Portals** (ECPPs) connect users not only with all the information they need, but also with everyone they need. ECPPs consolidate groupware, e-mail, **work flow**, and critical desktop applications under the same gateway as decision-processing and content-management applications. ECPPs are characterized by "virtual project areas" or communities.
- **Enterprise Mission Management Portals** (EMMPs) provide a "digital expertise-oriented workplace," a highly specialized and personalized Web site where everything a user team needs (such as access to ERP applications, productivity and analysis tools, and relevant internal and external content) to effectively manage mission-critical management activities such as customer relationship management (CRM) is consolidated and made accessible via the Web.
- **Enterprise Extended Services Portals** (EESPs) do everything the first three types do, but they focus on providing comprehensive job support from the standpoint of "virtual enterprises" by creating communities and "virtual service spaces" of channel partners, suppliers, distributors, and customers.

The convergence of the first and second EIP waves will occur within 1.5 years. This time will be spent on extending architectural frameworks that guided technology from the search-based, first-wave portals to a fully functional architecture capable of enabling expertise- and service-based, second-wave portals.

work flow: the defined series of tasks within an organization to produce a final outcome.

SOURCE: Excerpted from Davydov, Mark M., "The Second Wave of EIP," *Intelligent Enterprise*, March 1, 2000.

- **Knowledge producer interface** allows the knowledge worker to gather, analyze, and collaborate with peers or colleagues to generate new knowledge.
- **Knowledge consumer interface** facilitates the dissemination of knowledge across the enterprise. A key feature is a sophisticated personalization facility that takes into account the consumer profile before providing customized results.

Key Characteristics

enterprise knowledge portal: an electronic doorway into a knowledge management system.

Enterprise knowledge portals distinguish knowledge from information. They provide a facility for producing knowledge from data and information. They also provide a better basis for making decisions than do other portals. Gaining knowledge means competitive advantage over those with mere information. A summary of the key characteristics of enterprise information and enterprise knowledge portals is shown in Table 5-1.

Table 5-1
Knowledge portals versus information portals

Enterprise Information Portals	Enterprise Knowledge Portals
• Use both "push" and "pull" technologies to transmit information to users through a standardized, Web-based interface. • Integrate disparate applications including content management, business intelligence, data warehouse/data mart, data management, and other data external to these applications into a single system that can "share, manage, and maintain information from one central user interface." • Access external and internal sources of data and information and support a bi-directional exchange of information with these sources.	• Goal-directed toward knowledge production, knowledge acquisition, knowledge transmission, and knowledge management. • Focus on enterprise business processes (e.g., sales, marketing, and risk management). • Provide, produce, and manage information about the validity of the information it supplies. • Include all EIP functionalities.

Source: Firestone, J., "Enterprise Knowledge Portals," White Paper 8, www.dkms.com. Accessed March 2003.

To illustrate, take the case of the army knowledge online portal. The objective of this portal is to transform the army into a networked organization that leverages its intellectual capital to better organize, train, equip, and maintain a strategic land combat force. More specifically, the army needs quick access to its enterprise information at a low cost, and it must be able to use information technology to leverage army-wide innovation in services, processes, and knowledge creation.

Screens 5-2, 5-3, and 5-4 show the capabilities of the army knowledge portal as well as communities of practice that were created and their features. Among the key features are the following.

- User-customizable messages on the Web page.
- Directory search.
- Knowledge channels.
- Powerful search engine.
- Acquisition knowledge center.
- Officer career announcement and management knowledge center.
- Calendar and Frequently Asked Questions (FAQs).
- Career contact points.

Search Engines

As mentioned earlier, portals were mere search engines. For the purpose of distinguishing between the two, it would be useful to briefly cover the functions and role of search engines in e-commerce. E-merchants depend on search engines as sources for large volumes of Web traffic. **Search engines** are like yellow pages for online businesses. Many search engines have been created, and they vary in database size, navigation format, and collection method. Engines can collect Web site data by employing a traditional crawler, a human editor, or a paid subscriber.

search engine: software agents whose task is to find information by looking at keywords or by following certain guidelines or rules.

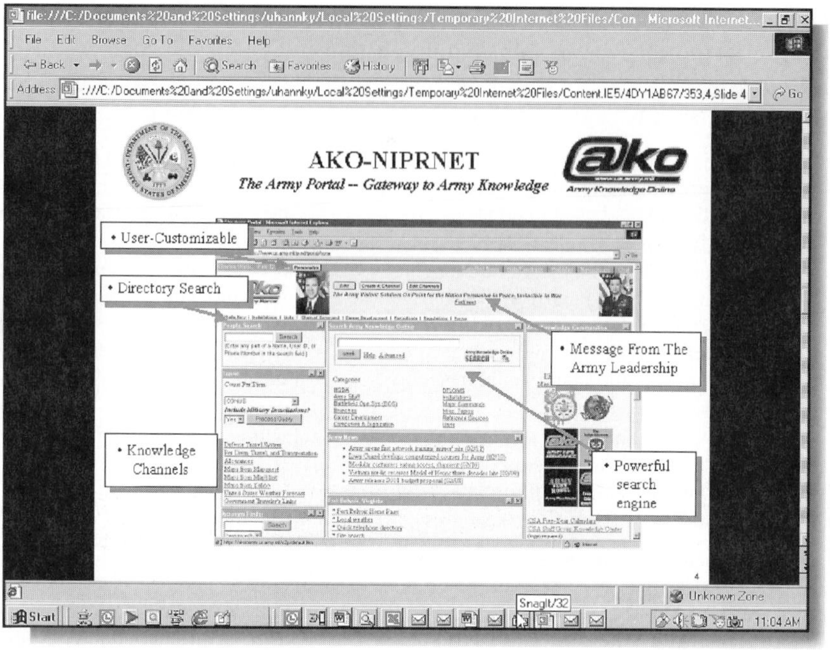

Screen Capture 5-2
The army knowledge portal

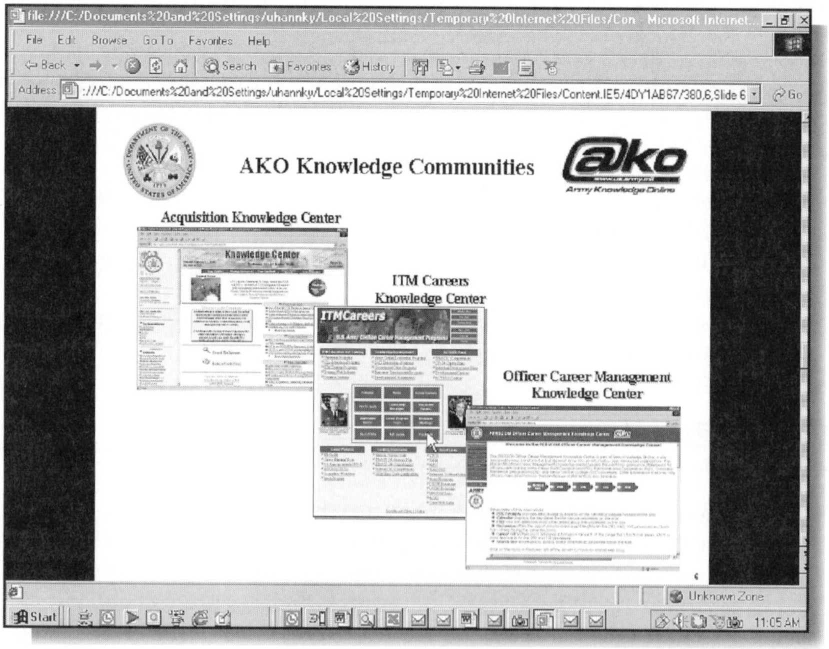

Screen Capture 5-3
The army communities of practice

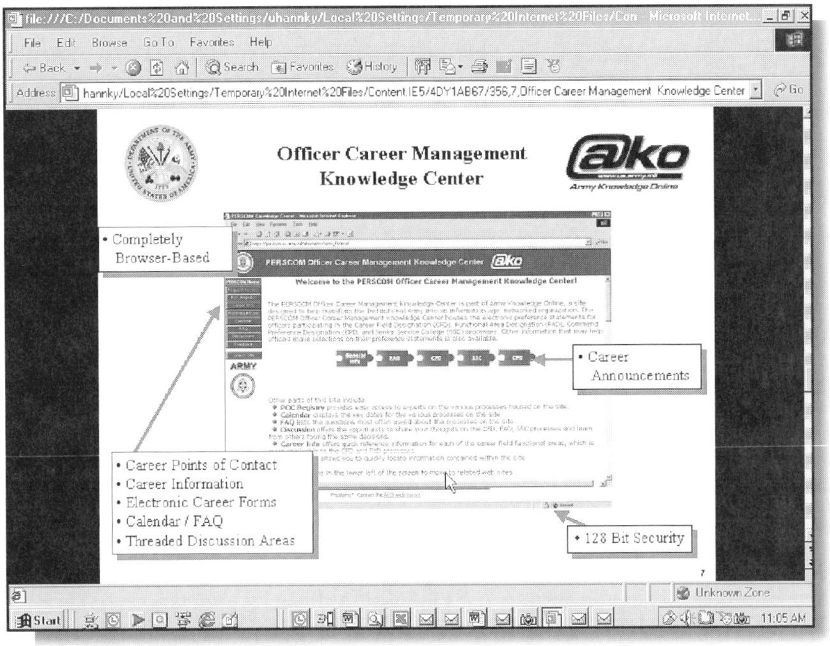

Screen Capture 5-4
Features of Officer Career Management Knowledge Center

Crawlers are computer-automated programs that scour the Internet for Web links. These links are added to a database and categorized by keywords and relevancy for future reference. The human method also employs Web surfing to find links to be added to a database but is subject to human analysis. Search engines that operate by paid subscribers will add a Web site to their database with the understanding that they will be paid for each Web surfer who clicks on a link to the business's Web site. Webmasters who understand and can take advantage of each type of search engine will be more successful in gaining exposure.

Historically, search engines were first implemented in small units that searched only one site or at most a handful, but their usefulness was soon recognized as the Internet grew. Various methods were used from searching the titles of Web pages to counting the number of keywords that showed up on the page. As the technology of indexing Web pages matured, one search engine—Google—rose in prominence above all others.

Most of Google's success is attributed to its unique way of ranking pages. PageRank is an algorithm that assumes that the more links a page has, the better it is. The page with the most links to it from relevant outside sites gets the highest ranking; the more pages that are linked to those linking pages, the better. The algorithm considers every link from an outside page as a vote of confidence in that particular page by the linking page.

Search terms are then determined by content and links instead of a simple word count. Domain names and the text of a hyperlink are important determinants of ranking and keywords. Googlebot, the crawler program, is fast, efficient, and objective in its categorization of Web pages. As a result, in October 2002, it had more than 2,469,685 Web pages indexed, and 13 million surfers have searched on Google. (See www.google.com.)

Getting listed in this massive directory is not a problem, but getting a good ranking is a different story. Because Google ranks mainly by recording the number of links that go to a Web page, any prospective Webmaster has to be able to spread the word about its Web site, especially among relevant sites. This might mean cooperating and trading links with a powerful competitor or first getting listed with specific directories.

Site content and relevance are integral parts of automated search engines. Consolidation of themes can help with the overall keyword searches that are so popular now. Crawlers use a combination of URL text, titles, keyword densities, meta-tags, and descriptions to extrapolate an overall theme for a Web site. If one is selling paper clips, it would help to have a large selection of all different types of paper clips and to have relevant information and facts about paper clips.

To illustrate, when searching for "money," CNN's Financial News Web page shows up as the top site. More than 150 Web sites link to CNN, including AOL, CompuServ, *AsiaWeek*, *TIME*, and the *Wall Street Journal*. The second-ranked Web page, Smartmoney.com, has more than 800 Web pages linked to it, but they are relatively obscure listings or directories. Furthermore, the 100th-ranking Web site, Moneynet.co.uk, is a bank in the United Kingdom that focuses on loans and mortgages. It has more than 120 linked pages but clearly does not have the breadth of coverage on the subject of money. As this example shows, the PageRank and content algorithms operate in a clear and logical manner.

It should be noted that no search engine is free of drawbacks. Yahoo! is the largest directory, but it gave up on maintaining its human-edited monstrosity in favor of simply reshuffling results from Google and Dmoz. Likewise, although Google dominates the Web, its reach is still limited. For marketers interested in promoting their items, the best plan of action is to thoroughly test and streamline the site based on set criteria. Exposure can be gained by simply joining forums, small directories, e-mail lists, and the like. Then, the Webmaster can submit not only the main site, but a few major subcategories within the Web site, as well. It is also good practice to submit the URLs of referring sites in order to increase rankings.

After the site is more or less optimized and has a somewhat mature feel, it is time for submissions to human-edited directories. Because the chances of rejection are high and the backlogs are extremely large, it is best to optimize the site as much as possible before attempting admission. At this point, one should know what keywords and terms are most popular, and most of the editor-distracting errors should have been smoothed over, thus increasing the chances of success when the editor comes around.

The Business Challenge

Today's organization is evolving from product- to customer-centric organization. At the same time, there is inherent pressure to optimize the performance of operational processes to reduce costs and enhance quality. Customer-centric systems allow companies to understand and predict customer behavior and offer the right product at the right time, while commercializing products at the lowest price.

Portals and Business Transformation

The challenge stems from two fundamental aspects underlying the current computing environment. First, the explosion in the volume of key business information already captured in electronic documents has left many organizations losing grip on information as they transform into new systems and process upgrades. Second, the speed with which quantity and content are growing means rigorous internal discipline to mine and integrate the sources of enterprise knowledge.

Consider the pressures faced by today's typical organization.

- **Shorter time to market:** New products and services have to be conceived, developed, and delivered in months or even weeks.
- **Knowledge worker turnover:** When a pivotal person leaves, the pain is felt widely and quickly. Organizations that do not tap into their employees' minds and take advantage of the knowledge within will fall behind quickly.
- **More demanding customers and investors:** For virtually every organization, the squeeze is on customers wanting to pay less while investors want more value from their investment. That means all the resources to which an organization can lay claim, including its intellectual resources, must be managed for the best results.

Today, more companies realize that they must develop strategies and processes designed to best utilize intellectual resources at strategic and operational levels. Ten years ago, companies began using groupware (e.g., e-mail, discussion forums, document libraries) for coordinating activities. Now, they are inundated with new tools for communicating, sharing knowledge, and interacting electronically. They are deploying next-generation information and application platforms (e.g., enterprise portals) and real-time tools (e.g., instant messaging, Web conferencing, streaming audio/video) but struggling to manage process engineering across partners and suppliers as another aspect of collaboration.

Research from International Data Corp., for example, indicates that 50 percent of companies adopting data warehousing are planning or already implementing knowledge management. According to a survey by Cambridge Information Network (a division of Cambridge Technology Partners), of its 3,500 member CIOs, 85 percent believe that knowledge management generates competitive advantage. Figure 5-2 reports reasons for launching KM projects.

Organizations are looking for solutions to support their new e-business models. As a result, the demand for tools to negotiate, plan, decide, and collaborate more effectively has increased dramatically. Unfortunately, most organizations meet collaboration requirements on a piecemeal basis, fulfilling requests as they emerge from business units or partners without an overall strategic plan. "The result is a hodgepodge of overlapping and redundant technologies" (Meta Group, Business Collaboration,1). See www.metagroup.com/cgi-bin/inetcgi/commerce/productDetails.jsp?oid=29277. Accessed June 2003.

The benefits companies are expecting from their enterprise portal initiatives are shown in the Figure 5-3.

Market Potential

Knowledge portals have emerged as a key tool for supporting the knowledge workplace. There is no doubt that portals are big business. More than 85 percent of organizations plan to invest in portals during the next 5 years, with a median expenditure of $500,000. As the world becomes more networked, these estimates are bound to climb. Portals can provide easier, unified access to business information and better communications among customers and employees. See Box 5-3 for sample pressures facing portals.

The portal market is comprised of several infrastructure components: content management, business intelligence, data warehouses and data mines, and data management. An example of portal in action is summarized in Box 5-4.

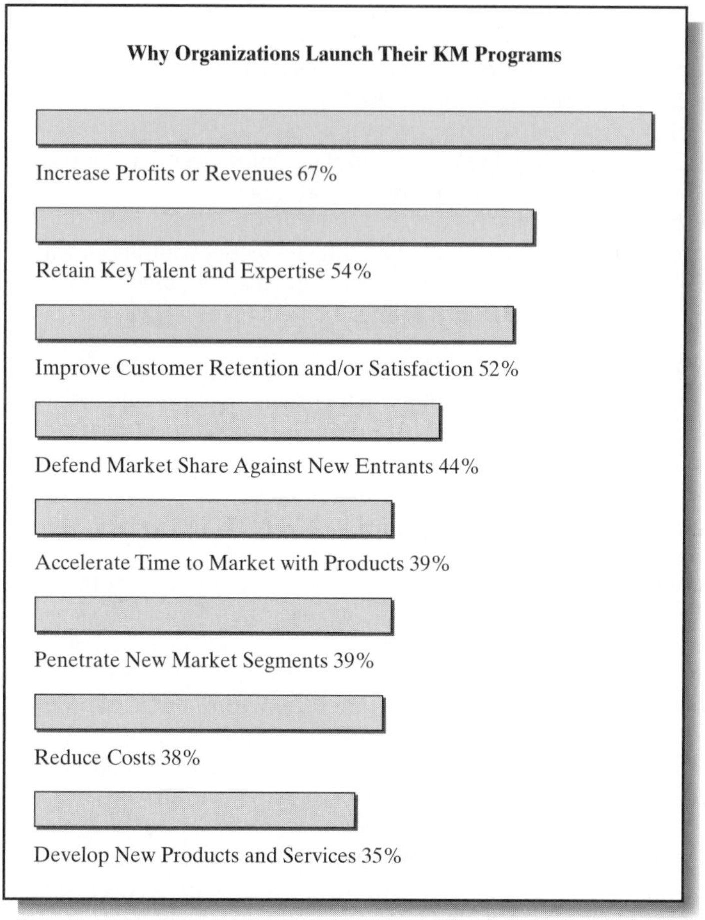

Figure 5-2
Main reasons for launching KM projects

Source: Cambridge Information Network, Knowledge Management Survey 1999.

Enterprise Portal Technologies

Key Functionalities

The main goal of a portal is to provide a single point of access to all information sources. Hence, portals must be the ultimate tools for universal integration of all enterprise applications. At the same time, because organizational staff members have different information needs and knowledge uses, portals have to deliver a personalized interface. Given the complexity of this challenge, portals must include the following seven functionalities.

1. **Gathering:** Documents created by knowledge workers are stored in a variety of locations (e.g., files on individual desktops, Web sites on the network, databases on servers, and so on). In order to be accessible, data and documents need to be captured in a common repository.
2. **Categorization:** This functionality profiles the information in the repository and organizes it in meaningful ways for navigation and searching. Portals are expected to support categorization at all levels, including the employee, partners, and customers.

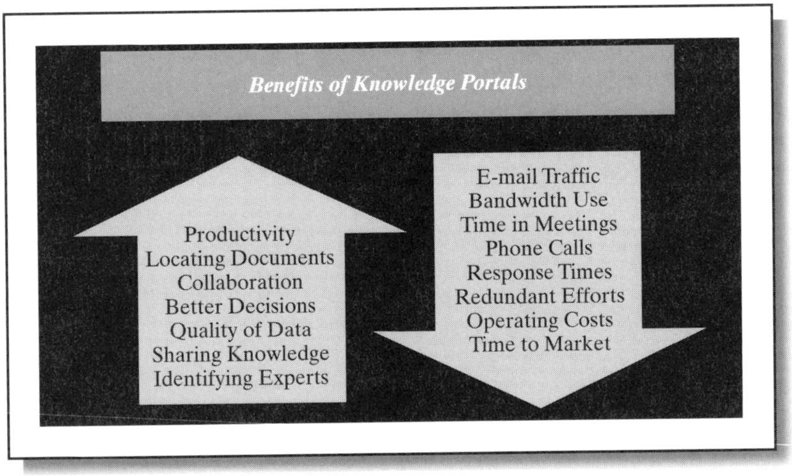

Figure 5-3
Knowledge portals increase productivity and performance in managing knowledge. They also decrease e-mail traffic and other time wasted in meetings and phoning.
Source: Metagroup Business Collaboration 2000.

BOX 5-3
The role of portals in facing business pressures

- **Business Integration vs. Information Integration or Application Integration:** Integrating information and applications are first steps to support business integration. A portal can support application and information integration, but the weakness at this point can be a lack of providing business context, or meaning, to the information. Business integration is the integration and translation through the metadata layer of information and applications to provide context.
- **Process Integration:** In addition to providing context, the portal solution should support process integration. Process integration includes work flow, categorization, and taxonomy services. These services provide the foundation for context. Information with work flow, categorization, and taxonomy equals context.
- **Application and Information Integration:** This is a strict reference to source systems from which information is generated. It also includes the data administration layers, such as cleansing, transformation, and extraction.
- **Enterprise Metadata Repository:** Metadata are vital as the mechanism for context. The repository should not include every piece of information that exists, only the information that will be utilized to provide meaning. The repository then becomes the "single version of understanding," not just the "single version of the truth."

SOURCE: Excerpted from Bolds, Robert, "Enterprise Information Portals: Portals in Puberty, Best Practices in Enterprise Portals," *KMWorld*.

BOX 5-4
Portal in practice

A BUSINESS-TO-EMPLOYEE PORTAL AT FORD MOTOR COMPANY

Ford Motor Company's use of the Plumtree portal is an example of a business-to-employee (B2E) Internet Portal. This case study example won DCI's Annual Portal Excellence Award for the Internet portal category, announced in January 2001.

Ford used the Plumtree to implement an expansive framework for its ambitious business-to-employee e-business strategy. The world's second-largest automaker chose Plumtree to create a single, simple, Web destination for 200,000 employees enterprise-wide to find and share the content and services they need to support customers and speed products to market. Ford is deploying the Plumtree corporate portal as part of an initiative to modernize the world's largest Intranet, hub.ford.com, which spans 800 Ford facilities and 150 manufacturing plants worldwide. The portal enables Ford to integrate the hundreds of thousands of Web pages that comprise hub.ford.com into one enterprise-wide Web destination. Now, Ford employees anywhere can draw on a common base of best practices, market news, product specifications, performance metrics, and policy and procedures for the information they need to make confident business decisions and act quickly on revenue opportunities. Information is available for customer relationship management, for order fulfillment, customer satisfaction, sales and volume tracking, economic assessments, competitive information, and Ford community initiatives.

FEATURES OF FORD'S B2E PORTAL

Personalization: Each hub.ford.com user tailors the portal experience to his or her role. To assemble a complete view of the business, Ford employees can select gadgets for embedding e-mail, real-time news feeds, stock reports, sales histories, personnel directories, self-service travel booking, corporate expense reporting, and pay and benefits in personalized portal pages.

Collaboration: The portal enables Ford employees to use a Web-based workplace for drag-and-drop file sharing, multithreaded discussions, real-time messaging, and polling that Ford is deploying enterprise-wide. Now, paint shop workers from manufacturing departments on different continents can share skills and ideas easily, shortening development cycles and increasing product quality.

Community of practice: To foster collaboration, project mangers at Ford will create community pages of content and services shared by entire business units.

BENEFITS TO FORD

Increased ROI on information technology: The Plumtree-powered hub.ford.com organizes scattered Intranet sites into a framework that everybody can use, anywhere, and broadens the audience for applications previously limited to specialists, increasing the return on Ford's electronic assets. Ford will integrate multiple data sources into the Plumtree corporate portal, including Documentum, whose content management platform is deployed throughout the enterprise.

Increased Productivity: A single, personalized destination for corporate content and services helps focus everyone on company strategy, brands, and competitors, increasing the impact of every employee. The hub.ford.com users know what is happening across the enterprise, and can stay on top of their customers, products, and markets to help drive sales. The portal is also the framework for a broad e-learning initiative to foster employee competency, leadership, and advancement.

BOX 5-4
Continued

Close Collaboration: Desktop access to digital workplaces is driving business-to-employee and business-to-business collaboration across Ford's enterprise. Now, Ford engineers can easily communicate with one another and with suppliers and product design, and executives can conduct secure meetings across time zones and borders.

SOURCE: Adapted from Finkelstein, C., "Building Enterprise Portal Using XML," TDWI Conference, Amsterdam, 2001.

It also should support categorizations in various dimensions, including the process, product, and service dimensions.

3. **Distribution:** Portals must help individuals acquire knowledge, either through an active mechanism (search interface) or a passive mechanism (push). This functionality supports the distribution of structured and unstructured information in the form of electronic or paper documents.
4. **Collaboration:** Collaboration is achieved through messaging, work flow, discussion databases, and so on. This functionality expands the role of portals from passive information provider to an interface for all types of organizational interactions.
5. **Publish:** The goal of this functionality is to publish information to a broader audience, including individuals outside the organization.
6. **Personalization:** A key component of the portal architecture is to allow individuals to enhance their productivity. Personalization is becoming a necessity for successful portals, due to the proliferation of information available through the portal. To take advantage of this functionality, knowledge workers must be able to manage and prioritize the delivery of information on a task function or an interest basis.
7. **Search/Navigate:** This functionality provides tools for identifying and accessing specific information. The knowledge worker can either browse or submit a query.

Figure 5-4 illustrates the most common features and business benefits of portals.

Figure 5-5 sketches the Microsoft portal architecture. Briefly, the key components are the following.

- The knowledge management platform offers a typical, but extended, three-layered architecture that allows a company to build a flexible, powerful, and scalable knowledge management solution.
- The knowledge desktop layer consists of familiar productivity tools, such as Microsoft Office, and integrates tightly with the knowledge services layer.
- The knowledge services layer provides important knowledge management services such as collaboration, document management, and search and deliver functionality, with modules for tracking, work flow, and data analysis.
- The system layer is a foundation that includes administration, security, and directories for managing the knowledge management platform. All services run on the system layer and benefit from the integrated communication services that connect with external solutions, platforms, and partners.

Common Features	Business Benefits
Search	Quick access to hidden information to **facilitate business processes**
Categorization	Ability to organize information assets by business process, group, or job category thus **promoting access to relevant information**
Query, Reporting, and Analysis	**Better decision support** as well as information dissemination and sharing
Integration of Information and Applications	Ability to access through a single interface, all applications and information required for **increased job throughout**
Publish and Subscribe	Maturation of business processes by collaborating with others, sharing information, and **improving business performance**
Personalization	Arranging the interface to meet an individual's needs and desires for **increased job productivity**

Figure 5-4
Portal features and their corresponding benefits

asynchronous collaboration: human-to-human interactions via computer subsystems having no time or space constraints.

synchronous collaboration: computer-based, human-to-human interaction that occurs immediately (within 5 seconds) using audio, video, or data technologies.

push technology: technology that places information in a place where it is difficult to avoid seeing it.

pull technology: technology that requires one to take specific actions to retrieve information.

Collaboration

Collaboration is a fundamental starting point for e-business transformation. The goal of the collaboration tool is to support information sharing. It means two or more people working together in a coordinated manner over time and space using electronic devices. In a well-designed collaborative environment, knowledge flow can be captured easily in e-mail, stored in document and discussion databases, and be available in a knowledge management system for later use.

Collaboration is distinguished by whether it is synchronous or asynchronous. **Asynchronous collaboration** is human-to-human interactions via computer subsystems having no time or space constraints. Queries, responses, or access can occur at any time and in any place. In contrast, **synchronous collaboration** is computer-based, human-to-human interaction that occurs immediately (within 5 seconds). It can use audio, video, or data technologies. Figure 5-6 summarizes the requirements for successful collaboration.

Another important distinction is whether to use push or pull technology. **Push technology** places information in a place where it is difficult to avoid seeing it. E-mail is a classic example of a push technology. **Pull technologies** require you to take specific actions to retrieve information. The Web is a good example of a pull technology. An electronic mailing list that uses push technology of e-mail is extremely powerful

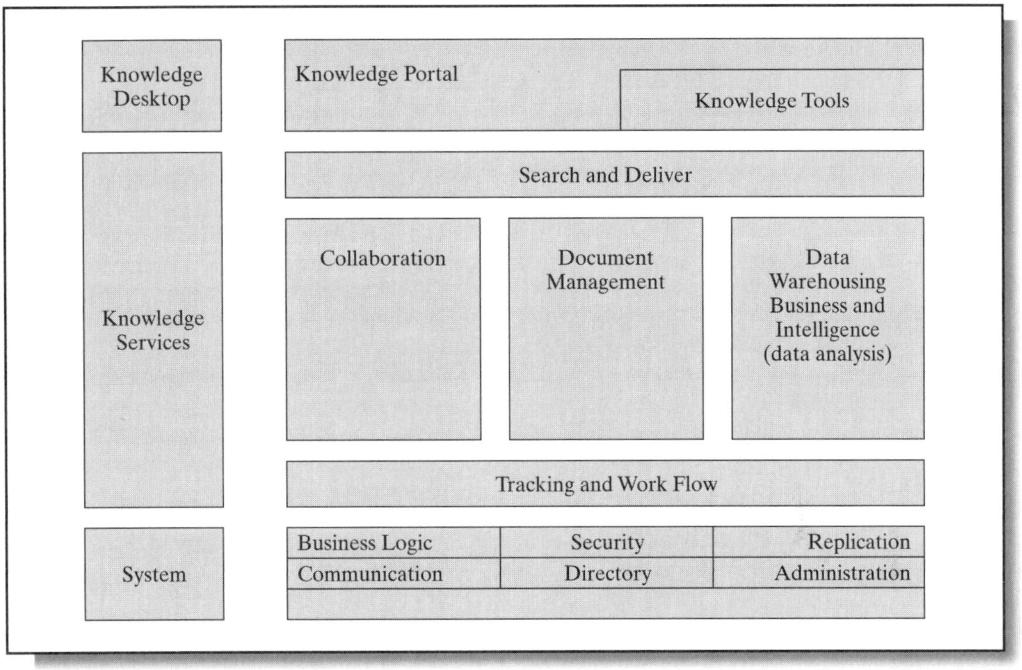

Figure 5-5
Layers of the portal architecture
Source: Honeycutt, Jerry, "Knowledge Management Strategies," *Microsoft*, 2000, 167.

1. E-mail systems that support collaborative services such as shared calendars, task lists, contact lists, and team-based discussions.
2. Web browser for browsing and presenting the documents to the user.
3. Simple search functionalities such as file services integrated with the operating system or search services integrated with an application (e.g., e-mail, discussions).
4. Collaboration services with a multipurpose database for capturing the collaborative data.
5. Web services for providing the access layer to documented knowledge.
6. Indexing services for full-text search of documents.
7. Well-organized central-storage locations such as file, Web servers, and documents databases.

Figure 5-6
Requirements for successful collaboration tools
Source: Honeycutt, Jerry, "Knowledge Management Strategies," *Microsoft*, 2000, 176.

as a collaborative tool, because it requires little learning or behavioral change on the part of the user.

Table 5-2 shows the technologies available to perform asynchronous and synchronous collaboration.

Table 5-2
Advantages and disadvantages of synchronous and asynchronous collaboration tools

Synchronous Collaboration	Asynchronous Collaboration
Teleconferencing Used extensively by senior management and staff, conference telephone calls represent an effective (if relatively expensive) collaboration technology use for a number of years and represent an extremely cost-effective collaboration technology. *Advantages*: personal, immediate feedback. *Disadvantages*: expensive, often doesn't work well across time zones.	**Electronic Mailing Lists** Lists have been in use for a number of years and represent an extremely cost-effective collaboration technology. *Advantages:* cheap. *Disadvantages:* limited communication medium.
Computer Video/Teleconferencing Computer-based **teleconferencing** and video-conferencing are rapidly evolving technologies that have tremendous potential for distributed organizations.	**Web-Based Discussion Forums** A number of different online discussion forum applications are in use. *Advantages*: same as electronic mailing lists except requires slightly faster Internet connection. *Disadvantages*: cultural resistance.
Online Chat Forum Such forums allow multiple users to communicate simultaneously by typing messages on a computer screen.	**Lotus Notes** Lotus Notes is a comprehensive collaboration tool that includes e-mail and groupware. *Advantages*: comprehensive collaborative solution employing state-of-the-art technologies for communication, document management, and work flow. *Disadvantages*: expensive to deploy when compared with other collaboration technologies.

teleconferencing: conferring with a number of people via telephone or computer systems.

Content Management

Content management requires directory and indexing capabilities to manage automatically the ever-growing warehouse of enterprise data. This component addresses the problem of searching for knowledge in all information sources in the enterprise. This knowledge includes structured and unstructured internal information objects such as office documents, collaborative data, Management Information Systems (MISs), Enterprise Resource Planning (ERP) systems, and experts, as well as information from outside sources. This component ensures that knowledge assets get into the knowledge management information base. This new complexity is handled by building sophisticated knowledge management taxonomy based on **metadata** (data that describe other data). Metadata are needed to define types of information.

metadata: data about data, such as indices or summaries.

Another issue handled by content management is the way documents are analyzed, stored, and categorized. Once the documents have been gathered, they must be analyzed so that their content is available for subsequent business queries, retrieval, and use by the end user. As documents enter the portal system, they are stored for later retrieval and display. Systems typically analyze the document content and store the results of that analysis so that subsequent use of the documents will be more effective and efficient.

As the number of management documents grows, it becomes increasingly important to gather similar documents into smaller groups and to name the groups. This operation is called categorizing. All automatic categorizing methods use features to determine when two documents are similar enough to be put into the same cluster.

Because document collection is not static, portals must provide some form of taxonomy maintenance. As new documents are added, they also must be added to the taxonomy. As the clusters grow, and the conceptual content of the new documents changes over time, it might become necessary to subdivide clusters or to move documents from one cluster to another. A portal administration, using the taxonomy editor, can monitor and implement these suggestions, in general, and can periodically assess the health and appropriateness of the current taxonomy and document assignments within it (Mack, Ravin, and Byrd, 2001).

In the publishing process, several things should be considered concerning the knowledge management taxonomy. Although tagging documents with metadata is important for the quality of content in the stage of document publishing, it is a burden to submit information if tagging the metadata is a time-consuming process. This is where the **Extensible Markup Language (XML)** comes in. See Box 5-5 for a brief description of XML.

Extensible Markup Language (XML): a specification developed by the W3C designed especially for Web documents.

Intelligent Agents

Intelligent agents are tools that can be applied in numerous ways in the context of enterprise portals. As a tool, intelligent agents are still in their infancy. Most applications are experimental and have not yet reached the efficient commercial stage. However, there is no doubt that they will play a crucial role in all aspects of enterprise portals, especially in intelligent searches and in filtering the right documents according to some criteria.

intelligent agents: programs, used extensively on the Web, that perform tasks such as retrieving and delivering information and automating repetitive tasks.

Consider the relationship between companies and their customers. As these relationships are becoming more complex, organizations need more information and advice on what the relationships mean and how to exploit them. Intelligent agent technology offers some interesting options for addressing such needs.

Customers are known to set certain priorities when purchasing products and services. Intelligent agents master individual customers' or customer groups' demand priorities by learning from experience with them, and can quantitatively and qualitatively analyze those priorities. Agents are software entities that are able to execute a wide range of functional tasks (such as searching, comparing, learning, negotiating, and collaborating) in an autonomous, proactive, social, and adaptive manner. The term *intelligent* in this context means only that we are dealing with entities that are able to adjust their behavior to the environment. In other words, they are able to learn from previous situations and replicate the behavior of the customer if we want to predict that customer's purchasing pattern.

Customers require a vast range of services that intelligent agents can address. Some of these services might include the following.

- Customized customer assistance with online services: news filtering, messaging, scheduling, making arrangements for gatherings, ordering, and so on.

BOX 5-5
What is XML?

XML is a subset of the Standard Generalized Markup Language (SGML) defined in ISO standard 8879:1986 that is designed to make it easy to interchange structured documents over the Internet. XML files always clearly mark where the start and end of each of the logical parts (called *elements*) of an interchanged document occurs. XML restricts the use of SGML constructs to ensure that fallback options are available when access to certain components of the document is not currently possible over the Internet. It also defines how Internet Uniform Resource Locators can be used to identify component parts of XML data streams.

By defining the role of each element of text in a formal model, known as a *Document Type Definition* (DTD), users of XML can check that each component of a document occurs in a valid place within the interchanged data stream. An XML DTD allows computers to check, for example, that users do not accidentally enter a third-level heading without first having entered a second-level heading, something that cannot be checked using the HyperText Markup Language (HTML) previously used to code documents that form part of the World Wide Web (WWW) of documents accessible through the Internet.

However, unlike SGML, XML does not require the presence of a DTD. If no DTD is available, either because all or part of it is not accessible over the Internet or because the user failed to create it, an XML system can assign a default definition for undeclared components of the markup.

XML allows users to:

- bring multiple files together to form compound documents.
- identify where illustrations are to be incorporated into text files, and the format used to encode each illustration.
- provide processing control information to supporting programs, such as document validators and browsers.
- add editorial comments to a file.

It is important to note, however, that XML is not:

- a predefined set of tags, of the type defined for HTML, that can be used to mark up documents.
- a standardized template for producing particular types of documents.

XML was not designed to be a standardized way of coding text: In fact, it is impossible to devise a single coding scheme that would suit all languages and all applications. Instead, XML is formal language that can be used to pass information about the component parts of a document to another computer system. XML is flexible enough to be able to describe any logical text structure, whether it is a form, memo, letter, report, book, encyclopedia, dictionary, or database.

SOURCE: Bryan, Martin, "An Introduction to the Extensible Markup Language (XML)." SGML Centre, 1997, www.personal.u-net.com/~sgml/xmlintro.htm. Accessed June 2003. www.personal.u-net.com/~sgml/xmlintro.htm.

- Customer profiling, including inferring information about customer behavior based on business experiences with the particular customer.
- Integrating profiles of customers into a group of marketing activities.
- Predicting customer requirements.
- Negotiating prices and payment schedules.
- Executing financial transactions on the customer's behalf.

These examples represent a spectrum of applications from the somewhat modest, low-level news-filtering applications to the more advanced and complicated customer

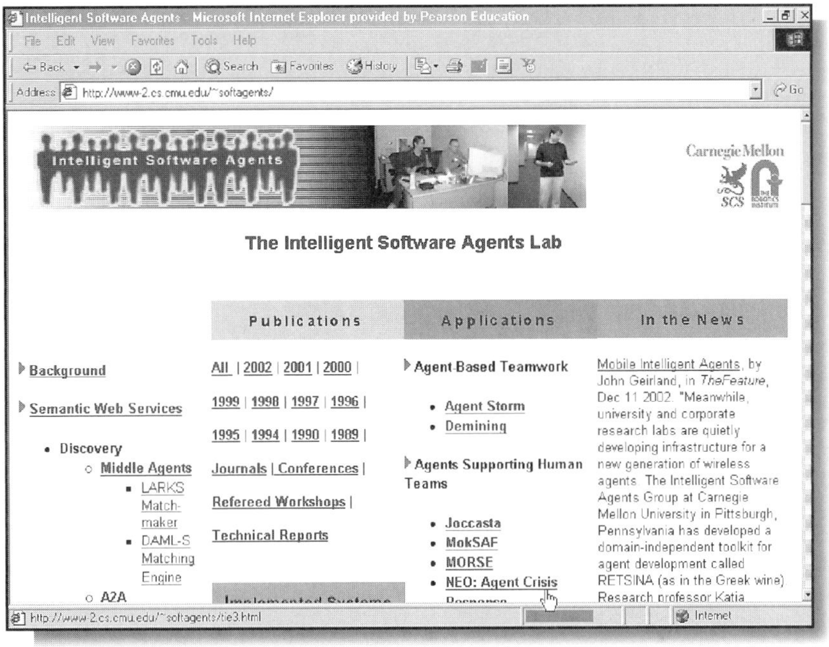

Screen Capture 5-5

Source: Used with permission of www-2.cs.edu/softagent/.

relationship management applications that focus on predicting customer requirements. The main point is that an intelligent agent is an intermediary between the enterprise and its customers, and a source of effective, utilitarian information encountered at different virtual destinations.

In terms of the future, Figure 5-7 shows new technology trends in implementing portals. The emphasis is on collaborative technologies to create communities of practice, advanced human computer interaction to enhance performance, and intelligent agents to automate the search function.

PORTALS AND WEB SERVICES

A major goal of software vendors is to employ Web services for seamless integration of applications into portal software. To explore this possibility, the difference between the business perspective and the technology perspective of Web services needs to be clarified. The business perspective centers on delivering software as a utility or a service, like electricity or telephone service, over the Web. Today's Web technology is capable of providing the platform for delivering software as a utility. In contrast, the technology perspective focuses on a set of specifications that will allow software system functions to be executed by other programs over the Internet, an Intranet, or an Extranet, regardless of location.

Many of today's so-called Web services have yet to make use of Web service technology. Instead, they adhere to the business definition of a Web service (Harris-Jones 2002). What makes the situation more confusing is that portal vendors tend to use the business and technology perspective interchangeably. The components delivered by portals (called portlets) are sometimes called Web services.

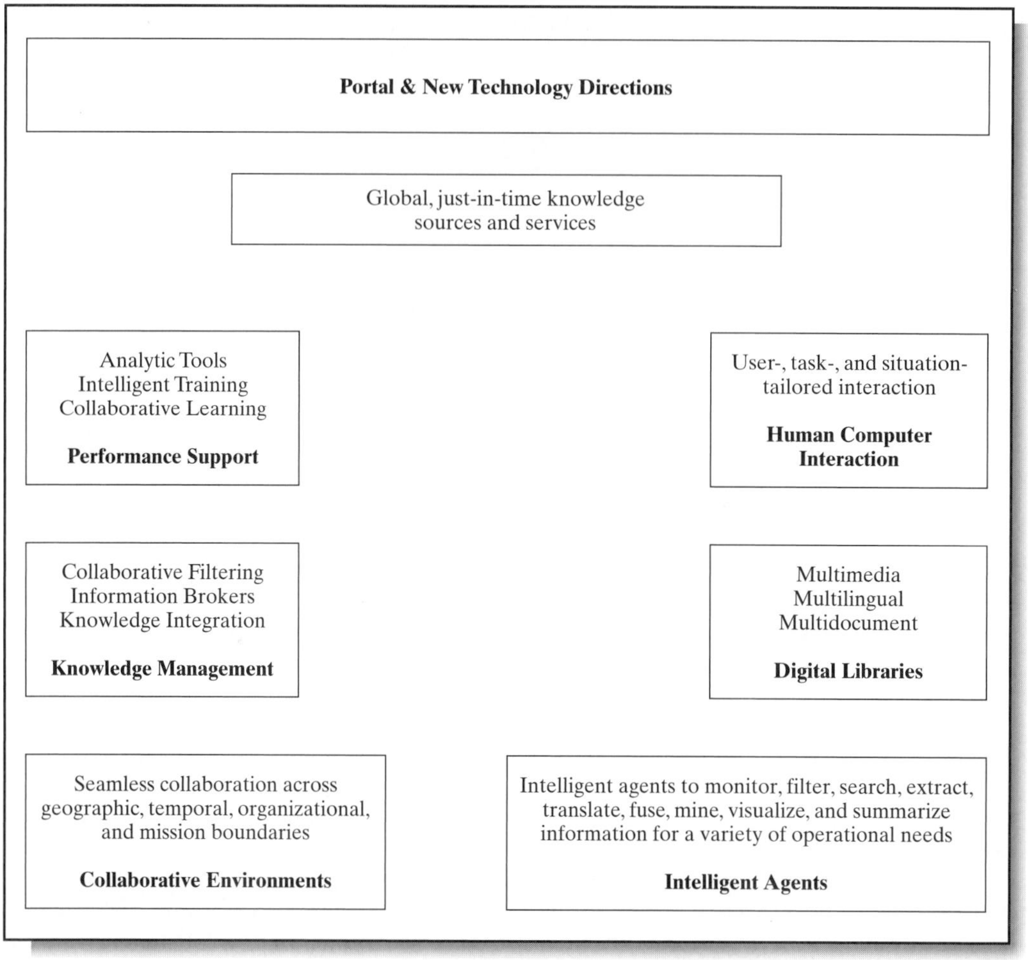

Figure 5-7
New trends in portals technologies
Source: Conover, Joan, "Using Portal Technology to Fuse Corporate Information Knowledge Management, Information Management, Data Warehousing," New Technology Digital Library, www.c3i.osd.mil/km/proceedings/53.ppt. Accessed June 2003.

Web service technology is a simple packaging technology accessible over the Internet that does not require any technology tied to a vendor's platform. It makes it possible for portal connectivity. This means that applications and content, external information, and trading partner applications can be brought together in seamless integration.

Using Web services to connect to content is an encouraging first step. The next step is to provide functionality within existing portals that can allow multiple Web services to assemble unique business processes. Once completed, it should be easy to define business processes by generating the underlying work flow for each business process. Web services can be great candidates for such functionality. Every indication from portal vendors suggests that Web services have a constructive future within the portal software. It will make it possible for portals to connect multiple functions together in a predefined complex business process (Harris-Jones 2002).

IMPLICATIONS FOR MANAGEMENT

Who Is Building Enterprise Portals?

META Group recently conducted a survey of 350 organizations (respondent organizations had at least 500 employees) to find how widely enterprise portals are being deployed, how the portals are utilized, and which services and vendors organizations use for portal deployment. More than 80 percent of the respondents knew of the term *portal*, and one in three currently either have a portal installed or have one in the development stage. Large organizations (more than 10,000 employees) have a significantly higher portal installation rate.

Who Sponsors Enterprise Portals?

New portal sponsorship is shifting away from IT—dropping from 63.3 percent of sponsorship of existing portals to 46.6 percent for planned portals—and toward the marketing/sales group (20.6 percent versus 6.7 percent), which is a strong indicator of the influence of e-commerce on portal development. The line of business has increased from 2.5 percent of share to 9.2 percent, and corporate staff sponsorship has remained the same.

Implementation Issues

Although technology issues can be categorized in many different ways, the codification versus collaboration paradigm also provides a particularly useful structure for understanding current trends in information technology. For globally distributed organizations (i.e., most international development organizations) that rely on the Internet as a medium for the sharing of knowledge, the issue of **bandwidth** is fundamental. At this point in the evolution of the Internet, bandwidth is a chief constraining factor for many applications. The determination of an organization's overall KM strategy will provide guidance for the implementation of appropriate technology. Hansen, Nohria, and Tierney 1999 present a valuable model to help guide thinking about managing organizational knowledge by distinguishing between codification and personalization strategies. This dichotomy is useful in informing the critical decisions required to ensure the right technological mix.

bandwidth: how fast a network connection is; a fast connection allows the user to view images and videos, and interact with remote sites as if they were a local computer.

Codification focuses primarily on computer use, whereby "knowledge is carefully coded and stored in databases" for easy access (see Chapters 7 and 9). By contrast, the personalization KM strategy makes use of computers "to help people communicate knowledge, not to store it". The emphasis is on knowledge sharing via direct, person-to-person contacts.

Bandwidth

Current trends point toward a steady decrease in the cost of Internet access. The rapid and pervasive spread of Internet communication coupled with the evolution of faster and cheaper technology is resulting in improved access to the Internet at lower costs. This trend has been slowest at manifesting itself in Africa. However, even there Internet access is spreading rapidly and is becoming much less expensive, especially in capital cities.

Given the importance of collaboration and the creation of communities of practice as a method for knowledge sharing, it is worth investigating the costs of a significant increase in bandwidth for regional offices that could support (1) desktop videoconferencing, (2) Internet telephony, (3) improved access to information systems based at headquarters, (4) other collaborative tools, and (5) access to more sophisticated information resources.

Most of the technological tools now available tend to help dissemination of know-how but offer less assistance for knowledge use. Tools that assist in knowledge creation are even less well developed, although collaborative work spaces offer promising opportunities. Such work spaces enable participation, across time and distance, in project design or knowledge-base development, so that those most knowledgeable about development problems—the people who are dealing with them on a day-to-day basis—can actively contribute to their solutions. Some of the more user-friendly technologies are the traditional ones: face-to-face discussions, the telephone, electronic mail, and paper-based tools such as flip charts. Among the issues that need to be considered in providing information technology for knowledge-sharing programs are the following.

- **Responsiveness to user needs:** Continuous efforts must be made to ensure that the information technology in use meets the varied and changing needs of users.
- **Content structure:** In large systems, classification and cataloging become important so that items can be found easily and retrieved quickly.
- **Content quality requirements:** Standards for admitting new content into the system need to be established and met to ensure operational relevance and high value.
- **Integration with existing systems:** Because most knowledge-sharing programs aim at embedding knowledge sharing in the work of staff as seamlessly as possible, it is key to integrate knowledge-related technology with preexisting technology choices.
- **Scalability:** Solutions that seem to work well in small groups (e.g., HTML Web sites) might not be appropriate for extrapolation organization-wide or on a global basis.
- **Hardware-software compatibility:** This is important to ensure that choices are made that are compatible with the bandwidth and computing capacity available to users.
- **Synchronization of technology with the capabilities of user:** Such synchronization is important in order to take full advantage of the potential of the tools, particularly where the technology skills of users differ widely.

Portal Product Selection

Creating an enterprise portal vendor shortlist can save time and effort typically devoted to large-scale market scans. Once a portal vendor shortlist has been created, each vendor should be evaluated through the use of scenarios that test key business functionality, based on architectural fit, vendor viability, and product features. Table 5-3 shows the features of some products and the best way to use them.

Table 5-3
Select portal vendor

Vendor	KM Portal Product	Feature Summary	Best Uses
Lotus/IBM	Lotus Raven 1.0 (in beta)	• Intelligent taxonomy builder automates document clustering, learns your preferences. • Expertise Locator links authors to content. • QuickPlace collaboration tool for instant messaging, app sharing, and virtual meetings. • Assigns value to data based on how often they are used. • Portal replication.	• Self-creating and refining taxonomies. • Personnel resources linked to data sources. • Advanced collaboration. • Easy portal repurposing. • Rapid application development with associated KM packages.
Open Text	MyLivelink Portal 1.0 with Livelink	• Facilitates content management. • Integrated work flow and project management with Task Lists and Java-based process maps. • Quick integration of features from other apps via widgets.	• Integrated KM. • Document management and work flow. • Custom collaboration spaces (personal, project, or enterprise).
Plumtree	Plumtree Corporate Portal 4.0	• Quick portal deployment with more than 600 syndicated application component gadgets, which can be freely distributed. • Automatic population of mapped taxonomies with filtered content. • E-mail, voice, and wireless notification of content updates. • Integration with LDAP directories. • E-room tools for collaboration and virtual communities.	• Easy and extensive content and application integration. • Scalability. • Advanced security and access control. • Trainable taxonomies. • Voice and wireless data access. • Customization and extensibility.
Woolamai	WebMeta Engine 1.0	• Quick integration of corporate portals with data and other apps without specialized training. • Intuitive, flexible portal interface. • Knowledge taxonomy adapts to data views, provides relevance filtering. • Data mining functionality. • Web site statistics monitor site activity.	• Usability. • Tracking site statistics. • Content streaming to wireless devices.

SUMMARY

1. Portal is a secure, Web-based interface that provides a single point of integration for and access to information, applications, and services for all people involved in the enterprise including employees, partners, suppliers, and customers.
2. Born with search engines such as Yahoo! and Alta Vista, portals have made their way into enterprises, bringing together not only information from the Internet, but in-house data, as well. These portals, which are known as enterprise knowledge portals (EKPs), aim to offer a single, uniform point from which all of an enterprise's data sources can be accessed.
3. The term *data sources* encompasses structured data (databases, Lotus Notes, and so on) and unstructured data (e-mails, files, archives, and so on), but also includes the data resulting from specific processes and enterprise applications (ERP and CRM tools, and so on). Today, the EIP market is thriving, and many vendors are betting big on portals' well-founded ability to fulfill enterprise needs.
4. Content management in the EKP context requires directory and indexing capabilities to manage automatically the ever-growing store of structured and unstructured data residing in data warehouses, Web sites, ERP systems, legacy applications, and so on. Using metadata to define types of information, good content management can serve as the backbone for a system of corporate decision making where business intelligence tools mine data and report findings back to key role players in the enterprise. Content management also can involve going outside the enterprise; employing crawlers that find pertinent data via the Internet; incorporating it into existing systems; indexing it; and delivering it to appropriate analysts, knowledge workers, or decision makers.
5. The collaborative functionality of EKPs can range from tracking e-mail to developing workplace communities. Some EKPs might allow workers in different parts of the world to create virtual meeting rooms where they can conference by chat, voice, or video communication.

KEY TERMS

- asynchronous collaboration, 146
- bandwidth, 153
- browser, 147
- content management, 132
- enterprise information portal, 135
- enterprise knowledge portal, 136
- Extensible Markup Language (XML), 149
- horizontal portal, 134
- intelligent agents, 149
- knowledge portal, 135
- metadata, 148
- personalization, 132
- portal, 132
- pull technology, 146
- push technology, 146
- search engine, 137
- synchronous collaboration, 146
- teleconferencing, 148
- vertical portal, 132
- work flow, 136

TEST YOUR UNDERSTANDING

1. Why are portals needed? How are portals similar to the concept of data warehouses and data marts?
2. What are the advantages and disadvantages of having your portal on the Internet instead of an Intranet?
3. List the differences between knowledge and information portals. Discuss the benefits of each.

4. Discuss the strategic and technological fit required for an organization to implement a portal.
5. Discuss the advantages and disadvantages of purchasing a portal from a vendor. Make sure you explore vendor Web sites such as Viador (www.viador.com/) and Autonomy (www.autonomy.com/).
6. Discuss the differences between static and dynamic portals. When would you use each one?
7. Discuss how you can use content management to sort knowledge from external and internal sources. Illustrate with examples.
8. Discuss the implementation issues that can arise from implementing a portal. Focus on technology, management, corporate strategy, and end users.
9. Give examples and uses of portals for the following: B2B, B2C, B2G, C2C, and C2G.
10. List the number of possible ways a portal can be made accessible, given current technological trends. Focus on five of these technologies, and discuss their strengths and weaknesses (Hint: Web browsers, cell phones, info kiosks, and so on).

Discussion Questions

1. In the past, companies used to use Electronic Data Interchange (EDI) to communicate with suppliers and customers. Discuss how portals can be used to replace the functions of EDI. Give examples.
2. An audit firm needs to develop a system that allows auditors and public accountants to search accounting standards, share knowledge, communicate, and share Word and Excel files between the head office and clients' sites. As a consultant, you have been asked to recommend such a system. What would you suggest?
3. A hardware retailer wishes to offer real-time support to customers via the Internet. Suggest how a knowledge portal, equipped with chat and CRM, can be used to accomplish this. What additional support can the hardware retailer offer? What information from the portal can be given to the manufacturer?
4. A multinational conglomerate has a centralized human resources department in Cleveland, Ohio. The human resources director wants to launch a new set of multilingual policies to all employees, according to their function, category, and grade. The HR director also wants to have employees interact, and fill out and give feedback on the policies. Suggest a computerized solution to this.
5. Discuss how synergy between different strategic business units can be harnessed and utilized by knowledge portals.
6. Discuss how portals can offer a solution to the centralized versus decentralized information dilemma. What forms of knowledge can be collected centrally, and what should be left decentralized? Why?
7. How can personalized portals use data-mining techniques? Suggest how knowledge management and data mining can be integrated on a portal and give supporting examples.

Web Exercises

1. 1NCR www.ncr.com

Challenge

Establish e-learning portals for customers and partners to help those audiences succeed with their NCR products and to generate new revenue for NCR.

Strategy

Use THINQ e-learning solutions to launch and track courses and provide community features—such as chatrooms and message boards—around the courses.

Results

NCR has extended nearly 4,000 online and classroom courses to more than 2,000 registered users, and is meeting its e-learning revenue goals.

NCR turns to THINQ to power customer and partner e-learning portals

NCR has come a long way in the 117 years since it introduced the first mechanical cash register, but the $6 billion company's tremendous success still hinges on the individual customer relationship. Today, NCR helps companies harness the vast amount of customer information they collect at the sales counter, over the phone, at the ATM and on the Internet. With this information, businesses can satisfy each customer's unique needs, often automatically, and transform customer transactions into rich customer relationships.

From the dawn of the cash register through NCR's leadership in data warehousing, the company's offerings have always been sophisticated. Accordingly, it has always been important for NCR to help customers learn how to reap the full potential of their NCR hardware and software. It is also important for NCR partners to completely understand the company's products so they succeed in selling and implementing them.

NCR has traditionally offered classroom training for customers and partners to achieve these goals. Recently the company started offering courses over the Internet. These classes combine the incisive content of NCR's classroom training programs with the reach and efficiency of the worldwide network, letting students anywhere in the world take a class any time they can access a Web browser. In addition to helping customers and partners succeed, this e-learning program also generates new revenue for NCR.

NCR evaluated a number of e-learning tools for the job of powering its two customer and partner e-learning portals. One portal is the Teradata Education Network (TEN), an e-learning Web site for the company's data warehousing customers. The other is the external NCR University (NCRU), which extends award-winning NCR employee e-learning to partners. After a rigorous review, NCR selected THINQ to build and power the portals, which offer customers and partners web-based, self-paced training, course tracking, employee-learning reporting, live virtual classes, hosted educational chats, a reference library, message boards and instructor-led courseware registration.

"Employee training is important, but it just scratches the surface of e-learning's potential," said Janet Perdzock, Program Manager, Global Learning Operations of NCR. "These initiatives improve our customers' and partners' businesses, enrich our relationships with those audiences and generate significant new revenue for us. THINQ provides a bridge to our courses, content and other back-end systems and is a key ingredient in our success."

NCR chose THINQ over other e-learning vendors because of THINQ's long experience in the learning industry, its integrated product, reputation, flexibility, affordability and ability to interoperate with NCR's existing infrastructure. THINQ's satisfied customers also tipped NCR's decision.

The NCRU portal for partners went live in July 2001 and offers 3,600 courses, including 859 NCR proprietary web-based training courses, NETg information technology courses, NETg desktop computing courses, multi-language courses; CDs, books, tapes and classroom courses; all filtered based on each company's profile. Since the launch, NCRU has signed up 766 users at 49 companies who have completed 375 courses. They can create individual learning plans, register online and view their entire training histories. Counting users who registered for a previous "interim" site prior to July 2001, the NCRU portal for customers and partners has 1,528 authorized users.

NCR's Teradata Education Network learning environment went live March 30, 2001 to its membership-based Learning Community. Teradata Education Network is exceeding all projections with more than 1,300 members, more than 1,000 user sessions every week, and more than 660 course completions in the first six months. One-third of all Teradata companies have an associate who is a member of TEN, and TEN is on track to meet its revenue goal for 2001. A 13-month membership to the site comes in many shapes and sizes, depending on the customer's need. An individual membership can cost as little as $895, and a Corporate Membership can cost as little as $6,795. Not only do members receive access to the learning community, but they also are provided with access to over 50 Teradata courses. Members get into message boards, access white papers, take virtual classroom courses and review recorded virtual classroom presentations.

Unlike most online training programs, Teradata Education Network allows students from around the globe to communicate with other students and make direct contact with instructors. One of the most powerful aspects of the network is the access to knowledgeable Teradata professionals worldwide, giving students a chance to stay current in an ever-changing market.

In the future, NCR plans more curriculum mapping/skill building capabilities and additional, customized portals for specific customers or partners. It also plans thorough profiling of individual users and corporations to better meet their e-learning needs.

"Customers were asking for an alternate way to train without leaving the office that would supplement their classroom learning," said Adam Zaller, program manager, e-learning, Teradata Customer Education. "Our customers say the Teradata Education Network learning community is like having 'Partners,' our annual user conference, 365 days a year. It's a community of customers helping each other, a revenue stream for the company, and a great way to help our technology solve critical business problems in the real world. Our customers and our prospects are now a lot more aware of education and what we have to offer. We anticipate usage to continue to grow, revenue to expand and the program to eventually cover the globe."

Questions

a. Discuss the advantages of Teradata as a learning option. What advantages does it give over conventional learning in terms of content delivery, convenience, growth opportunities etc.?
b. Discuss the possible disadvantage of having a purely electronic learning solution. How can the human element be incorporated?
c. Suggest ways in which NCR can incorporate curriculum mapping/skill building capabilities and customized portals for specific customers or partners, as mentioned in the case.
d. Suggest ways in which Teradata can be used to train some of its divisions and departments. Can Teradata be used to also train line, middle and upper management? If so how can they go about this, and what content can they use?

2. In the Know: Portal Power

With the help of a corporate portal, the U.S. Postal Service delivers quality KM.

At many organizations, corporate portals are seen as a convenient way to centralize proprietary information and make it easily accessible to employees. As such, portals can serve as an ideal knowledge management tool where employees can tap into a wealth of corporate know-how. Unfortunately, many portals fall short. Instead of serving as sleek KM vehicles, all too often portals resemble black holes where information gets dumped, never again to see the light of day.

For those striving to dust off their dormant corporate portals and transform them into a KM tool, John Gregory has a few sound words of advice. Gregory, a market research analyst for the United States Postal Service in Arlington, Va., is in charge of MarketTracks, a knowledge retrieval and competitive intelligence portal used by 1,000 sales and marketing employees.

Since 1994, the Postal Service has offered employees centralized sales and marketing information, first in the form of a client/server system and then, beginning in 1997, on the Web. Over the years, the organization has honed a practical strategy for creating useful, relevant online resources that actually work as advertised — they help employees do their jobs rather than hinder them.

As Gregory sees it, there are few mysteries to solve when it comes to figuring out how to create and sustain a useful portal. When considering content, Gregory assembled focus groups of users and asked them what they want to get out of a portal. In most organizations where 1,000 employees are the target audience, not everyone needs or wants to see the same information. As a result, personalization of content became an important criteria.

Once he examined the content issues, Gregory turned his attention to vendors and specific technologies. Vendor selection, Gregory says, is an area ripe with pitfalls, yet one that often gets short shrift. As a result of lackadaisical vetting processes, many companies are saddled with software that doesn't fit their needs or vendors that don't work well with them. The end result is money down the drain. "It can be enormously expensive to roll out a full-featured portal," Gregory says. "But it doesn't have to be that expensive."

For example, Gregory ruled out Plumtree's portal software because the Postal Service didn't need its entire suite and balked at the prospect of paying for add-ons as they were introduced. Instead, the Postal Service served as a beta tester for Epicentric, trying out the company's enterprise portal software among a small group of employees.

"There's a lot to be said for being an early adopter," Gregory says, adding that the chance of having a good relationship with a vendor is greatly enhanced by doing so.

Even with careful vendor choices, Gregory says the odds are against most portals. "A major flaw is design," he says.

Gregory says that good design means first figuring out what people are going to do with a portal by focusing on function rather than content. Essential to function is navigation that is well-planned and efficient. "Navigation isn't just a box marked 'search,'" he says. "There's got to be the taxonomy, links, site map and a help feature as well."

The navigation should never become static, however. As an organic entity, portals need to change and adapt as the organization does, a lesson that the United States Postal Service is putting to good use.

"People think of a portal as a database and end up putting up everything that they've got instead of what users need," Gregory says. "A portal really is an organic corpus of knowledge."

Source: www.cio.com/knowledge/edit/k021902_portal.html. Accessed June 2003.

Questions

a. Suggest ways in which content can be managed so that it can be personally available to an employee.
b. Discuss the advantages and disadvantages of being an "early adopter," and how it may impact organizations such as USPS.
c. Discuss the advantages and disadvantages of designing a portal on the bases of functionality instead of content.
d. What does the author mean by "navigation should never become static"? Explain with recommendations.

Chapter 6

Internet Service Providers—Hosting Your Web Site

Contents

Summary
Key Terms
Test Your Understanding
Discussion Questions
Web Exercises

IN A NUTSHELL

Before you complete the design of your Web site, the first important step is to find a way to put it up on the Internet. To support the exponential growth in commercial Internet traffic, an entirely new industry called **Internet Service Providers (ISPs)** has emerged. In 1969, only four hosting companies existed. In 1985, there were 1,960 companies; by 2002 there were more than 6,000 ISPs in the United States and more than 10,000 worldwide (www.isp.com/res/r2002-00.html).

virtual hosting: a company with its own domain name, hosted by an ISP to conduct business via the Internet.

virtual domain: a company with its own domain name, hosted by an ISP to conduct business via the Internet.

domain name: a company's identifier in cyberspace; a cross between a company's real name, a company's address, and a billboard displaying the address; a routing address on the Internet; a convenient way of locating information and reaching others on the Internet.

For a fee, the ISP gives you a software package, a user name, a password, and an access phone number. Equipped with a modem, you can then log onto the Internet and browse the World Wide Web, send and receive e-mail, and download software packages or text files. Nearly every ISP today offers what is called **virtual hosting,** or a **virtual domain,** as well. This allows you to have your own **domain name,** such as www.yourcompany.com, rather than using your ISP's domain name with a subdirectory designating your site, such as www.isp.com/yourcompany/.

More than half of today's *Fortune* 500 companies design and maintain their own Web sites, but more than one third of medium-size to small organizations turn to ISPs for many reasons.

- Companies often need a full-time staff and a Webmaster to handle day-to-day changes and enhancements to the site. In most cases, such specialization is not one of the company's core competencies.
- ISPs generally offer headache-free management of Web sites, operations, automated backup, and security.
- ISPs often have high-speed connectivity, multiple T1s, and even T3 lines to main Internet hubs. A T1 line transmits long-distance data at 1.5 megabits (million bits) per second. Large corporations employ a T3 line with the capability of transmitting 44.7 megabits per second. Smaller firms with limited resources often cannot afford the cost of the hardware and communications equipment required to run their own sites.
- ISPs can handle real access and real physical security, from power supplies and airconditioning to network links.
- ISPs often have the latest technology and are responsible for thousands of customers. Most organizations could not afford the constant

costs associated with updating and upgrading the technology necessary to keep their Web sites current.

With a good ISP, things can go smoothly for a marketing campaign; with a poor ISP, many difficulties will arise. This chapter focuses on (1) what an ISP does, (2) what services to expect, (3) how to choose an ISP, and (4) how to choose and register a domain name.

How ISPs Really Work

The better companies understand how an ISP works, the more easily they can select one. For an initial investment of a few thousand dollars and a few thousand more per month, you can connect directly from your business to an Internet backbone and never see an ISP. You become the ISP. You will have to run your own e-mail, Web hosting, DNS (domain name server), and so on. The following is a rough guide regarding what it takes and how much it costs to host your own Web site.

1. **Hardware**—A Web server, communication gear, and a special router: $5,000 to $18,000 per year.
2. **Communications**—Typically a T1 or fractional T1 line: $8,000 to $12,000 per year.
3. **Staff**—At least a Webmaster, a Web designer, and a help desk: $45,000 to $80,000 per year. More on what it takes to start an ISP is covered later in the chapter.

The minimal operating cost can run between $60,000 to $120,000 per year for the first year and $50,000 to $100,000 each year thereafter. You also shoulder full responsibility for keeping the connection going 24 hours a day, 7 days a week.

Screen Capture 6-1

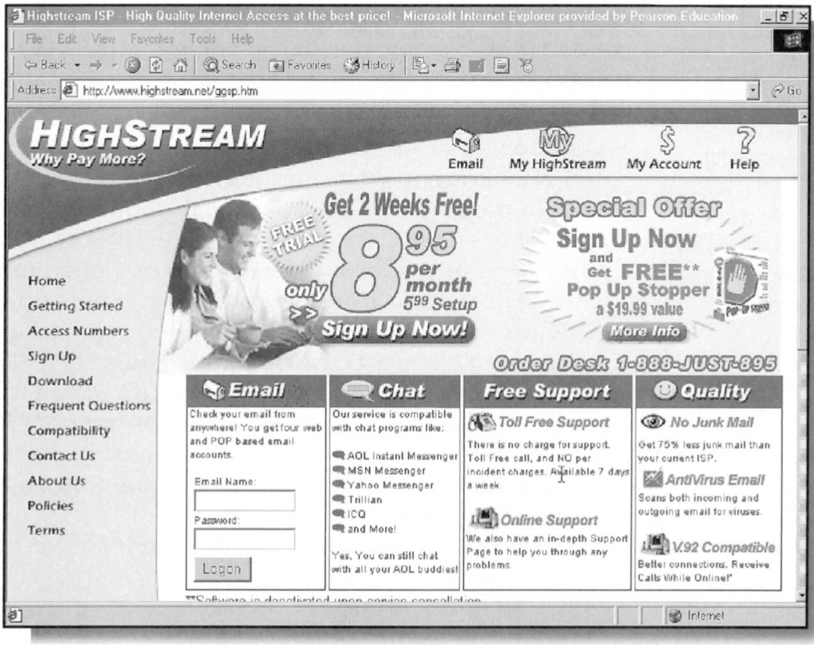

The Infrastructure

Unfortunately, a reliable ISP involves more than the three items previously noted. ISPs are cheaper, more reliable, and provide services that are difficult to match with a corporate in-house equivalent. The average cost of a hosting service (ISP) runs between $1,200 and $5,000 per year. The service manages storage, tracks Web traffic, and maintains the Web server on a day-to-day basis around the clock. All hosts promise security and privacy for your data, but they cannot guarantee it. Some uncertainty also arises in Web hosting billing, including hidden charges and sudden "nickel and dime" increases. (A section on how to choose an ISP is included later in the chapter.)

For others to access your company Web site, it has to be stored on a Web server that is always connected to the Internet by a high-speed link. The infrastructure includes the following (see Figure 6-1).

1. Standby electric power as backup to keep the site available in the event of a blackout.
2. Redundant *fault-tolerant* servers to ensure that your Web site will continue in the event a hard drive or a server breaks down.
3. Redundant communications lines to keep your site active in the event a phone line or a router goes down.
4. One or more firewalls to protect your Web site from hackers or unauthorized access.

Types of Service Providers

There are four types of service providers.

Internet Service Provider (ISP): a specialized company that connects customers with PCs and browsers to the Internet.

1. The **Internet Service Provider (ISP).** An ISP is simply a specialized business that offers Internet access. ISPs like AOL offer Internet service to millions of customers. They allow PC users to access the Internet via modems using a voice telephone network or directly via cables. An ISP provides an interface between the public phone system and Internet digital phone lines, which carry packets instead of voice conversations.

Figure 6-1
Web site infrastructure

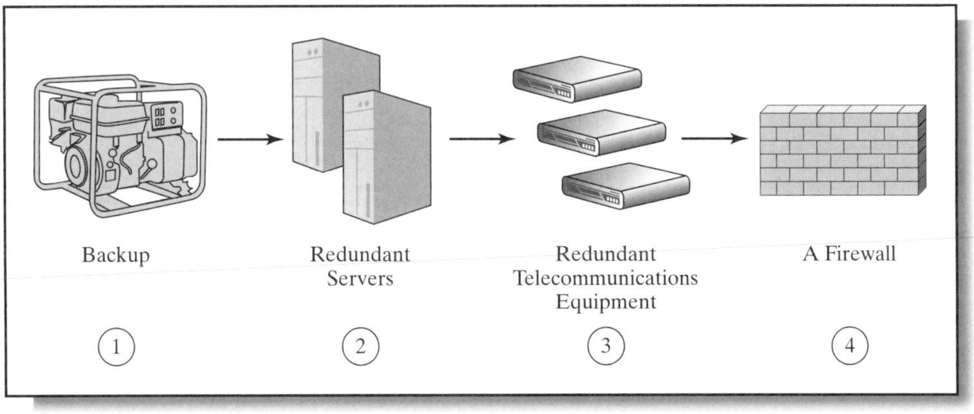

Application Service Provider (ASP): a company that offers packaged software for lease online.

2. The **Application Service Provider (ASP).** An ASP is an application renter. It offers packaged software for lease online, and generally focuses on high-end applications like databases and enterprise resource planning (ERP). These applications are expensive, take a lot of time to install, and are labor intensive to manage. Upgrades mean prolonged downtime and additional costs. Training also can be costly. ASPs allow small to midsize businesses to choose from a menu of applications without having to invest in either the staffing or infrastructure to support them.

Wireless Application Service Provider (WASP): a company that offers untethered applications; hosting, developing, and managing applications are similar to that of an ASP.

3. The **Wireless Application Service Provider (WASP).** These service providers handle untethered applications; their responsibilities involve hosting, developing, and managing applications similar to that of an ASP. However, there is one real difference. WASP infrastructure requires integration between the Web and wireless networks. This means that WASPs have to deal with a wide range of hardware and mobile devices, and wireless networking protocols. It makes the job more complex.

Business Service Provider (BSP): an Internet service developer that rents only its own proprietary applications via the Web.

4. The **Business Service Provider (BSP).** A BSP is an Internet service developer that rents only its own proprietary applications via the Web. Generally, the software is specific in function.

Wholesale Service Provider (WSP): a service provider that packages a selection of BSP applications for distribution online.

5. The **Wholesale Service Provider (WSP).** This is a new category of service provider that packages a selection of BSP applications for distribution online.

These service providers generally cater to small to midsize businesses and can be an important addition to large IT operations.

ISPs fall into one of three categories: the large wholesale access providers, the smaller Internet backbone providers, and the local ISPs. Although it might seem that the number of smaller providers would decrease as a result of acquisitions by larger providers, just the opposite is taking place. Larger wholesale providers have been finding themselves the targets of consolidation and acquisition, while the ranks of the smaller providers have been growing and growing. This trend is beginning to shift, though, with the emergence of firms such as OneMain.com, which is being formed as a conglomerate of several local ISPs.

The idea behind the combination of these smaller firms is that the conglomerate will combine "local marketing, content, and customer service . . . with the cost savings associated with a large-scale enterprise and a common operating platform." This trend has brought big business into the world of smaller, often less experienced, local ISPs, which have survived thus far based on their local expertise and appeal. It puts larger participants on a local level and might bring about the faster demise of thousands of poorer performing local ISPs.

Types of Web Hosting Services

Web hosting: providing, managing, and maintaining hardware, software, content integrity, security, and reliable high-speed Internet connections.

There are four types of **Web hosting** services: dial-up access, developer's hosting, Web hosting only, and industrial strength hosting. Thousands of local dial-up access providers handle Web page hosting for businesses. Developer's hosting usually involves hosting the Web pages of a business. This kind of hosting is usually customer focused, although at a high price. Some companies specialize in business Web site hosting. They allow no dial-up access but provide a wide variety of services to their customers. Finally, businesses with high-traffic sites find maximum reliability with the

Screen Capture 6-2

largest national industrial service providers, who supply coast-to-coast, 24-hour staffing and redundant connections to the Internet backbone at hefty prices.

Packets, Routers, and Lines

Those who have had a course in data communications will find this section a breeze. On the Net, information is sent and received in packets. A packet is small in size, usually just a few hundred bytes. When e-mail messages are sent, the TCP/IP layer breaks the message into tiny packets and writes the destination address on each packet to make sure it doesn't get lost. As a result, packets can be sent separately over the Net, like thousands of cars on a superhighway, each holding up a sign like "Orlando or Bust."

Packets can even take a different route across the Net. From Washington, D.C., to San Francisco, for example, one packet of an e-mail message might go through Houston, but another might pass through Denver. They may arrive at their destination at different times and even out of sequence. The receiving computer rearranges them into a form just like the original message (see Figure 6-2).

In practical terms, assume you are the ISP and a customer wants to send an e-mail message to a merchant somewhere in the United States. The Winsock Program running on her PC splits her e-mail message into Net-sized packets. The packets are then sent through her modem, which converts them into analog signals across an ordinary voice telephone line to an ISP. A modem is needed to receive incoming messages and convert analog signals to digital and back. An ISP needs many lines to absorb the volume of data transmission coming from thousands of customers without delay.

Once the packets are received, the ISP needs to send them from its computer, with a dedicated connection to some bigger ISP. Such a computer performs login procedures,

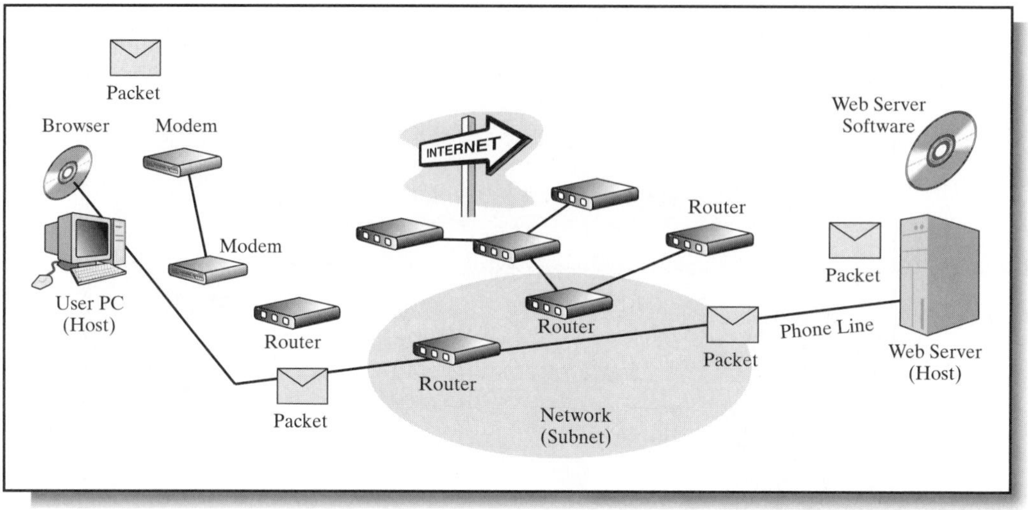

Figure 6-2
Packets, routers, and routes on the Internet

authenticates customer IDs, and manages the traffic using special software. This is the primary function of an ISP.

There is one point worth noting about communication lines. Because conversion from analog to digital and vice versa introduces noise, it is the noise that limits certain modems to 33,600 bits per second. If the packets coming from the ISP to the phone lines could remain digital all the way to the customer, data could be sent at 56,000 (56 K) bits per second from the ISP to the customer. The way to do this is for customers to get an Integrated Services Digital Network (ISDN) line to their phone company, so that the transmitted data will remain in digital format and transmission is possible at the 56-K rate. The ISP also must connect to the phone system with a digital circuit like an ISDN line. We assume the customer is not too far from the phone office (around 3 miles) for 56 K to work fast.

access server: a server that combines a modem and a terminal server into a single integrated box.

The 56-K digital modems are integrated into **access servers,** which combine a modem and a terminal server into a single integrated (and expensive) box. Many access servers like Sun Microsystems boxes handle up to 48 dial-up connections. Therefore, if the ISP has 4,800 customers and if 20 percent of the customers dial at the same time, the ISP will need approximately 10 access servers ($48 \times 0.20 = 9.60$).

The Connection

As Figure 6-3 shows, when you dial into an ISP, you dial into a router owned by the ISP. The ISP also has a router connected to the larger ISP. This second router is the gateway to the Internet. For this connection and other services like an e-mail mailbox, customers pay a set monthly fee.

backbone: cluster of competing companies called Network Service Providers.

The **backbone** of the Internet is a cluster of competing companies called Network Service Providers (NSPs) that work together to provide total interconnection. To connect to an NSP, the ISP must pay the NSP a monthly fee. The money comes from fees collected from the ISP's subscribers. A portion of the fees goes to manage the ISP's internal opera-

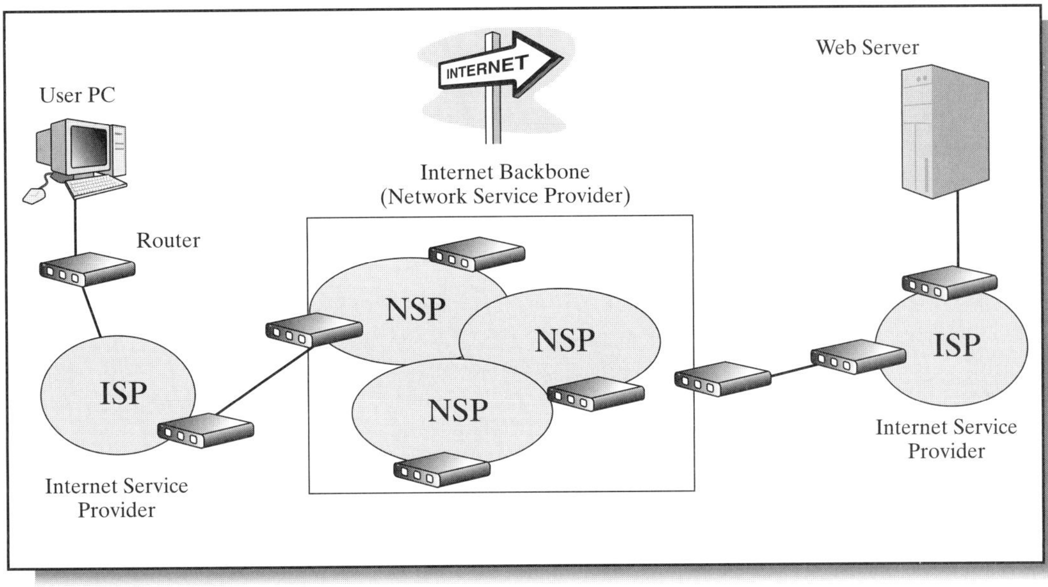

Figure 6-3
Internet Service Providers

tions and part to pay the NSP. Routers work together regardless of who owns them and how the charges are handled. They connect networks, filter bad packets, direct packets, and isolate traffic. See Table 6-1 for the main connection types, and their features and speeds.

Table 6-1
Selected connection types, features, and speeds (costs are estimates)

Connection Type	Theoretical Speed	Hardware	Connection Cost/Month	Provider Setup Cost	Provider Cost/Month
Regular phone line	33.6/56 Kbps	Modem	$25–40	$0–50	$15–30
Frame relay	56 Kbps to 1.544 Mbps	DSU/CSU	$200–4,500	$75–500	$40–400
T1 line	1.544 Mbps	T1 mux	$900–3,500	$500–3,000	$400–1,400
Direct PC	400 Kbps	Satellite dish	$10–130	$0–50	$15–30
Cable modems	10–30 Mbps inbound, 700 Kbps outbound	Cable modem, adaptor card	$35–45	Varies	None
T3 line	44.7 Mbps	T3 mux	$15,000–45,000	None (you are your own provider)	None (you are your own provider)

Becoming an ISP

There is no question that the demand for a reliable ISP continues to grow. To start an ISP business, one needs to consider the type of provider to be, the market(s) to target, the services to offer, and equipment requirements. Once these issues are addressed, an assessment can be made regarding whether it is worth investing in an ISP.

The Internet business model is based on distribution of bandwidth. The market consists of several National Service Providers (NSPs)—MCI, AGIS, Sprint, UUNet, PSI, Netcom, and ANS. Each company operates networks of high-speed lines across the United States and on a global basis. Current backbones are 45-Mbps DS3 or T3 circuits, being upgraded to 155-Mbps circuits. Most ISPs get their initial T1 (1.54-Mbps) Internet "feed" from the NSPs. Then they resell connections at 56 Kbaud to dial-up customers.

facilities-based ISP: a company that owns dial-up access servers or switches.

virtual ISP: a company that provides Internet service using equipment of a facilities-based ISP.

ISPs are facilities based or virtual. **Facilities-based ISPs** own dial-up access servers or switches. **Virtual ISPs** provide Internet services using equipment of a facilities-based ISP. They offer the services of a real ISP under their own company or brand name.

Facilities-based ISPs have significant start-up costs associated with hardware and software purchases and Internet access leases. Operating costs are also high, because they need a technical support staff 24 hours a day to manage the network and ensure reliable service. By contrast, virtual ISPs do not have either of these costs. Hardware, software, and technical support are provided by the facilities-based ISP. Capital expenditures can be focused on marketing and sales, which improve the chances of generating new customers.

In terms of control, being a facilities-based ISP allows 100 percent control of one's business. Because the ISP controls the speed of rolling out new technology, it could be faster to the market with the latest dial-up enhancements. One potential limitation of being a facilities-based ISP is limited flexibility. The leases and commitments to a telephone company usually carry high penalties for early termination. Becoming a virtual ISP means being somewhat out of control. The business will be depending on the facilities-based ISP to respond to customer needs and problems.

Target Market

Before deciding on hardware and software requirements, a prospective ISP should decide on the type of consumer to be targeted. ISPs have three major target markets, each with their own pros and cons.

- **Residential** market, which is the fastest-growing segment, as more and more households are connecting to the Internet every day. One advantage lies in the many new Internet-connecting devices available to residents such as handheld organizers, data-enabled mobile phones, and Web TV. As household personal computer use continues to rise, the residential market also should continue to be a major revenue source for ISPs. Yet, with such a crowded market, a potentially successful ISP must differentiate service offerings, such as guaranteed uptime record, attractive fees, and so on.
- **Commercial** market, which includes new and established businesses surging toward e-commerce and e-business. The most critical services to provide include a high level of quality service, dedicated connection, Web hosting, Web design and maintenance, and the like. Because costs can add up quickly, a new ISP must monitor costs on a regular basis.

- **Public** market brings up the example of the Internet Café, or "Cyber" Café. They have a basic setup, are easily managed, and can provide good income on a regular basis. Other examples of public market network infrastructures include clubs, motels, and schools. Each can be just as easily managed and arranged as a Cyber Café. One trick is to try hard to persuade customers to stay connected as long as possible. To do so means providing reasonable prices as well as a clean, friendly, and comfortable environment.

Services

An ISP is expected to provide a variety of services, most of which are expectations of any customer. The key services—required and optional—include the following.

Domain Name Server (DNS): a repository where the domain name for each ISP is stored.

- **Domain Name Service (DNS):** The DNS is where the domain name for each ISP is stored. It also identifies the mail server to be used for mail delivery from the Internet and stores information about any backup name and mail servers. ISPs must have at least one DNS server operating in their network, but two servers are common, each operating at opposing ends of the network.
- **E-Mail:** This is the most commonly used service on the Internet. It means an ISP must dedicate a separate server for e-mail. The key issues to consider are mail storage capacity per user and the maximum size the server will allow. The depth of e-mail service the ISP chooses to offer customers is up to the ISP, but all consumers must have reliable e-mail access available, no matter what type of customer they are.

Radius server: a network access server that authenticates a user's ID and password and triggers accounting to complete the customer's chargeable session.

- **Radius Server:** A Radius server is required to authenticate users and record accounting data for user authentication. A Network Access Server forwards a request to the Radius server's database to authenticate a user's ID and password combination. If the combination is valid, the request is accepted; otherwise, it is rejected and the connection is dropped. Authenticated connections trigger accounting, which is where IP addresses are returned to the dial-in client and a record is made of the start time of the session. When the session ends, accounting data and traffic statistics are transferred from the Network Access Server to the accounting process to complete the customer's chargeable session.

Optional Services

The primary optional services include the following.

- **World Wide Web Server:** This can be run on the same hardware as the DNS, e-mail, and Radius systems. Nearly all ISPs offer Web access.
- **File Transfer Protocol (FTP):** An FTP is a widely accepted file transfer standard on the Internet. It usually is restricted to a select group or individual. It is a client/server application that accepts connections from clients trying to connect to its server. FTP servers can be run on most server machines on the ISP's local network and require careful configuration to ensure safety and security at all times.

Internet Relay Chat (IRC): a text-based chat service, where users connect to a local server as part of a larger network of IRC servers.

- **Internet Relay Chat (IRC):** This is a text-based chat service, where users connect to a local server as part of a much larger network of IRC servers. To install an IRC server, the ISP must apply to the administrator of the IRC network, which might require a minimum amount of Internet bandwidth dedicated for IRC services. The ISP has the option of establishing its own IRC server to provide local chat services. See Figure 6-4 for an ISP network with IRC services.

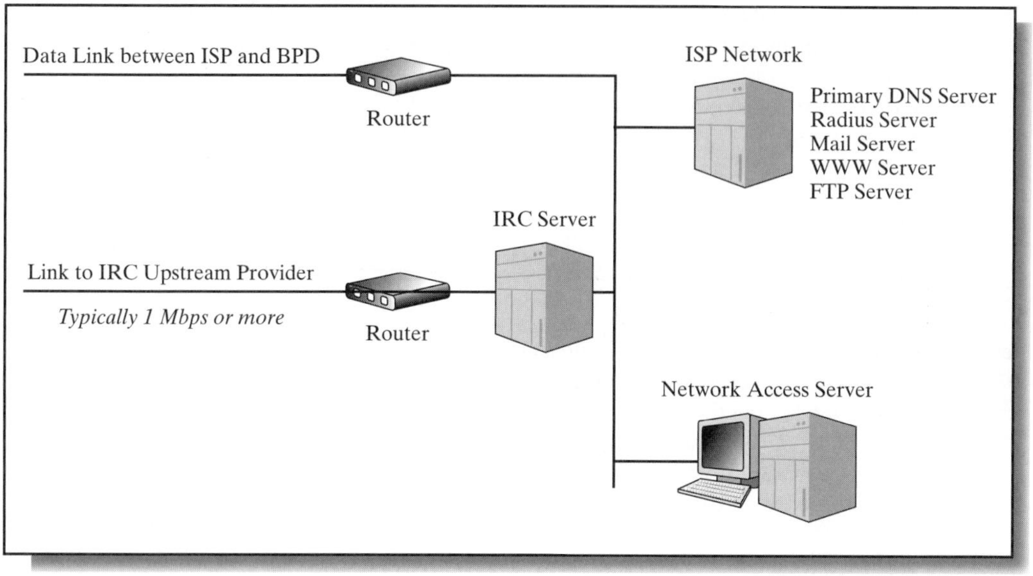

Figure 6-4
A typical ISP network with IRC services

- **News Server:** Internet Network News is becoming increasingly popular. Because there is so much data traffic for news, the cost for this type of service can be more than $100,000 a month. This is why many ISPs restrict the number of news groups to carry or offer a "suck" feed from another news server. A "suck" feed involves drawing news from an upstream news server upon request. This alternative is relatively inexpensive, simple, and can increase the functionality of an ISP as customers access any news article over the Internet 24 hours a day.
- **HTTP Proxy Service:** A proxy server generates and manages a local store of Internet objects such as Web pages, images, or FTP files, and delivers the objects when requested (called **caching**). For example, when a Web page is requested, the proxy server examines its internal database to see if the page is stored in the cache. If the page is not found, the request is passed on to the Web site and the page is returned. HTTP proxy servers are best run on independent hardware. They serve to minimize data traffic control costs and speed up requests as more and more users join the ISP over time.

caching: Internet objects delivered by a proxy server when requested.

Technical Requirements

Once the target market and services have been determined, a prospective ISP can focus on the technical needs of the business. The main components are access to Internet backbone, high-capacity lines, and servers.

Internet Access

The first thing to do is to purchase Internet access from a regional or national backbone provider. The connection between the provider and the physical location is the local loop. The cost depends on the size of the pipeline and the distance (in air miles) from the provider and the local telephone company central office. A charge is assessed for the size bandwidth required. With that in mind, several cable-based options are available.

- **T1 line**, sometimes called DS1 line, is a digital carrier line capable of transmitting a digital signal at 1.544 Mbps. This is the "raw" bandwidth needed for fast data and video transmission traffic on a 24-hour basis. It is also commonly used to connect LANs to the Internet. The line is split into 24 individual channels, each of which supports 65 K bits per second. A T1 line is known to serve up to 3,500 subscribers at a minimum cost of $1,000 per month.
- **T3 line**, sometimes referred to as DS3 line, transmits a digital signal at 44.736 Mbps, which is the equivalent of 28 T1 lines. A T3 line is split into 672 individual channels, each of which supports 64 Kbps and serves up to 100,000 subscribers. The lease cost starts at $18,000 per month.
- **Fiber-optic based** Internet access usually is reserved for businesses with large bandwidth requirements. The speed of fiber-optic networks is designated by Optical Carriers OC-3, OC-12, and OC-24. The main difference among the three types is speed. OC-3 line serves up to a half million subscribers at 155 Mbps at costs upwards of $50,000 per month. OC-12 line serves up to 2 million subscribers at 622.08 Mbps at costs upwards of $200,000 per month. OC-24 line can support 10 million subscribers at 1.244 Gbps at costs starting at several hundred thousands dollars per month.
- **Servers** begin with a minimum of two servers of each type to launch a start-up ISP. The servers include DNS servers, e-mail servers, and Radius servers. Optional servers may be considered for FTP, development and testing, registration, billing, tape, news, and proxy servers.

Beyond the basics, an ISP should consider multiple routers and switches to make forwarding decisions for data packets within the network, firewalls to increase the network's security, cables, tools, test equipment, printers, equipment racks, furniture, shelving, and cold spares. As can be sensed, quite a bit of financing needs to be considered in such an operation.

CHOOSING AN ISP

Web sites are becoming the foundation for critical interaction with customers, partners, and suppliers. Site performance, reliability, and speed of network service are prerequisites for the viability and integrity of the site and the business itself. ISPs are increasing in number, size, and services. They range in size from the giants, like industry leader America Online (AOL), to thousands of tiny companies dotting the landscape.

Some ISPs are local, and others are national and international, depending on their connection to the Internet backbone and the technology they use. Increasingly, companies that specialize in Web site hosting allow no dial-up access, which ensures that bandwidth (speed of connection to the Internet) is not compromised by competing traffic, such as customers accessing chat rooms. Ideally, a business putting up its Web site for the first time would want to look into industrial-strength Web hosting, where high nationwide traffic is handled quickly and responsibly, and where 24-hour staff and redundant connections to the Internet backbone are provided at competitive fees (see Box 6-1).

What to Consider

Your ISP has become indispensable. As you spend more and more time surfing the Web, you become sensitive to e-mail, network brownouts, and fluctuations in performance—to say nothing of busy signals. The proliferation of big-name national ISPs with tempting access networks causes you to do some thinking. With an open field of evenly priced ISPs

BOX 6-1
E-commerce trends: ISP and data center selection

You should consider your special needs as important criteria in your selection process. Selecting business partners from among the plethora of ISPs, application service providers (ASPs), and collocation data centers is always a challenge. Just when you think you've found the ideal partner, the company gets bought or grows so explosively that the new staff members can no longer supply the service you were receiving.

One problem to avoid is assuming that because you buy from competing sources that you automatically have redundancy. . . . If you buy network circuits from three separate top-tier IP networking providers, it's very likely that all of your traffic will ride the *same* fiber from your data center to a telephone company central office (CO). . . . [T]he major IP circuit providers that sell you bandwidth must in turn buy circuit capacity from companies that own or lease the fibers in the street. . . . In most cases, there's only one fiber tap from which your building can have fiber "lit up" and therefore a cut along the critical single fiber run from the tap will cause all IP providers' circuits to fail. Fiber outages between you and the CO will bring down all or most of your circuits. . . . Be clear in stating your requirements when you select your vendors. Put the required terms in your contract and service level agreements. Clearly outline the "remedies," or consequences, if your vendors do not fulfill their stated service levels.

Another problem to avoid is what I call the "small fish" syndrome. When selecting your vendors, be careful that you're not the smallest, least important customer on their lists. When one of your vendor's biggest customers—who might be one of your competitors—has an emergency, your problems might be ignored, even if this would be a breach of your service level agreement. Therefore, try to "pick on someone your own size" or select a vendor that has . . . very skilled, capable people in the operational areas of its organization, particularly the systems and network administrators, and a 24/7 staff. . . .

SOURCE: Wyle, Mitch, "Preparing Your Site for Speed and Reliability," *Web Techniques*, January 2000, 67–70.

to choose from, how do you select which one to use? For example, area code 804 has 324 ISPs. Shopping for a Web- hosting ISP is not easy, but here are some things to look for.

1. **Size of the pipeline or bandwidth.** High-speed T1 and T3 lines connect the ISP to the Internet backbone. As shown in Table 6-1, a T1 line carries up to 1.5 Mbps (megabits per second), and a T3 line carries up to 45 Mbps. Smaller ISPs often have ISDN connections or *fractional* T1 connections. These connections (*network plumbing*) are what expedites or hampers the connection between the Web server and the Internet.

Depending on the volume of your Web site traffic, it might pay to have a T1 line that connects you directly to the Internet. The cost is high, but so are the charges via the ISP. It is no longer safe to assume that a Web site is made up of HTML documents using a few kilobytes. The increasingly media-rich content of more and more Web sites requires high bandwidth to ensure speed and Web site readiness.

Network bandwidth growth is related to ISP growth. Bandwidth refers to the size of the *pipe* that feeds information across the network. In 1969, bandwidth was 9.6 kilobits per second (Kbps); in 1985, 56 Kbps; in 1990, 45 megabits per second (Mbps using T3 speed); in 1995, 155 Mbps, and in 2000, 2,048 Mbps. See Box 6-2 for more information on bandwidth.

BOX 6-2
E-commerce trends: How much bandwidth?

. . . [E]ven "mom-and-pop" small businesses, when moving to the Web, need to consider how to handle their rich media and downloads. One example, perhaps more appropriate to the *Fortune* 1000 crowd, is the use of high-bandwidth media on corporate recruiting sites. One of the more interesting fads on these job boards is the use of streaming video interviews with key executives who describe the corporate culture and why you should want to work at these companies. Considering the popularity of the Web for job searching, we can well imagine that these videos will use up a lot of bandwidth if job seekers or others curious about the company view them often. They may need a different type of service from the traditional functions of a job board, such as forms for submitting resumes or a system to search all the open jobs at the company.

News and sports sites are becoming more and more media-intensive. People want to see the "play of the day" with as much resolution as possible. People want to hear the rumble of those earthquakes or the howling winds in those hurricanes. Personal Web sites, the traditional home of family snapshots for grandma to view with her Web TV, are sprouting streaming and digital videos. Finally, look at home appliance, home improvement, and technical equipment sites. To cut down on expensive customer service, they're all publishing as much detail as possible about their wares on the Web. These details include huge documents, usually in PDF format with complete owners' reference manuals, specifications, and troubleshooting guides. They also include, where appropriate, very high-resolution color graphics of exactly what that tile will look like in your kitchen or exactly how that carpet will appear in the afternoon on your living room floor.

For these applications, the problem is usually more a matter of optimizing end-to-end bandwidth than handling large transaction loads. So what techniques are available for getting this fat media content to your customers? . . .

SOURCE: Wyle, Mitch, "Preparing Your Site for Speed and Reliability," *Web Techniques*, January 2000, 68–69.

Companies that sell Internet connections are fast struggling to survive the broadband competition. Cable and telephone companies that control "the last mile" of wire going to the homes make up about 90 percent of broadband connections (Angwin 2003). Dial-up services are enticing customers to keep their dial-up accounts by offering features such as spam filters and pop-up advertising blockers. In contrast, broadband providers like America Online (AOL) are aggressively marketing exclusive access to magazine articles, videos, and music from Time Warner as a way to discourage customers from "jumping ship." Eventually, the success of the dial-up services' broadband content focus will depend on how well the providers offer a subset of services at an affordable price; for instance, below $14 a month (Angwin 2003).

2. **Connection availability and performance.** In a 1999 study of 6,000 business users by *Inter@active Week*, it was found that connection availability and network performance are the most important criteria in evaluating an ISP. An ISP is viewed as a utility that should always be available. In terms of performance, the number of clients assigned to each of the ISP's computers and the space allotted on the computers are factors in ISP performance. Many successful ISPs use fast Pentium computers to ensure performance. ISPs also assign a certain amount of server space on their computers for your Web site traffic.

Five to 10 MB of ISP computer space is considered normal for most business Web sites. Yet, e-mail, log files, and system programs can use up considerable space.

3. **Virtual hosting.** This feature is commonly offered by most ISPs. You are allowed to have your own domain name, such as www.yourfirm.com, rather than using the ISP's domain name with a subdirectory designating your site (e.g., www.isp.com/yourfirm.isp.com/). A business registers its own domain name for a nominal charge of $100. It is a good investment should the business decide to switch ISPs at some time in the future. This means that in any commitment to go with an ISP, a provision should be included that you are free to choose an ISP and are not being locked into a long contract. Make sure when registering your domain name that your name is listed as the *administrative contact* with InterNIC (the domain name registration agency). This way, you're on your own and able to switch ISPs. You can see who is listed by checking your domain name at http://rs.internic.net/cgi-bin/whois.

4. **E-mail aliases.** An ISP allows a certain number of e-mail addresses per account. Larger businesses might want to have multiple e-mail boxes at the Web-hosting ISP, which gives flexibility and independence, especially if the company has branches scattered all over the globe. Three to five addresses is a good number in a typical business environment.

5. **Stability and staying power.** The term *stability* refers to the longevity of the ISP's customer base. That is, how often do customers switch from one ISP to another? This is referred to in the industry as the **customer churn rate.** It is estimated that, on average, large ISPs can expect a monthly churn rate of approximately 4 percent. For a company the size of America Online (AOL), this amounts to 800,000 customers per month. This movement of customers gives the smaller ISPs a chance to add to their own customer bases. *Staying power* refers to the ISP's ability to continue to provide reliable service during downturns or during times when its business is not doing well. This has a lot to do with the ISP's cash flow and backup plans. The continuing mergers and acquisitions mania that has seized the industry provides even more reason for looking into the longevity of the ISP in question (see Box 6-3).

customer churn rate: how often customers switch from one ISP to another.

6. **Local access.** Is the phone number the ISP is providing you going to be free of long-distance charges? A local telephone number is always a safe bet, but an 800 number is not. Your monthly phone tolls could exceed the ISP fee, because the 800 numbers are not free. On the other hand, a local access number will not do much good if you are going to need the connection while traveling a lot. In any case, you need to know how many local access (also called **point of presence,** or **POP**) numbers an ISP has and how they are available for your use.

point of presence (POP): physical location on the premises of a local exchange carrier at which messages are transferred or linked to other carriers.

7. **Customer service and technical support.** *Support* is the key word in customer service. Whether you need to install a Web site or simply access the Internet, setting up your browser for a new ISP can range from straightforward to daunting, depending on your level of expertise.

If you're new to the Internet, you definitely should look for an ISP that will be there to help you set up. Many offer free software that will automatically configure your computer to work with their service. Does your ISP have a 24-hour support line that you can call? Does it have the answers to your questions when you call? ISP customer service is key. Other questions to ask pertain to upgrades, customization, security, and scalability. For example, Who decides when to upgrade? How much customization can the ISP do? What kind of security does it offer? Can the ISP's software and support staff handle your growth?

BOX 6-3
E-commerce trends: Yahoo! posts a loud message: We're not next

After America Online Inc.'s earth-shaking announcement of plans to buy Time Warner Inc., all anyone in Silicon Valley and on Wall Street wanted to know was which giant would swallow or be swallowed by the Web's other blue-chip player, Yahoo! Inc.

The speculation was rampant: Would it be Walt Disney Co., whose own Internet effort has been one stumble after the next? Perhaps Rupert Murdoch's News Corp., another Internet laggard with whom Yahoo! has a large adver-tising relationship? Or, in the most delicious dreams of investment bankers, would Microsoft Corp. decide to scoop up Yahoo!, widely seen in the industry as the most likely threat to AOL's Steve Case, who is the longtime nemesis of Microsoft's Bill Gates?

But Yahoo! poured cold water on all that. "We are not changing our strategy in light of this [AOL-Time Warner] deal," said Tim Koogle, Yahoo!'s famously laid-back chief executive. "We have created a distribution platform that is hugely valuable, and that path is not wavering." Indeed, for all of its short history, the Santa Clara, Calif., company has loudly proclaimed its independence, even as it has emerged as the Web's leading "portal," or central destination point for e-mail, shopping, and data searches. The words behind its very name—Yet Another Hierarchical Officious Oracle—are a kind of fierce, ironic declaration that Yahoo!, down to the marrow of its corporate skeleton, will always be its own creation.

SOURCE: Swisher, Kara, "Yahoo! Posts a Loud Message: We're Not Next," *The Wall Street Journal*, January 12, 2000, B1.

8. **Reliability.** The question regarding reliability is this: Does the ISP you are considering have the capability to handle all the customers it is taking on? If not, you can expect delays, busy signals while trying to log on, or slowdowns. It is proper to inquire about the ISP's call-failure or call-success rates. How quickly you can go online depends on the time of the day. According to one report, 9 P.M. is the busiest time on the Internet on any day. By contrast, early risers have few problems logging in. Winter months usually attract heavier traffic. Other barometers of ISP reliability include network capacity and relationships with other ISPs.

9. **Price.** Some ISPs offer free service or other seemingly great deals, but remember that this is a *service*, not a *commodity*. These deals are not always the best for you or for your Web site. They might offer bare-bones access at no cost, but they come under attack for the heavy banner advertisement load that comes with the deal.

Prices vary with ISPs and with the type of service offered. Most providers offer unlimited access for about $20 per month. A different algorithm is available for occasional users, and discounts might be offered for long-term commitments. Before signing on, it is helpful to know whether a provider offers a free or low-cost trial membership so you can determine whether it is a provider you like. See Table 6-2 for an idea of the pricing policies of the top five portals.

Questions to Ask

If you are serious about choosing the right ISP, here are important questions to ask.

Internet Access

- Do you offer complete or partial access to the Internet?
- How do you connect to the Internet backbone?

Table 6-2
Estimated pricing policies of some large portals

Element	AOL	CompuServe	Microsoft Network	Prodigy	AT&T WorldNet
Web address	www.aol.com	www.compuserve.com	www.msn.com	www.prodigy.com	www.att. Com/worldnet
Setup fee	None	None	None	None	None
Monthly fee basic access)[a]	$9.95	$9.95	$9.95	$9.95	$4.95
Hours included	5	5	5	10	Long-distance customers 5
Each additional hour fee	$2.95	$2.95	$2.50	$2.50	$2.50
Unlimited access fee	$19.95	N/A	$19.95	$19.95	$19.95
Direct TCP/IP connection	Yes	Yes	Yes	Yes	No
Browser support	Proprietary	Internet Explorer	MSN program viewer	Internet Explorer	Internet Explorer/ Navigator
Free Web page space	2 MB	5 MB	N/A	2 MB	None
E-mail addresses/ accounts	5	1	1	1	1
Technical support	Y	Y	Y	Y	Y
Hours	24 hours, 7 days	7:00 A.M.–1:00 A.M., M–F; 1:00 P.M.– 10:00 P.M. Sat., Sun.	7:00 A.M.–2:00 A.M., M–F; Noon– 10:00 P.M. Sat., Sun.	24 hours, 7 days	24 hours, 7 days

[a] Rates or fees are subject to change.

Features

- Do you offer any proprietary services such as chat lines or informational databases?
- How many mailboxes can be offered with my account?
- Which e-mail utility do you offer? Can I attach through my e-mail account?
- Do you offer spam filters to help cut down on junk mail?

Hardware

- How many phone lines do you have?
- Which modem speeds are supported?
- Which leased line services are available?
- Do you offer ISDN? Which router do you use to support this?
- Do you use a full T1 line or better?
- What is the speed of connection to your regional provider?

Service

- What kind of setup help do you offer?
- Can I see my account status online?
- Is there an 800 number I can call from out of town?
- How many help desk staff do you employ full-time?
- During which hours do you offer help desk support?
- How many subscribers do you have?

Fees

- Are any initial setup charges assessed?
- What is the monthly charge?
- What is the charge to set up a Web page?
- If I go over my monthly allowance, how much is charged for additional time?
- In what increments of an hour do the charges accrue?
- Is the call to use your service a local or a toll call? (Cohen 2002)

Rating ISPs

Several agencies regularly rate ISPs and publish the results. For example, Visual Networks makes more than 100,000 online calls per month to major ISPs to assess how often connections to the first Web page are made quickly. For each category, ISPs are graded from A (excellent) to D (poor). The industry average is somewhere in the B range. The results are updated regularly and posted on Visual Network's Web site, www.visualnetworks.com. Another ISP rating site worth reviewing is CNET, http://home.cnet.com/category/0-3765-7-285302.html?ex.ws.isp.ros.fd.gp. To find an ISP, the most complete site, with more than 6,000 ISPs, is *The List: The Definitive ISP Buyer's Guide* at http://thelist.internet.com.

How exactly do you balance all these criteria? Some quick questions over the phone should give you an idea of the basic philosophy, structure, and kind of service an ISP provides.

1. Find someone with experience who's been using the ISP for at least 3 months and ask how good they find the service.
2. Find out the number of users the ISP has in your area and the number of modems in use at the ISP. Pick one that has a ratio of about 20 users per modem.
3. Find out what kind of pipe each ISP uses to the Internet (56-K, T1, 10-Mbps, and so on) and, with the information collected so far, pick the ISP with the largest pipe.
4. Find out how many employees the ISP has and what range of services it offers. In general, the wider the base is, the more likely it is that your service levels will remain high.

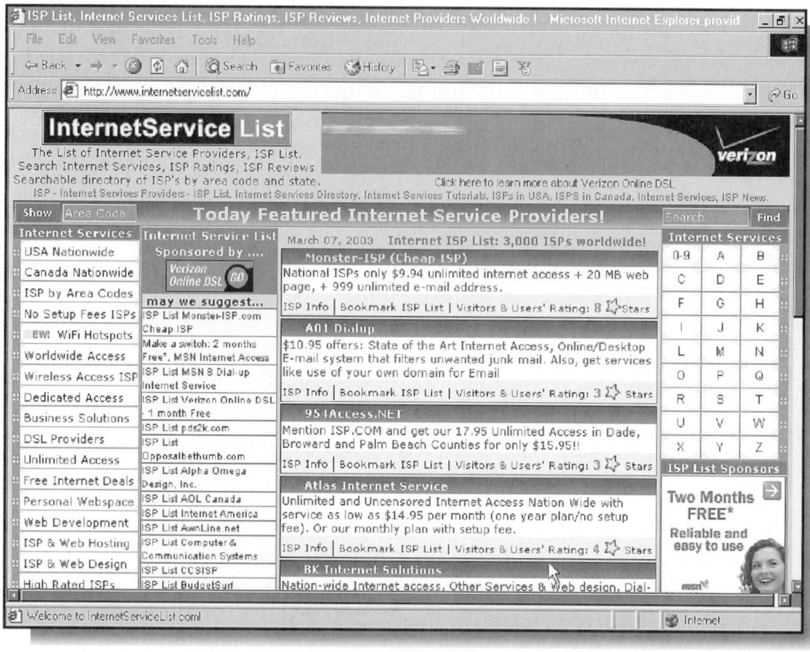

Screen Capture 6-3

Trends

A growing trend is toward no-fee and cut-rate Internet services that challenge existing ISPs like AOL. Giveaways such as Microsoft's Hotmail free e-mail service have caught on substantially worldwide. The largest free provider, NetZero Inc., has close to 2 million registered users and is growing. Others have begun offering no-cost Net access, as well.

The business of free ISPs is uncertain. With the heavy cost of supporting telecommunications networks and no monthly subscription revenue to cover costs, it is questionable how well or whether such companies can make up for the difference through advertising alone. Several free ISPs ran into trouble in 2000 and 2001. This is where the quality, reliability, speed, and integrity of a company's Web site should be weighed against those of the ISP under consideration.

ISPs currently are following three basic trends in their attempts to lower customer churn rates: building a brand identity, providing broadband service, and focusing more on business users. To build brand identity, ISPs are giving customers personal Web sites to provide a personal connection between the customer and the ISP. Experience has shown that this increased loyalty translates into a lower churn rate.

Another approach to building brand loyalty centers on the ISP's Web site. To create customer dependency, an ISP can allow personalization for each customer from this Web site. It might want to include easy links to local weather forecasts (a popular use for the Internet) or stock quotes. Some ISPs also are beginning to experiment with offering proprietary services such as interactive gaming in order to build their brand identities.

In terms of broadband service, speed is what everyone wants. As customers continue to demand faster and faster access and download times, ISPs are beginning to look into broadband service, which currently is available to only 2 percent of home Internet connections. By 2002, the number should be about 25 percent.

Today, businesses are focusing more time and funds on developing an Internet presence. This is important for ISPs because it allows them to expand into higher-profit services such as Web design, Web hosting, e-commerce support, and multiple e-mail accounts. By providing these services to corporate customers, an ISP will find itself with significantly lower customer churn in a segment of the industry that will be growing faster than the individual access segment. See www.witcapital.com.

ISP Requirements

Now that you have decided on an ISP, you can expect a basic package of software and services. Remember that choosing an ISP for online access is different from choosing one for online marketing. For online access, all you need is a reliable connection to the Internet. Changing an ISP, in this case, is simple. For online marketing, you need an ISP that can do the following.

1. **Register your domain name.** You can register your domain name yourself, but it is more convenient to have an ISP do it, although it could cost you more. In either case, make sure the registration is legally in your name rather than the name of the ISP, which can charge you a hefty fee for full ownership later. (See discussion of domain names later in the chapter.)
2. **Capture and forward e-mail.** Receiving and sending mail are important activities for an online merchant. The procedure is simple—your ISP receives your e-mail and routes it to you.
3. **Host your Web site.** Any ISP you choose should have the capability of hosting your Web site for a reasonable fee. To decide what is considered reasonable, check items like the basic rate, disk space charges, charges for hits, charges for number of visitors, fees for reporting statistical data, and fees for storing the Web site.
4. **Give technical and managerial support.** This can be an extremely important service in terms of the availability of technical talent to help troubleshoot your Web site or to assist in upgrading, enhancing, or improving your presence on the Internet.
5. **Give on-the-road support.** Although not a mandatory feature, an ISP can make life enjoyable when you are able to access your e-mail or other information through a local access number, regardless of location or time of day.

Choosing and Registering Your Domain Name

Internet domain names are everywhere. If you advertise and your advertisement does not remind potential customers of your products or services, the problem might not be in the advertisement, but more likely in a poorly chosen domain name. The trick is to choose a domain name that people will recognize and type easily and quickly. In addition, care should be taken to ensure that the domain name is easily interpreted in different languages and cultures.

domain name: unique Internet address that represents a Web site.

What Is a Domain Name?

Domain Name Server (DNS): Web server that stores registered domain names and their numerical equivalents.

A **domain name** is a unique Internet address designed to represent a Web site. The **Domain Name Server (DNS)** was developed to translate between the numeric Internet Protocol (IP) address used by the computer and the less technical name identifier that users can understand.

For example, the numeric IP address 193.231.72.31 might be the address of an organization called Kroger, Inc.

All Web access traffic and Web IP addresses operate at the Internet's TCP/IP layer. (See Chapter 4 for a detailed discussion of layers.) This layer is like a postal service that offers a set of rules called protocols for delivering messages between and among networks. This is how it works: Suppose you have a computer attached to the Internet via an ISP and you're assigned a unique physical address, called an IP address. To send a message to another computer on the Internet, four steps are involved, as shown in Figure 6-5.

1. The sending PC has a unique IP address that takes the form xxx.xxx.xxx.xxx, where each set of xxx's is between 0 and 255.
2. TCP breaks the message into specific bits called packets for easy transmission and handling. Each packet has the sender's IP address so it won't get lost in transit.
3. The IP packets are sent to their destination via a router that reads the destination address and sends it along the fastest available route. Like a traffic officer at an intersection after a football game, the router feeds traffic via several routes to minimize congestion and keep things moving. The sending computer does not have control over the route the message takes. It is up to the router to look over the total volume and available routes and make an intelligent decision on the optimum path.
4. On the receiving end, TCP checks to make sure all packets are assembled correctly to present the message intact (Panko 2003, 19–20).

Importance of a Domain Name

A successful real estate agent once said that the most important thing to consider in buying a house is "location, location, location." A domain name is the Web site's "house," the place where it handles its e-mail and other e-commerce transactions. It will appear in newspaper ads, on business cards, and on company stationery. All employees will learn it, hopefully with pride. Every time a company advertises, it is effectively communicating its presence or location to the public at large. The company's Web URL should be easy to remember and should represent what the company is all about. If it is not found or

Figure 6-5
TCP/IP and message transmission

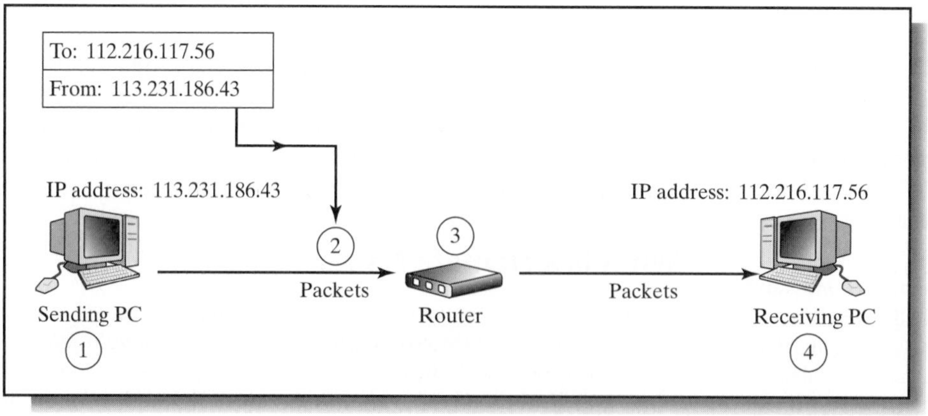

remembered quickly, visitors will surf elsewhere and find the competition. It is as simple as that.

As noted before, ensure that the domain name is officially in your name. You don't want visitors to go through your ISP to get to your Web site. There is a difference between www.isp.com/yourpoorcompany and www.diamondjeweler.com. The first choice shows that the company has an inexpensive presence and that its fees are low. It is as bad for the company's image as handwriting the e-mail address on existing stationery or business cards rather than printing a new batch.

Choose a good domain name or one that an average visitor will find easy to guess. Sometimes the best names are taken, which means you will need to think a bit harder to find an alternate name that will be a good fit. Consider registering the following kinds of domain names.

One or two close names. Think of one or two close alternative domain names for your company or names that visitors might think of. If available, register them as alternatives. The problem with so many alternative names is that look-alike Web addresses could funnel Web traffic to the wrong place. The Internet is awash in Web sites that trick people into visiting by using addresses that vary by one or more characters, a hyphen, and the like.

Unique product domain name. If a company has a product under development or a new product about to be released on the market, it is helpful to register a domain name that is the best fit for that product. Doing this should be part of strategic planning.

Ideal company domain name. Think of the ideal representation of your company for a company domain name and then don't wait: Register it at once. Remember, though, the domain name is not a chance to rename the company or to be funny or interesting. The focus is on a name that is easy to guess. See Table 6-3 for a list of some of the most profitable American firms, their best domain names, and their most logical alternative names.

How Does a Domain Name Work?

Take a look at the following URL, which is the address of the University of Virginia, and find the domain name in it: www.virginia.edu/schls.html.

Table 6-3

Domain names, alternatives to names, and actual registered names

Company Name	Ideal Domain Name	Alternate Name	Actual Domain Registered
BankAmerica	bankamerica.com	bankofamerica.com	bank-america.com, bofa.com
Coca-Cola	cocacola.com	coke.com	cocacola.com, coke.com
General Motors	gm.com	generalmotors.com	gm.com
Exxon	Exxon.com		exxon.com
IBM	ibm.com		ibm.com
Intel	intel.com		intel.com
Wal-Mart Stores	walmart.com	wal-mart.com	wal-mart.com

The URL has three major parts.

1. **http://**Internet protocol (http or hypertext markup language) and separator (://).
2. **www.virginia.edu** The domain name. www means world wide web; Virginia is the second-level domain, and .edu is top-level domain.
3. **/schls.html** A subdirectory of the file (/schls.html), which is the list of schools at the University of Virginia that will be retrieved.

The first part is the Internet protocol name. The World Wide Web uses HyperText Transfer Protocol (HTTP). A colon and a double slash follow the acronym as separators. The Internet protocol name always begins with http://.

The second part is the domain name. It includes the second-level domain (*virginia*) and the top-level domain (*.edu*). The third part is the subdirectory and file name that simply identify the specific file that the user needs (in our example, a list of schools).

However, reading a domain name is not that easy. It actually is read backwards. In this example, the address reads: I want the names of schools at the University of Virginia.

Here are the top-level domains.

.com	Commercial organizations and businesses in general
.edu	Educational institutions (4-year colleges and universities)
.gov	U.S. government agencies (nonmilitary)
.mil	U.S. government military agencies
.net	Companies that support the Internet
.org	Organizations such as nonprofits, etc.
.uk, .ca, .sy, etc.	Country codes formalized by an IOS (International Organization for Standardization) committee. For a complete list, visit the GeoCities Web site at **www.geocities.com**.

Choosing a Domain Name

In the world of the Internet, it is the *.com* at the end of the MyBusiness.com address that is the most desirable for Internet business. The *.net* domain is considered far less desirable. Unfortunately, the name that you most want might been taken by someone else already. Domain-name speculators register domain names that come close to trademarked terms in the hope of reselling them at a huge markup.

The following procedure is suggested when choosing a domain name.

1. Jot down on a piece of paper all the possible domain names you can think of that fit your organization's image, products, or services. End each name with .com if it is a business, .edu if it is an educational institution, .org if it is a nonprofit organization, and so on.
2. Ask friends, peers, employees, and others who use the Web to suggest domain names for your company. Inasmuch as most people will guess at a name, some of the choices will be surprising.
3. Narrow the list to a few favorites. This should be based on the relevance of the names to your business and how easy it will be for Web visitors to guess the name.
4. Go to the InterNic Domain Services Web site, www.internic.net, and enter the domain name(s) you want to check for availability.
5. Enter all the domain names on your list. You might be lucky to find that 1 out of every 10 names entered is available.
6. For the available domain names, enter each name as a URL in your Web browser to see if the name is in active use. If not, then proceed with domain name registration.

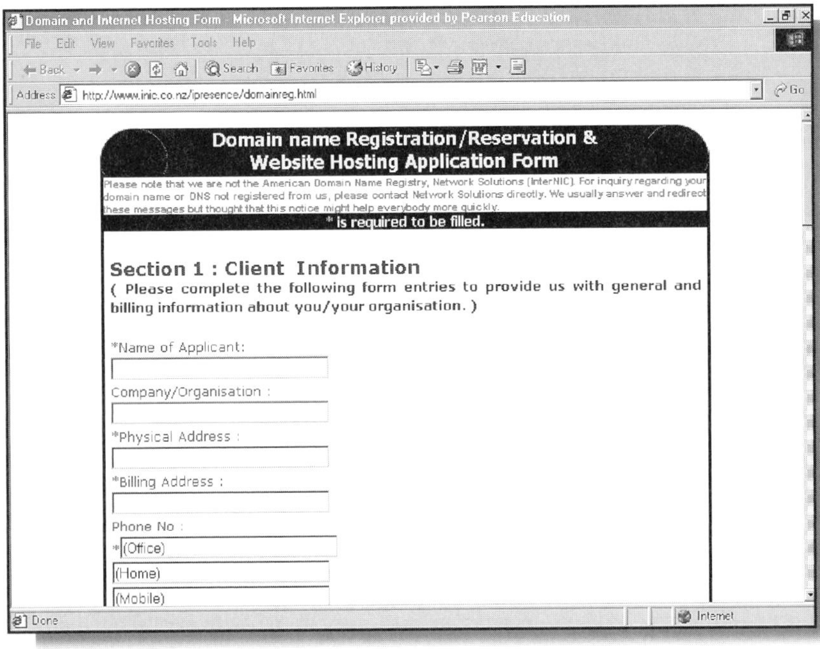

Screen Capture 6-4
An InterNic form
Source: Copyright © 2003–2004. Used with permission of ICANN. All rights reserved. www.internic.net

In choosing a domain name, legal implications must be considered, especially concerning the issue of trademarks.

1. Determine if the proposed domain name infringes on trademarks. Trademark infringement is a problem not only with existing trademarks, but also with names similar enough to cause confusion for consumers.
2. Make sure the proposed domain name does not adversely affect any famous trademark. The federal Trademark Dilution Act prohibits weakening or tarnishing famous trademarks.
3. Once cleared of potential claims of infringement or dilution, the proposed domain name should be registered as a federal trademark with the U.S. Patent and Trademark Office.
4. Register the proposed domain name with InterNic or Network Solutions (NSI). This quasi-government agency assigns domain names in North America on a first-come, first-served basis.
5. Look for expanded top-level domain names and registries. The International AdHoc Committee (IAHC) was created by the Internet Society in 1997 to study revisions in the domain name system. Its proposed final plan will create the following eight new generic, top-level domains.

   - **.arts** for entities emphasizing art, culture, and entertainment
   - **.firm** for businesses and firms
   - **.info** for providers of information services
   - **.nom** for individuals
   - **.per** and **.nom** for personal sites

- **.rec** for entities emphasizing recreation/entertainment sources
- **.store** for businesses offering goods
- **.web** for businesses emphasizing Web activities

Registering a Domain Name

Once a domain name is selected, the next step is to register it. The process of registering a domain name is as easy as filling out a Web-based form.

There are two ways to register: on your own or through an ISP. On the surface, registering on your own seems simple. Go to the Network Solutions Web site, www.networksolutions.com, and follow the instructions online. You will pay a fee of $70 to register your domain, but your ISP cannot use the name until you contact them and inform them that you have registered. The ISP, in turn, will transfer the domain name to its DNS server for a transfer fee. The problem with this approach is the headache for a first-time registrant. You have to make sure when you register that you have the registrant and the administrative and billing contact at Network Solutions. This is why the alternative of having an ISP do the job is preferable.

The ISP goes through a similar procedure, although it will charge about $50 for processing in addition to the $70 fee for registration. However, the ISP must demonstrate responsibility for your online presence. Here are some pitfalls to keep in mind.

1. **Overcharging.** ISPs in general have their own algorithm of fees, including setup fees, transfer fees, monthly fees, special services fees, and so on. Shop around for a reliable ISP with experience and a reputation for quality technical support at a reasonable charge.
2. **Domain name status.** The "don't ask, don't tell" concept applies in situations where, if you don't ask to make sure the domain name is registered in your name

Screen Capture 6-5

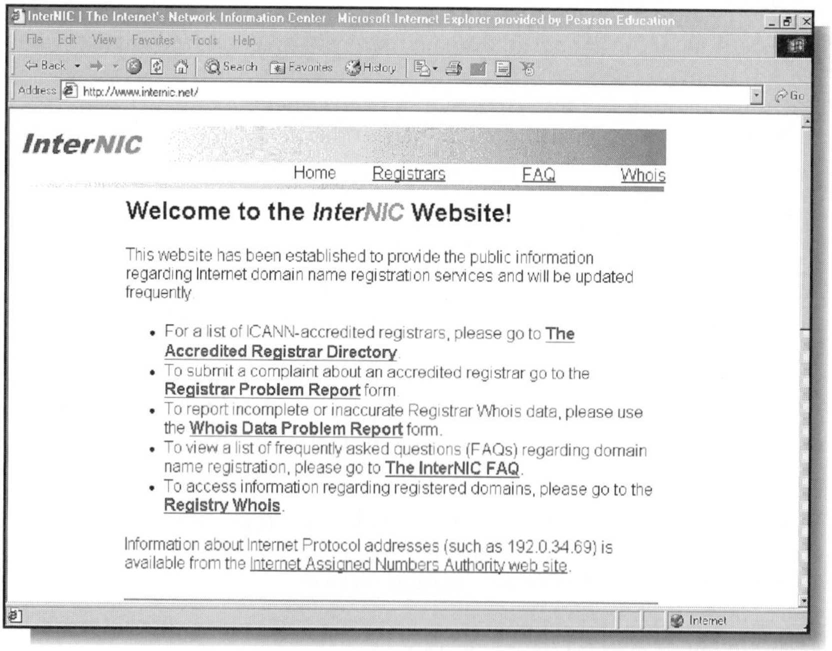

rather than in the name of the ISP, it is likely the ISP won't volunteer details. Make sure you own the exclusive right to your domain name.

3. **Backup.** When connection problems occur, does your ISP have another Internet connection for a backup? Surprisingly, many ISPs operate on a shoestring. Backup also has to do with how likely the ISP is to stay in business. Changing ISPs is neither pleasant nor convenient.
4. **Contractual language.** Before committing, read the agreement the ISP expects you to sign before your Web site is formally and legally on the Internet.

In 1999, the U.S. Department of Commerce opened up a new domain naming process to a California-based nonprofit organization known as the Internet Corporation for Assigned Names and Numbers (ICANN). This was done in response to the growing demand for domain names. The controversy over hogging names continues. Those who own them view hogging as a protective strategy. For example, MoveCentral Inc., a start-up, registered more than 60 domain names before settling on MoveCentral as its company name and the domain name *movecentral.com* for its homepage. The company's ownership of the remaining names ensures it has eliminated the likelihood of copycat sites (Emigh, September 27, 1999, p. 86).

Three FAQs

Here are three frequently asked questions about the domain name process that are worth considering.

1. What is involved in registering a domain name in .com, .net, or .org?

   To register a domain name, you need to provide the registrar of your choice with the contact and technical information that makes up the registration. The registrar stores the contact information and submits the technical information to a central directory called the "registry." The registry, in turn, provides other computers linked to the Internet with the information to send you e-mail or to find your Web site. You also will have to enter a registration contact with the registrar that specifies the terms of your registration and how it will be maintained.
2. How long does a registration last? Can it be renewed?

   The original registration is for 2 years, renewable 1 year at a time. Beginning January 15, 2000, a registrar can offer initial and renewal registrations in 1-year increments, with a total registration period not to exceed 10 years.
3. Can the registrar be changed after registering a domain name?

   Yes, but only after 60 days from initial registration. Make sure to contact the new registrar before disconnecting from the current one. For details on other FAQs, visit the InterNic Web site at www.internic.net/faqs/domain-names.html.

Application Service Provider (ASP)

The advent of the ASP industry spawned out of a desire to meet the changing needs of business of all sizes and structures quickly. Those who do not have the time, financial resources, or manpower to purchase and maintain their own software can now turn to other companies to do it for them. Currently, more than 500 ASP firms provide services to different businesses, large and small. Most of these firms belong to an organization called the ASP

Industry Consortium—an advocacy group that sponsors continuing research on the ASP model and promotes the ASP industry around the world. The consortium experienced 1,900 percent growth during its initial year of operation. More than $300 million has been spent on ASP services, and it is estimated that the market for ASPs will exceed $22 billion by 2003.

With experience in time-sharing, outsourcing, and packaged software, going the ASP route is proving wise for many businesses, large and small. ASPs are companies that lease application software to customers via the Internet. They allow businesses to lease software on a monthly or yearly basis. The applications are hosted on the ASP's remote site, and the ASP also is responsible for updating and maintenance. In addition, the ASP provides technical support to its users.

A complete application service package consists of two unique service components.

- **Web site hosting and delivery**—physically storing software applications on centralized servers and then leasing them to other companies. The ASP provides the operating hardware and software to support a customer-developed Web site.
- **Application technical support**—providing end-to-end connectivity support.

How Do ASPs Work?

Although many models would fit an ASP (e.g., airlines), most companies denote ASP as services provided through the Internet. Here are some of the most common features of an ASP. The ASP:

- Owns and operates a software application.
- Owns, operates, and maintains the servers that run the application.
- Employs the staff to maintain the application.
- Makes the application available to customers everywhere via the Internet, normally in a browser.
- Bills either on a per-use basis or on a monthly/annual fee basis. In many cases, the ASP can provide the service for free or even pay the customer.

ASP Benefits

Several benefits are distinct to ASP.

- Outsourcing to an ASP lets the firm concentrate on its core competencies, strategic projects, and generating revenues and serving customers rather than on managing technology. ASP handles IT staffing, upgrades, and backups.
- Quicker access to the latest functionality and services. ASPs can keep their technical environment up-to-date as part of their agreement with the client.
- Low cost of entry and short setup time. Using an ASP can cut monthly costs of application ownership by as much as 50 percent.
- Shifts Internet bandwidth to the ASP, which can provide it at lower cost.

With these benefits come some concerns. The main concerns are as follows.

- **Security and loss of control.** The use of ASP may raise fears about the safety of data from external tampering. Because the provider hosts the application software, companies cannot be sure that confidential and critical information is not being viewed and used by outsiders.
- **Reliability and quality of service.** There is some debate about using the Internet as a medium for secure transfer of critical data. Viruses and hackers are rampant over

the Internet, and it is not the best method of transferring certain data. There is also the question of the quality of service provided by inexperienced ASPs and their ability to deliver on their promises.

- **Ambiguity.** Another barrier to decision making is the difficulty of drawing up clear service level agreements. There is no room for ambiguity when the client is totally dependent on the support of the ASP.
- **ASP quality and financial stability.** Not every ASP is the best for every organization. Because no standard form of pricing has been established, the client needs to decide whether it should be cost per transaction, database size required, or number of PCs.
- **Standardization.** ASPs discourage customization to keep costs down.
- **Application performance.** To counter this concern, top ASPs offer service level agreements (SLAs) with performance guarantees and penalty clauses (Hayes 2001).

Shaking Hands Is Not Enough

service-level agreement (SLA): a contract between the user and the ASP vendor, stating the vendor's commitments to ensure reliable delivery of information.

When it comes to a point where an ASP has been selected, a rewarding relationship with the provider begins with a clearly written, well-defined **service-level agreement (SLA)** outlining the client's performance expectations. It is a contract that defines the technical support that an ASP will provide to clients. Learning how to interpret the business and technical aspects of an SLA can make the difference between a mutually rewarding relationship and one headache after another in trying to navigate with an incompetent ASP. Box 6-4 summarizes some of the key issues to be included in an SLA. The conclusion is that successful outsourcing of any application will require accountability, performance, and remediation to be spelled out and agreed upon by all parties.

In conclusion, in a business climate where the IT budget is scarce, the value of ASPs starts making sense. Hiring a staff to build and implement internal systems is costly and time consuming. Many IT managers have been forced to take a harder look at ASPs. Even with some of the potential pitfalls, ASPs do offer cost efficiency and implementation benefits. If a company needs to be cutting edge but does not have the funds to spend on a huge IT initiative, ASPs are increasingly becoming the only place to turn. Internet reliability and efficiency will first have to improve, but this is happening gradually. Carrier-class routers and switches are much more intelligent than before, with built-in quality-of-service features.

BOX 6-4
Service-level agreement (SLA)

Working with an application service provider (ASP) can be a risky proposition, especially for established companies that entrust the care and management of core business applications to small or emerging companies. In its march toward becoming a legitimate and permanent fixture in the IT outsourcing landscape, the ASP industry has promulgated service-level agreements (SLA) as a means of mitigating these concerns.

Last spring, the American Cancer Society Inc. (ACS) in Atlanta decided to find an ASP to host its Siebel Systems Inc. customer relationship management system. CIO Zachary Patterson says he believed that the ASP model would free his organization from IT delivery, since technology isn't the organization's core business but is a critical enabler. The SLA ACS

(*continued*)

BOX 6-4
Continued

reached last fall with Annapolis, Maryland-based Usinternetworking Inc. to host the Siebel suite would be one step in outsourcing.

ACS's top priority is customer satisfaction, and its SLA reflects this business imperative. "Uptime on a router means nothing to a business." Patterson worked hard to make certain that Usinternetworking understood what ACS's service meant to its cancer patients, volunteers, and donors.

Most ASPs promised 99.9 percent uptime. Although the math appears fuzzy and the second decimal unimportant, 99.99 percent reliability means only 5 minutes of downtime per month, while 99.95 percent availability allows for 45 minutes of downtime. For certain applications, it is completely unrealistic to tell a customer that it will be down for only 5 minutes per month.

"Weasel words" is a point of contention in SLAs. ASPs have to feel some pain for falling down on the job. Typically when an ASP does not meet its performance agreement, it pays the customer in either additional service or dollar credits. But one SLA guaranteed 99.9 percent uptime but didn't count the first 15 minutes of downtime. 15 minutes of downtime during peak buying hours represents a huge problem for online retailers, but 15 minutes of downtime at 2:00 A.M. probably has fewer consequences.

SOURCE: Excerpted from Patterson, Zachary, "Service-Level Agreements," *Computerworld*, January 22, 2001, 53.

SUMMARY

1. Internet Service Providers (ISPs) are attractive to many companies for several reasons including the following: specialized staff to manage Web sites, high-speed connectivity to main Internet hubs, real physical security from power outages, and the latest technology.
2. ISPs can belong to one of three categories: the large wholesale access provider, the smaller Internet backbone provider, and the local ISP. Larger wholesale providers have been the target of consolidation and acquisition, and smaller providers have been growing.
3. Hosting a Web site involves three major items: hardware, communications network, and qualified staff. Minimum operating costs can run from $60,000 to $120,000.
4. There are four types of service providers: ISPs, ASPs, BSPs, and WSPs.
5. The backbone of the Internet is the group of Network Service Providers that work together to provide total interconnection. ISPs connect to NSPs and pay a fee to do so.
6. Shopping for a Web-hosting ISP involves several factors: size of the pipeline or bandwidth, connection availability and performance, virtual hosting, number of e-mail addresses allowed per account, ISP stability and staying power, free local access, customer service and technical support, and ISP reliability and cost of service.
7. For online marketing, an ISP should be capable of registering your domain name, capturing and forwarding e-mail, hosting the Web site, technical and managerial support, and on-the-road support.
8. Your domain name is the "house" for your Web site, e-mail, and other e-commerce transactions. Make sure it is officially in your name. It should be easy to guess the name. Register a domain name that comes close to your product or company name.

9. The Wireless Application Service Provider (WASP) handles untethered applications, with responsibilities involving hosting, developing, and managing applications similar to that of an ASP. Mobile commerce is covered in more depth in Chapter 7.
10. ASPs are services provided through the Internet. They own and operate a software application, maintain the servers that run the application, employ the staff to maintain the application, and make the application available to customers everywhere via the Internet.
11. To consider becoming an ISP, it is important to consider the target market, the services to provide, the technical requirements, and the type of provider to be. Quality lines and bandwidth choice are extremely critical to a high-performance setup.

KEY TERMS

- access server, 168
- Application Service Provider (ASP), 166
- Backbone, 168
- Business Service Provider (BSP), 166
- caching, 172
- customer churn rate, 176
- domain name, 161, 181
- domain name server (DNS), 171
- facilities-based ISP, 169
- Internet Relay Chat (IRC), 171
- Internet Service Provider (ISP), 165
- point of presence (POP), 176
- Radius server, 171
- service-level agreement (SLA), 189
- virtual domain, 163
- virtual hosting, 163
- Virtual ISP, 169
- Web hosting, 166
- Wholesale Service Provider (WSP), 166
- Wireless Application Service Provider (WASP), 166

TEST YOUR UNDERSTANDING

1. In what way has the World Wide Web brought back the old concept of time sharing? Explain.
2. What reasons drive medium-size to small organizations to Internet Service Providers?
3. Cite statistics that support the growing trend in commercial Internet traffic.
4. How do ISPs work? Give an example.
5. How much do you think it costs to host a Web site? Contact a local ISP and find out.
6. What infrastructure represents a typical ISP?
7. Explain briefly the various types of Web-hosting services.
8. List and briefly explain the five elements needed to be an ISP.
9. The backbone of the Internet is a cluster of competing companies called Network Service Providers or NSPs. How do they work?
10. If you were looking for an ISP, how would you choose one? Be specific.
11. What is bandwidth? How does it affect Web site performance?
12. What is a domain name? Why would one need to be careful about choosing one?
13. How would a company with a new Web site choose and register a domain name? Be specific in terms of procedure.
14. Given what you now know about choosing a domain name, what procedure would you follow in choosing one?

15. What is so distinctive about the Wireless Application Service Provider?
16. Summarize the key services of an ISP. Which one is the most popular? Why?
17. Distinguish between facilities-based and virtual ISPs.
18. How would you explain the difference between T1 and T3 lines?What questions would you ask before choosing an ISP? Be specific.
19. How would ASPs work? Give an example.
20. What concerns would one consider in deciding on an ASP?

Discussion Questions

1. When you contact an ISP to determine whether its services are appropriate for your new Web site, what questions would you ask or what type of information would you need to make up your mind?
2. Look up www.findanisp.com and determine the ratings of two local ISPs and one national ISP (e.g., AT&T). Elaborate on the fees, features, and ratings of each ISP.
3. Do you think free Web services will last? Discuss in detail.
4. The chapter talks about trends that ISPs are currently following to lower customer churn rates. Discuss.
5. Two businesses want the same domain name. How is the situation settled?
6. Newspapers, TV, and the media have made known the rivalry between Netscape and Microsoft for dominance in the Web browser market. Is this beneficial or harmful for the average consumer?

Web Exercises

1. Several domain name disputes arose in 2000 and 2001. Search the Netscape site for some of the domain name controversies. *Hint:* In the subject area, enter a subject such as *domain name disputes, domain name controversy*, and so on.
2. Choose a domain name and check it at the InterNic Web site, www.internic.net, to see if it is taken. If it has been taken, who has it?
3. Interview a local business with a Web site. Write a report showing the procedure the business followed to decide on its domain name and how the business registered it.

Chapter 7

Mobile (M) Commerce—The Business of Time

Contents

In a Nutshell

In today's society, it is rare to walk down the street without seeing people talking on a mobile phone or checking their schedules on a Palm Pilot. Living life on the go, Americans and Europeans are searching constantly for ways to keep in touch with anyone, anywhere, and anytime. Wireless technology is all things to all people. From garage door openers to cellular phones, cordless keyboards to Palm Pilots, wireless devices have become commonplace. In the business world, wireless technology is a necessity, and it is gaining ground everywhere. In Silicon Valley or any European capital, the cell phone is a tool of the smart-working elite—a way to squeeze more value-added time to long commutes, to check with clients, or to verify stock prices on the run. The new solution is wireless communication. The term *wireless* means "transmitting signals over radio waves instead of wires" (see Box 7-1).

A relatively new addition to e-commerce and to physical media like coaxial, twisted-pair, and fiber-optic cable is wireless data transmission—the backbone of mobile or **m-commerce.** Going wireless is like scuba diving wearing lightweight gear and not being linked by a long umbilical cord to a ship for air. It is data communication without physical attachments—microwave,

m-commerce: business transactions and payments conducted in a non-pc-based environment.

BOX 7-1
Microsoft furthers hardware reputation

Microsoft released one wired and one wireless optical mouse, a tiny optical mouse for notebook computers, one regular and one "natural" split-design keyboard and two wireless desktop mouse-and-keyboard combo sets. You can plug the transmitter into your keyboard and mouse ports on the back of your computer, or into a USB slot. You'll get smoother mouse movement, although it'll take up one of those precious plugs. The keyboard and mouse need two AA batteries, since they require power to send signals to the transmitter. After plugging in everything and pressing reset on each device, Windows XP saw them and it all worked.

The two devices have a roughly six-foot range and use radio waves so you don't need a direct line of sight. The mouse doesn't have a ball inside to get gummed up. You don't need a mousepad either. As long as you use them on a surface with a visible texture, the tiny camera inside tracks movement and creates smooth strokes.

The keyboard is appealing too. Microsoft has changed the multimedia keys across the top again—the volume keys are very smart and useful. The Notebook Mouse is perfect for his hands and designed to replace a laptop pointing device. Some people like the little eraserhead mouse, or trackpoint as some manufacturers call it. I prefer trackpads but I don't think anyone really likes either.

SOURCE: Hopper, D. I., "Microsoft Furthers Hardware Reputation," *Richmond Times Dispatch*, October 27, 2002, E8.

radio wave, and infrared. It is a convenient alternative to network cabling connections and is quickly becoming the network of choice for an increasingly mobile workforce, due to the flexibility and freedom such technology offers.

wireless LAN (WLAN): a standard for wireless networking.

Wireless LANs already have gained acceptance in a wide range of vertical markets, including the health care, retail, manufacturing, warehousing, and academic circles. The technology has increased the productivity of these industries through the usage of handheld terminals and mobile computers to transmit data in real time to centralized hosts. Because this technology is easily applicable to other industries, the worldwide wireless LAN market is expected to grow to $1.6 billion by 2005 (3COM 2002).

Mobile phones are wireless. They are different from PCs. Other than size and portability, people use mobile phones in a unique way. A connected PC is used to check e-mail or to shop on the Internet. It is not possible to tell when messages are checked or orders are placed. In contrast, a mobile phone is carried with consumers wherever they go. It is kept on all the time, waiting for calls or ready to send messages. Yet, it continues to be a problem doing business via the mobile phone due to its limited interface and technical problems. An insufficient built-in security system is another problem. Yet, for end users, wireless networks are just as effective as wired systems. They have a transmission range of several hundred feet, allowing users to connect with the network from anywhere within most facilities and even from outside. In short, wireless networks are affordable, easy to install and operate, and eliminate the cost of cabling.

As wireless networks expand, m-commerce will follow. It is analogous to the growth of the Internet and the World Wide Web, respectively. The current growth of wireless and mobile networks has brought vast changes in mobile devices and user acceptance. According to one source, more than 350 million mobile devices are in use worldwide, 80 million of them in the United States (Cellular 1999). The Gartner Group, a market research firm, predicts that by 2004, at least 40 percent of consumer-to-business e-commerce will be generated from smart phones using wireless application protocol or WAP (Haskin 1999, Varshney et al. 2001).

In this chapter, we cover the essence of m-commerce: benefits and limitations, m-marketing, m-payments, languages, applications, security and legal issues, and emerging models for m-commerce. The goal is to provide a comprehensive coverage of this fast-emerging technology and its potential for enhancing trade, personalization, and customer service.

What Is M-Commerce?

Imagine receiving an important e-mail while you're out to lunch or away on business, or checking your stock portfolio on the way to the airport. What about this: Your pharmacy sends you a short note telling you that you're about to run out of your medication for diabetes and asks you if you want a refill. When you click "yes," the medication will be ready in minutes and you can pick it up on the way home or have the pharmacy deliver it here. Although these seem like futuristic visions, they already can occur through m-commerce or mobile commerce. Until recently, mobile data referred to any nonmobile voice, such as a portable telephone, a pager, or even a garage door opener. Today's focus on services and applications on the mobile phone is what m-commerce is all about. This means that messages from one person to another are not m-commerce, but messages from an information service provider that are charged a rate constitute m-commerce.

M-commerce is the transmission of user data (e.g., e-mail, spreadsheet) without wires. It is also the management of the processes that handle the product or service needs of a consumer via a mobile phone. It is also the use of wireless devices to facilitate the sale of products and services, anytime, anywhere. This technology takes into account a viable relationship between a mobile phone and a person to generate a business opportunity that normally does not exist in traditional e-business.

M-commerce also refers to business transactions and payments conducted in a non-PC-based environment. These are carried out via radio-based wireless devices that can access data networks and conduct business-to-business and business-to-consumer transactions over wired, Web-based, e-commerce systems. The first thing to remember is that m-commerce is not about selling products or services on a mobile device. They are part of m-commerce but do not include the personal role of a mobile phone.

Several categories of services comprise m-commerce.

- Information-based consumer services like searching the Web for restaurants or movies using a data-enabled cellular phone. Sending e-mail also is included.
- Transaction services, where consumers download and listen to digital music in a wireless setup, make purchases by a cellular device and have the price added to the phone bill, or carry out "buy and sell" business transactions wirelessly.
- Location-centric, personalized services that anticipate your purchases based on your location and data stored in your "profile," by product, time of the year, and so on (Hamilton 2000, R3). See Figure 7-1. This unsettling possibility means that companies can beam advertisements, coupons, and other electronic pitches at consumers depending on their location at the time. Related to this category is tethering employees via wireless devices that can track their movements and communications (see Box 7-2).

Figure 7-1
Business in the air

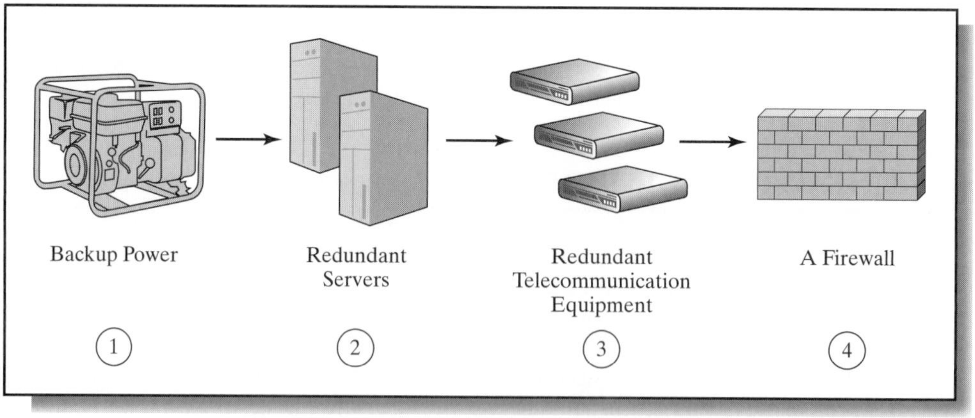

Source: Hamilton, D. P., "Making the Connections," *The Wall Street Journal*, December 11, 2000, R3.

BOX 7-2
Wireless advertising

. . .Wireless advertising is real and here to stay. Whether it's the national advertiser promoting its brand, or the local merchant attempting to drive store traffic, wireless advertising provides convenience, efficiency, and customization. It enables consumers to access important information and take advantage of advertising promotions when and where they want them. A sample of potential avenues for wireless advertising include:

- Wireless yellow pages, where advertisements are placed within the "yellow page" content. For example, a consumer may be scrolling through the wireless yellow pages to find a listing of Italian restaurants. When the consumer receives the requested information about Italian restaurants, they also receive a series of embedded advertisements or promotions linked to that content.
- "Search-and-Pitch" channel which dynamically targets and sends advertisements based on the search criteria entered by the consumer. For example, the consumer types in Italian cuisine and both content and appropriate ads are delivered to the device.
- Content-driven wireless advertising is similar to traditional Internet banner advertising, in that ad content is directly related to the content of the site being viewed by the consumer. For example, when a consumer accesses sports scores on their device, the accompanying advertisement may be from Nike or the local professional sports franchise.

To consumers and privacy advocates, wireless advertising can be considered an invasion, especially when considering the personal nature of the device itself. The fear is that everywhere you go and everything you do will be monitored—or that you'll be bombarded with advertising while you walk down the street. Today, wireless carriers simply do not possess the technical capabilities to track every single one of their subscribers all the time. In the future, this capability may become more technically feasible and cost-effective. However, if the privacy issues are not addressed, then governments are sure to step forward with legislation.

Ultimately, consumers want to exert influence and choice over wireless advertising. They want to receive value-added information and direction on products and services. They want something dramatically different from what they receive in today's Internet advertising. Guidelines must be established. Targeted, permission-based advertisements must be the focus.

SOURCE: Excerpted from DePriest, Tim, "Wireless Advertising: Opportunities and Challenges," *Computerworld*, May 5, 2003, 42ff.

In the mid-1990s, companies realized that going online was more than replicating static brochures in HTML format or developing interactive Web sites. Likewise, today, companies are beginning to realize that going wireless is more than reformatting HTML into Wireless Application Protocol or WAP (to be explained later). The best way to understand the difference between the two technologies is to look at the physical size of a PC monitor (200 inches) versus the display device on a mobile device (approximately 10 inches, which limits the amount of information shared). In terms of the bandwidth, the typical 9,400 bits per second (bps) is what a PC modem used several years ago. Finally, trying to enter text with a 12-key keyboard on a mobile phone can be frustrating.

Other differences exist, as well. Think of paying airtime for wireless Web use but having to put up with banner ads and other distracting news without your permission. Once wireless becomes commonplace, trying to combat invasions of privacy or junk e-mail will become a challenge. Finally, although PC-oriented e-commerce employs HTML technology, m-commerce and the wireless Web use two distinct development languages: Wireless Mark-up Language (WML) and Handheld Device Mark-up Language (HDML). These languages, which require different browsers loaded on mobile phones, will be explained later in the chapter.

WHY WIRELESS?

The wireless Web is a technological frontier, open and growing. The technology already has taken off in Finland and Japan, where schoolchildren watch cartoon characters on their Web phones and businesspeople on the run participate in lotteries and pay for soda from vending machines using their Personal dgDital Assistants. Web phones in the future will be used to deliver information such as stock quotes, flight delays, and news items. According to an InfoWorld Wireless Survey of 500 readers, more than 95 percent currently use a cell phone and 69 percent use a standard pager. The projection for exponential use of Web-based phones is obvious (Orubeondo 2001). Another source estimates that the number of mobile telephone subscribers will exceed 1 billion in 2004 and will account for an annual value of $13 billion or 7 percent of all electronic commerce transactions.

Wireless communication traces its roots to the invention of the radio by a young Italian named Guglielmo Marconi in 1894. He successfully transmitted radio waves without using wires. By September 1895, Marconi had built equipment that transmitted electrical signals through the air. Known as the true "grandfather of wireless communication," Marconi went on to win the 1909 Nobel Prize in Physics for his contribution to the

Screen Capture 7-1

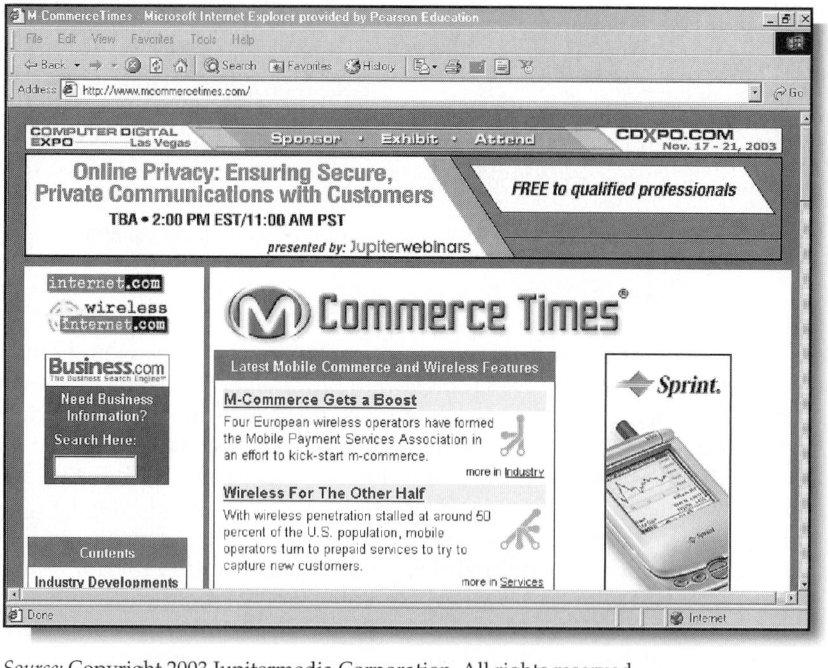

www.mcommercetimes.com

development of wireless telegraphy (San Filippo 1999). Cellular planning continued during the mid-1940s,after World War II, but trial service did not begin until 1978, and it was not until 1984 that full deployment began in America (Farley 2003).

Wireless technology means cutting the cord (cables) that forms today's computer network. Wireless networking makes it possible to connect two or more computers without the bulky cables, giving consumers the benefits of a network with little or no labor (Gomes 2001, R16). Accessing events is easy, but knowing when important events will take place is totally different. In the way of analogy, if a car crashes into a tree and no one sees it crash, did it make a sound? It must have. The same applies in day-to-day business. Just because consumers were not informed of a price change, it does not mean the change did not occur. It did. It all means that time is a factor everyone is trying to minimize. We live in a dynamic business world where information changes by the minute, and value-added decision making is all about having the right information at the right time. Certain information must be delivered in real time, regardless of location.

The wireless initiative is launching a new battle against time. Compared to the Internet, which has demonstrated information availability *anytime*, wireless mobile technology makes such availability *anywhere*. When using the Internet, you are online (direct) with information as long as you are connected to the network. If you are not connected, you are out of luck. The problem is that users are committed to other activities and cannot be wired constantly to the Internet. Wireless technology frees users to be able to access any information anywhere, which brings up the time issue again. With wireless technology, information can be accessed as it happens. Employees would be empowered to make decisions faster, customers can ask questions more spontaneously, and business owners will be plugged to the heartbeat of their business, regardless of their location.

Key Benefits

Given these differences, one wonders how the wireless Web benefits the consumer. The most obvious benefits are time and money, which give computing legs. It is the facilitator between the e-world and the real world. Think of being airborne at 32,000 feet over the Atlantic and being able to put the 8-hour flight to good use. As reported in Box 7-3, you can do e-mail and maintain Web links at affordable rates. It is not necessary to wait out a connection with your business, customers, suppliers, and others. Employees can make decisions faster. Customers can ask more questions, and businesses can respond more accurately. Managers can control what happens at any time, because they are plugged into the heartbeat of the business. As a result one needs the *anywhere* functionality to stay competitive (Dushko 2002, 14).

Consider the case of the U.S. army using mobile technology and a satellite link to track supplies during the 2003 war with Iraq. Sixty-four mobile units were used to scan information about combat and supply vehicles and send the data via a secure satellite link to an authorized central asset-tracking system. The equipment can be stationed virtually anywhere—roadsides or intersections—to scan vehicles in army columns and convoys as they approach (Songini 2003).

Another benefit relates to shopping. Think of a situation where a consumer is on a lunch break and has limited time to shop for various products and prices. Instead of making several cell or phone calls to identify which business carries the belted leather briefcase for the right price, the consumer can use wireless (M) commerce to quickly check the selection at various stores and obtain the best price for the product in a matter of seconds. This benefit goes beyond products. Airlines, movie theaters, and even restaurants should soon begin to deliver special discounts for mobile users to generate store traffic.

BOX 7-3
Airlines bring the Web in-flight

After years of ordering passengers to go offline upon takeoff, a number of airlines are set to make it possible to e-mail or even surf the Internet while mile-high. Early next year, Lufthansa will become the first airline to offer high-speed Internet access to passengers. British Airways will follow suit soon after. Verizon, which now owns GTE (General Telephone), started rolling out JetConnect on carriers including Continental Airlines. The service allows passengers to plug their laptops into the Airfones and play games or send instant messages. Airfone plans to eventually add high-speed e-mail to the mix. JetConnect currently is priced at a flat fee of $5.99 for the entire flight.

Boeing's Connexion service uses satellites to send and receive data from Web surfers onboard the aircraft. Passengers will be able to plug their laptops directly into seat-mounted jacks. Boeing claims the hookup will be simple enough that anyone can do it. But just in case, the first few flights on Lufthansa and British Airways will have techies on board just to be sure of a smooth implementation.

Boeing and the airlines are still working on the most critical part of the puzzle—pricing. A Boeing official says surveys suggest that travelers would be willing to pay $25 to $35 for access on a flight of about 7 hours.

SOURCE: Lieber, Ron, and Lunsford, J. Lynn, "Totally Wired at 32,000 Feet," *The Wall Street Journal,* October 24, 2002, D1ff.

The number of two-way wireless messaging and cell phones for wireless Internet functions has skyrocketed everywhere. Today's emphasis is on applications that are location-centric. Location is a key ingredient for creating a personalized user experience for the wireless Internet (corp.cellmania.com 2002). It allows users to pay bills, check their credit card balances, and bank over the wireless Internet. Just as the Internet has changed the way business is conducted, the wireless Web is expected to have similar or greater impact. According to the Gartner Group, within 4 years, 40 percent of all e-commerce will be conducted wirelessly. McKinsey & Co. also projects that by 2005, e-commerce over mobile devices will be between $10 billion and $15 billion worldwide. With the advent of "smart phones" that allow the Internet to be taken "on the road," these projections are likely to become a reality (Gartner Group 2002).

Location is a critical factor in m-commerce. Managers of physical stores would value technology that helps bring foot traffic to their location. The wireless channel for promotions can target promotion campaigns for their individual stores, whether they are hotels, movie theaters, or restaurants that have perishable items to sell. Think of a restaurant that uses technology to attract local customers during a slow week. This would allow them to match prices, offer specials, or unload excess inventory. For example, a local theater can offer 30 percent discount on tickets for a particular show. As the show draws near, the discount can increase right up to the beginning of the show. Box 7-4 shows examples of companies that made progress on location-centric commerce.

Another benefit of location-centricity is in location tracking of products, services, and even people, which allows providers to focus more accurately on delivery times and improve customer service. For example, stores can track multiple trucks carrying a large amount of inventory and divert them to unload specific merchandise just in time for ready sale. This aspect saves time and minimizes inventory space. As shown in Figure 7-2, a handheld device works through a satellite-based wireless system to communicate with trucks that have

BOX 7-4
Examples of companies making progress on location-centric commerce

OfficeDepot (www.officedepot.com)—This site is personalized by postal code. The site displays the product availability at the store, which covers the customer's postal code. The customer can also order products and choose either to pick up the products at the local store or have them delivered.

Circuit City (www.circuitcity.com)—This site's store locator lets customers find all the stores in the vicinity of a given city or postal code. Customers can then select up to three stores to check for product availability.

Go2Online (www.go2online.com)—This mobile site allows users to search for directions and phone numbers for a variety of local establishments such as restaurants, shops, theatres, hospitals, police stations, and gas stations.

Autoweb (www.autoweb.com/)—In this site's used car section, users can look for a car from a particular manufacturer, with a certain price range, and within a certain distance from the user.

Ecompare (sprint2.ecomparewireless.com)—This mobile site allows users to compare the price of a particular product at one store with the same product at another store. This mobile site allows users to compare the price of that product with prices at other sites online.

SOURCE: http://corp.cellmania.com/newsroom/whitepapers/whitepapers_local.html.

onboard intra-truck communication (Varshney et al. 2001). Assembly plants, supermarkets, airlines, and other mass-transit corporations are candidates for location tracking systems.

In addition to mobile inventory management, another benefit of mobile commerce benefits the consumer. A consumer uses a mobile unit such as a palm pilot to access a database of particular products, the stores that sell them, and their respective prices. Rather than going from one store to another, the customer sends a signal (called a query) to the database that searches each vendor's inventory system and recommends the nearest location where the customer could purchase the product (see Figure 7-3).

Overall, the main benefits of m-commerce are convenience and flexibility with true anytime, anywhere access. There is also the advantage of efficiency for the store and the customer.

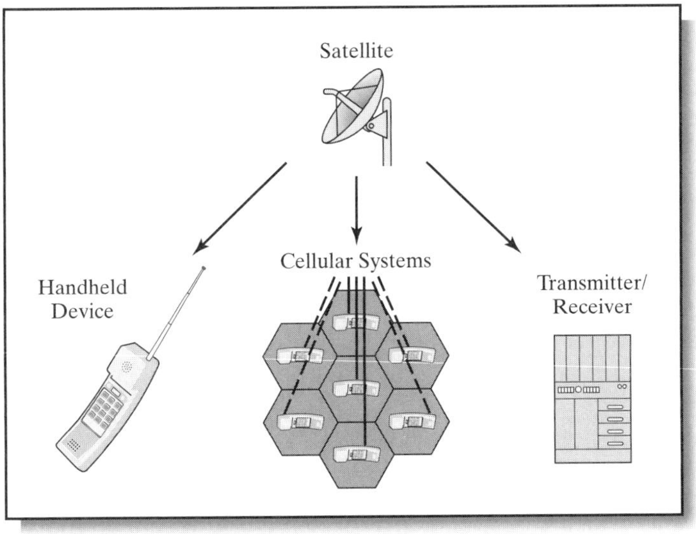

Figure 7-2 Location tracking of goods

Source: Varshney, U., Vetter, R. J., and Kalakota, R., "Mobile Commerce: A New Frontier," *Computer*, Oct. 2000, 32–38.

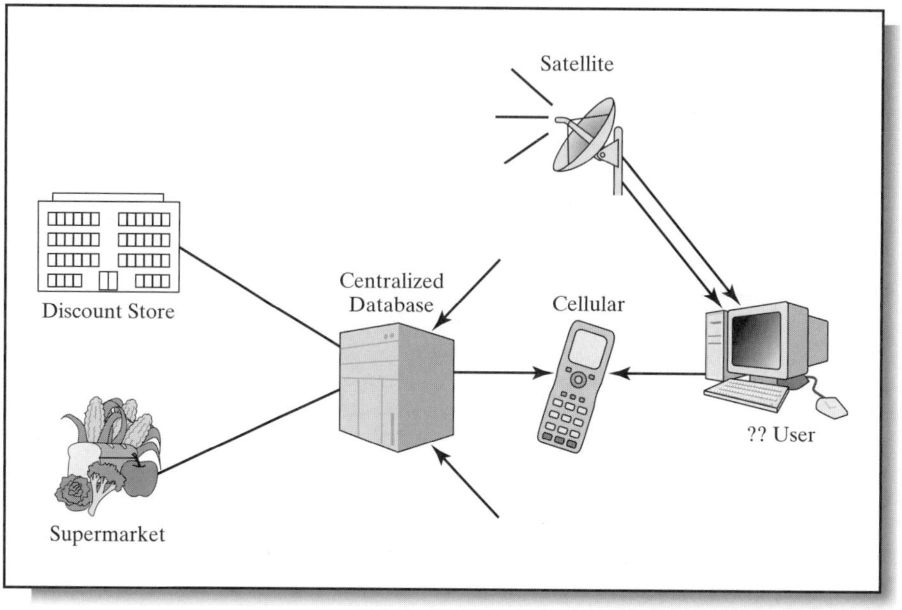

Figure 7-3
Product location—A conceptual view
Source: Adapted from Varshney et al. (op cit., 3).

Wireless Application Protocol (WAP): open, global, industry-wide mobile specifications for wireless network architecture; application environment and a set of communication protocols.

The key service is mobility. The road map to wireless Web growth began in 1998, with the first release of a standard, called **Wireless Application Protocol (WAP).** This standard is designed to deliver messages and data traffic to mobile phones within a geographical area. A year later, Japan introduced I-mode, which attracted 5 million users by year-end. More progress was made between 2000 and 2002, leading to the introduction of new third-generation (3G) networks that operate at more than 30 times the speed of earlier systems. Analysts forecast about 200 million users by late 2003 (Reinhardt 2001, 27).

Wi-Fi Is the Key

The key to the growing surge of wireless Internet access is Wi-Fi (wireless fidelity), which represents a collection of related wireless technologies. It speaks to the Internet's powerful allure of an "always-on" connected world, which makes it possible to share things anytime that otherwise might cost money (*Washington Post* 2003). It is an emerging industry standard that makes it possible for hardware firms to create wireless products that communicate with one another. It also sends Web pages and phone calls via radio waves, bypassing the expense of cables and high-speed Internet service in the United States. In Iraq, for example, the rebuilding effort since the end of the war in 2003 could be to skip the build-out of traditional phone and cable networks altogether. According to one source, Wi-Fi equipment makers such as Cisco Systems are discussing with government agencies the possibilities for Wi-Fi in Iraq. Meantime, Wi-Fi has already been proved in remote places such as Mount Everest, Indonesia, and Native American reservations. On Mount Everest, Yaks carry Wi-Fi gear to the mount base camp at 17,000 feet at a cybercafe that opened in April 2003. Climbers and support personnel use the technology for e-mail and phone calls round the clock (Kessler 2003).

The appeal of Wi-Fi is for home users as well as in business. For home users, going wireless means sharing a high-speed Internet connection with many computers without having to connect them by wires everywhere. The heart of a home wireless infrastructure is a device called an *access point*. The device plugs into a home owner's Internet connection, which spreads Internet access to the rest of a house, up to 300 feet. Similarly, in a business, Wi-Fi makes the work environment more mobile and easier to shift work spaces around offices within the firm. Likewise, business travelers at airports or airport lounges can access e-mail while waiting for flights (Wingfield 2003).

On the international scene, with speed a major challenge, a new version of the popular Wi-Fi standard (Wireless G) was introduced in 2003 that works with the older one (wireless B) and is five times as fast. This development can now zip music files between computers and let laptop users surf the Web from coffee shops to airport stops at impressive speeds. The new product can stream a number of high-quality videos simultaneously, while the older standard can barely handle one stream under normal conditions (Henderson 2003).

Despite progress made on Wi-Fi, security remains a major concern. Hackers have been able to crack data-scrambling software that comes with most wireless hardware, making it easy to snoop on private exchange transmitted through the air. So far, the benefits have far exceeded the limitations, especially when an effort is being made by a major firm to address the security factor for home or business use.

E-commerce continues to grow at phenomenal rates, although most of the development involves wired infrastructures. As wireless networks grow, m-commerce is bound to offer new avenues for growth and new opportunities in this emerging frontier. Plunging prices and easier deployment already are paying off. Even small companies can justify wireless systems once available only to giants such as United Parcel Service Inc. Device makers continue to come out with smarter and smaller handhelds. As exemplified in Box 7-5, the wireless Web works in four major areas.

- Wireless work environments, such as offices that transmit data from a company's Intranet to employees on the move. Several hospitals and family practice facilities have designed a wireless network for staff to check charts and patient data, which eliminates handwriting errors. In one case, the respiratory therapy group of one hospital cut staff by 20 percent, saving $1.5 million a year, and the group handled 13 percent more patients.

BOX 7-5
Why wireless?

Ten years ago, U.S. Fleet Services considered building a wireless network for its drivers, but soon decided against it. Customizing mobile devices and developing software was too hard, and the company didn't have computer systems robust enough to make it worth the hassle. Then, last year, U.S. Fleet revisited the technology—and this time it put the pedal to the metal.

In hospitals, offices, and factories, a standard called Wi-Fi (aka 802.11b) that connects devices to wireless networks is simplifying installations. This year, employees using Wi-Fi network are expected to more than double, to 12 million, according to Gartner Inc. Another boost: Tiny radios can now track parts in warehouses or alert techies when machines are on the blink.

The biggest action is in reaching out to field personnel. In years past, Pepsi Bottling Group Inc.'s 700 soda fountain technicians spent too much time on the phone instead of time fixing

(*continued*)

BOX 7-5
Continued

the company's 1.3 million vending and fountain machines. Customers called in problems, then a call-center employee paged a technician, who would ring for details about the job. At the end of the day, repair workers would fax in forms detailing their visits—with results not available on Pepsi's intranet until 5 days later.

That system is on its way to the trash heap. Pepsi's technicians now have off-the-shelf handheld devices. Dispatchers today retrieve from Pepsi's intranet everything the technicians need to know about a job and zap it off to the paperback-sized handheld. When the job's done, the technician sends an electronic bill to headquarters. At the same time, the handheld automatically tells the stockroom which parts were used so when the technician stops in for supplies, replacements are waiting for pickup.

The payoff? Pepsi answers calls 20 percent faster than it used to and has saved $7 million—meaning the project will pay for itself in just 2 years. "When we tried to figure out why customers switched to our competitors, part of the answer was customer service and equipment failure," said a senior vice president of Pepsi.

SOURCE: Green, Heather, "Winging Into Wireless," *BusinessWeek*, February 18, 2002, EB9.

- Employees on the move help companies reach suppliers and improve customer service. Through a wireless network, service response time can be cut dramatically. Errors from the once-popular fax machine are all but gone.
- Smart environment, where wireless devices in a warehouse or a manufacturing facility can be programmed to automatically collect from neighboring computers data about workflow, status of inventory or parts availability, and so on. This means no more handwritten reports or bills and missed deliveries.
- Wireless devices open new shortcuts to stock trading, banking, and more. It is now possible to have direct access to and control over one's personal finances. Bankers, brokers, and others are pushing custom-tailored financial services by advances in communications and trading technologies.

Key Limitations

No technology or system exists without limitations. One limitation is distance. For desktop computers, access points can reach up to 1,800 feet. For laptops, it is much shorter. Even though wireless signals go through walls and other barriers, they attenuate (weaken) en route. The network's range can be extended through repeaters that refresh the weak signal before sending it anew.

Speed is another limitation. The wireless network that uses the 802.11b standard runs at 11 megabits per second. This is one-ninth the speed of the wired network. This means it takes longer to send a large file by wireless. A third limitation of wireless technology are the security and privacy factors. As we shall explain later in the chapter, wireless security requires special technical safeguards to protect the integrity of e-mail and other data broadcast via radio waves. When wireless networks transmit data as radio signals, virtually anyone in the vicinity can tap into the data with the right software. To address this threat, every wireless product comes from the vendor equipped with built-in encryption (Gomes 2001, R16).

Finally, there is the question of privacy. The ability to track users is the number one privacy concern related to the growth of the wireless industry. Do you really want your cell phone to disclose to anyone where you are all the time? As explained in Box 7-6, con-

BOX 7-6
Location-centric issues

Privacy advocates say the ability to track users—the crucial element for many visions of mobile commerce—is the number one privacy concern related to the growth of the wireless industry. "This is as close as we've ever come to Big Brother," says Andrew Shen, policy analyst for the Electronic Privacy Information Center in Washington, D.C. "It creeps people out."

Wireless carriers are hoping that phone customers won't have the same concerns as Mr. Shen. Triangulation, one technique that will be used, locates callers by measuring how far they are from at least two or three communications towers, by tracking the length of time it takes for the signal to reach the different towers. Another technology matches patterns created as radio waves are emitted by cell phones and then bounce off buildings and other obstacles to a communications tower where the waves are matched against a database of thousands of pattern variations that can indicate the origin of a call.

BUILDING A PROFILE

Once location systems are up and running, location companies and carriers "will be able to build an enormous profile of a person's physical movements. And if you couple that with the browsing and purchasing profile Web sites, such as DoubleClick or Amazon.com, we already have, it could be an Orwellian nightmare."

The risk of treading on customers' privacy is huge. Paul Reddick, vice president of product management and development for the Wireless division of telecom company Sprint Corp., says carriers are working hard to preserve their customers' privacy, being careful about which vendors they set up partnerships with. He adds that Sprint is looking at contractually obliging vendors to maintain privacy.

SOURCE: Sullivan, Allanna, "Someone to Watch Over You," *The Wall Street Journal*, December 11, 2000, R8.

sumers should be able to control who sees their location information. Yet, when consumers receive valuable services, they must be willing to give up their privacy.

Unfortunately, Wi-Fi is vulnerable to hackers. While setting up a wireless network gives people freedom to access the Internet without their PCs being tethered to cables, most of such networks are unprotected and vulnerable to hackers who could steal data, launch spam, or attack other PCs. According to Poole's 2003 survey, unprotected wireless systems remains above 60 percent (*Washington Post* 2003).

CRITICAL SUCCESS FACTORS

For m-commerce to be successful, four critical factors are monitored.

- **Mobility:** Most people consider their mobility critical to their lifestyle. Any m-service offered must take into account people's mobility and profile of usage if it is to benefit financially through m-sales and m-services.
- **Personalization:** This means identifying and following up on each customer's market segment and determining the best options for them. This is considered individualized service, similar to what they would get in a reputable brick-and-mortar store.
- **Global standardization:** This critical success factor has two aspects. First, for m-commerce, customers want to continue moving around without having to change services or worry about taxation, legal rules, or other constraints that are unique to

each country. Second, customers look for standardization in terms of one bill, one password, and one user interface. This will make it easier and quicker to transact business in a mobile environment.

- **Customer profiling:** This area of specialization addresses customer needs over a time period via certain behavior such as advertising, promotions, or special offers. This attempt takes into consideration personalization features, as well as customization.

When m-commerce was new business, the network was a major key success factor. Hearing quality and availability were the key concerns. Today's concentration is on customer satisfaction, which means paying greater attention to customer needs for services and quality. That is why customer control management is increasing in importance. A separate section is covered in Chapter 10.

How Wireless Technology Is Employed

Bluetooth™

Bluetooth: a universal, low-cost, wireless connection standard.

A growing wireless connection standard, **Bluetooth** is a universal, low-cost, wireless technology designed for short-range radio hookup for wireless connectivity among computers, scanners, and printers. It allows any Bluetooth-enabled device to communicate with other similar devices, regardless of manufacture. It is a type of wireless networking that allows electronic devices to communicate and share information without action from a user, wires, or cables. These devices include cell phones, Palm Pilots, computers, home appliances, headphones, and keyboards. Bluetooth communicates on a radio-frequency band of 2.45 gigahertz radio spectrum to wirelessly connect devices within 10 to 100 yards. Steps have been taken to prevent any interference with other systems (see Figure 7-4).

The concept was initially developed by Swedish mobile phone maker L. M. Ericsson in 1994 to make it possible for laptops to make calls over a mobile phone. Bluetooth is named after King Harald "Bluetooth" Blaatand II of Denmark (940–981 A.D.). He earned his nickname from the blueberries he ate that stained his teeth. Bluetooth unified

Figure 7-4
International radio frequency allocation

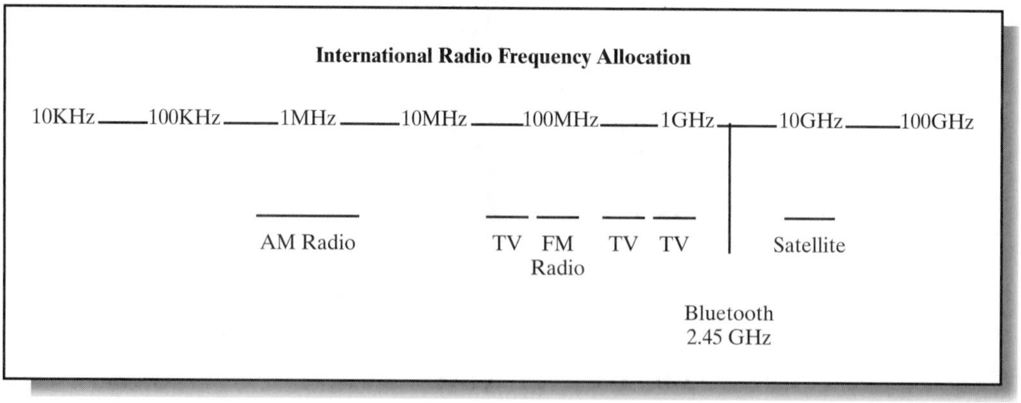

Denmark and Norway during his reign. Ericsson hoped that the new standard would unite the telecommunications and computing industries, as well.

Bluetooth SIG

In February 1998, Ericsson, IBM, Intel, Nokia, and Toshiba formed a Bluetooth Special Interest Group (SIG) to develop standards for the technology, hoping to expedite its development and final adoption. One of the SIG's goals is to gain global acceptance so that Bluetooth devices can be used anywhere in the world.

The SIG divides itself into two categories: Promoter members and associate companies work together like a board of directors to make decisions for the SIG. The associate companies are members of different work groups, and each has a charter outlining the work group's goals. For instance, the scope of the Car Profile working group is to ensure device interoperability in the car environment by wirelessly connecting portable and car-embedded devices using the technology defined in the Bluetooth specification (www.bluetooth.com/sig/sig/sig.asp. Accessed May 2003, since deleted). Companies work within these work groups to develop standard devices for universal adoption by manufacturers.

Main Capabilities

Bluetooth uses short-range radio links to allow wireless communication between computers and all types of portable, electronic devices, forming small, private networks. In one respect, it is an enabling technology. It creates a common language between various electronic devices that makes it possible for them to communicate and connect with one another.

The key Bluetooth features include low cost, low power consumption, low complexity, and robustness. As shown in Figure 7-5, Bluetooth-enabled laptops can communicate

Screen Capture 7-2

Source: Bluetooth logos and trademark are property of Bluetooth SIG Inc. and are used under the license of Prentice Hall. Copyright © 2003–2004. All rights reserved.

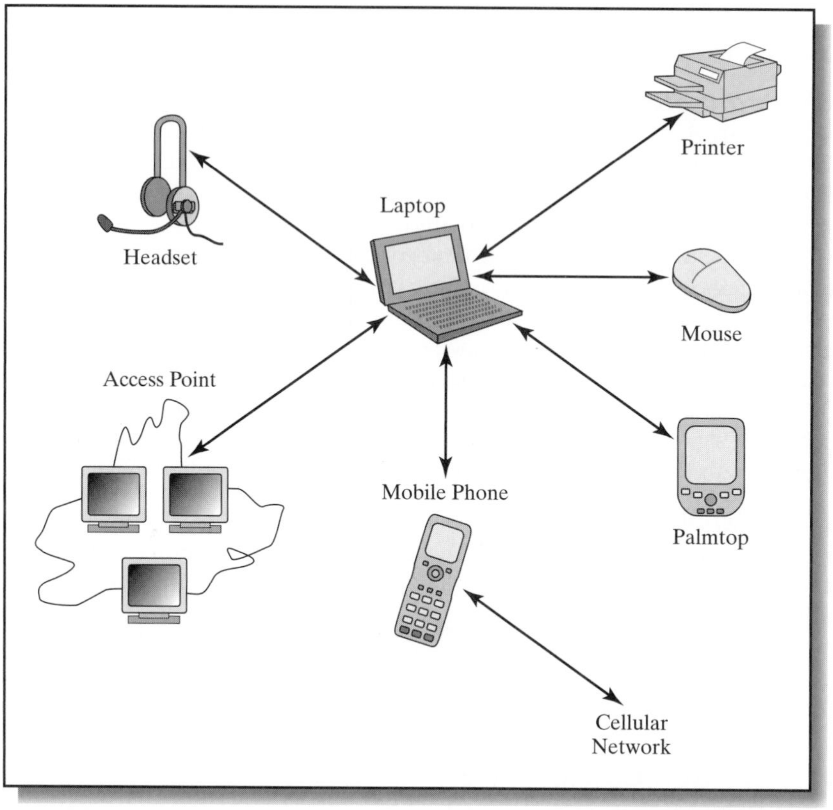

Figure 7-5
Wireless connections using Bluetooth

with palmtops and mobile phones to synchronize schedules and contacts. Bluetooth-enabled printers and mice can communicate without the tangle of serial port cables. Bluetooth also enables wireless access to LANs, the mobile phone network, and the Internet for a variety of portable handheld devices and home appliances (Kansal 2002).

Bluetooth devices send out weak, 1-milliwatt signals that limit their ranges in order to avoid interference. It is possible to have multiple devices in a room, because Bluetooth makes frequency overlapping unlikely with a technique called spread-spectrum frequency hopping. This "hopping" refers to a device changing regularly between the use of 79 randomly selected frequencies within an indicated range. With Bluetooth transmitting change frequencies 1,600 times per second, it is improbable that two would be operating on the exact same frequency at the same time.

radio layer: primary layer in Bluetooth architecture.

piconet: group of devices connected to a common channel, identified by its unique hop sequence.

Protocol Architecture

Bluetooth SIG has released specifications for various Bluetooth architecture layers to speed the development of devices and applications. A primary layer, called **radio layer,** forms the physical connection interface that oversees transmission within a small network called piconet. A **piconet** is a group of devices connected to a common channel, identified with its unique hop sequence (see Figure 7-6). In addition, this

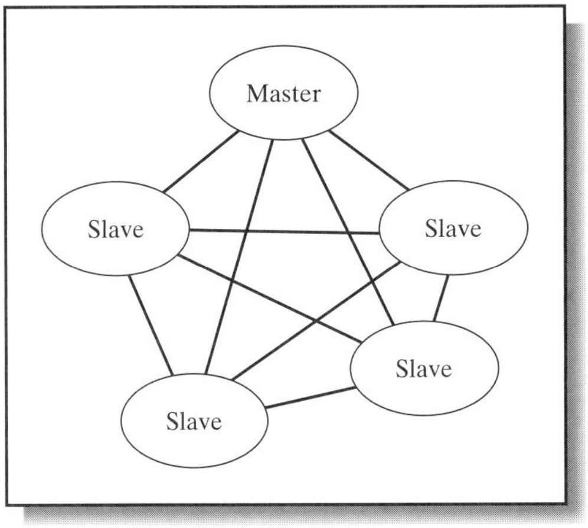

Figure 7-6
Two Bluetooth devices connected together create a network called a piconet. A single master device controls from one to seven slave devices.

baseband: second layer in Bluetooth architecture; converts the data into signals that the radio interprets and converts to a frequency of 2.4 GHz.

Link Manager Protocol (LMP): a Bluetooth layer that sets up ongoing link management with Bluetooth devices.

logical link control and adaptation protocol (L2CAP): is layered over the Baseband Protocol and resides in the data link layer.

layer specifies frequency, modulation scheme, and transmission power as a core protocol (see Figure 7-7).

The second layer is **baseband,** which with a radio and an antenna makes up the physical transmission component of a Bluetooth device. The baseband processor converts the data into signals that the radio interprets and converts to a frequency of 2.4 gigahertz. The signal is then transmitted through the air by the antenna and is received by the antenna of another Bluetooth device, which receives the data and processes it in the reverse order. The devices must be within 30 feet of each other, as radio signals suffer propagation (loss) effects at distances of greater length (www.darwinmag.com/learn/curve/column.html?ArticleID =12. Accessed June 2003).

After the baseband layer, the next stack is **Link Manager Protocol (LMP).** This layer sets up ongoing link management with Bluetooth devices. This includes security features such as authentication and encryption. Upper layer protocols are adapted to the baseband layer via **logical link control and adaptation protocol (L2CAP)**. See Figure 7-6.

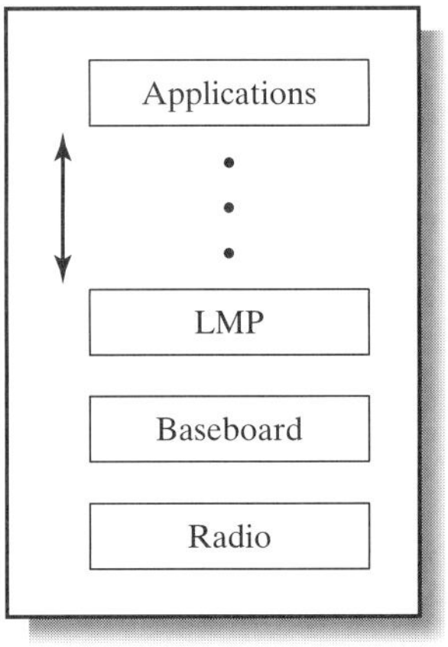

Figure 7-7
Basic protocol architecture components

Unfortunately, Bluetooth is not the only technology operating within the 2.4-GHz region. HomeRF and 802.11, as well as the militaries of France, Spain, and Japan, transmit within this band, and officials wonder if the technologies will interfere with one another and cause errors (Bethoney 2001). Bluetooth combats this problem through the use of frequency "hopping," which reduces the number of frame collisions using short data packets.

Link Management Protocol (LMP) performs three important functions.

- **Piconet management:** A group of devices are connected to a common channel with a unique hop sequence. In this arrangement, an initiating device (master) and the receiving device (slave) are linked and detached by the LMP and can switch their roles, when necessary.
- **Link configuration:** The LMP ensures that the Bluetooth device does not operate below specified performance limits. If a device sits idle for a specified time period, LMP minimizes power consumption by transferring the device to a "parked" state and also allows another device to join the piconet.
- **Security functions:** LMP controls various security functions in Bluetooth transmission. It monitors authentication of other devices trying to make a connection and manages the encryption keys used to establish secure links.

Bluetooth Applications

Application development is the responsibility of the individual work groups within the Bluetooth SIG. Current projects include car kits to allow for hands-free operation while driving, headsets to access devices stored away (cell phone in a purse), and synchronization software to keep schedule and contact data on personal devices up to date (www.ee.iitb.ernet.in/uma/~aman/bluetooth/tut2.html. Accessed June 2003). In terms of distance, the range of each radio is 10 meters (30 feet), which can be extended to 100 meters with a special amplifier.

Although the technical aspects of the Bluetooth standard enable easy and efficient wireless communication between devices, the technology will be effective in everyday life only if the products have a true impact on the consumer. As the technology gains greater acceptance by end users, production and innovation should improve in kind. A study by Cahners In-Stat Group predicts up to 1.4 billion Bluetooth-enabled devices by 2005 (www.inquiry.com/pubs/infoworld/vol22/issues51/001218hnenable.asp. Accessed June 2003.).

Products

Most of today's products feature wireless networking. Companies such as 3Com, Socket Communications, and Brainboxes have developed products that enable computer components to communicate with each other automatically (www.Palowireless.com/bluetooth/products.asp. Accessed June 2003). These products include printer modules that remotely connect computers within the personal area network to printers, and wireless networking devices that remotely connect computers to a broader network and to the Internet.

Bluetooth development is finding early success with wireless phones. Motorola, Ericsson, and Nokia have all developed Bluetooth-enabled phones that make the "wireless personal area network" more of a reality. For example, Motorola's Timeport 270 was designed to work with the Bluetooth Smart Module accessory and the Bluetooth PC card to allow all of a user's electronic devices to communicate seamlessly (www.beststuff.com/articles/737. Accessed June 2003.). Additionally, Motorola has developed a hands-free car kit for use with Bluetooth phones, which will make use of a wireless phone while driving much safer and more user friendly.

One factor that greatly limits the volume of Bluetooth devices is the technology itself. The technology has undergone significant changes in the past few years, making development much more difficult due to the lack of a stable platform for testing new products. The rapid development of application suites and the solidification of standards by the SIG should help counteract this problem.

The true potential of Bluetooth lies in applications that have yet to be developed. Bluetooth's ability to link multiple devices together holds limitless possibilities. For instance, Cambridge Consultants developed two Bluetooth products for day-to-day, less tech-savvy individuals. One device, called the "e-mail pen," enables users to read and write e-mail anywhere in their home without using a computer. The pen translates handwritten messages into computer text, which it then sends to the "pod" to create the e-mail and send it out over a phone line.

Another product is a car key to allow secure remote entry and possibly allow for fingerprint identification. It is capable of activating personal settings, displaying fuel status and mileage, generating diagnostic information, and much more (www.cambridge-consultants.com. Accessed June 2003.).

Security Issues

Even though each piconet link is encoded against eavesdropping and interference, security issues could stall Bluetooth development. One flaw could allow a hacker to obtain the encryption key to a device and "listen in" on communication between two devices or pretend to be a device and send false messages to the other party. Another issue is to allow unwanted individuals to track a device as it moves and eavesdrop on the other device's conversation. However, each case requires specialized skills on the intruder's part to succeed.

Screen Capture 7-3

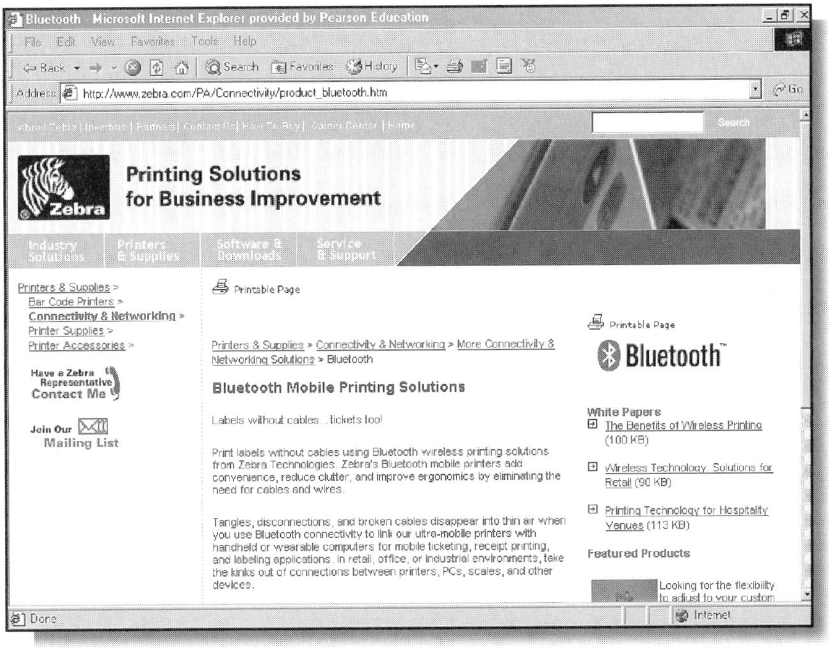

There two basic concerns in wireless security.

- The transmitted message must be protected all the way to its destination host to ensure that it is delivered intact.
- The host system must verify or authenticate the user it is communicating with. Without such a security move, the host system is left vulnerable to all kinds of wireless hacking

Wireless security centers on wireless Ethernet networks using Wi-Fi (Wireless Fidelity) at speeds up to 11 million bits per second over 100 meters (Kay 2002, 38). As a wireless network standard, Wi-Fi is growing in popularity, especially in colleges and universities throughout the United States. It is ideal for frequent transmission of high-bandwidth files or for devices needing constant network or Internet connectivity www.3com.com (see Box 7-7).

Wi-Fi equipment works like a cordless telephone. It invisibly extends a fast Internet connection up to 1,500 feet to any laptop or computer equipped with a wireless receiver. This makes it ideal for a business with officers to share the same stationary Internet connection, paying for only a single hookup (Drucker and Angwin 2002).

Wired Equivalent Privacy (WEP): part of Wi-Fi security mechanism that makes it possible to encrypt messages before heading for their destination.

Other security standards exist, but most of today's wireless networks depend on the 80211b standard. Part of Wi-Fi is a security mechanism called **Wired Equivalent Privacy (WEP),** which makes it possible to encrypt messages before heading for their destination. Even then, concern still looms about the adequacy of security. An attacker

BOX 7-7
Wi-Fi in schools despite insecurity

Many universities are enthusiastically turning to Wi-Fi, including Buena Vista University in Storm Lake, Iowa, where 145 Wi-Fi access points are installed across the 1,400-student campus.

The rollout in mid-2000 was originally secured with 40-bit WEP encryption, but security has been enhanced with WEP-plus technology. To lessen the chances of student hackers changing their grades or reducing their tuition bills, Buena Vista has kept its registrar and business offices on the wired Ethernet LAN. The university will eventually upgrade to more secure protocols such as 802.11a but so far hasn't installed firewalls behind the wireless access points as some analysts recommend.

"We have, in general, the sense of security here," Clipperton, managing director of information systems at Ayaya, Inc. in Basking Ridge, New Jersey, noted that the wireless network cost less than $400,000, about one-third of the cost of wiring classrooms and other buildings.

Boingo Wireless Inc. in Santa Monica, California, boasts that it has 500 "hot-spot" Wi-Fi WLANs ready to serve the public in hotels and airports nationwide. Users can download free Boingo sniffer software that lets them find Wi-Fi networks. The cost is up to $75 per month for unlimited service. An additional $30 provides a personal VPN for users.

Although the company can't be sure if concerns over Wi-Fi security have cut into sales of its service, Boingo decided to provide the personal VPN if a customer's company doesn't have one, because "we knew customers needed a solution to overcome the widely publicized shortcomings of Wi-Fi," says Christian Gunning, director of product management.

SOURCE: Hamblin, Matt, "IT Rolls Out Wireless LANs," *Computerworld*, March 25, 2002, 48.

can access a wireless network from outside the organization with no physical connection, which compromises the security infrastructure (see Figure 7-8).

Briefly, WEP uses a secret key to encrypt messages transmitted between a mobile station and a base station connected to a wired network. The mobile station accepts each message after verifying its authenticity. A 40-bit key is standard but vulnerable to security threats. Even the latest 128-bit key is not fully secure. In 2001, Ian Goldberg, a Canadian cryptologist, broke WEP. However, it takes know-how and practical experience in cryptology to break down a seemingly secure standard (Kay 2002, 38).

Satellite Technology

repeater: a device that extends the distance of a physical link.

Most of today's "long-haul" data transmission is made possible via satellites circling Earth. A **repeater** in a satellite receives the signal representing the data and "repeats" the signal to another location—normally to an Earth station. A special frequency band is used to transmit to the satellite. The satellite regenerates the signal and transmits back to an Earth station at a different frequency band. Repeating a signal from one Earth station to another takes approximately 250 milliseconds (Ciampa 2002, 5).

To illustrate, a nationwide fresh produce truck might be equipped with a satellite communication system to accept data from headquarters or relay customer data directly to its truck. One technology revolves around a smart wireless computer terminal

Figure 7-8
The threat to wireless security

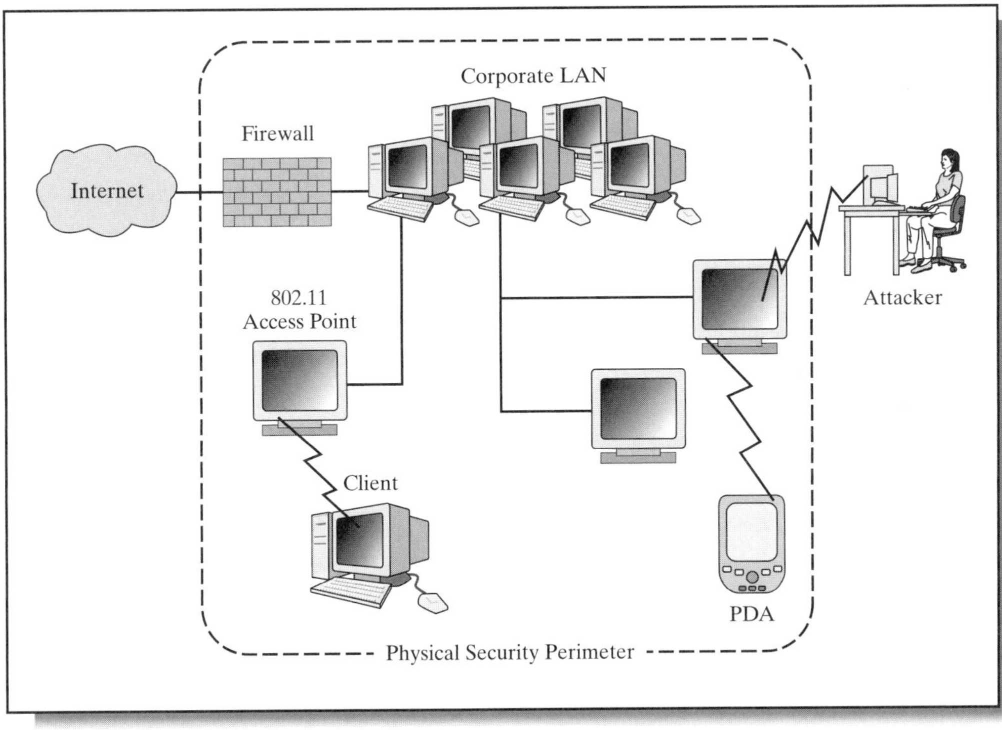

Source: Kay, Russell, "Wireless Security," *Computerworld*, June 24, 2002, 38.

installed in the steering wheel of the truck. Time-sensitive pickup orders, route alerts, or changes in pickup schedule are transmitted from headquarters to the truck via satellite. The truck makes appropriate adjustments on the proper route to destination without delay (see Figure 7-9).

2G Digital Cellular Technology

Once the information is received by the online truck terminal, the driver drives to the address where the pickup is available. The driver leaves the truck with a handheld device, called **Personal Digital Assistant (PDA).** After the vendor fills out the shipping form (name of sender, produce in the box, and the grocer's name and address), the driver enters a preprinted tracking number into the PDA, which has a scanning facility and a keyboard. Once complete, the PDA prints out a routing label and pastes it onto the box before loading it onto the truck. The information stored in the PDA is transmitted instantly to the terminal in the truck via a cellular tower using wireless digital cellular technology.

Personal Digital Assistant (PDA): handheld device that scans information and transmits it to a terminal in a vehicle via wireless digital cellular technology.

Palm Pilot

PDAs are one of the fastest-selling consumer devices in history. Computer organizers originated in the 1990s, but they were too big, expensive, and complicated. In 1996, the original Palm Pilot was introduced, and it was a hit with consumers. It was small enough to fit in a shirt pocket, ran for weeks on AAA batteries, was easy to use, and could store a lot of information. The two types of PDAs are handheld computers and palm-sized computers. The major differences between the two are size and display.

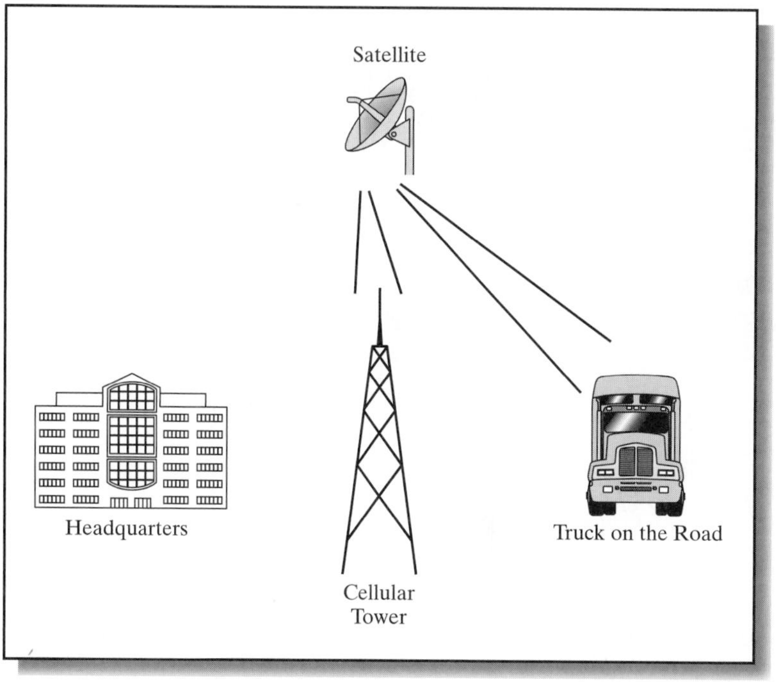

Figure 7-9
Basic satellite network

No matter what type of PDA you have, they share the same major features. Both store basic programs in a read-only memory (ROM) chip and are powered by batteries. Both have some type of LCD display screen that is used for output and input. The handheld computers have input devices that typically use a miniature keyboard, and the palm-sized computers use a touch screen exclusive in combination with a handwriting recognition program. This program allows the user to draw characters on the touch screen, and the software converts the characters to letters and numbers. Figure 7-10 sketches the parts that can make up a PDA.

data synchronization: the communication between a PDA and a personal computer.

Mobile Telecommunications Switching Office (MTSO): cellular switch that places calls from land-based telephones to wireless customers.

Palm Pilots function similarly to cellular phones. The communication between a PDA and a personal computer is referred to as **data synchronization.** This is done mostly through a serial number connecting to an infrared light to beam information. These devices are all located in the microprocessor, which serves as the brain of the PDA. The microprocessor coordinates all of the PDA's functions according to programmed instructions stored in the operating system. In order to gain Internet access, the microprocessor also must connect to the **Mobile Telecommunications Switching Office (MTSO)** to be located in a certain cell site (Freudenrich 2002, 1).

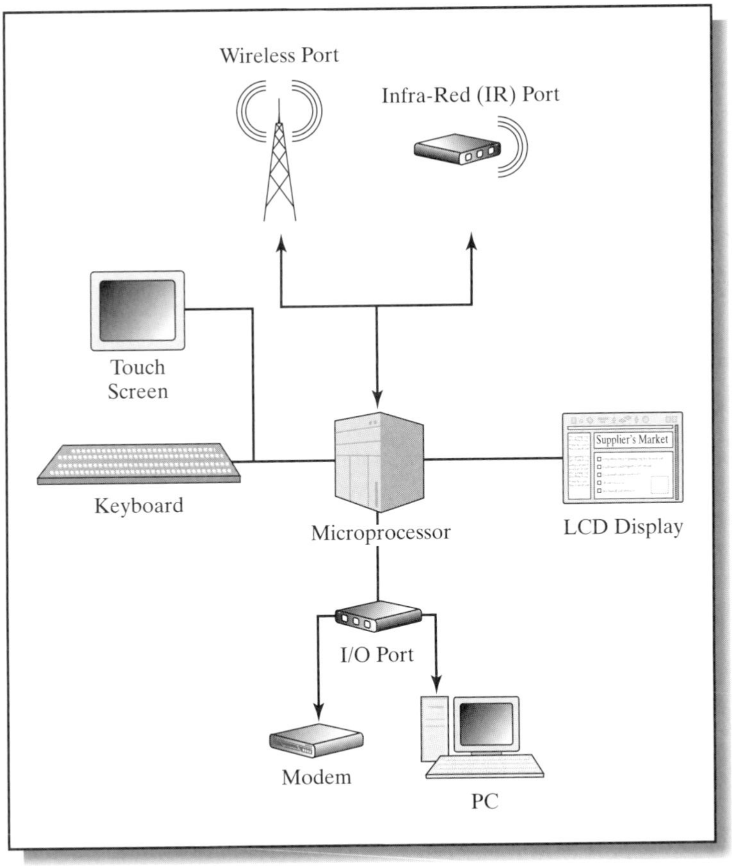

Figure 7-10
Key parts of a PDA

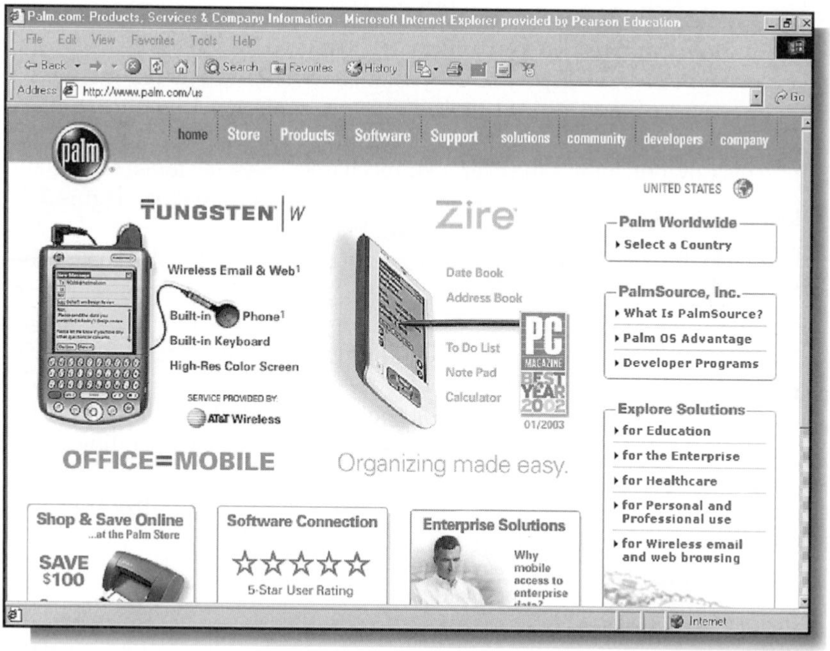

Screen Capture 7-4

Cellular Phones

Wireless communications work around specific cells or geographic areas. When you are in a certain cell, you can access wireless communications. Cellular radio provides mobile telephone service by employing a network of cell sites distributed over a wide area. A cell site contains a radio transceiver and a base station controller, which manages, sends, and receives traffic from the mobiles in its geographical area to a cellular telephone switch. It also employs a tower and antennas and provides a link to the distant cellular switch, the Mobile Telecommunications Switching Office. This MTSO places calls from land-based telephones to wireless customers, switches calls between cells as mobiles travel across cell boundaries, and authenticates wireless customers before they make calls.

Here is briefly how a cell phone works. When you power up the cell phone, it listens for a System Identification Code (SIC) on the control channel. The control channel is a special frequency that the phone and base station use to talk to one another about things like call setup and channel changing. If the phone cannot find any control channels to listen to, the user gets the annoying "Out of Range" or "No Service Found" display on the cell screen.

When the cell phone receives the SIC, the phone compares it to the SIC programmed into the phone. If the SICs match, the phone knows that the cell it is communicating with is part of its home system. Along with the SIC, the phone also transmits a registration request, and the MTSO keeps track of the phone's location in a database. This way, the MTSO knows which cell site you are in when it wants to ring your phone.

Once the MTSO gets a call, it tries to find you and your phone. It looks in the database to see which cell site you are in. The MTSO then picks up a frequency par that your

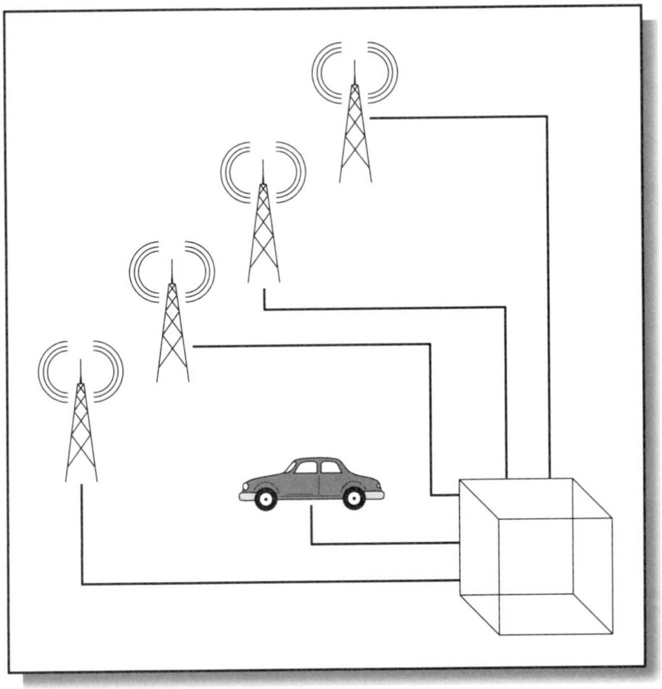

Figure 7-11
Signal passing from cell to cell during travel

Source: Adapted from Brain 2003, 1.

phone will use in that cell to take the call. It communicates with your phone over the control channel to tell it which frequencies to use. Once your phone and the tower switch to those frequencies, the call is connected (Brain 2003).

Once you move toward the edge of your cell site, your cell site's base station notes that your signal strength is diminishing. Meanwhile, the base station in the cell site you are moving toward sees your phone's signal strength increasing. The two base stations coordinate with each other through the MTSO. At that same point, your phone gets a signal on a control channel telling it to change frequencies. This hand-off switches your phone to the new cell (see Figure 7-11).

On the other hand, when the SIC on the control channel does not match the SIC programmed into the phone, the phone knows it is roaming. The MTSO of the cell site that you are roaming in contacts the MTSO of your home system, which then checks its database to confirm that the SIC of your cell phone is valid. Your home system verifies your phone to the local MTSO, which then tracks your phone as you move through the cell sites.

2G digital voice networks have earned respect since their introduction in 1990. The technology was updated in 1997, with a focus on improved speed and performance. The number of users of 2.5G standards reached 400 million worldwide in 2000. 3G voice and data technologies were introduced in 2001 and are expected to expand globally during the next 2 to 3 years (Biggs 2001). Despite promise, 3G technologies have a ways to go before adoption. The primary reason is that the mission-critical applications that sit in a corporate network use too much bandwidth to be accessed by wireless technology. These and other restrictions are expected to be worked out in the near future (Schwartz 2001).

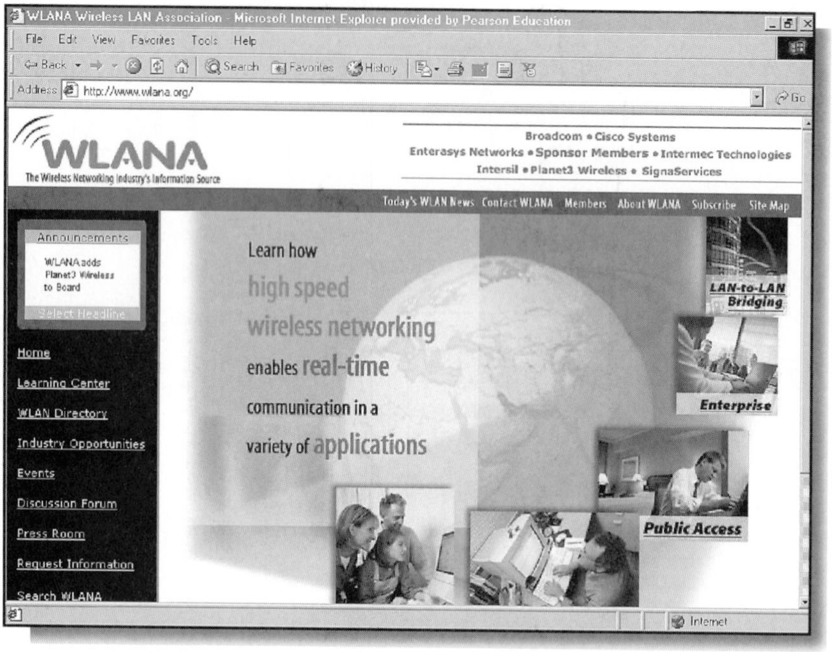

Screen Capture 7-5

WIRELESS LAN

Wireless Network Interface Card (WNIC): a card that interfaces between the wireless device and an access point for data or voice transmission and reception.

access point (AP): when a wireless station sends a frame to a server, an access point acts as a bridge that passes the frame over the wired LAN to the server.

The most common standard for wireless networking is Wireless Local-Area Networks (WLAN). The technology uses radio waves instead of a cable to connect laptops and other electronic devices to a LAN, using Ethernet connections over the air (Brewin 2002, 50). A WLAN is identical to a regular LAN, except that the devices are wireless. Each computer has a **Wireless Network Interface Card (WNIC)** with an antenna built into it. Signals from the WNIC are sent through radio waves to an **access point (AP).** The access point is bi-directional. It is designed to receive the signals and transmit them to the WNIC (see Figure 7-12).

WLAN design is flexible and is becoming cheaper to deploy. However, it only travels 150 feet. Most wireless LANs lack built-in security, leaving business networks open to potential hacking (Chen 2002). Security can be strengthened by adding higher-level encryption, depending on the sensitivity of the information transmitted and the security requirements of the users. The problem today is that user name plus password is weak. It is too easy, stuck on the wall, or borrowed from someone. In contrast, a strong password is difficult to deploy, requires frequent change, is too long to remember, or has too many "odd" characters. New algorithms should be available that will assure security and privacy of the communications transmitted.

Factors to Consider

For an organization to adopt wireless LAN technology, several factors must be considered.

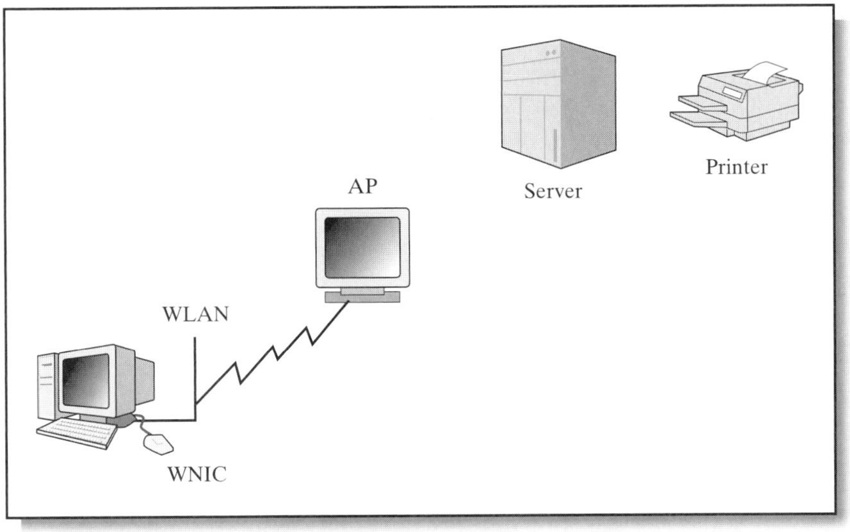

Figure 7-12
A typical WLAN in a business environment

- **Range and coverage:** The interaction between the airwaves and objects can affect how the energy propagates, which influences the coverage and range a particular wireless system achieves. Most WLANs use radio frequencies to allow the penetration of most indoor walls and objects. A typical WLAN infrastructure has a range from less than 100 feet to more than 300 feet. This coverage can be extended to allow roaming through the use of microcells.
- **Throughput:** The actual throughput or performance of a WLAN varies from system to system, but propagation effects significantly affect it and the type of WLAN technology implemented. The throughput of most commercial WLAN configurations is 1.6 Mbps and now more commonly 11 Mbps. These data rates provide enough throughput for most productivity applications such as e-mail exchanges, access to shared accessories (printers), Internet access, and the ability to access files and data from other users.
- **Security and integrity:** Wireless technology originally was developed for military applications to provide a secure and reliable means of communication. Current wireless technology provides connections that are far stronger and more reliable than cellular phone connections and has data integrity equal to or better than wired networks. WLANs already have security measures built in, making them more secure than most wired LANs. Security provisions such as encryption make it extremely difficult to gain unauthorized access to network traffic. In most WLAN configurations, individual nodes must be security enabled before they can access network traffic.
- **Cost and scalability:** The cost of a WLAN includes infrastructure cost (access points) and user cost (WLAN adapters). Infrastructure cost depends on the number of access points used and ranges in price from $1,000 to $2,000. The number of access points needed is based on the required coverage area and the number and type of users participating in the wireless network. The coverage area is proportional to the square of the product range ().

- User costs depend on the number of wireless LAN adapters (one per client device) and the cost of installing and maintaining a WLAN. Fortunately, WLANs are scalable and range from simple to complex systems. These networks can support a large number of nodes and large open areas by adding additional access points to increase or boost coverage.
- Standardization of WLANs: Widespread acceptance of wireless infrastructure depends on industry standardization to provide compatibility and reliability among vendors and manufacturers. In September 1999, IEEE ratified the 802.11b (High Rate) standard, which provides data rates of up to 11 Mbps. WLANs can now open new markets by achieving performance, availability, and throughput comparable to wired Ethernet.

Wireless Application Protocol (WAP)

With our lives becoming more dependent on personal electronic devices, we consider Internet viewing options on cell phones and Palm Pilots of greater value today. Wireless Internet services are in high demand as the digital cellular network continues to be a rapidly growing market. To address the challenge, a group of cellular phone companies agreed that a universal standard was vital for positive wireless Internet implementation. This was especially the case, because the HTML Internet standard is not efficient enough to allow communication via a wireless data network. As a result, they collaborated and created a Wireless Application Protocol, better known as WAP.

WAP Forum: an industry association; develops the world standard for wireless information and telephony services on digital mobile phones and other wireless devices.

WAP is the basis for the mobile Internet. It is a result of the **WAP Forum's** efforts to come up with industry-wide specifications for technology useful in developing applications and services unique to wireless communication networks. The objectives of the forum are to:

- Embrace existing standards and technology wherever possible.
- Create worldwide wireless protocol specifications that will work across differing wireless network architectures.
- Bring Internet content to digital cellular phones and other wireless terminals and devices.

The WAP concept is straightforward. Cellular devices are connected permanently to a wireless network. By adding an Internet protocol layer to the network, these devices and millions of users can be connected permanently to the Internet without having to dial in. With this protocol, one is able to access the Internet and keep in touch with anyone, anywhere, anytime via a micro browser–equipped wireless phone. Imagine you are in a meeting with a customer who wants to know the balance of her account. You call up her account through a secure connection and find out that she has just overdrawn her checking account. You alert her to use your cell phone to authorize an online transfer from her savings to checking to cover the balance before the account is charged a penalty.

This type of interactive electronic exchange marks the dawn of the Mobile Internet Revolution. The world of information is available not just on our desktops but at our fingertips, and the possibilities are truly endless.

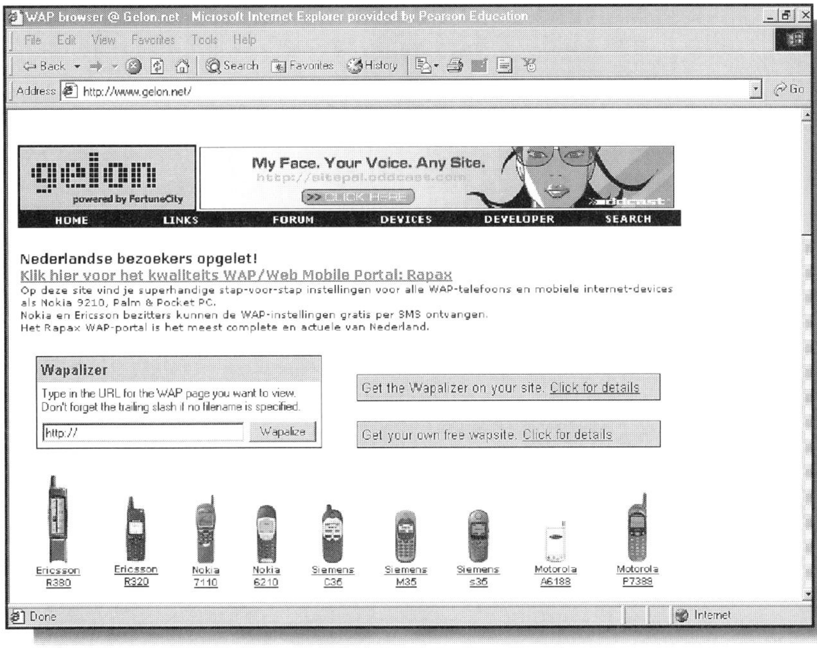

Screen Capture 7-6

How WAP Works

When one accesses a Web site from a PC Web browser, the user requests data and the server sends that data in the form of HTML over an IP network (see Chapter 3). The Web browser converts the HTML data into text and graphics. In contrast, on a mobile device, a WAP browser performs the role of a PC Web browser. It requests data from a Web site via a WAP gateway that acts as a "go-between" for a Web browser and a Web server. It translates the Web Markup Language (WML) to or from HTML. A markup language is a way of adding information to content that tells the device receiving the content what to do with it. It specifies the format and presentation of text and the hierarchies of pages, and it links their pages.

Wireless Application Environment (WAE): a WAP element that establishes an interoperable environment to allow operators and service providers to build applications and services for a large variety of wireless platforms.

Wireless Markup Language (WML): is based on XML, a markup language that has garnered enormous support due to its ability to describe data; in contrast with HTML, which is used to describe the display of data.

Figure 7-13 is a schematic of the WAP model. The architecture follows the OSI layering model covered in Chapter 2. The protocol gateway converts user requests from the WAP protocol stack to the Web protocol stack (HTTP and TCP/IP). Encoders and decoders convert WAP content into compact encoded formats to reduce the size of data sent over the network. Here is a brief summary of the functions of each element of the stack.

- **Wireless Application Environment (WAE)** is based on a combination of Web and mobile telephony technologies. Its job is to establish an interoperable environment to allow operators and service providers to build applications and services for a large variety of wireless platforms. It uses **Wireless Markup Language (WML)** optimized for use in handheld mobile terminals (see Figure 7-14).

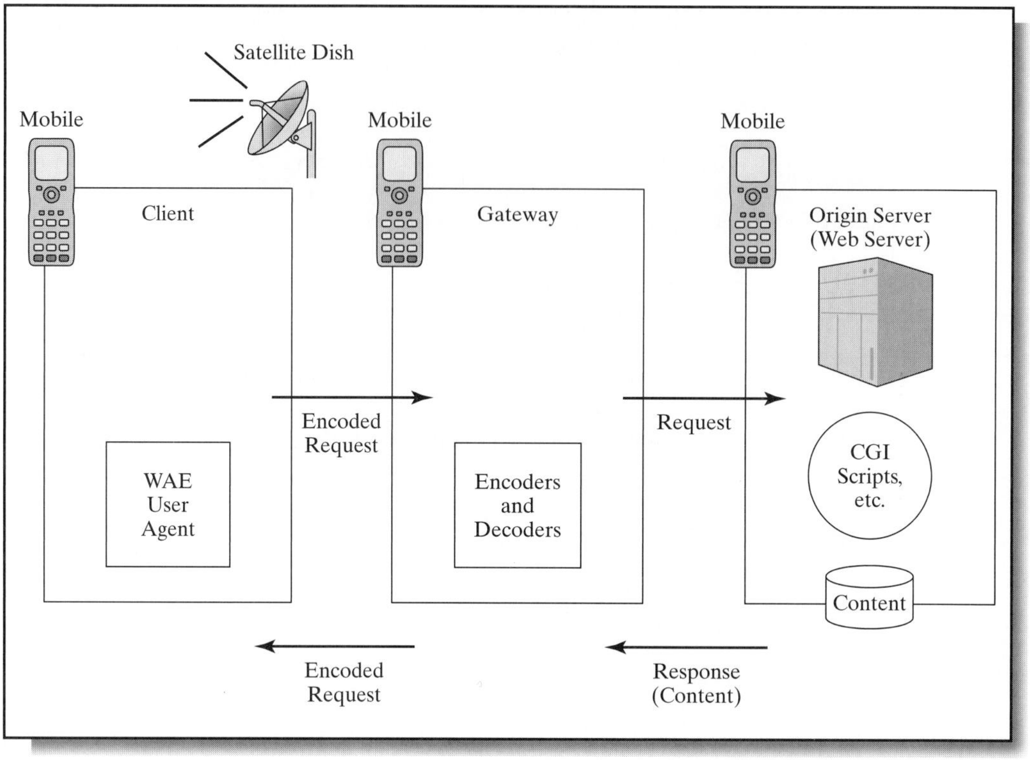

Figure 7-13
Schematic of the WAP model

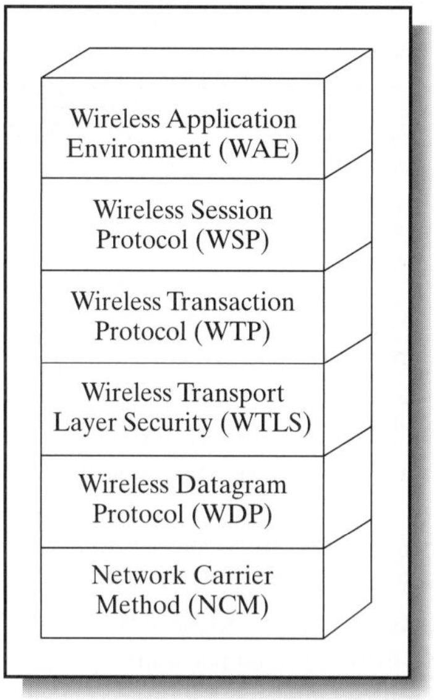

Figure 7-14
WAP protocol stack

Wireless Session Protocol (WSP): a WAP element that decides whether a network and a device will communicate back and forth or whether data will be transmitted straight from a network to the device.

Wireless Transaction Protocol (WTP): a WAP layer that ensures that data flow from one location to another efficiently based on a request/reply paradigm.

Wireless Transport Layer Security (WTLS): a WAP element that gives security to the system via encryption, data integrity verification, and authentication between the user and the server.

Wireless Datagram Protocol (WDP): a WAP feature that confirms easy adaptation to the WAP technology.

Network Carrier Method (NCM): a technology that a wireless provider uses.

- **Wireless Session Protocol (WSP):** WSP is an application layer with a consistent interface for two session services: whether a network and a device will communicate back and forth, a connection-oriented session, or whether data will be transmitted straight from a network to the device, which is a connectionless session. If the session is connection oriented, the data will go directly to the next layer down, the Wireless Transaction Protocol (WTP) layer. Otherwise, the data will be transmitted to the Wireless Datagram Protocol (WDL) layer.
- **Wireless Transaction Protocol (WTP):** This layer serves to ensure that data flow from one location to another efficiently based on request/reply paradigm. WTP is equivalent to the TCP layer of the TCP/IP OSI architecture and is responsible for packet segmentation, reassembly, and acknowledgement of packets.
- **Wireless Transport Layer Security (WTLS):** WTLS gives security to the system through encryption, data integrity verification, and authentication between the user and the server. It also provides denial-of-service protection. The security aspect is important for providing secure connections for services, such as e-commerce. To optimize security, dynamic key refreshing was developed to allow encryption keys to be updated on a regular basis during secure sessions.
- **Wireless Datagram Protocol (WDP):** WDP confirms easy adaptation to the WAP technology. It provides a common interface to the upper-layer protocols, and hence they function independently of the underlying wireless network.
- **Network Carrier Method (NCM):** Carriers are any technologies that a wireless provider uses. The information passed through the layers is received by WAP clients and relayed to the mini browser of the device.

In m-commerce using WAP, the design idea underlying WAP is to use a gateway at the intersection of the wireless mobile network and the conventional wired network to conduct e-business. For example, when a customer places an order with an e-merchant, three parties are involved: the Mobile Service Provider (MSP) that acts as a WAP gateway to connect between the wired and wireless Internet, the customer who uses a WAP-enabled cell phone, and the e-merchant's Web site, which is connected to the Internet (see Figure 7-15) (Christian and Jorgensen 2002).

As can be seen, WAP bridges the gap between the desktop and the small-screen mobile device environments. The strength of WAP is that it is an open and free standard. Any manufacturer can produce WAP-enabled devices, and any Internet site can output WAP-readable Web pages. Currently, the most promise for WAP lies in its potential. Some of this potential for WAP-enabled phones is currently being realized in Europe where users are able to buy books or CDs from Amazon.co.uk or Amazon.de. (www.cio.com/archive/071500/wireless_content.html. Accessed June 2003.). WAP also helps standardize the applications that will proliferate using wireless communication technologies.

WAP Benefits

Most WAP benefits are reflected in wireless applications. The critical benefit of wireless applications is the reduced reaction time of mobile professionals. Greater mobility and

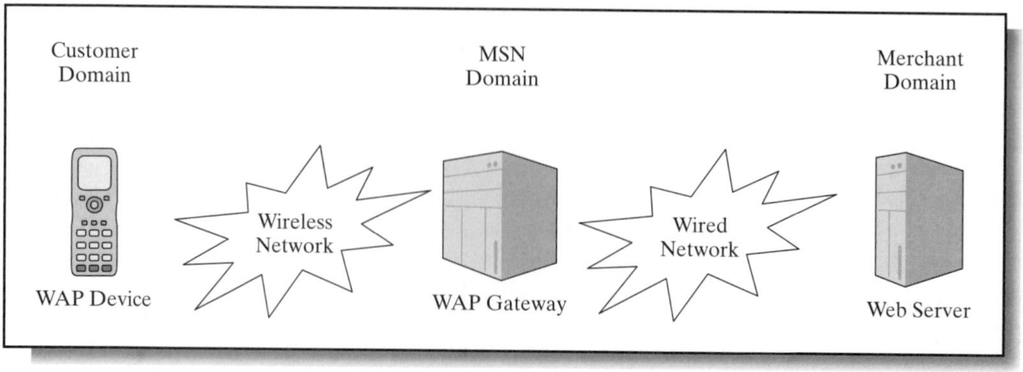

Figure 7-15
M-commerce: A typical WAP architecture

instant access to critical information mean taking immediate action and dramatically increasing productivity from anywhere at any time.

Many WAP applications that are tailored for the business community are currently being developed. For example, some of these applications include ones that enable business people to use their WAP devices to buy their own airline tickets and hotel reservations. Many experts believe that the first WAP applications designed specifically for businesses will come from enterprise software vendors that incorporate WAP functionality into their products. As long as the client handheld device has a WAP display, all of these applications are possible.

Experts envision WAP applications to capture micro payments, such as parking fees and vending machines payments. Other experts believe that WAP applications will link business transaction systems to other machines in the future. In this respect, handheld devices would act like smart devices that could interact with a central application system, such as vending machines, storage tanks, materials handling equipment, vehicles, and the like. Box 7-8 summarizes some of the known WAP applications in business.

WAP Limitations

In adopting WAP architecture, one needs to be thinking about the limitations of mobile devices and mobile networks, such as the following.

- Low-power central processing units (CPUs).
- Small screens with questionable clarity, especially during a bright day. The number of pixels and lack of color variety make it difficult for the user to read the pages from a Web site.
- It is a challenge to explore the Web using small keypads and no mouse.
- Limited device memory.
- Questionable connections for reliability.
- High latency or delays before making the connections. Because most Web sites have detailed graphics and take time to load, handheld devices cannot load pages in a reasonable amount of time.

Yet, despite the limitations, there are good reasons why WAP should be used to implement mobile Web browsing.

BOX 7-8
Select WAP applications

- Computer Sciences Corporation and Nokia are working with a Finnish fashion retailer who plans to send clothing offers direct to mobile telephones using a combination of cursors, touch-screen technology, and WAP to allow would-be shoppers to hot-link to order-entry pages on the Web.
- In Finland, children already play new versions of competitive games such as "Battleship," via the cellular networks. In the music world, Virgin Mobile in the UK offers to download the latest pop hits to customers in a daily offering.
- Scala has developed several WAP products for small to medium-sized companies which would allow, for example, a field sales force to access customer order information and stock availability details via a WAP handset.
- A key growth area for the technology will be business-to-workforce, with companies using WAP applications to reach employees at any time. Scala is currently working on time-sheet applications and techniques for entering and filing expense claims via the mobile phone.
- Nokia says applications that will benefit from WAP include customer care and provisioning, message notification and call management, e-mail, mapping and location services, weather and traffic alerts, sports and financial services, address book and directory services, and corporate intranet applications.
- A new Internet service called ePhysician helps doctors in how they do their jobs. This technology runs on a standard Palm Pilot and allows the doctor to order prescriptions and lab tests, schedule appointments immediately, and verify drug interactions, all from the palm of his hand. Doctors can request a prescription promptly and the patient will have medicine waiting for them right when they arrive at the pharmacy. Another advantage is providing this service to doctors reduces prescription errors by 55 percent, as miscommunication between doctors, pharmacists, and staff is more common than we want to believe.

SOURCE: Adapted from www.mobileinfo.com/WAP/. Accessed June 2003

- WAP already has earned wide acceptance from major players such as Motorola, Nokia, and Ericsson.
- WAP development and implementation are simple. Wireless Markup Language (WML) offers just about everything that a mobile Internet application needs. The programming part is also easy to learn and implement. WML is an integral part of WAP architecture.
- WAP security algorithm works on lines similar to Web security. The key security measures include public key cryptography and digital certificates. They are adequate for most any transaction using WAP.

Security Issues

The emerging world of wireless connectivity presents multiple security threats to IT infrastructures. Even wireless Internet is under attack by hackers. In WLANs, there is something called the WAP gap—the small window of time between decrypting and encrypting information when there is vulnerability. However, the chances of a security breach are low. The most significant risk is to LANs. The 802.11 family of specifications used for wireless LANs relies on a protocol that has been broken. Without the proper security measures in place, a wireless LAN can be accessed by anyone with cheap equipment and hacking skills (Hamblin 2002).

Serious weaknesses also have been found in the encryption system known as Wired Equivalent Privacy (WEP), which is built into the wireless networks. One research report described WEP's use of encryption as fundamentally unsound (Fraudenrich 2002). However, this fundamental lack of security will not slow down the adoption of wireless technology. Consumers will still continue to purchase cell phones and Palm Pilots. Security professionals currently are focusing on limiting the gap between desired and achieved levels of control. They hope that within the next 2 years, wireless technology will be as secure as it can be (Connolly 2001).

Legal Issues

With the growth of wireless transmission, companies are beginning to consider the liability issues. For example, Smith Barney, an investment banking firm, has paid $500,000 to settle a lawsuit brought by the family of a motorcyclist who died after being hit by a car driven by one of its brokers, who was talking on the phone while driving. Because the broker was conducting business on the way to work, the jury concluded that his company was liable for damages (Glater 2002).

Many more such cases are likely to come up as more employees travel on the job, contacting the home office and customers by cell phone while driving. Employers have been liable for decades, but the application of negligence doctrine to wireless transmission and m-commerce is still new in day-to-day business. Civil lawsuits against employers, however, continue. In the Smith Barney case, the broker served less than a year in a work-release program after pleading guilty to manslaughter. Legal issues are covered in greater depth in Chapter 12.

Managerial Issues

Adoption of any technology can be chaotic and traumatic. Designing technology for m-commerce requires a well-thought-out strategy, which considers many different aspects of a business organization. The procedure for implementing wireless infrastructure is straightforward but requires careful and methodical steps. The key steps are as follows.

- **Evaluate corporate needs.** Survey employees or users to find the benefits a wireless network will provide for their jobs, their productivity, and their interpersonal relations. In other words, figure out how the corporate environment will be affected by the change.
- **Evaluate the wireless needs.** Find out the best wireless technology that will meet corporate needs. Planning in advance can eliminate a number of unanticipated headaches later on, especially during testing, training, and deployment.
- **Send out a "Request for Proposal (RFP)."** This is a proposal in which wireless vendors are requested to bid on the project. Included in the RFP are the organization's specifications to be met by the vendor.

- **Request a demo of the proposed wireless system.** After evaluating all vendors' proposals, select the best two vendors based on criteria such as vendor reliability, quality of the product, customer support, price, and so on. Then, ask each vendor to demonstrate a "look-alike" system before placing the order.
- **Install and test the wireless system.** Once you have decided on the top vendor, the system can be installed, and every component should be tested in line with every other component for integrity and reliability. Members of the company IT staff should be involved.
- **Employee training.** Prior to the final installation, employee training should be launched, so that when the system is ready to use, company employees will be ready for the challenge. More importantly, members of the IT staff should be trained to maintain the infrastructure and ensure 24-hour service.
- **Ongoing maintenance.** Ongoing network maintenance and monitoring mean the IT staff never has to say "I'm sorry" when the system fails. All sorts of electric, hardware, software, and personnel backup are implied in this critical phase of system operation.

We can conclude that wireless technology in terms of hardware and software is all well and good when the wireless system operates effectively. The most important element in such an operation is the human staff that will address problems as they come up, the way they maintain and upgrade the system in line with changing corporate and employee needs, and how well they stay abreast of the technology to meet the demands of the wireless system they manage. Without the combined contributions and support of top management, the whole concept and adoption of wireless technology and m-commerce could be a bad experience.

Finally, the best practice to reduce support costs is to standardize wireless devices, predict wireless user problems in order to increase the efficiency of the help desk, and understand the limitations of wireless, such as transmitting data only for short distances as opposed to the speed and bandwidth requirements of company applications for today and down the road (Ware 2002). In the final analysis, no m-commerce manager should promise more than what can be delivered. It is the only honest way of running a business—any business.

Trust Issues

We have known for years that customers have an inherent resistance to sharing personal or private information with technology, especially Web sites, because they lack trust in the site. Gaining trust in mobile commerce can be a daunting task because of its unique features (Siau and Shen 2003). As a concept, trust is a psychological state involving confident positive expectation about another person's motive with respect to a given exchange or a relationship entailing risk. From a customer's view, their trust in e-commerce is built on the Internet vendor's expertise and operational abilities. There is also goodwill trust involving trust in the Internet vendor's honesty. Until such trust is solidified based on experience in the field, customers continue to have problems with trust that freely allows the exchange of personal information over the Internet.

In order to enhance trust in mobile commerce, security must be designed into the entire mobile system. Encryption, digital certificates, and specialized private and public keys are among the measures that could help meet future security requirements in the mobile environment (Siau and Shen 2003).

Finally, there are ways companies can consider to initiate customer trust in mobile commerce. According to Siau and Shen, they include:

- Enhancing customer familiarity with the company and its business
- Building vendor reputation that suggests certainty and less risk in doing business—helping foster customer trust
- Providing attractive rewards such as free trials or gift cards to attract potential customers
- Maintaining company integrity on the basis that a mobile vendor's action must match its promises
- Strengthening security controls via methods such as digital signatures and authorization functionality to relieve customer security concerns and enhance trust in wireless commerce
- Using external auditing to monitor operations

Regardless of the method(s) used, customer trust is crucial for the growth of mobile commerce. Building trust in general is a complex process of attitude, perception, practices, and policies. Only time can determine how likely or in what way customers are going to trust in the mobile environment.

IMPLICATIONS FOR MANAGEMENT

All indications point to the growing future of m-commerce. It will change business and consumer relationships, shift value chains, and create opportunities for healthy competition. Management should keep in mind, though, that the approach is long on technologies but short on standards. There are also other limitations. For example, how many consumers would be willing to pay a fee for accessing their checking balance or bank accounts? Like the ATM, however, the time will come when mobile commerce and access to self-service functionality will become as common as the telephone. It will become an expected service rather than a distinct differentiator (Henderson and Harrison 2002).

Mobile commerce opens doors to new ways of doing business. For example, location-based services will find a vacancy at the nearest hotel and will search for the best rate within one's price range. Another way is in B2C, where organizations can now understand more fully their customers' preferences and movements. Mobile phones carried 24 hours a day are convenient personal channels for banking and instant communication from any location.

A third way mobile commerce will dominate is in mobile payments, mobile advertising, and other areas where they have a time-based and location-based value. Imagine your local electric company having to have a representative come and read the meter for billing. The information is copied or stored for at least 1 day before it is reported to headquarters for processing. Now imagine this information being sent directly to the company IT computer or server via a wireless network for instant update and billing. Bills can be transmitted directly to the customer's bank account for online payments by prior arrangements.

With all of these benefits and all of this potential though, serious problems need to be addressed. With "push" advertising messages, special offers to mobile users, and so on, there is the potential to annoy rather than accommodate consumers with unwanted information, especially at the wrong time. They may react by switching off the device or filtering out messages based on source, content, and the like.

Here are three important issues that management must address.

- Consider the cultural and location-based issues that arise from introducing a mobile environment. A company with geographical locations must establish local expertise in each core location to address local demands or problems unique to the mobile practice.
- Prepare the company to offer mobile services at some point that will be strategically advantageous to the business, the product, or the manufacturing process. As mobile commerce matures, there is bound to be increasing customer demand to use mobile technology to competitive advantage.
- In any case, an organization must experiment with the new m-technology and view the whole effort as an investment in tomorrow's way of doing business. Experimentation generates awareness and understanding of how best to put wireless communication to good and effective use.

The future of wireless lies in faster, more reliable methods of transferring data. Increased use of voice commands and audio improvements, as well as consolidation between devices, will be the next step in allowing easier communication. Secure connections also will prove to be more stable in this industry. Most importantly, speed and constant connectivity will play a vital role in the future of wireless communications.

There is no question the future of wireless technologies lies in 3G, which is known as the next generation of wireless applications. This technology will include multimedia functions in addition to high-speed data transmission and system connections. 3G enables wireless networks to be connected at all times, compared to the old way of dialing into a network using circuit-switched communications. This generation of wireless is high speed with transmission rates up to 5 Mbps, has packet-based networks, and allows advanced roaming abilities (Dunne 2003). 3G will model the increased connectivity capabilities and improved reliability that we are looking for in the future of wireless technology.

Logic suggests that placing the Internet on mobile phones will create enormous wealth and treasure chests of business opportunities. Based on the experience to date, however, this has not yet happened (Chouinard 2002). Mobile commerce still is struggling with the relatively slow Internet access speed. Faster networks are underway to correct the problem. Once successful, m-commerce will take on a different meaning. Some mobile devices will act as payment cards in stores. For example, a repair store won't give you an invoice after repairing an appliance. You will simply use your payment-enabled phone and the payment will be fully taken care of.

Overall, the risks in m-commerce still include merchant reliability, data integrity, user authentication, and dispute resolution between customer and merchant. These are not simple situations to resolve. Between now and 2005, there is hope that the payment card industry will solve these and other problems related to doing business via mobile.

SUMMARY

1. M-commerce is the transmission of user data without wires. It also refers to business transactions and payments conducted in a non-PC-based environment. The main categories are information based, transaction services, and location-centric.
2. The wireless Web is a technological frontier, open and growing. It traces its roots to the invention of the radio back in 1894. Wireless networking makes it possible to connect two or more computers without the bulky cables, giving the benefits of a network with little or no

labor. The whole wireless initiative is launching a new battle against time. The focus is on *anytime*.

3. M-commerce offers several benefits: a facilitator between the e-world and the real world; easy and convenient shopping; and location-centricity to conduct business and tracking of products, services, and people. Overall, the main benefits are convenience, flexibility, and efficiency with anytime, anywhere access.
4. Wireless limitations address distance, speed, crawling pornography, security, and security factors. Tracking users is the number one privacy concern.
5. In m-commerce, four critical success factors need to be monitored: mobility, personalization, global standardization, and customer profiling. Today's concentration is on customer satisfaction, paying greater attention to customer needs for services and quality.
6. A growing wireless connection standard, Bluetooth is a universal, low-cost, wireless technology designed for short-range radio hookup for wireless connection among computers, scanners, and printers. In one respect, it is an enabling technology, creating a common language between various electronic devices that makes it possible for them to communicate and connect with one another. The key features include low cost, low power consumption, low complexity, and robustness.
7. The key layers of Bluetooth are the radio layer, baseband layer, and link manager protocol. The devices must be within 30 feet of each other, as radio signals suffer propagation effects at distances of greater length.
8. To have security in a wireless environment, the transmitted message must be protected all the way to its destination, and the host system must verify or authenticate the user it is communicating with. Wireless security employs wireless Ethernet networks using Wi-Fi at speeds up to 11 million bits per second over 100 meters. Other security standards include WEP, which makes it possible to encrypt messages before heading for their destination.
9. 2G digital cellular technology expedites vehicles in motion. Information is received by the online truck terminal, and the driver drives to the address where the pickup is available. A handheld device, called PDA, captures the information related to that address. Once complete, it prints a routing label and pastes it onto the box before the driver loads it onto the truck.
10. A cell site contains a radio transceiver and a base station controller, which manages, sends, and receives traffic from the mobiles in its geographical area to a cellular telephone switch. It employs a tower and antennas, and provides a link to the distant cellular switch called a Mobile Telecommunications Switching Office. This MTSO places calls from land-based telephones to wireless customers, switches calls between cells as mobiles travel across cell boundaries, and authenticates wireless customers before they make calls.
11. Once you move toward the edge of your cell site, your cell site's base station notes that your signal strength is diminishing. The base station in the cell site you are moving toward sees your phone's signal strength increasing. The two base stations coordinate with each other through the MTSO. At that same point, your phone gets a signal on a control channel telling it to change frequencies. This hand-off switches your phone to the new cell.
12. The most common standard for wireless networking is Wireless Local Area Networks, or WLAN. It is identical to a regular LAN, except that the devices are wireless. WLAN design is flexible and is becoming cheaper to deploy, but it travels only 150 feet.
13. For an organization to consider wireless LAN technology, it must consider range

and coverage, throughput, security and integrity, cost and scalability, and standardization of WLANs. Related to WLAN is wireless application protocol, or WAP. It is the basis for the mobile Internet. The WAP concept is straightforward. This type of interactive electronic exchange marks the dawn of the Mobile Internet Revolution. The world of information is available not just on our desktops but at our fingertips, and the possibilities are truly endless.

14. Most WAP benefits are reflected in wireless applications, which reduce the reaction time of mobile professionals. Because of greater mobility and instant access to critical information, productivity can be increased dramatically from anywhere at any time. Experts envision WAP applications to capture micro payments, such as parking fees and vending machines payments.

15. WAP has the limitations of low-power central processing units, small screens with questionable clarity, limited device memory, small keypads and no mouse, questionable connections for reliability, and high latency before making the connections.

16. With the growth of wireless transmission, companies are beginning to consider the liability issues, as well as managerial issues. To implement wireless infrastructure requires careful steps, which include evaluating corporate and wireless needs, sending out an RFP, requesting a demo of the proposed wireless system, installing and testing the system, training employees, and ensuring ongoing maintenance.

KEY TERMS

- access point, 218
- baseband, 209
- Bluetooth, 206
- data synchronization, 215
- Link Manager Protocol (LMP), 209
- logical link control and adaptation protocol (L2CAP), 209
- m-commerce, 194
- Mobile Telecommunications Switching Office (MTSO), 215
- Network Carrier Method (NCM), 223
- Personal Digital Assistant (PDA), 214
- piconet, 206
- radio layer, 208
- repeater, 213
- WAP Forum, 220
- Wired Equivalent Privacy (WEP), 212
- Wireless Application Environment (WAE), 221
- Wireless Application Protocol (WAP), 202
- Wireless Datagram Protocol (WDP), 223
- wireless LAN (WLAN), 195
- Wireless Markup Language (WML), 221
- Wireless Network Interface Card (WNIC), 218
- Wireless Session Protocol (WSP), 223
- Wireless Transaction Protocol (WTP), 223
- Wireless Transport Layer Security (WTLS), 223

TEST YOUR UNDERSTANDING

1. Define m-commerce in your own terms.
2. Briefly explain the main categories of m-commerce.
3. Explain the justification for introducing or adopting wireless Web.
4. Summarize the key benefits and limitations of m-commerce.
5. What areas does a wireless Web work in?
6. When we talk about critical success factors of m-commerce, what do we mean?
7. Distinguish between:
   a. personalization and customization.
   b. WLAN and WAE.
   c. Wi-Fi and WEP.

8. Explain briefly the main capabilities and limitations of Bluetooth.
9. Sketch out the configuration of a piconet.
10. What is the difference between L2CAP and LMP?
11. What is a repeater? Illustrate.
12. What should an organization consider in deciding on wireless LAN technology?
13. Is there a difference between Bluetooth and WAP? Explain briefly.
14. In your own words, describe how WAP works.
15. Distinguish between:
    a. Bluetooth and piconet.
    b. WTP and WTLS.
    c. WDP and NCM.
16. Briefly cite the key benefits and limitations of WAP.
17. What security issues are involved in WAP?
18. Summarize the legal and managerial issues in wireless transmission.

Discussion Questions

1. Go on the Internet and look up recent developments in the adoption of Bluetooth in banking. What were your new findings?
2. If you were a consultant to a major firm interested in wireless transmission, what advice would you give the firm? How would you proceed before you recommend or do not recommend the technology? Be specific.
3. Security and privacy have been "drummed up" in virtually every area of the Internet and e-commerce. Do you think there are good reasons for this much sensitivity to the areas of concern? Discuss.
4. Having used a cell phone by now, what is your opinion about companies funneling advertisements to your cell phone? Are there any benefits to you as a student? Can you think of any drawbacks? Write a three-page report explaining your thoughts.

Web Exercises

1. Search literature or the Web and address the features and capabilities of the latest Palm Pilot on the market.
2. Form a group of three to four peers and brainstorm the pros and cons of wireless transmission for a major bakery in your town. Write a two-page report summarizing your decisions.
3. Write a five-page report on the latest developments in wireless transmission for the academic area. For example, some schools already have installed wireless labs, and others have implemented a wireless environment for students to access their e-mail or authorized files.

Chapter 8

Designing Web Sites

Contents

IN A NUTSHELL

In the previous chapters, we discussed the role of the Internet, how to launch a business on the Web, and the technology that supports e-commerce. In this chapter, we focus on the critical component of e-commerce: the Web site as the interface between the e-merchant and the Web consumer. Remember that e-commerce is a unique way of doing business. It is available 24 hours a day, 7 days a week, anywhere, and it is accessible to anyone. It allows a business to not only display products and services, but also to sell online.

Building a Web site is a major step to doing business on the Internet. A Web site is the gateway to the Internet. Deciding how to design the site, what to include in it, how to organize its contents, and what security measures to incorporate are critical aspects of building an e-commerce infrastructure.

Take CDNow.com as an example. This e-merchant is a veteran in e-commerce and is the leading online music store. The Web site was launched in 1994 and averages 3 million visitors per day. Orders more than tripled in 2002 over 2000 during the holiday season. Reviewers praise the site for four attributes: straightforward navigation, sophisticated search functions, clearly displayed pricing and product descriptions, and customization features. Visitors can search easily for the item they want from the 500,000 items available on the site. Repeat customers can customize their visits with shortcuts to favorite artists, a wish list, and their current order status. The site has minimum graphics to ensure that it runs faster. CDNow is going global, with versions in different languages (German, Spanish, Portuguese, French, Italian, and Japanese) and alterations to accommodate the cultural, economic, and social constraints of the different regions in which it will do business. See Exhibit 8-1 for an example of a workable Web site.

Another aspect of Web site design is the match between what a business is trying to sell and the customers the site attracts. Most current Web sites fall short of meeting user needs. For example, buyers returned about 10 percent of all products bought online during the December 1999 holiday season, which is double the rate of returns of products bought at stores. Many customers found the return process tedious compared with going back to an actual store. A good Web site is flexible and intelligent enough to anticipate customer needs and accommodate them. For returns, something as simple as a downloadable return label would be a good start.

This chapter is about designing Web sites, from page design to stage or final display. We begin with the life cycle of design, then elaborate on plan-

The Goodness of Design Fit

A veteran in e-commerce, CDNow.com Inc. was launched nearly 6 years ago and averages 3 million unique visitors a day. Orders were up 225 percent in 1999 over 1998 during the holiday-shopping season. Based on traffic, CDNow.com is the leading online music store, and reviewers praise the site's consistent and straightforward navigation, sophisticated search functions, clearly displayed pricing and product descriptions, and customization features.

The search function lets visitors look for items by artist, title, record label, and more—a must for a site where the number of available items exceeds 500,000. Keeping clicks to a minimum is no accident. Everything is based on user or visitor experience. Visitors can also choose to customize their visits. CDNow offers features that repeat customers want: shortcuts to favorite artists, a wish list, and information on current orders.

Graphics are kept to a minimum, so response time is good. The firm is moving into global e-commerce with versions of the site in various languages, but there are still some snags that need to be worked out. For example, the French version of the site pitches products in the right language, but quotes prices in dollars.

Exhibit 8-1
An example of a workable Web site
Source: Excerpted from Sonderegger, Paul, "CDNow.com," *Informationweek*, February 14, 2000, 156.

ning and organizing the site, ways to build it, design tips and criteria, issues in site development, and how to evaluate site developers. In the next chapter, we focus on Web site maintenance and evaluation, site performance, traffic management, and Web staffing.

What Does a Web Site Do?

Think of a Web site as a storefront. It has the name of the store, representative product displays, and special offers. The only difference is that a Web site is a virtual storefront, and the customers are cyber-customers. The emphasis is on speed, efficiency, good response time, and availability of procedures that expedite a sale.

A Web site is basically a series of pages with links to other pages or other sites. The pages contain text, banners (ads), graphics, and sometimes audio and video. The four key components of a site are the following.

homepage: the first page of a site; page that appears when visiting a URL address.

Web page: carrier of specific information reached by clicking a button on the homepage.

link: a connector that makes it possible to go to another Web page.

banner: a graphic display on a Web page, usually for advertising.

- **The homepage:** This is the first page of a site that appears when visiting a URL address. It contains links that take the visitor to specific areas within the site and buttons to help the person navigate (get around) the site. It also contains general information about the e-merchant and its policies.
- **Web page:** A **Web page** is a carrier of specific information reached by clicking a button on the homepage. A Web page is related to a homepage like a series of paragraphs is related to a heading in a text chapter.
- **Link:** A **link** is a connector that makes it possible to go to another Web page on the site or on the Internet, or to go back to the homepage. A link has a specific title and directions for use.
- **Banner:** A banner is a graphic display on a Web page, usually used for advertising. The banner generally is linked to the advertiser's Web page.

A Web site has some special benefits over a brick-and-mortar storefront.

1. **Reaching millions of customers quickly and reliably.** In 2000, more than 200 million people worldwide were connected to the Internet, and more than 40 percent of them were well educated. These customers look for convenience, ease of finding services or products, and the ability to order directly from their computer.
2. **Establishing a presence in cyberspace.** The entry-level goal of a new Internet business is presence. The new Web site displays "who we are" information, which may include office hours, location, a map showing how to get to the brick-and-mortar location, and perhaps featured products. Thousands of companies begin at this level before they turn the site into an interactive trading place.
3. **Leveraging advertising costs.** Unlike radio, TV, or newspapers, where limited time or space is available at high cost, advertising on the Internet is cheaper, quicker, and limitless. Including a company's Internet address in a small print ad or a 30-second TV or radio spot should direct thousands of customers to the company's Web site to do business.
4. **Reducing the cost of serving customers.** A Web site can offer a variety of labor-saving services—application forms, information via links or e-mail, and order handling and shipment without human intervention. Answering frequently asked questions on a Web site cuts down on phone calls. Asking for feedback from customers via e-mail also can provide information while the experience is fresh in the customer's mind.
5. **Promoting public relations.** A Web site on the Internet is like passing business cards to thousands of potential customers. It is like saying "Here is what I do, what I am, and what I can do for you. You can reach me anytime, from anywhere, and I'll be available." The Web site also allows for the timely dissemination of information about a new product or a special sale.
6. **Reaching international markets and customers.** The Internet is populated by millions of prospective customers all over the world. The main constraint is collecting payment for products and services.
7. **Test-marketing new products or services.** One or more Web pages can display changes in your product or service faster than you can feed a fax machine. In an increasingly time-sensitive environment where strategic thinking is critical, the time gap between manufacturing and retailing is becoming increasingly narrow.

The Life Cycle of Site Building—From Page to Stage

Site building is the science of figuring out what you as a site designer want the site to do and then creating a blueprint for the building process. The building life cycle is shown in Figure 8-1. Planning begins with developing the site's goals and collecting client opinions. The next step is to define the audience and the competition. The third step is the creative phase. The designer begins to build the site—forming a skeleton, picking the metaphors, and mapping out the navigation. The final step is the visual design.

Planning the Site

The planning phase of site building is the foundation for great Web design. It is the blueprint for designing form, function, navigation, and interface. Planning means defining the site's goals. Think of how many sites are on the Internet: Some are good, more are

Screen Capture 8-1

Source: Copyright © 2003–2004. Used with permission of www.arabnews.com.

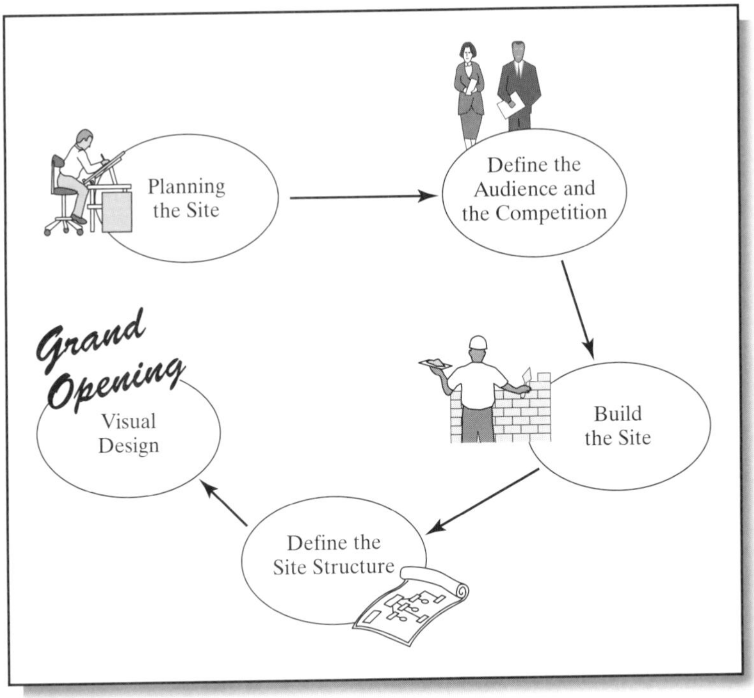

Figure 8-1
Site building life cycle

bad, and hundreds are ugly. In a 1999 article called "Why Do So Many Web Sites Suck?" user interface guru Don Norman pointed to software as the main culprit. Mr. Norman criticized Microsoft for including so many features that the result is "bloated, confusing products that no user in her right mind would have asked for" (Swaine, p. 55).

The overall objective of a customized Web site is to:

1. Speed up the interactive process.
2. Reduce human intervention to a minimum.
3. Save time.
4. Make buying and selling through the site cost-effective.

The aim of the planning stage is to provide for quick application development and deployment. Doing this means organizing the site—creating an efficient structure for the files and folders that make up the site. Ideally, the content should be finalized first.

Defining a site's goals involves two things: determining who will be involved in defining the goals and whether there is time or a need for formal definition. The scale of the Web site project is a major factor in deciding whether a formal process is necessary.

Another aspect of the planning phase is asking questions to decide on the site's mission, the short- and long-term goals of the site, who the intended audience is, and why people will want to visit the site. Once the questions are agreed upon, they should be prioritized and passed on to involved personnel for conversion into goals. The hard part is to distill the final list into a master list of goals that are acceptable to all participants.

Define the Audience and the Competition

In this phase, the key question is: How can you design a site if you don't know who will be visiting it? Determining who the audience is can pay handsome dividends. Defining the audience includes not just who the users are, but their goals and objectives, as well. The first step is to generate a list of intended audiences. If the list gets too long, then divide it into categories.

Let's say a bank wants to put up a Web site to promote its services, with a focus on loans. Audience categories might be current brick-and-mortar customers, cyber-customers, young adults looking for auto loans, new commercial companies looking for commercial loans, contractors looking for lines of credit, and new home owners looking for mortgage loans. Within the auto loan category, one can find people who need a car loan right away, those who need a car loan for the next season, and those who are just shopping. The audience list is ranked and agreed on before the final list is produced.

Another way of looking at defining the audience is to identify what prospective customers want. Here is what retail cyber-surfers look for when they shop online, according to research by BizRate.com, a firm that judges e-commerce Web sites using customer feedback (www.bizrate.com/ratings_guide/guide.xpml. Accessed June 2003).

1. Competitive product prices.
2. Well-designed product representation.
3. Good product selection.
4. Reliable shipping and handling.
5. On-time delivery.
6. Easy ordering.
7. Valuable information about products.
8. Posted privacy policy.
9. User-friendly navigation tools.

Any way you look at Web site design, the goal is to enhance site visitors' experience by escorting them quickly to the merchandise that best suits them. Speed and responsiveness are crucial. Remember the 8-second rule: If visitors wait more than 8 seconds, they most likely click out and try the competition.

In addition to defining the audience, you need to create scenarios or design test cases of customers accessing the site for various reasons and see how well the site matches their needs. Another way of testing the site design is to select a representative set of users. Write up a scenario about each type of user to see how well the site will deliver what they're looking for. This exercise is part of defining the overall cyber-environment.

The second part of this step is competitive analysis. The idea is to be aware of what other sites are doing. Make a list of your competitors' Web sites, evaluate them, and see where your site needs work. Start with evaluation criteria such as personalization, consistency, and ease of navigation. (Web site evaluation is covered in detail in Chapter 9.) User experience, defining the audience, creating scenarios, and evaluating the competition are part of the *design document*—a prerequisite to moving ahead to the actual design.

Build Site Content

This phase pinpoints what the site will contain. The focus is this phase is on gathering the pieces for creating and organizing the structure of the site. The pieces represent the content. For example, if I were building a Web site for a bank, the homepage would contain basic information about each department (loans, customer service, trust, checking, and savings) as well as basic company information such as privacy policy, location, banking hours, and names of officers.

Here is what one company's boss suggested as a list of necessary items.

1. Company logo.
2. A catalog of products, with pictures.
3. A bio of the company, including a picture of the boss.
4. A page of testimonials from loyal customers.
5. A form for placing an online order.
6. A counter showing that the site has gotten a high number of hits so far.

To harness ideas about the prospective Web site, it is helpful to create a list of the content and functional requirements. Pass the list by key department heads or through a committee to make sure there is support and consensus before you proceed with the actual design. Another approach is to have each department create its own list of content, and present the resulting integrated list for all to approve. You now have a **content inventory,** which can be used to launch the actual construction phase. Box 8-1 illustrates this process.

content inventory: a list of the company activities (contents) that make up the Web site.

When the content inventory list is final, determine the order of priority of each function or department. If the focus of the Web site is loans, then the loan function should be prominent. This ties into the goal of the site and the audience for which the site is being designed. After this step is completed, the designer needs to determine the feasibility of each function. For example, are technology and money available to buy or build the function? If money is limited, you may have to drop some functions in order to meet budget constraints and deadlines.

The result of this phase is a new addition to the design document, which could be labeled *content and functional requirements*. It should include a brief description of how the content inventory was gathered and finalized. This type of documentation will come in

BOX 8-1
Sample content inventory for a typical commercial bank

Home Page

1. Bank services
2. Personal deposit accounts
3. About loans
4. Trust and investment services
5. What's new?
6. Contact us

Bank Services

1. Automated teller machines (ATMs)
2. Basic commercial checking accounts
3. Certificates of deposit (CDs)
4. Foreign currency exchange
5. Money market accounts
6. Regular commercial checking accounts

Loan Department

1. Personal loans
2. Home equity line of credit
3. Commercial deposit accounts
4. Commercial loans
5. Money market checking

Trust and Investment Services

1. Investment management
2. Personal representative
3. Guardianship
4. Living trusts
5. Life insurance trusts
6. Escrow
7. Testamentary trusts
8. Trust services

handy later on when you need to maintain the Web site if someone other than the original Web designer does the work.

Define the Site Structure

In this phase, the focus is on creating a good site structure, exploring various metaphors to represent content items, defining the architectural blueprints, and deciding how the user will navigate the site. Once a **site structure** is created, everything else should fall into place. This step ensures easy site navigation and well-laid-out pages and templates. Think of the structure as a skeleton that holds the entire site together. It promotes order, discipline, organization, and trust.

site structure: an organized layout of a merchant's departments or functions that becomes the basis for the Web site.

Exploring metaphors as a way of trying to visualize the site's structure generates ideas and alternative ways of approaching site design. Metaphors can be organizational or visual. Organizational metaphors usually rely on the company's existing structure. For example, if you are creating a bank Web site focused on loans, your metaphor could be a commercial bank where services are grouped logically by type (mortgage loans, commercial loans, bridge loans). Visual metaphors rely on graphic elements that fit the nature of the site. For example, if you were designing a Web site to sell music products, which allows users to play music, you would include icons like "start," "pause," and "stop." This way, users don't have to learn anything new. Instead, they can rely on their experience with CD players.

Defining the architectural blueprint involves diagrams showing how elements of the site are grouped and how they relate to one another. Figure 8-2 illustrates architectural blueprints for our banking example. It is easy to understand the proposed design of the

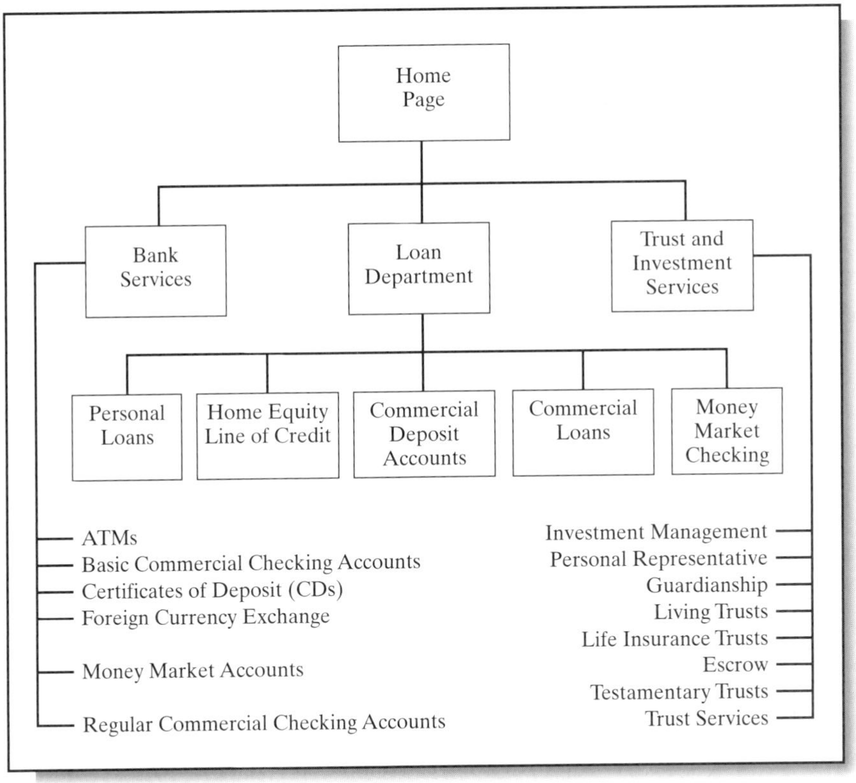

Figure 8-2
Architectural blueprints of site contents listed in Box 8-1

site and the order in which it is being planned. The client can see it and comment on it before it is adopted as the final blueprint.

In this phase, you also will define site navigation. How will visitors use the site? How will they get from one page to another? How do we make sure they don't end up on a competitor's site? Local navigation can take a number of forms. It can be a list of topics like the ones found on Yahoo! (www.yahoo.com). It can be a menu of choices such as that found on the Bank of America Web site. It also can be a list of related items such as loans, checking, and savings on a bank Web site. For examples of Web site navigation, see this book's Web site, www.prenhall.com/awad. (Look up the Webmonkey site at www.webmonkey.com for information on navigating a multipart article via links to each section.)

Visual Design

The final phase of a site-building life cycle is developing the visual design. The goal is to give visitors a mental map of the Web site: where they are, where they have been, and how to proceed. The first step is to use a layout grid to show how well the icons, buttons, banners, and other elements fit together. Like the format of a letter, a layout grid is a template that shows the focus of every page. The company's brand should appear on each page to reinforce the company's image. An example of a layout grid is shown in Figure 8-3.

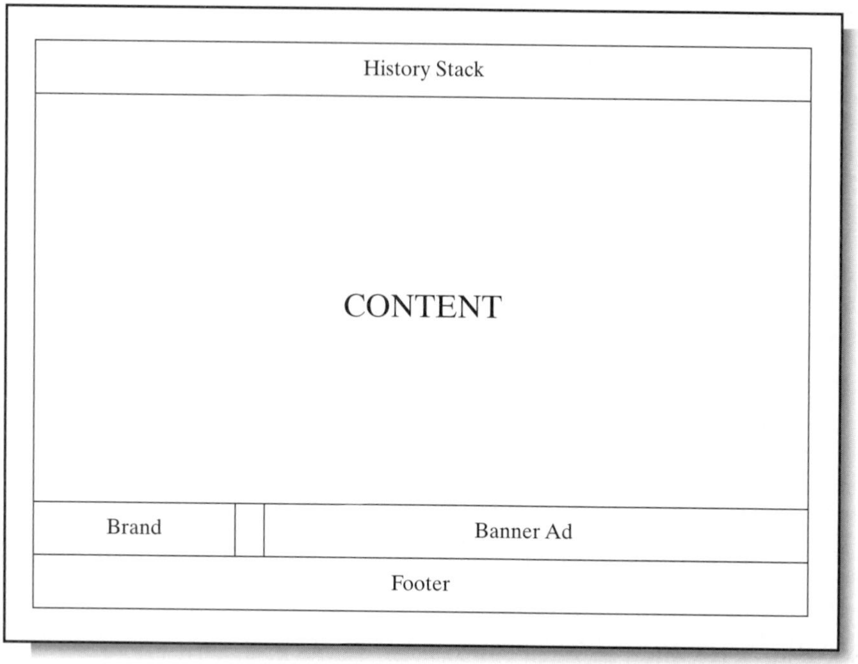

Figure 8-3
Layout grid

Source: Adapted from Shiple, John, "Information Architecture Tutorial," *Webmonkey*, www.hotwired.com/webmonkey/98/28/index4a_page2.html.

One way of getting started is to see how many page types can be generated from the site structure listing. Page style and form should be consistent throughout the site. Content is the critical part of a page, and that's where to start. Then add other elements like branding, advertising, navigation buttons, page titles, and headers and footers.

Another aspect of the design phase is establishing the look and feel of the site via page mock-ups. Mock-ups integrate the design sketches with the layout grids. Once completed, the visual design also is incorporated into the design document. The design document is now complete. It shows how to construct the site, add content, and revise after the site is up and running.

Web site design has, as its main goal, attracting and retaining visitors. Personalization is critical: The designer should tailor Web content directly to a specific user. Tracking the user's behavior on the site will help in doing this. Software on the site then can modify content to fit the needs of the particular user. With personalization, users can get information quickly and more reliably than on traditional sites. **Cookies** may be the most recognizable personalization tools. Cookies enable a Web site to greet a user by name.

cookie: bits of code that sit in a user's browser memory and identify the visitor to the Web site.

Design Languages

The early years of Web site design began with Hypertext Markup Language (HTML). It is the first tool used to help in the designing of a user's Web site. The military as well as academic institutions were the first groups to use the Web. The goal was simply to exchange information. Tim Berners-Lee created HTML as we know it today. In 1990, he imagined a simple hypertext language that could be used to transform documents onto the Web. Initially, it was used to indicate whether a paragraph was needed, a title was in place, or to describe the content of a Web site. Because HTML was also text based, anyone could master the language.

Inevitably, the demand for more stylized, highly colorful Web sites emerged. A graphical browser, called Mosaic, soon appeared. With it came increased demand from Web designers for color text, color background, pictures, fonts, and so on. To respond to the increasing sophistication of what can be done with a Web site, a talented college student, named Marc Andreessen, added "<img>" to his product, the Mosaic Browser.

Andreessen eventually went to California and formed Netscape. Bill Gates, the chairman of the board and founder of Microsoft, saw the endless possibilities of Web design and began to add different tags to his browser, the Internet Explorer. The <marquee>, <iframe>, and <bgsound> tags eventually were supported by the Internet Explorer, which posed an interesting question. If the current trend continued down its intended path, Internet Explorer and Netscape Browser would support two completely different versions of HTML 3.0, and there would be no way anybody could view all the sites the Web had to offer. Either the browsers would have to come together and form a single, compatible form of the current version of HTML or Web surfers eventually would have to choose between browsers. Another solution would be for Web designers to create multiple versions of their Web sites. Such a solution would be prohibitive to provide.

Screen Capture 8-2

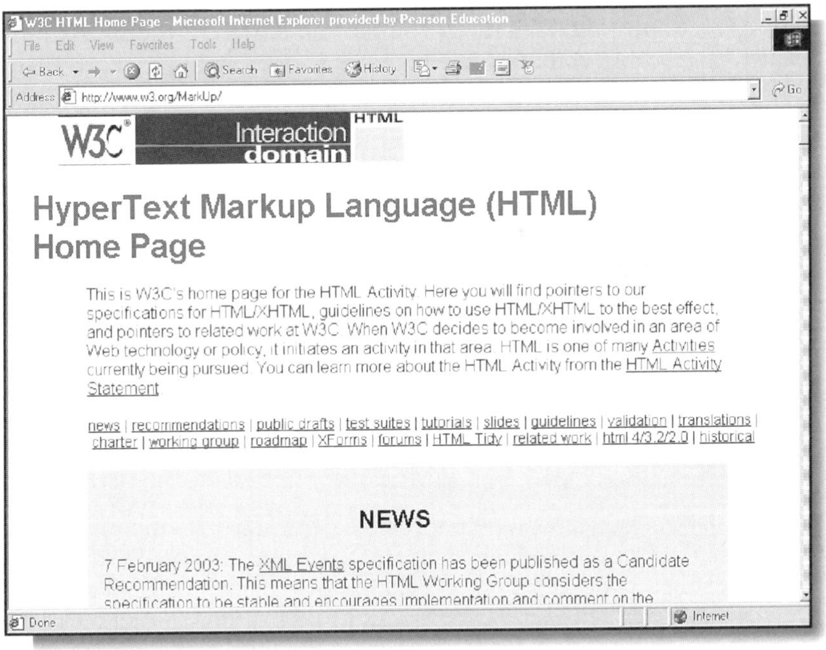

Source: Copyright 2003–2004 World Wide Web Consortium. Massachusetts Institute of Technology, European Research Consortium for Informatics and Mathematics, Keio University. All rights reserved. http://www.w3.org/Consortium/Legal/2002/copyright-documents-20021231, www.we.org/MarkUp/.

Java became another popular language for designing Web sites. When John Gage of Sun Microsystems and Marc Andreessen of Netscape announced that their browser was going to be using Java exclusively, the language became a reality. Primitive applications of Java could no longer satisfy the public's need for bold, multimedia-enriched content. Out of this need rose the popularity of such technologically advanced utilities as Macromedia Flash and Shockwave, and next-generation languages like Extensible Markup Language (XML) and Vector Markup Language (VML). These advances increased visual pleasure exponentially without a comparably large increase in file size or loading time.

New age languages have given designers more room for creativity and imagination. The offspring of Internet cornerstones HTML, XML, and VML integrate graphics with documents so much better than earlier versions did. Because they are developed by software giant Microsoft, XML and VML figure to be a big part of Web design in the near future.

How to Build a Web Site

Like any brick-and-mortar site, a cyber-store needs a good location, a good look and feel, and a secure site to attract and engage customers. The question is: How should you build an ideal store? The range of choices is anywhere from having a Web-based service such as Yahoo! Store build a small-scale operation in a hurry, to enlisting the help of an Internet Service Provider to start small and grow, to doing it yourself with off-the-shelf software loaded on your own Web server.

Storefront Building Service

A new class of dot.coms will help you build a customized online store quickly and cheaply. Most such Web-based services offer a Web catalog of up to 100 products and ensure the proper linkup to an online merchant account. The service includes giving your store a Web address, managing the Web traffic, and maintaining the store on its Web servers. The main drawback of this approach is the standardized nature, color scheme, and look of the site.

Services on the Internet allow you to build your own sites—and some of them are also free. For example, Bigstep.com provides an easy-to-build site environment, where you can sell as many products as you like. Getting a merchant account that will allow you to accept credit cards requires paying a nominal monthly fee plus a small fee per transaction. The downside is that Bigstep uses its logo on your site to advertise its presence. The logo links back to Bigstep's Web site (www.bigstep.com), which may compete with the products you sell. There is also the question of how well the ISP manages traffic spikes (see Box 8-2).

The ISP (Web-Hosting) Service

One advantage of enlisting an Internet Service Provider (ISP) to build and maintain your site is the support you get and the chance to grow your site as your e-business expands. An ISP is generally experienced in store-building technology that is more sophisticated than that available on sites like Bigstep. More and more ISPs license versions of their e-commerce software to help you build your own store. Other Web-hosting services such as Verio (www.veriostore.com) help you establish a merchant account and build shipping and sales tax calculations into the site. See this book's Web site, www.prenhall.com/awad, for some examples of these services.

BOX 8-2
Traffic spikes

Your Web servers are humming along peacefully, doling out Web pages at a leisurely rate as Internet users from around the globe request them. Then something happens that drives hordes of visitors to your site. Your Web servers buckle. Visitors endure tedious waits for each page—or worse, "server unavailable" errors.

Traffic spikes can be broken into two broad categories: the ones you expect and the ones you don't. Those you expect you can prepare for in advance. On September 11, 2001, news-hungry users from around the world flocked to CNN.com for the latest headlines about the terrorist attacks in New York City and Washington, D.C. On an average day, the site serves about 40 million page views. On September 11, that number climbed to more than 162.4 million page views, then to 337.4 million the following day.

"The first step we took was to slim down the page. We took off the graphics and the pictures and kept the most relevant information out there," says CNN.com spokeswoman Elizabeth Barry. But streamlined content wasn't enough. Without additional hardware, CNN.com could never have handled its increased load. Even so, CNN.com did all it could to reduce the load on its servers by routing visitors to alternate information channels.

Cache servers can also make a difference. This is hardware that sits between the Web server and Internet connection, caching and distributing frequently accessed content to reduce the load on the server. Good site design and proper configuration of your Web servers can also help ease the workload during traffic spikes. Tweaking your Web application is very critical. In the hands of a good system administrator, a well-configured server can double the amount of content you can serve.

Availability and cost are two competing issues in dealing with traffic spikes. You have to have enough availability to service your users. You don't want to give them a bad experience when trying to get your software. You can reduce the cost and frustration of badly timed spikes by using a hosting provider that doesn't lock you into tiers of project bandwidth needs.

Think of preparing for traffic spikes like preparing for a flood; as long as you've got a disaster kit tucked away in the garage and the family has agreed on what to do during an emergency, things will probably go smoothly. You may not know exactly when the flood is coming or how deep the water will be, but you can be sure you have the resources to manage when it does.

SOURCE: Excerpted from Savetz, Kevin, "Managing Traffic Spikes," *New Architect Magazine*, November 2002, 24–26.

Do It Yourself

Setting up your own e-commerce Web site costs more; requires experience; and forces you to worry about security, management of Web traffic, and responding to technical and procedural details 24 hours a day. Costs are incurred for site development, hardware, bandwidth, and full-time Web administration. The main benefits are unlimited upgrades, customization, better control over performance, and potential for growth.

Over the long haul, this approach is worth the effort for a large business that is committed to online business. For a small business, it is usually cheaper and quicker to hire a Web designer to do the job, but a company employee also should be trained to become the Webmaster to maintain the site on a daily basis.

Web Navigation Design

Designing successful Web navigation is an art and a science. The best way to approach Web design is to put yourself in the shoes of the prospective visitor. The merchant's goals and those of the user are often different. Profiling the user up front can help predict problems in the way the Web site will be navigated.

Take the bank example. A Web developer helps a commercial bank set up a Web site. In the early stages of discussion with upper management, the developer asks managers what they expect to get out of the site. What are their needs and concerns? In few weeks, the designer creates a site that meets these needs. The bank is happy. However, when the site debuts on the Internet, e-mail includes comments from unhappy customers and new visitors. The number of hits is low, and visits to the site hardly go beyond the homepage. Four months later, the site is virtually abandoned. The bank management has the impression that the whole idea of being on the Internet is a bad joke.

In reality, no one stopped to consider the visitor's goals and how those goals differed from those of the bank (see Table 8-1).

Conflicting goals and poor communication can spell doom for the site. When visitors can't achieve their goals, the bank eventually suffers the most in lost customers and substantial development costs. The Web developer, the bank, and select users should sit down and think through goals and expectations. Creating profiles and conceptualizing site design in terms of possible scenarios goes a long way toward avoiding such problems.

Screen Capture 8-3

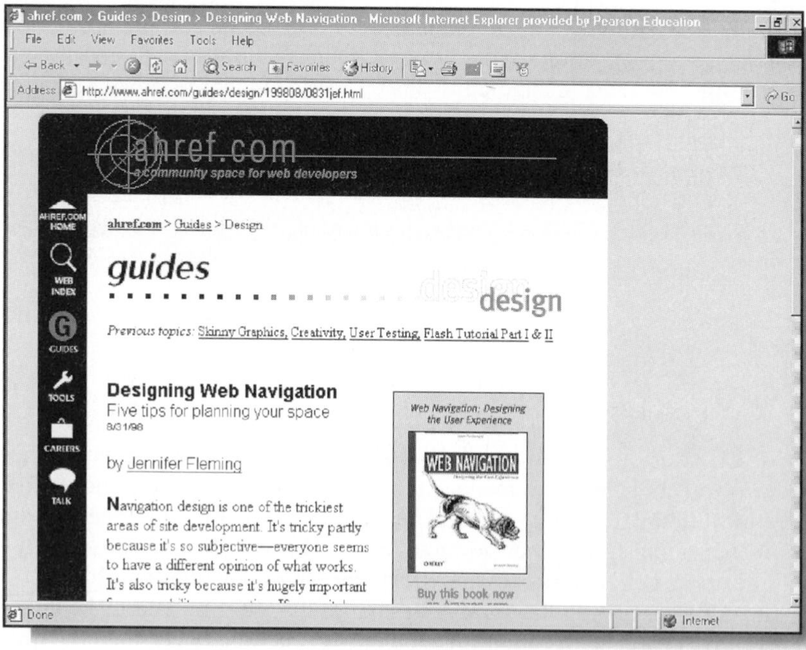

Table 8-1
Goals

BANK	VISITOR
Wants to know more about customer	Wants to surf the site with privacy
Wants to generate revenue via the site	Wants to save money via the Internet
Coaches visitor to click first on the loan button	Annoyed at having to start with loans
Rushes visitor to take a virtual tour of the bank	Irritated because other information is more important
Asks for personal information about banking needs	Feels personal information is none of the bank's business

Creating User Profiles

You are the vice president of operations of a medium-sized commercial bank near a major university. You're best known for customer service and stability. You develop an idea for a Web site that reflects this image. Think of the type of customer you attract and how unique the customer base is compared to the competition across the street. The area where your bank is located is competitive. Each competing bank has a Web site and is trying to attract new customers. You must answer the following questions. What do people want from a bank like yours? What are their goals, besides opening a basic checking account? Some customer profiles can be helpful in answering these questions.

customer profile: brief study of the type of person who might visit your Web site.

Customer profiles are brief studies of the types of persons who might visit your site. Here are profiles of two customers who might represent part of your target audience.

Gary

Gary is an assistant professor in his early thirties. He is recently divorced and has custody of two children. Because of the divorce settlement, he is sensitive about his financial privacy. He has been living in a small community for more than 2 months and is interested in a bank that values customer service, in a location within a few miles of the university or his residence. In a couple of years, when he hopes to get tenure at the university, he plans to build a large home, replace his 1996 Toyota Corolla with a new Lexus, and open a trust fund for each of his two children.

Since he moved to town, Gary has been trying various banks based on newspaper ads and recommendations from colleagues. He complains to associates that most banks are impersonal and have high charges for checking, use of the ATM, and overdrawn accounts. Gary is not sure about finding his ideal bank on the Internet, but he'd rather try that than ask more people the same questions.

Monique

Monique is a 22-year-old, fourth-year student at the same university. She is a member of a sorority. She comes from a close-knit family and has always valued personal contacts and attention. She heard about your bank's site from another student. Because she has 1 full year before she graduates, Monique hopes she can handle her personal and financial needs on the Web from the university computer lab. Being able to open a checking and a savings account could easily attract the rest of her sorority to do business with your bank. Monique worries that cookies and other snooping devices might invade her privacy, and that she might end up with a lot of junk mail. She is willing to try a Web site that looks conservative, presents a nice appearance, has value-added content, and might have a phone number that can be answered by a human voice.

The two profiles are not the same, but you can sense shared concerns that alert you to the patterns you should incorporate into the site. In this case, privacy, warmth, personal attention, and responsiveness should be central items in designing your bank Web site. You also can predict that being in a university-oriented community, reasonable or low service charges to students might make a hit.

Using Scenarios

scenario: situation that helps you view the navigation process and the site as a point of entry.

Another way of conceptualizing prospective site users is through scenarios. A **scenario** helps you view the navigation process and the site as a point of entry. To illustrate, take Monique's user profile. How would she be likely to move through the site? What problems might she encounter? How would she handle such problems? When you add predictions or likely actions to a user profile, it becomes a scenario. For example, Monique is interested in accessing the bank's Web site. She's already got a browser on her PC, although she lacks confidence about navigating on the Internet. The first thing she looks for is easy-to-follow instructions, icons, or layouts to take her where she wants to go on the site. Because she is sensitive about privacy, the privacy statement button should be easy to access. Also, because she is more interested in information about opening a checking account, an icon that will take her to this function should be visible on the homepage.

If Monique cannot find these two key items on the homepage, she might lose interest and simply go elsewhere. This means that you need to build flexible navigation capabilities into your site if you want to attract Monique and her sorority sisters.

In Gary's case, the first thing he looks for is ease of navigation, a strong privacy statement, warm color that gives an impression of personalization and security, and trust. Because he is sensitive about privacy, the privacy statement should be easily accessible from the homepage. Because he is interested in setting up a trust fund for each of his children, the homepage should have trust funds listed as one of the bank's specialties. Without these two features, Gary will likely click away to another bank's Web site.

What About Cultural Differences?

In designing Web sites for conducting business in different countries, the focus should go beyond just providing sites with different language versions. Someone remarked, "It doesn't matter that your site sells diapers or offers tips on American quilting patterns—disregard cultural differences and your site will be doomed" (Chau et al. 2002).

One aspect of culture is color. As we shall see in Chapter 9, different colors mean different things to different people. For example, the color white represents purity in the United States, but the Japanese think white represents death. To the Chinese, a red background represents happiness; in the United States, red represents danger. The bottom line is that people in general learn patterns of seeing, sensing, and feeling from living within their social environment in the country of their birth. This means that people with different cultural backgrounds react differently to a globally generic Web site (Chau et al. 2002). In a Web site, unique features must allow the targeted consumer to feel at home. This includes the use of the native language, the country's national flag, or color as cues to attract a wider pool of visitors to the site.

User-Friendly Site

A major conclusion from profiles and scenarios is that you must design user-friendly Web sites. In fields such as Web architecture, a lot of effort is spent understanding user behavior and preferences. The same is true when assessing site navigation. The trick is to make your site as easy to learn and navigate as possible. Another trick is to anticipate problems. Remember what it was like the first time you accessed a Web site? I remember my first class in speech, when the instructor tried to help us design a framework for making a speech: Stand up, speak up, and shut up. The problem with this three-step process is that it lacks detail. A better framework would be: Walk to podium, lay your notes on the lectern, greet the audience, present your speech, provide meaningful conclusions, end with a summary of sorts, recognize applause, take your seat, and so on.

Providing guidance for Web site visitors is much the same. The easier it is for first-time visitors, the more likely they are to return. Remember, the stability, reliability, and security of a Web site are paramount. Sites that leverage the power of the Web in developing unique solutions to common problems will be way ahead of other sites in the same industry.

Design Guidelines

Several tips regarding Web site design are worth considering. Each idea can be as good as others, because design means integration of color, content, layout, speed, and the like. See Box 8-3. for a select list of Web design tips based on the author's experience. Remember, with no standard guidelines, it is rare that a Web site does everything right. No one even knows what that is. Luxury retailers have yet to learn that glitz is great, but not online. See Box 8-4 for more details.

Remember that no Web site is perfect. Some of the best sites continue to have problems like inconsistent graphics and outdated information, but with smart design, a less-is-more attitude may be all that is needed to drive up your company's Web traffic.

Design Criteria

In designing Web sites, the primary goal is for visitors to experience the site as you intended them to. If the site presents information, distributes, or sells a product or service, the visitor must view the site as having credibility. Quality and reliability also must be assured. A Web site is a part of an e-business strategy that should be designed and managed effectively. Design criteria such as appearance and quality assurance, public exposure, consistency, scalability, security, performance, and navigation and interactivity are among the key factors to consider.

Appearance and Quality Design

The key question here is: Is the site aesthetically pleasing? Most site developers agree that mixing text with graphics adds interest to the site. Allowing text to flow around graphics or varying the margins also tends to make the content more attractive. The goal is to make the site easy to read, easy to navigate, and easy to understand.

quality assurance (QA): a process used to check the readiness of a site before it is loaded on the Web.

How attractive a Web site appears to a visitor has a lot to do with quality assurance. **Quality assurance (QA)** is a process used to check the readiness of a site before it is loaded on the Web. Visitors want to *trust* the site and be assured that it is reliable and has no glitches or blips, regardless of the frequency of access.

BOX 8-3
Design tips

1. Keep the site simple.
2. Web design involves problem solving. Clearly define the problem that needs to be solved.
3. Users come to your site for content. Give it to them fast and simple. Keep content current and structure it into simple hierarchies.
4. Transmission speed is an important aesthetic matter. You have 3 seconds to convince a user not to use the Back button. Something should be displayed on the screen immediately, and it better be interesting.
5. Everything on the screen should load in 30 seconds. The display should be fast.
6. Site performance is critical. Response time should not be more than 8 seconds.
7. Site availability can make the difference between a one-time visitor and a loyal customer. Brownouts and outages cost time, money, and nowadays, a drop in stock valuation. The site should be available 24/7.
8. The organization fielding the e-business application needs to know what kind of traffic the site can handle. Victoria's Secret's experience was an example of successfully driving visitors to a site, and then not being able to serve them.
9. Make sure the company's name and logo are clear and visible on each Web page.
10. Be careful not to waste too much effort on bells and whistles. Keep graphics and other bandwidth-intensive design items to a minimum.
11. If you use animation, make sure it has a theme, story, or point. Otherwise, avoid gimmicky pages with animation that walks across the page.
12. Make it a habit to save your work periodically.
13. Remember to use color carefully. (Color is covered in detail in Chapter 9.)
14. If a visitor leaves the homepage to go elsewhere within the site, make sure he or she can easily return. Each page should have a link back to the homepage.
15. When designing a complex site, identify the decision makers, define the goals, and sketch a way for the design team to solve the design problems.

style guide: a template designed to measure the materials used to build the Web site.

To live up to this level of quality, a Web developer must live up to a set of standards that will inspire trust in the site's visitors. These standards are established through a **style guide.**

To create a style guide, a Web developer pulls together all the existing information about the Web site design. The style guide includes corporate guidelines for maintaining the company image, such as how to use logos, slogans, and images; acceptable fonts; and so on. The goal is to provide the site with visual consistency. An extreme example of inconsistency in site design is using wild fonts for one page and conservative ones in the next page, without regard to how they blend with the content or the flow of messages.

Public Exposure

E-business is public. Any mistakes, redundancies, misrepresentations, oversights, or unauthorized content or links are immediately displayed for the world to see. These problems all have legal, marketing, and public relations implications. The Web designer should verify that content as well as form are credible and reliable at all times.

BOX 8-4
Selling strategies

When Neiman Marcus opened shop online in the spring of 1999, the company worried about how to translate the selling points of its real-world stores to a humdrum computer screen. Like lots of luxury merchants, Neiman Marcus decided a flashy presentation was the key. Pretty snazzy stuff. And today, it's all gone. Neiman Marcus.com no longer features any clever animation—or other flashy effects, for that matter. But it does have far more merchandise, neatly arranged by category and designer.

Customers just didn't want all the special effects and they don't miss it at all. In fact, revenue tripled at the site last year. The consumer wants a secure shopping experience, to know that her credit-card information is protected. She wants to find key brands and the newest trends. And she wants the navigation to be convenient and the search easy.

While most luxury retail sites focus on exclusivity, extravagance, and entertainment, affluent online shoppers demand convenience, confidence, and control. Take Tiffany & Co., which ranked sixth in Forrester's survey of 30 luxury Web sites. Tiffany's site is well-stocked with jewelry and gift products—and on selection alone, Tiffany is given high marks. But in its effort to set itself apart, Tiffany's special features can make shopping there frustrating.

A visitor to Tiffany.com, for instance, is immediately offered a choice: the homepage asks if you want to visit the HTML site or the Flash site. Neither of these are explained, though you are told that the Flash site recommends you use a Flash 4 plug-in—whatever that is. The Tiffany's problems are common to many sites. The Flash feature—which makes for pretty animation but confusing menus and tricky navigation—bogs down many luxury sites. Moreover, Tiffany has increased the selection on the site: There are now some 2,000 products available, up from 200 two years ago.

So, what do the critics think a well-designed luxury site *should* look like? The top finisher in Forrester's convenience survey, Nordstrom.com, has few gimmicks or gadgetry—no Flash interfaces, streaming videos, or travel sites. Just tons of merchandise shown in big clear pictures and categorized in a simple, straightforward manner. Nordstrom.com also gets high marks for customer service.

SOURCE: Excerpted from Zimmerman, Ann, "Keep It Simple," *The Wall Street Journal*, April 15, 2002, R10–R11.

Public exposure includes site availability—uninterrupted service 24 hours a day, 7 days a week. The visitor in Saudi Arabia who just logged on to your site does not care if it is midnight here. To ensure availability, the networking and technology infrastructure must support this type of demand.

Viewability and Resolution

The key question here is whether the site is viewable in different browsers. The two major browsers are Netscape Communicator and MS Internet Explorer. Also, everyone uses different resolutions and screen sizes. Although a certain site will look best at a certain resolution, it should be viewable in 800 × 600 without a side-scroll and also be viewable in 1,024 × 768 and higher without the backgrounds tiling horribly.

Consistency

The key questions under the consistency criterion are whether the fonts and font styles are consistent. Will the Web site and contents appear the same on all visitors' screens?

Depending on the design tools used and the browser, a site might appear restricted on Netscape but not on Microsoft Explorer, or vice versa. To prevent this from happening, a Web designer programming in HTML needs to fine-tune the final draft of the site, or the site should advise the visitor as to the best browser to use before accessing the site. Fonts and font styles are a problem in most sites. A site should have not only a design theme, but a text theme as well. If you like Arial, stick to Arial for all of your text. This excludes your title and button graphics. The easiest way to ensure consistency is to make sure your site uses Cascading Style Sheets.

Scalability

The key questions in scalability are these: Does the site provide a seamless growth path, and does it have the potential for enhancement or upgrade in the future? **Scalability** (ability to upgrade the site) is an important consideration with new Web sites because it is difficult to determine the number of future visitors. A Web site should be capable of being expanded as usage increases and as needs change. This means protection of the initial investment in site construction.

scalability: potential for enhancement or upgrade.

Security

Protecting a site from hackers is a tricky business, especially when it comes to deciding on the security software, encryption algorithm, and methodology to ensure secure trading online. The site should show only what the visitor wants to see. Web sites where access security is critical should run on a dedicated secure server. In banking, passwords may be required to allow customers access to their bank accounts. E-security is covered in detail in Chapter 13.

Performance

Security has a direct relationship to performance. The more security is embedded into a Web environment, the more a Web designer worries about performance. It is like catching a flight on a busy evening. The more checkpoints that must be passed before boarding a flight, the longer it takes to board.

From the end user's view, performance is judged based on the answer to the question: How long does it take for the page to appear? Sites that are heavy on text often download instantly. Graphics take time and can bring downloading of the page to a halt. Most search engines have a 45-second timer: If the site takes longer than 45 seconds to download, it displays the message "can't find" or "can't access site."

Navigation and Interactivity

A Web site must be logically linked and allow visitors to get to another page that is of interest to them and then back to the homepage. Icons or buttons should be formatted and laid out to expedite **navigation.** Sometimes an explanation is given to describe the function of each icon and where it will take the visitor.

navigation: synonymous with "surfing"—how a visitor gets from one page in a Web site to another.

Think of navigation as a house with multiple entrances. The classic metaphor is that a house has only one entrance. In reality, there is a back door, a garage door, a dog door, or a window ajar on the second floor. Navigation must allow for a variety of access points, depending on the visitor's experience and needs.

BOX 8-5
The surge of unwanted ads

Tired of animated banner ads prompting you to click on the monkey or inviting you to win free money in overseas casinos? Fear not, software entrepreneurs are on your side, with a series of programs designed to eliminate the clutter that Web advertisers have pasted under, over, and next to the information you're looking for. In addition to making many Web pages easier to read, stripping out advertising can make many of them load faster, an important consideration if you're surfing over a dial-up connection.

One of the longest-lived and most popular ad blockers available on the Internet, AdSubtract mostly lives up to its reputation. It blocks banner ads just about everywhere it encounters them, without noticeably affecting the display of the pages. This software does far more than block banner ads, though. It can be configured to block pop-up windows; manage cookies; and eliminate animated graphics, background images, and the music that some Web sites start playing automatically. It can even prevent some sites from forcing your browser to refresh itself regularly. The only drawback is that the free version works for only 30 days. A permanent version costs $29.99, although downloading the demo and providing your e-mail address in the registration got you, at the time of this writing, an offer to buy the software for $19.99.

SOURCE: Excerpted from Hamilton, David P., "Tossing Out the Pitches," *The Wall Street Journal*, October 21, 2002, R7.

Navigation and interactivity are closely related. Easily navigable sites promote interactivity. In banking, for example, a Web site may offer customers a variety of investment products described in a number of pages. After making a selection, customers click on a navigation bar to calculate the rate of return for that investment. Based on the results, they can change the investment decision and navigate accordingly. Customers also may be allowed to make investment decisions directly using funds in their checking or saving accounts.

The bottom line is for the Web site to reach the intended audience and build an image of integrity, reliability, and quick accommodation around the clock. Sites like Web Site Garage can help you analyze your site. They provide the total file size and download time of the pages. For more examples of these sites, see this book's Web site. Another test is to select a sample from the competition. Find some sites you consider competitors and see how they stack up in terms of file size and performance limits.

One thing that works against navigation and customer focus is excessive Web advertisements. If you consider such a route, you can expect a clutter of advertisements pasted over, under, and next to the homepage you're looking at. These distractions can reduce the surfer's interest in what your Web site has to offer. As summarized in Box 8-5, ad blockers are now available to eliminate distraction.

HIRING A WEB DESIGNER

Now that you're ready to do business on the Internet, you need a skilled designer to build the storefront and the Web site. You could teach yourself to build your own site if you have time and some knowledge; many Web sites offer tutorials and easy-to-follow procedures. For examples of such sites, go to this book's Web site, www.prenhall.com/awad.

A great site is www.hotwired.com or www.webmonkey.com.

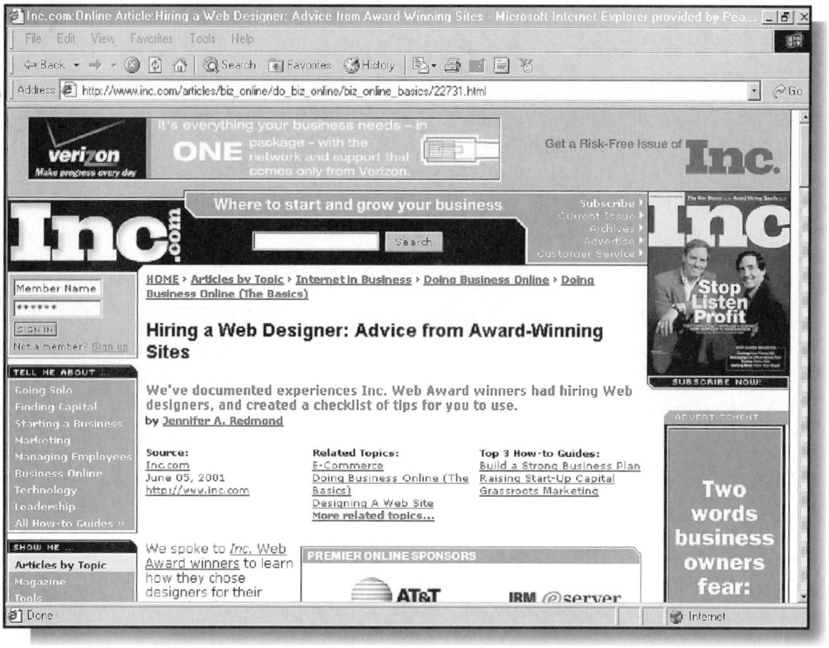

Screen Capture 8-4

Unfortunately, although this approach might save you money, it is neither safe nor prudent for serious online business. If you want your site to attract visitors and beat the competition, and if you want a unique site and one that actually sells products online, you need to hire someone to build that site. In large site projects, a committee consisting of representatives from various departments works with the site developer to ensure the overall quality of the resulting site.

The Budget

In addition to hiring costs, you need to budget for the costs of running a Web site, maintaining and upgrading the site, monthly hosting fees, and a dedicated Webmaster to keep the whole infrastructure on course. The challenge is to prepare a budget that incorporates all aspects of direct and indirect costs for a year and get top management approval so that as the site is being developed, the key decision makers can track its progress.

What to Look for in a Site Developer

A critical issue to consider in Web site design is the developer. That individual or company must not only have extensive Web design experience, but also be experienced with a variety of databases, security standards, and programming languages.

Competition for qualified Web developers has caused many companies to go out of their way to attract potential employees (e.g., Microsoft furnishes temps with cars and condos). Based on the surge of sites today, demand is growing faster than supply. It used to be that mainly high-tech firms hired Web employees. Now, almost every company from bank to bakery is looking for site developers to help them create a presence on the Internet.

What's the best way to find a Web designer? As a starting point, look at a site that you like and try to contact the Web designer who built it. Contact Web developers in the area and put together a short list to choose from. Look up their sites and draw up a list of the features you like and don't like. Find out what services the firms offer. Learn about logo design procedures, database development, animation, user testing, site hosting, language used in site design, and so on. Send out bids to a select few.

If you're having trouble deciding on the design shop, try visiting a few: Meet the designers, and check their competence and capabilities. Do you like working with them? Do they share your thoughts about what the proposed site should look like? Do they have what it takes to reach your visitors?

Many professionals often wonder why Web site projects fail. Here are some of the reasons that culminate in Web site project failure.

Web site designers agree to a completion date when they have no idea how to meet it. In trying to meet such unrealistic deadlines, the team pushes for an aggressive schedule to accelerate the work, only to encounter one error after another that delays the whole Web site project. To make up for lost time, testing begins to degenerate, which invariably cause problems after installation.

- Incompetent or inadequate staffing. When the project team is short-handed, lacks competency, or is under pressure to produce miracles, motivation is the first victim of such arrangements. For example, two designers working 14 hours a day to produce a Web site cannot be as reliable as two qualified designers working 7 normal hours a day to do the same work. Tight deadlines have been known to burn two ends of the candle unnecessarily, knowing that there are only two ends to burn.
- Poor quality design. When quality suffers, it is either because of incompetent staff or trying to meet unrealistic deadlines. In the latter case, quality reviews, inspections, and thorough testing take a back seat, especially when pressure comes from top management.

Changing requirements of the client. This problem has been known for decades to cause delays in the completion and quality of Web site design. We have seen this problem in designing information systems since the 1960s. First, the client was not shown the product until after it was ready to use. The clients complained, because they had no chance to see it sooner. Then, a new approach was tried, whereby the client became part of the design team. Still, the client who keeps making changes could drive the design team batty (Humphrey 2002).

Box 8-6 presents ideas that ensure a successful Web design partnership.

Filling Web Positions

Because of the increasing demand for developing and maintaining Web sites, companies are creating full-time positions for this purpose. Hiring a Web development team means creating unique job descriptions. The employer needs to recognize this special talent with a successful career path. In deciding on the right person for the job, the employer needs to realize that the most experienced candidate might not be the most qualified. The candidate needs to demonstrate the capacity to learn from experience and the ability to manage projects and communicate well. Capable employees with limited experience may see the job as an opportunity to learn and work harder at staying abreast of the technology.

Another way to attract Web talent is through an internship program. Interns get exposure and training, and generally leave with positive things to say about their experience with the firm. They might return at a later date and become permanent employees. In return, the company gets good public relations for the firm and good future employees.

Another path is in-house training of employees with potential for Web design work. This can be done through classroom meetings or presentations. A technical library with the latest technical and design-building information is also helpful. Classes employees take at community colleges or universities are also positive moves. The company reaps the benefits of more highly trained employees with the potential to do Web design work.

BOX 8-6
Deciding on an outside design team

All managers want to ensure their Web projects run smoothly, meet corporate needs, finish on schedule, and are ultimately successful. Unfortunately, not every company manages to work well with its chosen design team. There are several techniques that companies can use to foster solid, successful relationship with their design firms.

1. Define the problem. That is, outline the problem the design firm needs to solve. Not all design firms will gel with your company's personality and objectives, This is why the second point is important.
2. Choose your design firm carefully. Find the consultants who can best meet your needs, but be wary of design firms that promise everything. Look for a firm that is strong in your greatest areas of need.
3. Help designers evolve your vision. Involve the designers in the process early enough that they can have an impact on the project. If you bring them in too late, they won't be able to come up with real solutions for your business needs. Remember that design doesn't always mean architecture. Be ready to provide a lot of information to your designers when you start a project.
4. Do preliminary user research. When you're hiring designers to do a project, you probably know the business imperatives behind what you want to build. But do you know what your users' needs are? Good designers will want to get in touch with your users and see firsthand how they think and interact with your site.
5. Set clear goals and success criteria. Sample criteria for project success include launching in time for a big sales meeting or trade show, increasing sales by a certain percentage, or winning an award or write-up for your site design.
6. Map out project modules. By modularizing your project, you have the opportunity to assess how well your efforts advance company strategy as you go along.
7. Demand clear documentation. A good firm will give you templates that let you build and grow the design they created for you.
8. Express communication preferences. Tell your designers how you prefer to communicate—daily, in-person check-ins?
9. Designate a single point of contact. To keep your project running smoothly, give your designers the name of one go-to person in your company.
10. Rally key stakeholders. Large companies need to juggle different internal opinions and imperatives when working on Web projects. One approach is to build a small, trusted steering committee of project stakeholders. You should also know who could trip up your project—and how.
11. Get results. Always raise concerns as soon as they appear on your radar.

SOURCE: Excerpted from "Steenson, Molly W., "Ten Steps to a Perfect Design Partnership," *New Architecture Magazine*, November 2002, 29–30ff.

SUMMARY

1. Because a Web site is the gateway to doing business on the Internet and is the primary interface between a business and its prospective cyber-customers, deciding how to design the site, what to include in it, how to organize its contents, and what security measures to incorporate are the most critical aspects of building an e-commerce infrastructure.
2. The benefits of building a Web site for a business include reaching millions of customers quickly and reliably, establishing a presence on the Internet, leveraging advertising costs and reducing the costs of serving customers, and reaching international markets and customers.
3. Building a Web site includes the following steps: Planning the site, defining the audience and the competition, building site content, defining the site structure, and visual design.
4. Defining the audience includes knowing who the users are as well as their goals and objectives. The assessment includes creating scenarios or design test cases.
5. In defining a site structure, the focus is on exploring various metaphors, defining the architectural blueprints, and deciding how the user will navigate the site.
6. There are several ways to build a Web site. One way is via storefront building services. Another way is to enlist a Web-hosting service that also maintains the site. The third way is to do it yourself, which requires experience in Web design, hardware and software, and Web administration.
7. Several design criteria should be considered: appearance, accuracy (because any mistakes are immediately displayed for the world to see), consistency, scalability, security, performance, navigation, and interactivity.

KEY TERMS

- banner, 235
- content inventory, 239
- cookie, 242
- customer profile, 247
- homepage, 235
- link, 235
- navigation, 252
- quality assurance (QA), 249
- scalability, 252
- scenario, 248
- site structure, 240
- style guide, 250
- Web page, 235

TEST YOUR UNDERSTANDING

1. Briefly summarize the benefits of having a Web site for e-commerce.
2. A Web site can offer a variety of labor saving services. Do you agree? Give examples.
3. How does a Web site promote public relations?
4. Explain the major stages of building a Web site. Is one stage more important than all the others? Elaborate.
5. What goes into planning a Web site? Discuss.
6. What is involved in defining the audience and the competition? Be specific.
7. According to research by BizRate.com, what do retail cyber-surfers look for when they shop online? Explain.
8. What should one consider in building site content? Explain.
9. In what way are architectural blueprints related to navigation?
10. How would you explain visual design in Web site development?

11. What is the difference in function between a storefront building service and a Web-hosting service?
12. What is involved in creating user profiles? Elaborate.
13. Is there a difference between performance and scalability? Explain.
14. If you were in a position to hire a Web designer, how would you proceed? What would you look for?

Discussion Questions

1. Can one safely design a Web site without going through the planning phase? Discuss in detail.
2. In Web design, how much of the work can you do yourself without professional help?
3. If someone came to you and said, "Look, I know nothing about the Web, but my competitors are all on it. How about designing a Web site for my jewelry business in the next few days?" What would you say? What questions would you ask?
4. How would you go about analyzing a small retail business that wants to launch itself on the Internet?
5. What might be competitive strategies for an organization trying to launch a clothing business?
6. Select some of the better-known online travel agencies (priceline.com, cheaptickets.com, expedia.com), review their Web site features, and report your findings.
7. Check three search engines (e.g., Yahoo!, Excite, Hotbot). Compare and contrast their sites.
8. Explain how a shoe repair shop can take advantage of a Web presence for its business.

Web Exercises

1. A medium-size bank is in the process of installing a Web site that would allow it to interface with the larger global community on a full-time basis. The bank has 89 employees, $189 million in assets, 20,000 checking accounts, 11,000 customers, and intense competition from neighboring banks for the marginal customer. The bank is customer oriented in the classical style of hand shaking and greeting people by name. The trend, however, is for the younger, computer-literate customer (such as students at a neighboring university) to want a different kind of customer service. The bank wants to be part of the Internet community and wants to grab the cyber-customer for information access, issuing small loans, and other services.

   As a consultant:

   a. What questions or information would allow you to advise the bank on its readiness to make use of a Web site?
   b. What would you emphasize that the bank must do, and how would you sell any change to the bank's president?
   c. What type or level of planning is involved?

2. Access the following Web sites:
   www.ibm.com
   www.microsoft.com
   website.oreilly.com.

They should display three e-commerce packages, respectively:

- IBM's Net.Commerce 2.0
- Microsoft's Commerce.2.0
- Oreilly & Associates, Inc.'s Website Pro 2.0

Answer the following questions.

a. Which attributes are unique to each package? What features does each package offer?
b. Which attributes are common across the three packages?
c. Which package would you select for a small to medium-size financial institution? Why?

Chapter 9

Web Site Evaluation and Usability Testing

Contents

In a Nutshell

In the previous chapter, we discussed the basics of Web design—how to build a Web site, navigation design, and design criteria. It is tempting to think that the work is done once the site is designed and on the Web, but in a rapidly changing Web environment, day-to-day maintenance and evaluation are needed. Systematic evaluation of your Web site is like checking its pulse: It tells you if you're fulfilling the site's mission, suggests format or layout improvements, and makes sure the site evolves along with your company and the Web.

Web site evaluation means considering graphic identity, navigation quality, functionality, and content. Remember that a site built using solid design principles need not have lots of bells and whistles to grab a visitor's attention. The key is usability and performance.

Part of Web site evaluation is managing Web traffic. When the site was initially planned, the designer must have done some competitive research to determine the kinds of sites your competitors have. These sites should be revisited periodically to see what changes competitors have made and what changes your site needs. As you evaluate your site, think about how any changes might fit into what is already on the site. You need to keep the site user friendly, fresh, and cohesive.

Anatomy of a Site

A Web page's design is basic to its ability to communicate information. The Web world is crowded with books on building "successful" Web sites, "killer" Web sites, "Web sites that work," and so on. Perhaps the best way to focus on building successful Web sites is to learn about how to build lame sites. Box 9-1 addresses just such a topic—chasing customers away and baffling them with "Cyberbull."

The number one issue in Web site design is how it comes across to the visitor. Here are some questions to consider in evaluating a Web site.

- Are any elements placed incorrectly?
- Does the *Search* field on the existing site look as if it refers to all of ZDNet?
- Is the information hierarchy properly arranged?
- Should the heads that relate to ZDNet be enlarged?
- Should the fonts for the headings be made more readable?

Color and Its Psychological Effects

A site visitor has formed a first impression of your site within the first 8 seconds of clicking on. Appropriate design involves matching the demographics and content of expected visitors to appropriate colors, shapes, and typefaces.

Color is arguably the most important design element in a Web site. Theoretically, a designer has a 216-color scheme to consider (Muler 2002). Realistically, far fewer colors are used in most Web sites. Before using color, ask yourself this question: What

BOX 9-1

Be careful not to end up with a lame Web site

Let's look at the major goals of a lame site:

- Drive away customers.
- Confuse people about the company, so they have no idea what kind of services you offer.
- Ensure that the Web site loses the maximum amount of money possible, perhaps even bankrupting the whole company as a long-term goal.

Every customer is different and, therefore, there are innumerable ways to drive them away. But, certain tried-and-true methods are practically guaranteed to yield results.

- Force your visitors to register before they enter your site. You nip the traffic in the bud by making them fill out a lengthy form, giving you a lot of detailed information that you will never use, and make every field a required field.
- The first item on your homepage should be a huge graphic that is totally meaningless until it is completely downloaded. Do not make it interfaced. Make the title of your document something meaningless like "Homepage" or "Welcome to our Site."

Clear, concise information is the bane of lame sites. Keep this site wordy, vague, and confusing. Extravagant promises are fine. Keep these tips in mind:

- Always have a "vision" and a "mission" statement, and a "goals" or "objectives" statement.
- If you must include a contact e-mail or address, bury it deep in your site, linked only from some irrelevant and seldom-visited section.

It never ceases to amaze me that even some of the smallest, most unknown companies on

Screen Capture 9-1

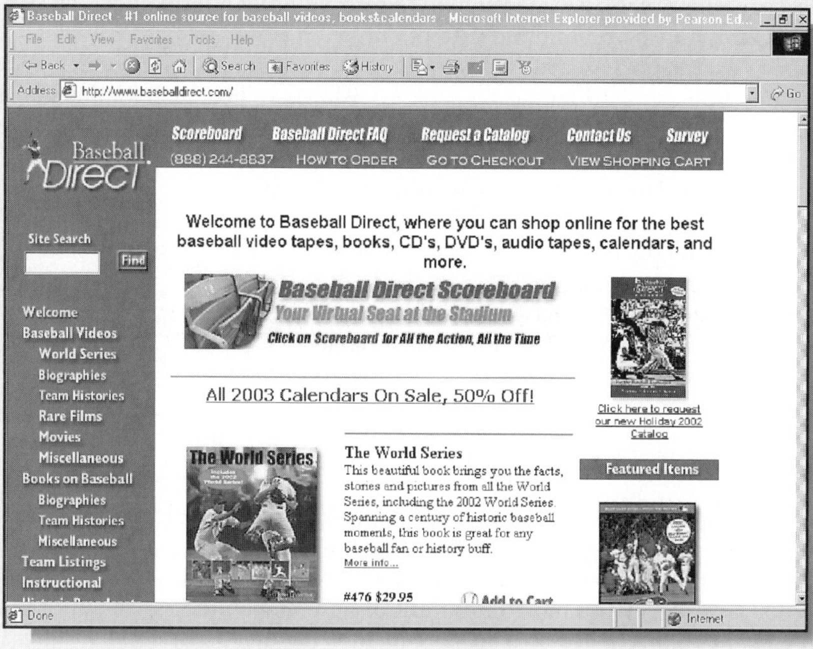

Source: 2003–2004 Baseball Direct. All rights reserved.

BOX 9-1
Continued

the Web create excellent-looking sites to a high standard of professionalism, while the giants of commerce run circles around them in the field of creating awful amateurish sites. Here are a few things you can do to keep your site down to a remedial level:

- Pay careless attention to improve typography. Always use lots of exclamation points and, be sure to put commas, where they don't belong !!!!!!!
- Bad spelling is easy. You don't even have to misspell words—just use them improperly. Always mix up "it's" with "its" and "their" with "they're."
- Punctuation and grammar are two other good areas to point. Let sentences run on, and participles dangle! Infinitives? Split 'em like peas!
- Page layout is one of the easiest things to do badly on the Web. Always use plenty of horizontal rules and make columns either narrower than 1" or wider than 4".

The following techniques will ensure that your company's Internet project stays in the red.

- Promise the Moon. Tell senior management that the Web will double the company's sales, halve expenses, and guarantee Steve Forbes elected president of the United States, all within 6 months.
- Buy a bunch of hardware and software and hire lots of staff.
- When you've spent your budget, return to step A. Blame someone else for the failure.

Remember, a little more money will solve any problem that may come up. Keep these tips in mind as the red river swells:

- Don't submit your new site to the search engines, as it will only result in increased traffic.
- Make sure your site stays the same. Establish an elaborate maze of red tape for any changes that anyone might want to make.
- Don't use log-analysis packages to track your site traffic. In fact, don't even bother to back up your server logs.

SOURCE: Excerpted from Morris, Charlie, "How to Build Lame Web Sites," Media Group, Inc. 2001, 1–12. http:// webdevelopersjournal.co.uk/books/booklead.html. Accessed June 2003.

is the goal of the Web site? Entertain? Inform? Sell? The first consideration is to set up the Web site so that color appears immediately. If the purpose of the Web site is to inform, choose colors that are simple and not distracting. Choose colors that reflect your audience's values and cultural preferences. For example, if the site represents a community bank, then choose warm colors. Colors and their psychological effects are listed in Table 9-1

When designing a Web site, remember that one of the benefits of Web site marketing is to minimize interaction cost. Web site content that is wordy, verbose, or stuffy can kill the site. Visitors look first and read later. The site should talk, not preach. The old saying "good engineering is simple engineering" certainly applies in Web design.

It is worth repeating that colors take on different cultural hues. The trick is to use a color that is acceptable to various cultures, while simultaneously representing the product or service. Most global firms load their unique Web site on a server in the country where it is viewed by that country or region. See Box 9-2 for examples of the relationship between color and culture.

Table 9-1
Summary of major colors and their psychological effects

Color	Psychological Effects
Red	No doubt, red creates attention, but tends to overtake other colors on the page. The recommendation is to use it as an accent, not as a background. Red also can be viewed as power, energy, warmth, passion, aggression, danger. Red with green is a symbol of Christmas. Examples:www.Wesleyan.edu
Blue	Trust, conservatism, stability, security, technology, order. Used in the United States by many banks to symbolize trust. Examples:www.Ford.com, www.Wachovia.com
Green	Nature, health, good luck. Does not do well in a global market. Has been successful in attracting investors in the Middle East versus the United States. Green is underused on the Web. Certain shades symbolize youthfulness and growth. Examples: www.Firstunion.com
Yellow	Optimism, hope, dishonesty, cowardice, betrayal.
Purple	Spirituality, mystery, royalty, cruelty, arrogance. Appears very rarely in nature.
Orange	Energy, balance, warmth. Signifies a product is inexpensive (in the United States and outside of Halloween and St. Patrick's Day).
Brown	Earth, reliability, comfort, endurance.
Gray	Intellect, futurism, modesty, sadness, decay. Easiest color for the eye to see.
White	Purity, cleanliness, precision, innocence, sterility, death. It reproduces freshness and is a quite popular color at luxury Web sites that cater to the upper middle, because it gives the sense of "pristineness." According to Muller (2002), "pages with a white background print the quickest and are therefore employed when a company thinks users may need to print pages on a regular basis."
Black	Power, sexuality, sophistication, death, mystery, fear, unhappiness, elegance. Signifies death and mourning in many western cultures. It is definitely not a good background for printing. The color is used often at fashion Web sites and works well as background for many photo shots.

Source: Adapted from Color Voodoo Web site at www.colorvoodoo.com. See also Muller, Thomas, "Shades of Meaning," *The Wall Street Journal*, April 15, 2002, R4.

Site Evaluation Criteria

In evaluating Web sites, several criteria can be used. The following criteria are not listed in order of importance: All are considered important for site evaluation.

- **Color:** Color and general layout have a definite psychological impact on site visitors. An ideal layout is one with minimal text on a page and lots of white space. The Web site should be easy to navigate, with navigation bars on each page. Pictures should be chosen and placed carefully, not just scattered throughout the site.
- **Shape:** Shape is an extremely powerful (but overlooked) tool. It can motivate consumers, inspire visitors, and make a visit to the Web site enjoyable. A circle represents connection, community, wholeness, endurance, and safety. It refers to feminine features like warmth, comfort, and love. Rectangles represent order, logic, and security. Triangles represent energy, power, balance, law, and science. A circle and triangle in combination can result in an energetic, dynamic impression. A circle and a rectangle can convey warmth and security. Check the FedEx logo (www.fedex.com) as an example.

BOX 9-2
Color and culture

What makes Red Square red? Any visitor to Moscow can see that the venerable square is predominantly gray, notwithstanding the blood-red crenelated wall that surrounds the Kremlin. The red in Red Square is a particularly striking example of the way color can shed light on how different cultures see the world. Where English-speakers might associate red with danger or rage, in Russia it is linked to the word for beauty.

Red (*hong*) also carries positive associations in China, where it connotes happiness and is used on festive occasions. A Chinese bride is more likely to wear red than white, flaunting her joy the way a traditional white-clad Western bride flaunts her alleged virginity. White, in fact, is most definitely out on Chinese wedding days. It is the color of mourning. And in France, a bride won't be wearing white if hers is a *marriage blanc* (white marriage), that is, a marriage of convenience for reasons like obtaining working papers.

In France, meanwhile, when someone's seriously frightened, he'll say he has *une peur bleue* (he's scared blue). If he's got the blues, on the other hand, get out the bug spray—he'll tell you he's got *le cafard* (the cockroach). Red hair in France is not *rouge* but *roux*, and to call *une rousse* (a redheaded woman) *une rouge*—"a Red"—could produce an unpleasant reaction. Blond, of course, is easier—the French gave the world the word—but the line between *blond* and *chatain clair* (light brown) is not that easily discernible, even to the French.

SOURCE: Excerpted from Bortin, Meg, "When Colors Take on Different Cultural Hues," *International Herald Tribune*, September 28–29, 2002, 9.

- **Type:** Type should be appropriate and used carefully. For example, a serif typeface (like Times Roman) expresses organization and intelligence. It is also elegant and conservative. Sans serif faces like Helvetica and Arial are warm and friendly type styles. They are excellent choices for screen fonts because they are clear and easy to read. Decorative fonts are best used for titles and display; they should not be used for body type.
- **Content:** Companies new to the Web think that once they put up a site, people flock to visit it. This is far from the truth. Studies have found that users don't want to scroll up and down the page looking for information. This means that Web sites should provide valuable, timely information—not lots of text. Popular sites include updated information, interactivity, fun, and freebies. Well-organized, edited, and timely original content set in an attractive and consistent format are traits of great Web sites.
- **Services Offered:** What unique services does the site offer? It is not enough for a bank to simply list its services. It must provide some detail on those services, along with contact information in case of questions or a need to follow up.
- **Primary Focus:** Every Web site should have a primary focus. Take Oakley, Inc., maker of designer sunglasses, for example. The company's main focus is making glasses, yet it also produces shoes and watches. It is the same with banks. All banks have a primary focus, whether it is home equity loans, auto loans, or CDs. They also might offer personal checking accounts or savings and investment plans, but these may not be their primary focus.

ancillary: supportive services or features of a product.

- **Ancillaries:** In Web design, it is important to have links to ancillaries that do unique things for the visitor. For example, one banking ancillary is to evaluate current mortgage loans or help answer questions such as whether the visitor qualifies for an auto loan. These ancillaries have been known to attract customers who want more services or advice that is freely available.
- **Site Classification:** Web sites also can be evaluated based on five categories: category 1 (mere presence) to category 5 (multimedia, interactivity). Category 1 sites offer the bare essentials such as hours, location, directions to the company, and a list of services; these sites are purely informational. Category 2 sites offer more detailed information (forms, applications) and options that allow visitors to send in data for services like loan applications on a bank site. Category 3 sites involve greater interaction and use video and color to guide the visitor to primary buttons, links, or services. Category 4 sites use multimedia as well as workflow tools, and begin to show personalization. Category 5 sites are highly customized and offer advanced services that stretch across the Internet. They also coach the visitor in making decisions, ordering products or services, and using electronic cash to consummate transactions.
- **Professionalism:** This criterion considers how professional the site looks to a visitor. It includes neatness, spelling, and grammar.
- **Speed:** The critical question here is how long it takes the visitor to click from one page to the next. A page that takes more than 8 seconds to come up rates low. Pages that come up within 1 second are considered fast (see Box 9-3).
- **Consistency:** This criterion looks at how similar Web pages are in layout and design. If the site doesn't have a theme, it will not attract many visitors.
- **Personalization:** Sites that are high on personalization use cookies, which keep track of repeat visitors and their preferences, and respond to them as though the interface is one-on-one. Sites that have no personalization also have no log-in screens and little interactivity with the user as an individual.
- **Security:** Sites with firewalls and digital certificates, as well as SSL for information and transaction processing, would rate high on the security scale. (SSL is a protocol for transmitting private information over the Internet.)

scalability: how easily a Web site can be updated.

- **Scalability:** This criterion is related to how easily a site can be updated. A site high on scalability has a simple structure, uses frames and Extensible Markup Language (XML), and has a design that lends itself to easy maintenance.

Sample Evaluations

To illustrate the extremes in Web site evaluation, let's look at two Web sites. The first is www.mediterraneanbakeryanddeli.com. It is a good example of how putting little thought into implementation can compromise a Web site. First, the light blue and dark gray colors are unappealing. Beyond that, they do not promote a feeling of being invited. The opening page is text intense, although the owner's picture represents small, private business. If I were a visitor, I would not spend much time accessing such a homepage every time I logged on. When you click on six of the nine options, you face graphics unrelated to the product.

The site is a category 2, which offers detailed information about products with text and some graphics. Among the complete list of products and recipes that might be of interest to customers, it offers no links to the outside world.

The other extreme of Web site design is the Wachovia Bank site, www.wachovia.com, which is an excellent site. Not only is it full of information and useful ancillaries, but it also is well organized and easy to navigate. The company uses dark blue, light blue, and

BOX 9-3

E-commerce trends: Turbocharged Web pages

Start-up vendor Fireclick Inc. aims to render the 8-second rule obsolete with server software that downloads Web pages even before visitors have a chance to point and click. Using real-time and historical clickstream analysis, Fireclick's Blueflame software continually primes the browser cache one step ahead of an online user's actions. By downloading "most likely" page elements directly to a user's browser cache, the software can reduce page download times from 20 seconds to as little as 1 second.

As a result, e-businesses can improve browse-to-buy ratios; increase the number of completed transactions on their sites; and cultivate more loyal, repeat visitors, Fireclick said. Currently, online users consume bandwidth only when they request a Web page. During page views, modems sit idle.

Blueflame's proprietary content-delivery algorithm uses this idle time to retrieve pages that are most likely to be requested. The software decides where users are likely to head based on general site traffic patterns as well as macrostatistics on how users transition from one Web page to another. For instance, it is known that 80 percent of Amazon.com visitors request the top 10 best seller list early in their site visits, so when someone enters the site, Blueflame would automatically download the list page.

Screen Capture 9-2

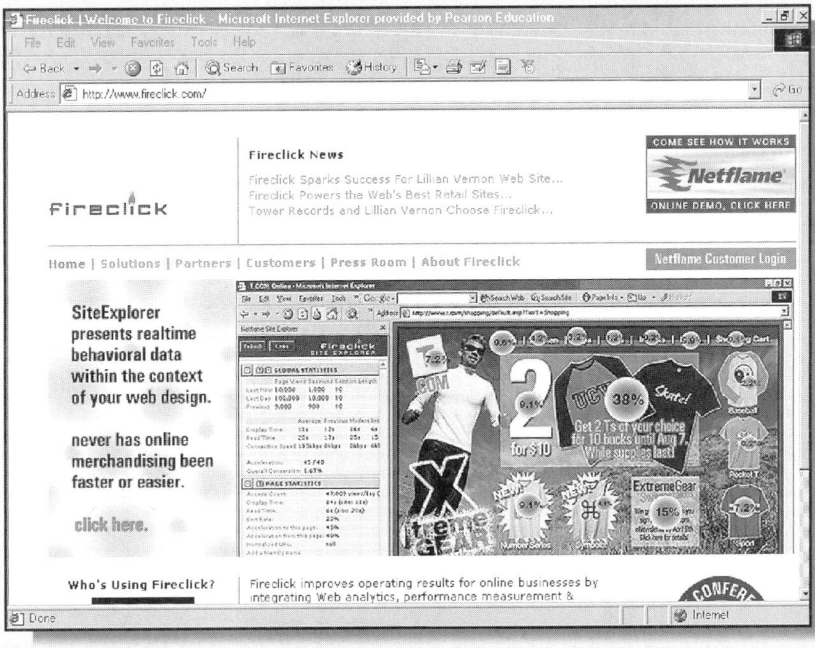

Source: 2003–2004 Fireclick, Inc. All rights reserved.

SOURCE: Zimmerman, Christine, "Web Pages Turbocharged," *InternetWeek*, March 20, 2000, 1ff.

beige as the primary colors. The color scheme helps organize a wealth of information. In addition to good use of color, the site employs slightly rounded, rectangular tabs to aid navigation and organization.

Concise frames with Java script pop-up menus provide viewers with subjects they can then investigate at increasing levels of depth and complexity without being overwhelmed with too much plain text and too many numbers. The site focuses on personal finance (all types of lending, investing, and typical banking services), as well as corporate services (accessing capital, managing risk, enhancing productivity). The site does a good job of demonstrating the company's overall focus on providing total solutions for personal and corporate banking.

Wachovia's Web site falls within the category 4 classification, because customers can apply for loans and services and conduct various business transactions through the site. The site gives an extremely professional impression, with an easy-to-follow layout and presentation of services in addition to consistent use of tool bars and organization schemes. These factors all contribute to quick navigation and convenient exchange of information.

No apparent personalization exists on the Wachovia site, but it does offer a login. The bank is able to compile a database of customer preferences and transaction behaviors so that it may someday take advantage of cross-selling services. Crucial to this endeavor is the clear presentation of privacy and security policies. Secure connections are made whenever any kind of personal information is transferred to and from the company. Although the Web site is complex, with an extensive number of services, the organization should mean improvements can be made with minimal difficulty.

Web sites are evaluated in various ways, using all kinds of criteria. The problem to date is lack of guidelines or standards with which to evaluate Web sites. Waller (2001) proposes "60 Ticks" for a good Web site (see Box 9-4). The important point to remember is that a Web site is evaluated best by coordinating preset criteria that are unique to the nature of the firm, its products, its audiences, and its mission. Cultural factors continue to be important.

Web Personalization

In designing a Web site, the question that lurks in the back of a developer's mind is: Are we getting the most out of the Web? Web personalization allows users to get more information about themselves and their interests, although it could mean giving up some privacy. The idea is to tailor Web content directly to a specific user by having the user provide information to the Web site either directly or through tracking devices on the site. The software can then modify the content to the needs of the user (see Box 9-5).

It is important to note the difference between personalization and customization. With customization, the focus is on direct user control. The user decides to click between options (e.g., headlines from CNN, the *New York Times*, the *Wall Street Journal* from a specific portal), and enter the stock symbol that the customer wants to track. Personalization is driven by artificial software that tries to serve up individualized pages to the user based on a model of that user's needs (past habits, preferences, and so on). Personalization of a Web site assumes that the computer infrastructure can address the user's needs. With users having different preferences at different times, personalization is not all that perfect. In any case, attempts have been made to use artificial intelligence to match the product with users' needs.

Personalization requires more than a software package or a tool and mining a Web site's data. The e-company's technical Web staff extracts, combines, and evaluates data taken from multiple sources and integrates the results into custom-facing channels before personalization becomes operational. It is costly and highly technical (see Figure 9-1). It also requires knowledge of the product, human behavior, and marketing strategies.

BOX 9-4
Statements that represent a good Web site

Impressions on first entry **YES** **NO**

- The URL/domain name is appropriate and meaningful.
- The surfer sees something meaningful within 8 seconds.
- The site name and product/purpose come up instantly.
- The first page is less than 20 K, and images are kept small.
- Text is visible while graphics are loaded.
- Graphics are named with useful text content.

The homepage is exciting, interesting, attention grabbing **YES** **NO**

- There is useful information on the homepage.
- The homepage looks good, and has a clean, uncluttered look.
- Important information is "above the fold" (top 600 × 300).
- Not distracted by excessive animation or flash.

The homepage contains the key facts **YES** **NO**

- Name of organization (preferably in H1 text heading).
- Shows business, products, where based.
- Style appropriate for target audience.
- Shows the sort of information available in the site.
- Shows name, address, telephone, fax, e-mail.
- Title is meaningful.
- META statements are correct.
- If frames are used, correct text links and METAs are provided.

Shopping Experience **YES** **NO**

- Friendly and quick route to buy.
- Secure handling of credit card information.
- Order acknowledged with delivery date stated.
- Order tracking provided.
- Delivery reliable.
- Returns policy stated.
- Certificates obtained from trade bodies.
- Privacy of data statement.
- Appropriate use of cookies.

The following is a list of the remaining headings in the paper. For details regarding the "ticks" under each heading, e-mail the author atwaller@waller.co.uk:

- Back office support.
- Links are clear and meaningful.
- The whole site has a structure.
- All the pages obey the same rules.
- Long Web pages have their own structure.
- All Web pages have a reference.
- Useful external links are provided.
- The Web site achieves its purpose.
- Browser compatibility and accessibility.

SOURCE: Excerpted from Waller, Richard, "60 Ticks for a Good Web Site," *Website Creation, Training and Consultancy*, West Sussex, United Kingdom, April 24, 2001, 1–4.

Figure 9-1 shows the processes required to operationalize Web personalization. It also specifies the components and hardware that support the processes. The four key steps are:

- **Customer interaction:** Visitors interact with the Web site and gradually provide information that profiles the visitor in terms of shopping preferences, likes, dislikes, and so on. In many cases, the site requests visitors to fill out a form, stating their preferences.
- **Data collection and integration:** This process activates primarily ETL (extraction, transformation, loading) unique to each e-merchant's goal. Some companies might only

BOX 9-5
Personalization and revenue

Personalization technology is helping plenty of Web retailers create customized electronic shopping boutiques whose inventory and pricing can vary from shopper to shopper online. At Cabela's Inc., a sporting goods retailer in Sidney, Nebraska, it's also helping to boost supply chain efficiencies across all three of the company's sales channels: stores, catalog, and online. The same technology that tracks individual customer preferences and shopping habits is increasing inventory turns and revenue, all within the context of building a branded experience.

The focus on personalization technology fits with Cabela's overall strategy of one-to-one customer service. This applies in its eight stores as well as at its call center, which handles catalog orders placed over the telephone plus all customer queries, regardless of where or how the customer shops. Tim Miller, director of Cabelas.com used established application programming interfaces to link the call center and catalog sales information with customer information generated via the Web site and other back-end information, such as order fulfillment data.

For online shoppers, the automated e-commerce system can alert them when particular items in their sizes are priced at closeout. As a result, Cabela's is able to cut costs and clear out excess and odd-lot inventory by advertising via e-mail rather than the U.S. Postal Service. Advertising sent via the U.S. mail doesn't reflect real-time inventory conditions as the e-mail ads do.

The personalization technology involves the products as well as the customers. For example, because there are many government restrictions on the sale of hunting paraphernalia, the ability to tailor product data based on customers' geography helps Cabela's provide shoppers with the appropriate information.

The bottom line is that personalization technology can enhance the customer experience and deliver operational efficiencies like increased inventory turns. What the Cabela's example shows is that getting those returns involves fully integrating the technology with the overall retail experience, not just your e-commerce site.

SOURCE: Excerpted from Fox, Pimm, "Getting Personal Boosts Revenue," *Computerworld*, June 17, 2002, 38.

want to capture Web site visitors' clickstream data, try to make sense out of customer interests, and make proper enhancements or changes to the Web site. Other companies want to go deeper into customer analysis, bringing certain data from multiple databases and storing it on a customer information repository. **Clickstream** refers to lines of code stored in a file every time a surfer views a Web page. Clickstream data make it possible for a company to track surfers as they navigate through the company's Web site—the pages they click on, how long they stay on each page, the ads viewed, and so on (Hall 2002).

clickstream: lines of code stored in a file every time a surfer views a Web page.

- **Business intelligence:** Company analysts rely on artificial intelligence packages and other techniques to figure out customer preferences based on the data collected in the customer information data warehouse or repository.
- **Customer interaction personalization:** In this process, the results of business intelligence help in generating personalization rules, which are integrated into the e-merchant's Web site personalization engine. The rules serve to target surfers with specific content based on preestablished behavioral profiles in the customer information repository or data warehouse.

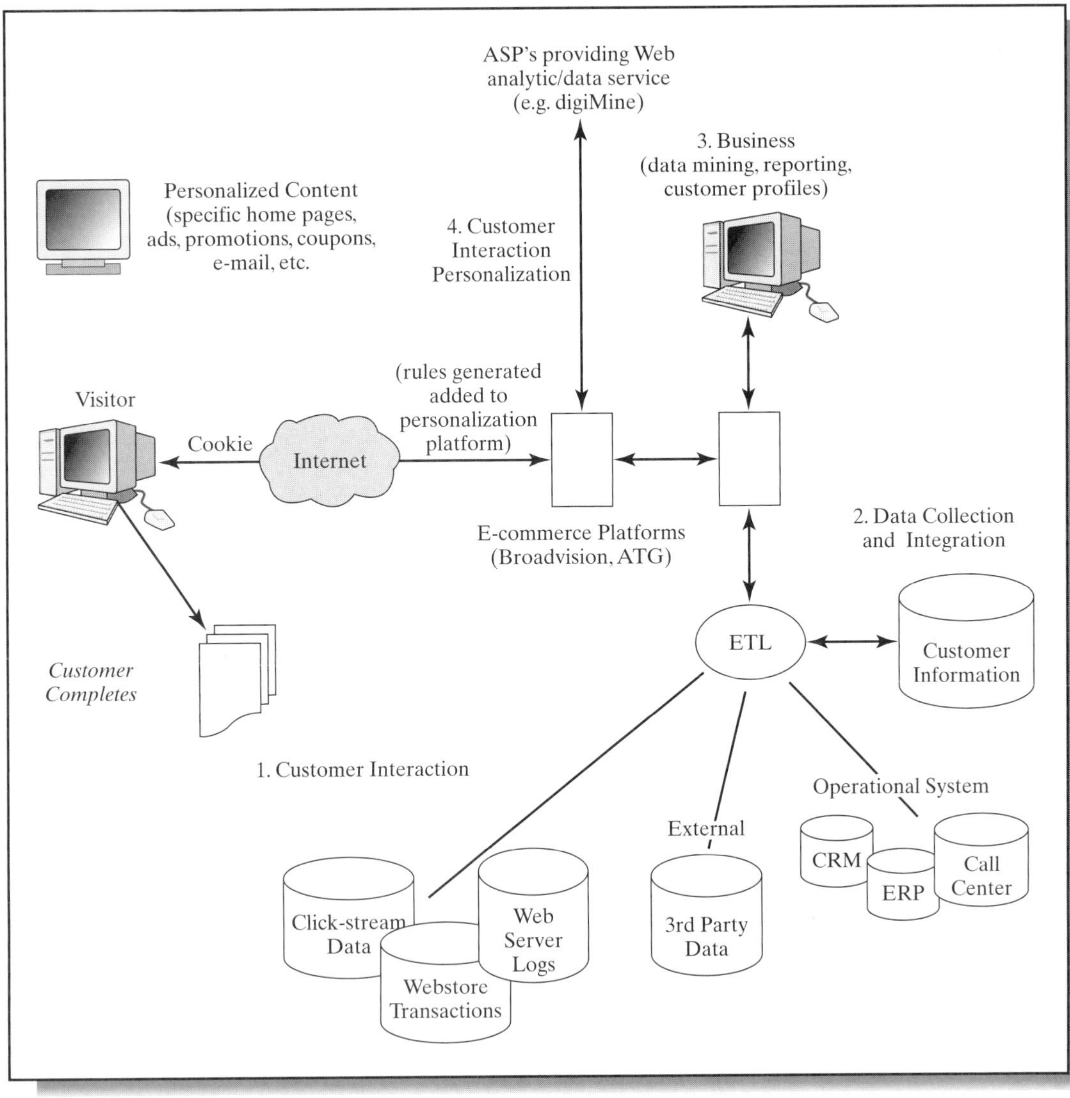

Figure 9-1
Components of personalization

Source: Adapted from Hall, Curt, "The Personalization Equation," *Software Magazine*, April 1, 2001, 27.

Because our focus is on e-commerce, personalization should be customer-centric in that it should be looked at from the consumer's viewpoint and driven by Internet users themselves. An example of user-driven personalization is my.yahoo.com, where anyone can create a personal profile of the information resources that you want to see displayed on the homepage every time you connect to the Yahoo! site. The Web server tailors the displayed content around the specifications of each user's profile. This type of personalization is used for filtering content rather than for the one-to-one e-marketing of products via the Internet (White 2001).

inference-based personalization: a technique that tracks a Web user's behavior, identifies other people with similar behavior, and uses such people to recommend to the surfer their products.

For e-business applications, a popular technique, called **inference-based personalization,** tracks a Web user's behavior, identifies other people with similar behavior, and uses such people to recommend to the surfer their products. For example, the well-known Amazon.com waits for customers to commit to a product (e.g., book), and then they are shown a list of other products purchased by people who purchased the same product.

Approaches to Web Personalization

Four general approaches can be taken to Web personalization. Each approach is adopted for a reason.

- **Cookies:** Cookies are probably the most recognizable personalization tools. They are bits of code or a text file that sits in a user's Internet browser memory and identifies that person to a Web site when they return. In a way, a cookie allows the site to greet the user by name. It is also a way to communicate information about you to Web sites that you visit. An example is Yahoo! Inc.'s My Yahoo! pages. Technically, a cookie is a message a Web server sends to a Web browser. The browser stores the message in a text file. The message is returned to the server every time the browser requests a page from that server.
- **Collaborative filtering software:** This software keeps track of users' movements across the Web to interpret their interests. It views their habits, from how long they stay on a page to the pages they choose while on the Web site. The software compares the information about one user's behavior against data gathered about other customers with similar interests. The result is a recommendation to the customer. A good example is Amazon.com's "Customers who bought this book also bought . . ." feature.
- **Check-box:** In this user-controlled process, a visitor chooses specific interests on a checklist so the site can display the requested information. The approach is less obvious than cookies.
- **Rule-based personalization:** Users are divided into segments based on business rules that generate certain types of information from a user's profile. For example, BroadVision (www.broadvision.com) asks visitors to fill out a form to determine the type of product or information it can provide. The information on the form becomes the visitor's profile, which is stored in the database by user segment (community, income, sex, age, and so on). The decision to give personalized information is based on business rules. The database looks up the visitor's profile and triggers a business rule to fit the profile. For example, if the person lives in California, then deliver travel information about California; if the person's income is greater than $100,000 per year, then send information about first-class airfare to Bermuda and product information about Hartman luggage.

WHAT'S THE BIG FUSS OVER COOKIES?

cookie: information about a Web site visit deposited in the visitor's browser.

When it comes to monitoring Web site traffic, it is impossible to differentiate among visits to a site unless the server can somehow *mark* a visitor. In order to do this, the Web site deposits a piece of information in the visitor's browser called a **cookie.** It's like a claim check at the dry cleaner. You drop off a suit or shirts and get a claim check. When you return with the claim check, you get your clothes back. A site uses cookies to personalize information, to help with online sales/service as on Amazon.com, or to track popular links or demographics as on DoubleClick.

Technically, a cookie is an HTTP header with a text-only string placed in the browser's memory. The string contains the domain, path, how long it is valid, and the value of a variable that the Web site sets. If the user spends more time at the site than the lifetime of this variable, the string is saved to file for future reference.

Several myths about cookies continue to bother the layperson. Among the popular ones are the following.

transient cookies: cookies that contain information about the user that the Web server can access until the browser is closed—occupy no hard drive space.

persistent cookies: cookies that contain information that the Web server retains on the hard drive of the user's computer. They carry with them an expiration date and remain on the hard disk until the date expires.

- *Cookies clog the hard disk.* **Transient cookies**—cookies that contain information about the user that the Web server can access until the browser is closed—occupy no hard drive space. In contrast, **persistent cookies**—cookies that contain information that the Web server retains on the hard drive of the user's computer—carry with them an expiration date and remain on the hard disk until the date expires. Transient cookies lack expiration dates and last only for the duration of the session.
- *Cookies can put a virus on my computer.* Because cookies are always stored as data in text format instead of an executable format, they cannot do anything hostile. Even then, a virus would not be able to spread automatically until the user opened the file. Based on www.cookiecentral.com, making a cookie that could spread a virus would be virtually impossible.
- *Cookies give companies access to my personal file.* Cookies can store any information the user provides to a Web site. Unfortunately, depending on the ethics standards of each company, whatever personal information is offered to a company's Web site may be spread, but laws limit the details that can be released. Legal and ethical issues are covered in Chapter 12.
- *Disabling cookies in my browser will prevent any Web sites from gathering information about me.* According to a U.S. government report, the data that cookies collect also can be recorded in a Web server's log files. Cookies just make it easier (http://content.techweb.com/wire/story/TWB19980316S0015).

The original purpose of cookies was to save users' time. This has continued to be one of the major benefits of this technology. Disabling certain cookies might disable the service that identifies you as a member. For example, the author has a free portfolio account on www.quicken.com. To access the account, Quicken asks for the user ID and password, which have been stored in advance (a cookie on my PC). Deleting the cookie in cache memory prompts Quicken to ask you for the same information, as if you're a new entrant.

There are other benefits, as well. A case can be made that the consumer is actually the winner, as cookies can help reduce the distance from consumers to the product(s) they seek, because cookies automatically provide access to goods consumers might be interested in. If used properly, marketing information contained within cookies is a quick and convenient means of keeping site content fresh and up to date. (See www.cookiecentral.com/faq.)

If one is looking for limitations or cause for concern, cookies utilize space on a client's hard drive for a Web site's purposes. They do so without permission to use space or capture the information. The most prolific argument against cookies is that they threaten our privacy as Internet users. They know which Web browser you are using, which operating system you are running, and even your IP address. They also track which Web site you came from and which Web site you are going to without permission. In most cases, you are not revealing your information to just one Web site but to multiple sites. A marketing company can track your movements on all pages containing its advertisements. They can follow only which pages you are looking at and for how long, but not what you do within those pages like the host site can. What makes this whole business disconcerting is that companies combine and share information into one large database and, many times, sell it to telemarketers, who then attempt to push their products to you in the middle of your dinner. Laws have been instituted to bar such practice during certain hours, but the whole idea is another nuisance to cope with.

Deleting and Rejecting Cookies

Cookies can be deleted or rejected at will. To do so, you need first to close your browser, because cookies are held in memory until you close your browser. If a cookie is deleted with the browser open, it will make a new file when you close it and you won't be able to get rid of it. Remember that if you delete a cookie, you start from scratch with the site that once recognized you through the cookie. Instead of deleting all cookies, you probably should open the cookies folder and delete the ones from servers that you don't want to keep.

Netscape and Microsoft Internet Explorer provide features that can alert you every time a cookie is being added to the browser. For example, Netscape 4.7 allows an *alert before accepting cookies* feature to be set. Through the **Edit/Preferences/Advanced** menu, a user has the following choices: (1) accept all cookies, (2) accept only cookies that are sent back to the originating server, (3) disable cookies, or (4) warn me before accepting a cookie.

In Microsoft Internet Explorer, cookies can be disabled by using the **Tools/Internet Options/Security** menu. Microsoft saves cookies in the Temporary Internet Files folder, which takes up approximately 2 percent of the hard drive. Netscape limits the total cookie count to 300. (The average size of a cookie is from 50 to 150 bytes.)

Privacy Concerns

Are cookies a threat to privacy? The sad truth is that you are as anonymous as you want to be. Revealing any information through the Web makes it public information, except for the safeguards available to the user in the PC browser. Some companies abuse the information they receive from visitors, resulting in that most hated product of Internet commerce—**spam.** Because of spam, people are becoming increasingly skeptical about what happens to the information they provide to certain Web sites.

spam: online or e-mail equivalent of junk mail.

Recent high-profile breaches of Web users' privacy have raised public concern about data collection through cookies and other techniques. Many companies are revisiting their privacy policy statements because the privacy issue has become so explosive. For example, the privacy statement on Intuit's popular Quicken.com Web site makes it clear that customers have the option of not accepting cookies used to gather information and that the company "will not willfully disclose customer data without their permission."

Despite the publicity regarding the privacy issue, Web sites continue to collect an unprecedented volume of data about customers. Oracle reported building a data warehouse for Amazon.com that holds up to 3 terabytes (billions) of customer sales data. The warehouse has the capability of scaling up 1,000 times to 3 petabytes (trillions) in 5 years.

Some companies are reevaluating their reliance on cookies as a way to collect customer data, but unless an alternative is adopted, lawsuits will continue to be filed. In

2000, Yahoo.com and Broadcast.com were the targets of a $50 billion lawsuit in Texas, where the use of cookies is considered a violation of the state's anti-stalking law (*USA Today*, March 31, 2000, B1).

WHAT MAKES A WEB SITE USABLE?

What good is a Web site if no one can use it effectively? On the Internet, it is survival of the easiest. If visitors cannot find what they're looking for, they can't buy it. The sad truth about doing business on the Web is that most Web sites rebuff more than 70 percent of the customers who visit them, which means passing up millions of dollars in potential sales (Lais 2002). A lost customer is lost for good. The cost of flipping to another Web site is so low it does not make sense to go back to a site that failed once or twice. In Web design language, this is called **churning.** It is a basic measure of visitor dissatisfaction with online products or bad interface design.

churning: basic measure of visitor dissatisfaction with a site.

The key to attract customers back to one's Web site includes high-quality content, ease of use, quick downloads, and frequent updating. The fact is that searching for information can be an experience. It can be a good experience when users find what they're looking for quickly and painlessly. This is what usability is all about. It can be a bad experience when the information is elusive. It does not matter whether the user is a novice or an expert: No amount of information can overcome a poorly designed Web site.

The goal of effective Web site design, then, is to give users a good experience that will turn them into frequent and loyal customers. The main difference between a person's behavior in a physical store and on the Web is related to **switching costs.** In a physical store, a customer goes to the store, finds the merchandise, and begins the purchase with a salesperson. In this case, switching costs are high. Once we find a product, most of us will go ahead and deal with a rude salesperson rather than go to another store and possibly encounter the same behavior. In contrast, switching costs on the Internet are low. If visitors do not find what they are looking for, the competition is only a mouse click away.

switching costs: the time it takes a visitor to switch from one Web site to another.

Studies of user behavior on the Web have found low tolerance for inefficient designs or slow sites. People simply do not want to wait or learn how to navigate a cluttered site. Most Web sites are tough to use. Usability studies consistently find less than 50 percent of Web sites usable (Nielsen and Norman, 2000, 66). Bloated graphics, cluttered text, and minimal useful information leave little for visitors to work with, so they go elsewhere and are unlikely to return.

To illustrate the usability factor, suppose you want to buy an ink jet printer for home use. In checking out the leading Web sites, you find Hewlett-Packard (www.hp.com), Canon (www.canon.com), and Epson (www.epson.com). You click on Hewlett Packard's Web site, only to find no mention of printers. Being a novice surfer, you click on "home and home office." There, you find a graphic of a young couple romantically watching a show on a computer monitor. Below the image, you find a generic text heading "Printing and Multifunction" in fading blue against a gray background. You say to yourself "I thought I was looking for a home printer, not an entertainment center." When you click on "printing and multifunction," you are faced with further choices of printers. You choose one option regarding the printing type before you begin to see a selection of printers with a brief summary of the features of each HP printer. None of the descriptions helps you choose a printer to buy. You don't even know what the product numbers mean.

So, in frustration, you click away to the Canon Web site. The total time you have spent is more than 3 minutes (Author's experience, January 3, 2003).

When you visit Canon's Web site, the site makes no mention of and displays no interest in selling printers. Its homepage has a link to "products" that requires you to click on a specified country before it allows you to go any further. Then, you click on "office product"; then on "printers" on the left task bar; then to whether you want network printers, non-network printers, or office printers. You click on "office printers," which finally brings up the page that shows Canon's jet printers. The descriptions are brief and the frustration continues.

Finally, on the Epson site, you have a list of Epson America Inc.'s printers, with a short, easy-to-understand description, in two clicks. One more click on any of the printers and you get a list of features and technical information to help you make a decision. In the meantime, the whole process from Hewlett Packard to Epson took close to 15 minutes. You click on Amazon.Com as a last resort, and all you have to do is enter "ink jet printer" in the search window on the top-left corner (first thing the human eye sees) and voila! You have a list of all the ink jet printers that you can choose from. This time, you have access to all the information you need in *one* click. It is quick, accurate, and reliable.

Usability Guidelines

Designers strive to make a Web site as inviting and easy to navigate as possible, but for one reason or another, many forget to follow some basic guidelines (see Box 9-6). In checking for usability, a number of questions need to be addressed (see Box 9-7).

If you forget everything else, remember the three most important criteria for successful Web sites: conciseness, scanability, and objectivity. Meeting them results in a well-written, easily navigable, pleasantly interactive, distinctive, and thoroughly tested Web site (see Screen Capture 9-3).

CNN (www.cnn.com): A high volume of information displayed on the surface; all stories are available in a clear format.

EBay (www.ebay.com): This site provides a unique feature: It gives the visitor the impression that the site's purpose is strictly buying and selling.

BOX 9-6
Web shopability

- Show the full product cost as soon as possible.
- Explain why you need to collect personal information.
- Use opt-in rather than opt-out policies to give the shopper more control over data sharing.
- Don't overemphasize promotional products.
- Cross-reference products.
- Ensure that images are big and show features that are important to buyers.
- Put the search box on every page.
- Make "All" the search list default (so it searches the whole site).
- Avoid jargon and clever or made-up names.
- Have the customer select options before the product goes in the shopping cart.
- Expect users to hit the Enter key when filling out forms.
- Offer a toll-free number for placing phone orders.

SOURCE: Lais, Sami, "How to Stop Web Shopper Flight," *Computerworld*, June 17, 44.

BOX 9-7
Usability checklist

- **Is the site engaging?** That is, do visitors enjoy the experience? Do they feel in control of the site tour?
- **Is the site efficient?** Is response time fast enough to keep visitors on the site? Does the site make it easy for visitors to understand what each page is about?
- **Is the site supportive?** When visitors make a mistake, is it easy for them to undo their mistake? Does it offer help, advice, or directions when necessary?
- **Is the site consistent and reliable?** Does the site respond consistently throughout a visitor's tour?
- **Decide on a writing style and stick to it.** For example, don't use a variety of forms for the same term, like *e-commerce, E-commerce, ecommerce*, and *EC*. Consistency is critical. Do a walk-through with someone else to edit all pages before posting. At least run a spell check. Remember that errors erode visitor confidence.
- **Give visitors what they're looking for.** Give visitors a reason to visit. For example, if you're selling office supplies, show visitors how to purchase them. The site should be designed to reflect what visitors want to buy rather than what the merchant wants to sell.
- **Identify your business.** When the homepage comes up on a visitor's screen, it should show your business in a unique light. This is called **branding.** Take time to create your own brand.

branding: placing a logo on every Web site page to distinguish your business from the competition.

- **Keep the big picture in mind.** Good design should result in a usable and easily navigable site. Designers, marketers, and technical people should work together to come up with a site that results in a positive user experience.
- **Make the site easy to navigate.** Like good software, an effective Web site should not need a tutorial or a user's manual. A visitor who gets lost in the middle of the site will most likely leave out of frustration. Remember the 8-second rule.
- **Focus on content before graphics.** Content should be useful and usable. Good content should guide, educate, sell, and make a hit with the visitor. Graphics and animation are no substitute for content. Use fewer words, because it is *painful* to read online. Users read 25 percent more slowly online than in print because of the poor resolution of most monitors.
- **Make your text scanable.** According to Nielsen's research, 79 percent of Web users scan rather than read. Only 21 percent read word for word. When visitors were presented with a scanable version of a site, their performance improved by 47 percent (Nielsen, August 18, 2000, 1ff). To improve scanability, consider bold text, large type, highlighted text, captions, graphics, contents lists, and bulleted lists.
- **Be careful about flashy marketing language.** Present information without boasting, and minimize any subjective claims. Hype is not attractive in Internet marketing. People do not appreciate being misled. If users do not like what they see or read, they'll click to another site.
- **Encourage visitor feedback.** The Web site should incorporate an opportunity for visitors to offer praise, criticism, suggestions, and the like. Make it easy for them to reach you via the Web, by phone, fax, or e-mail.
- **Test, test, and test again.** Remember the two levels of testing: First, see if the Web site is technically right, then see if the site is right in the eyes of the visitor. Simply analyzing site logs (records of how many hits each page got, the paths users took through the site, and so on) is not a reliable way to test the Web site. The site should be tested on people.

Screen Capture 9-3
An example of a successful Web site: CNN (www.cnn.com)

Fidelity Investments (www.fidelity.com): This site is unique because it gives visitors the impression that the information they want is easy to find. The material is displayed in a clear and concise format.

Disney (www.disney.com): Visitors knew why they went to the site but tended to get lost easily.

Motorola (www.motorola.com): When this site was tested for usability in 1999, users had a hard time getting to the pages because of Web server errors.

MSNBC (www.msnbc.com): This news agency presents essentially the same stories as CNN, but the way the site is designed forces users to work around ads, which often makes it irritating to navigate (Millard, October 1999, 7).

Perhaps the most critical factor in customer loyalty is fostering *trust* through Web site design. Customers must believe that an e-merchant will follow through on an order, protect the privacy of the e-customer, and assure end-to-end transaction integrity. For online stores, trust means profits, especially when most of the traffic is generated by repeat customers. Also, more and more people complain about the download time, not because of the 8-second rule, per se, but because they are having trouble completing a task. This means that designers must develop navigation efficiency and clear content together.

Reliability Testing

The Internet's increasing role as a medium for commerce has placed new emphasis on reliability. Reliability is related to usability. If the scanners at a local grocery store go down, the cashiers will be hard pressed to do business—but they can still manage. If the

reliability: the percentage of time the Web site is available.

Web server of a store like Best Buy crashes, the whole operation stops. For a Web administrator, the core of **reliability** is availability. For example, 98 percent reliability per year means the Web site is not available roughly 7 days out of the year.

The three components to Web availability are system availability, network availability, and application availability. A system might be available, but if the network is down, the system is not available and, therefore, not usable. If the system is up and running, but not the application, the system is still down.

To ensure Web site reliability and usability, these ideas are worth noting.

- **Provide system backup.** The system that supports the Web site should be coupled to a second system that can take over in the event the first system fails.
- **Install a disk-mirroring feature.** This device allows you to add or replace hardware while the system is in operation.
- **Ensure that the system hardware is *fault-tolerant*.** Have a specially designed operating system that keeps the Web site or any application running, even when the Central Processing Unit (CPU) goes down. The goal is to eliminate unplanned or unexpected shutdowns.
- **Be sure applications are self-contained.** If the Web server uses other applications such as Domain Name Service (DNS) or e-mail, provide a dedicated server for those jobs.
- **Be sure there is adequate hard disk space.** Enough hard disk space must be available to handle unexpected surges in Web traffic.
- **Buy everything from a single vendor.** Unless the company is adept at buying hardware and technology from various vendors, reliability, integrity, and maintainability of the total system are best served by buying everything from a single vendor.

User Testing

The churning problem is best corrected early in the process by simply asking prospective visitors or customers what they want before finishing the design. Once the design is complete, user testing is crucial before loading the site on the Internet. To test, invite people who will most likely be using the product. Try to eliminate bias by selecting users who have no preconceived notion about the product. For example, if you're building a site for Sears, don't invite people who work for Kmart (see Box 9-8).

Once the sample has been determined, the next step is to decide what to look for during the test. This type of testing is not a matter of statistics. It is tempting to think that if 6 out of 10 users say they like the company logo on the homepage, that 60 percent of the potential audience likes the logo. Unfortunately, this is not necessarily true because Web site evaluation is essentially subjective. It depends on the visitor's perception of appearance, color, layout, navigation, and so on.

In most cases, you do not need statistics to tell if something is not working well. If every user testing the site finds it difficult to locate certain buttons, there is a good chance that the wider audience will have the same difficulty. The bottom line is not to take test users' choices literally. It is better to look for trends in the way the site is succeeding or failing to reach users.

In conducting user testing, remember that your subjects are not the most reliable source of information, especially for subjective items like color, format, or page integration. It is still critical that the designer present the site with a description and an explanation of

BOX 9-8
Role of user testing

At American Airlines Inc., a recent Web site overhaul included new servers and increased network capacity in the data center. It also meant new standards for Web designers on such things as the sizes of GIF image files and the breadth of color choices to minimize performance slowdown.

Despite stress-testing the new site with tools before it went live in the spring, the company rolled out the site incrementally—to 50,000 of its best customers at a time—during the ramp-up to the site's formal launch. This way, the company could see real-world loads and ease the internal team into the new site. During the ramp-up, the developers could see how people navigated through the site and how applications performed. But because most users were still using the old site, the team wasn't hanging on the edge of the limb. It gave the developers a chance to fix a few minor problems before the full-scale rollout.

The result? AA.com Web pages now average load times of 1.7 seconds, down from 5 seconds.

SOURCE: Excerpted from Hall, Mark, "Find Those Bottlenecks," *Computerworld*, August 19, 2002, 29.

the layout. Then if you place the site in front of users and let them try it (review it, place orders), their reactions can give you a good sense of the underlying patterns in their responses.

Managing Images and Color

A company can optimize its Web site in a number of ways. The main areas include images and color, speed, format, layout, and links. Images are appropriate when they are in the right location and are the right size. Experience has shown that bigger images are not always better. Unattractive images can be a serious problem. In one consulting job, the client wanted a large picture of the bank on the homepage. When the site was loaded on the ISP's Web server and launched on the Internet, it took 45 seconds to download and the result was simply ugly. After receiving quite a few complaints from site visitors, there was a quick retreat to the drawing board. The large image was replaced with a much smaller one.

In terms of color and contrast, the key question is: Do the colors you pick work well with the goal(s) of your site? The main point for the Web designer is to be smart about the colors. It is not a good idea to think in terms of favorite or least favorite colors. Just make sure the color supports your message and presents your story in the best light. Most Web site designers agree that dark text on light background is most appropriate. The trick is to have enough contrast between text and background.

Readability Testing

Readability is more than just contrast. As we have discussed earlier in the chapter, font type and size, color of background, length of line, and layout of text when combined with graphics are each important contributors to readability. White type on a black background is readable, but light gray type on black is easier on the eye. The safest combination is black type on a white background. It might not be the flashiest combination, but it is safe. The larger the type is, the more readable the text is, but the longer the line is, the more difficult it is to read. Long lines and narrow margins just don't work well.

Images: GIFs Versus JPEGs

It is inevitable that some images or graphics will appear on your Web pages. Adding graphics is a little complicated, but it is easier when you understand the basics. The best method is to put the graphic in a separate file and then reference that file in your Web page so the browser retrieves the graphic and displays it on the page.

GIF: a popular bit-mapped graphics format used on the World Wide Web.

JPEG: a popular bit-mapped graphics format ideal for scanned photographs.

To optimize the page, you need to decide whether a given image ought to be in a **GIF** or a **JPEG** format. Either format can be used. The main difference between the two is the compression technique. The GIF format is perfect for smaller graphics that should look crisp and bright, like simple company logos, icons, small buttons, and navigation bars or images with large page areas of solid color. Using GIFs for large pictures often leads to huge file sizes and long download times.

JPEGs display thousands of colors and can be compressed into smaller file sizes than GIFs. They're ideal for scanned photographs or multicolor images because they handle true color well. One problem with JPEGs is that they do not handle large areas of solid color or sharp edges well. Some older browsers do not handle JPEGs at all. In contrast, all graphic browsers handle the GIF format.

Caches

cache: high-speed storage on a PC for frequently used instructions and data and infrequently changed pages.

Images that repeat throughout a Web site, such as logos or navigation bars, do not need to download again and again. Netscape and Microsoft Explorer set aside a memory **cache** to store recently used images in RAM and on the hard disk by default. Once stored, a browser recognizes the file name and pulls the image straight from cache rather than downloading it. This makes images appear to download faster and is a performance boost to the Web site.

How It Works

Figure 9-2 is a general layout of how cache works. Briefly, it involves the following steps.

1. A user requests a Web page
2. The user's browser checks cache to see if the request is in. If in, then no more request is necessary; otherwise, the browser asks the local server.
3. The server checks cache to make sure it is not stored there. If in, then it serves the browser.
4. Server requests from Internet.
5. Server checks location of request and refers it to the closest distribution server.
6. Distribution server delivers the request to local server.
7. Request delivered to local server.
8. Local server sends it to original requesting user. Browser now caches object (Kay 2002).

How Many Links?

As part of site navigation, links and cross-links are inevitable. The critical question is how many? The more links that appear on a page, the less likely it is that any link will be read. Visitors tend to tune out and just read the text. Also, links can take up as much as half of a page's HTML and, like logos, images, and icons that reside in cache, they are downloaded repeatedly with every page. Minimizing the links will help speed up site performance. Screen 9-4 shows the extensive number of links on the Webmonkey homepage.

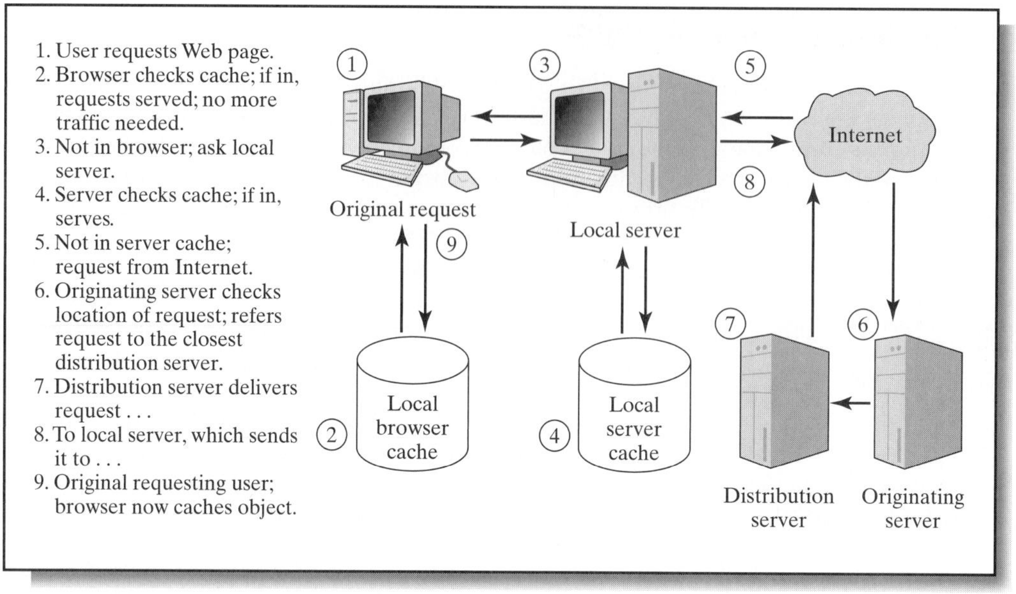

Figure 9-2
How cache works

Source: Kay, Russell, "How It Works," *Computerworld,* August 19, 2002, 36.

Screen Capture 9-4
A Web page with many links: Webmonkey (www.webmonkey.com)

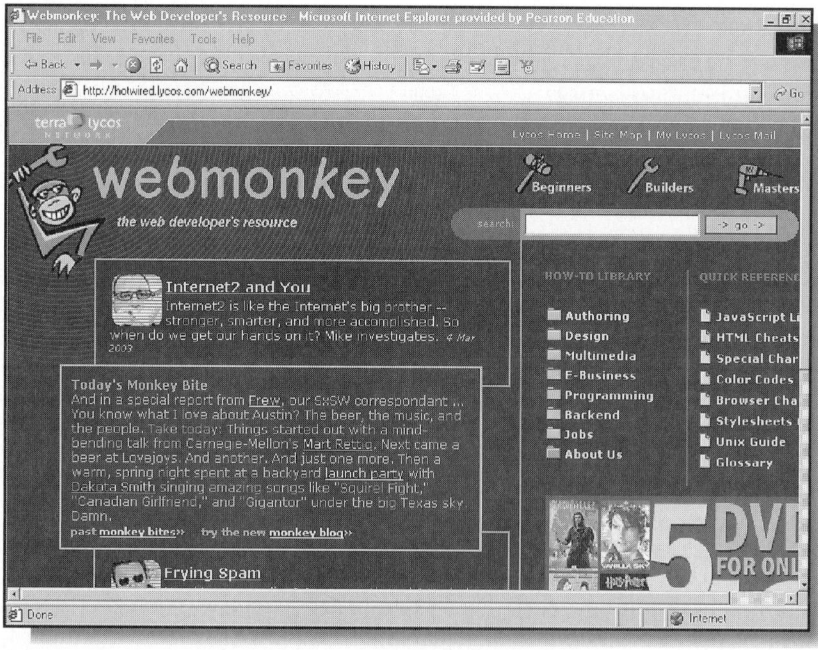

The Role of the Web Server

It is not just the links, images, color, or format that can affect the performance of a Web site. It is also the speed of the servers and the network connection. Review the status of your ISP's Web server, the bandwidth used, the Web sites it hosts, and the nature of the Web traffic the ISP handles. If you are hosting your own Web site, revisit the server software to ensure that it is tuned for speed. In the meantime, test your site against the competition to see how well it fares in terms of speed and overall performance.

WEB SITE CONTENT AND TRAFFIC MANAGEMENT

Now that you have a Web site in operation, the next step is to learn how to manage its content and traffic.

Content Management

Web content management: collecting, assembling, publishing, and removing content from a Web site.

Web content management is the process of collecting, assembling, publishing, and removing content from a Web site. The focus is on version control, content security, and visitor approval. Web content management differs from Web site management, which focuses on easy navigation, availability, performance, scalability, and security. Web content management makes sure a site eliminates waste and clutter. Stuff gets tucked away on a Web site until a visitor hits it and finds dated, irrelevant, or incorrect material. Managing content means promoting the reliability and integrity of the site.

Web Traffic Management

In terms of traffic management, the idea is to monitor the volume of business coming into the site and interpret its impact on sales, productivity, and inventory turnover. This is based on the philosophy that speed thrills. Never let your visitors get lost. Purge outdated content and never let your visitors see dead links, which sap your credibility. The most common tool for this kind of management is usage statistics reports generated for the client by the ISP. A sample report is shown in Figure 9-3. The report contains a monthly physical count and graphic representation of the total hits (per hour, per day), total pages, total visits, total kilobytes, and usage by country.

One important point to make in reviewing such reports is caution regarding the reliability of the numbers. For example, many reports will specify the total time the user spends on your Web site but cannot tell you whether the user was lost for 10 minutes on the credit-card verification screen before clicking away in frustration (see Box 9-9).

How quickly visitors browse a Web site is another statistic many tools measure. This measure is often falsely associated with speed. In practice, the speed with which visitors move around the site has little to do with their usage patterns. In one study, Spool found that visitors rated the Amazon.com site faster than About.com (Spool, 1). Paradoxically, Amazon.com's pages took an average of 36 seconds to download over a 56-bit modem, but About.com's pages were downloaded successfully in 8 seconds. His conclusion from watching how users traversed the site is that "speed equals ease of information retrieval." To improve the perception of how fast your site loads, take visitors more quickly to the information they're looking for.

Summary by Month										
	Daily Avg				Monthly Totals					
Month	Hits	Files	Pages	Visits	Sites	KBytes	Visits	Pages	Files	Hits
Feb 2001	10360	8718	430	175	3335	1214720	4909	12044	244124	290092
Jan 2001	8217	6799	422	181	3484	1264175	5614	13086	210791	254749
Dec 2000	9287	7376	489	197	3889	1424863	6124	15178	228686	287904
Nov 2000	9171	7592	537	216	3711	1433696	6499	16129	227763	275145
Oct 2000	9703	8002	557	219	4092	1540738	6799	17282	248077	300809
Sep 2000	7548	6073	544	226	3364	1086662	6780	16330	182200	226459
Aug 2000	7509	6003	532	211	3500	1084247	6551	16492	186112	232794
Jul 2000	7216	6206	474	211	3482	1121731	6872	14699	192409	223711
Jun 2000	7497	6445	491	231	3376	1055889	6707	14249	186932	217434
May 2000	8338	7054	526	241	3741	1169288	7479	16312	218682	258487
Apr 2000	7198	5695	580	260	3634	1089009	7800	17414	170858	215966
Mar 2000	5922	4831	458	218	3488	1105460	6773	14207	149779	183601
Totals						14590478	78907	183422	2446413	2967151

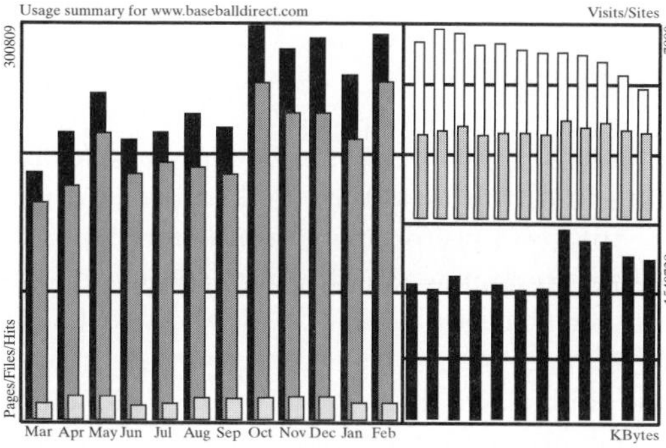

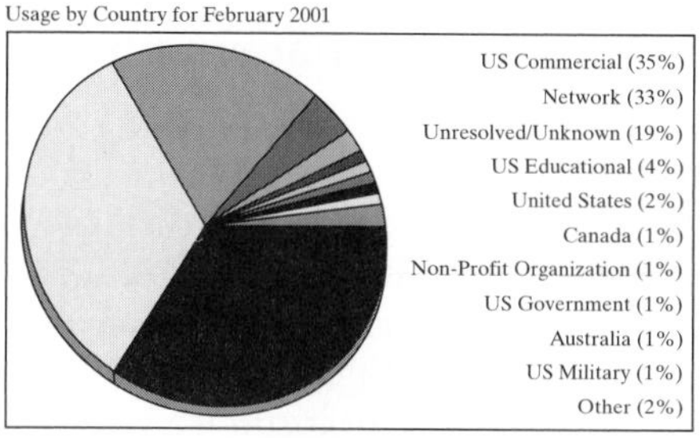

Top 30 of 42 Total Countries							
#	Hits		Files		KBytes		Country
1	101210	34.89%	77819	31.88%	434080	35.73%	US Commercial
2	95978	33.09%	84948	34.80%	375673	30.93%	Network
3	54121	18.66%	46808	19.17%	237494	19.55%	Unresolved/Unknown
4	10193	3.51%	9655	3.95%	47436	3.91%	US Educational
5	6387	2.20%	5027	2.06%	25436	2.09%	United States
6	4093	1.41%	3212	1.32%	17017	1.40%	Canada
7	4054	1.40%	3883	1.59%	18936	1.56%	Non-Profit Organization
8	2559	0.88%	2213	0.91%	9686	0.80%	US Government
9	1683	0.58%	1677	0.69%	6330	0.52%	Australia
10	1467	0.51%	1395	0.57%	6660	0.55%	US Military
11	1376	0.47%	1373	0.56%	6644	0.55%	United Kingdom
12	1131	0.39%	1035	0.42%	4080	0.34%	Japan
13	1070	0.37%	691	0.28%	1798	0.15%	Old style Arpanet (arpa)
14	510	0.18%	505	0.21%	3907	0.32%	Germany
15	454	0.16%	446	0.18%	2315	0.19%	Sweden
16	443	0.15%	223	0.09%	1044	0.09%	Czech Republic
17	418	0.14%	358	0.15%	1198	0.10%	Mexico
18	340	0.12%	339	0.14%	2118	0.17%	Argentina
19	315	0.11%	315	0.13%	2170	0.18%	France
20	292	0.10%	292	0.12%	1325	0.11%	New Zealand (Aotearoa)
21	220	0.08%	219	0.09%	1369	0.11%	Taiwan
22	197	0.07%	115	0.05%	377	0.03%	Belgium
23	191	0.07%	191	0.08%	1146	0.09%	Austria
24	162	0.06%	162	0.07%	780	0.06%	Netherlands
25	160	0.06%	158	0.06%	722	0.06%	Italy
26	145	0.05%	145	0.06%	682	0.06%	Switzerland
27	118	0.04%	118	0.05%	675	0.06%	Ireland
28	98	0.03%	98	0.04%	658	0.05%	Dominican Republic
29	92	0.03%	92	0.04%	539	0.04%	Finland
30	89	0.03%	87	0.04%	281	0.02%	Macedonia

Figure 9-3
Usage statistics report

BOX 9-9
Assessing site traffic

In the beginning, there were hits. Today, hits are largely discredited as a measure of Web site traffic, since they count individual files served up. A single Web page can account for a dozen or more hits if it has a lot of photos, while a text-only page could generate just a single hit.

What counts as a page view? Is it when a Web page is first requested? When content has completely finished loading? Or when a tracking pixel—a tiny file placed on a page specifically for counting page views—is called? Such distinctions are important to Internet ad buyers, because the numbers can differ depending on the definition used. Consider the impatient user who requests a page but then hits Back or surfs elsewhere before that page—and its ad—loads.

One of the softest Web numbers is the tally of unique visitors per month. For sites that require registration and login, it's fairly simple. But the rest must depend on other devices, ranging from analyzing server log files to using cookies that can be accessed by a Web site the next time that user visits.

Web site operators usually get information about site traffic from their own server logs, an outside online advertising company such as New York-based DoubleClick Inc., or a third-party rating service. Major sites typically use a combination of sources. In addition to using outside rating services, log file analysis is also quite useful, says Jeff Julian, president and publisher of IDG.net, a *Computerworld.com* sister site. It lets him see what people do after they arrive at a site. Server logs usually record each visitor's domain or IP address, browser type, and files requested. Web site staff can then use commercial log analysis software or home-brewed code to sift through the raw data and pull together the statistics they are seeking.

SOURCE: Excerpted from Machlis, Sharon, "Measuring Web Site Traffic," *Computerworld*, June 17, 2002, 42.

The Web Site Administrator

On the Web, success is measured in terms of increased traffic, which can quickly slow down a site. The resulting performance drop can discourage visitors and cause problems in attracting repeat customers. Rising traffic is not the only problem site designers face. Site technology and infrastructure are also becoming increasingly complex. They involve front-end Web servers, middle-tier application servers, back-end databases, and a number of special-purpose servers. The result is increasing stress for the Web site administrator.

Successful site administrators understand the business value of fast performance. They also understand that they must be proactive and correct situations that can affect the speed with which content is delivered to the site visitor. The situations range from Internet congestion at the ISP to sluggish database performance on the Web site's end. Web site administrators have to evaluate the architecture and figure out which problems they have enough control over to correct and which ones have to be addressed through outside sources or services.

As Figure 9-4 shows, several aspects of a company's Web architecture are the responsibility of the Web site administrator.

- **Database server:** The administrator's main concern is efficient use of the database server and how well the database can scale up to meet rising traffic. A lot of sites rely on client/server technology that is not designed to handle thousands of simultaneous users. The upgrade can be expensive and difficult to do. Some database managers are now opting to distribute their databases over several low-cost machines to support the Web site.

- **Application server(s):** The main concern with application servers is having sufficient power and good-quality components. Servers should not be overloaded. Jobs such as sending automatic e-mail to many destinations do not have to be done in real time. A batch approach could save CPU time and leave real time for end-user traffic.
- **Web server(s):** The main problem here is not having enough servers to accommodate high-volume simultaneous users. Low-cost servers can be added to ease the handling of the total traffic generated by the Web site.
- **Special-purpose servers for encryption, security checks, and so on:** The main concern for the Web site administrator is CPU-intensive encryption slowing down special-purpose servers. Also of concern is the importance of monitoring the server-to-server switching infrastructure to ensure the viability, continuity, stability, and integrity of the entire technology-based environment.
- **Internet bandwidth:** Bandwidth is the Web site's connection to the rest of the world. The main question is whether there is enough bandwidth to expedite the Web traffic for the site. Unlike the past, when site managers had to decide how much bandwidth to have, today every Web site can be provided with a co-location service to be assured of adequate Internet connectivity. Once connected, your site can bank on additional bandwidth in seconds to accommodate a sudden increase in site traffic.
- **Internet performance status:** The administrator's main concern is how badly backbone congestion, distance, and the many hops affect traffic performance. Most site managers measure site performance from the inside out: They track how long the system takes to handle content and requests during peak periods. This approach does not reveal anything about the user's experience because the traffic could be on different ISP infrastructure connected to the Internet at different times and speeds and using PCs with different

Figure 9-4
Main elements of Web architecture

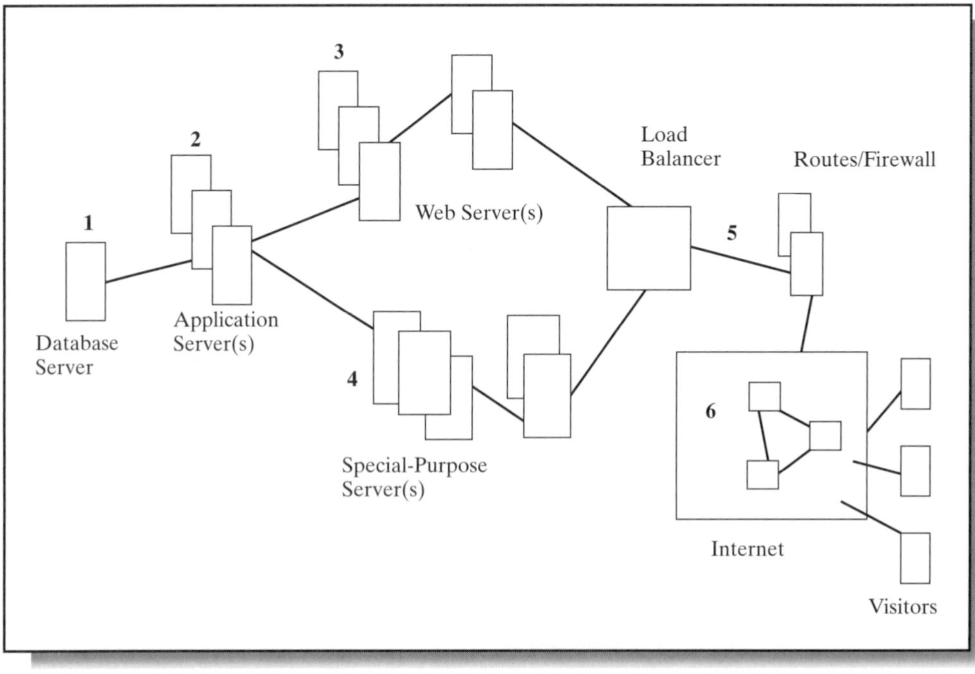

capabilities. The new alternative is using specialized services that regularly check URLs from different points or locations around the Internet. The resulting statistics help site managers determine how badly their sites are suffering from performance problems.

With good control over all these technology-based elements, site managers should have a grip on the performance and integrity of the Web site. Other than financial problems and budgets, one other problem should be addressed—people. Technology that must function round the clock requires experienced, highly trained people to manage it. With more and more visitors entering the Internet, the demand for site use and site management will continue to increase. The increase in demand for technical people poses serious challenges for the site manager. Ensuring an adequate staff requires planning, professional recruiting, and attractive financial packages to retain qualified help.

SUMMARY

1. Web site evaluation means considering graphic identity, navigation quality, functionality, and content. It also includes managing Web traffic.
2. Appropriate site design means matching the demographics and content of a Web site to appropriate colors, shapes, and typefaces.
3. Several criteria have been established for evaluating Web sites: use of color, layout, minimal text, timely information, unique service, speed of performance, consistency in design, protection from invasion and hackers, and scalability.
4. There are four general approaches to Web personalization: cookies, **collaborative-filtering software**, **check-box personalization**, and **user-based personalization.**
5. Cookies are the primary means of tracking visitors and personalizing the site experience for the repeat visitor.
6. A Web site should be as inviting and easy to navigate as possible. In checking for usability, a number of questions need to be addressed: Is the site engaging? Is it efficient? Is it supportive? Is it consistent and reliable? Reliability testing means checking for availability: What percentage of the time is the site available?
7. In user testing, the first step is to determine the sample of users and then decide what to look for during the test. It is important to remember that people in general are not the most reliable source of judgment, especially for subjective items like color, format, or page integration.
8. Web content management means collecting, assembling, publishing, and removing content from a Web site. Without Web content management, the site will have serious problems from waste and clutter.
9. In terms of traffic management, the idea is to monitor the volume of business coming into the Web site and interpret its impact on sales, productivity, and inventory turnover. The most common tool is usage statistics reports generated for the client by the ISP.
10. Web site management involves good control over the technology-based elements of the site to maintain a high level of site performance and integrity.

collaborative-filtering software: software that keeps track of users' movements across the Web to interpret their interests, and views their surfing habits from how long they stay on a page to the pages they choose while on the Web site.

check-box personalization: a user-controlled process; a user chooses specific interests on a checklist so the site can display the requested information.

user-based personalization: a Web design approach in which users are divided into segments according to rules that generate certain types of information based on a user's profile.

Key Terms

- ancillaries, 266
- branding, 277
- cache, 281
- check-box personalization, 287
- churning, 275
- clickstream, 270
- collaborative-filtering software, 287
- cookie, 272
- GIF, 281
- inference-based personalization, 272
- JPEG (Joint Photographic Experts Group), 281
- persistent cookies, 273
- reliability, 279
- scalability, 266
- spam, 274
- switching cost, 275
- transient cookies, 273
- user-based personalization, 287
- Web content management, 283

Test Your Understanding

1. What are some key questions to consider in evaluating a Web site? Explain.
2. How does color have an impact on the site visitor? Be specific.
3. List and briefly elaborate on the criteria for Web site evaluation.
4. Distinguish between: page content and personalization, category 1 and category 5 Web sites, personalization and scalability, cookies and collaborative-filtering software, and check-box personalization and user-based personalization.
5. Elaborate on the general approaches to Web personalization.
6. In what way is a cookie considered a personalization tool? Explain.
7. What makes a Web site usable?
8. The main difference between a person's behavior in a physical store and that on the Web is switching costs. Do you agree? What is switching cost? Explain.
9. If you were to recommend a set of guidelines for effective usability testing, what would you include?
10. What is the difference between (a) reliability and user testing and (b) reliability and readability testing?
11. What is involved in Web content management?
12. What is involved in Web traffic management?
13. What is the role of the Web site administrator?

Discussion Questions

1. Is Web site design an art or a science? Explain.
2. In your own words, what would you say are the two most important measures of a Web site's performance?
3. How does the Internet keep track of a person's preferences between browsing sessions? Are there security restrictions that a browser could impose that would force a change in the way information about users is recorded?
4. If you were consulting a first-time client whose main products are perishables (fruits, vegetables, and so on), what Web site features would you recommend? How much emphasis would you place on the concept of usability?
5. Color and graphics are important in Web site design. How do you know how many graphics or what type color to incorporate in a Web site? Be specific.
6. If you were asked to test a new Web site for usability, how would you proceed? Elaborate.

7. It has been said, "Graphic design neither helps nor hurts." Do you agree? Discuss.
8. There is a lot of discussion about navigation and content being inseparable. Do you agree? Expound.

Web Exercises

1. Evaluate the following sites.
   - www.statefarm.com—State Farm Insurance
   - www.wachovia.com—Wachovia Bank
   - www.fedex.com—FedEx

   Questions:
   a. Evaluate each site in terms of color scheme and the profile of the organization as perceived by the visitor.
   b. Does each site follow the use of proper color for psychological effect or impact? What changes would you make? Why?
   c. Is there a relationship between color and how conservative an organization is? Elaborate.
2. **Team assignment:** Review the bank sites assigned to your team and answer the following questions.
   a. What is the size of the bank (large, medium, small)?
   b. What is the category of the site? Here are the five categories.
      - Category 1: Homepage, who we are, and so on
      - Category 2: Electronic catalog, data collection
      - Category 3: Interactive, business transactions
      - Category 4: Multimedia, workflow/BPR integrated
      - Category 5: Delivery platform expansion, individualization
   c. In what language is the Web site written? (Hint: Right click on the screen and select Source view.)
   d. Does the site accommodate a shopping cart? Security features? Tally the number of hits per hour?
   e. When you bring up the homepage, what is displayed first, second, and so on?
   f. Is the site business-to-consumer, business-to-business, or both? Why? How do you explain it?
   g. How well designed is the site? How user friendly is it? Elaborate.

Team Number	Site Assignment	Name
1.	www.bankofamerica.com	Bank of America
2.	www.fnbsm.com	First First National Bank of South Miami, South Miami, Florida
3.	www.banknd.com	Bank of North Dakota
4.	www.fmtulsa.com	F & M Bank, Tulsa, Oklahoma
5.	www.countynationalbank.com	County National Bank, Hillsdale, Michigan
6.	www.mortgagesfbhp.com	First National Bank of Highland Park, Ill.
7.	www.kawvalleybank.com	Kaw Valley State Bank, Topeka, Kansas

3. Specify a Web site topic of your choice, and follow these three steps.
   a. **What did you set out to do?** Exactly what is the title or topic of the project? What benefit do you foresee in taking on this topic? This is more like a justification step.
   b. **How did you proceed?** That is, what steps did you take to do the work? For example, if you were assessing shopping carts, did you first begin setting criteria as a step for the evaluation? How did you choose or decide on the product? How was the work organized and executed?
   c. **What did you end up with?** What results did you get? How reliable were the results? That is, how did you test the Web site? What do the results mean for the client, for the business, for business in general, for the industry, and so on?

   What problems (if any) did you encounter while on step 3b? How did you correct them?

   What do you conclude from your work? Be specific and complete.

   Sample topics:
   - Web site design of a small jewelry store
   - Designing a Web site for your sorority or fraternity
   - A personal Web site—friends and family

Chapter 10

Marketing on the Internet

Contents

IN A NUTSHELL

The Internet will transform every organization in the world. It will create winners and losers, and force corporations to rethink strategies and directions. In the Internet world, companies either evolve or get eliminated. As Lou Gerstner of IBM said, "We're not selling a Web server or a 3-D engine for your PC. We're selling ways for companies to make money."

The Internet offers a high degree of interaction and affords consumers unprecedented benefits, from convenience to bargain prices. Shopping is as easy as searching the Web. Selling on the Internet affects two key areas of e-commerce: business-to-consumer (B2C) and business-to-business (B2B). Both areas involve connecting people and processes to suppliers, customers, and business partners. The connection is the Internet, or the Information Superhighway, and the process is reaching people to consummate a transaction or to deliver a product. Online marketing is direct marketing. It is securing transactions, paying for business services in a secure way, sales force automation, and having the proper network to finalize a sale.

The bottom line is reaching people, making money, growing with technology, and improving the corporate core process. For example, Chrysler reduced operating costs by $1 billion per year by collaborating with suppliers electronically. The state of Connecticut reduced the number of delinquent taxpayers by 30 percent by publishing the names of delinquents on the Internet.

Marketing is "the art of the possible." It is the process of planning and implementing the conception, pricing, advertising, and distribution of goods and services to meet the demands of the market for which the product or service is intended. When it comes to reaching people online, the opportunities are virtually unlimited.

It is important to know that online marketing is about business, not just technology. The goal is leveraging an existing investment, starting simple and growing fast, anticipating where you're going with the product, understanding what is unique about the product, attracting and promoting a repeat customer base, and keeping the lines of communication with the customer or supplier open and operational around the clock. Internet marketing is unique in its approach, process, and protocols, but everything must work together in the interest of the corporation, its customers, and its suppliers. This chapter covers online marketing: It sets guidelines and clarifies the rules of the process.

One of the areas covered in this chapter is the role of personalization in online marketing. Marketing on the Internet is unique because it is personal.

It is not enough for e-commerce to be fast and cheap. An online business must know its customers, their habits, behaviors, and potential. Almost everything the customer does on a Web site can be used for a profile. Unless the customer is studied and tracked carefully, it will be difficult for the business to know what to offer in the way of products and how such offerings will lead to growth and profitability, but this kind of tracking often raises ethical and legal issues. These are covered in Chapter 13.

THE PROS AND CONS OF ONLINE SHOPPING

The Internet is a meeting place where shoppers and buyers conduct business. The number of shoppers and the volume of business continue to surge. Study after study points to the exponential growth of online shopping. For the online merchant, it is important to understand why people shop, the pros and cons of online shopping for the customer, and the business justification for doing business on the Internet.

The Pros of Online Shopping

From the consumer's viewpoint, the Web as a whole is empowering, because consumers can opt to click away to the competition any time they wish. The Web is about choice, and the options are endless. Three factors make online shopping attractive.

1. **Choice:** Consumers in general enjoy having choices before they decide whether to buy or what price they are willing to pay for a product.
2. **Vast selection:** Online, products can be displayed, reviewed, and compared at no cost in time or funds. This feature makes online shopping much more efficient than having to visit store after store.
3. **Quick comparison:** Consumers can quickly compare products in terms of price, quality, shipping terms, and so on before making a final choice.

Online shopping boils down to a supply of information. By offering extensive product information, online merchants can help people make the best choice. What does all this mean? Strong evidence suggests that online shopping has inherent advantages that will attract consumers to the Web (even if prices are slightly higher than those of brick-and-mortar stores), due to the availability of information and the speed of information access. Less legwork is needed for shopping on the Internet.

The Cons of Online Shopping

With all the good features of online shopping come a few drawbacks: Certain buying decisions require information that can best be found in traditional, brick-and-mortar stores. For example, when buying personal items like perfume or clothing, the consumer needs to see, feel, smell, or test. Products that require in-store help continue to be bought at traditional stores. For example, Lowe's Home Improvement Warehouse, whose employees advise consumers about products and tools and how to use them, would not do as well on the Web as Barnes and Noble, which sells books with virtually no in-store help. Certain other products do not sell well on the Web because of delivery problems. For example, large items like lumber, fencing, or furniture are best sold in local stores.

Unfortunately, most Web sites do not provide a consumer experience that feels like real *shopping*. Instead, consumers continue to search on their own, which is not the goal. Worse, the tools available on the Web site to help the user reach the right product are inflexible. They generally are designed without any consideration regarding how real consumers approach shopping (Nielsen and Tahir 2001). Yet, brick-and-mortar stores aren't perfect, when one thinks of parking, obnoxious salespeople, waiting in line to check out, and so on. A shopper can walk out of one store, but going to another store for a price difference is another hassle (see Box 10-1).

Justifying an Internet Business

The first question a merchant should ask before plunging into Internet marketing is this: Is the Internet right for my business? To answer this question, you need two pieces of information: a clear picture of the business and an understanding of the forces that might threaten its survival.

BOX 10-1
Brick and mortar versus online shopping

Here is an area of e-commerce design that could exceed the capabilities of real people in physical stores in terms of speed, accessibility, and comprehensiveness. In reality, search is one of the most common, and one of the least successful, ways that users look for things on the Web. Customers can't ask to speak to search's manager, although we've often seen users go to outside search engines such as Google when they have no success using a site's own search engine.

Tell customers what you don't have. A salesperson in a brick-and-mortar store generally tells you if the store doesn't carry what you're looking for. Search engines, on the other hand, often tell you nothing in this situation. When a search returns no hits, users struggle to understand what it means. Does the site not have the item? Is it called something else? Did you misspell the name? Think of the horror of a salesperson staring dumbly as you repeatedly ask for an item using different names, vocal inflections, anything to get your point across.

People like to comparison shop. Without comparison tools on Web sites, users must drill down to get information on a product, grasp the most important details, and either remember them or print them out, back up, find another item, and start the process again. Often users can't remember key features of one product once they've gotten to another, so they're forced to compare based only on what they do remember.

Filtering through the good and the bad can overwhelm them if they don't get any help from the Web site. In physical stores, good salespeople listen to what a customer is looking for, and then point the customer to a selection of stock that meets the criteria. Similarly, when you have a large number of products or a lot of content on your Web site, you need to provide ways for your customer to narrow down the choices. We saw an interesting behavior in our study. No matter how Web sites displayed their product listings, users stopped looking at product listings after two or three pages. This means that if you have a large number of products, you need to help your customers narrow down the list to fit on two or three pages. We use the term *winnowing*, which originally meant "separating the wheat from the chaff," to refer to this process.

SOURCE: Excerpted from Nielsen, Jakob, and Tahir, Marie, "Building Sites With Depth," *Web Techniques*, February 2001, 46ff.

Several reasons can be given for going on the Internet.

1. **To establish a presence.** Many companies provide just basic information (general company information, name, history, location, shopping hours, and so on), products for sale, today's specials, methods of payment, special discounts or offers, and the like. Their Web sites have basic links, are simple to navigate, and can be quite responsive. A comment page usually has an e-mail button that the surfer clicks to send a message. The overall goal is to tell customers why they should do business with you.
2. **To serve customers.** In marketing, one of the first things to do is make customers aware that you're available to serve them. Many brick-and mortar-stores use online marketing to attract new customers. The level of service offered depends on the type of business and the product. For example, making a form available to prequalify for a loan would be considered entry-level Internet marketing for a bank. The consumer fills out the form online and clicks on the "submit" button to send it via e-mail to the loan department for processing. It is quick, safe, and saves having to drive to the bank.
3. **To heighten public awareness.** With a company Web site, anyone who accesses the site and learns about the company and what it has to offer is a potential customer. No alternative marketing medium can do the same job this quickly or this well.
4. **To share time-sensitive information.** When it comes to timing and availability of information, the Web has no equal. For example, a quarterly earnings statement, merger news, or the name of the grand-prize winner can be made available in a matter of seconds for the world to know. Also related to this feature is the availability of color, graphics, video, and audio to go with news releases, interviews, or special announcements. No brochure can do this as well.
5. **To sell goods.** This attraction carries high priority in Internet marketing, but before getting serious about selling, it is important to consider the other features listed previously. That is, before online customers begin to order, they need to know about the business.
6. **To answer important questions.** Every day organizations spend time and money trying to address customer queries, most of which are repeat questions. Among the roles of the Web site is to compile frequently asked questions (FAQs) that customers can access. This will remove another time-consuming task from the company's staff.
7. **To stay in touch with field personnel.** The sales force occasionally needs information from the home office about a product, a procedure, or a special situation. Using the Web to provide such information is the most efficient and effective way to do business from afar.
8. **To market at the international level.** With a Web page, a company can reach international customers just as easily and quickly as it can reach the customer next door. In fact, many companies have learned that before going on the Web, they must have a plan in place to handle the surge of orders.
9. **To serve the local market.** Local or global, Web access is everything. A local restaurant, a movie theater, or an auto repair shop can benefit from Web marketing. No matter where the business is located, the customer should be able to access it on the Web.
10. **To market specialized products.** Specialized products or services, from baseball caps to flying lessons, are ideal for Internet marketing. For example, how about a briefcase made of African ostrich skin for $1,100? (See www.africa-exotic.com/clothing.htm.) With millions of surfers on the Web, the smallest interest group could turn out to be a sizable number of customers for the product.
11. To reach the youth market. The "under 25" surfer is fast becoming a formidable segment of the Web market. With offerings from athletic products to specialized international tours, start-up firms catering to that market segment are reaping dividends.

Someone summarized the justification for entering online marketing by suggesting that if you answer "yes" to your business being local and dependent on face-to-face customer contact, chances are the Internet is not for you. On the other hand, if you have an unusual product and the product can be shipped by mail, then you should seriously consider Internet marketing.

INTERNET MARKETING TECHNIQUES

banner: advertising with links to a merchant's Web site.

pull marketing: passive Internet marketing, where the user takes the initiative requesting specific information from the Web site.

push technology: a technique where the Web site "pushes" the information onto the customer, irrespective of his or her interest.

The Internet allows for a continuum of marketing techniques ranging from strictly passive to aggressive. The passive tack comes down to viewing the Web as a variation on television and the visitor as a variation on the TV viewer. Take **banner** Web ads. With sound, animation, and other techniques, these messages try to get a visitor to quit surfing long enough to read or click on them.

Passive Internet marketing is called **pull marketing,** because it requires the user to pull the information from the site. The user must actively seek out the site. Currently, most people access Web site content by pulling. Each time a user clicks a link, the browser sends a request to the Web server (a pull) asking for a specific page. The browser downloads the page and displays it on the user's screen (see Figure 10-1).

In aggressive Internet marketing, the Web site seeks out potential customers. This is called **push technology,** because the Web site "pushes" the information onto consumers, irrespective of their interest. The Web server does not wait until the consumer requests a page. When the content the consumer has signed up for is ready, the server delivers (pushes) it automatically to the consumer's PC so it can be read, reviewed, or watched. As shown in Figure 10-1, most Internet marketing techniques fall somewhere in between these extremes.Table 10-1 shows examples of pull and push activities.

Not all products translate well online and, therefore, may not need anything beyond the passive-type site. Forrester Research came up with the following formula to decide whether a product justifies a Web presence.

Figure 10-1
Range of Internet marketing techniques and applications

PULL TO PUSH CONTINUUM			
PASSIVE	MODERATELY	MODERATELY	AGGRESSIVE
Providers of information (mere presence) advertising	Site registered with many search engines Specialized services to users requesting information Specialized e-mail to users requesting periodic information	Off-line advertising Banner advertising Targeted e-mail to past customers	Spam Mail Chain Mail

Source: Adapted from Greenstein, P., *E-Commerce*, New York: McGraw-Hill, Inc. 2000, 368.

Table 10-1
Examples of push and pull technology

Pull Technology	Push Technology
You turn on your computer and begin to read the electronic newspaper personalized around your favorite subjects or headlines.	You receive a note from Barnes & Noble that your spouse's favorite novel has just arrived. You click on the bookseller's Web site and order a copy.
Around 9:30 A.M., a window pops up from your stock brokerage house displaying the ticker tape of NYSE and NASDAQ stocks.	You are alerted by your brokerage house that the two stocks you want to sell have just been rated "strong buy" by Merrill Lynch.
Before going home, a news flash from your airline reminds you to be at the gate 1 hour early because the flight is booked solid.	Amazon.com sends you an e-mail to remind you that the impact wrench you hesitated to order on 6/3 is now on sale plus a $20 coupon if total order within the next 10 days is $100 or more.

$$\text{SNI} = \frac{\text{Price}}{\text{Purchase Frequency}} \times \begin{array}{c}(\text{Sale viability} + \text{Research intensity} + \\ \text{Configurability} + \text{Service level})\end{array}$$

CONSIDERATION GAP (Intensity of prepurchase deliberation)

SITE-TO-PRODUCT AFFINITY (Ability to deliver online experience correlated to the product or service)

Where:

Price = How expensive is the product compared with other household purchases?
Purchase frequency = How often does the household purchase the product?
Service level = How much customer service does the product need online?
Research intensity = How research intensive is the purchase decision?
Configurability = How customizable is the product?
Sale viability = How viable are online sales of the product?

Applying the formula and using a 1 to 5 score (1 = low and 5 = high), here is an example of the SNI of two extreme products.

$$\text{Ketchup} = 1/5 \times (1 + 1 + 1 + 1) = 0.8$$
$$\textbf{\textit{Home mortgage}} = 5/1 \times (5 + 5 + 4 + 3) = 85$$

According to the standard, a site index score lower than 25 indicates no need for a site; 25 to 49 means the brand will benefit from a site; 50 or more indicates a definite need for a site (adapted from Cohen, 1999, 125).

Registering with search engines and directories is one way of trying to attract visitors. Getting information about specialized services to users who request it usually is done by e-mail. This is a way to attract visitors to a site that requires action by the Web site and the visitor. Interested visitors usually sign up for the service. Because the visitor requests the information, this type of Internet marketing is more pulled than pushed by the customer via the Web site.

Off-line advertising, such as on radio or television or in magazines and newspapers, although expensive, is necessary to promote a Web site. This is more push than pull marketing. Web sites don't just attract business the moment they are on the Internet. It takes repetitive ads locally and nationally, which means a hefty budget and a professional marketing effort.

Online banner advertising is a service offered (for a fee) by Internet marketing firms that install advertising banners on popular Web sites (like search engines) with links to a merchant's Web site. This is more costly than other methods, but it is also more effective in attracting visitors.

aggressive marketing: a marketing technique where the Web site seeks out potential customers; push technology.

Targeted e-mail to past customers is **aggressive marketing** because past visitors do not expect further contacts with the online merchant. This method is effective, because it discontinues the advertisements if past visitors do not return to the site within a designated time period. *Cookies* are used to identify and track customer responses to e-mail advertisements.

spamming: sending out millions of e-mails to recipients who never asked for them.

The most aggressive (and abusive) Internet marketing technique is spamming. **Spamming** is sending out millions of e-mails to recipients who never asked for them. E-mails are sent to individuals and organizations that have never visited the merchant's Web site. Addresses are purchased, swapped with other businesses, or obtained via software robots that scan the Web and collect addresses from Web sites, Web pages, mailing lists, and other public sources. Spamming is the online equivalent of junk mail (see Box 10-2).

Pop-Up Advertising

The increasing need for getting consumer attention to online products and services has led to the well-known, annoying pop-up: an advertisement that "pops up" in a new browser window regardless of the user's wish to open such a new window (see Box 10-3).

BOX 10-2

Ways to combat spamming

The increasing pain of dealing with unsolicited bulk commercial e-mail is prompting new moves to stamp out the unwanted messages. Some service providers have had enough. For example, Fairport, New York-based PaeTec Communications Inc. last week said it had disconnected a direct e-mail marketing company from its broadband network after a New York appeals court overturned an injunction that had prevented it from doing so.

Most companies don't want to disclose what spam costs them on the receiving end. It is kind of like admitting your network has been hacked. Neither here nor there, the incidence of spam is doubling every 6 months, according to David Ferris, an analyst at Ferris Research Inc. in San Francisco. Its antispam software measured 4.3 million spam blasts last month, up from 1.7 million in October.

Two bills that would set federal antispam provisions have been introduced in the U.S. Senate this year. But those measures could actually "legitimize" some of the most egregious spam being sent. Any legislation that gives individuals and companies the ability to fight the onslaught of spam would be very welcome. Even if it scares off 10% of the spammers, that would help.

SOURCE: Excerpted from Disabatino, Jennifer, "Spam, Efforts to Fight It Both on the Rise," *Computerworld*, May 13, 2002, 22.

BOX 10-3
Pop-up ads

Nothing annoys some Web surfers more than the ads that pop up on, or under, the sites they're viewing. But like it or not, these intrusions are spreading from the margins of online advertising to the mainstream, for one good reason: They just might work.

Perhaps the best-known—and most publicly reviled—pop-under advertiser is X10 Wireless Technology Inc., a Seattle-based maker of surveillance cameras that was a pioneer in the use of the format. X10 wouldn't comment on its Internet strategy, but after the company began using pop-under ads last year, its site became one of the most visited on the Web. It was estimated in May that X10's site had achieved a remarkable 32.8 percent reach—meaning that about a third of the people online that month visited the site. Everyone claims to be annoyed by the ads, but they also know what it is, so in that sense, the advertising is effective.

In recent months, pop-up and pop-under advertising has spread to more-established marketers, with companies such as American Airlines, Amazon.com Inc., and Orbitz LLC using the format. Orbitz won't disclose figures on how effective the ads have been, but the company's click-through rate (the number of viewers who click on the ad to reach the Web site) matches the experience of other companies that have used pop-ups.

By and large, consumers understand that advertising is necessary to support free Web sites. There is annoying advertising in every medium. Think about TV commercials or about the menus that restaurants stick under your door. The question is, where do Web publishers draw the line?

SOURCE: Excerpted from Rosenbaum, Joshua, "Annoying . . . but Effective," *The Wall Street Journal*, April 15, 2002, R8.

They have been viewed as the most frustrating feature on the Web. Pop-ups are an effective form of advertisement because they are relatively cheap and can be tailored to individual consumers. These new pop-ups have quickly spread throughout the Internet. Unfortunately, there are no standards on which to judge their usage. According to Nielsen/NetRatings data, there were 11.3 billion pop-up advertisements on the Internet between January and July 2002, 9 billion of which (80 percent) were from 63 of the 2,208 firms using pop-up advertisements (Lemke 2002).

Among the largest companies to capitalize on the easy mass production of pop-up ads are travel sites such as Orbitz.com, Expedia.com, and Travelocity.com. Orbitz.com, for example, created 687 million pop-up impressions between January and July 2002, second only to X10 Wireless, which created more than one billion pop-up impressions in 2002 alone.

From the surfer's view, in addition to slowing down the human side of Internet use, pop-ups can sometimes slow down software on surfers' computers by the creation of another window and crowding the World Wide Web with excess packets and bundles of information. If left unchecked, in time, the Internet could become considerably slower to the presence of these unwanted ads.

From the ISP's view, pop-up ads are a major source of revenue. After receiving numerous consumer complaints, some ISPs have made adjustments to the onslaught of this form of advertising by simply eliminating or regulating pop-up ads. One such ISP is Earthlink, which in 2003 began providing its 5 million users with free pop-up blocking software. In doing so, ISPs could charge their clients a monthly fee for eliminating such online interruptions.

The adverse impact of pop-up ads was so pronounced in 2003 that some computer programmers have taken the time to create programs with the sole purpose of eliminating pop-ups. One example of anti-pop-up software can be found at www.intermute.com, which also includes programs to eliminate spam-mail.

Are there ethical implications to pop-up ads? Many Internet users, including this author, feel that pop-up ads are intrusive and even violate privacy issues as well. Some advertising agencies have become so invasive that they place a shortcut icon to the company's Web site on users' desktops without their consent. From the cyber world to the real world, this is tantamount to a firm intruding into one's home and placing their number on speed dial without permission of the household. It is obvious that some regulation is long overdue, but who should be responsible for this regulation? No single person or agency owns the Internet or its content, so regulating it will prove to be a daunting task, regardless of the regulator(s).

The E-Cycle of Internet Marketing

Like any business venture, Internet marketing follows a life cycle that begins with planning, followed by the four P's: product, pricing, place (distribution or delivery), and promotion. (Customer personalization is unique to marketing on the Internet and is discussed later in the chapter.) See Figure 10-2.

The Business Plan

business plan: a written document that identifies a merchant's business goals and how to achieve them.

Whether you are an experienced business owner or a start-up organization, the basic steps for starting an online business are the same. The first is a business plan. A **business plan** is a written document that identifies your business goals and how you will achieve them. It can be as simple as laying out the things you want to do and matching them

Figure 10-2
The e-cycle of Internet marketing

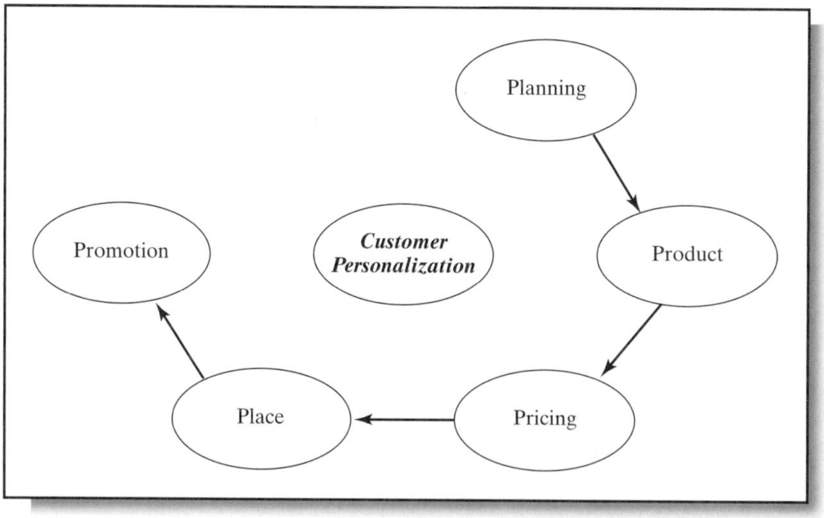

against other products on the market, the competition, the constraints, and the cash flow requirements. In virtually every case where an online business failed, it was either because of poor planning or poor management. A business plan is critical for an Internet business.

For a small business, it is a good idea to check with the local Small Business Administration office; call the national toll free number (1-800-697-4636), or visit its Web site www.sbaonline.sba.gov. The SBA has generic business plans and can help you make your own. For a large business, planning is more elaborate and can take weeks and months to complete. A committee of experienced staff usually look at the entire life cycle of the business, do simulations to see how well a Web site operates using sophisticated software, and match all the alternatives against set goals before generating the master plan. Elaborate planning involves attorneys, accountants, and strategists, in addition to business owners and managers.

The content of a business plan varies with the type and size of the business, but generally includes the following elements.

vision: perception or insight into what can happen or take place in the future.

1. **Mission:** What is your business is trying to achieve? Missions are related to the **vision** of the owners, which is also considered.
2. **Product:** What are you selling? What makes it unique?
3. **Competition:** Who are your competitors? How well established are they? Analyze their Web sites and review the unique features they offer customers.
4. **Target audience:** Are prospective customers likely to use the Internet at work or at home? Do they use e-mail? News groups? AOL?
5. **Marketing:** How do you plan to reach your customers? What advertising media do you plan to use?
6. **Sales plan:** What sales methods (telemarketing, agents) do you plan to employ? What about distribution channels, pricing, and fulfillment processes?
7. **Operation:** What equipment, location, and size of facility are you planning to start with? What about the size and quality of staff that will support the operation? Who are your suppliers? How reliable are they? How many of them are on the Internet? What experience do they have? Do they deal with your competitors? What about customer service and support? How will customers reach you?
8. **Technology:** What hardware/software and other technology do you need? Which ISPs are available? How reliable are they? What are their charges?

The Product

When it comes to product, the emphasis is on viability, quality, reliability, dependability, and integrity. Quality products mean fewer headaches in the way of returns, repairs, or customer complaints. This is especially important in Internet marketing, where customers look for reputable merchants with quality products at competitive prices. Products may be physical goods or services. Physical goods are tangible, like grocery items, shirts, and automobiles. Service products are the work performed by professionals such as doctors, certified public accountants, and travel agents, along with information like real-time stock quotations. Identifying the unique features of either type is critical in Internet marketing.

Pricing

Once the product is identified, the next step is to decide how much to charge. Web-based pricing strategies differ with the merchant, the market, and the type of customer. For example, ParenthoodWeb.com (www.parenthood.com) offers a free service for visitors in order to develop a community. It is devoted to offering families and those about to become parents Web sites that are most likely to be of interest. Other sites, such as those offered by the airlines, use frequent purchase plans to reinforce customer loyalty and encourage repeat purchase, or Web-only specials to encourage online purchase. Online auctions are another approach to selling goods on the Internet. An auction item starts at an attractive minimum price, allowing purchasers to bid up the price. A fourth approach is exemplified by www.priceline.com, which asks customers to offer a price that they would be willing to pay to fly to a given destination, stay at a favorite hotel, rent a car, and so on. In this case, Priceline's pricing process *is* its product.

Place

Electronic commerce facilitates the exchange of information between businesses and delivery companies to ensure prompt and timely delivery of physical goods to customers. More and more companies align their fulfillment phase with delivery companies like Federal Express so that direct deliveries are made to the customer from the supplier, bypassing the need to stock many items in a warehouse.

The Internet itself can be viewed as a delivery channel for digital products. Thousands of software packages and applications can be ordered online and downloaded directly onto the customer's PC. Some Internet merchants deliver online news services and stock trading services electronically. This is a new distribution channel for sellers of digital products that is cheap, fast, and effective. The only drawback is the possibility of tapping or theft of digital data.

Screen Capture 10-1

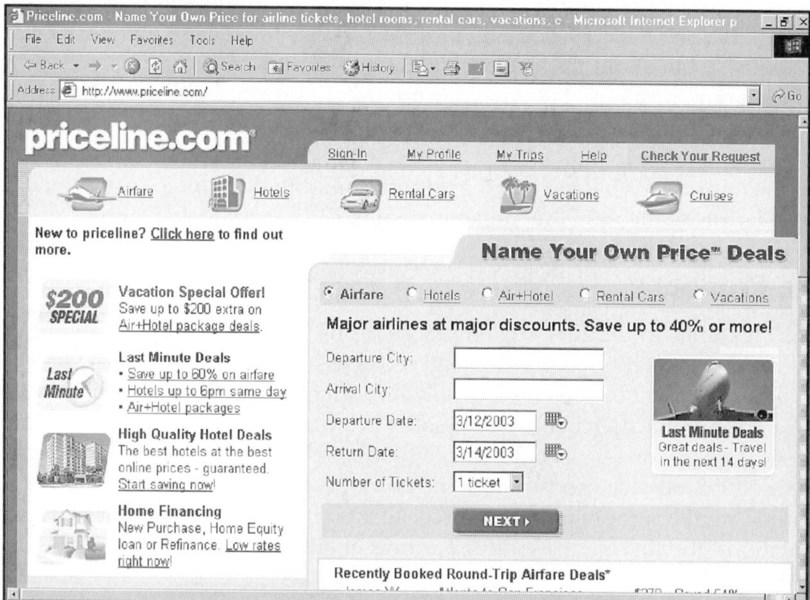

Source: All material herein © 1998–2003 priceline.com Incorporated, all rights reserved. PRICELINE.COM and PRICELINE are registered service marks and are service marks of priceline.com Incorporated. (CST2040530-50) ws-31.

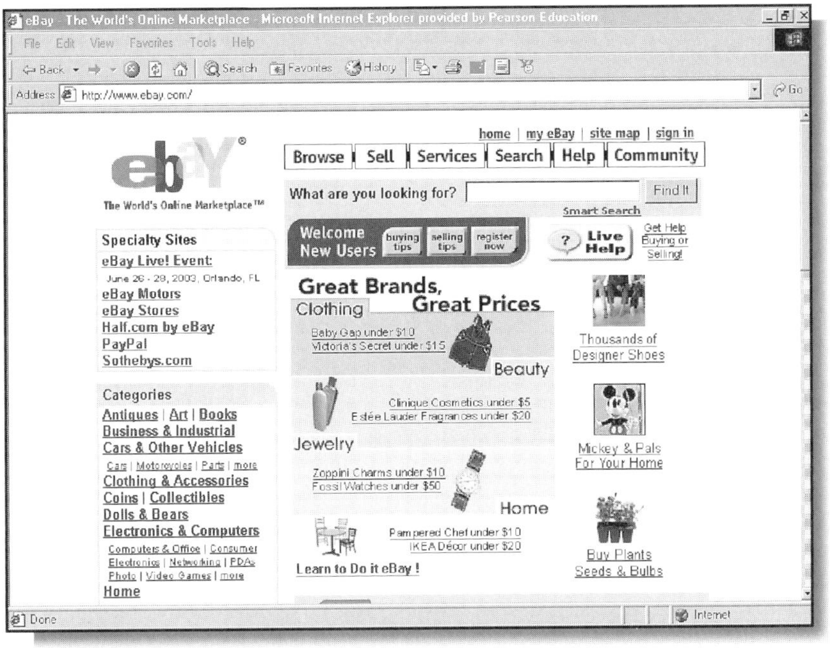

Screen Capture 10-2

Source: These materials have been reproduced with the permission of eBay Inc.

Promotion

Internet marketing is about promoting a product to get the attention of prospective customers. Internet marketing follows the AIDA (attention, interest, desire, and action) guidelines for direct mail marketing. The first goal is to get the *attention* of the prospective visitor. Web site quality, ease of navigation, and personalization are important, because attention is the entry point or the front of the marketing process. Good graphics, attractive banners, and proper use of color are essential to draw visitors to the Web site (see Box 10-4).

Banners are the most popular type of Internet ads. They continue to be the staple of Web advertising. They are to the Internet what 30-second commercials are to television (Rewick 2001). A banner is a rectangular strip that is placed horizontally across the top of a Web page. Some flash and others blink. The idea is to attract the consumer to click on the banner as an entry point to the Web pages to follow. However, consumers quickly became click resistant. Being relatively crude, less than 0.5 percent click through them.

Banner ads are also the most controversial. Critics view them as window dressing that can easily be tuned out by surfers. Supporters say that banners are cheap and fit the traditional ad agency formula. According to the "Ogilvy on Advertising" ad manual, five times as many people read the headlines as read the copy. Leading Web marketers think that enough banners will create a footprint—a reminder of the product or service that is available (see Box 10-5).

The use of banners is not as easy as it may seem, as click-throughs hover below 1 percent. There are numerous ways to make them used for awareness or advertising. Banners should be small and fast loading. If animation is used, it should be actions in horizontal movements, as evolution has trained the human eye to be very alert to such motions for

BOX 10-4
E-commerce trends: Sites not worth seeing

When Louisa Melcher, age 18 months, lost her beloved doll last month, her mother turned to the Internet for help. The Melchers live in California, but Dolly had been purchased at F.A.O. Schwarz in New York. Louisa's mom figured this would be a quick fix: Log on, order Dolly II, pay extra for FedEx, and maybe only one night of sleep would be lost in the household.

But the Melcher family hit on a practice that is likely to be the undoing of many a retailer with a bricks-and-clicks strategy. Faoschwarz.com is not all of F.A.O. Schwarz off-line. In fact, it only has a smattering of the toy store's merchandise. And Dolly was not among them. "I no sooner finish telling her 'Don't worry, Dolly will be back tomorrow' than I find out the Web site is FAO Schwarz.Lite.com," says Louisa's mother, Amanda Biers-Melcher.

This is all too familiar. Traditional retailers, looking for a quick way to get online and compete with the rising tide of e-tailers, are routinely putting up Web sites that pale in comparison with their real stores. They do it, they say, because a smaller selection of merchandise online is much easier to keep in stock and cyber-shoppers will be less disappointed by inventory outages. The last statement is wishful thinking on the part of the retailers. Customers get irritated when they find their favorite online store less satisfying than the real thing.

Limited or no merchandise may make for a more manageable Web operation, but it doesn't advance a retailer's brand. In fact, it can do it damage. Companies that would never dream of letting one store site get away with sub-par performance will let their Web site lag. Most traditional retailers still view the Internet as a side business rather than as part of their core strategy, says consultant Wendy Liebmann, president of WSL Strategic Retail.

SOURCE: Excerpted from Neuborne, Ellen, "Sites Not Worth Seeing," *Business Week E.Biz*, May 15, 2000, EB16.

survival. A banner text should also be used wisely by using the largest font possible and a simple readable font like Courier or Times New Roman. Business marketers should test their banners by getting a number of different designs and trying them in different ad networks. This way, they can learn where customers are and what makes them respond best.

In any case, once the site gets the visitor's attention, the next step is to create *interest* in the product(s) displayed. The display is like bait. Quick response time and ease of navigation make a difference in how quickly a visitor is guided through the choice of products. Information creates interest in a site. Web pages have to be updated constantly and provide excitement to keep visitors interested.

The interest phase should lead to the next step—building a *desire* for action. Interactivity through navigation generates a desire to continue or to click away. In most cases, the visitor clicks back and forth, reviewing and assessing every product before making a decision. That decision is the *action*—placing the order or the sale. This is as easily done as filling out an online form. Once completed, the visitor clicks on a button to e-mail the form to the company for processing. Once received, the company initiates the fulfillment phase of the marketing process.

Promoting a product requires persistent online presence. Many off-line brands do not always translate to the Web. One strategy is to combine online and off-line marketing in a consistent, continuous way. Messages across multiple media should work together.

BOX 10-5
New format brand ads

There are different approaches to designing Web ads. The ones worth noting are the skyscrapers, bulky boxes, buttons and big impressions, pop-up ads, and e-mail.

SKYSCRAPERS

Banners represent a lot of the real estate on a Web page. So perhaps it isn't surprising that one of the latest offshoots is known as the "skyscraper." It is simply a tall, skinny banner ad, and it can take up even more space than the pioneering top-of-the-screen rectangles. Because a typical personal computer monitor is wider than it is high, a skyscraper ad can perch on either side of the screen without infringing too much on the page itself. But, text in vertical ads is harder to read. And if an ad sits too far off to the side, a viewer may never even scan it.

BULKY BOXES

On the News.com Web site of San Francisco's Cnet Networks Inc., banner ads are about the size of a CD case and sit smack in the middle of the page. Instead of being taken to another site, readers who click on the ad get more information without having to leave the page. News stories wrap right around the ad box. This makes the ad a lot harder to ignore. But the reader's eye has to track around it in order to see the content.

BUTTONS AND "BIG IMPRESSIONS'"

Not all banners are so aggressive. Walt Disney Co.'s Web sites, including ESPN.com and ABC.com, now run business-card-size banners on the upper-right-hand corner of the page. Disney calls this format "the Big Impression." The nice part about this design is because the Disney ads sit off to the right side, they aren't interfering with other material on the screen and can remain there for a long time. Yet, because the ads are off in a corner on the right side, they might get overlooked. After all, people read from left to right.

POP-UP ADS

Some ads don't hesitate to get in your face. So-called pop-up ads appear in a second window that pops up on the screen while a Web page is loading. These speedy connections allow for what online ad types call "rich media" ads, which use animation, sound, and streaming video. Banner ads can include rich media and are getting livelier these days, but flashy content is found more often in the pop-up ads. These lively ads are more intrusive and memorable because they pop up and have to be clicked on to be gotten rid of. They are used primarily as a brand-building tool by automakers, consumer-products companies, and movie studios. Yet, many people banish the box from their screens even before they see the ad. They can be incredibly annoying, precisely because they are so intrusive. They often slow down the loading of the site you are trying to view.

E-MAIL

Because recipients have to subscribe to receive e-mail, marketers are guaranteed a highly targeted audience. Response rates can run as high as 5 percent to 15 percent. The positive part is that e-mail marketing has proved to be a cost-efficient way to acquire new customers. There are no postage fees and no hassle of pickup and delivery. But, as e-mail surges, so will the clutter in customers' in boxes. The challenge will be to retain high response rates and low "unsubscribe" rates.

SOURCE: Excerpted from Rewick, Jennifer, "Choices, Choices," *The Wall Street Journal*, April 23, 2001, R12.

With surfers ignoring online marketing, advertisers are trying creative new approaches. Among the changes are the following.

- Smarter ads, with Web sites using improved tracking software to decide which demographic category surfers fit into, their likes, dislikes, and so on. From there, the ads the surfers see do a better job of matching their interests. Some of the ads even ask surfers to recommend products they might like.
- Forcing ads to appear smack in the center of the monitor before the surfer's eyes. Some companies have devised huge, animated mega-banners that dominate a Web page. Some even keep reappearing on other pages within the Web site even after the site is shut down.
- Advertisers creating their own "information-heavy" Web sites, on the basis that it is easier to get surfers to read or listen to a sales ad if offered free content in the bargain (Hwang 2001).

Personalization

personalization: a technique that combines product and promotion for customers to receive information customized to their needs.

The fifth P in e-marketing is **personalization.** The technology combines two P's—promotion and product—so customers receive personalized information or visit a homepage customized for them (for example, a customer's favorite stock quotes displayed on his screen). The role of personalization in e-commerce has been on the increase. The personalization software provides the one-to-one recommendation of products and services and direct access to personally relevant news, and it collects information about user interests for customer relationship management (CRM) activities. Three main ideas make up the personalized presentation of information.

- Technically detailed descriptions are presented to the level of the user's knowledge.
- Product presentations are customized to suit the user's interests.
- The user's expectations regarding the amount of relevant information to be presented are met (Ardissono et al. 2002).

Important Rules

Online personalization is a new field, and its practice is a new art. Based on experience in the field, common practices have been established for this area of specialization. Several rules are worth noting.

- **Keep resistance away from personalization.** Customers do not like to fill out forms or participate in surveys about themselves or about product preferences. Use subtle ways to draw them in little by little.
- **Consider any source of information.** The sources include data warehouses, databases, and data mining performed on data warehouses.
- **State preferences of users through forms or similar procedures.**
- **Focus on privacy in every way possible.** Customers do not mind sharing personal information if they can be sure they trust you. The last thing you can afford to do is share their information or sell it.
- **Make an effort to learn from every move.** Infer from customers' action or inaction. Study it and mine it for future use. A satisfied customer is best shown the moves that worked last time.
- **Jump-start a personalization relationship by posing the user a set of questions.**

- **Sell the goodness of personalization.** This can be done after you start asking surfers what they need. Then, demonstrate how your personalized environment can meet their needs.
- **Make life easier for users to tell you what they want and what they hate.** Provide an optional, brief questionnaire that customers can respond to "on the fly" whenever they feel in the mood.
- **Make sure there is no delay in a personalization environment.** Nothing is worse for the user than to encounter unnecessary or unwarranted delays, especially when they know the interface is personalized.

In most personalized interfaces, a bit of *artificial intelligence* is incorporated into Internet marketing. For example, if you visit Hallmark's Web site, its database can store information about your visit so that it can provide personalized, free service such as "Mr. Jones, next Tuesday is your wife's birthday. Consider our new card # I-34A, which shows a sketch of Nancy, her favorite cat." Amazon.com does something similar. After the first visit, the homepage greets you in person, will automatically bring up your credit card number to verify, and while you're still deliberating on the book, bring up information from people you know or from reviewers about the book you're considering. This is true personalization. It crosses promotion and product and enhances both in the process.

Marketing Implications

A power shift has occurred from the merchant to the consumer in terms of accessing and controlling information that leads to a buy–no buy decision. The consumer has acquired additional power that today is called *knowledge*. At the core of this knowledge is the information at one's fingertips 24/7. At anytime, from anywhere, the consumer can access any information on virtually any topic. Consumers are now actively participating in jobs that were once the domain of the marketer. In the past, consumers were limited to purchase and consumption. Today, they can design the product they want from their own homes. Technology is changing the marketing game and altering the way marketers interact with consumers.

Another marketing implication behind the power shift is the unique Internet marketing strategy that today's online merchant must adopt. Such a strategy follows common-sense rules like these.

1. **Content:** Don't bore your customers with unnecessary content or detail. Make the site simple and get to the point.
2. **Dynamic and attractive sites:** Make your Web site attractive using technology that personalizes information to fit the visitor's profile.
3. **Brands:** A merchant's Web site should be his or her most important brand. From the banner to the buttons, links, graphics, text, audio, and video, the site becomes the storefront of the business.
4. **Get to the point:** Conciseness, clarity, and ease of navigation are important criteria to keep in mind for a Web site. Customers do not like clutter. They have a low tolerance for reading a lot of text. Information should be in short paragraphs, spread over several pages.
5. **Promotion:** Don't expect customers to line up for your Web site just because you have one. Promote your site everywhere—local newspapers, radio program, mass mailing, and so on.

6. **Online events:** Events such as a new product offering or a 2-day discount on hot items create customer awareness, especially when they are presented on the site's homepage.
7. **Free giveaways:** This can be a great reinforcer for loyal customers. Amazon.com has a program that evaluates the frequency of customer traffic and recommends a series of enticing giveaways for customers who suddenly stop placing orders.
8. **Consistency:** The Web site's pages should have consistency in layout and overall flow. Content also should be distributed consistently across pages in an easy-to-follow format.

MARKETING YOUR PRESENCE

Millions of Web sites are on the Internet. You are a newcomer. How do you market your presence? How quickly does your Web site begin to get hits? How do you promote your Web site elsewhere on the Web? A marketing colleague once commented: "When you find something that works, don't fix it!" It is obvious that Web site promotion takes planning to draw attention, interest, and interested visitors. Visitors won't come unless they know where to find you and why they might want to visit. For ideas on how to generate traffic, check www.submit-it.com The goal is not just to get the greatest number of hits; it is to generate business and increase profits.

Promoting Your Site on Your Site

Self-promotion begins with your domain name. Most domain names are company names or names that remind the visitor about the product (e.g., IBM), the founder, or something that will encourage a click to that site. One way to increase the number of hits is to encourage repeat visits. Over time, visitors begin to sense stability, reliability, and availability of products and service. For existing customers, the risk of dealing with an unknown merchant has been removed.

Many first-time merchants arrange with a software developer to distribute its browser with the logo (trademark, trade name, company name, seal) in it whenever a visitor boots up the software. This type of promotion can be mailed to existing customers with an invitation to visit your site with giveaways or special prizes to the nth visitor. Other ways include bartering an ad exchange, accepting paid advertising, recruiting sponsors, or negotiating reciprocal links. For example, a bank that receives a query through its Web site about a loan that it cannot handle has a button on its homepage that will link the customer directly to a designated bank for follow-up. If the latter bank issues the loan, the initiating bank earns a commission or a flat rate based on a prior arrangement.

One comment should be made regarding hit rates. The raw hit rate alone does not tell you (1) how many computers visited the site or the page, (2) feedback from users by e-mail, (3) the number of times a specific file was accessed, (4) the number of repeat visitors from the same address, (5) how long users spent on the site or page, (6) the number of unique addresses from which calls were made, or (7) the frequency of requesting whole pages. Most ISPs can provide this information so that hit rates can be evaluated properly.

Updating site content is important for attracting return visitors. Every time something new is added, repeat the announcement via your site, e-mail, or other sources that have worked well for your e-business. It is also important that visitors have no problem finding new information quickly. A *what's new* button on each page is an effective way to expedite traffic. For example, the Federal Express homepage has a button for new material that highlights a current activity FedEx is sponsoring.

Another area worth considering is sharing with visitors any awards or recognition from the media your business has received. In other words, "toot your own horn." This goes beyond putting out a local press release. It is a testimonial to your viability and should bring repeat visitors.

What about promotional giveaways, contests, and games? The whole idea behind these marketing tools is to remind visitors that you are there. They can be enticed by reminding them of future promotions and the date(s) when they are offered. Visitors need a reason to come back. Use your mailing list to remind visitors when a new game will be available online and when they can see if they have won in a drawing. This momentum can get visitors to broadcast the news to others who might then look up the site.

Promoting Your Site on the Web

Search engines and directories are the most frequently used vehicles to locate sites on the Web. A search engine uses logic search to find the site you want based on a combination of keywords. A directory, like the traditional telephone directory, is an organized listing with specific categories such as yellow and white pages. Sometimes hundreds of matches are found in response to a search on a particular topic. Some search engines list the top 10 sites, with a probability (e.g., 85 percent) that it is the site you're looking for.

directory: an organized listing with specific categories such as yellow and white pages in a telephone directory.

spider: a program that explores the Web, collects keyword information, and stores it on a huge database.

Your site must be available to these search engines and directories. Keep in mind that the best search engine can look up no more than 35 to 40 percent of the hundreds of millions of Web pages. Lycos, for example, uses a robot, called a **spider.** This is a program that explores the Web, collects keyword information, and stores it on a huge database. In contrast, the well-known search engine Yahoo! requires you to submit information to include in its database.

Regardless of where your site is included, it must stand out from other sites. You want your site to top the list, because most surfers click only on the top three or four sites before they click away. Choice of keywords makes a difference. The more extensive and accurate the list you include in your homepage, the more often your site will be selected as a result of a robot search. For example, one commercial bank coded 42 keywords into its homepage (e.g., *commercial, small loan, personalized, prompt service, people oriented, independent, student loan, low interest rate*). Brainstorming among staff for the best keywords is a great idea.

More than 25 major directories and search engines can be found on the Web. Some of the more popular ones are listed in Table 10-2. With most search engines and directories, the registration procedure is simple. Fill out an online form including your name, URL address, and a brief description. In the case of one bank, the paragraph is "Customer-oriented, full-service bank highly rated for quality service, security, and solvency. Bank offers Dade County residents automated services, lobby and branch facilities for prompt, courteous service. Annual statement available." Many search engines limit the number of keywords you can include. Some sites allow only a single URL address, a single description, and a single keyword. Other sites allow several pages as long as the description, URL, and keywords are different.

Should you submit your address to search engines and directories before launching the site? In most cases, a new online business should ensure that the site's design is flawless before launching. Many things can go awry, especially the quality of the graphics. To

Table 10-2
Sample search engines and directories

Name	URL Address	Brief Description
Alta Vista	www.altavista.digital.com	Keyword search engine
AT&T	www.att.com/directory	Directories
Excite	www.excite.com	Web
Infoseek	www.infoseek.com	Largest commercial directory
Lycos	www.lycos.com	Spider
Magellan	www.mckinley.com	Search engine; business related
Web Crawler	www.webcrawler.com	Natural language spider
Yahoo!	www.yahoo.com	Hierarchical search engine; most organized on Web

illustrate, one client organization spent more than a year before it agreed on the Web site's content, layout, colors, and so on. Then, the president decided that he'd better get the site loaded on the Internet overnight. He did. A few days later, a customer called to tell the president what a shoddy picture she had on her screen and how long it took to appear. In addition, the site included typos and other errors that no one caught during the final meeting of the company's Web committee.

Promoting Your Site on the Internet

The Internet can be used in different ways to promote a Web site. The most common is to use e-mail to contact registered customers to remind them of changes or new content on the site. Smaller businesses and first-time online merchants can use an automatic service that allows visitors, registered or not, to request e-mail when site changes take place.

Another way to reach Internet customers with news about your site is through news groups and mailing lists. News groups can be used to test the viability of your site. A mailing list discussion allows site presence, leaving your URL address virtually everywhere.

Check out some of the more often-accessed topical news groups for details. Most news groups allow only new or revised Web site addresses. Other news groups (regional, event oriented, or industry specific) might be appropriate for your type of business or product. Usually, most of their addresses end in ".announce." A list of news groups can be found on List (www.list.com). On any of these sites, a photo, video, or a sound file in addition to your announcement or press release would add value.

A relatively new way of reaching customers on the Internet is what is referred to as mobile-marketing (M-marketing). Wireless advertising is real and here to stay. With location-based technology proliferating, advertising to wireless devices is on the rise. Wireless advertising provides efficiency, customization, and convenience. It makes it possible for consumers to take advantage of advertising sales when and where they may be.

One potential avenue for wireless advertising is via wireless yellow pages. In this design, ads are placed within the "yellow page" content. For example, a user can scan through wireless yellow pages to locate a Chinese restaurant. Once the user receives the requested information, the content comes with special promotions or discounts linked to that content.

As we gain experience with M-marketing, we will realize that the advertiser, consumer, and the service provider benefit. Advertisers increase sales opportunities by reaching more targeted consumers. The wireless consumer saves time and money by receiving the right ad at the right time. It is also a highly personalized experience for the consumer. To the seller of advertising space, it means additional revenue stream and value-added promotion to subscribers.

Attracting Customers to Your Site

E-commerce is booming. Online merchants are selling everything from yachts to diapers. The question is How does one lonely Web site attract customers in a vast Internet? In many cases, it takes effective marketing and a hefty budget. However, between off-line and online TV ads, radio spots, and online banner ads, sooner or later your site will become known and visitors will begin to come.

Guidelines for Making a Site Attractive

Attracting customers to your site involves the following.

1. *Keep the site content current so visitors continue to return for news.* After a site was on the Web for several months, one merchant was reluctant to make changes. His argument was that because mere presence was the goal, it was not worth the expense of updating. As a result, the number of hits and the volume of business began to dwindle. So much for this merchant's online business.
2. *Offer free information or products.* Like it or not, customers tend to swarm toward sites that have something to offer. Giveaways like mouse pads are a low-cost attraction. Once visitors register, greeting them by name the next time they visit is a great reinforcer. When they order things, they should not have to reenter information given in previous visits. For business-to-business e-commerce, *offering a free service* as a way to entice customers online is an attractive marketing tool. Once an online company offers a tool to help another company run its business free of charge, it makes it difficult for the recipient not to patronize the business.
3. *Implement a cross-selling strategy* designed to assist the visitor to make a final decision. For example, in online bookshops like Amazon.com, the customer is presented with other books by the same author or on the same topic that other customers have bought after buying that particular book. This marketing technique applies to other online businesses, as well.
4. *Ensure easy and quick navigation* and incorporate technology that anticipates the needs of the customer based on past purchases. This is called customer **profiling** or **personalization.** The Web site should be designed so that any piece of information can be accessed with no more than three clicks. (Personalization is covered in more detail later in the chapter.)

profiling: Web site technology that anticipates the needs of the customer based on past purchases.

5. *Introduce event marketing.* Special events on an online merchant's Web site attract new customers and encourage repeat visitors. For example, one day Victoria's Secret broadcast its fashion show live on the Internet. RealPlayer was used to transport the streaming media. More than 250,000 copies of the software were downloaded per hour on the day of the event. The idea was a great success, but unfortunately, the technology was not designed for real-time media. As a result, the server crashed.

6. *Enlist affiliates.* Web site owners can be affiliates of an online merchant by advertising the merchant's products for a fee or a commission. Amazon.com has about 260,000 such affiliates, who earn between 5 percent and 15 percent commission for any sales on their sites. The added exposure is free.
7. *Try out viral marketing as a tool for getting noticed.* Viral marketing is sending a message via e-mail and making it so compelling that recipients want to pass it to everyone they know. Like any other tool, viral marketing has drawbacks. Like banner ads, the problem is its potential to explode in volume to the point where it would be tantamount to spam. To date, most viral campaigns have targeted high school and college students going directly to their campus e-mail. This, in itself, raises privacy concerns (see Box 10-6).

Implied in the guidelines is the criticality of managing content quality. Regardless of the tool, message management is to e-marketing organizations what total quality manufacturing is to the industrial community. The focus is on improving the value of the message and the quality of writing. With major e-organizations, it involves a set of strategic principles to apply content quality, the actual development process, and an implementation process to leverage the strategic principles. A summary of the message management life cycle is covered in Box 10-7.

Cultural Differences

Cultural differences play a definite role in what the Web site displays and how marketing comes across to the local customer. Take the case of Kellogg's highly successful British TV

BOX 10-6
Woes of viral overload

Advertisers are hot on the tactic, and the idea of putting consumers to work spreading the word about a brand or service seems sound. But like most good ideas, viral marketing has its drawbacks—and we may see them very soon. There are some high-profile viral success stories, however. Take Hotmail. By simply sending e-mail, consumers hawked the service because every message contained a Hotmail ad. That helped it grow to 12 million accounts in its first year, 1996. The 1999 hit film *The Blair Witch Project* benefited from similar contagion. By the time the movie opened, even I had heard that it was a true story. I'd been bitten.

My in box occupies an ever bigger slice of my hard drive. If viral marketers have their way, in addition to my daily dose of e-mails from companies pitching junk, I'll get another pile passed on by friends. It'll be cute once, maybe twice. But there's a viral traffic jam lurking just a few clicks down the Information Highway. Even good friends can be as annoying as marketers if they bombard me too much. Companies think viral marketing will cut through the clutter, but if they come en masse, they'll be the clutter.

Viral marketing is a powerful theory. It attempts to harness the strongest of all consumer triggers—the personal recommendation. In the Net age, it may well be possible to include consumers in marketing and let them spread the word to global millions. But as companies pursue this latest tactic, they would be wise to remember it's no miracle cure for their marketing ills. At best, it's a way to support a broad marketing program. At worst, it's an awful little bug spread by desperate marketers and their unsuspecting consumers. I already feel a chill coming on.

SOURCE: Excerpted from Neuborne, Ellen, "Viral Marketing Alert!" *BusinessWeek e.biz*, March 19, 2001, EB8.

BOX 10-7
Managing content quality

There are three building blocks that enable message management:

- A set of five strategic principles that drive content quality and effectiveness.
- A structured content planning and message development process.
- An implementation process that leverages the five strategic principles.

FIVE STRATEGIC PRINCIPLES

The first principle is to **adopt a 360-degree view.** Taking a 360-view means managing public and private content, including content contained in enterprise systems like CRM, in a coordinated and systematic fashion. A second principle is simplifying the message combined with a less-is-more philosophy. This puts a premium on textual efficiency and managing content in smaller, more logical chunks for more effective electronic delivery.

A third principle is to transfer knowledge, not disseminate information. The knowledge transfer perspective is closely aligned to a less-is-more philosophy, with profound implications on the way content is created and delivered and how marketing and sales organizations gather and share sales intelligence. A fourth principle is to increase channel value. Companies need to ensure that the channels are one step ahead of the market, saying the right things at the right time, and adding value in the customer's eyes. A fifth principle is to keep content current and relevant.

The content planning and message processing is essentially to develop a comprehensive content plan that defines an integrated content framework and establishes a formal positioning and message development process that generates a central positioning and message knowledge base.

Message management implementation is the third and final building block that enables message management. The goal is to implement the content plan and leverage the five strategic principles.

SOURCE: Excerpted from Schmonsees, Bob, "The Quest for Content Quality," *Kmworld*, October 2002, 12–14.

ad featuring a child wearing a Kellogg's T-shirt displaying the vitamins and the iron in the product. The ad was banned in the Netherlands because advertising vitamins and iron content is considered a claim to medical benefits, which is forbidden. The same ad was disallowed in France because French law forbids using children for product endorsements.

Another issue is one of local habits and how online marketing should adapt to them. For example, an American hotel could offer a reservation service that includes pets, because it is common for Americans to take pets on trips. However, if the pages are translated into Arabic, it would not make sense to have a pet option, because it is unlikely that Arab visitors would take pets, let alone to an American hotel. An example of a company that observes local habits is Amazon.com, which is Amazon.de in Germany. The online bookseller uses a German domain name, the site is in German, the books are German, and the people who run the business are Germans who know the culture and how to conduct business in Germany.

A company that plans to expand into foreign countries must get to know the local customs, habits, and behaviors. The first step is to go to local Web sites and see how they do business. This includes Web site design; use of color, banners, size and type of links; and so on. If you plan to do business over a long period, consider hiring local talent to handle customer service. One source of information about cultural differences is the National Forum on People's Differences (www.yforum.com). It offers answers and solutions to a variety of situations that are unique to different cultures. This can be a good starting point for planning an online venture.

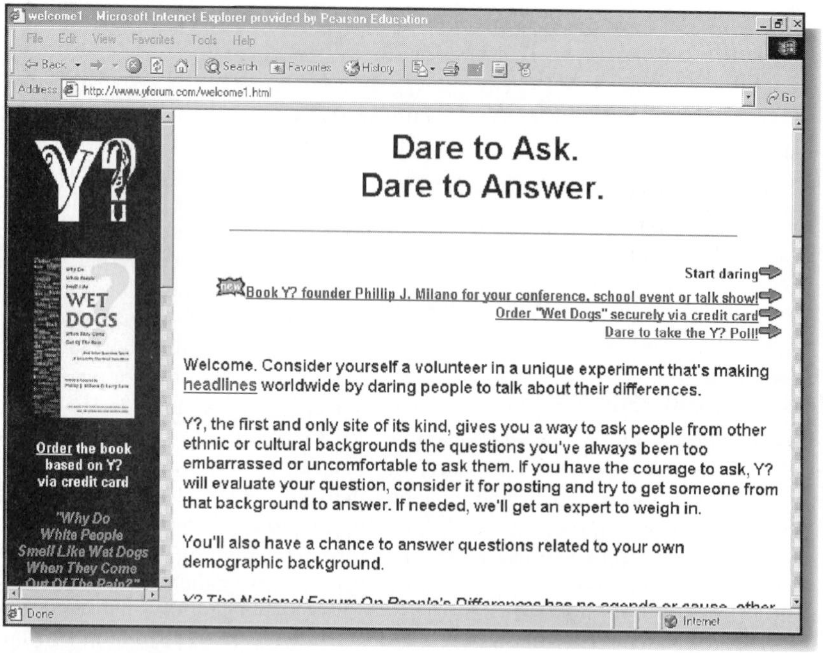

Screen Capture 10-3

Source: © 2003–2004 www.yforum.com. http://www.yforum.com//welcom1.html.

Predicting Buying Behavior

Consumers worldwide can shop online day and night, year -round. With projections that the Internet will generate sales in excess of $294 billion by 2002, online merchants may wonder how to market on the Net (Bellman 1999, p. 32). The key question is, What factors influence online shopping? The Wharton Forum on Electronic Commerce (ecom.Wharton.upenn.edu) sponsors ongoing research on Web consumer attitudes about online shopping and predictors of online buying behavior. Here is a summary of the major findings.

1. The online population is relatively younger, more educated, and wealthier than the overall U.S. population.
2. The median age of the Web consumer is 29, and educational attainment is "some college" compared to "high-school graduate" for that of the U.S. population overall.
3. The median household income is $50,000 to $74,999.
4. Eighty-five percent of the U.S. online consumers are white, and more than 21 percent reported spending more than 20 hours per week browsing on the Web from home.
5. The most common regular use for the Internet (more than once per week) is for work—at home (52.3 percent) and at work (37.8 percent).
6. The Internet is used regularly at home to read news (19.1 percent) and for entertainment (10.8 percent).
7. A total of 4,368 respondents (42.9 percent) said they have never bought anything online.
8. Approximately 30 percent of the respondents reported spending between $150 and $400 per year via the Web.

The study concludes that Web consumers shop online or use online services to save time (Bellman 1999, p. 38). The Web site should make it convenient to buy items (like the one-click-to-purchase approach at Amazon.com), and the checkout process should be smooth and flawless. Customers are increasingly valuing time savings over cost savings, which may be the key benefit offered by successful online stores.

Personalization

Imagine looking up a Web site that sells books. It welcomes you. It is no coincidence that it lists the last two books you bought. The site proceeds to make you special offers on a book you have been thinking about buying. You're so taken by the offerings that you click on the submit key. Two days later, the book arrives. Your VISA or MasterCard has already taken care of the payment. This type of marketing (also called marketing to one or one-to-one marketing, profiling, or personalization) is the wave of the future because it addresses individual needs. The idea is to gather information about consumers and send the right message at the right time.

The first step is identification. Information technology is used to identify a customer. Digital certificates also can be used to authenticate a customer because they contain information about the user, usually stored in the browser or in a smart card. After identification, the server looks up the user's personal record in the database to determine his or her buying pattern and presents attractive products, information, or services to the customer. This type of automated assistance promotes differentiation, which means that customers are treated on a personal basis. The merchant's system addresses the needs of every single customer in a unique way. Digital techniques make it easy to track customers, store their information in the database, and create special offers on the Web site.

The World Wide Web is not a mass medium. It is a personal medium. Unlike television, newspaper, or radio, which deliver to a mass audience, the Web is delivered continuously and is experienced differently by each visitor to the site. Personalizing the experience of each customer—giving a customized view of your content or product offerings—is done by enticing customers to give you information about themselves and their habits. The information is then run through a database for analysis and profiling. The transformation process is not cheap, but it is easily justified when it works. It can lock in a repeat customer and promote long-term customer relationships.

There are three ways to add personalization to a Web site: keywords, collaborative filtering, or rule-based personalization. In *keyword-based* personalization (see www.my.yahoo.com), users are presented with a set of categories of information on the Web site. After they register and click on categories, they are offered information within these categories for future sign-ups for products or services. This is a straightforward approach to delivering a personal experience without much expense. To deliver information from a keyword-based system, users enter their names and passwords, which are matched to a list of keywords they entered on previous visits. The data linked to these keywords are drawn instantly through a format that embeds HTML codes for headings and other details.

In *collaborative filtering* (e.g., www.netperceptions.com the input of many users is compared before the program comes up with a recommendation to the visitor. The process begins with a user database like that of a keyword-based system, but with extensive demographic information (age, sex, education, economic status, and so on) and detailed user preferences that are then matched against other user preferences in the database. The preferences also can be matched against the demographic data before the final recommendation is displayed. This approach is more expensive and requires a lot of information from many people to make recommendations reliable. The software alone can run upwards of $50,000.

In *rule-based personalization* (see www.multilogic.com, www.kodakpicturenetwork.com and www.broadvision.com), the system matches user input to a set of rules about user behavior. If you input to a Web site that you are a retiree and like travel in a Third World country where accommodations are cheap, the Web site might suggest Armenia or Uzbekistan for starters. Like collaborative filtering, however, this software is expensive. It takes time and know-how to set up and maintain. The rules used to generate recommendations are more valid and reliable the more information is collected from people.

One issue in using personalization is the nature of the database used to create the recommendations. In collaborative filtering, user preferences are first aggregated and then queried to produce the answers. In rule-based personalization, large volumes of data have to be captured before the program comes up with the rules that are later used to generate the recommendations.

Mobile Agents

Early online retailers saw advanced technology as the silver bullet and believed that once the e-business is built, customers will flock to it. Today's dot.com survivors learned to focus on basics, such as attracting customers to the site and making them satisfied. The current push is to integrate Web site activities and brick-and-mortar operations. There is also a continuing drive toward wireless and Web site personalization.

Part of the trend is the dawn of mobile agents and artificial intelligence (AI) software. As summarized in Box 10-8, AI mimics real-life consumer behavior by tracking patterns

BOX 10-8
AI in e-commerce

An experimental software at Microsoft lets your PC help manage your workload. It can learn about what you're doing at any given moment and make decisions about how to give you incoming information or messages. Here is how the AI program does it:

- Scans the sender and text of all incoming e-mail and gives each one a score from high priority to low. An e-mail from someone new asking for lunch next week would earn a low score. An e-mail message from the boss with words such as "due today" or "fired" would get a high score.
- Tracks your keyboard and mouse movement, and learns that how much you're typing could mean you're busy on a deadline, which means no incoming messages are welcome.
- Watches your calendar and contacts. If you were in a meeting outside the office or town, your PC would forward high-priority messages to your cell phone.
- A video camera on the PC tracks your movements. If your facial look means you're thinking, then the software takes the gesture that you should not be disturbed.
- If there has been no movement on your part, the software interprets it that you're dozing or taking a nap.
- An audio sensor would know whether you're talking on the phone or are holding a session with people in the office.
- The software builds a database about the e-mail you read and respond to and the ones you delete, trying to learn what you consider important. With all this information, it learns to screen incoming messages and decide on the ones to forward to you at the appropriate time.

SOURCE: Adapted from Maney, Kevin, "How AI Could Work," *USA Today*, June 20, 2001, 2A.

of movements and the like. These mobile agents are beginning to change the shape of e-commerce and e-business, with new concerns regarding who really owns information (Wagner and Turban 2002).

As can be seen, mobile agents are beginning to make changes in the e-world. The key question is whether mobile agents partners or predators. Ebay made headlines in 1999 when they won a court case against third-party predatory search agents or intelligent agents that would access the auction site, search for items that address a customer's query, and notify the customer about prices and other attributes unique to the query. This is a process performed by shopbots—intelligent agents that aggregate information from various databases and recommend the product and the store that has the best price.

Ebay's response suggested that agents are predators, not partners (Wagner and Turban 2002). Despite the court ruling, third-party companies are still evaluating the legality of eBay's stand. In any case, intelligent agents fall into many categories and carry out numerous problem-solving tasks such as planning, negotiation, diagnosis, and the like. As mentioned earlier, they answer and screen e-mail messages, act as a secretary screening phone calls, and even provide recommendations to the "boss" about how efficiently he or she is running the show.

TRACKING CUSTOMERS

From an e-marketing point of view, attracting visitors to a Web site is just the first step. The next is to track their movements to ensure that as many visitors as possible are converted into purchasers and repeat customers. For this reason, e-marketers need quick insight into the activities that affect the Web site—who is visiting the site, the number of page hits, number of visitors, number and type of purchases, how visitors behaved, and how to reinforce or influence consumer behavior. Customer tracking is the future of Web marketing. It allows marketers to gain important information about customers including demographic profiles and likely future purchases. Certain procedures, benefits, and issues are related to this ever-growing need to manage customer needs and expectations. From all indications, tracking customers with ads in mind is growing rapidly via wireless (see Box 10-9).

Gathering Web Data

There are three main ways of collecting data on Web site visitors: log files, forms, and cookies. Each is briefly explained in the following paragraphs.

log files: files on the Web server that keep track of domain types, time of access, keywords used, and search engines used.

Log Files

Log files are files on the Web server that keep track of domain types, time of access, keywords used, and search engines used. The keywords, for example, tell the merchant what visitors were looking for when they came to the Web site.

Forms

Registration and purchase forms are the two most effective ways of gathering Web site visitor information. They capture customer-provided personal information (name, address, birth date, sex, zip code, e-mail address, and so on). Web retailers place links and contests on the Web site homepage to capture visitor preferences via forms. The more interaction there is with customers, the more information there is that can be gathered about their tastes and preferences.

BOX 10-9
Ads on wireless

Advocates of wireless advertising say cell phones and handheld computers are perfect deliverers of ads, especially since the devices are carried by consumers virtually everywhere they go. But skeptics argue that consumers will spend hardly any time scrolling their mobile devices for ads. Only a small subset of advertisers—local vendors, restaurants, and entertainment complexes—will find the ads cost-effective.

Still, few analysts doubt that there will be revenue from wireless ads. The wireless providers charge about $40 to $50 per 1,000 clicks for a wireless ad, compared with the $25 per 1,000 clicks for ads placed on Web sites. By 2005, some analysts project that money spent by advertisers on wireless ads worldwide will soar to as high as $17 billion. Even skeptics such as Mr. Nail at Forrester forecast the market to reach $800 million in the same period.

Having tried different wireless service providers and the ads they promote, my verdict: It may be fun to surf some wireless ads—especially those with interactive elements—if you have some downtime. But if I'm busy and on the run, I'd rather return to my old routine: Get the information I need from my Palm and simply ignore the ads altogether.

SOURCE: Excerpted from Tam, Pui-Wing, "Show of Hands," *The Wall Street Journal*, April 23, 2001, R14ff.

Cookies

As noted in Chapter 8, a cookie is a small piece of information that is sent to the visitor's browser when the visitor accesses a particular site. When it arrives, the browser saves it to the hard disk. When the visitor returns to that site, some of the stored information will be sent back to the merchant's Web server along with the new request. Cookies are standard components for tracking visitor activities on most Web sites. They tell retailers who is a first-time visitor and where repeat visitors having been within the Web site.

In general, cookies are harmless. Some cookies have expiration dates, and when that date comes, the visitor's browser simply erases it from the hard drive. Cookies with an expiration date generally are referred to as *persistent cookies*. Cookies that will last as long as the browser stays open are referred to as *session cookies*. When the browser is closed, session cookies simply disappear.

Any way you look at it, cookies make a lot of people uncomfortable. They invade people's privacy. Unlike e-mail, cookies are hidden from the visitor's view. They allow the merchant to recognize individual users instead of just machines. There are, however, a number of things that a cookie cannot tell anyone—whether more than one person uses the same computer to view a Web site; whether one person uses more than one computer to visit a Web site; and the person's name, age, and the country from which they are accessing the Web site.

Clickstream Data Analysis

clickstream data: a Web site visitors' clicks, which leave footprints representing their behavior.

When visitors go on a site, their clicks leave *footprints*. This type of information is called **clickstream data.** It includes any measure that helps observers learn how visitors navigate a site and why. Today, nearly every Web site collects and evaluates clickstream data in one form or another. The data can be used to learn how to design better customer-friendly sites, where to spend Internet advertising dollars, how to run successful e-marketing campaigns, and even how to personalize Web pages.

Clickstream data can pinpoint a host of customer behaviors. Online retailers began analyzing clickstream data to figure out why customers might leave the site prematurely and abandon shopping carts. These data are then compared with similar data from other carts to determine the following.

1. Whether the products in the abandoned cart were high-profit or loss-leader items.
2. The value of the products in the abandoned shopping carts.
3. The volume of products in the abandoned carts.
4. The number of different product types in the abandoned cart.
5. The average and total value of the products in the abandoned shopping carts compared to those that cleared the checkout process.

Customer satisfaction is the most sensitive and gratifying goal for an online retailer. Treating the customer differently based on these findings is bound to improve customer satisfaction. Software packages help retailers analyze clickstream data to help them do just that. Box 10-10 shows a case in point.

Based on a number of studies, the common data to track include the following.

1. Where a visitor first landed on the site.
2. How the visitor got to the site (typing in a URL address vs. a subject name, clicking on a banner ad, and so on).
3. The number and sequence of pages viewed.
4. The number and cost of each product purchased.
5. The length of time the visitor stayed on each page and on the entire site.
6. The total cost of each visit.
7. The point on the site where the visitor clicked away.

These are only guidelines, because the key is to decide what specific information an e-merchant considers important to the marketing business plan. A sample of clickstream products is listed in Table 10-3, one of which is DoubleClick. It combines data on Web surfers—such as IP address, operating system, and sites visited—with off-line data—such as name, address, and a customer's purchase history taken from the separate databases—to

BOX 10-10

E-commerce trends: Getting help from Clickstream data

For weeks, the site administrator of CVS.com waded through his company Web site, trying to make sense out of the number of pages that were called up, the order of pages viewed, the products purchased, where the visitor left the site, and so on. He invested in new clickstream technology to figure out how to help customers wade through its 15,000-item inventory. He wanted to decrease the rate at which visitors abandoned the site before completing a purchase.

Clickstream analysis showed there was a high drop-off rate from the site's checkout page. There were some inefficient paths and procedures that were also confusing to the visitor. He rectified these problems by rewriting directions on the checkout pages, adding "messages" to the visitor like "You are now on step two of the four steps to check out," reducing the total number of steps in checkout, and redesigning some pages to look more user-friendly.

SOURCE: Adapted from Dahir, Mubarak, "Just for Clicks: It Pays to Follow Your Customer's Every Move," *The Industry Standard,* May 15, 2000, 305ff.

Table 10-3
Sample Clickstream tools

Watching You

Company	Product Function	Pricing
Accrue Software www.accrue.com	Analyzes clickstreams to refine content, sales efforts, pricing, and merchandise placement	Starts at $15,000
Doubleclick www.doubleclick.com	Full-service ad-management solution for content providers	$1.25 per 1,000 page views to 45 cents per 1,000 page views
IBM www.ibm.com	SurfAid Analytics includes site reporting, traffic and content categorization, decision support, and advanced data mining	Setup fee: $2,000-10,000; monthly begins at $750
Macromedia www.macromedia.com	Real-time Web site analysis and reporting, so Web content can be personalized and dynamically updated	Prices start at $100,000
WebTrends www.webtrends.com	Scalable Web analytics, marketing and campaign analysis, and integration of visitor data with other data sources, including enterprise	Typical deal costs $50,000 and up.

Source: Excerpted from Dahir, Mubarak, "Watching You," *The Industry Standard*, May 15, 2000, 310.

target customers with impressive precision. From a marketer's viewpoint, the process is attractive. Its technology can tell where customers have been on the Internet and where they are going. If the Web can be used as a surveillance device, then the marketing opportunities are virtually endless.

The Reliability of E-Intelligence

It is clear that e-marketing means more than just putting up an attractive Web site. The goal is to identify and retain repeat customers, especially for high-margin products. This requires e-intelligence or information that helps the merchant understand who their customers are and what entices them to buy. This is where artificial intelligence is used to mine the Web to answer people's questions (see Box 10-11).

Clickstream analysis tools alone do not elicit much behavioral information about Web site visitors. We need to know the following.

1. What Web site content most often gets people to buy online?
2. Why do people abandon their shopping cart and click away?
3. How do e-sales compare to those on other channels?

Finally, one should be careful how much of the data collected are reliable. Different log analysis tools produce different results for reasons. Industry measurement standards are lacking. Log analysis software vendors have their own definitions of how to handle open visits, errors, search engines, and the like. Questions still arise about how to identify a unique visitor or how to count visitors. Is it by cookie? By IP address? To make things

BOX 10-11
E-intelligence

If you ran into him online, you might first be struck by the kid's prodigious memory. He calls himself "SmarterChild" and can recite a litany of facts—this season's entire baseball lineup, every word in the dictionary, and the weather in major cities across the country. SmarterChild, a computer program, is part of a new species of "chatterbots" that are renewing debate about the extent to which computers can achieve intelligence. The electronic personalities of this generation use the vast repository of information on the Web as their memory bank, not just some rigid database.

The company that conceived Smarter Child, Active Buddy Inc., created the bot as a marketing tool that would engage people in conversation and then tell them about various products or services. The idea that computers might serendipitously comb through troves of data to produce useful bits of information faces numerous political, economic, and social hurdles, such as privacy concerns, not to mention enormous technical obstacles. And skeptics abound.

For the most part, bots like SmarterChild are able to talk only about certain established topics. But some have been able to reach a touchstone of artificial intelligence—passing the Turing Test, in which researchers ask humans to guess whether they are communicating with a person or a machine. If people can't tell the difference, the machines are deemed to have passed the test.

SOURCE: Excerpted from Cha, Ariana E., "Web May Hold the Key to Achieving Artificial Intelligence," *The Wall Street Journal*, September 6, 2002, A9ff.

worse, the data-gathering software often comes with bugs that distort the accuracy and reliability of the statistics generated from traffic analysis.

Role of the Shopbot

Since online shopping began, the quest has been on to help customers find the best price. Even though online shopping is quicker than bricks-and-mortar shopping, customers still don't want to spend too much time surfing sites to buy a particular item. For this reason, shopping **bots** were created, whose software searches several sites and will tell you what each site charges for the same item and where the best buy is located. Bots are a bargain hunter's dream. The consumer decides on an item, sets a price, and sends a bot into cyberspace on a search mission; the result is finding the consumer's favorite item at the best available price.

bot: short for robot; also called a shopping agent.

Bots have been part of Web technology since the beginning of Web business. Historically, bot technology first appeared in the form of spiders and crawlers that search engines still use to locate Web sites. More recently, the technology has become more intelligent. Bots sit on Web servers. First, they try to learn your preferences and specific needs, and then they go to work for you. It is like telling the bot, "Hey, I am looking for a 1994 BMW 325i convertible with less than 30,000 miles, and I want to spend no more than $3,000, period."

Are bots a threat to e-merchants' tenuous foothold in a shifting digital marketplace? Turning off a shopping bot could deprive a merchant of an important visitor—the bot that could recommend the merchant's product. Because more than 80 percent of online shoppers comparison shop before they buy, search-and-comparison tools like bots are the perfect way to bargain hunt. Bots also give equal airtime to large and small Web sites.

This helps the consumer as well as the merchant. They force retailers of every size to keep their prices competitive, which helps the consumer. Merchants complain that bots consume bandwidth on the merchant's site, and that can be a big problem. Each hit from a shopping bot is like one user, and the requests can run into the thousands at once, often overloading sites and slowing traffic for other users.

Today's newer bots are more intelligent and more efficient. They store information on a site's thousands of products in a local cache (storage) and refresh them only every 3 days, rather than every 10 seconds as older bots did. They gather data about a merchant responsibly, search during off hours, and give merchants the option to release direct data regarding product prices rather than spidering their way through the sites with each request. They also compare customer service, delivery options, warranties, and the like. In the end, e-merchants that give the customer a satisfying experience will prevail over those with simply the lowest price.

Customer Service

For all the positive and promising things that e-commerce provides, it continues to suffer from the nature of its business: the automation that removes the human contact between buyer and merchant. Impersonal business has rarely been a plus with the consumer. Therefore, anything that can be done to improve the contact between the seller and the buying public will build bridges of confidence that can have a lasting effect on the business. In the final analysis, it is customer support and customer service that will pay dividends.

Don't Annoy the Customer

Consumers face the never-ending problem of trying to buy a product at the lowest price and with the best customer support—good warranties, quick response to repairs, minimum wait time at the phone, replacement of defective products within days, and the like. Unfortunately, merchants must make a minimum profit if customer support is to survive. The author remembers several consulting situations where negotiations with the vendor reached a point where one vendor commented, "I don't mind selling you our system at near cost, but that leaves me nothing to support the product or, in fact, the business." In every transaction (off-line or online) where quality of customer service is a given, the price is usually not the lowest or the best.

Regardless of the combination of price and customer service, rule number one in Internet marketing is "Don't annoy the customer." There must be improved logistics to keep the customer happy. From the time the order is placed to the time the product is delivered, a mechanism should be in place to keep the customer informed about the status of the order, where it is in transit, and whether it is being shipped on schedule. There must be minimum wait time over the phone. According to a survey of 10,000 computer owners, the average time spent on hold, waiting for technical support, is 17 minutes. Staffing phone help lines during that year cost software companies worldwide about $11 billion of the nearly $18 billion spent on support services (Mullaney 1999p. 54).

Because of price competition on the Web, many national organizations are reconsidering support services. For example, free house calls for PC repair by IBM and Packard Bell have already dropped from 1 year of free in-house service to 90 days. One software maker now sells support for $199 that buys 10 phone calls or $1,600 per year for unlimited calls. The aim is to move customer support traffic away from high-cost services to manufacturer-run Web sites, which are cheaper to staff. At that level, the customer has a choice of sending a fax or an e-mail message, hoping to get a response the next day. In the meantime, the system is idle, generating customer dissatisfaction and complaints.

Regardless of the reasons or the procedures followed in e-commerce, botched logistics can spell disaster. Order taking is the easy part; fulfillment is where the merchant promotes or destroys customer satisfaction. In a study reported by Hanrahan, among the 10 reasons why e-shoppers come back to a merchant's Web site are "level and quality of customer service" and "on-time delivery" (Hanrahan 1999, p. R20). Seasoned e-retailers know they need a good system for order fulfillment and delivery. In most online shopping, when a customer initiates an order, it triggers an automated process that sends the order from the merchant's Web site to a distributor via electronic data interchange (EDI) or over the Internet. The merchant updates the customer by e-mail on the status of the order, how long it will take, and when the order should arrive. More and more merchants now give the customer the procedure for tracking the status of their orders online (see Box 10-12).

Salespeople and Internet Marketing

One of the critical side effects of Internet marketing is the role of the salesperson, who is accustomed to controlling the information the customer receives. All of a sudden, the

BOX 10-12
E-commerce trends: Price isn't everything

For online shoppers, low prices don't count for everything. Just ask Shopping.com. When the Corona del Mar, California, online retailer—which sells a range of products—got a torrent of orders last Christmas, it simply couldn't handle the volume. Its systems broke down, and employees were left scrambling to fill what orders did get through.

The results were quick and harsh. Angry customers clogged online message boards with complaints about billing errors, busy signals, and missing orders, and the local Better Business Bureau received nearly 270 complaints.

What happened next was just as dramatic. Compaq Computer Corp. acquired Shopping.com for $220 million soon after the holiday shopping season. It immediately moved to make peace by offering a $250 gift certificate to anyone with a complaint against the retailer on file with the Better Business Bureau. And in May, Shopping.com began a "125 percent satisfaction guaranteed" program, pledging to refund the purchase price, plus 25 percent, to any dissatisfied customer. The overtures to customers seem to be working, judging from the letters received from customers who got the $250 certificates.

Customers lured online with low prices and one-click ordering still demand the same level of customer service as they do in the real world. They expect orders to be filled on time, complaints to be addressed, and employees to help them with questions.

But customer service isn't cheap. How can sites living off razor-thin margins keep customer satisfaction high? Many firms are turning to a process called "up-leveling": beginning with low-cost, automated customer service, and providing real-time service only as a last resort. A customer with a question is guided to a Frequently Asked Questions (FAQ) page on the retail site, then given the chance to send an e-mail message if he or she can't find an answer. Only if the e-mail reply doesn't satisfy the customer is he or she given a phone number to call for a live rep.

SOURCE: Excerpted from Hanrahan, Timothy, "Price Isn't Everything," *The Wall Street Journal*, July 12, 1999, R20.

customer has that information over the Internet. In industries like real estate and insurance, which are salesperson heavy, resistance to new technology continues. For example, Nationwide Insurance, which is planning to get its 15,000 agents to use the Web through a Siebel System 99 customer relationship management suite, is already getting resistance from the initial users. Understandably, most agents come from the "old school," but the firm has no choice. Traditional systems can no longer distribute leads to agents effectively, and the firm has to cut operating costs to remain competitive.

Many other companies are trying to convince their sales staffs that using the Web to improve efficiency does not mean eliminating the human touch or replacing the sales force. Take the case of Oracle Corporation and its attempt to automate sales processes. Based on a late 1999 report, Oracle's automated Web-based software installation encountered similar resistance. Its sales force is now being used as educators and in customer support.

To date, no matter how much automation technology provides in direct marketing, customers will still rely on human salespeople before making complex purchases. Even at the highest level of e-commerce, the need for live sales help continues. E-commerce today is eliminating administrative sales work, letting human salespeople focus on providing value to customers. Companies must find a way to forge a balance between e-commerce operations and sales force operations. Personalization tools can be made available for salespeople to check on their progress, their commissions, and their standing in the sales department at their convenience.

Management Implications

Another implication for management is return on investment. With the huge investment that most of today's successful Web sites have made, it is important to look into tools that can analyze what visitors have done and predict what they will do. They also should be capable of providing insight into where customers are coming from and how they behave on the Web site. This means continuous analysis and handling data about thousands of visitors interactively. By providing online, real-time solutions, e-businesses can react in time to stay alive and to grow.

Finally, with the increasing concern about customer service, companies that have gone all out to solidify a successful future on the Web should reconsider their approach to customer support. Software is available that businesses can use to manage all aspects of customer encounters. Software can handle field service and dispatch technicians, and call centers can handle all channels of customer contact including voice and self-service via a Web site.

E-commerce without e-service can be suicidal for a business. When a customer order goes awry, the customer won't come back. Talking to your customers is not only good for business, it is also good for name recognition. It is healthy for your brand. Trusty phrases like "Thank you" and "We apologize" still work in most cases. The only taxing part is dealing with events beyond your control. Then you have to handle customer complaints on a case-by-case basis. This is where quality customer service becomes the lubricant of e-commerce.

Successful Internet marketing means high-level executive involvement and thinking fresh about a new way of selling, advertising, delivering merchandise, and knowing your market, which means exploring your customers, competition, and supply sources. It also means defining, selecting, and prioritizing the things it takes to implement the company's e-business vision.

Summary

1. Marketing is the process of planning and implementing the conception, pricing, advertising, and distribution of goods and services to meet the demands of the market. Online marketing is about business, not just technology. The approach, the process, and the protocols in Internet marketing are unique and must work together for the merchant, the customer, and the supplier.
2. Three factors make online shopping attractive: quick sorting through choices, vast selection of products, and quick comparison of products.
3. Online shopping has some drawbacks: Certain products like tools are still best bought through brick-and-mortar stores, bulky products like lumber do not sell well on the Internet, and certain buying decisions require experiential information.
4. The Internet provides a continuum of marketing techniques, from passive (pull) techniques where visitors seek out merchants, to aggressive (push) techniques, where the Web site seeks out the customer.
5. Internet marketing is made up of an e-cycle that begins with planning followed by the four P's: product, pricing, place, and promotion. Personalization is a unique e-marketing feature.
6. One marketing implication behind the power shift from merchant to consumer is a unique marketing strategy that follows rules that make sense. They include simple content, dynamic sites, conciseness and ease of navigation, effective promotion of the Web site, free giveaways, and consistency.
7. To promote a site on the Web, it must be available to search engines and directories. The site must stand out from other sites. Choice of keywords makes a difference.
8. Attracting customers to a site involves keeping site content current, offering free information or products, implementing cross-selling strategies to assist visitors in making a final decision, quick and easy navigation, introducing event marketing, and enlisting affiliates.
9. The first step in personalization is customer identification. The three ways to add personalization to a Web site are keywords, collaborative filtering, or rule-based personalization. The three ways of collecting data on Web site visitors are log files, forms, and cookies.
10. Successful Internet marketing means high-level executive involvement, thinking about a new way of selling and delivering merchandise, and finding what it takes to implement the company's e-business vision. The test of successful e-marketing is customer service and customer satisfaction.

Key Terms

- aggressive marketing, 298
- banner, 296
- bot, 321
- business plan, 300
- clickstream data, 318
- directory, 309
- log files, 317
- personalization, 306
- profiling, 311
- pull marketing, 296
- push technology, 296
- spamming, 298
- spider, 309
- vision, 301

Test Your Understanding

1. Marketing is "the art of the possible." Do you agree? Explain.
2. From the consumer's view, what makes online shopping attractive? What are some of the drawbacks?
3. How would a merchant justify going on the Internet? Elaborate.
4. What is spam? How does it differ from virtual marketing?
5. In what respect is customer personalization unique to Internet marketing? Be specific.
6. What are the phases that make up the e-cycle of Internet marketing?
7. What are banners? In what way are they controversial?
8. Define personalization. Give an example of your own.
9. What is involved in attracting customers to a Web site? Explain briefly.
10. How is customer tracking carried out? Of the ways covered in the chapter, which one is the most common?

Discussion Questions

1. Do you think e-businesses are more concerned about presence than brick-and-mortar businesses? Why?
2. From a marketing view, what Web design mistakes do first-time e-firms make?
3. In what way(s) is promoting a product on the Web different from using mass media (TV, radio, newspaper, and so on) and word of mouth? Explain.
4. How can passive and aggressive (pull/push) ads work together for a given firm? Discuss.
5. What managerial implications can one draw regarding Internet marketing?

Web Exercises

1. As a network administrator of Shenanigan's, a retailer of children's products, you have seen the business expand from 1 specialty store in a downtown location to 11 stores throughout the Commonwealth of Virginia. The company hired a marketing research firm that found that most of its customers are females between 23 and 30 years of age and are avid users of the Internet. These customers would not mind ordering children's products (clothing, toys, and so on) on the Web.
   a. Design a business plan that can be used as a step for Shenanigan's to go on the Internet. In the plan, make sure to consider the elements covered in the chapter.
   b. Write a memo to Shenanigan's CEO, explaining things like customer tracking, banner advertising, and the like, that relate to the recommended site.
2. Interview a senior manager of a company that uses electronic marketing or e-commerce about his or her experience in this area of operation. Is the company making money? How costly has the building and maintenance of the electronic system been? What performance criteria does he or she use to determine success or poor performance? Write a short news release to your college newspaper to report your findings.

3. Go on the Internet and evaluate three companies that have recently announced their first Web site. How much e-marketing is there? How effective do you predict it will be?
4. Access two business Web sites and review their homepages. Evaluate the goals of the sites. Are they primarily used for advertising new products? General awareness? Special product sales? Career opportunities? How much overall e-marketing does each Web site offer?
5. Look up the following Web sites and evaluate the uses and issues related to banner ads.
   a. Coder.com (www.coder.com)
   b. doubleclick.net (www.doubleclick.com.)

Chapter 11

Business-to-Business E-Commerce

Contents

IN A NUTSHELL

It should be obvious by now that the Internet is changing the face of the worldwide economy. Its greatest impact is on business-to-business (B2B) commerce because of its effect on the way companies form strategic alliances and supplier relationships. The increased volume and speed of the Business-to-Consumer (B2C) e-commerce surge and the promise of supply-chain efficiencies is driving B2B demand in companies that have to reduce operating and handling costs while accelerating the supply-chain process. Companies that take advantage of B2B efficiency stand to become market leaders in their industries. The savings they realize from supply-chain costs can be passed along in improved IT operation and, ultimately, to B2B clients.

The differences between B2C and B2B e-commerce are far greater than those between retail and wholesale purchasing. From a business viewpoint, it means savings behind the scenes, ready and convenient alliances with suppliers, meeting cost-cutting objectives while delivering goods and services on a just-in-time basis, and fine-tuning complex procurement collaboration, timely delivery collaboration, and electronic payment systems within the alliance.

In one respect, B2B is collaborative commerce. Companies forge long-term alliances while reducing the cost of doing business. Collaborative commerce requires that information such as product pricing, inventory, and shipping status be shared among business partners. One user of collaborative commerce is Ensco Inc., a company that hauls hazardous chemical wastes from manufacturing plants. Each plant requires Ensco to keep it briefed on the disposal process, because the plants have legal responsibility for the disposal of waste material. Ensco's system shares this information with all of its customers—information that was not available before (Alexander 2000, p. 45).

The B2B market is estimated to be more than 10 times larger than the B2C market. Web-based B2B companies profit in a number of ways. They can help other companies set up sites where goods or services can be sold. They can act as brokers at auctions and get a percentage of each sale. They can earn revenues by allowing companies to advertise on their Web sites. The search engine Yahoo! has entered the B2B business, hoping to ride the wave of success.

Yahoo! provides users with access to a rich collection of online resources including forums and shopping services. More recently, it introduced auctions and a B2B facility where companies can find products of all varieties for their businesses from other companies trying to sell to Yahoo!

This chapter focuses on the concept and mechanics of B2B, how it differs from B2C, the pros and cons of this emerging strategy, the technology supporting B2B, and implications for the integration of B2B and B2C for the enhancement and profitability of the business process.

WHAT IS B2B E-COMMERCE?

Historically, business has always been about exchange. Back in the days of barter, a seller exchanged an item with a buyer for a different item. In one remote Syrian village in the 1940s, for example, the only cobbler made a new pair of shoes for two dozen eggs if the soles were made from car tire rubber or 10 kilos of wheat if the soles were made from cow leather. When money is introduced to represent economic value, it eliminates barter.

Supply chains have existed since business was organized to deliver goods and services to the customer. The silk route between India, China, and West Asia and the English and Dutch East India companies are early examples of global supply chains. However, the concept of competitive advantage and supply-chain management (SCM) are relatively new. There are reasons for the emerging events.

- Today's customer has become more cost conscious and value-conscious, and is in a position to demand quality products in a timely manner.
- The maturation of information technology and networks makes it possible to design a supply chain to meet customer demand.
- The global dimension, involving distance, costs, time, variety, and uncertainty, makes it almost mandatory that the long supply chains be managed efficiently around the clock (Kumar 2001).

In today's digital world, money is exchanged by the invisible transfer of funds between businesses via computers, regardless of distance or location. E-business uses the same process. Companies continue to form business relationships. The unique contribution of B2B e-commerce is in the way these relationships are established and maintained. They are established for the mutual benefit of all parties. When hundreds of businesses are connected, the Web eliminates distance and creates a market where price and time are the main constraints.

As can be seen, B2B activities are critical to any enterprise, regardless of size, volume of sale, or type of product. A company almost certainty has relationships with other businesses. The nature of the relationship is both operational and strategic. The operational activities of a B2B process support those relationships based on strategy. The software helps track operational activities that are moved through the B2B information pipeline (McGoveran 2001).

Defining B2B

B2B: alternative ways of executing transactions between buyers and sellers that are business organizations; a network of independent organizations and long-term trading partners.

B2C: alternative ways of executing transactions between buyers and sellers in which the buyers are individual consumers.

The literature provides a number of definitions of B2B. E-commerce refers to alternative ways of executing transactions or activities between buyers and sellers. **B2B** implies that both sellers and buyers are business organizations. **B2C** implies that buyers are individual consumers. With or without the Internet, commerce between business and consumer is different from commerce among businesses. B2B involves complex procurement, manufacturing, and planning collaboration; complex payment terms; and round-the-clock performance agreements.

E-business is not information technology, and information technology is distinctly separate from e-business, although they are intertwined with each other. With today's increasing emphasis on "just-in-time" processing, e-business cannot survive without technology. It is considered the backbone of the supply chain that keeps businesses operating together. This involves ease of product return, timeliness of delivery, product availability, product information, and Web site navigation (Fogarty 2002). A proposed list of technologies that qualify for satisfying B2B processing needs is summarized by Morgenthal (2001). It includes the following.

- Messaging products for facilitating secure, reliable data movement between trading partners.
- Work flow and process flow products for implementing conversational logic.
- Trading partner management products for helping identify where the data need to go and how they should get there.
- Directories for assisting businesses in locating other businesses that provide a particular service or product.

Traditional B2B e-commerce involves negotiations and contractual commitments between long-term trading partners (suppliers, manufacturers). The nature of the commitment is clearly defined and highly repetitive. It is about buying and selling commodities such as paper, plastics, and even cows. Ben Zaitz traded in his farm boots and acquired a laptop to develop the Cattle Offerings Worldwide (COW) Web site at a time when the idea of using the Web to trade cows was unheard of. After the concept caught on, the site attracted 40,000 visitors per month and held in excess of $2 million worth of auctions of livestock and commodities.

B2B is more than a mechanism for taking orders online. It is a network of independent organizations involved in a business area or an industry such as chemicals, plastics, automotive, or construction. It is also a new way to view products, production, and pricing. It is delivering customized services and goods, and managing inventory for business partners. This means extending the supply chain so companies will be able to respond on a minute-by-minute basis.

It all boils down to the concept of exchange. For example, Alliant Foodservice Inc. had long followed the traditional way of handling food distribution. Distributors controlled how suppliers funneled products to restaurants and other businesses. Now,

Screen Capture 11-1

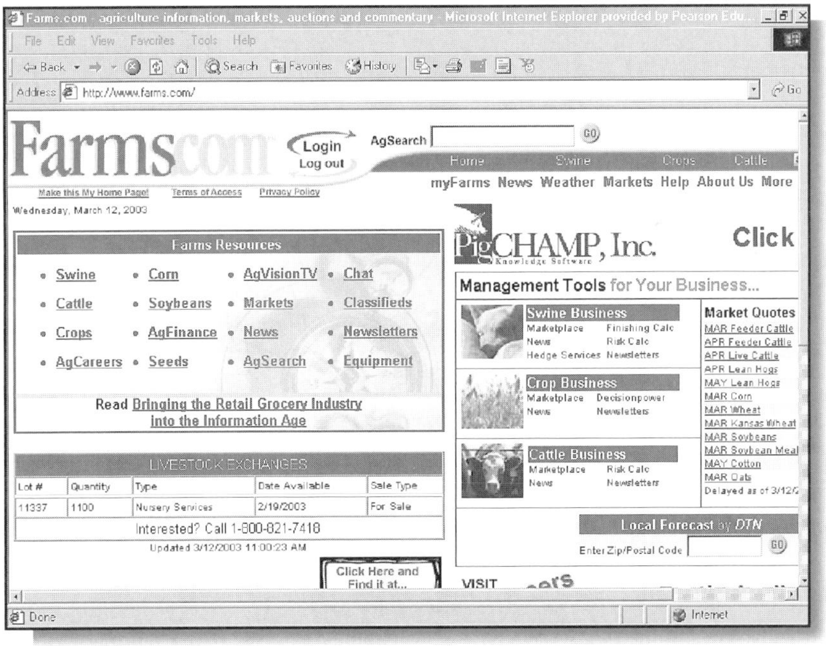

through its Web site (AlliantLink.com), Alliant lets users such as restaurants and hotels order goods without using catalogs, faxes, or phones (see Box 11-1).

In addition to direct communication and speed, the efficiency factor must be considered. In the case of Alliant, the company ships about 1 million cases of food and supplies per day. Under the traditional method, the process offered many opportunities for errors. Now the company is using the Web and wireless technology to reduce errors by more than 60 percent (Crockett 2000, p. EB90). For example, when orders were entered by fax and phone, an average of three ordering errors occurred per 1,000 cases of food shipped. Ordering directly via the company's Web site cut the error rate to less than two errors per 1,000 cases. Similar error reductions also appeared in handling out-of-stock queries, delivery returns, and inventory mis-picks.

BOX 11-1

E-commerce trends: The Alliant exchange process

By linking 4,000 restaurants with 75 food suppliers and a national distribution service via its AlliantLink.com Web site, Alliant is making the ordering and delivery of food more efficient. Here's how:

STEPS FOR RESTAURANT OWNERS

1. A restaurant that decides at the last minute to sell Memorial Day barbecue specials can place an order for an extra truckload of chicken wings with a few quick clicks at the AlliantLink.com Web site.
2. Rather than calling an Alliant salesperson who checks with a few warehouses to see if supplies are available, one touch at AlliantLink.com zaps the restaurateur into a Web site listing 165,000 products—saving customers hours of tracking time.
3. Packers at the nearest Alliant warehouse with the right inventory receive the electronic order. They load trucks and send them out for delivery within 24 hours.
4. While customers can see what they owe on the Web site and even print their bill out, it's still little more than a convenience. In a year, Alliant hopes to do electronic billing and receive e-payments. Alliant expects to get paid 3 to 5 days faster and save more than 10 percent in processing costs.

STEPS FOR THE FOOD SUPPLIERS

1. With Memorial Day approaching, a supplier like Nabisco can promote its A1 Steak Sauce to specific restaurants on the AlliantLink.com Web site. Before, Nabisco would have had to offer rebates through middlemen.
2. Alliant charges suppliers about $400 an hour to prepare data about the restaurants that buy the most steak sauce this time of year. With a few keystrokes, Nabisco can retrieve this data from AlliantLink.com.
3. Nabisco can then buy an ad on AlliantLink.com for $60 to $80 per 1,000 page views that targets the restaurants most likely to buy the sauce. Alliant controls the ad so that it pops up when the selected buyer arrives at the order screen.
4. Alliant analyzes the restaurants that click on the ads and determines how many of them actually bought. The analysis is passed on to the supplier who can then prepare a marketing campaign targeting those restaurants.

SOURCE: Excerpted from Crockett, Roger, "Chow (On)line," *Business Week E.Biz*, June 5, 2000, EB86.

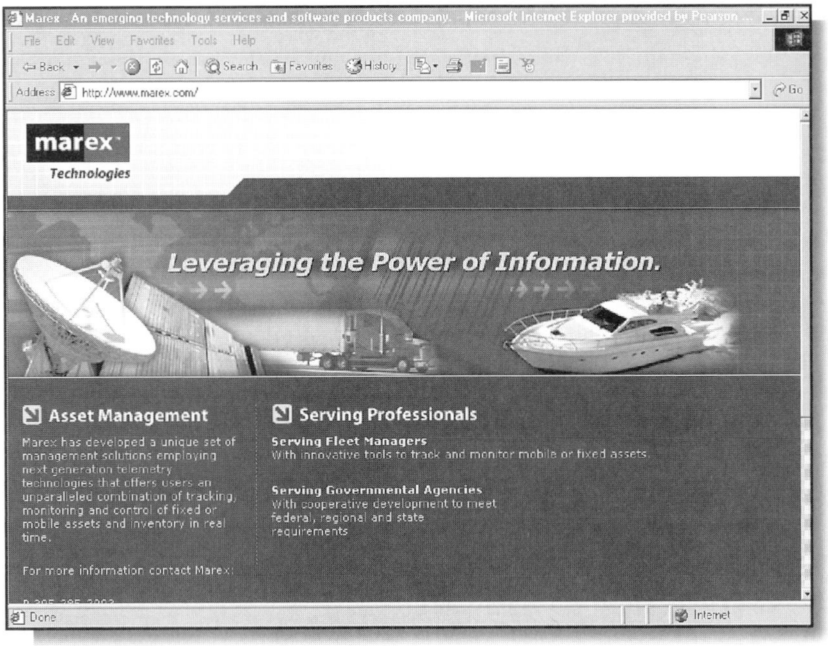

Screen Capture 11-2

The traditional approaches to communication (phone, fax, face to face, and mail) are being replaced by Web-based models—auctions and exchanges. In geographically dispersed markets, buyers who cannot find the right suppliers end up paying more or settle for inferior products. With B2B e-commerce, supply-chain participants are directly connected. For example, marex.com, a marine exchange, links boat builders, dealers, and yacht brokers who buy and sell wholesale.

Figure 11-1 presents the following specific elements of B2B.

1. **Buying company:** Focus on procurement in terms of reduced purchase prices and cycle time. The buying company announces a request for purchase of a certain product on its Web site, and the participating suppliers in the B2B network send their bids.

2. **Selling company:** Focus on marketing and sales. The seller attracts the buying organization to its Web site for business. Each seller has its unique catalog, pricing policy, and discount schedule.

3. **Intermediating service provider:** Focus on ensuring order fulfillment. Such a service provider mediates between the buying company and the supplier (seller), usually for parts and unique products. For example, GM plays the role of intermediary between its dealers and the hundreds of suppliers that provide spare parts.

4. **JIT deliverer:** Focus on just-in-time delivery. This phase of B2B is critical because ensuring delivery of items just when they are needed means savings in time and money.

5. **Web-based platform:** Focus on the Internet, Intranets, and Extranets. An Intranet connects islands of information on separate computers within the firm. An Extranet is a dedicated network between business partners on the Internet. (Intranets and Extranets were covered in detail in Chapter 4.)

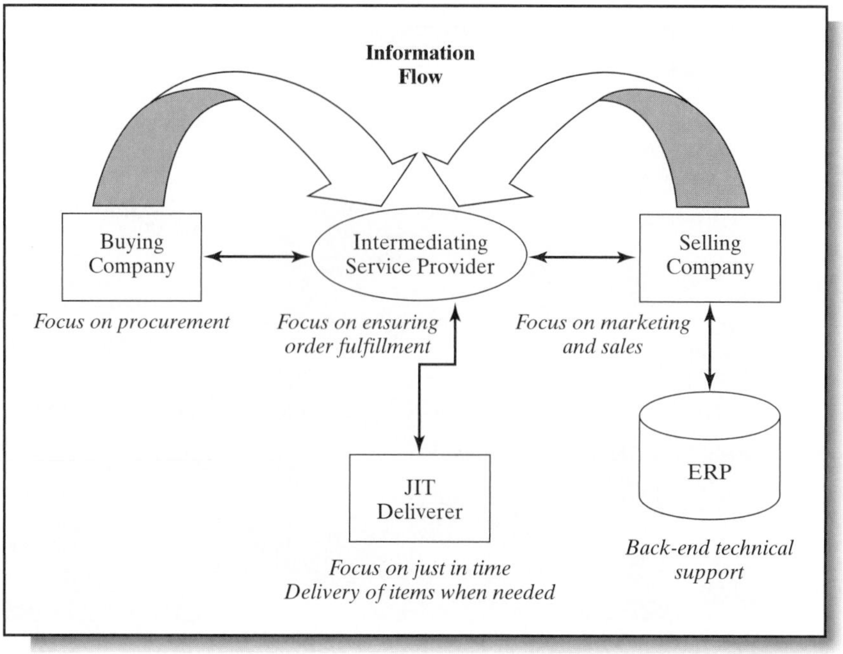

Figure 11-1
Key B2B entities

Electronic Data Interchange (EDI): electronic exchange of business documents such as bills, orders, and shipping notices between business partners.

6. **B2B Tools:** Focus on **Electronic Data Interchange (EDI)** and software agents. EDI is the electronic exchange of business documents like bills, orders, and shipping notices between business partners. EDI is designed to convert proprietary data into a format that can be transmitted electronically. EDI is covered in more detail later in the chapter.)

7. **Back-end technical support:** Focus on Enterprise Resource Planning or ERP. Integrating B2B with technical infrastructure such as ERP, database management systems, and Intranet data flow means keeping most information traffic on the supplier's servers.

B2B Versus B2C

Table 11-1 summarizes the key differences between B2B and B2C. Essentially, the following characteristics differentiate them.

1. **The connection mechanism:** In B2C, the connection mechanism is consumer-to-system. In B2B, one business uses a Web browser to interact with a Web server application of another business.

2. **Type of relationship:** The relationship in B2C mainly involves placing orders and executing payments. In B2B, the relationship focuses on online procurement, order fulfillment, and work-in-process tracking for high-volume transactions.

3. **Nature of control:** The control mechanism in B2C is unidirectional. The seller controls the relationship with the consumer. In B2B, control ranges from one-sided control to peer-to-peer setups, depending on the nature of the relationship between the two businesses.

Table 11-1
Contrast between B2C and B2B

	B2C	B2B
Type of connection	**Consumer-to-system—** Consumers use their PC browser to order products via the merchant's Web site	**Business-to-business—** Representatives of a business use their company's Web browser to order products or to inquire via another business (e.g., supplier) Web site
Type of relationship	1. Placing orders 2. Executing payments 3. Fulfilling orders 4. Browsing of merchant's catalog 5. Sending feedback or e-mail messages	1. Online procurement 2. Tracking order status 3. Executing payments 4. Managing promotions, returns, catalog information 5. Fulfilling orders
Nature of control	Unidirectional—relationship defined by the merchant	Ranges from unidirectional to peer-to-peer (mutual agreement) among businesses
Level or nature of needs-based segmentation	**Moderate to low**	**More focused than B2C** (e.g., Boeing buys only aircraft parts, not garden tractor or automobile parts)
Sales complexity	**Moderate**	**Complex**

4. **Nature of needs-based segmentation:** Needs-based segmentation is more focused in B2B than in B2C, which tends to drive down costs and procurement. For example, GE has developed a Web-based TPN (Trading Process Network) that allows suppliers to bid on component contracts. This $1 billion per year business reduced procurement time by half and processing costs by at least one third.

5. **Sales complexity:** The level of sales complexity is higher in B2B than B2C. Many products are purchased as parts for other products, making the relationship more like a partnership. Bigger purchases mean bigger discounts, and prices are nearly always negotiable. Large businesses also use sophisticated computer systems to exchange invoices with suppliers, whose Web sites must be integrated to do business.

Advantages and Disadvantages of B2B

B2B e-commerce is a worldwide bazaar where one can buy anything, from paper clips to live elephants to oil tankers that are two football fields long. The goal is to save money on purchases that are negotiated instantly. Suppliers use the purchaser's Web site to respond to bids and sell excess inventory. Replacing a purchasing bureaucracy with online links means savings, improved efficiency in ordering material, many fewer errors, and a just-in-time environment that minimizes inventory sitting in the warehouse. As Box 11-2 mentions, GM and Ford entered B2B, and both companies realized all these benefits.

Electronic alliances with distributors, suppliers, resellers, and other partners generate information for businesses regarding customers, products, suppliers, transportation, inventory, competitors, supply-chain alliances, and marketing and sales. Businesses have access to customers' sales history; product sales history; terms and discounts; product offerings and availability; and promotions, sales, and marketing information. They also can get shipping costs and terms, shipping schedules, inventory locations, carrying charges, and response time for inventory replenishment. They can learn about roles and responsibilities in supply-chain alliances and available partners, along with competitors' products and market share.

There are also drawbacks. B2B e-commerce sites were exploding in number in early 2000. Hundreds were launched to support major buyers in the automotive, chemicals, pharmaceutical, retailing, and other industries, with the goal of getting supplies more cheaply and quickly. Yet, like any other new process, they have faced major obstacles. According to Downs (2000), despite the hype about B2B e-commerce, it has been slow to catch on. More than 600 Web exchanges introduced during 1999 and 2000 have yet to make money. In a 2002 report by Coltman et al. (2002), e-business does not fit every business (see Box 11-2).

BOX 11-2
E-business in retrospect

Despite the media attention, e-business among consumers is still in a formative stage. The few successful examples we have of B2C businesses—say, Amazon or eBay—are arguably in specialized categories of goods and attract a minority of customers.

There are several reasons why businesses are more willing than consumers to communicate, negotiate, buy, and sell online:

- Large companies are generally better equipped to communicate electronically. For example, Dell's online catalog-based competencies—quick response, low-cost fulfillment system characterized by direct customer interactions and made-to-order manufacturing—easily translated to the Web.
- Companies are more cost conscious. Every dollar saved in procurement is equal to a dollar of profit. For example, the opportunity to standardize procurement systems and capture cost savings has been the driving force behind joint exchanges involving Ford, General Motors, and others.
- As corporations develop online strategies aimed at reducing costs and increasing efficiency, network effects have a particularly strong impact. Organizations that have invested substantially in developing IT supply-chain infrastructures have a strong incentive to encourage others to do the same and thus make further efficiency gains from a more complete network.

A common belief was the low set-up costs associated with e-business technology would enable a one-person business to make its virtual storefront available to as many consumers as the big players—representing a major potential threat to established brands. This threat would be amplified by the consumer's use of intelligent agents and comparison software. However, the evidence indicates these predictions have yet to reflect reality.

The main impact of e-business is its ability to reduce the cost of exchanging and processing information, thereby reducing the overall costs of customization—either between a producer and a supplier, or a customer and a product/service provider. The potential is not that the bottle of Coke will be cheaper (although this might occur in some circumstances), but the cost of getting the right item to the right customer will be reduced.

SOURCE: Excerpted from Coltman, Tim, Devinney, Timothy M., Latukefu, Alopi S., and Midgley, David F., "Keeping E-Business in Perspective," *Communication of the ACM*, August 2002, 69–73.

BOX 11-3
B2B and antitrust

Experts say B2B exchanges will run into antitrust trouble if they do any of the following.

1. Form a cartel to fix prices or allocate markets.
2. Allow competitors to see one another's prices in an electronic catalog, bid, or auction.
3. Allow competitors to signal future price increases or discounts.
4. Unfairly restrict who can join the exchange or prevent members from participating in other exchanges.
5. Allow competitors to discuss their prices, outputs, costs, or strategic planning.

SOURCE: Betts, Mitch, "FTC Keeps an Eye on B-to-B Online Markets," *Computerworld,* July 10, 2000, 20.

One problem with B2B is possible antitrust violations resulting from doing this type of business. For example, owners of major e-markets may conceivably shut out smaller, competing exchanges. The electronic open-bid process itself might lead to questionable price signaling. Here is one scenario: Buyer A wants to buy 100,000 linear feet of lumber for a housing project. He posts a proposal at an online exchange. One supplier bids on the project, and competing suppliers see the bid and undercut it. This process continues until the nth supplier provides the lowest bid, which Buyer A accepts. Meanwhile, Buyer B and other suppliers watch the process and have a good idea of how the bidding takes place.

This part of the process was once done more discreetly using paper, phone, and face-to-face meetings. Price signaling may be smart business, but it is being questioned as a violation of antitrust laws (Nash 2000). During a 2-day workshop on exchanges, FTC officials and legal experts said the key to avoiding antitrust problems is to allow an open Web exchange and keep the prices and trade secrets of all suppliers in the B2B system confidential (see Box 11-3).

To date, no one has figured out a formula that will ensure success in B2B commerce. Most Web exchanges charge a small percentage of each transaction as a fee for doing business. To make money, billions of dollars in transactions must be handled each month, which is not easy. One reason is the competition. Also, companies as well as suppliers that dominate a specific niche are building their own exchanges tailored to their products and industry.

THE SUPPLY CHAIN

supply chain: the process of moving goods from the customer's order through raw materials, supply, production, and distribution of products to the end user.

In terms of the relationship between businesses, the B2B environment can best be explained using the supply-chain process. **Supply chain** represents all the events associated with the flow and transformation of goods from the raw material stage to the end-user customer. It is the process of moving goods from the customer's order through raw materials, parts supplier, production, wholesaler, and retailer to the end user. This process includes order generation, order taking, status feedback, and timely delivery of goods and services. Traditionally, many of these processes have been done with paper transactions such as purchase orders and invoices requiring verification and signatures. B2B is beginning to replace these time-consuming activities.

B2B supply-chain collaboration involves a group of manufacturers, retailers, and suppliers using the Internet to exchange business information and work jointly at forecasting

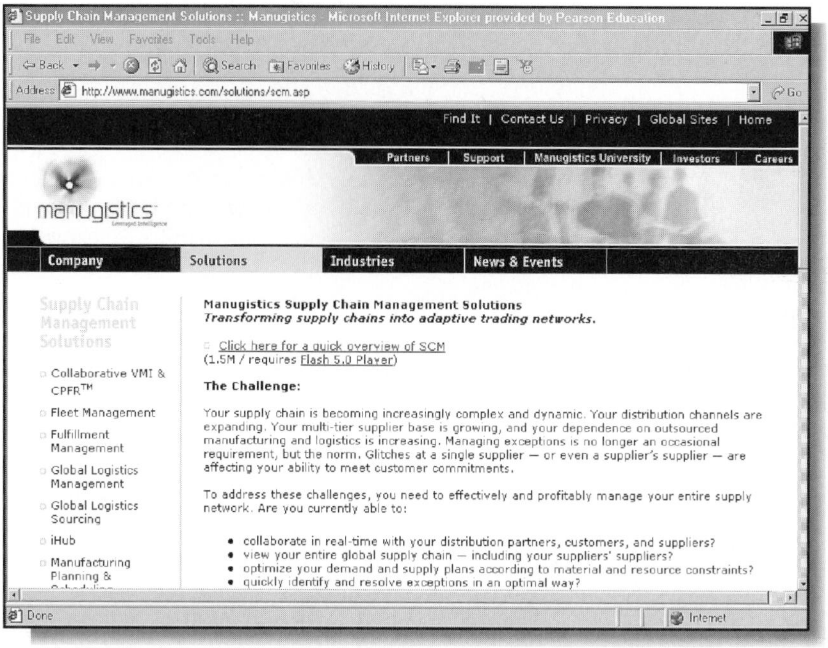

Screen Capture 11-3

Source: Used by permission of Manugistics.com. All rights reserved.

demand for their products, developing production schedules, and controlling inventory flow. There are many benefits: reduced inventory, higher sales, improved ability to customize products for different business buyers, and reduced production costs. The main challenge is establishing trust among partners to share sensitive business information and upgrading business applications that will advance collaboration. Partners also have to agree on a common standard for exchanging information and transactions. (Initial attempts to impose such standards were made possible through EDI, which is covered later in the chapter.)

Several elements make up the supply chain.

- **Production:** A decision is made on the products to create at a specific plant, the supplier(s) that will service the plants, and how goods will find their to the ultimate customer.
- **Inventory:** To keep the supply chain in operational order, each link in the chain must keep a certain inventory of raw material, parts, and partially manufactured products as a hedge against uncertainties. This way, in the event of a momentary delay in any of the links, the process continues uninterrupted.
- **Location:** It is critical that production facilities, warehousing points, and initiation points are known in advance. Once known and assured, the supply chain as a process begins to operate reliably around the clock.
- **Transportation:** This step simply determines how materials, parts, and products logistically get from one point in the supply chain to another. Deciding on how to ship often is a trade-off between shipping cost and timing of availability. High-priority parts that are sorely needed will likely be shipped by air rather than rail or truck (Kay 2001).

Knowledge management has become a critical element in the supply-chain system. KM is the process of capturing and making use of a firm's collective expertise anywhere in the business—on paper, in documents, in databases (called explicit knowledge), or in people's heads (called tacit knowledge). In the supply chain, knowledge management provides the ability to manage decision points and areas where human expertise is required. The new focus of a supply chain is *collaboration, coordination, and cooperation* of all parties involved so that organizational processes, technology, and experienced people assure the necessary integration for the good of the chain. The emphasis on collaboration involves all partners from the supplier to the retailer. Box 11-4 summarizes how knowledge management helps manage the process.

B2B Building Blocks

B2B e-commerce operates on a technology-based e-business platform. Functions that are typical to B2C, such as personalization and content management, are also relevant to B2B architecture. An e-business platform for B2B services consists of five key components: the application server infrastructure, the B2B integration server, the personalization software, the content management facility, and the e-commerce package.

1. **The Application Server:** The function of this component is to develop, manage, and execute B2B services and traffic for high-performance, nonstop service. The application server manages connections and applications, makes services available during upgrades, detects dead connections, monitors security, and ensures a fault-tolerant B2B environment

BOX 11-4
Knowledge management and the supply chain

The supply chain is a 24/7 operation, and there is a need for visibility across time zones and cultures. That requires extremely tight document management and work flow processes. One major trend is the use of knowledge management to manage exceptions in the supply-chain process.

"Every company has schedules and plans. The tough job is to figure out how unplanned changes affect schedule," says Lorne Jones, director of global product marketing for supply chain for SAP (http://sap.com). "If a drug company has a big purchase order come in from Wal-Mart, for example, how big an impact will that unexpected order from Wal-Mart have on the production of aspirin?" The ability to manage events and exceptions—which is really knowledge management—is key to supply-chain success.

Security issues are also having an impact on knowledge management in the supply chain. Jones says, "We are going to be required to identify what we're shipping in real time. Officials need to know who is shipping, who is receiving. This is going to be a fundamental part of commerce going forward."

Efficient document management practices can shave days off the process of clearing customs. For example, according to Harry Sangree, VP of product management for INTTRA (inttra.com), "It is all about making sure that the documents are accessible when the shipment makes it through various checkpoints. A truck picks up a shipment to take it to the pier or terminal, where it might wait for some paperwork. The idea is for the paperwork to arrive ahead of the package. Through our next release, we're adding the ability to manage the bill of lading, a process that can take 6 to 7 days to catch up with the shipment. Through electronic means, we can cut the wait time to half of that."

SOURCE: Excerpted from Zimmermann, Kim Ann, "Linking Partners in the Supply Chain—KM Helps Manage the Process," *Kmworld*, September 2002, 22–23.

around the clock. This means that users should have no difficulty accessing the system anytime (Smith 2000, p. 40).

2. **The B2B Integration Server:** Because so many systems and protocols must work together to support B2B e-commerce, the integration server joins company, external, and application data or documents for quick, reliable, secure service. For example, a purchase order is acknowledged as an incoming document. The integration server then directs the document handler to forward it to an order desk. Once the system processes the order, the document handler queries the inventory database before it schedules a shipping date.

3. **The Personalization Software:** The personalization feature in B2B is similar to that in B2C. It makes it possible for a company with multiple buyers (called partners) to display or provide only the content that is unique to the partner. The software takes into consideration factors like stored partner profile, purchasing behavior, and user privileges. The goal is to allow a tightly focused B2B interface and interaction with each partner.

4. **The Content Management Facility:** This special facility is the deliverable of B2B e-commerce. Comprehensive content management supports a work flow process that facilitates B2B content review and approval. The content manager's main responsibility is to ensure that the content reaches the designated user or online system. It also taps the personalization software to serve the content to the appropriate user, whether another server or an online system.

5. **The E-Commerce Package:** This set of programs plays a role similar to that of the one it plays in B2C. It includes customer service and product management, a storefront for direct delivery, a shopping cart, and order-fulfillment modules (Smith 2000, p. 40).

To do its job, the e-business platform must run on open standards. This means that when companies integrate with buyers and suppliers, the B2B architecture must run on any hardware or any operating system. Security is also a serious issue. The security protocol might need to cover an entire application, parts of an application, or even specific components of an application.

Quality of service is an important consideration. As in traditional business, highly valued and long-term business partners get special treatment. Once they log in and are verified, the B2B system diverts them to a premium-level server, but other partners are routed to the regular server. Quality of service also might improve when partners increase their business.

Finally, for e-business to achieve maximum efficiency, its infrastructure must meet several criteria.

- The technology must accommodate evolving needs. This implies flexibility and adaptability.
- Performance must be ensured in terms of rich and superior user experience.
- The infrastructure must be reliable and available 24 hours a day, year round. The cost of downtime can be staggering in terms of lost business.
- The infrastructure must have *scalability,* which is a term that means "the capability of the current system to upgrade to standards to meet the growing needs of the e-business."
- Because e-business means global business, it must be technically capable of reaching as many as 550 million Web surfers over more than 12,000 ISP networks covering hundreds of countries each hour of the year.
- The system must be easy to use and consistent. Sometimes this is achieved by leveraging the capabilities of a reliable third-party vendor to pick up the slack.
- The system must be secure and protected from cyber-fraud, denial-of-service attacks, viruses, and the like.

To keep track of supply-chain operations, special tools are available. Referred to as Supply Chain Event Management (SCEM), such software lets users analyze, monitor, and control functions in the supply chain. As illustrated in Figure 11-2, a retailer sends an order to a supplier for 500 cans of driveway sealer. When the order is processed, the supply warehouse finds out it is short 150 cans. The shortage is fed back to the supply-chain server attached to a SCEM system. SCEM automatically orders the 350 cans from an alternative supplier, who ships the cans directly to the retailer's warehouse. In this case, SCEM acts as a watchdog.

B2B Integration Challenges

B2B integration means coordinating information among partners and their information system infrastructures. B2B integration has been subject to many interpretations. Some technology people view it as mere electronic data interchange (EDI). Others see it as an application integration extended outside a business organization. A third view sees it as putting a Web front end on applications so that suppliers, customers, and business buyers can share information for making deals. Each interpretation makes sense but misses the fundamental meaning of B2B integration (see Olsen 2000).

B2B integration means spanning independent businesses, each with its own set of applications and users. Some applications are Enterprise Resource Planning (ERP) packages;

Figure 11-2
Supply chain event management

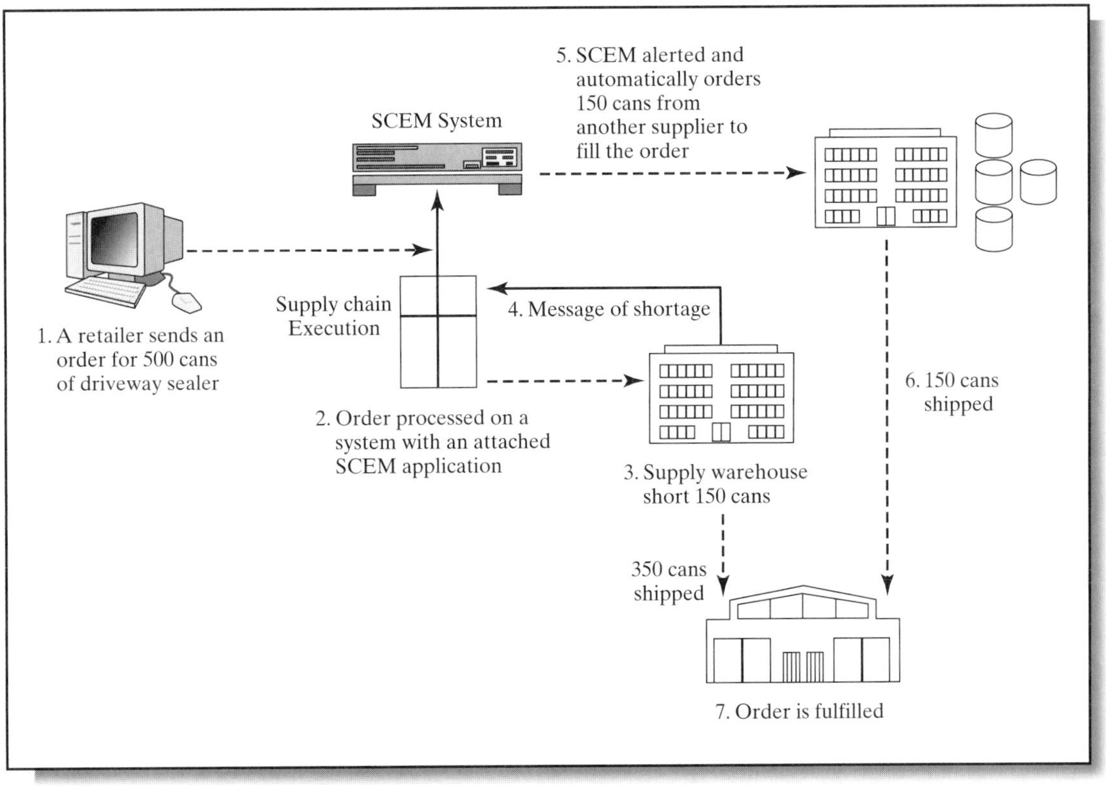

Source: Adapted from Songini, Marc L., "Policing the Supply Chain," *Computerworld,* April 30, 2001, 55.

others are traditional systems running on a mainframe. In each firm, transactions are processed differently. Orders, production scheduling, and other internal processing also are handled differently. B2B integration means being able to interact with these heterogeneous systems without being tied to one specific system technology (see Box 11-5).

Several solutions are available to the problem of B2B integration. One obvious one is to use a Web site as a front end for information sharing among partners. One partner uses its Web browser to interact with the Web server of another partner, and so on. Another solution is to extract information from one partner's application and convert it into a format amenable for transmission via EDI, File Transfer Protocol (FTP), e-mail, or HTTP. A third approach is for two companies to use common technology to coordinate data exchange between their respective applications.

The criteria used for B2B integration depends on how close a relationship an organization wants to establish with another, how much agreement is required between them, and how complex the integration must be and whether it threatens their autonomy.

Standardization has been an ongoing issue. One problem with standards such as TCP/IP, HTTP, and EDI is that they take time and effort to develop. Business conditions among partners also change, and many businesses find it necessary and attractive to form an agreement before standards are available. In most cases, the cost of developing standards is justified when there is high-volume demand or use. Standards are ideal for products and interactions that are stable over a long period of time, but finding candidates is neither easy nor predictable.

Eventually, for any B2B agreement, the key question is whether a B2B agreement specifies an exchange protocol. Are agreements industrywide, national, or international? Are they

BOX 11-5
Integrate to collaborate

An integration solution that enables effective processes and further enables seamless information flow to support those processes is a critical requirement for an effective e-business infrastructure. To foster collaboration, business processes must be fast, responsive, proactive, change rapidly, and provide instant visibility for confident decision-making.

Manufacturers are best served by an integration framework designed specifically for manufacturers—one that incorporates key business processes unique to manufacturing and provides all systems a continuous view to the plant floor via automated data collection. The system should support application-to-application processes plus human intervention. It should provide intelligent notification, alerts, and alarms based on user-defined workflow and specified business processes as the foundation of application integration. The system should enable companies to visualize their business processes, spotting bottlenecks and eliminating redundant steps. Streamlining business processes results in reductions of both cycle times and costs.

You cannot fully realize the promises of true collaboration throughout the value chain without basing your integration on the foundation of a noninvasive, complementary, component-based architecture. In manufacturing, it is critical that the integration starts from the plant floor, where the collection and dissemination of accurate, timely strategic data begins its journey—serving decision-makers across the enterprise and throughout the supplier network and setting the foundation for a solid e-business information infrastructure.

SOURCE: Business-to-Business in Manufacturing. Excerpted from Hamlin, Ken, "Integrate to Collaborate: The e-Business Infrastructure for Manufacturing." *eAI Journal,* December 2002, 32–34.

agreed upon in advance or on an ad hoc basis? All these issues, including managing e-business alliances, have to be resolved before B2B integration can be considered stable and lasting.

Embedded in any agreement among partners is the availability of a way to manage partners in a supply chain. Called Partner Relationship Management (PRM), this system is a new phase in B2B integration. It focuses on how partners engage each other on a regular basis. For example, we could have collaborative processes such as product design that are under serious consideration. Without PRM, no organization can expect to have an effective value chain.

The Trust Factor

Regardless of the design, arrangements, and manageability of a supply chain, the core of collaborative relationships over time is trust. A key trust question is whether the vendors connected with your organization are trusted allies or corporate spies. Much can be known about a vendor relationship by the level and quality of experience over time. One view is that vendors are in the business to make money. They will do whatever they can that is ethically acceptable to help them achieve their goals. If they are on the premises and hang around and talk to people, they will likely know more than they should know. This means that the more inside information a vendor gathers, the more the vendor can use that information to advantage, especially during negotiations.

Every vendor wants to know three things: company budget, the area where critical operations have the highest priority, and who in the organization makes the final decisions? Any of these factors could circumvent the procurement process. See Box 11-6 for the pros and cons of a trusting relationship. Ethical or not, vendors should be handled with care. The happy medium is to share with vendors only whatever is relevant to business. Employees should be selective in terms of what they may or may not share with a vendor. A security protocol also should be established on every project. As someone remarked, "You don't get people in a plane and do security checks at 30,000 feet. You do it before you take off" (Melymuka 2002).

With B2B relationships on the Internet, trust takes on a unique meaning.

For example, how do you know you're dealing with a legitimate and trustworthy business? Also, how do you know electronic exchange is secure and that your trading partner on the other end is who he says he is? Concerns of trust have kept many organizations away from B2B trade. B2B buyers worry that they won't receive the right merchandise, the right quality, and at the right price from a certified vendor in the right quantity and time. The same feeling goes for the seller. Sellers often worry about getting paid on time and extending credit to questionable buyers (Violino 2002).

What If the Chain Snaps?

With so many suppliers, vendors, retailers, financial institutions, and intermediaries making up the supply chain, what happens when one of the links snaps or is temporarily inactive? For example, UPS Logistics Group was caught unprepared and braced for a supply-chain disaster following the September 11, 2001, terrorist attacks. It found itself without a key distribution center that kept critical repair parts flowing to customers (Hicks 2002). That center was destroyed only 150 yards away from the World Trade Center. An alternative UPS LG service parts hub in Manhattan was written off because of safety concerns after the terrorist attacks. A third alternative hub could not be reached, because the roads were closed. This is an example of a situation in which a company is truly in a crisis mode.

BOX 11-6
Pros and cons of trust in supply chain

PROS

A Trusting Relationship Brings Results

"I treat my Siemens manager the way I treat my Genzyme manager," says Mimi Moran, director of IT client services at Genzyme. "I don't make the distinction that he works for someone else; he works for me."

The 30 Siemens workers in her 51-person client services group go through Genzyme's orientation. They have the same unfettered physical and virtual access as most Genzyme employees so they can repair and deliver equipment to desktops throughout the company. They eat at the cafeteria and attend IT-sponsored events.

Recently, the CIO decided to give IT personnel a denim shirt with a newly developed IT logo. "We were going to put a little 'Genzyme' on some and 'Siemens' on the others, but the CIO said, 'No, everybody is IT,'" Moran recalls. "We will trust them to perform just like everybody in the organization," she says. "We don't hold things back."

It seems to be working. When the group started the engagement 3 years ago, it had a customer satisfaction rating of 3.8 on a scale of 8. Today, it's more than 4.4 "I know it's business, but they do an awful lot for us, because we have a good relationship," Moran says. "If we didn't, would they go that extra mile?"

CONS

The Vendor That Knew Too Much

Once, while working on a project for a client, Phil Bode's International Computer Negotiations IT team was doing preliminary planning for a wide area network. "We were trying to figure out how to do it," he recalls. "There were charts up on the wall."

An employee of the company's long-distance carrier who had access to the facility came in and saw the charts. "He knew the time line, and he got a pretty good idea of the budget from talking to people," Bode says. With this information, the vendor put together a proposal, and the sales rep approached the CIO, a golfing buddy. He talked the CIO into awarding his company the contract rather than following the request-for-proposals (RFP) process.

Inside information and a too-friendly relationship with the CIO enabled the vendor to circumvent and control the customer's procurement process, and things went downhill from there. Because there was no RFP, the project requirements were never nailed down properly. Because multiple bidders weren't heard from, no new ideas or approaches were considered, and there was no competition over price. "It was over time and over budget, and we wound up spending more in service charges each month than we thought we would," Bode recalls. "It was one of the worst projects I ever saw."

SOURCE: Excerpted from Melymuka, Kathleen, "Know Your Partner," *Computerworld*, November 11, 2002, 45–46.

One of the aftereffects of the September 11, 2001, terrorist attacks has been a growing awareness of the need for disaster planning so that the chain can keep operating. Without such a plan, the mere announcement of a disruption in production or shipment could be costly. According to a Georgia Institute of Technology study, after such an announcement, the company's stock price can fall an average of 8.62 percent on the day of the announcement and can drop as much as 20 percent within 6 months (Hicks 2002).

disaster planning: taking specific steps to ensure the flow of products and services during a disaster.

Disaster planning means taking specific steps to ensure the flow of products and services during a disaster. The first step is to work with the highest-risk customers and collaborate on a contingency plan to suit their needs in the event of a disaster. Pricing should be stable during such a disruption, and alternative inventory sources should be identified and guaranteed without any costs of delivery. Finally, it is important to empower employees on supply-chain disruptions and how to communicate effectively to minimize unnecessary delays.

B2B Models

Several models have been established for B2B e-commerce based on who controls the marketplace: buyer, supplier, or intermediary. Each model is explained in the following sections.

Buyer-Oriented B2B

buyer-oriented B2B: a buyer purchases thousands of products and uses the Internet to open a marketplace and a Web site for suppliers to do the bidding.

In the **buyer-oriented B2B** model, a buyer like General Motors that normally purchases hundreds of thousands of products each month uses the Internet by opening a marketplace on its own server and opening the window for suppliers to do the bidding. As shown in Figure 11-3, the buyer loads products via a catalog or a directory, with specific requests regarding make, model, size, price, and so on. Outside suppliers access the catalog, decide what product they want to bid on, send the information to the buyer, and hope to be the lowest bidder.

supplier-oriented B2B: a supplier invites individual consumers and business customers to order products via its electronic market store.

Supplier-Oriented B2B

The **supplier-oriented B2B** model is close in design to the B2C model. A manufacturer or a supplier invites individual consumers as well as business customers to order products via its electronic store (see Figure 11-4).

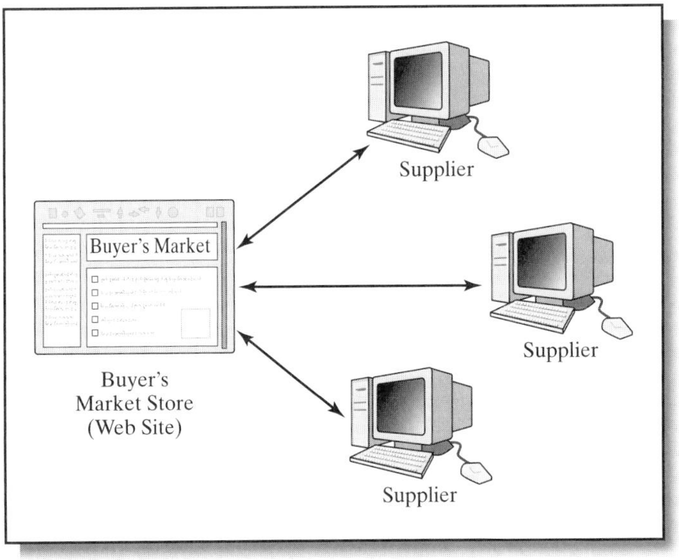

Figure 11-3 Buyer-oriented B2B model

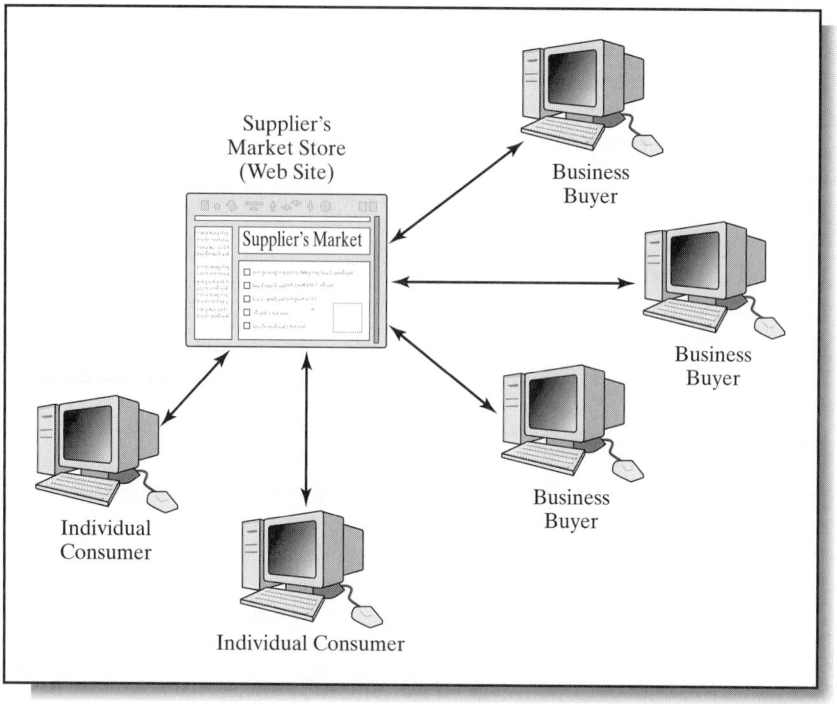

Figure 11-4
Supplier-oriented B2B model

Well-known examples of supplier-oriented B2Bs are Dell and Cisco. Dell's sales to business buyers represent 90 percent of its computer sales. Likewise, in 1999 Cisco sold more than $11 billion worth of routers, switches, and other networking devices to businesses via the company's Web site.

Electronic Auctions

One of the Internet's unique features is bringing together people with narrow interests who are geographically dispersed. Web auctions can cater to such groups by providing an auction site.

In an auction, a seller offers a product or an item for sale. This is called "putting an item up for bid" because the seller does not put a price on the item. Interested buyers get information about the item and offer bids—prices they are willing to pay. An auctioneer, who handles the whole process, keeps the auction going until the bids are closed.

electronic auction: auctions carried out on electronic Web sites such as eBay.

A unique version of supplier-oriented architecture is the **electronic auction.** The Internet is booming with all kinds of auctions from e-Bay to hundreds of smaller imitators with questionable reputations. There have been reports of fraud, where purchasers got less than they bargained for from auction sites. In some cases, the product was misrepresented, and in others the product was never delivered (see Box 11-7).

Electronic auctions can be of three basic types: forward auctions, reverse auctions, and Internet exchanges. Each has unique features and promises.

BOX 11-7
Questionable integrity of auction sites

Joan Spingelt, an elementary school teacher, got less than she bargained for in her first purchase from auction site eBay. She bought a Palm Pilot V Personal Digital Assistant from Tec Computers to organize her addresses and schedules. The company never sent her the unit. Instead, she says she received excuses—and soon no replies at all to her e-mails.

The Federal Trade Commission filed charges related to auction fraud against the company. In all, some $90,000 in goods ordered from the company were never delivered. Ms. Spingelt will likely receive only about $40 from the settlement, her first return on that $361 money order she mailed 3 years ago.

Law-enforcement agencies have the power to elicit information from money-wire services and credit card companies—something the defrauded consumer cannot do alone. Still, most law-enforcement agencies don't yet have experienced Internet investigators, and many don't investigate frauds if only a small amount is lost. Florida's Department of Law Enforcement will only probe cases of fraud involving $50,000 or more, although the agency's Computer Crime Center recently lowered the floor to $10,000 in cases of suspected Internet fraud.

And if scammers are tracked down, victims often won't receive full restitution. Suing probably won't help much, either. The best thing to do is probably to hire a professional. Experts emphasize that you should not take the law into your own hands with any information you might dig up. Give it to the professionals investigating your case.

SOURCE: Excerpted from Bialik, Carl, "Getting Your Money Back," *The Wall Street Journal*, September 16, 2002, R7.

Forward Auctions

forward auction: an auction where a seller entertains bids from buyers; an auction used to liquidate merchandise.

A **forward auction** generally is used to liquidate merchandise. One seller entertains bids from many buyers. This seller-controlled model allows the seller to post products or services it wants to sell via its auction Web site. Buyers view the offer and submit competing bids. Sometimes, buyers can see other buyers' bids and respond to them. Sometimes the auction is *blind*, and bids are sealed from competing buyers. After the expiration date, the seller reviews the bids and selects the highest one. Payment and fulfillment are handled through normal electronic channels (see Figure 11-5).

Forward auctions are used most often for surplus merchandise, last year's models, and so on. They are ideal in situations where supply and demand are unpredictable and a time factor is pushing the seller to unload the merchandise. Sellers have more control than in traditional liquidation sales.

Reverse Auctions

reverse auction: an auction used to solicit bids; the lowest bidder wins.

A **reverse auction** generally is used to solicit bids, and the lowest bidder wins. It is buyer controlled: Buyers post the goods they want to buy, and sellers compete to provide them. The buyer pits suppliers against one another in a bidding war. The buyer reviews the bids and considers factors such as the location of the seller, cost of delivery, and whether the seller can deliver on time. When the auction expires, the lowest bidder is selected. The buyer produces the money, and the seller ships the goods (see Figure 11-6).

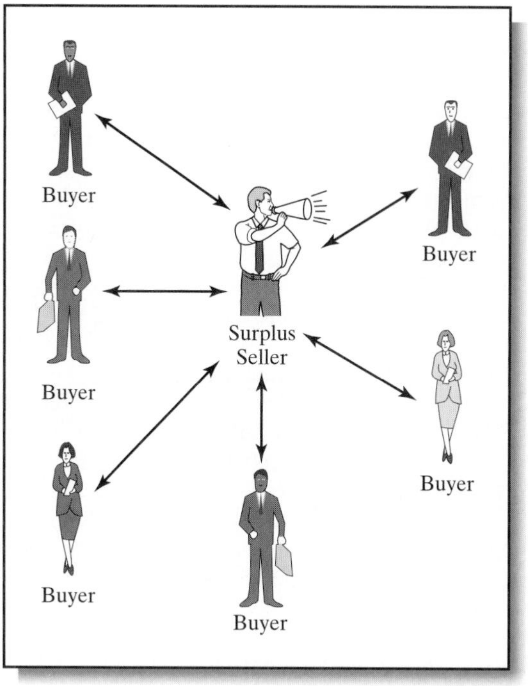

Figure 11-5
Forward auction model

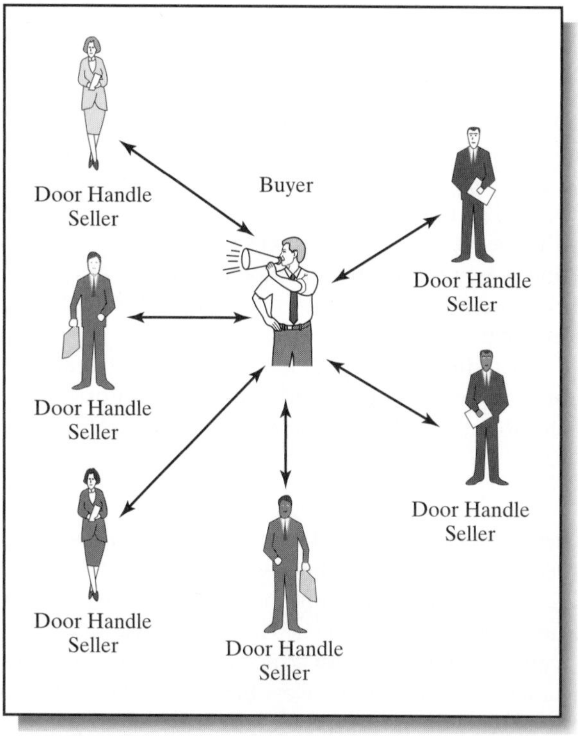

Figure 11-6
Reverse auction model

Reverse auctions are typical of large corporate purchases, for example, GM buying rearview mirrors or John Deere buying mower blades. This model tends to drive down prices and expand the buyer's zone of choice among suppliers.

Internet Exchange Auctions

Internet exchange auction: an electronic auction involving many buyers and sellers who trade bids and offers until an agreement is reached to exchange product for payment. A third party often operates the exchange.

An **Internet exchange auction** involves many buyers and sellers who trade bids and offers until an agreement is reached to exchange product for payment. A third party operates the exchange. All kinds of companies, trading products from airplanes to livestock, are included. A company first places a bid to buy or sell a product. Buyers and sellers work interactively with the bids and offers. When a deal is made, it is a match between a buyer and a seller on variables such as price, volume, and delivery costs. Third parties often help in the exchange process. They have the responsibility for credit verification, quality assurance, and prompt delivery of the goods (see Figure 11-7).

One issue involved in this model is exchange ownership. There are three kinds of ownership. One manufacturer or broker can set up the exchange and run it; a third-party intermediary can set it up and promise to run it fairly; or several industry leaders can put it together so no one dominates and all can benefit. Visionaries have been touting the concept of linked exchanges that form a "true network economy" (Dalton, March 13, 2000, p. 95). One concept is to combine competing exchanges into one, similar to the exchanges operated by General Motors and Ford. Another concept is wiring different exchanges so that the B2B part includes many similar markets connected by bridges. Either way, many

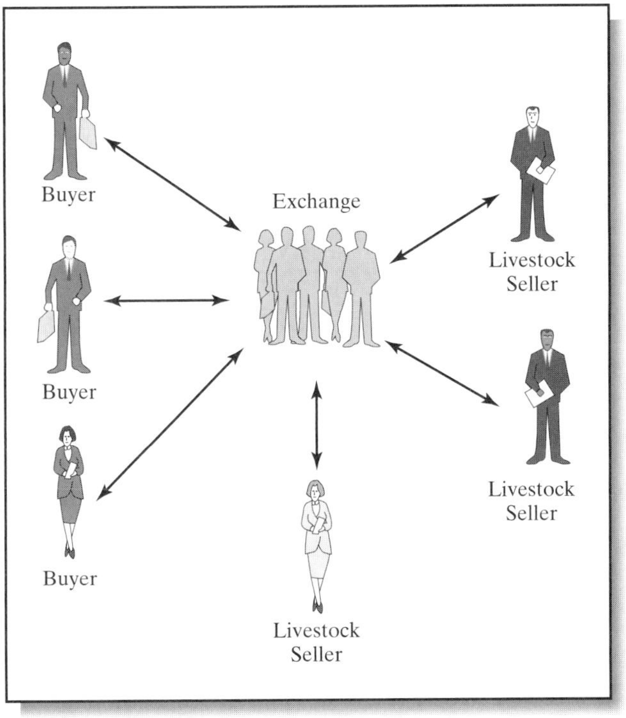

Figure 11-7 Internet exchange model

more connections will exist than we have today, which eventually will contribute to the reshaping of today's economy.

Intermediary-Oriented B2B

intermediary-oriented B2B: an intermediary company establishes an exchange market where buyers and sellers can make deals.

The **intermediary-oriented B2B** setup revolves around an electronic intermediary company that establishes an exchange market where buyers and sellers can make deals (see Figure 11-8). Typical of this type of exchange are intermediary malls like www.Grainger.com and http://Procure.net, a large industrial distributor that handles maintenance, repair, and operations (MRO) purchases. This Web site has an electronic catalog containing more than 100,000 products and 30 seller sites, and it averages more than 60,000 hits per day.

MRO is where most B2B product sales take place. Every industry has its own MRO needs. Quantities purchased range from 1 to 1 million units. The more a business buyer buys, the more savings it realizes on purchases. Companies that succeed in an MRO business specialize in a specific industry to minimize potential competitors and offer customers information vital to their business growth and success.

informediary: a firm that facilitates the transformation of the traditional industrial economy to a new, information-based economy.

With the likely surge of B2B and B2C through the decade, a major segment of the revenue is likely to be claimed by a new breed of company, referred to as the information intermediary. Informediaries facilitate the transformation of the traditional industrial economy to a new information-based economy. According to Grover et al. (2002), **informediaries** are companies whose main job is to match the needs of a large consumer base and a large supplier base, requiring analysis of an enormous amount of information (see Figure 11-9).

Figure 11-8
Intermediary-oriented B2B

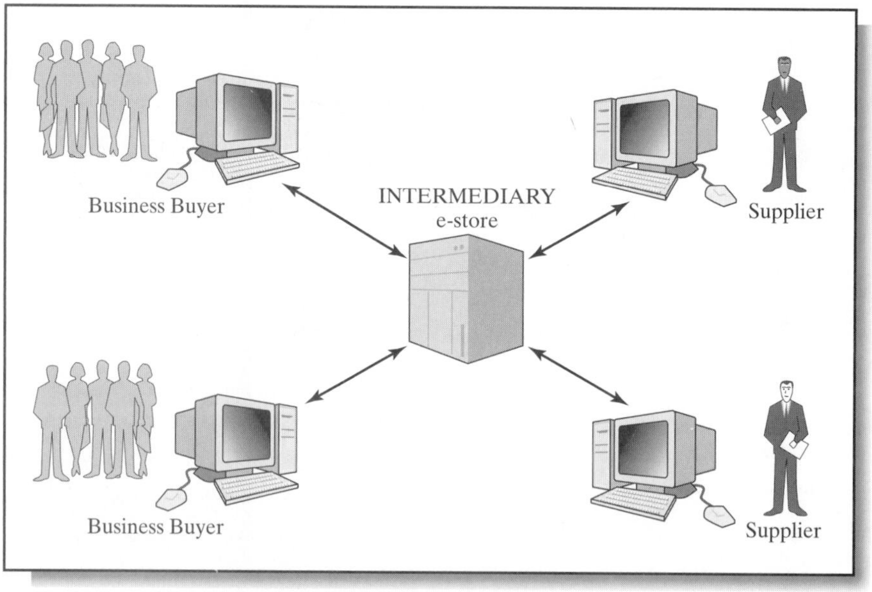

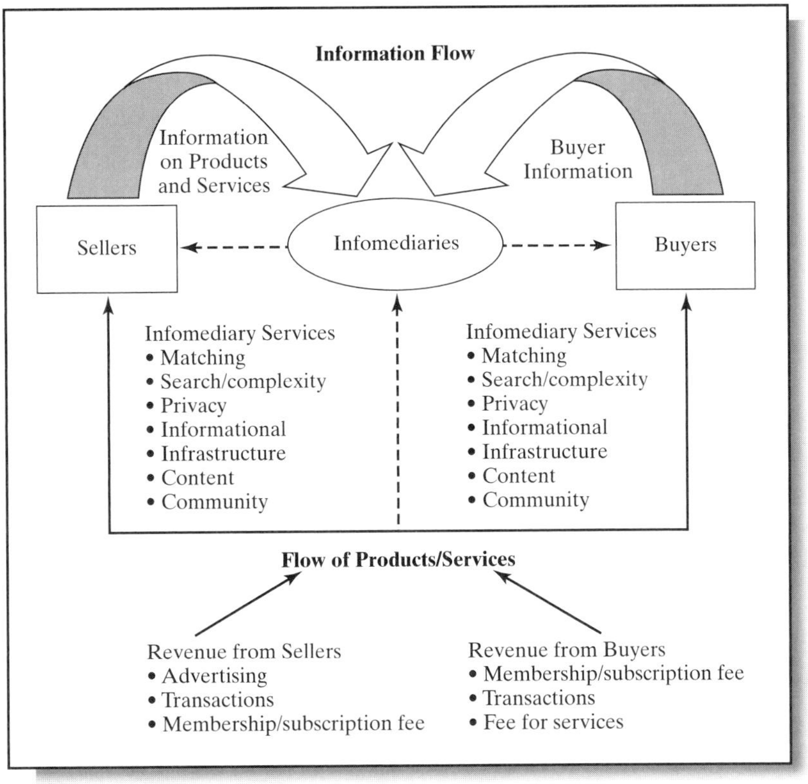

Figure 11-9
Informediary model

Source: Adapted from Grover, Varun, and Teng, James, "E-Commerce and the Information Market," *Communications of the ACM,* April 2001, 81.

B2B Tools—EDI

Most B2B traffic is handled by a communication tool called Electronic Data Interchange (EDI). EDI allows one computer system to communicate with another computer system using a standardized electronic form. It is a computer-to-computer transfer of business information among businesses that use a specific standard format. The information exchanged could be transaction data, requests for quotes (RFQ), order acknowledgments, shipping status or schedule, and so on. This type of data represents more than 75 percent of the total EDI traffic between businesses.

EDI has four components.

1. **Interbusiness:** Transmission of data between businesses. Because there is little standardization, most companies using EDI use a third-party service provider or value-added network (VAN) as a communications intermediary. Such a provider handles the various communications protocols, line speeds, and performance on a regular basis.
2. **Computer-to-computer:** Data communication from one computer to another. This means providing online links between a buyer's and a seller's business applications, with no human

intervention at the receiving end. Delivery to the receiver is by electronic transactions. The receiver simply passes the transaction to the receiving computer application for processing.

3. **Standard transactions:** Electronic versions of standard business forms. In EDI, a computer program, not a human being, processes all data. EDI is designed to allow the receiver to handle a standard business transaction (e.g., bill a customer) in machine-readable (not human-readable) form between trading partners' computers.

4. **Standard format:** Transactions must be transmitted in a predefined form.

How EDI Works

Prior to EDI, purchase orders, acknowledgments, invoices, and purchase order changes depended on communication between trading partners for limited hours each day, using phone or fax. Today, computers enhance communication between trading partners, regardless of time, place, or distance. Figure 11-10 shows the general configuration of information flow without EDI. A request for a product is sent to purchasing for action. The purchasing department places a purchase order, which is sent to the seller via regular mail or by fax. A copy of the purchase order is sent to the finance department for payment upon receipt of the product. On the seller's part, the purchase order goes to the sales department, which fills the order through manufacturing or the warehouse. The product then is sent to shipping, which delivers it to the buyer's receiving department. Once received, it goes to the warehouse. This triggers payment of the invoice by the finance department.

As you can see, the process is labor intensive, and promotes delays and waste throughout the entire purchase cycle. The alternative is EDI (see Figure 11-11). With EDI, a buyer makes a decision to order a product. The buyer's EDI computer generates the purchase

Screen Capture 11-4

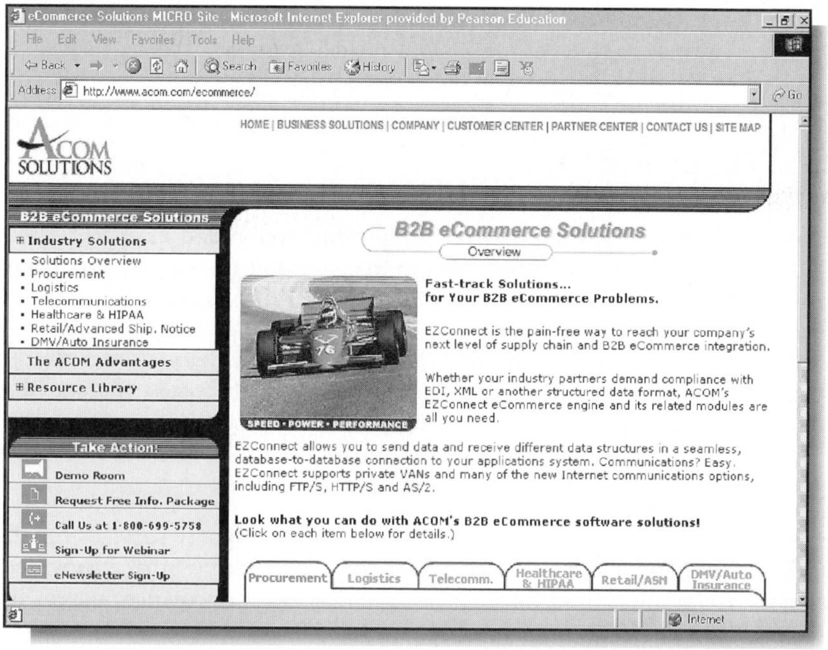

Source: ©2003 ACOM Solutions.

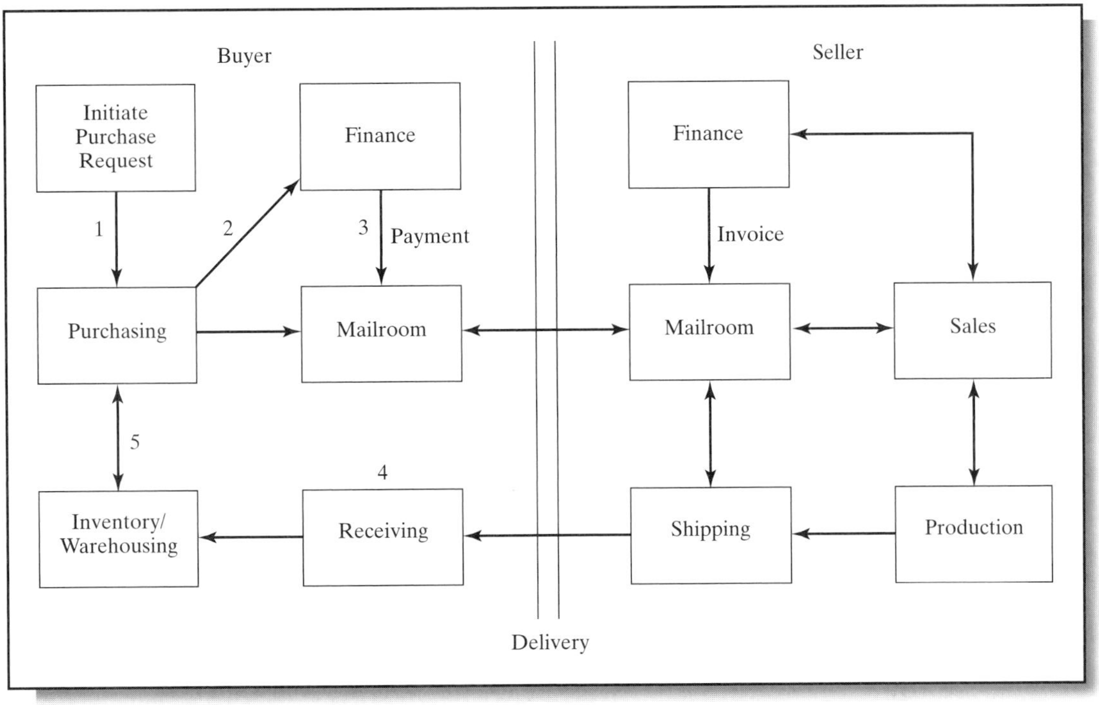

Figure 11-10
Traditional information flow between buyer and seller

order transaction in its purchasing application (the same step it took in the traditional method; see Figure 11-10). The purchase order transaction is transmitted directly to the seller's EDI system in machine-readable EDI standard generated by the buyer's EDI system.

The seller's EDI system sends an acknowledgment notice to the buyer's EDI system after it passes the order information to the receiving order entry application for processing. The processing is handled like any incoming purchase order. The seller's EDI system communicates with the company's network to activate shipping and billing. It also generates shipping confirmation to the seller and a copy to the buyer. The buyer's EDI system sends an electronic payment to the seller's computer.

EDI is a fast and efficient way of handling business transactions such as purchase orders, shipping notices, invoices, and other documents. All communications occur through the interactive EDI servers of the buyer and the seller. EDI contributes to competitive advantage in the way it expedites transactions, information flow, and payments. It speeds up the business exchange between buyer and seller as well as between seller and seller. The latter benefit is unique to B2B e-commerce. Well-known retailers like Wal-Mart, Proctor and Gamble, and Levi Strauss could not have been successful without the quick response, fast product delivery, speed, data integrity, and standardization that EDI offers.

EDI and Standards

EDI has been around since the early 1970s. After a decade of attempts, a number of industry groups got together to develop cross-industry standards for widely used mechanical and electronic items. In the United States, the most popular standard is the American

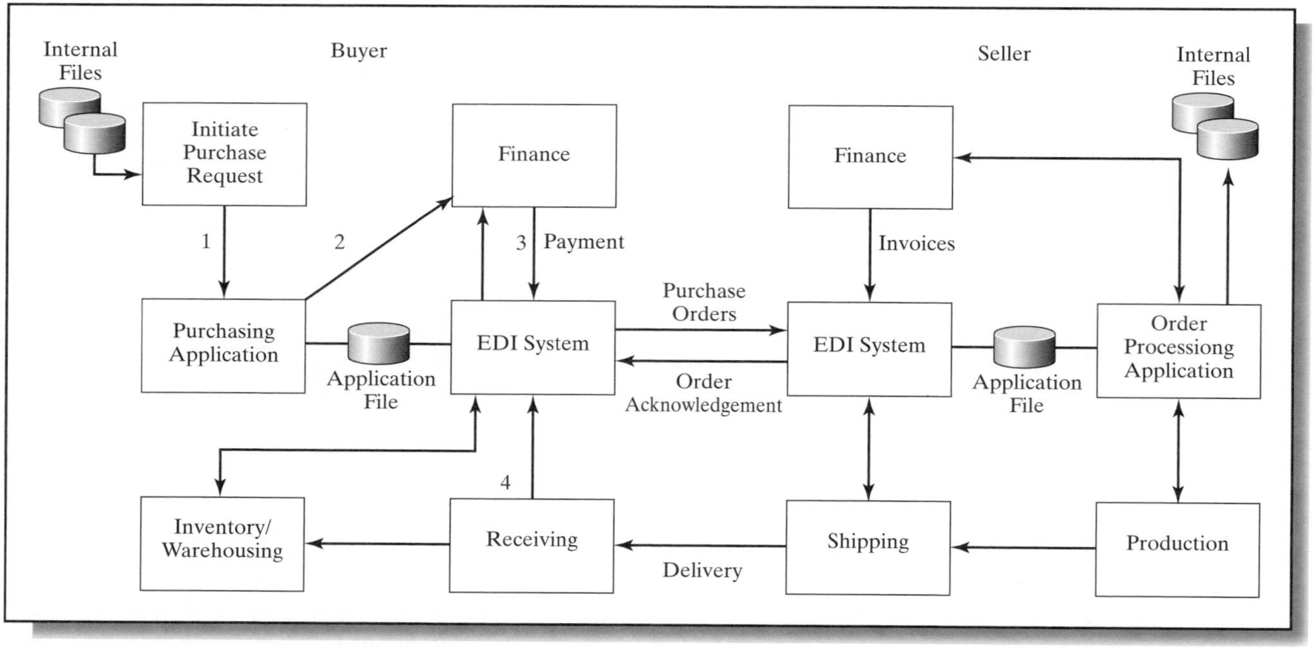

Figure 11-11
Information flow between buyer and seller with EDI

National Standards Institute (ANSI X.12). Most *Fortune* 500 companies use dedicated telephone lines or a VAN run by companies like AT&T or IBM to carry EDI data exchanges. In 1989, the United Nations published its first standards under EDI for Administration, Commerce, and Transport (EDIFACT, or UN/EDIFACT). See Table 11-2.

EDIFACT is destined to gain strong support from the United States, Western and Eastern Europe, and Pacific Rim businesses because it was developed prior to the businesses in different areas developing their own systems to the point where they could not change them. EDIFACT got a tremendous boost in 1988, when the U.S. Customs Service said it would support the EDIFACT standard. Australia and the United Kingdom then followed suit.

Advantages and Drawbacks

EDI has three tangible benefits.

1. **Cost reduction and time savings:** By eliminating unnecessary paperwork, information flow becomes more efficient. The seller's EDI computer sending acknowledgments and electronic billing eliminates the paper invoice, for example.
2. **Improved B2B problem resolution:** EDI responds quickly to business inquiries and transfers of documents with an automatic audit trail to ensure accuracy and consistency. This improves trading partner relationships. In most cases, partners cooperate on how to set up EDI and its various applications. The result is improvement in information sharing and cooperation between trading partners.
3. **Accuracy with integrity:** Eliminating data entry means improved accuracy in the way data are processed. This contributes to the integrity and reliability of the business process. The receipt of more accurate and complete business transactions through EDI improves information processing in the affected application. For example, the receipt of an EDI purchase order invariably improves the accuracy of the order entry application of the seller.

Table 11-2
Sample UN/EDIFACT transaction sets

AUTHOR: Authorization	IFTMAN: Arrival Notice
BOPCUS: Balance of Payment Customer	INVOIC: Invoice
BOBDIR: Balance of Payment Declaration	INVRPT: Inventory Report
COARRI: Container Discharge/Loading Report	ORDCHG: Purchase Order Change Request
CONITT: Invitation to Tender	ORDERS: Purchase Order
CONPVA: Payment Valuation	ORDRSP: Purchase Response
CREADV: Credit Advice	PAXLST: Passenger List
CUSDEC: Customer Declaration	PAYORD: Payment Order
CUSRES: Customer Response	QALITY: Quality Data
DEBADV: Debit Advice	QUOTES: Quote
DELFOR: Delivery Schedule	REQOTE: Request for Quote
IFTDGN: Dangerous Goods Notification	STATAC: Statement of Account

Despite the benefits, EDI has definite drawbacks.

1. EDI has yet to catch on as the perfect solution to information flow or for doing business. With millions of businesses in the United States, fewer than 200,000 have adopted EDI. EDI is expensive and requires a heavy investment to launch and maintain the technology.
2. EDI is point to point. Every contact requires special hardware and software.
3. EDI requires expensive VAN networking to operate at peak efficiency. Only high-volume, large trading partners can afford this investment.
4. As a system, EDI is not easy to use, learn, or implement.

Justifying EDI

Given the pros and cons of EDI, the next question is: Under what conditions could a business justify EDI? We know that EDI is a candidate if the business situation is paper intensive, people intensive, and requires fast information processing or delivery of goods. In terms of business documents and forms of messages such as telephone and fax, realistic criteria justify EDI implementation.

1. **Volume of data:** Companies that handle a large of volume of data on a regular basis find EDI a welcome relief. Also, if the nature of the information stored (such as a catalog) is large but requires frequent access, the business is a candidate for EDI. EDI will eliminate the manual handling of the catalog, along with the error rate in updating it.

2. **Frequency of document transmission and reception:** Because of the heavy installation and maintenance expense of EDI, most companies have found that EDI is justified when documents are sent and received frequently.

3. **Content sensitivity:** Another criterion is the sensitivity or critical nature of the information contained in the document. Documents involving international contracts or orders make the content highly sensitive for accuracy and integrity.

4. **Time sensitivity:** This criterion addresses the time and speed factors. EDI can ensure quick delivery, provided the firm's internal information processing procedures are also quick and accurate.

Rating the business based on these criteria should give a clear indication of whether it can justify the EDI investment. In doing the rating, it is important to evaluate the overall results rather than each criterion alone. For example, inventory queries are short in content (mostly product number, quantity, and a descriptor) but might be high in frequency. The important point is to think of the long term and use realistic criteria along with heuristics (the experience of the business) to make the final commitment to go with EDI.

One alternative is to opt for Web-based EDI. As an open communication channel and publicly accessible network, the Internet can bring online B2B trading to virtually every organization. It can cut communication costs in half, and complement or replace existing EDI applications. Web browsers and search engines are also user friendly and require little training (see Figure 11-12).

Financial EDI

This specialized area of EDI centers around the electronic transmission of payments between a payee and a payer via their respective banks. Financial EDI is part of B2B because it allows businesses to replace the labor-intensive activities of collecting, disbursing, and processing payments with an electronic system. It also improves the certainty of

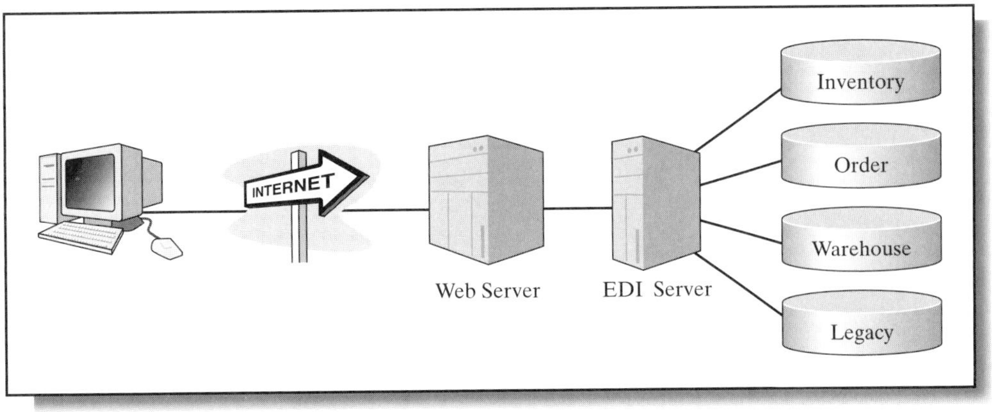

Figure 11-12
Web-based EDI

payment flows between trading partners' bank accounts. By prior protocol, a payee's bank can electronically credit the payee's account, and the payer's bank can debit the payer's account on the scheduled day of payment.

Three main types of noncash payment procedures are presently in use for B2B payments: bank checks, Electronic Funds Transfer (EFT), and Automated Clearinghouse (ACH). Checks are used worldwide; they are instruments of payment by which payees collect funds from payers. The life cycle of check processing is an established routine. If payee and payer have an account with the same bank, the bank's check processing system simply debits the payer's account and credits the payee's account by the same amount. This is done instantly via a teller, and the process is called *on us* check processing. If payee and payer have accounts in separate banks, the procedure is more complicated.

The payer mails a check to the payee, drawn on Bank A. The payee deposits the check in his or her account at Bank B. Upon receipt, Bank B sends the check to the IT department, where the amount of the check is entered on the bottom-right corner of the check using magnetic ink character recognition or (MICR). This process uses special ink that can be read easily and accurately by a check sorter/reader. The check is read by an electronic sorter/reader, which recognizes that the check is drawn on Bank A. It is stacked in a special pocket for clearance later.

In the evening, the *not on us* checks are processed through an automated clearinghouse (ACH)—a computerized system that clears checks drawn on other banks. ACH notifies the payer's bank electronically to verify the payer's account and the amount drawn against the account. If the payer's bank says the account against which the check is drawn is invalid, closed, or overdrawn, ACH returns the check to the payee's bank marked "insufficient funds," "account closed," and so on. If the payer's bank acknowledges the account and the amount as valid, ACH instantly processes a debit to the payer's account and a credit to the payee's account. This transaction, plus millions of others, is processed in a matter of minutes and hours.

EFT is the transfer of credit between banks, where payments flow electronically from the payer's bank to the payee's bank. Banks settle their payments either by having accounts with one another, through the Federal Reserve's system called Fedwire, or through the Clearing House Interbank Payments System (CHIPS). FedWire is a Federal Reserve board system and the largest funds transfer system in the United States. It is used by banks to transfer funds from one bank to another. CHIPS is a huge operation, processing more than 90 percent of all international dollar transfers. With the Federal Reserve guaranteeing Fedwire funds, transfers cannot be revoked once the receiving bank is notified that its account has been credited by a reserve bank.

EFT is one of the earliest examples of online payment systems in banking. Although funds transferred account for a small portion of the total noncash payments, they account for more than 85 percent of the value of all noncash payments. EFT is used when a high priority is placed on timeliness and certainty of payment. For lower-priority payments, ACH is usually the alternative mode of payment processing.

ACH, unlike EFT, processes a high volume of relatively small-value payments for settlement in less than 2 days. The two primary ACH services are:

1. Preauthorized credits, for example, a university depositing payroll in faculty/staff's respective banks.
2. Preauthorized debits, such as bill payment.

To provide these services, banks have shared ACH systems with other bank systems, such as FedWire and CHIPS.

Beyond B2B: A2Z

Separating the business world based on who is buying and who is selling somehow lacks meaning in the real world, where a complex set of interactions called the *value chain* takes place. As we noted in Chapter 1, the value chain includes B2B processes like manufacturing as well as B2C processes like retailing. It is called the value chain because the strength of the chain depends on the strength of each link. For example, it does not make sense to improve a consumer product and then distribute it through old-fashioned retailers.

Downes (2000) suggested combining B2B and B2C into an "A2Z" approach that would connect all the links of the value chain via partnerships. The link would then be transformed from physical connections to digital ones. Take the case of a Wisconsin dairy that followed a non-digital version of A2Z. The family-owned business has cows, a processing plant, and trucks that deliver milk and dairy products directly to the consumer. With no information to indicate how each phase of the cycle can be optimized, the business ultimately fails due to higher transaction costs than the traditional cycle from farmer to wholesaler, to grocery store, to consumer. It turns out that home delivery was too costly.

With an A2Z strategy, the business has a clear picture of each stage of the process—"movement of raw materials, location of product in transit and in warehouses, and a snapshot of consumer demand broken down to ever-smaller market segments" (Downes 2000). A feedback loop moves backward from the consumer up the chain to the supplier of the raw materials. This loop brings consumer experience with the product, not just what they bought and how many units. This information becomes a new source of value at each step in the product life cycle. It affects product customization, product development, and targeted advertising. Those who control the information flow also will control the product flow and, therefore, the value.

Role of Leadership

From all evidence, e-business is maturing. Business strategies contribute to e-business strategies, which require a long-term commitment to product development; innovation; and effective execution of products, services, and information with partners and others alike. To do all this requires a high order of discipline and close adherence to business and communication fundamentals. The so-called Net-ready leaders must have a set of qualities, skills, and experience to see e-business navigate as part of the supply chain and ensure strength in the value chain.

To create traction in B2B, each e-business in the chain must develop traction around leadership, management, and technology. This means leaders who can empower rather than delegate and sell goodness of fit rather than impose. Cisco, Dell, Amazon, and Charles Schwab are names that consistently appear on any list of leading e-businesses. According to one source, they are successful not because of cool technology, but because they use technology to achieve business objectives.

Management Implications

B2B e-commerce is creating an opportunity for the greatest change in corporate efficiency and performance since the invention of the telephone. The technology riding on the Web enables unprecedented improvement in the buyer/seller relationship. It is affecting all kinds of information flows (see Box 11-8).

As we have seen, there are supplier-oriented B2B, buyer-oriented B2B, and third-party intermediary B2B models. The goal is to line up partners, work with them, and allow them to compete for the lowest price to help the buyer improve profitability. The power of the buyer is putting pressure on the suppliers to be more customer oriented and to demonstrate value-added deals for competing buyers. With intelligent agent software, customized and personalized information is now available to attract and retain suppliers around the clock.

The changes in B2B e-commerce are so intense that technology has become a mere enabler, not a solution. The real issue is managerial—how to handle privacy, taxation, and security, and how to make the Web safe for its participants. On the human side, as complex and timely as B2B is, IT talent is the critical component that makes this technology reliable.

Compensation is a major issue and always will be a high priority. Employees know what they are worth and what the competition is paying. Beyond compensation are intrinsic factors that promote a professional's career including utilization of abilities, creativity, security, good working conditions, competent supervision, autonomy, independence, and recognition. These elements are all part of the package that employees feel is job related. Job loyalty does not come cheap: Employers must look at the elements that enrich employees' professional life and add benefit to the business, from flexible work hours to taking a Spanish course.

Finally, IT employees should be involved in the decision process, especially in projects that affect their jobs. Taking ownership of one's career is attractive to any employee. Assuming a proactive role in deciding what one wants to do is also a strong motivator. In 1999, Allstate went all out to sell its policies via direct call centers and its Web site. It offered a series of job opportunities for employees to consider. Allstate.com is "our biggest-priority, number one project with a number one focus," according to a senior official (Copeland 2000, p. 66). Apparently, it's an attraction for prospective employees who want to know what the company is looking for. In the end, success, profitability, and growth become joint ventures between the business and those who run it. No better combination is available to handle B2B e-commerce.

BOX 11-8

E-commerce trends: Managing e-commerce alliances—a checklist

TEN SUCCESSFUL FACTORS IN DEVELOPING YOUR PARTNERSHIP:

1. **Are you socializing enough?** When you want to attract partnering attention from firms much larger than your own, do everything you can to reach them on a personal level. When you start, be willing to take on any job, no matter how awful.
2. **Are you compatible?** Partners need to have compatible business practices in order to effectively sell and deliver solutions. That single-mindedness covers everything from employing a common engagement methodology to agreeing on the same technical definitions.
3. **Are you flexible?** Partnerships can't afford to be bureaucratic, given the fast pace of e-commerce and the rapid evolution of business models.
4. **Have you put someone in charge?** Establish one partner as the project leader. Usually, whoever lands the customer should be the one to run the show, because the deliverables are a continuation of the sales cycle.
5. **Are you managing project transitions?** You could have e-anarchy on your hands without a clear road map of each partner's roles and responsibilities. That includes managing the handoffs that occur when one phase of a project melds into another.
6. **Have you decided on a billing method?** Most customers would rather have a single bill than multiple invoices. Figure out who is going to do the deed (the prime contractor is the likely choice).
7. **Are you electronically linked?** Electronic links between business systems can further ease the administration burden. Some partners also have opted to create a common repository for software code. Just be sure to protect your intellectual property.
8. **Have you minimized partner overlap?** Minimize the overlap between your skills and services, and those of your partners. Choose partners whose specialties are outside your own where you're unlikely to step on each other's toes. It also cuts down on employee raiding.
9. **Are you maintaining a healthy skepticism?** Don't trust your partners unquestioningly. When push comes to shove, a larger partner may choose you as the scapegoat. Document everything to ward against this. And keep in close communication to ensure that everyone's expectations are understood and met.
10. **Have you considered unlikely sources?** These days, even companies that have traditionally ignored the channel are looking for partners. VA Linux, for example, sells most of its products via the Web. But the company also sells to Web integrators and will need to partner as it grows its own service offerings.

SOURCE: Moore, John, Schindler, Esther, and Sperling, Ed, "Managing E-Commerce Alliances: A Checklist," *Smart Reseller*, April 17, 2000, 36.

SUMMARY

1. B2B involves complex procurement, manufacturing, planning collaboration, payment terms, and round-the-clock performance agreements. In one sense, B2B is collaborative commerce. Companies forge a long-term alliance and reduce the cost of doing business.
2. B2B and B2C have distinctive characteristics: In B2C, the connection mechanism is person to person; in B2B, it is the Web

browser of a business interacting with a Web server application of another business. In B2C, the business is placing orders; in B2B, it is online procurement and order fulfillment. In B2C, the control mechanism is unidirectional; in B2B, control ranges from one-sided control to peer-to-peer setups.

3. Among the advantages of B2B are suppliers using the purchaser's Web site to respond online to bids and sell excess inventory. B2B also allows business firms to form electronic alliances with distributors, suppliers, resellers, and other partners. On the other hand, most of the B2B Web exchanges have yet to make money. The question of antitrust violations resulting from alliance types of business also arises.
4. B2B is part of the supply-chain process. Supply-chain collaboration involves a group of manufacturers, retailers, and suppliers using the Internet to exchange business information, develop production schedules, and control inventory flow.
5. Among the models in B2B e-commerce are buyer-oriented B2B, supplier-oriented B2B, the electronic auction, and intermediary-oriented B2B.
6. B2B integration is about coordinating information among partners and their information system infrastructure. One solution to B2B integration is via a Web site. Another is to extract information from a partner's application and convert it into a format for transmission via EDI, File Transfer Protocol, e-mail, or HTTP. A third approach is for two companies to use common technology to coordinate data exchange.
7. Most B2B traffic is handled by EDI, which is computer-to-computer transfer of business information between two businesses that use a specific standard format. A specialized area of EDI centers around the electronic transmission of payments between a payee and a payer via their respective banks. The three main types of noncash payment procedures in use today for B2B payments are bank checks, EFT, and ACH.

Key Terms

- B2B, 330
- B2C, 330
- buyer-oriented B2B, 345
- disaster planning, 345
- electronic auction, 346
- Electronic Data Interchange (EDI), 334
- forward auction, 347
- Informediary, 350
- intermediary-oriented B2B, 350
- Internet exchange auction, 349
- reverse auction, 347
- supplier-oriented B2B, 345
- supply chain, 337

Test Your Understanding

1. What is B2B e-commerce? What makes it so unique?
2. In what way is B2B considered collaborative commerce? Elaborate.
3. B2B is more than taking orders online. Do you agree? Explain.
4. Compare and contrast B2B and B2C e-commerce.
5. Cite the pros and cons of B2B e-commerce. Do you think the advantages exceed the drawbacks? Justify your answer.
6. What is price signaling? Give an example of your own.
7. What red flags could run B2B exchanges into antitrust trouble? Explain.

8. Identify the distinctive characteristics and give an example of each of the following electronic auctions:
   a. Forward auction.
   b. Reverse auction.
   c. Internet exchange auction.
9. In what way is the application server different from the B2B integration server? Be specific.
10. What management implications can one consider for B2B e-commerce?

Discussion Questions

1. With all the activities and developments in B2B e-commerce, address the implications for a career in e-business.
2. B2B has been changing rapidly during the past decade. Review the literature (via the Internet) and cite five factors in the B2B sector that have contributed to key changes.
3. Locate a major organization in your area and conduct an interview to elicit the following information.
   a. The type of e-business environment available.
   b. The level of sophistication of business-to-business technology.
   c. The return on the investment.
4. Work with your team and discuss B2B integration challenges in detail. Specifically, identify the concept of B2B integration and the various solutions to B2B integration.

Web Exercises

1. Go to www.fedex.com on the Internet and investigate the type of support available to customers (e.g., checking the status of deliveries).
2. Go to www.dell.com and evaluate the site from the business buyer's perspective. Is there a procedure that would allow ordering in the supplier-oriented marketplaces?
3. Access www.ibm.com and evaluate the services offered. For a first-time business on the Internet, which service would you recommend the new e-merchant consider? Why?
4. What can one foresee beyond B2B e-commerce? Surf the Internet and address new events or developments in the area.
5. Surf the Internet and choose a software agent application or package. Write a 300-word report summarizing its features, where it would best be used, and the technology required for optimum performance.

Chapter 12

Legal, Ethical, and International Issues

Contents

IN A NUTSHELL

An international airline's Web site cost the company a $14,000 fine. It advertised an attractive fare for seats that were never available, a violation of U.S. airline regulations. Customer complaints poured in, which triggered the fine by the U.S. Department of Transportation. When it comes to the legal implications of Internet business fraud, the U.S. Department of Transportation is one of many government watchdogs including the FBI, the Federal Communications Commission (FCC), and the Federal Trade Commission (FTC), among others. Even the U.S. Postal Service has an interest in Net fraud, especially in the areas of vacations, prizes, or rigged contests by fictitious Web merchants.

The legal and ethical implications of the Internet are attracting a lot of attention among industries and governments around the world. There are international implications, as well. Diverting one's income to an overseas bank account to evade taxes is considered illegal. In contrast, an employee submitting an inflated expense report is unethical. Ethics deals with honesty, trustworthiness, and fairness. *Legal* means "abiding by established laws for certain acts."

Law enforcers from Canada, the United Kingdom, and other countries are loosely organized in terms of monitoring and enforcing the punishment of illegal acts. The rapid development of communications technology and the heavy use of the Internet for business present many challenges for the law everywhere. According to Stewart Taggart, the Internet has promoted "fast, cheap, and out of control tax evasion and privacy issues that are causing a nightmare for the law. As long as there have been borders, people crossed them in search of the most advantageous legal environment. The borderless Internet is pushing the matter that much quicker" (Taggart 2000).

Here is a case in point: A professional front man provides "sovereign services," where he will put your business or personal affairs in the best mix of global jurisdictions to keep the authorities at bay. Such services involve exploiting differing rules in different jurisdictions—for a profit. Over time, all this border hopping could lead to a showdown between businesses and the forces of control at all levels. It is an open question whether more than 200 governments can coordinate such traffic. In any case, given today's open electronic borders, the possibilities look limitless. As one attorney remarked, "It's difficult to arrest an electron" (Taggart 2000).

Taxation, especially sales tax, is another hot issue. No single place owns the Internet, but every state and country tries to control it. Norbert Elbert of Hackensack, New Jersey, was sentenced to 2 years in prison for child pornography, convicted by a federal court in Tucson, Arizona. Elbert has never been to Arizona, but a federal investigator in Arizona was able to retrieve the evidence from Elbert's computer in New Jersey via the Internet. He had violated a new Arizona law against pornography. This means that today an e-business can easily break the law anywhere. Copyright and trademark laws differ from one country to another. Even the idea of sending an encrypted message to someone in a country where encryption is prohibited could cause a legal nightmare.

Like all business, e-commerce operates in a legal environment. Some traditional laws apply, but other laws must be developed to address the unique way business is conducted in a borderless world. This chapter addresses various practical legal, ethical, and privacy issues for Internet commerce. It covers the primary issues faced by law enforcement agencies, businesses, and the consumer—privacy rights, tax policies, Net tort law, and liability.

When we look at the Internet as global, as involving a multitude of different cultures and governments that cannot agree on most things, the issues of legal and ethical environments become truly daunting. Despite these differences, legal disputes and case law are beginning to surface. The author is not an attorney, and this text does not replace attorneys' opinions or state the law. It is merely an overview of the problems, processes, and implications of this important subject and how they affect business and the consumer.

ETHICAL ISSUES

IT professionals and those in disciplines such as medicine and law subscribe to codes of ethics that govern the way they behave with clients, customers, and the public at large. Trust is linked to the expectation that a professional will behave ethically. This is essential in business because society depends on fairness and good judgment. Businesspeople are expected to tell the truth and warn customers when a fault is discovered in a product.

The inclusion of ethics in e-commerce is the current challenge confronting U.S. organizations. It is easy to see how businesses have become accustomed to lower standards of ethics and a rising insensitivity to IT glitches. Consider a recent IT conference that offered tutorials on how to act without morality, how to leave decency behind, and how to seize the future by the throat and make it cough up money—all for a fee of $2,340 for each tutorial (Strassmann 2000). How about the well-known case of *Microsoft versus the U.S. Justice Department*, where late in 1999 a key Microsoft executive provided a misleading demonstration of Windows 98 before a federal judge, or the America Online release of Version 5.0 without alerting users that it interfered with Internet Service Providers and disabled competing software?

This type of arrogance attests to the increasing tendency of IT software developers to show a smug disregard for problems affecting businesses and consumers alike. As technology advances, users and developers have a responsibility to consider the ethical implications that may arise.

What Is Ethics?

ethics: justice, equity, honesty, trustworthiness, equality, fairness; a subjective feeling of being innately right.

Ethics is not easy to define, but to discuss ethical issues we need a common definition. **Ethics** is one or all of the following: fairness, justice, equity, honesty, trustworthiness, and equality. Stealing, cheating, lying, or backing out on one's word all describe a lack of ethics. Something is ethical when a person feels it is innately right, which is a subjective judgment. For example, "thou shalt not steal" is a belief held by most people, but a parent who steals a loaf of bread to feed four starving children may be forgiven for this behavior.

Figure 12-1 is a conceptual model of acceptable behavior, with ethics as a factor in each quadrant. For example, if a person falsely reports a donation to a charitable organization, it

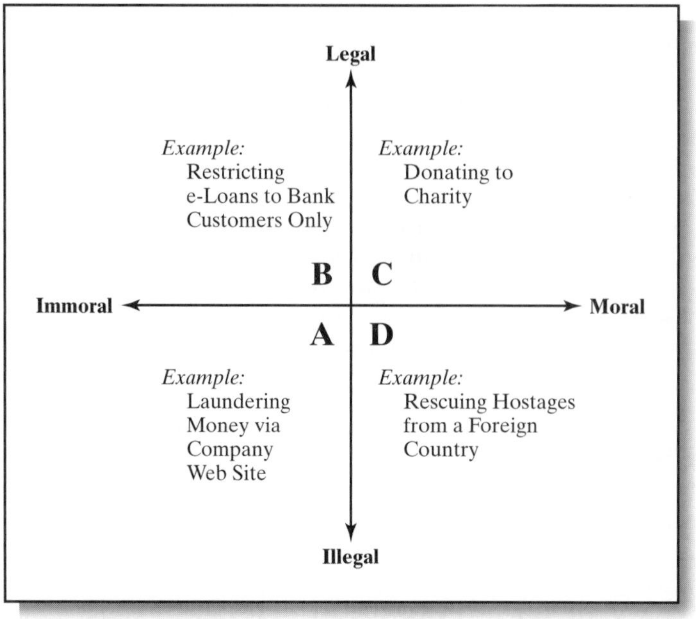

Figure 12-1
A model of acceptable behavior

is considered both illegal and immoral (quadrant A). This action implies a lack of ethical standards and personal values. In quadrant D, rescuing hostages from a foreign country might be illegal (and dangerous) by that country's laws, but it is moral (and implicitly ethical) under U.S. laws. Deciding what is moral, legal, or ethical is a constant struggle.

An unethical act is not the same as an immoral or an illegal act, although one may lead to the other (see Box 12-1). For example:

1. Cheating on a federal income tax return is more *illegal* than immoral, although it is implicitly unethical.
2. Cheating on a friend is more *immoral* than illegal, although it is tacitly unethical.
3. Sending a padded bill to a client is *unethical* and possibly illegal.

Incidents such as these are related to value systems, beliefs, and culture. Laws often are created to combat unethical acts that threaten a society's survival. They also are used to reinforce existing systems of ethics. Codes of ethics also create a strong sense of professionalism. A **code of ethics** is a declaration of the principles and beliefs that govern how employees of a corporation or an association are expected to behave.

code of ethics: a declaration of the principles and beliefs that govern how employees of a corporation or an association are expected to behave.

To illustrate, take the case of a loan advisor function built into the Web site of a commercial bank that uses 17 criteria to determine whether an applicant qualifies for a loan. For several years, the bank has been criticized by state auditors for not granting enough loans to minorities or to people living in minority districts. A review of the software package revealed that most loans favor applicants who are white and married rather than those who are single, separated, or divorced.

When the discriminating rules were pointed out, the Web designer said: "I developed this application based on the vice president of mortgage loans' requirements. He reviewed several prototypes and cleared the final version to be tagged to the bank's Web site. Why don't you talk with him?"

BOX 12-1
The saga of a yacht

During a board of directors meeting of a small commercial bank, the first agenda item was a review of the Statement of Condition (expenses, revenues, and so on) of the bank for the previous month, which was January. John, a new member of the board, noticed a line item under "entertainment" for $12,000. He thought to himself, "Here's a local bank of 140 employees. What kind of entertainment is going on at the bank or by the bank to add up to this much expense?"

Out of curiosity, he raised the question at the meeting: "Mr. Chairman, I'd like to know a little about the entertainment expense item. Could this be from the Christmas party, reflected as a January expense?" The bank's president, sitting next to John, replied: "Well, as you know John, the bank incurs all kinds of entertainment expenses. Why don't you stop by my office after the meeting and I'd be happy to explain it further. Mr. Chairman, I move that we take the next item on the agenda as listed . . ."

After the board meeting, the president explained, "John, the entertainment item is the bank's monthly contribution to the chairman's entertainment of customers and officers of the bank. A chairman has certain privileges." John then asked, "How long has this been going on?" The president, his face turning red with irritation, said: "I really don't want to elaborate further on this. Remember, you are new on the board. I wouldn't advise asking the chairman about it. I'd let it go. The bank is making enough money. The chairman's family owns 78 percent equity in the bank. What more explanation do you want? How about taking you out to lunch today?"

John later discovered that the monthly charge of $12,000 was a dockage fee for the chairman's 140-foot yacht. As a board member, he had a responsibility to review the integrity of the information reported. This type of expense is questionable, especially when, for the past 6 years, there has been no bank-related entertainment aboard the vessel. He is now in a quandary whether he should stay on the board or resign.

SOURCE: Anonymous.

In addressing the equity question, the vice president replied: "I make decisions on loans based on guidelines from the board of directors. Our chairman is a major stockholder of the bank. He does not live in the area and wants to make sure we approve secured loans. Why don't you talk to the president about it?"

In a meeting with the president the next day, the president said: "I'm surprised you're bringing up bank policy. We paid a Web designer to write the loan program and make it work on the bank's Web homepage based on our requirements. So, what's the big fuss all about?" The question raised here still remains: Whose behavior is unethical?

A more recent finding that questions ethics points to companies that make money with employees' life insurance when they die. As summarized in Box 12-2, hundreds of banks take out insurance policies on employees with the company as the beneficiary. Some have received as much as 15 percent of their net income from the tax-free interest they get from premiums they pay on the policies. The ethical question is whether the bank should notify the spouse or the parent up front about the practice. Should the bank share in the proceeds when the employee dies?

One of the problems with ethics in business is that many firms overlook ethics issues. From 1988 to 1993, Arthur Andersen LLP, one of the Big Five U.S. accounting firms,

BOX 12-2
A question of ethics

Many American banks, taking advantage of relaxed restrictions by federal regulators, are getting a boost in their profits from tax-free income they earn from life insurance policies they take out on their employees. Most employees at the hundreds of companies that buy janitors' insurance have no idea their employer stands to cash in upon their death. After heavy lobbying from the insurance industry, states began permitting the practice in the late 1980s.

Companies enjoy tax-free gains on the money they put into the policies. And when employees die, the death benefit to companies is also tax-free. The Internal Revenue Service in 1996 began disallowing even more lucrative deductions that companies were taking on the interest on loans against life insurance policies. But in 1997, bank regulators loosened their own rules on insurance coverage. Thanks to lobbying from banks, the Office of the Comptroller of the Currency, which regulates federally chartered banks, relaxed restrictions on banks' janitors' insurance.

Because the gains are tax free, "the profit falls to the bottom line. I can't imagine a more profitable loan that they could make," says Eric Connerly, a financial services analyst and principal at Boston Partners, a money manager in Boston.

Sovereign Bancorp carries on its books some $659 million in "bank-owned" life insurance, which includes policies on executives and other employees. That figure reflects the amount it has paid for the insurance, plus past investment gains but minus fees and death benefits. Earnings from these assets contributed $18.2 million, or 15.6 percent of the bank's net income for last year.

SOURCE: Excerpted from Francis, Theo, and Schult, Ellen E., "Many Banks Boost Earnings with Janitors' Life Insurance," *The Wall Street Journal*, April 26, 2002, A1ff.

invited 10 well-known ethicists and spent $5 million developing an ethics program. The real ethics question is, How did this firm end up being convicted of obstructing justice through corrupt auditing in the Enron fiasco? (Dadurka 2002).

Have you ever been ensnarled on a Web page that won't let you go back or get out, or one that diverted you to an X-rated Web site? On the Web, dirty tricks are everywhere. One of the most annoying aspects of Web surfing is that you do not always go where you want, and if you do end up in a place you did not want to go to, it is not always easy to get out. The ethical question centers on whether it is ethical or moral to trap people in one spot, especially if it is a pornographic site.

Ethical issues also have moral implications. Take the case of Colonel Kassem Saleh who was stationed in Afghanistan during the war against the Talibans. He could count on e-mails from his women—more than 50 fiancees who he met via Internet dating services, such as tallpersonals.com, match.com, and christiansingle.com. His scheme fell apart in May 2003 when a local Washington television station broadcast a story about a woman who was engaged to a "Saleh." Before too long, other women who thought they were Saleh's fiancées called the television station (*Times* Report 2003).

Major Threats to Ethics

Ethics in e-commerce is more openly discussed as a serious concern today than ever in the past, because the threats have steadily increased. Today's e-businesses face ethical dilemmas of dimensions not imagined 10 years ago. The main threats are the following.

1. Faster computers and more advanced networks.
2. Sophisticated global telecommunications.
3. Massive distributed databases.
4. Ease of access to information and knowledge bases.
5. Transparency of software.
6. The idea that captured information can be used as a competitive weapon.

Technological advances have resulted in the need to reevaluate ethical standards and their implications for privacy, confidentiality, and integrity. Software copyright infringement, unauthorized e-mail access, and the sale of competitive data are serious issues. High-speed, low-cost data transmission is raising new questions about property rights, piracy, and plagiarism. All of this is forcing a reevaluation of the e-merchant's code of ethics.

Faking a Hard Day

Ethics is having a hard time with white collar slackers who get help from e-mail and Internet technology. Think of a manager lingering over coffee and a doughnut. He could actually open windows and work with documents on his screen via the hand-held phone, giving every impression to those around him or her that John is somewhere around at this late hour.

Spencer 2003 reports that the tactics are not new, but the tools are. Think of the old trick of leaving a jacket on the back of the desk chair or keeping the lights on to show presence. The new options allow people to operate the office computer by remote control. One feature in Microsoft Outlook allows e-mail to be sent at any specific time, day or night. In Microsoft Outlook, under options, one feature "do not deliver before" will allow the system to send e-mail at the designated time during your absence. Is this considered ethical?

Improving the Ethical Climate

E-businesses can take a number of steps to improve ethical behavior in their IT departments, which is where Web sites are updated and programs are written.

1. To promote ethical behavior throughout the organization, top managers should act as role models.
2. The company should establish a code of ethics that takes into consideration the state of technology (Intranets, Extranets, local area and wide area networks, and so on). Goals should be realistic, achievable, and agreed upon by all employees. Each organizational level should create its own customized ethics program, using the company's code of ethics as a framework.
3. Unethical behavior should be dealt with promptly according to criteria and procedures set in advance.
4. The company should set up and support a strong ethics training program for all new employees and reinforce the training on a regular basis.
5. The company should motivate employees to focus on honesty, integrity, fairness, and justice as goals that are just as important as money or the bottom line.

Once the code of ethics has been agreed upon, the next step is to decide who is going to lead the ethics movement. Organizations have used two approaches: bottom up and top down. The *bottom-up* approach inculcates ethics behavior at the employee level with the full support of top management. The other approach, called *top down*, suggests that company attitudes start with the CEO. By virtue of personal acts, decisions, and overall behavior, the top corporate officer sets the tone for the kind of image the company will have.

Take the case of Boeing Aircraft's former chief executive, William Allen. After World War II, in September 1945, he resigned from his law firm to lead Boeing. Allen had served as a company attorney for 20 years and as director for 14 years. He is remembered as a man of great sincerity, honesty, and integrity. When he accepted the job of president, he offered the following resolution as a reflection of his personal values.

1. Do not be afraid to admit that you don't know.
2. Be definite—tell it like it is.
3. Try to promote honest feelings toward the company around Seattle.
4. Don't talk too much . . . let others talk.
5. Be considerate of your associates' views.
6. Above all, be human—keep your sense of humor and learn to relax.

Under Allen, Boeing acquired a reputation as a highly ethical firm whose employees had strong values and integrity. His time as CEO is remembered as a period of "uncompromising high standards and clean ethics." Employees always knew where they stood.

With today's heavy use of the Internet by company employees, an ethics question is What should a company do about employees who spend much of their time on nonproductive or nonbusiness-related Internet browsing? Is it ethical for a company to track employee e-mail? Is it ethical for one business to get the lowdown on a business rival? Any of these issues is a threat to ethics, because they involve privacy.

Regarding the first question, the general opinion is that employees are expected to devote 8 honest hours of service on the job. When they spend nonbusiness-related time on the Internet, it is viewed as cheating the employer. There is also the liability problem, because any business transacted on the Internet makes the company liable. Because the business owns the Internet line and the equipment, the employer is entitled to determine when, for how long, and for what reason the Internet can be in use. This happened to be the case when a brokerage firm's agent hit a pedestrian while using the cell phone to do business with a company client.

Ever since e-mail began in the mid-1990s, companies have questioned whether they should scan employee e-mail or monitor the traffic that is leaving or coming into the company files. Companies are stepping up measures to police it, especially as they realize they can be held legally responsible. Like the telephone, using e-mail for limited personal business is acceptable, but some controls must be in place.

Managers can have problems in controlling unproductive Internet surfing. The ideal approach is for managers to limit cyberslouching, while at the same time not offend employees. Ultimately, the best way to conduct electronic monitoring is a combination of feedback and control monitoring. For example, one company monitors all Internet usage and logs all traffic. However, logs are reviewed only at the request of the human resources department to investigate an employee productivity problem (Ubaczewski and Jessup 2002).

Electronic monitoring for pornography and sexual harassment has increased in recent years among most firms. For example, in one case at one of the author's institutions, an IT specialist was fired on the spot when caught exchanging information related to child pornography after having been given one written warning. The university employee manual clearly states that such exchange may result in immediate dismissal.

In terms of one business "spying" on another, whether it is legal or ethical depends on the procedure followed. As explained in Box 12-3, a company crosses the line if it anonymously coaxes proprietary information from an unsuspecting competitor (Warren 2002). The alternative is to use legitimate Web sites to gather useful information. Examples are http://Altavista.com, http://Anonymizer.com, www.Epinions.com, and Netsol.com.

BOX 12-3
Spying on others

The explosion of company Web sites, chat rooms, and e-commerce has produced a gold mine of information just waiting to be unearthed by resourceful businesspeople eager for the scoop on a competitor. In corporate-speak, it's called gathering competitive intelligence. But let's not mince words. We're talking about good old-fashioned spying with a big plus: You never have to leave your desk.

ETHICAL CONCERNS

Sound shifty? Actually, business-ethics experts agree there's nothing wrong with learning what you can about your competitors from the wealth of public information available on the Web. Where you cross the line is if you anonymously coax proprietary information from an unsuspecting competitor. You should never misrepresent yourself when gathering information. This does not mean you have to identify yourself. Dropping anonymously into a competitor's Web site is akin to the time-honored business practice of wandering into a rival's store to look over his merchandise, how he's priced it, how he's advertised it, and how he's displayed it.

You can judge your competitors by the company they keep. At Altavista, the search string link://www.companyname.com will reveal who has Web sites that are linked to those of your rivals. (Also check link://companyname.com—some companies are cataloged with the three w's, and some aren't.) That list will give you an idea of how well connected your competitor is in the Internet community.

You cannot neglect the obvious. Start broadly. Evaluating the design and layout of the Web site can give you clues to the company's sophistication and the image the firm is trying to project. For a publicly traded company, comb through the investor-relations site, which lays out the company's financial details, including quarterly reports on profits, losses, and unusual expenses. All this is required by law to be public.

SOURCE: Excerpted from Warren, Susan, "I-Spy," *The Wall Street Journal*, January 14, 2002, R14.

Codes of Ethics and Other Tools

Business ethics is closely tied to corporate culture and values, which means that a code of ethics should represent all that the company stands for. The code should be all encompassing and stable over time. It does not make sense, for example, to change the code for every new situation that comes up.

Once a code of ethics has been posted and approved by management and employees, it becomes a commitment to behave within its guidelines on a day-to-day basis. Box 12-4 provides excerpts from the code of ethics of the Association for Computing Machinery (ACM), whose international membership exceeds 80,000.

An honest workplace, where managers and employees are held accountable for their behavior, is the best environment in which to promote ethical corporate behavior. To keep the ethical climate healthy, an organization must stress regular self-assessment and encourage open debate within the workplace. **Self-assessment** is a question-and-answer procedure that allows individuals to appraise and understand their personal knowledge about a particular topic. In the case of ethics, it is not an exercise to satisfy others. The goal is to think about ethics and adjust one's behavior accordingly. It should be an educational experience for the participant.

self-assessment: a question-and-answer procedure that allows individuals to appraise and understand their personal knowledge about a particular topic.

BOX 12-4
E-commerce trends: ACM code of ethics

GENERAL MORAL IMPERATIVES

1. Be honest and trustworthy.
2. Avoid harm to others.
3. Honor property rights including copyrights and patents.
4. Access computing and communication resources only when authorized to do so.
5. Respect the privacy of others.
6. Honor confidentiality.

MORE SPECIFIC PROFESSIONAL RESPONSIBILITIES

1. Acquire and maintain professional competence.
2. Know and respect existing laws pertaining to professional work.
3. Give comprehensive and thorough evaluations of computer systems and their impact, with special emphasis on possible risks.
4. Improve public understanding of computing and its consequences.

ORGANIZATIONAL LEADERSHIP IMPERATIVES

1. Articulate social responsibilities of members of an organizational unit and encourage full acceptance of those responsibilities.
2. Manage personnel and resources to design and build information systems that enhance the quality of working life.
3. Acknowledge and support proper and authorized uses of an organization's computing and communication resources.
4. Articulate and support policies that protect the dignity of users and others affected by computing systems.

SOURCE: Excerpts from *Association for Computing Machinery*, "Code of Ethics," October 2001, 1–6.

One self-assessment procedure asks a participant to assess a scenario and judge whether an ethics issue is involved. The response is recorded on a special form and later compared to the judgment of a panel of experts. The following is an example.

Company XYZ has developed the software for a computerized voting machine. Company ABC, which manufactures the machine, has persuaded several cities and states to purchase it. On the strength of these orders, ABC is planning a major purchase from XYZ. XYZ software engineer Smith is visiting ABC one day and learns that problems in the construction of the machine mean that 1 in 10 is likely to miscount soon after installation. Smith reports this to her superior, who informs her that it is ABC's problem. Smith does nothing further.

QUESTION: Is an ethics issue involved?

OPINION: Participants nearly unanimously agreed that doing nothing further would be unethical. Use of inaccurate voting machines could invalidate elections and potentially harm the general public. Responsible (ethical) behavior and good business practice are not inconsistent. The software engineer should pursue the matter further.

The Privacy Factor

Privacy is a basic American value. It is also one of the most pressing concerns of computer users today and an issue that is inadequately addressed in e-commerce. Cyberspace, originally intended for scientists, is now dominated by marketers seeking information—the lifeblood of e-business. What makes information so valuable is that most of it is gathered discreetly. E-companies are taking advantage of their ability to obtain information without the customer's knowledge or permission. Such private information is being documented, sold, and used to promote e-business. E-businesses have an ethical responsibility to inform users of what information is being captured and how it is being used.

The thought of being watched is unsettling. Hidden video cameras, phone taps, and surveillance bugs are all examples of technologies that are considered to be unethical (and sometimes illegal), because they allow data to be collected about individuals without their knowledge. Web sites have been developed whose only business is selling information about people who visit their sites. Some businesses use game sites to attract children and then gather personal information from them.

Senator Ernst Hollings (D-SC) proposed the Online Personal Privacy Act, on April 18, 2002, with the goal of creating uniforms laws across the United States relating to Internet privacy. The bill covers two types of information: sensitive and nonsensitive. Sensitive information is "any financial, medical, ethnic identification, religious affiliation, sexual orientation, or political data." Companies must seek the consent of users they are collecting sensitive information about through a procedure called "opt in." Companies also must allow users to "opt out" of any data collection of nonsensitive material. They must inform users of how their information will be used and who will have access to it. The Federal Trade Commission (FTC), the state's attorney general, and the user can sue companies that release sensitive information in federal court (Mariano 2002).

A new federal law created a new precedent, in which federal authorities may monitor Internet users. The USA Patriot Act, passed in response to the terrorist acts of September 11, 2001, gives federal authorities the right to tap into what you are doing on the Internet and e-mail. Also, Internet service providers must make themselves more susceptible to wiretaps by the federal government. This act drew many concerns from civil libertarians, in that the surveillance powers give law enforcement agents too much leeway to collect private information on people who are on the periphery of investigations (Olsen 2002).

The FTC has identified the following five principles of privacy protection, which are widely recognized in the United States, Canada, and Europe.

1. **Notice:** Consumers have the right to be told in advance about any personal information being gathered.
2. **Choice:** Consumers should have the final say regarding the use of personal information, other than the processing of such information.
3. **Access:** Consumers should be able to access and correct any personal information captured in files or databases anywhere.
4. **Security/integrity:** Consumers' personal information should be processed, stored, and transmitted in a secure way so as to assure integrity at all times.
5. **Enforcement:** The courts should back consumers if any of the aforementioned principles are violated.

Three categories of concern arise regarding information privacy. The first involves the electronic data that businesses store about consumers. Who owns such data? The second is the security of electronic data transmission. Encryption has been promoted as a secure way to transmit data over the Internet. The third concern is the unauthorized reading of personal files. Public key architecture (PKI) and other technologies are used to control unauthorized access.

The FTC has been watching a number of e-commerce companies closely, such as Amazon.com. In the past, the FTC has sided with businesses, favoring self-regulation over legislation, but because the public at large is worried about surrendering personal data online, the likelihood of government intervention to protect the consumer is on the rise. Watchdog groups such as Junkbusters, the Electronic Frontier Foundation, Privacy International, and the Online Privacy Alliance are pushing for government oversight to protect the public. E-merchants, on the other hand, continue to prefer self-restraint to legislation (Perine 2000).

With Net privacy in its infancy, sites, including the following, have been established that serve as building blocks for the next generation of privacy protection.

- www.spybot.com—This site helps scan your computer to advise you whether it is vulnerable to hidden programs that lurk in the background.
- www.privacy.org—This site offers a collection of Net privacy articles derived from top news organizations.
- www.junkbuster.com—A great site for assisting consumers in their fight against unsolicited advertising practices, from spam and junk mail to cookies and the like.
- www.freedom.net—This is an Internet privacy software package designed to protect your personal information. It can block junk mail and stop online tracking. The package sells for less than $50 per copy.
- www.epic.org—This site contains a massive collection of news, links to software, guidelines, and a report on the privacy policies of the top 100 U.S. firms.

The Professional Ethicist

As the Internet has dominated e-commerce, e-business, and society in general, ethics in the use of technology to protect one's privacy has generated a new breed of professional ethicists to help firms navigate the moral gray areas of the Web. More and more firms are hiring people with integrity; who are well grounded academically; and who practice ethics, morality, and objectivity in problem solving.

Ethics consultants perform a number of important functions. They hold workshops and meetings, and advise executives on setting ethical guidelines for the day-to-day operation of their firm. They conduct surveys and talk to employees to figure out where the ethical loopholes are and how to correct them. The idea usually works for most firms, but it is not a guarantee that the company will become ethical in attitude or practice. As mentioned before, Arthur Andersen's $5 million investment in an ethics program did not deter it from the audit scandal with Enron. Whether an ethics program works depends largely on the commitment and support of top management, and honest maintenance of ethics on a daily basis.

A typical ethicist holds a graduate degree in the humanities, psychology, behavioral science, communications, or human resources. The ethicist holds values designed to put integrity, trust, and honesty into corporations, especially in terms of their relationships with employees, the community, and local government. Communication skills, training, and facilitating skills are critical. Business knowledge and basic legal understanding are helpful.

Some of the ethical core values to consider include putting funds and resources back to the community, striving to play the business game in a way that it is a win-win endeavor, treating employees to enrich the feeling of belonging, providing recognition, and giving a share of the company wealth to those who have added value to the firm's productivity. Ethics consultants can earn as much as $9,000 per day at corporations or close to $200,000 as full-time specialists.

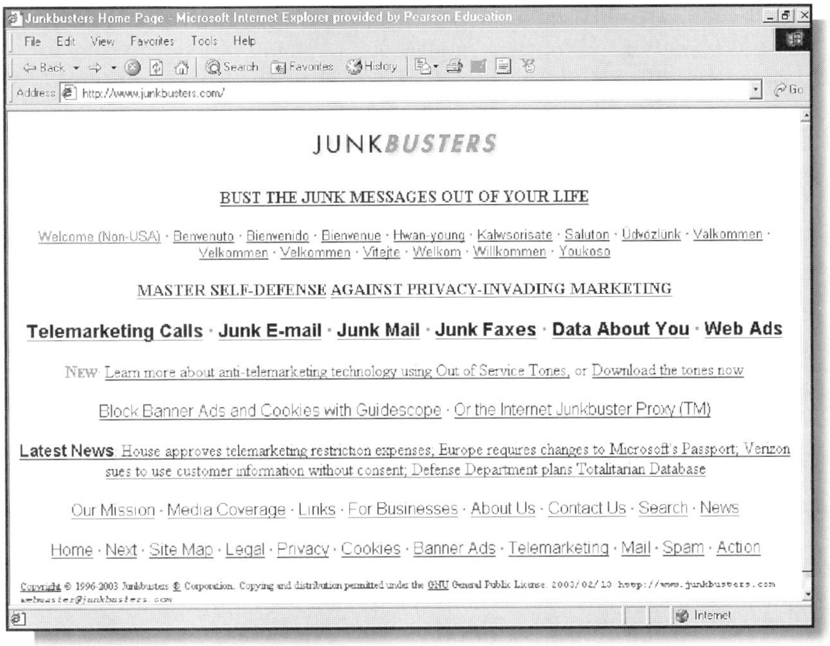

Screen Capture 12-1

Source: Copyright © 1996–2003 Junkbusters® Corporation. Copying and distribution permitted under the GNU General Public License. 2003/06/20 http://www.junkbusters.com.

Legal Issues

Every legitimate business, whether it is brick –and mortar or online, operates in a legal environment. Contracts, taxation, and copyrights are among the legal issues that all face. Many of the legal questions that arise from e-commerce are not settled, but new laws can change the rules and plug loopholes. In an age of prolific litigation, online shoppers and e-merchants should be aware of the legal ramifications of e-commerce. Consider the following situations.

1. Via its Web site, a large computer firm sells a server to a client, with proper configuration, ready to go. When the server is installed, the user discovers that the configuration is faulty and the server, as it stands, is worthless. The company operates out of Europe, and the cost of shipping the unit for repairs would be prohibitive. It also would bring the user's business to a standstill.
2. A customized computer system used by an architect incorrectly determines the stress requirements of a new multimillion-dollar public building. Unknown to the architect, the software, acquired via the Internet, had definite bugs. As a result, the completed structure soon collapses, killing or injuring dozens of people.
3. A radiation machine bought over the Internet by a young doctor calculates the dosage in the treatment of cancer patients. Two years after treating hundreds of people, four die due to radiation overdose. The problem was faulty programming. The e-merchant denies responsibility.

4. Software has been used recently by online services to divert online sales commissions that would otherwise be paid to small Web merchants by big sites like Amazon.com and eToys. This "stealware" is considered legal, because the users agree to the diversion. The diversion involved is estimated to be in the hundreds of thousands of dollars and probably will continue, because most users are unaware that the software is operating on their computers or it might be too costly to contest (Schwartz and Tedeschi 2002).

Each of these cases is real. Who is liable in such situations and for what reasons?

The Question of Liability

When a product is bought over the Internet and found to be defective, liability becomes an issue. The blame may fall on the merchant or the vendor that shipped the merchandise. Depending on how the warranty is worded, liability could fall on the manufacturer. Tort and contract laws present challenging questions for organizations and the legal community. If a product produces the wrong solution, which causes injury to others, the resulting damage often leads to litigation. Each entity involved in the process (e-merchant, vendor, shipper, manufacturer) is potentially vulnerable to legal action.

product liability: a tort that makes a manufacturer liable if its product has a defective condition that makes it unreasonably dangerous to the user or consumer.

strict liability: a seller is liable for any defective or hazardous products that unduly threaten a user's safety.

The nature of the Internet and its technology have not yet reached a point at which new legal remedies are required for e-commerce. The old, familiar liability issues are still applicable. Tort law and **product liability** are the two major (and often overlapping) areas of concern, with the issue of warranties falling under the first area, and **strict liability** and negligence falling under the second.

One area that is attracting attention in M-commerce is doing business by cell phone. The use of two-way pagers, mobile phones, and other m-tools now means that business can be conducted anywhere, but it might make companies liable if employees using these gadgets are involved in accidents, usually car accidents (see Box 12-5).

Tort Law on the Internet

tort: a wrongful act subject to civil action.

tort law: a special area of law focused on remedying wrongs between parties.

Torts are wrongful acts subject to civil action. **Tort law** is a special area of law focused on remedying wrongs between parties. In e-commerce, it can mean settling contract problems between the e-merchant and the ISP. ISPs have yet to be regulated by any federal or state agency. That is why each ISP can decide on prices, quality, speed, reliability, and the like. Internet tort cases already have been brought against businesses and clients. Most of the cases relate to fraud, negligence, false advertising, misrepresentation, and trademark violations.

fraud: the intent to deceive.

Fraud is the intent to deceive. It is knowing a material fact about a product in advance, but covering it up in a sale. This applies to the e-merchant as well as to the consumer. For example, if a customer gives an unauthorized or stolen credit card number over the Internet, that customer is liable for fraud. If a merchant advertises a product on a Web site and makes false claims about what it will do, the merchant can be liable for fraud. In many countries, watchdog organizations as well as government agencies watch closely for Internet fraud (see Box 12-6).

negligence: failing to take a certain action, which in turn causes injury or material loss to another.

Negligence is failing to take a certain action, which in turn causes injury or material loss to another. For example, a person who drives at

BOX 12-5
The liability question with cell phones

Smith Barney, the investment banking firm, has paid $500,000 to settle a lawsuit brought by the family of a motorcyclist killed in Pennsylvania by one of its brokers who was talking on the phone while driving, according to a lawyer for the victim's family. But in Minnesota, where a psychiatric nurse reached for her cell phone while driving home and rammed another car, the jury concluded that answering the call was not part of her job.

The resulting confusion over the law is one reason that employers and their lawyers will be closely observing the outcome of a suit filed in Virginia against a law firm whose associate was driving and, the plaintiffs contend, talking to clients when she killed a teenage girl in the summer of 2000. That trial is scheduled to begin next week.

Employers have been liable for negligence for years, but the application of the negligence doctrine to our technological society is in fact relatively new. The Virginia lawsuit against Cooley Godward, the employer of the lawyer who ran over a 15-year-old girl, could help set a precedent in this fuzzy area. The lawyer, Jane Wagner, pleaded guilty to a felony and has already completed a 1-year work-release program, according to her lawyer. Now the civil suit against the law firm is about to begin.

SOURCE: Excerpted from Glatten, Jonathan D., "Doing Business by Cellphone Creates New Liability Issues," *New York Times*, December 3, 2002, Technology 3.

high speed on an icy road, skids into a car, and kills its occupants would be sued for gross negligence.

false advertising: advertising the availability of a product or a service when, in fact, no such thing is available.

misrepresentation: a tort area that tags to fraud.

False advertising is simply advertising the availability of a product or a service when, in fact, no such thing is available.

Misrepresentation is another tort area. Like false advertising in intent, claiming that a product will perform certain functions when in fact it cannot is misrepresenting the product. Likewise, salespersons who fail to disclose the negative aspects of a product when they know all along about such weaknesses would be subject to prosecution.

Related to this area is a heading in the April 14, 2003 at Msn.com, "Does Pfc. Jessica Lynch Own the Movie Rights to Her Life?" Jessica Lynch is the rescued American POW during the Iraqi war in 2003. NBC is planning to make a movie about her life. In one respect, legal sources suggest that facts about particular people are not exclusively owned by anyone and copyright law (explained later) only protects creative expression, not facts. Yet, the so-called "disclosure of private facts" tort or right of privacy allows people to block publication of certain intimate facts about their life. Ms. Lynch might be able to sue if NBC gets certain facts wrong or if an error in the TV movie harms her reputation (Volokh 2003).

Web Site: Product or Service?

Opinions vary on the question of whether a Web site is a product or a service. One legal opinion suggests that if the software is sold off the shelf as a mass-marketed item, then it is a product. If the software is custom designed, then it is viewed as a service. According to the same legal source, software that is custom designed but affects a large number of customers could be treated as a product.

BOX 12-6
A fraud case in question

Some popular online services are using software to divert sales commissions that otherwise would be paid to small Web merchants by big sites such as Amazon.com and eToys. Critics call the software "parasite-ware." The sites that use the software, which is made by nearly 20 companies and used by dozens, say it is legal because their users agree to the diversion.

"It is painful when someone walks in and takes sales right from under me," said Shawn Collins, who runs a number of Web sites that feed customers to Amazon and other merchants. "I probably saw a drop-off of 30 percent in income for the past 6 months."

The diversion begins when consumers get free software from the Internet that helps them swap music or other files or find bargains online. As they install the software, they are asked whether they would also like to show support for the software maker by shopping through an affiliated Web site. These sites often give a percentage of each purchase back to the software maker as a commission.

What the consumers are not told clearly is that if they agree to participate, their computers may be electronically marked: Future purchases may appear as if they were transacted through the software maker's site even if they were not.

A successful affiliate Web site can make $60,000 a month from referrals, said Haiko de Poel Jr., chief executive of Abestweb, an online forum devoted to affiliate marketing, who has organized owners of sites to fight Morpheus and others using the diversionary software. Last week, Amazon cut off affiliate payments to Morpheus, one of the sites that employs the shopping software, said one online executive. Coldwater Creek, an online clothing store, has also blocked Morpheus.

SOURCE: Excerpted from Schwartz, John, and Tedeschi, Bob, "Software Diverts Online Commissions," *International Herald Tribune*, September 28–29, 2002, 16.

Uniform Commercial Code (UCC): a law drafted by the National Conference of Commissioners on Uniform State Laws, which governs commercial transactions.

The resolution of this issue is important for users and developers of Web sites. If a Web site is a *product*, the claimant does not have to prove that the Web site is negligent to hold the developer liable. Fortunately, the **Uniform Commercial Code (UCC)**—a federal law that defines the concepts of product law and contracts—allows the developer to limit liability for defective Web sites through a "disclaimer of warranties" (claiming in writing no liability before the sale) in the contract. Other than such an escape clause, the loss resulting from negligence falls on the developer as a cost of doing business.

If a Web site is a *service*, the contract law of the state in question applies rather than the UCC, and negligence principles should be used. Negligence is more difficult to prove because the plaintiff must show the aspect of the process that caused the defect and prove that failure to use sufficient care caused the defect.

Many legal experts want Web sites to be considered services in order to avoid the strict liability associated with products. For example, if a medical Web site mass-distributed to hospitals nationwide is classified as a product, then the product manufacturer may be liable without having to prove negligence. However, Web sites that require the user and the software behind the site to place an order or contact a patient most likely will be considered a service. A summary of these relationships is presented in Table 12-1.

Table 12-1
Web sites as a product or a service in litigation issues

PRODUCT	SERVICE
1. Off-the-shelf software.	1. Custom-designed software.
2. Mass-marketed software.	2. Negligence principles should be used.
3. Custom designed but affects a large number of customers.	3. Negligence cause of action more difficult for plaintiff to prove.
4. Proving negligence is unnecessary to hold developer liable.	4. For liability, law of the state applies rather than UCC.
5. UCC allows liability via disclaimer of warranties.	

Warranties

The Uniform Commercial Code (UCC) is the foundation of commercial contract law in all states except Louisiana. It contains provisions for computer contracts in the form of warranties. A **warranty** is an assurance made by the seller about the goods sold. An additional safeguard is the federal Magnuson-Moss Consumer Product Warranty Act, enacted in 1975, which clarifies the issues relating to warranty information disclosure requirements and regulates the limitation of implied warranties. Both the UCC and the warranty act identify the various types of warranties (express and implied) and serve as references for further information on the subject.

warranty: an assurance made by the seller about the goods sold.

There are two types of warranties. An **express warranty** is offered orally or in writing by the maker of the product and is usually part of the sale. The buyer purchases the goods in part because of a statement by the seller with respect to the quality, capacity, or some other characteristic of the package. An express warranty need not be a specific statement. It may be found in the seller's conduct.

express warranty: a warranty offered orally or in writing by the maker of the product.

An **implied warranty** arises automatically from the fact that a sale has been made and the assumption that the product will do what it is supposed to do. For example, a Web site should be fit for the ordinary purposes for which it is used. This implied warranty of *merchantability* indicates that the Web site should do what it is expected to do. The other aspect of implied warranty is one of *fitness*. A knowledge base should be fit for the particular use intended by the buyer. Violation of this warranty is probably not common among Web designers or software developers, although it might be more common among companies that do customized programming.

implied warranty: a warranty that arises automatically from the fact that a sale has been made and the assumption that the product will do what it is supposed to do.

Disclaimers and warranties are closely related. A **disclaimer** is evidence of the seller's intention to protect the business from unwanted liability. Many software packages are labeled "as is," meaning they are sold without warranty of any kind regarding performance or accuracy. Other disclaimers go so far as to state that neither the developer, retailer, nor anyone affiliated with the developer is liable for damages even if the developer has been forewarned of the possibility of such damages.

disclaimer: evidence of the seller's intention to protect the business from unwanted liability.

Even though disclaimers are clearly stated, their legal status is fuzzy. The main issue centers on whether the software in question is a product or a service. In either case, the courts are inclined to include warranty disclaimers for final judgment. Express warranty disclaimers are effective, provided they are conspicuously placed and in writing.

A Web customer can reasonably look toward warranties as protection if damage is caused through the use of a product purchased through a company's Web site. Showing a reason why a warranty exclusion should not be accepted is difficult. In fact, two states have enacted *shrink-wrap* laws, which hold that all warranties made or disclaimed on the license found inside the shrink-wrapping are legal and final. Cases involving warranties also require that the user shows who is at fault and why, which is a difficult task.

Strict Liability

Tort theory is based on several issues including the assumption that the producer of a product is in the position to reduce risks and insure against injuries that could result. As with warranties, a software package must be considered a product for the tort theory of strict liability to apply. If this criterion is met, developers, manufacturers, and distributors could all be held liable for injuries even though reasonable care standards have been satisfied. For example, even though no errors are found in a Web site, the Web designer still could be held liable under the tort theory of strict liability should damages or losses result from the use of the Web site. Imposition of this theory protects the Web visitor regardless of whether anyone is at fault, in a strict sense. The major legal issues are summarized in Box 12-7.

out-of-bounds error: an error that occurs because either the software did not have the expertise to address the particular problem or the designer improperly condensed the technology.

The Designer's Liability

In Web design or software development, the designer is often responsible for system accuracy and reliability. A variety of errors may become embedded in the system: Some are nontrivial and others are out-of-bounds errors. An **out-of-bounds error** is one that occurs

BOX 12-7
Legal issues of Web design

1. Web designers own their knowledge of the work if no prior agreement was established.
2. A preemployment contract or intellectual property agreement can limit the Web designer's liability for the Web site.
3. If a Web designer builds the Web site and a problem arises with the site, the Web designer is subject to charges of personal liability under the doctrine of *respondent superior*. If the Web designer is an employee of an organization, the organization also is involved in the negligence action.
4. If a Web site is a product, proving negligence is unnecessary to hold the developer liable. The UCC allows developers to limit liability for defective work via a disclaimer of warranties in the contract. For these liabilities, the loss falls on the developer, regardless of fault, as a cost of doing business.
5. If a Web site is a service, the contract law of the state applies, rather than the UCC.
6. Courts tend to be reluctant to exclude warranty disclaimers or attempts by the software house *to avoid their applications as unconscionable (corrupt).*
7. Cases involving warranties require that the user show who is at fault and why.
8. The software in question should be considered a product under UCC rules for warranties to be relevant or for the tort theory of strict liability to apply.

nontrivial error: an error that triggers other areas in the software to malfunction and is difficult to correct.

because either the software did not have the expertise to address the particular problem or the designer improperly condensed the technology. A **nontrivial error** is one that triggers other areas in the software to malfunction and is difficult to correct. This type of error has a large financial impact on the e-business, especially if the product is mass marketed. The consequence is decommissioning the system or facing litigation.

Because designers rely on their experience to develop the product or software, when a malfunction occurs, designers are vulnerable to charges of personal liability under the doctrine of *respondent superior* (an employer-employee relationship). If the designer is an employee of the organization that sells the software, the employing company is involved in the negligence action. In the end, the company is responsible for certifying the system before it is released for public use.

The User's Liability

Even end users of the product are not immune from lawsuits. They are directly responsible for proper use of the product. Users' ability to refuse to comply with the product directions will increasingly come into question. By not properly utilizing an available resource, users could be negligent by omission (what is called *passive negligence*). For example, the use of an intelligent system in medical diagnosis could place the responsibility for utilizing the system on the user as an *affirmative duty*.

Copyrights, Trademarks, and Trade Names

intellectual property: includes software, books, music, videos, trademarks, copyrights, and Web pages.

copyright: ownership of an original work created by an author.

copyright law: a law that gives the author or creator of a tangible product the right to exclude others from using the finished work.

The area of Internet copyright and trademark violations falls under intellectual property law. **Intellectual property** includes software, books, music, videos, trademarks, copyrights, and Web pages. Controversy is growing over who owns the intellectual property of domain names, programming, and Web sites. Even the HTML coding of the Web site is in question.

Copyright is ownership of an original work created by an author. It is a form of intellectual property protection that covers the look, feel, and content of printed media like articles and textbooks, as well as software programs and software packages. **Copyright law** gives the author or creator of a *tangible* product the right to prevent others from using the finished work. That is why authors and publishers place a copyright notice on the back of the title page. Copyright protection applies immediately upon creation of the manuscript.

Several kinds of works are protected—literary, musical, dramatic, pictorial, graphic, and sculptural works; Web sites; sound recordings; and architectural works. Computer programs and most compilations can be registered as literary works. Several categories of material are not eligible for copyright protection. For example, works consisting entirely of information considered common property and containing no original authorship are not copyrighted. Familiar symbols or designs, or mere listings of ingredients or contents are also not copyrighted.

A copyright is good for the life of its author plus an additional 70 years after the author's death. In the case of a joint authorship, the term lasts for 70 years after the last surviving author's death. Specific conditions and laws also protect people from copying someone else's work without permission. For example, a writer can quote up to 250 words without permission, provided recognition is given to the author of the quoted work. The same procedure applies to copying material on other people's Web pages. Beyond that, users need permission from the copyright holder to quote or to copy. A magazine that once copied only 300 words of ex-President Gerald Ford's 200,000-word autobiography was found guilty of copyright violation.

The Digital Millennium Copyright Act (DMCA) approved by Congress in 1998 extends copyright law to digital content. As explained in Box 12-8, it is intended to protect "the technological locks that content owners can put on any type of copyrighted content to prevent circumvention" (Thibodeau 2002).

In information technology, a database or a directory and the way it is organized are considered a compilation and are copyrightable. A compilation's copyright protects all components within it. An original compilation of names and addresses that are now in public domain is also copyrightable. The same applies for logos and trademarks. Copyright protection on the Internet has its own set of limitations. By international agreement, only an expression can be copyrighted, but not facts. The biggest problem on the Web is not the text content, but images and programs. Because JPEG images are so easy to download, cut, and paste on any Web page, images are not easy to protect.

BOX 12-8
DMCA

It wasn't until PCs were in wide use that Congress acted in a broad way to extend copyright protections to the digital domain. President Clinton signed the DMCA in October 1998. The law has many critics and challengers, who say it impinges on the right of consumers to copy content and creates a predicament for scientists conducting certain kinds of security research.

The Digital Millennium Copyright Act (DMCA) has survived one important test. The Motion Picture Association of America (MPAA) sued Eric Corely, the publisher of *2600: The Hacker Quarterly*, when the magazine sought to post De-Content Scrambling System code that circumvented DVD anticopying technology, arguing that First Amendment protection applied. New York District Judge Lewis Kaplan found for the MPAA. For now, at least, the courts have resolved this clash in the DMCA's and plaintiffs' favor.

The key points of the DMCA are:

- Makes it a crime to circumvent antipiracy measures built into most commercial software.
- Outlaws the manufacture, sale, or distribution of code-cracking devices that copy software.
- Permits the cracking of copyright protection devices, when necessary to conduct encryption research, assess product interoperability, and test computer security systems.
- Limits ISPs from copyright infringement liability for simply transmitting information over the Internet. However, they are expected to remove material from users' Web sites that appears to constitute copyright infringement.
- Requires webcasters to pay licensing fees to record companies.
- States explicitly that nothing in this section shall affect rights, remedies, limitations of defenses to copyright infringement, including fair use.

SOURCE: Thibodeau, Patrick, "DMCA," *Computerworld*, December 2, 2002, 41.

trademark: registration of a company's trade name so that others cannot use it; a word or a symbol that distinguishes a good from other goods in the market.

A word, a picture, or an image that identifies a product or service is intellectual property and is protected by a **trademark.** The term means "registration of a company's trade name so that others cannot use it." It is also a word or a symbol that distinguishes a good from other goods in the market. As shown in Screen 12-2, "For Dummies" is a trademarked name, "IDG Books" is a trademarked logo, and the icon on the left is a trademarked symbol of the same firm.

Trademark liability is well known among most firms. ISPs receive immunity from defamation and other tort claims committed on their hosted sites through the Federal Communications Decency Act (CDA). However, this protection does not include trademark infringement. When it comes to litigation, suing ISPs for trademark infringement is a tricky route to take. Take the case of fashion company Gucci's American subsidiary suing Hall & Associates, the owners of www.goldhaus.com, claiming that the online jewelry retailer infringed on Gucci's registered trademark. According to court documents, Gucci America twice warned Mindspring, the Atlanta-based ISP, that Hall & Associate's www.goldhaus.com was using Gucci trademarks illegally. Mindspring asserted that it was not liable for its client's infringement, because it is immune by the CDA. The court denied Mindspring's defense, because it found that the ISP contributed to trademark infringement by knowingly keeping the client on board (Prencipe 2001).

Who owns a trademark (or a copyright) is often a contractual matter. Trademark protection is a maze of federal and state laws that have to be reviewed carefully before securing protection. Some trademarks might be registered in one state but not in others, and some states have individual laws covering trademarks. An example of the difference between a copyright and a trademark is shown in Box 12-9.

Screen Capture 12-2
Trademarks

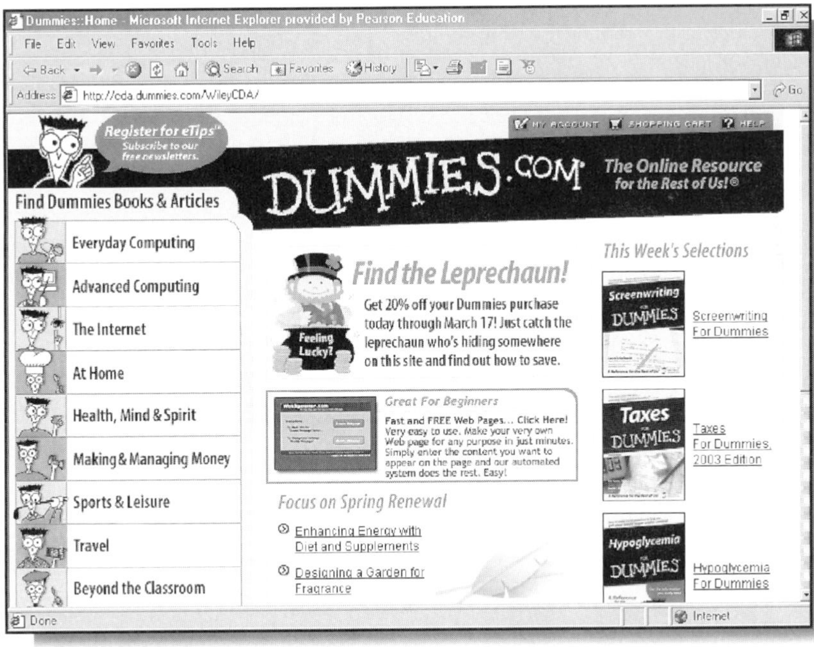

BOX 12-9
An example of copyright and trademark language

Welcome to Amazon.com. Amazon.com and its affiliates provide their services to you subject to the following notices, terms, and conditions. In addition, when you use any Amazon.com service (e.g., Friends & Favorites, e-Cards and Auctions), you will be subject to the rules, guidelines, policies, terms, and conditions applicable to such service.

COPYRIGHT

All content included on this site, such as text, graphics, logos, button icons, images, audio clips, and software, is the property of Amazon.com or its content suppliers and protected by U.S. and international copyright laws. The compilation (meaning the collection, arrangement, and assembly) of all content on this site is the exclusive property of Amazon.com and protected by U.S. and international copyright laws. All software used on this site is the property of Amazon.com or its software suppliers and protected by U.S. and international copyright laws. The content and software on this site may be used as a shopping, selling, and e-card resource. Any other use, including the reproduction, modification, distribution, transmission, republication, display, or performance, of the content on this site is strictly prohibited.

TRADEMARKS

AMAZON.COM; AMAZON.COM BOOKS; EARTH'S BIGGEST BOOKSTORE; IF IT'S IN PRINT, IT'S IN STOCK; and 1-CLICK are registered trademarks of Amazon.com, Inc., in the United States and other countries. PURCHASE CIRCLES, SHOP THE WEB, ONE-CLICK SHOPPING, AMAZON.COM ASSOCIATES, AMAZON.COM MUSIC, AMAZON.COM VIDEO, AMAZON.COM TOYS, AMAZON.COM ELECTRONICS, AMAZON.COM e-CARDS, AMAZON._COM AUCTIONS, zSHOPS, CUSTOMER BUZZ, AMAZON.CO.UK, AMAZON.DE, BID-CLICK, GIFT-CLICK, AMAZON.COM ANYWHERE, AMAZON.COM OUTLET, BACK TO BASICS, BACK TO BASICS TOYS, NEW FOR YOU, and other Amazon.com graphics, logos, and service names are trademarks of Amazon.com, Inc. Amazon.com's trademarks may not be used in connection with any product or service that is not Amazon.com's, in any manner that is likely to cause confusion among customers, or in any manner that disparages or discredits Amazon.com. All other trademarks not owned by Amazon.com or its affiliates that appear on this site are the property of their respective owners, who may or may not be affiliated with, connected to, or sponsored by Amazon.com or its affiliates.

USE OF SITE

This site or any portion of this site may not be reproduced, duplicated, copied, sold, resold, or otherwise exploited for any commercial purpose that is not expressly permitted by Amazon.com. Amazon.com and its affiliates reserve the right to refuse service, terminate accounts, and/or cancel orders in its discretion, including, without limitation, if Amazon.com believes that customer conduct violates applicable law or is harmful to the interests of Amazon.com and its affiliates.

COPYRIGHT COMPLAINTS

Amazon.com and its affiliates respect the intellectual property of others. If you believe that your work has been copied in a way that constitutes copyright infringement, please follow our Notice and Procedure for Making Claims of Copyright Infringement.

DISCLAIMER

THIS SITE IS PROVIDED BY AMAZON.COM ON AN "AS IS" BASIS. AMAZON.COM MAKES NO REPRESENTATIONS OR WARRANTIES OF ANY KIND, EXPRESS OR IMPLIED, AS TO THE OPERATION OF THE SITE OR THE INFORMATION, CONTENT, MATERIALS, OR PRODUCTS INCLUDED

(*continued*)

BOX 12-9
Continued

ON THIS SITE. TO THE FULL EXTENT PERMISSIBLE BY APPLICABLE LAW, AMAZON.COM DISCLAIMS ALL WARRANTIES, EXPRESS OR IMPLIED, INCLUDING, BUT NOT LIMITED TO, IMPLIED WARRANTIES OF MERCHANTABILITY AND FITNESS FOR A PARTICULAR PURPOSE. AMAZON.COM WILL NOT BE LIABLE FOR ANY DAMAGES OF ANY KIND ARISING FROM THE USE OF THIS SITE, INCLUDING, BUT NOT LIMITED TO DIRECT, INDIRECT, INCIDENTAL, PUNITIVE, AND CONSEQUENTIAL DAMAGES.

If a company hires an outside firm to develop its Web site, the contract should clearly give the company all intellectual property rights. The Web designer's contract is a "work made for hire." If the design is done in-house, the employment contract also should make clear that any creative work performed by employees belongs to the company. For a $30 fee, anyone can copyright their work with the Library of Congress. Its Web site address is www.loc.gov/copyright (see Screen 12-3).

Taxation Issues

One of the most controversial issues facing e-commerce and global tax authorities is taxation, especially sales tax. In every state, a business enterprise is required to pay taxes and collect taxes. In brick-and-mortar businesses, computers or electronic machines compute

Screen Capture 12-3
Library of Congress copyright Web site

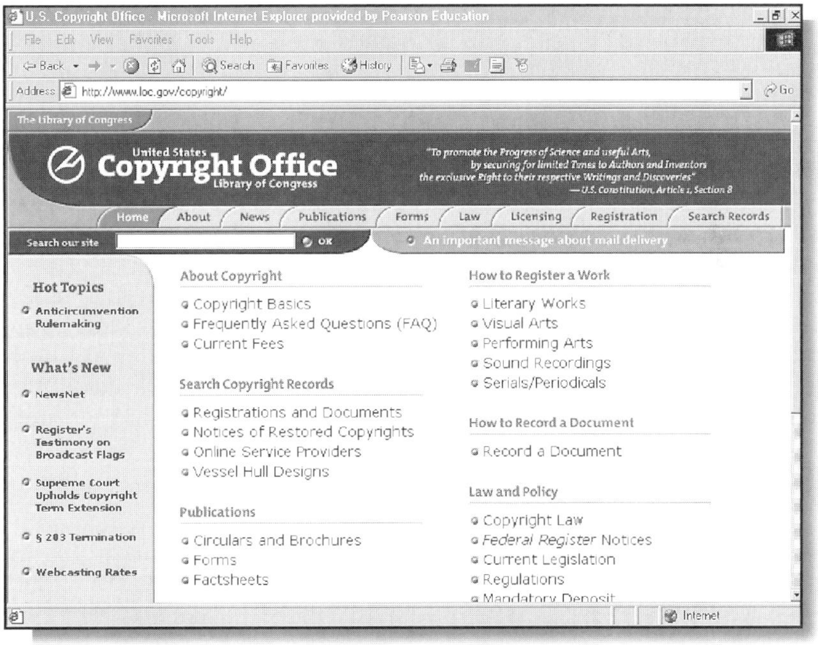

and account for taxes to comply with local, state, and federal tax laws. On the Internet, tax collection is not so easy. What is collected depends on the location of the e-merchant's business, the location of the buyer, the types of goods for sale, and so on. Each state and county has different sales taxes and different jurisdictions. The rules for taxation also differ by country.

To make the problem worse, quantifying the lost tax dollars has been difficult. States have had trouble collecting sales tax even for off-line purchases. If tax authorities are struggling with these tax issues, how will they deal with taxation via M-commerce? All indicators suggest that sales-tax revenue loss is projected to increase exponentially unless something is done to collect it. According to one source, the largest portion of the $51 billion online sales for 2003 is expected to go to major Internet-only retailers such as Amazon.com and Dell Computer that have shown little interest to collect sales taxes (Tedeschi 2003).

A survey of 8,900 online shoppers by Forrester Research reported that 33 percent of online shoppers don't care about Internet taxes. To them, shipping cost is more important. If the government passed a universal tax on Internet purchases, 33 percent of the respondents reported, "I would not change my online purchasing," and 32 percent replied, "I would significantly reduce online purchasing" (Mowrey 2000).

Internet Tax Freedom Act

To date, the most important bill passed by the U.S. Congress regarding Internet taxation is the Internet Tax Freedom Act (ITFA), written into law on October 21, 1998. The act established the following.

- A 3-year moratorium on special, multiple, or discriminatory taxes on the Internet that would be imposed by any state or local governments. Any goods or services sold over the Internet cannot be subject to new or special taxes that apply exclusively to Internet transactions.
- An advisory committee was created by Congress to explore different issues relating to Internet taxes. The role of the commission is to explore various issues regarding government Internet policy and its effects on e-commerce.
- The federal government is barred from taxing the Internet or any transaction that takes place through it.

Despite all this, many issues remain unsolved. For example, what would be taxed? Who would set a tax rate? Who would collect any taxes from the Internet? Would the collected taxes end up being used by local governments to compensate for lost sales tax? Who would regulate the system, and how would such a regulatory agency do so? How will a tax affect the profitability of e-commerce? Would such a tax affect consumers' purchasing habits on the Internet?

In April 2000, the advisory commission sent a formal report to Congress and recommended a moratorium, barring special or discriminatory Internet taxes for another 5 years (till 2006). The Internet Nondiscrimination Act of 2000, passed in May 2000 by the U.S. House of Representatives, extended the Internet tax moratorium set forth in the IFTA for 5 years. The commission also recommended permanently banning taxes charged on Internet access.

Legal Disputes on the Internet

In B2C, several kinds of disputes have legal implications.

1. The customer pays for the merchandise, but the e-merchant fails to deliver.
2. The customer pays in full but receives either the wrong merchandise or a partial order.

3. The customer does not like the product, but the e-merchant has no procedure for accepting returned merchandise.
4. The customer does not like the product, but the e-merchant refuses to accept returned merchandise or give credit to settle the dispute.
5. The e-merchant delivers, but the customer does not admit that he or she ever received the merchandise.
6. The e-merchant delivers, but the customer refuses to pay. The customer's 14 year old ordered the product using a parent's VISA card without authorization.
7. The customer receives the merchandise, but it arrives damaged. The carrier denies responsibility, the e-merchant claims it is the carrier's responsibility, and the vendor is located overseas with no customer service number.
8. The customer receives the merchandise, but it does not operate properly. The e-merchant asks the customer to ship the product to the manufacturer at the customer's expense. The manufacturer has no in-house service center.

In terms of recourse, a lot depends on the laws protecting buyers in the state in which they reside. It also depends on where the e-merchant operates. Legal costs often exceed the value of the contested merchandise, which leaves the customer with no choice but to abandon the product. Where the Web server or the business is located determines the rights of the customer to recover. Unfortunately, it is not always clear where the server is located, especially when the e-merchant has multiple Web servers in different countries. What makes the situation more difficult is the fact that no legal restrictions apply regarding where the top-level domain (e.g., ".uk") can be used and where it cannot be used. About the only thing that counts is the country where the e-merchant is located. That location determines the jurisdiction on the Internet.

One legal issue that has surfaced relates to products that are available in one country but are restricted in the country from which the customer is ordering. For example, Amazon.com was criticized by Germany's Simon Wiesenthal Center for selling books like *Mein Kampf,* which are banned in Germany. Although Amazon.com's German subsidiary does not offer these books on its Web site, the U.S. Web site does. If the product is confiscated in Germany, what recourse does the customer have to recover the product?

jurisdiction: the legitimate scope of government power.

This matter boils down to the legal issue of **jurisdiction,** or the legitimate scope of government power. A court must have jurisdiction over the litigants and the claims before it entertains a lawsuit. In the context of Internet commerce, this issue erupts when a dispute arises between businesses from different states. For example, is a customer in Chicago required to travel to California to defend against a firm that is suing him for breaking a sales agreement? Except in criminal cases, state and federal laws limit a court's jurisdiction over a defendant from another state. This means that e-commerce and ensuring security and integrity in e-business are still clouded by such legal issues.

Related to the issue of jurisdiction at the international level, in a landmark defamation decision for defamation law, Australia's high court in 2002 ruled that a Melbourne businessman can sue a U.S. publishing company (Dow-Jones & Co.) in Australia over an article published in the United States and distributed on the Internet (Rose 2002). According to legal experts, the decision could have wide-ranging implications for how information is disseminated on the Internet.

The final legal dispute relates to bots. Are bots legal? A shopbot is a software package that roams the various Web sites, accesses information related to a specific product, and produces the location of the seller or store that will sell the product at the lowest price.

The legality of the practice depends on the way one looks at the process. On the one hand, a Web site should be open to all surfers—customers and competitors, like a general brick-and-mortar store. On the other hand, how much business is this practice taking away from the Web sites visited? See Box 12-10.

Web Linking and Domain Name Disputes

hyperlink: text or image whose address can be linked to another Web page for reference.

The infrastructure of the Internet is designed around **hyperlinks**—text or image whose address can be linked to another Web page for reference. When you click on the link, it automatically goes to the attached location and the designated Web page. This jumping from one site to another raises legal issues that include the following points.

1. Referencing a linked site without permission from the site owner.
2. Retrieving or downloading information from a linked site without referencing or permission.
3. Unauthorized use of a company's registered trademarks.
4. Adding a Web program to a company's Web site without permission.

BOX 12-10
Bot practice

For a fee, Bargain Networks Inc. lets subscribers search its site for the lowest price on all sorts of merchandise, from cars and electronics to Pez dispensers. But how it gets those prices has put it on the front lines of an Internet legal war.

Automated search robots—known as bots, crawlers, spiders, or scrapers—to hundreds of online retailers and auctioneers are deployed so the best deal is just a click away for online shoppers. Some Web sites object to the practice, arguing that such unauthorized harvesting of data is effectively trespassing on their sites. To protect their turf, the sites being visited by bots are employing a legal doctrine dating back to the Middle Ages known as "trespass to chattels" and a law passed in the mid-1980s designed to prevent hackers from gaining access to government and corporate computer systems.

Online auction and other Internet businesses say bots cause them a host of harms, from draining their system capacity to undermining business partnerships that depend on strong brand recognition and enticing consumers to spend time rummaging around their sites. Moreover, they say, bots steal business from them by misleading and confusing customers. For the bot-using companies and their legal allies, however, restricting the use of search bots unfairly blocks competition by exerting monopolistic control over information that wouldn't ordinarily be subject to copyright protection.

Some legal experts say the court rulings favoring Web sites with no-trespassing protocols go too far and threaten the core principles of the Internet: If information is available to any surfer with a browser, the experts say, it should be available to companies using automated search robots to harvest information. The law shouldn't say a Web retailer can put up a sign on its homepage saying only people interested in buying products can visit, and competitors can't, just as we don't allow the owner of a store in a mall to forbid competitors to walk in and notice their prices.

SOURCE: Excerpted from Plitch, Phyllis, "Are Bots Legal?" *The Wall Street Journal*, September 16, 2002, R13.

Inappropriately referencing a Web site is not a clear-cut issue; it depends on the intent of the referencing. For example, one bank's Web site advertised online automobile loans. When a visitor entered the amount she would like to borrow (in this case, it was $47,000 for a Mercedes), the Web site asked her to click on the referral button, giving the impression that her application would get special attention. She ended up on the Web site of a large bank in another state that specializes in jumbo auto loans. The visitor was unhappy about this runaround and promptly clicked away from both sites.

One New Jersey bank Web site had this note on its homepage: "Want to compute your mortgage rate on a house? Click here." The software package that did the mortgage calculation was registered to a Chicago bank. The networking algorithm detected unauthorized use of the package by the New Jersey bank Web site and promptly sued for damages. The case was settled out of court, and the New Jersey bank had to delete the referral to the mortgage calculator.

Domain name disputes have existed since business hit the Internet. In 1992, the U.S. government contracted with Network Solutions, Inc. (NSI), which also goes by the name InterNIC, to manage the top-level domains. Initially, domain names were assigned on a first-come, first-served basis, but this caused companies and individuals to register domain names for which they had no use and hold them for future sale at exorbitant prices. Since 1995, the policy has changed so that domain names are still issued on a first-come, first-served basis, but applicants are reminded in writing that such issuance does not duplicate or replace the legal right of another party, such as one with a registered trademark, to use the name.

The low-cost registration fee of $70 for 2 years of registration has caused several individuals to register and hold known names hostage for big money. One poacher registered for 200 domain names, including his former employer's, but he kept losing cases filed against him by firms defending their right to use their trademark name. The general rule to resolve domain name disputes is to compare the date the claimant of a dispute first used a trademark or the effective date of a validated trademark registration. If the registered holder appears to have infringed on the registered trademark owner, then NSI assigns the registered holder a new domain name. The court is the only other avenue for seeking relief (see Box 12-11).

Here are some guidelines regarding domain names and trademarks.

1. Find out whether the proposed domain name infringes on any trademarks. The fact that someone registers for a domain name does not in itself give the owner the legal right to use it.
2. Secure federal trademark registration of the proposed domain name. Once the name clears against possible claims of infringement, it should be registered as a trademark with the U.S. Patent and Trademark Office.
3. Register the proposed domain name with InterNIC (Internet Network Information Center), the agency that represents the U.S. government in assigning domain names.
4. In the event of a poached domain name, bring a lawsuit to force InterNIC to reassign the name to the original owner—the owner of the same name or trademark.
5. Get permission before linking to other Web sites.

Encryption Laws

Encryption is not a pleasant word to use in certain countries. Some Middle Eastern countries, for example, prohibit any form of encryption for business or personal use within the country or across the border. Encryption poses a threat to the powers of many governments, but because of the impressive surge of traffic on the Internet, awareness of security has increased

BOX 12-11
The cost of poaching

In what is thought to be the first ruling on a potent provision of recently signed cybersquatting legislation, a U.S. judge has empowered Bell Atlantic Corp. to take possession of nearly 2 dozen Internet addresses. Under the ruling, verbally issued by a magistrate judge, Bell Atlantic can transfer the actual registered domain names, said Sarah Deutsch, chief intellectual property counsel for Bell Atlantic.

In entering his order, the judge relied on the Anticybersquatting Consumer Protection Act, which gives trademark owners a powerful weapon to combat cybersquatters, those who register various permutations of company names with "bad faith intent." Key to the New York telephone company's case was a provision that explicitly allows trademark owners to take legal action directly against domain name holders, without the necessity of hauling each alleged transgressor into court.

Trademark owners have praised the legislation, but critics worry that it goes too far and may end up snaring Internet entrepreneurs and others who innocently register names similar to a trademark. Individuals whose last name happens to resemble a corporate moniker, for example, are concerned they will be dragged into court and forced to pay a huge fine for registering an address with their own last name.

SOURCE: Adapted from Plitch, Phyllis, "Court Order Lets Bell Atlantic Wrest Domain Names From Cybersquatter," Dow Jones & Company, February 2, 2000, 1.

significantly within governments worldwide. In 1999, France abandoned its policy of disallowing encryption for message transmission. A summary of select countries and their encryption regulations is presented in Table 12-2.

Cryptography has had its share of attention over the past decade. Among the issues are these: What can be exported and what cannot be exported? How safe is the computer from Internet crime? In the United States, there tends to be a difference of opinion on encryption between federal agencies like the FBI and big business. Secure electronic payments require

Table 12-2
Select countries and their encryption requirements

Country	Encryption Use	Encryption Export
Australia	No restrictions	Qualified restrictions
China	Prohibited	No known exports
European Union (EU) countries	No restrictions	None
India	No restrictions	None
Israel	License required	Qualified restrictions
Japan	No restrictions	License required
Russia	License required	No restrictions
Singapore	No restrictions	No restrictions
South Korea	Prohibited	Prohibited
United States	No restrictions	None for software less than 56-bit

Source: Adapted from Amor, Daniel, *The E-business ® Evolution*, Upper Saddle River, NJ: Prentice Hall, 2000, 126.

secure lines. The belief is that encryption makes lines more secure. In 1997, the FBI made a strong pitch before a U.S. Senate panel on the need for stricter control over digital encryption products. Cases have already come up in which criminals and terrorists have relied on encryption to evade the law. The debate continues with no definitive end in sight.

INTERNATIONAL ISSUES

With the Internet cutting across countries around the globe, a number of international questions have arisen recently regarding controls of Web site contents and e-commerce in general. Two major questions come up when reviewing the international scene: What right does any one country have to determine the materials that should be available on the Internet? Can a country regulate an entity in cyberspace, but not on the soil of that country?

To address these questions, let's take the issue between France and Yahoo! Yahoo!'s legal counsel believes that because Yahoo! is a U.S. company, subject to regulation by the United States, it would violate domestic freedom of speech laws if the company were to block French users from accessing these materials. To extrapolate on Yahoo!'s position, it seems that if a French citizen could come to the United States to purchase contraband that is illegal in France, then that same citizen should be able to buy it over the Internet. Assuming that buying over the Internet is analogous to buying in person, it would be up to France to regulate which physical objects enter its borders. This idea would hold, regardless of where the goods originated.

As predicted, the issue between France, Yahoo!, and the United States is not that simple. Yahoo! seems to be skipping the crucial second question—where the transaction takes place. Yahoo! is assuming that the transaction must be taking place in the United States—a position that is not necessarily the case. Yahoo! wants the United States to step in and apply its laws to protect the company from international regulation, but it does not attempt to determine where the electronic transaction takes place. Without this information, it is impossible to apply an appropriate law based on current trade agreements or treaties with France. Nothing applies until the jurisdiction is determined.

A similar problem faced the German high courts, but it was dealt with on a domestic level. Germany prohibits certain material from being viewed on the Internet, and ruled that German ISPs were not to host any Web sites that published "restricted materials." Any German ISP that did not comply would be subject to prosecution. One can conclude that because no existing international laws apply to Internet commerce, legislation is best left up to individual countries and their ISPs.

Another important issue relates to the different laws in many countries. In an uncertain legal climate surrounding e-commerce, an online business often opts to let go of some customers in certain countries over leaving them vulnerable to possible libel or product liabilities in those countries. Years of litigation have failed to establish international legal standards to protect the rights of sellers and buyers on the Internet and prevent unauthorized copying of software or digitized products. Many online merchants today refuse to sell beyond their immediate home countries.

A summary of some of the major international rules—passed or pending—that relate to the Internet include:

- The World Intellectual Property Organization (WIPO). This organization succeeded in two treaties to adapt copyright rules for e-commerce. Not only do they cover physical copies and broadcasting, but books, songs, and films distributed online as well. Forty-one countries also committed to outlawing cyber-piracy of CDs and DVDs, hacking into online music and film subscription services. The ratification went into effect in 2002. See wipo.int/treaties/ip/wct/index.html and wipo.int/treaties/ip/wppt/index.html.

- The European Union's Electronic Commerce Directive gave online business firms assurance in 2000 that they would have to comply with laws only where they are based, not in any other country in the Union.
- The Digital Millennium Copyright Act of 1998 adapted U.S. legislation to the WIPO treaties. See copyright.gov/legislation/dmca.pdf.
- The European Union's Rome II Directive is hoped to allow consumers to sue e-businesses in their home country. Online business firms are concerned they will have to comply with 15 different laws on product liability and defamation.
- Hague Convention on International Jurisdiction and Foreign Judgments in Civil and Commercial Matters—a draft treaty in 1992 designed to set global standards for defamation, copyright, and libel on the Internet. The idea is that if one wins a judgment in one country, it will be enforced in other countries. An accord is sought after in 2004 (Newman 2003).

MANAGEMENT IMPLICATIONS

One conclusion from our discussion of legal and ethical issues is that the legal rules that define the Internet are yet to be clarified. The questions that constantly come up before various technical, academic, and government groups dealing with cyberspace are these: What rules should be instituted to govern the Internet? Who will make and enforce those rules? What shape should copyright protection take in the Web—a world of costless, instantaneous, and undetectable copying?

Communication networks are essentially defined by a set of rules—the network protocols that specify the characteristics of the messages to be transmitted, the medium through which they can travel, and how the messages are routed through the medium to their destination. Because the Internet is a set of relationships among networks, network protocols may be viewed as part of the "law of cyberspace."

Keep in mind that the Internet is not a physical object, but a set of protocols that has been adopted by a large number of networks to make the transfer of information among them possible. Physical location and physical boundaries are irrelevant, which means that the legal implications will continue to be a problem. Each country has to police its own portion of the Internet traffic and use its jurisdiction to enforce its laws.

Another area of concern is the long-range effect of Internet patents, especially those held by e-companies like Amazon.com that cover fundamental online business practices. Patents have become something that no company can comfortably ignore. For example, a federal judge's preliminary injunction in 1999 barred BarnesandNoble.com from using a one-click order-capturing system considered too similar to that of Amazon. These patents are bound to put companies at a significant competitive disadvantage.

So far, e-commerce has forced companies to differentiate themselves on the basis of what is unique and unavailable to competitors—knowledge, business methods, and the skills to implement the methods. A company's competitive advantage no longer stems from its market position, but from difficult-to-duplicate intellectual assets and how it deploys them. Take the example of Dell Computer. Its success comes not so much from the technological superiority of its products (most of its computer components are off-the-shelf components), but from its build-to-order, direct sale approach. To protect this advantage, Dell secured 42 patents that cover its customer ordering system as well as its business methods (Rivette 1999, p. 181).

Regardless of laws that might ensure integrity and protection for consumers and merchants, the ultimate goal in doing business on the Internet is to promote standards that everyone can accept or adopt. Those who do business on the Internet have a responsibility to monitor their employees' behavior and the traffic that their Web site generates to ensure a stable, lasting, and satisfactory relationship with clients, vendors, visitors, and distributors. Without such a commitment, the business could easily fail.

Finally, management must focus on legal and consumer protection issues surrounding B2C e-commerce. Ethics may be tangential to running a business, but lack of ethics could mean serious erosion of the company's customer base. That very problem sealed Value America's fate: It went bankrupt. In addition, ethics means different things in different countries. Companies need to develop a code of ethics tailored to each country or region in which they operate.

Finally, the privacy issue continues to haunt the e-consumer. With Web sites amassing vast amounts of information about their visitors, pressure is mounting for new laws. As Congress considers the legal route, new software, designed to give consumers control over how much protection they want from the e-merchant, is appearing. The stakes are high. Information about consumer activities has become necessary for the survival of the e-merchant. Yet, there is a consumer outcry about invasion of privacy. In a 2001 online survey about Internet privacy among 2,365 adults nationwide, almost two thirds said they were "very concerned" or "somewhat concerned" about threats to their personal privacy on the Internet. More than 60 percent have learned how to deactivate cookies to combat threats to privacy (Simpson 2001, p. B1).

Microsoft is working on a software package named Privacy for Protection Preferences (P3P) that lets consumers decide how much protection they want. When visitors look up a Web site, their Web browsers automatically load the P3P-encoded privacy policy and compare it with the visitor's preferences. If the site does not match, the browser blocks the transmission of personal information. As a result, the visitor may not have access to certain features offered by the e-merchant's Web site. On the surface, P3P functions only if the Web site makes its privacy policy *talk* in P3P's special language. It could be some time before either new laws or reliable software can address the sensitive issue of the consumer's right to privacy.

On the wireless end, the privacy of consumer location data is a key issue facing banks, airlines, and retailers as they send advertising to wireless users. The sanctity of location data is a business's responsibility, especially for wireless carriers. In the final analysis, consumers should be given an option to start services and to stop them (Hamblen 2000, p. 46).

SUMMARY

1. Legal and ethical implications of the Internet are attracting attention in industries and governments around the world. Taxation and sales tax are hot issues. Legal disputes and case law are beginning to surface quickly.
2. The question of ethics in e-commerce is the current challenge confronting U.S. organizations. Ethics is fairness, justice, equity, honesty, trustworthiness, and equality. An unethical act is not the same as an immoral or an illegal act, although one may lead to or imply the other.
3. There are several threats to ethics: faster computers and advanced networks, massive distributed databases, ease of access to information, transparency of software, and the view that captured information can be used as a competitive weapon.
4. Privacy is a basic American value. To formalize what constitutes privacy, five widely recognized principles of privacy protection are worth remembering: notice, choice, access, security/integrity, and enforcement. There are three categories of

concern: collection of electronic data by businesses about consumers, security of electronic data transmission, and unauthorized reading of personal files.

5. Many of the legal questions that arise in e-commerce are not settled due to lack of specific laws or legal guidelines. Situations involving products that produce the wrong solution, causing injury to others, fall under laws of strict liability or negligence. The basis of liability involves product liability and tort law. If an e-merchant advertises false or wrong products or a customer gives an unauthorized credit card over the Internet, he or she is liable for fraud. Fraud, negligence, false advertising, and misrepresentation are bases for litigation.
6. Internet copyright and trademark violations fall under intellectual property law. Copyright law gives the author of a tangible product the right to exclude others from using the finished work.
7. The question of whether a Web site is a product or a service elicits varied opinions. If a Web site is a product, proving negligence is unnecessary to hold the developer liable. If a Web site is a service, the contract law of the state in question would apply.
8. On the Internet, tax collection is not easy, depending on the location of the e-merchant's business, the location of the buyer, the types of goods for sale, and so on. Those who support taxing Internet commerce include many state officials who are concerned that taxing online shopping could put online merchants at a disadvantage.
9. Regardless of the laws that might assure integrity and protection for consumers and merchants, the ultimate goal of doing business on the Internet is to promote ethics through standards that everyone can accept or adopt. Management must focus on legal and consumer protection issues surrounding B2C e-commerce.

Key Terms

- code of ethics, 366
- copyright, 381
- copyright law, 381
- disclaimer, 379
- ethics, 365
- express warranty, 379
- false advertising, 377
- fraud, 376
- hyperlink, 388
- implied warranty, 379
- intellectual property, 381
- jurisdiction, 387
- misrepresentation, 377
- negligence, 376
- nontrivial error, 381
- out-of-bounds error, 380
- product liability, 376
- self-assessment, 371
- strict liability, 376
- tort, 376
- tort law, 376
- trademark, 383
- Uniform Commercial Code (UCC), 378
- warranty, 379

Test Your Understanding

1. Why are legal and ethical implications attracting attention around the world?
2. Give an example of an unethical act that is not necessary illegal.
3. Elaborate on some of the ethical issues surrounding the Internet. What single issue do you consider the most important? Why?
4. How can a company improve the climate for ethical behavior on the job?
5. The FTC identified five principles of privacy protection. Explain each briefly.
6. What is tort law on the Internet? What makes it so unique?
7. How is fraud different from misrepresentation? Be specific.
8. Distinguish between trademarks and copyrights.

9. What exactly is intellectual property law? Give an example.
10. Is a Web site a product or a service? Justify your answer.
11. Briefly explain the Uniform Commercial Code.
12. Give examples of your own of disputes on the Internet that have legal implications.

Discussion Questions

1. Why do you think companies adopt a code of ethics? Do they apply what they advertise?
2. The Internal Revenue Service acquires demographic data about tax-paying citizens in an effort to elicit relationships to their tax returns. In your opinion, is this effort an unethical act? An illegal act? An immoral act? Discuss.
3. Shoppers at a national retail chain are asked for their zip codes as part of the checkout process. This information is used to figure out the pattern of business coming from various regions in the community. As a result, the store decides on the products, prices, specials, and so on to maximize sales volume. Shoppers are not told why zip codes are solicited. Is the store's action ethical? How does it compare to the use of cookies in Web shopping?
4. E-commerce has generated much controversy regarding privacy. Why do you think this has happened?
5. Taxing Web shoppers has been a controversial subject for several years. Should Web shopping be taxed in the same way as brick-and-mortar shopping? Discuss this matter using recent evidence.

Web Exercises

1. An ongoing debate is taking place regarding taxing e-shoppers. Look up information on the Internet about the Internet Tax Freedom Act. Learn about it and write a report arguing against it.
2. Review the Medical Board of California Web site (www.medbd.ca.gov), where California reports data about doctors, disciplinary actions by hospitals, court cases and judgments against doctors, and so on. Do you think the information invades doctors' right to privacy? What about the consumer? Does the consumer have the right to learn about doctors' records before they commit their bodies for diagnosis, surgery, and so on?
3. Evaluate five Web sites of your choice. Review their respective privacy policies. What did you find common in all policies? What was unique in each policy? What important clauses were missing, if any?
4. Go to the Federal Trade Commission Web site (www.ftc.gov) or other Web sites and investigate types of scams on the Internet. Present your findings in class.
5. Visit the Cyberlaw Web site (www.cyberlaw.com) and learn about what you can and cannot represent on your Web site before you break the copyright law. Report your findings in class.
6. Go the Zelerate Web site (www.consumers.com). What services does this site offer? Write a two-page report.
7. Look up a Web site that explains how to prevent unsolicited e-mail. Summarize your findings for the class.

Chapter 13

Understanding E-Security

Contents

In a Nutshell

We have seen how e-commerce accommodates the increasing consumer appetite for online shopping and Internet trade using the World Wide Web as the enabler. The payment consummates a typical shopping spree, but the top considerations in a payment system are security, data integrity, and privacy. Transaction contents can be read, modified, or made up by anyone with sufficient experience or tenacity. Without proper security protocols, the potential for exploitation is great.

Call it the e-commerce paradox: E-commerce firms must be open and closed at the same time. They must be open to sharing information with customers and vendors, but closed to hackers and intruders. Creating a security culture and procedure that straddles this fine line can make the difference between success and failure. When it comes to e-commerce, security is the bottom line for everything a business wants to accomplish.

Internet security is not about protecting hardware. It is about protecting information. The risks inherent in e-commerce can be harnessed only through appropriate security measures and business and legal procedures that ensure the integrity and reliability of Internet transactions. Solving the security problem makes the Web storefront a reality.

The field of electronic security focuses on designing measures that can enforce security policies, especially when a malicious attack occurs. Security in e-commerce generally employs procedures such as authentication, ensuring confidentiality, and the use of cryptography to communicate over open systems. In this chapter, our focus is on electronic security, security design, server security issues and procedures, and how to achieve application security. The name of the game is security—security management, security update, and security maintenance. Without a regular program that monitors the status and integrity of the security of a Web site, unanticipated problems can occur. (Encryption, which is part of security, is covered in Chapter 15.)

Security in Cyberspace

The electronic system that supports e-commerce is susceptible to abuse and failure in many ways.

- Fraud, resulting in direct financial loss. Funds might be transferred from one account to another, or financial records might simply be destroyed.
- Theft of confidential, proprietary, technological, or marketing information belonging to the firm or to the customer. An intruder may disclose such information to a third party, resulting in damage to a key customer, a client, or the firm itself.
- Disruption of service, resulting in major losses to the business or inconvenience to the customer.
- Loss of customer confidence stemming from illegal intrusions into customer files or company business, dishonesty, human mistakes, or network failures.

One of the problems of security engineering is that subverted systems often function normally. Although e-commerce is surging by leaps and bounds, a variety of hurdles remain to the widespread acceptance of the technology and the entire process of shopping on the Internet. The recent growth of the Internet has focused worldwide attention on the growing problem of privacy, security, and the potential for fraud and deception unless security standards are implemented properly. For all parties to trade electronically, a way of verifying identities and establishing trust must be created.

Someone once said, "Network security is the most important thing on the planet," yet the first time it hinders performance, security is relaxed. The massive volume of traffic on the Internet and the staggering amount of personal, commercial, governmental, and military information in the networking infrastructures worldwide pose monumental risks. The missing step in most cases is a plan that considers security of the network as a whole.

Why the Internet Is Different

In traditional ways of doing business, merchants expect to be paid with real money. When they accept credit, they require personal signatures on credit forms. When they lock up at the end of the day, the alarm is set or the guards take over for the night, and the police come in case of a break-in.

Practical and legal differences exist between traditional store- and paper-based commerce and computer-based commerce. Signed documents have inherent security attributes that are lacking in computer-based files. Table 13-1 summarizes the differences. Some of the security attributes include the ink embedded in the paper fiber, the biometrics of signatures (pressure, slant, shape, and so on), unique letterhead, changes or deletions in the document, and the like. Computer-based messages are represented by a string of bits that reside in computer memory, using measured fractional volts that distinguish between zeros and ones. Computer-based records can be modified quickly and without detection. Sometimes all it takes to corrupt a record is a few simple keystrokes.

Unlike the traditional 10:00 A.M. to 6:00 P.M. store hours, an online store is open 24 hours a day, 7 days a week. It is unattended, except for the technology that performs the shopping and payment processes and the voice of customer service on an 800 number.

Remember, we're allowing anyone, anywhere, anytime to use these connected computers as long as they have the password that gives them access to the public network. As mentioned earlier, the Internet is the largest interconnected data network infrastructure in the world, with no central control and, therefore, not much security. Because of this

Table 13-1
Paper-based versus electronic commerce attributes

PAPER-BASED COMMERCE	ELECTRONIC COMMERCE
Signed paper documents	Digital signature
Person to person	Electronic via Web site
Physical payment system	Electronic payment system
Merchant and customer are face to face	No face-to-face contact
Easy detectability of modifications	Detectability is difficult
Easy negotiability of documents	Negotiable documents require special security protocol

and the lack of standards, the Internet gives thieves and hackers the opportunity to cause all kinds of problems.

Without good security, computer fraud is virtually untraceable. To make things worse, communications over the Internet seem impersonal and distant. Some people with little knowledge crank up enough courage to defraud a merchant, deface a Web site, or corrupt a database—feats they would not think of trying if they were dealing with a merchant face to face in a local store. The lack of laws punishing the intruder or protecting the innocent makes things worse. The legal system relies on physical evidence such as a canceled check, a person's original signature, place of residence, and similar details to determine whether the plaintiff has a case. What on the Internet substitutes for such evidence? Digital signatures identify the individual (signature) in the same way that DNA identifies the missing person at the crime scene.

Conceptualizing Security

Any way we look at security, it means addressing risk and protection from the unknown. Risk is a matter of degree. For example, banks require greater security than a store because of the risk of losing millions of dollars in nontraceable cash. The biggest risk in e-commerce is fraudulent credit card usage and the mishandling of personal e-mail information. Security concerns are about network and transaction security. Lack of transaction security has made many customers leery of making payments over the Internet. Network security means that lines and networks are protected from the threat of unauthorized third-party access to data and information.

The first issue in security is identifying the principals. They are people, processes, machines, and keys that transact (send, receive, access, update, delete) information via databases, computers, and networks. Security concerns generally involve the following issues.

- **Confidentiality:** Knowing who can read data and ensuring that information in the network remains private. This is done via encryption. See Chapter 14.
- **Authentication:** Making sure that message senders or principals are who they say they are.
- **Integrity:** Making sure that information is not accidentally or maliciously altered or corrupted in transit.
- **Access control:** Restricting the use of a resource to authorized principals.
- **Nonrepudiation:** Ensuring that principals cannot deny that they sent the message.
- **Firewalls:** A filter between corporate networks and the Internet to secure corporate information and files from intruders, but that allows access to authorized principals.

E-commerce began with Electronic Data Interchange (EDI) in the early 1980s, when banks and businesses electronically transferred funds and made payments to one another. It was interbusiness trading in many industries—manufacturing, retailing, automotive, and government—and security was an add-on expense. The network was a controlled digital infrastructure. With the advent of business-to-consumer e-commerce and the Internet in the 1990s, information security became paramount. Several factors are driving this change: global trading far beyond the scope of EDI, which was confined to U.S. industries, and online, real-time trading. With trading partners around the world, the reasons are obvious for exercising prudence through effective security measures to keep businesses out of foreign courts. Online, real-time trading means a limited amount of time for consumer and merchant to investigate each other. To delay online transactions, as was the case with delayed EDI business, defeats the whole purpose of real-time business. The availability of reliable security packages leaves no excuse for not ensuring information security in e-commerce, regardless of the size and type of business. This is especially true in transacting e-payments.

Changes in attitudes toward security have opened the door to serious consideration of security technology. In e-commerce, security can make or break a business; It already has become a strategic asset. It is the best way to protect information flow, ensure integrity, and reinforce customer confidence.

The time has come to get serious about secure electronic commerce. The technical part involves the use of cryptography and digital signatures to ensure the reliability of transactions over insecure networks.

The Privacy Factor

privacy: the ability to control who may see certain information and on what terms.

The lack of **privacy** has been more of a problem with the Internet than it has with any other medium invented to date. Incredible amounts of information are collected and stored every day, and no one knows what is done with it. It is getting to the point where, according to Dreazen, "in 10 years, the average person will be unable to run for public office unless they've been living in a monastery" (Dreazen 2002). Today, an array of sophisticated new tools is beginning to make a difference (see Box 13-1).

Every time the issue of security surfaces, privacy also is involved. A secure Web site implies a site that ensures the privacy and confidentiality of the visitor's transactions. This means a Web site should post the vendor's privacy policy for the consumer to evaluate.

Most people's fears with respect to the sharing of personal information in buying online can be handled through education. Companies should review the information by-products that result from a product purchase, observe good information-handling practices, and disclose privacy policies to give customers a reason to trust them.

In the absence of regulatory protection, experts urge privacy-sensitive surfers to take basic steps to protect their privacy while online.

- Send anonymous e-mail through remailers, which reduces the chance of the e-mail being read by hackers who might be monitoring Web traffic from sites like hotmail. An example of a remailer is www.gilc.org/speech/anonymous/remailer.html. Through such a site, the message bounces through a number of computers that forward it on, making it virtually untraceable.
- Improve security through your Web browser. One feature is to deactivate or block cookies. You also can set it to alert you when a site is trying to embed a cookie on your machine. The downside is that you might have difficulty visiting popular sites that require installing cookies on your PC.
- Use a secondary free e-mail service like Microsoft's Hotmail.com to prevent your main e-mail (personal or business) from spam.
- Stay away from filling out any form or questionnaire online. This is especially the case when the form is asking for personal information such as address, age, annual income, and so on. Investigate the site and see how much you trust them with such information.
- Consider using privacy software to give your files or PC contents some privacy. For example, Anonymizer@anonuymous.com offers a pay service that encrypts the content and address of the Web sites you visit to shield you from employers and other prying eyes. Other software, called Window Washer (www.webroot.com), washes off (erases) all files, cookies, temporary Internet files, and other garbage that might

BOX 13-1
Guarding one's privacy

Three years ago, as he was introducing a new online data-transmission technology, Sun Microsystems Inc. Chief Executive Officer Scott McNealy was asked if he thought the product needed more safeguards to make sure the transmissions weren't intercepted. His assessment was blunt. "You have zero privacy anyway," he said. "Get over it."

Much of what you put on the Net was more or less fair game for hackers and other unscrupulous characters—not to mention the e-tailers that were beginning to collect reams of personal data on you as you visited their sites. Today, an array of sophisticated new tools offer powerful protections against many of the most common online privacy violations. Used properly, they can drastically improve your chances of keeping your Web visits, e-mails, and instant messages confidential.

Such measures, experts warn, are crucial for Web surfers. Despite advances in computer security, hacking continues virtually unabated. Unknown attackers recently stole the Social Security numbers of 265,000 state employees in California by breaking into a state payroll system. Privacy threats lurk even in normal Web usage. Consider the cookies that are automatically downloaded to users' computers when they visit certain Web sites. They are designed to identify the users of a Web page and can store information about their identity and shopping preferences. This allows Amazon.com, for example, to recognize you when you return to the site and to recommend new products to you. But the cookies also allow Web advertisers to track, on behalf of their clients, the Web sites that individual computer users have visited and whether they clicked on online banner ads.

Several prominent cases have put the privacy issue in the spotlight in the United States. In August 2002, Double-Click Inc., one of the biggest online advertising firms, settled a 30-month probe by a coalition of 10 states into its data-collection practices by agreeing to pay $450,000 in fines, better disclose how it tracks consumers online, give individuals access to the profiles created about them, and allow an outside company to audit its privacy policy.

SOURCE: Excerpted from Dreazen, Yochi J., "The Best Way to Guard Your Privacy," *The Wall Street Journal*, November 18, 2002, R4ff.

have resided on your hard disk. A special feature of the software, called "bleach," goes over the erased material repeatedly to "bleach" your disk clean, depending on the number of times you set the feature.

- Install a firewall program to protect your computer from hackers. It can filter specific information leaving your computer or information coming into your computer. One example of a firewall is Internet Security Systems Inc. The software sells for about $40 (Dreazon 2002).

E-companies that take privacy seriously hire a full-time chief privacy officer as a first line of defense. Such a person would be expected to have a fundamental commitment to morality. A privacy officer looks at privacy as a human right that involves the global information infrastructure for most international firms. As Box 13-2 summarizes, once a chief privacy officer is aboard, that person's job includes a number functions, from setting up a privacy committee to conducting privacy reviews of all products and services regularly, consistently, and aboveboard.

BOX 13-2
Functions of a chief privacy officer

Jules Polonetsky has the power of life and death. Over contracts, anyway. As the chief privacy officer of DoubleClick, the biggest Internet advertising company, Mr. Polonetsky has the authority to rip up contracts with companies that do not comply with Double Click's rules for protecting consumer privacy. In recent weeks, Mr. Polonetsky says, he has cut off a half dozen clients whose sites did not meet DoubleClick's criteria, which include having a clear privacy page on the client's site and an easy way to opt out of data collection.

But DoubleClick, which distributes ads to consumers on thousands of Web sites, has taken a public beating from advocates for privacy rights, who contend that it tracks people's online wanderings too intrusively. The company has consistently denied that its policies violate consumer privacy; the Federal Trade Commission recently dropped an inquiry, but it still faces class action suits and lawsuits by state attorneys general. And so DoubleClick is redoubling its efforts to build a reputation as a company that protects privacy.

Chief privacy officers (CPOs), have been appointed at companies like IBM, AT&T, and Eastman Kodak. There are now at least 100 privacy chiefs in the United States, making $125,000 to $175,000 a year. Alan F. Westin, a former Columbia University professor who is now a corporate consultant on privacy issues, recommends that a chief privacy officer's duties include the following.

- Set up a privacy committee.
- Study and assess privacy risks of all operations involving personal data.
- Develop a company privacy code.
- Interact with concerned regulators and consumers, and provide a contact point for consumers.
- Create and oversee employee privacy training.
- Monitor privacy laws and regulations—and the company's compliance.
- Conduct privacy reviews of all new products and Internet service.

Companies court disaster by appointing a powerless CPO, simply for appearance. Lawrence A. Ponemon, who heads up privacy issues for Pricewaterhouse Coopers and runs privacy audits that help corporations find the weaknesses in their own policies and practices. "I'd say the majority—more than 50 percent of the companies that have established a CPO—don't allocate ample resources to get the job done right," Mr. Ponemon said. "Therefore, it's an empty promise. If you don't have the resources, you can't get the job done."

SOURCE: Excerpted from Schwartz, John, "First Line of Defense," *New York Times*, February 12, 2001, C1ff.

DESIGNING FOR SECURITY

For information security design, the key question is How do you know that the design will be secure? The answer lies in an effective design that should be part of the business-to-consumer installation from the beginning. Adding security mechanisms as an afterthought can be costly and ineffective. Designing for a secure e-commerce environment is a decision made with the future in mind. The design process begins with a chief security officer and involves five major steps: (1) assessing the security needs of the firm, (2) establishing a good policy, (3) fulfilling Web security needs, (4) structuring the security environment, and (5) monitoring the system (see Figure 13-1).

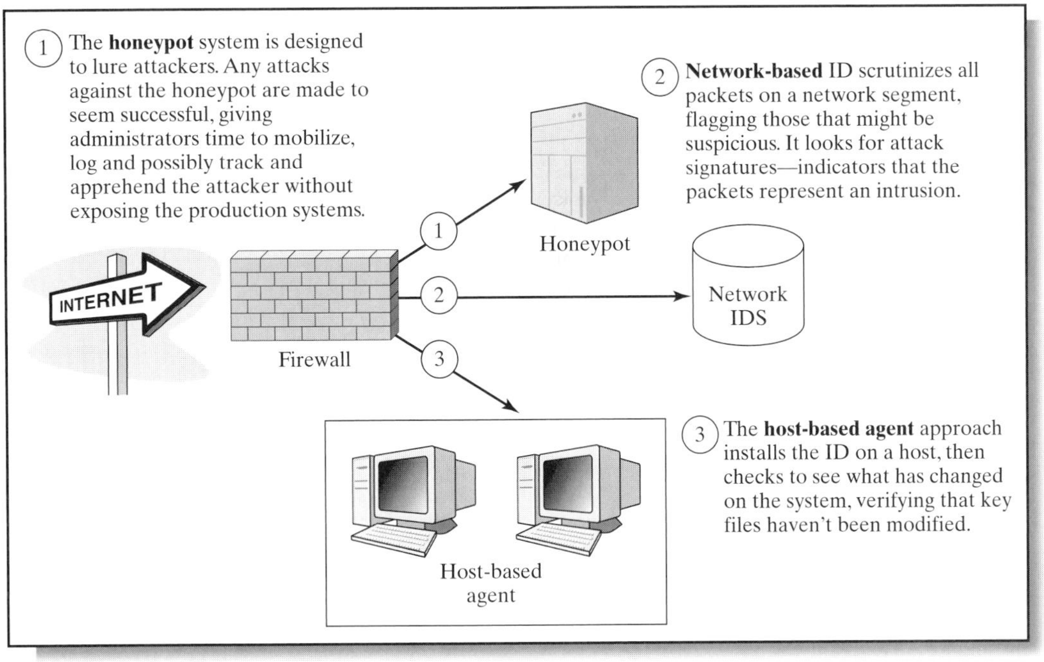

Figure 13-1
Logical procedure flow—An example

Box 13-3 addresses the importance of establishing a chief security officer to oversee the entire security setup for the firm. The security professional who is hired should be well versed in the technology as well as the nature of the business of the employer. In addition, the person must be able to pinpoint which security breaches threaten the company's bottom line.

Assessing Security Needs

Common sense tells us it is prudent to look for security vulnerability before it is too late. The cheapest and most effective way to fix problems is while they are in development. As shown in Figure 13-2, a system assessment life cycle begins with the development of a new system using security best practices. Then, the system should be tested to detect unforeseen security flaws before it is released for implementation. Finally, a running system should be monitored and maintained at all times (Dyck 2002).

Adopting a Security Policy That Makes Sense

One of the serious mistakes companies make when it comes to security is failing to establish good security policies and ensure that they are followed. Policies should cover the threats against which information must be protected in order to ensure confidentiality, integrity, and privacy. Unfortunately, policies are easier to write than to enforce. For example, a firewall cannot be installed and then forgotten. Every time technology is upgraded, a router is replaced, the volume of traffic increases, or incidents of unauthorized access occur, the entire e-commerce infrastructure should be reevaluated and software such as firewalls should be upgraded or replaced.

BOX 13-3
Importance of a chief security officer

Nearly all the security officers we spoke with said they agree that this year's number one issue—the adoption of international security standards—just might simplify some of the complexities of e-security. Security managers have a lot more work ahead of them: Threats from internal employees account for nearly 40 percent of all security breaches, according to a joint survey of 273 organizations that was released last March by the San Francisco-based Computer Security Institute and the FBI.

The problem is exacerbated by high employee turnover. The key to surviving these increasingly complex attacks will be creating security awareness campaigns. These programs should cover three areas: access-control management, root (Unix) and administrative (Windows NT) access, and information handling by both permanent and temporary employees.

It is important to keep security policies simple, follow up with refreshers, and use media coverage of security events to keep the issue on users' minds. The test this year will be to raise awareness with more creative viruses and Trojan horses than Melissa and "I Love You" to fuel user-assisted breaches.

In B2B exchanges, security becomes very big when you look at the chain of events that need to occur relating to a transaction. Each link has to be secure, because everyone in the chain is a potential competitor. Your chief security officer will be on the hunt for streetwise security experts next year. They will need to become more creative in their staffing efforts, finding most of their employees inside the organization and then mentoring and training them.

Last year, the leading industry-recognized training and certification program was the Certified Information Systems Security Practitioner, offered by U.S.-based International Information Security Certifications Consortium Inc. (www.isc2.org). Chief security officers also face a shortage of privacy experts this year, as the medical and final industries feel the squeeze of the Gramm-Leach-Bliley Act. Because these jobs are so regulatory driven, privacy officers will most likely originate from legal and consumer affairs departments.

SOURCE: Excerpted from Radcliff, Deborah, "Pick Your Security Officer's Drain Brain," *IT Agenda*, January 2001, S36ff.

The policies should cover the entire e-commerce system including the merchant's local area networks, hardware, software, firewalls, protocols, standards, databases, and the people directly involved in the e-commerce process. The policies should spell out Internet security practices, the nature and level of risks, the level of protection, and the procedure to follow to react to threats and recover from failure. Above all, policies must have the blessing of top management if they are to have a chance of succeeding.

Considering Web Security Needs

The second design consideration is for the company to list top vulnerabilities and take a close look at critical applications to decide risk levels. The amount of security a Web merchant needs depends on the sensitivity of its data and the demand for it. For example, if your site collects credit card numbers for access, you'd want the highest security possible for the Web server, the network, and the Web site. You would want to consult with your Web administrator or an outside security consultant to see what options are available and how to put them to good use.

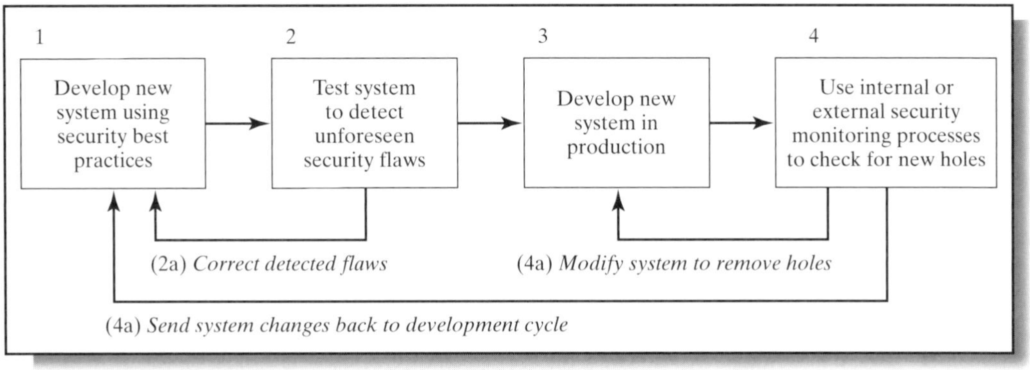

Figure 13-2
The security assessment life cycle
Source: Adapted from Dycke, Timothy, "A Vulnerability Scan Plan," *eWeek LABS*, May 20, 2002, 43.

Designing the Security Environment

The design begins with sketching out the stepping-stones—the sequence and parameters in the security network based on the security policy and requirements of the e-commerce system. Physical security design implements the logical design with a focus on hardware, PCs, operating systems, firewalls, security protocols, networks, physical location and layout, and the cables that will connect the merchant with the Internet Service Provider.

How much security goes into a system depends on how much risk the company is willing to take, the kind of security policy it is willing to adopt, and the present state of security practices in the workplace. For example, if an e-application is run by certified and authenticated operators, employing a strong physical system, the demand for further authentication and access control should not be that high. The same application managed by operators in branches and other remote locations would impose more stringent security requirements that include the network, the interfaces, and the physical environment in which business operations are conducted on a daily basis.

security perimeter: security boundary that includes firewalls, authentication, VPNs, and intrusion detection devices.

firewall: a system that enforces an access control policy between two networks.

authentication: the process of deciding the identity of a user attempting to access a system.

A **security perimeter** generally includes firewalls, authentication, virtual private networks (VPNs), and intrusion detection devices. Installing such software and devices is part of physical design. The challenge is to police the entire perimeter.

The first line of defense of a company's e-site is the **firewall.** Traditionally, firewalls included a host of applications and services such as File Transfer Protocol (FTP) support. Today's special-purpose firewall appliances hone in on security-related functions. This is a better approach because it reduces the chance of misconfiguration. The less there is to configure, the less chance there is that things can go wrong. (Firewalls are covered in detail later in the chapter.)

Another technology protecting the perimeter is **authentication.** Under the old EDI system, both sender and receiver had to sign up for the service with the value-added network (VAN) provider and agree on the format to be used before transactions were carried out. On the Internet, you don't know whom you are dealing with. To grant authentication, a hardware token generates a unique password every so many seconds. The password must match that on a central server that is synchronized with the token, and VPNs provide encryption for data transmitted across the wire, but companies must still worry about sensitive data stored in databases, such as credit card numbers and consumer profiles that have been searched over time.

Authorizing and Monitoring the Security System

Once the perimeter is secure and only authorized users are allowed access to the e-commerce site, the next step is to install a system that generates authorization to different users to handle different jobs. Most companies adopt a policy that denies access to all except those who are explicitly allowed. This policy, along with good security design, should keep a site reasonably secure. However, in situations where customers are routinely placing big-ticket orders, the security system should provide strong authentication for such orders and an audit trail. You must be able to prove that customer A at company X did, in fact, place an order on May 3 for $113,000 worth of diamonds. This is called nonrepudiation, and it is covered in the next chapter. Security design steps are shown in Figure 13-3.

monitoring: capturing processing details, verifying that e-commerce is operating within the security policy, and verifying that attacks have been unsuccessful.

These functions require that the security system be monitored via feedback mechanisms to ensure that the entire system is working properly. **Monitoring** means capturing processing details for evidence, verifying that e-commerce is operating within the security policy, and verifying that attacks have been unsuccessful. This system does not replace the human guard who checks the doors, makes the rounds on each floor, and makes sure badges and IDs are valid at all times. The guard and the electronic security system complement each other to keep an e-commerce site reliable at all times.

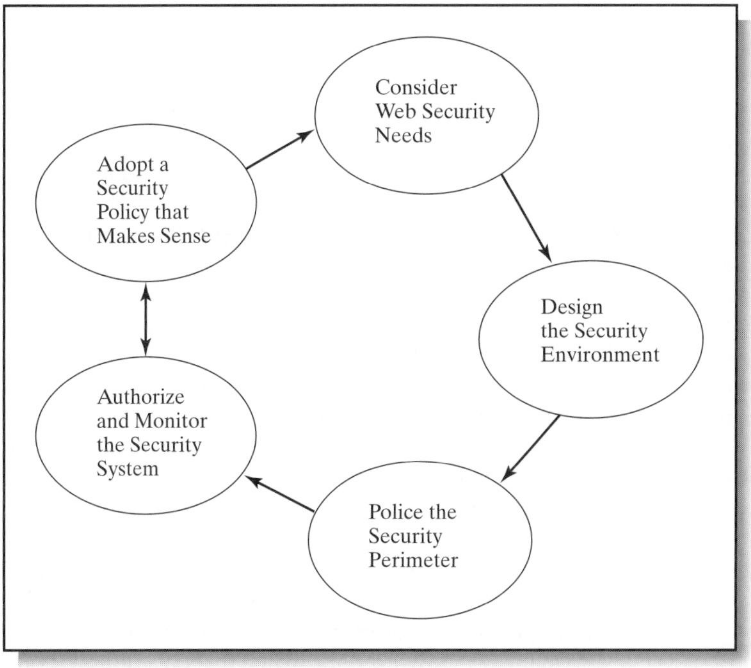

Figure 13-3
The security system design process

Raising Awareness of Possible Intrusions

With today's firms relying more and more on the Internet, they face an ever-growing spectrum of threats, which means an increase in protection against cyber-risks far beyond what traditional property and casualty insurance policies cover. Denial-of-service attacks already have targeted businesses such as Amazon.com, Buy.com, CNN.com, eBay, and E-Trade. Attackers have even tried to slow down the entire Internet (Nelson 2002).

Recognizing this growing need for cyber-insurance, as well as the complexity traditionally associated with the qualification for such coverage, Internet Security Systems, Inc. (ISS) and Marsh, Inc. have announced a joint program designed to aid companies in expanding their risk management strategies to include online exposures. ISS's program is composed of select managed security services, bundling managed firewall, intrusion detection, and antivirus services together with emergency response services, to provide clients with the peace of mind that comes with 24/7 protection and a lowered total cost of ownership. Such a program was designed specifically to provide the opportunity for its clients to contract with Marsh for cyber-risk insurance (Lexis-Nexis 2002).

User organizations and ISPs can ensure that traffic exiting an organization's site or entering an ISP's network from a site carries a source address consistent with the set of addresses for that site. This would allow tracing of attack traffic to the site from which it emanated, substantially assisting in the process of locating and isolating attack traffic sources.

Dial-up users are the source of some attacks, so stopping spoofing by these users is also an important step. ISPs, universities, libraries, and others that serve dial-up users should ensure that proper filters are in place to prevent dial-up connections from using spoofed addresses. Network equipment vendors should ensure that no-IP-spoofing is a user setting and the default setting on their dial-up equipment.

How Much Risk Can You Afford?

CIOs and other top management officials often ask two questions regarding their company's security and how it relates to e-commerce: How secure are we? How much will it cost to secure our e-system? Other questions arise as well: How secure do we need to be? What are we doing to monitor and improve security? What monitors do we have that tell us whether we've been hit and how hard? The level of security can be determined by the specific threats inherent in the system's design.

Another way of addressing the risk factor is to estimate the pain threshold your company and the attacker are willing to tolerate. In this case, the network administrator needs to know what is being protected, its value to the company, and its value to outsiders. The statements "When you have nothing, you have nothing to lose" and "There is not that much that they can steal" do not apply in network and Internet security. The goal of security strategies, methods, and procedures is to raise the threshold of pain an attacker must endure to access and cause damage to a system.

One of the key questions in designing a security policy is the level of protection required against the risks the merchant is willing to assume. It is like deciding on whether to put cash in a savings account with 100 percent security (up to $100,000) or invest in stocks that could go up or down in value. In any case, security risks address the adversaries that could wreck an e-commerce business. Professional attackers might view a site as a challenge and work day and night until they crack it. A casual attacker might just try hard enough to be a nuisance. In looking at security risks, the focus is on the determined attacker's intentions and resources.

Kinds of Threats or Crimes

Before promoting security, you must know what you are trying to prevent. Web merchants must consider three kinds of threats or crimes.

1. *Those that are physically related.* For example, a hacker might attempt to steal or damage inventory. Other examples include stolen credit card records, stolen computer hardware or software, and sheer vandalism. An attacker, often by guessing passwords, might succeed in gaining access to another user's account. The attacker might even be capable of drumming up unauthorized features such as discount coupons or specials in an effort to get merchandise free of charge.
2. *Those that are order related.* For example, a customer might attempt to use an invalid or a stolen credit card or claim no merchandise was received on a good credit card. Children might use their parents' credit card without permission. Insiders can do a lot to infect an order because they have access to sensitive systems and information. All it takes is a disgruntled or greedy employee to disrupt or divert an order to his or her advantage.
3. *Those that are electronically related.* A hacker might try to *sniff* e-mail information or attempt to steal credit card numbers and use them illegally at a later date. A **sniffer** (also called a cracker or a cyber-punk) might vandalize a site by replacing files, deleting files, or attempting to intercept and decode communications between the merchant and customers. Crackers often use off-the-shelf attack software from technical magazines with little knowledge or experience in its use or potential. Another example of an electronically related attack is damaging, defacing, or destroying a Web site and infecting the entire business-to-consumer interface with malicious software called a virus. (More will be presented on viruses later in the chapter.)

sniffer: a person or a program that uses the Internet to record information that transmits through a router from its source to its destination.

Other potential groups of attackers or criminals can threaten the e-commerce environment. How about payments from legitimate user accounts being diverted to an unauthorized person's account? Payment could go to the wrong party, with the real buyer completely unaware of what is happening. What about attackers creating a look-alike Web site to draw unsuspecting users?

Finally, some intruders attack the Web site a little at a time so that it is difficult to detect the continued drain on the system. For example, an attacker who succeeded in accumulating a large number of credit card numbers might opt to use one credit card at a time at small businesses, for small purchases, or during a time when traffic is heavy, without arousing any suspicion.

Client and Server Security Threats

Two types of security threats affect a company's Internet client-server environment: attacks on client computers—all the PCs attached to the local area server—and attacks on the server(s) itself. In either case, we need to know the types of attacks, how an attacker breaks in, and what the attacker does once in the system.

Client Computer Attacks

The literature on security and survey specialists in the security business indicates that three main reasons explain why client computers are attacked.

1. **Sheer nuisance:** This includes unsolicited mail, displays of advertisements on the Web site, or anonymous messages that are disruptive and potentially destructive. No malice is involved, but the mere inflow of this type of garbage causes irritation and loads up the person's PC hard disk.
2. **Deliberate corruption of files:** It's no secret that viruses can cause all kinds of problems with data integrity. Melissa, WORM, and hundreds of other viruses since the early 1990s show how vulnerable the PC is in an e-commerce environment. Protecting against a deliberate invasion of files means backing up files regularly so that a copy is available for updating or restoring what may have been lost.
3. **Rifling stored information:** This is a direct attack on the client computer—the PC attached to the server. In this case, vital information such as a file of credit card numbers, a school's file of student transcripts, or the mental health history of psychiatric patients is the target. Think of a situation where a program or a virus enters your PC, steals information, and transmits it through e-mail to the public at large. This kind of attack clearly has legal implications, which will be covered in the chapter on legal issues.

The next question is: How are client computers attacked? There are three ways.

1. **Physical attacks:** The first line of attack is through unattended computers during business hours, computers not logged off at night, or computers with easy-to-break passwords. Client computers should never be left unattended without appropriate security checks.
2. **Viruses:** Anyone who has used a Web e-mail service knows the potency of a virus. Hackers and crackers have little difficulty propagating Trojan horses or e-mail viruses. Horowitz (2001) highlights the top 10 security mistakes made (see Box 13-4). The good news is that new intrusion-detection systems and firewalls have done a lot to block security breaches and identify the sources of unauthorized access.
3. **Computer-to-computer attacks:** With client computers linked via the server, it is not uncommon for one computer to export or publish information to others in the network. In a corporate environment, where security protocols and procedures are lax, the adage "a chain is as strong as the weakest link" applies. One disgruntled employee can spam or **spoof** the entire network.

spoof: an imposter; someone who pretends to be someone else or representing a Web site as authentic when it is a fake.

Server Security Threats

In e-commerce, the execution software on the client side or the server side poses real threats to the security of all transactions. When security measures are weak, the adage "in the presence of obstacles, the path of least resistance is always the path of choice" applies. Good design is important for software quality. It is also important to think of security not as an add-on piece of software, but as part of the security system from the beginning.

All the reasons for attacking client computers apply to attacking servers as well, except that an attack on a server affects all the computers attached to it. The impact can be astronomical in terms of disruption of service, loss of information in transit, and the integrity of the files. Furthermore, because servers store security credentials for client computer users, it is all the more necessary to incorporate cryptographic schemes to protect such information from attack.

BOX 13-4
Security mistakes people make

People are more careless with computers than perhaps any other thing of value in their lives. The reason is unclear, but observers agree that end users—and even some IT departments—can be pretty dumb when it comes to protecting computers and their contents. The following are some notable, less-than-bright errors that people and IT professionals commit when it comes to computer security:

- **The not-so-subtle Post-it Note:** Yes, those sticky yellow things can undo the most elaborate security measures. Too lazy to remember their passwords, users place them where they—and everyone else—can see them.
- **We know better than you:** You may think that certain security measures are necessary, but not all end users agree, which leads them to do an end-run around you. Antivirus software is an example. They think it slows down their machine.
- **Leaving the machine on, unattended:** They simply walk away when done. Who needs a password?
- **Opening e-mail attachments:** Users open all their e-mail attachments before thinking.
- **Poor password selection:** If there is a bugaboo among security experts, it is poorly chosen passwords. A combination of letters and numbers is a better password than either alphabetic or numeric only. For example, the phrase "I pledge allegiance to the flag" can become "ipa2tf," which is very difficult to break.
- **Loose lips sink ships.** People often talk in public places about things they shouldn't. For example, at a bar, they will say, "I changed my password and added the number 2," and someone sitting two stools down will hear this.
- **Laptops have legs:** Everyone knows how common it is for laptops to be stolen in public places, but it is surprisingly common for a person to leave his laptop in his office, unsecured and unattended, and in full view of passersby.
- **Poorly enforced security policies:** The best-designed security plans are useless if IT fails to rigorously enforce them.
- **Failing to consider the staff:** It has been known for a long time that the greatest security threat is from in-house. Disgruntled employees can cause enormous problems.
- **Being slow to update security information:** Service packs are not kept up-to-date, which creates a window of opportunity for hackers.

SOURCE: Excerpted from Horowitz, Alan S., "Top 10 Security Mistakes," *Computerworld*, July 9, 2001, 38.

Other server (and network) security threats include the following.

- **Web server with a port active:** This indicates weak authentication (which is covered in the next chapter). This also makes it vulnerable for password sniffing, software attacks, and Web attacks. In password sniffing, an attacker eavesdrops on a communications line to intercept passwords being transmitted unencrypted. The attacker can then use the password to masquerade as a legitimate user.
- **Windows NT or Windows 2000 server not upgraded to act as firewall:** In this case, a hacker can take control of the server for software and virus attacks.
- **Anonymous FTP service available on the Web server:** A hacker can gain network access easily by logging on as a guest. This could make the server vulnerable to forgery attacks or spoofs and Web attacks.
- **Web server directories that can be accessed and indexed:** This indicates that files can be copied and replaced.

How are server attacks launched? Attacks range from those with limited objectives, such as access to a specific file or application, to access to a major application with the intent of running it like a legitimate user. The worst are **denial-of-service (DOS)** attacks, where users are bombarded with hundreds or thousands of messages that clog the Internet site so nothing can get in or out.

denial of service (DOS): attack by a third party that prevents authorized users from accessing the infrastructure.

The first step in an attack is to log in by guessing at a password. Unfortunately, the typical password is someone's street number, the last four digits of a social security number, a telephone number, or something similar. An attacker also might latch onto the client-server traffic using a sniffer virus and catch passwords as they whiz by. Unattended terminals are ready targets for attackers wanting to take over a network connection. Once user privileges are compromised, the attacker will have access to all kinds of files, applications, and the like. The attacker will have no difficulty embedding viruses, transferring files to computers located anywhere in the world, or simply rendering the terminal inoperable. Three years after the high-profile hits, DOS attacks are still a threat (see Box 13-5).

DOS attacks are hard to characterize, because what they have in common is their end effect, not the means by which they are carried out. Some DOS attacks flood a network with traffic or modify a router's configuration. One of the main reasons why DOS attacks are so hard to fend off is that on the surface, they appear like ordinary Web site traffic. The difference, though, is their intent, along with the volume, frequency, and source of the traffic (Henry-Stocker 2001).

Protecting e-mail is another aspect of server protection. Sending e-mail is a part of every workday. So is e-mail abuse. It is not only e-mail servers, but also the connections

BOX 13-5
DOS on the run

DOS attacks make computer systems inaccessible by flooding servers or networks with useless traffic so that legitimate users can no longer gain access to those resources. During a 3-week period in mid-2001, researchers from the University of California, San Diego, detected approximately 12,800 DOS attacks against more than 5,000 targets.

The threat is a lot worse today than 2 years ago. There are lots of indications that since September 11, the number of DOS attacks has greatly increased. Here are some tips to help prevent a DOS attack:

- Regularly review publicly available information on recent security vulnerabilities and incidents. It helps in configuring and updating your public Web server against new forms of attacks.
- Regularly update your DOS detection tools to discover new patterns or events (resulting from new or updated attacks taking advantage of new vulnerabilities).
- Update firewall-filtering mechanisms to deny new attacks.
- Temporarily disable specific services that might be vulnerable.
- Augment your alerting procedures.
- Work with your Internet service provider to understand what precautions have been taken to guard against DOS attacks.
- Get a configuration that uses multiple connections built from different network backbones. This will help switch public Web servers to another connection in the event of a DOS attack.

SOURCE: Excerpted from Vijayan, Jaikumar, "Denial-of-Service Attacks Still a Threat," *Computerworld*, April 8, 2002, 8.

between servers that must be protected. Devices such as S/MIME and SMTP over Secure Sockets Layer (SSL) are employed to combat attackers. S/MIME ensures that a message is encrypted and digitally signed by the client and then by the Web server it is leaving. SMTP SSL is installed between two e-mail servers to make sure all e-mail packets are encrypted. These devices are covered in detail in the next chapter.

Hackers

In early February 2000, a surge of attacks left "Top Gun" Web sites like AOL and Yahoo! few options for defense. Imagine a prankster arranging for thousands of people around the world to dial your home number continuously for hours at a time. This, in effect, is what happened to the Web sites of eBay, E*Trade Group, and Yahoo! They fell victim to what is commonly known in the Internet security business as a denial-of-service attack. As the name implies, the attack does not intend to harm anyone or any file, as is the case with viruses. Its aim is to prevent the Internet from performing its vital function of linking people and technology. These attacks take advantage of the Internet's open nature, and there is no surefire way to defend against them until after they're underway (see Box 13-6).

BOX 13-6
Stalking the hackers

The Federal Bureau of Investigation yesterday geared up to mount a worldwide hunt for the perpetrators of a wave of attacks against major Web sites, as the targeted companies assembled their own teams of sleuths to try to find the raiders. The FBI is working on reconstructing the attacks by examining the records of the target companies and their partners on the Web. Such a broad analysis of Internet traffic can help narrow the search to particular geographic regions or groups of related servers. The FBI is collecting logs from Internet service providers that can show where transmissions originated.

But that analysis is fraught with complications. One problem is that some ISPs don't retain such records. Because of privacy policies, companies can only turn over such records if the FBI obtains a subpoena. Even then, it isn't always possible to trace the traffic to an individual machine. Locating the servers is only a first step. Software designed for service-outage attacks is widely available across the Internet, meaning that just about anyone could have picked up a program and used it. In contrast, programmers who write viruses typically customize their code, making it possible to trace authorship in some cases.

What's more, the attacks themselves are typically waged from hundreds or thousands of otherwise "innocent" servers that have been infiltrated by hacker software. Even identifying those servers can be a challenge, because the software typically fakes the "return address" that would normally identify the origin of any data packet sailing across the Internet.

Guessing at the identities and motives of the attackers rapidly became a kind of cottage industry. Among the leading theories promoted by security gurus and Internet hangers-on are thrill seekers (high school students looking for excitement), cyber-gangs (gangs of hackers daring each other to greater feats of hackerdom), or hacker activists who protest against the growing commercialization of the Internet—thus the strikes against leading e-commerce vendors.

SOURCE: Hamilton, David, and Cloud, David, "Internet Under Siege: Stalking the Hackers," *The Wall Street Journal*, February 10, 2000, B1ff.

Despite the war on terror, the Internet continues to be a hacker's haven. More than 70,000 computer-security incidents were reported during the first 9 months of 2002, compared to 21,750 in 2000 (Panettieri 2003). One denial-of-service attack launched in October 2002 caused a flood of status requests to each of the Internet's major DNS root servers.

Denial-of-service falls under cyberterrorism—unlawful attacks and threats of attacks against computers, networks, and the information stored in them when done to intimidate or coerce a company or a government in furtherance of political or social objectives. Denial-of-service attacks against Yahoo!, CNN, eBay, and other e-commerce Web sites estimated to have caused over $1 billion in losses. It also shook the confidence of business and individuals in e-commerce. For example, during the Kosovo conflict in 1999 NATO computers were blasted with e-mail bombs and hit with denial-of-service attacks by hacktivists protesting the NATO bombings.

To activate a denial of service, the hacker breaks into a large number of less-secure computers and servers connected to a high-bandwidth network, usually corporate or government. The attacker installs stealth programs that are hard to spot and serve as electronic soldiers, lying undetected on the hijacked computers, waiting to attack a Web site. In and of itself, this stealth program does not harm a Web site, but because the program duplicates itself thousands of times, the hacker can create unimaginable congestion in network traffic.

From a remote location, the hacker (called remote hacker) specifies a target network such as eBay or Yahoo! and activates the planted programs with a brief command via the Internet to a number of computers. The command triggers the computers to start flooding target sites with bogus requests for information. This is when the attack begins. The victim's network is overwhelmed. The source of the deluge of network traffic has been intentionally masked, making the attack hard to trace. Legitimate users encounter the equivalent of a constant busy signal and are denied access to the site (see Figure 13-4).

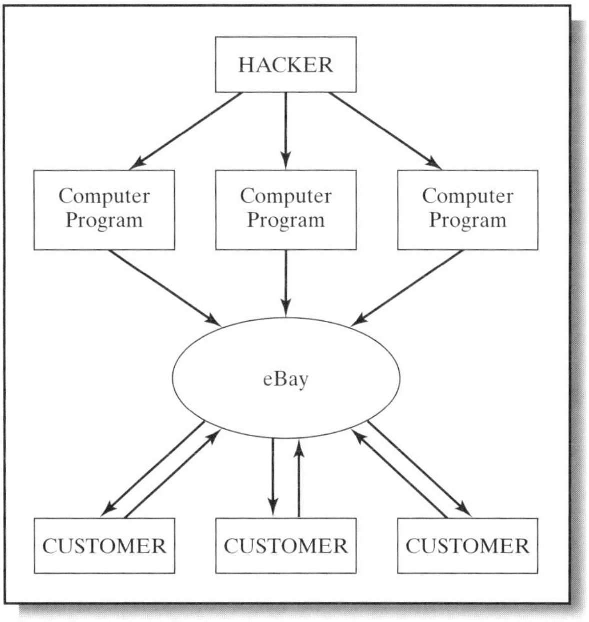

Figure 13-4 The hacking process

There are several ways a hacker carries out his or her trade:

- **Social engineering**. This approach tricks a person into revealing their password. Sometimes, this is carried out via a company executive's unsuspecting relatives to get access to sensitive information.
- **Shoulder surfing**. In this method, the hacker looks over an employee's shoulder while he or she types in a password.
- **Dumpster diving**. A hacker simply waits for a company's trash to be dumped in a container on a public street or in an alley and looks through it for sensitive information. The attempt is legal, unless there is a "no trespassing" sign.
- **Whacking (wireless hacking)**. All a hacker needs to have is the right kind of radio within the range of a wireless transmission zone. Once tapped into a wireless network, the hacker easily accesses anything on both the wired and wireless networks, unless the data is sent unencrypted.

The whole illicit effort is carried out with one mission in mind—information retrieval and misuse. Such information includes:

- Company Web sites
- Contract arrangements, pricing, etc.
- Customer information
- Company operations, wages, salaries, etc.
- Technological and manufacturing operations and processes
- Corporate strategies and business methods
- Program source code
- New products or product lines
- Personal information about employees or executives

Hackers and ethics do not mix. What is the remedy? First, site operators track a flood of information to a specific computer. Once they detect the source, they block any further requests from that computer. This is difficult when many computers are involved. To protect your computer(s) against hackers, check the Gibson Research Corporation Web site at http://grc.com for a free online security checkup. Another option is to download a free firewall from Zone Labs at www.zonelabs.com and install it on your computer workstation. If you are running a commercial site, commercial firewall software with intruder tracking is available from Black Ice at www.blackice.com (McCance 2000).

intrusion detection: sensing when a system is being used without authorization.

Intrusion detection is sensing when a system is being used without authorization. An intrusion-detection system is designed to monitor company systems and network activities. Using information collected from these activities, it notifies the authorities when it identifies a likely intrusion (see Figure 13-5).

Another way of fighting hackers is to hire one who works at foiling the efforts of the troublemakers. Under certain conditions, it is better to hire burglars than cops (Panettieri 2003). Hackers have a better understanding of technology infrastructure than a typical IT manager. Ethical or reformed hackers normally hire themselves out to break into a client's computer network with the client's consent in an effort to patch up security holes. See Box 13-7 for details on this new breed of hackers.

More recently, cyber–forensic investigations have been employed to combat cybercriminals. In many cases, large businesses use cyber-investigators to set up alarms and traps to watch and catch intruders and criminals within their networks. Box 13-8 describes a typical case in point.

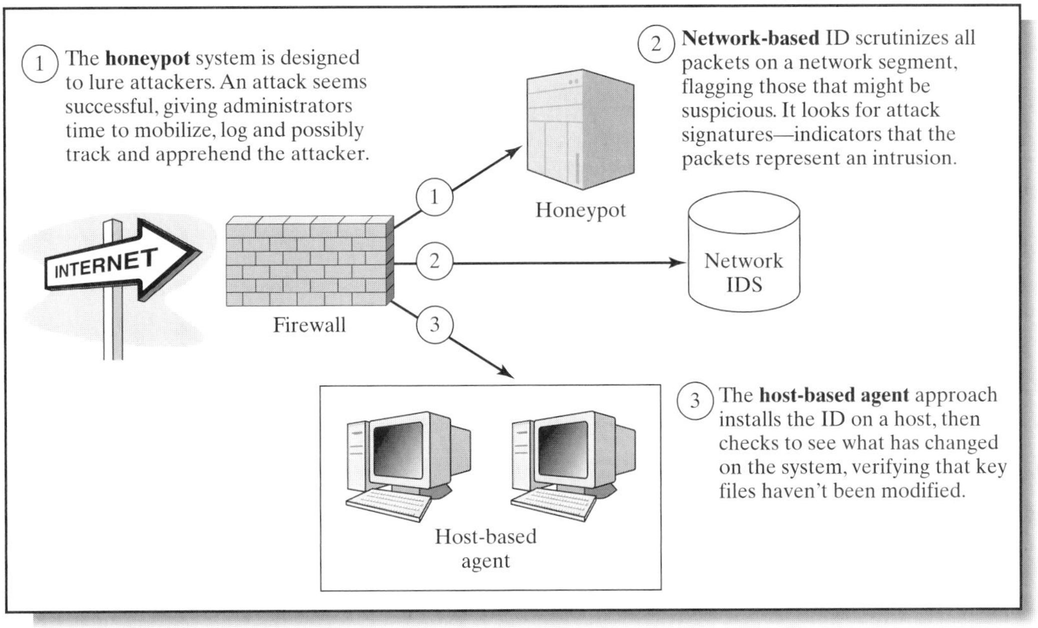

Figure 13-5
Intrusion-detection systems (IDSs)
Source: Adapted from Loshin, Pete, "Intrusion Detection," *Computerworld*, April 16, 2001, 62.

The trend is for more and more government agencies and private business to look with improved attitude toward the work of the benign or reformed hacker. For example, since the tragic September 11, 2001 attack, chronic security concerns have led Uncle Sam to deputize the country's hackers in the summer of 2003 to help fight the war on terrorism. The White House cybersecurity adviser encouraged hackers in an address to the annual Black Hat convention of hackers in Las Vegas that summer to probe popular computer programs and share any weaknesses they find with the software developers for tightening security. A White House official also suggested the government would look into legal protection for benign hackers (Dreazen 2002).

In the final analysis, no single entity is responsible for the interconnected computers, servers, routers, switches, and fiber optic cables that make up cyberspace. This means every Internet stakeholder must follow strict guidelines for cybersecurity. In February 2003, President George W. Bush released the 76-page final draft of *The National Strategy to Secure Cyberspace*. The policy statement calls for the creation of an emergency response system to cyberattacks and a reduction in the nation's vulnerability to such threats (Lemos 2003). Five major initiatives are involved:

- Create a cyberspace surety response system
- Establish a threat and vulnerability reduction program
- Improve security training and awareness
- Secure the government's own systems
- Work internationally to solve security issues (U.S Dept. of Homeland Security).

BOX 13-7
The ethical hacker

Ethical hackers are becoming a mainstay of the effort to make corporate networks more secure. Their appeal is simple: More companies are deciding it makes sense to pay the good guys to break into their networks before the bad guys do it and cause untold damage. The growth of the Internet has only added to the demand for vulnerability assessments, as companies have become more exposed to the outside world through the Web, and finding security holes has become easier for mischief-makers because of readily available online hacker tools.

Mr. Chapple, a computer scientist principal at Computer Science Corporation (CSC), says there are essentially two broad categories of computer security threats: external and internal. External threats range from industrial spies—who break into a company network over the telephone lines or Internet connections to steal trade secrets—to hackers, who mostly sneak in to commit sabotage. But the most damaging are internal threats—from, say, disgruntled employees who wipe out company databases or spies who infiltrate the company and steal sensitive information.

Team members use the HEAT (hydra expert assessment technology) program, developed by Mr. Chapple and others, to conduct broad scans of a client's network to identify all the hardware and software attached to it, from computer workstations to network routers to Web site servers. HEAT then automatically runs through a battery of vulnerability tests that identify and record security holes on the network.

Bad hackers routinely scan for such exploitable electronic loopholes—known as "exploits" in hacker jargon—and post software on the Internet that lets anyone scan for and take advantage of the vulnerabilities. SCS's security team updates the HEAT software as new loopholes are publicized on the Internet.

SOURCE: Excerpted from Wingfield, Nick, "It Takes a Hacker," *The Wall Street Journal*, March 11, 2002, R11.

Recent fears of terrorism have prompted the *The National Strategy to Secure Cyberspace*. The five initiatives are overseen by the Department of Homeland Security, passed by Congress in 2002. A select foreign terrorist organization list for 2002 are shown in Table 13-2.

The Virus: Computer Enemy Number One

virus: a malicious code that replicates itself and disrupts the information infrastructure.

The most serious attack on a client computer or a server in an Internet environment is the **virus.** What is a virus? It is a malicious code that replicates itself and can be used to disrupt the information infrastructure. Viruses commonly attack system integrity, circumvent security capabilities, and cause adverse operation by taking advantage of the information system or the network. They incorporate themselves into computer networks, files, and other executable objects, and replicate whenever those programs are executed or those infected diskettes are accessed. The replicates are not always exact and are often capable of spreading further in many different ways, including through e-mail attachment. Fortunately, 95 percent of viruses do not contain destructive codes that harm the system. They do no more than copy themselves and execute trivial codes that activate a beeping sound, display a message box, or simply do nothing. See Box 13-9 for a brief history of the virus.

BOX 13-8
Following the evidence

THE CASE OF THE SNEAKY ENGINEER

How Forensics Examinations of Many Machines Helped One Company Retrieve Its Intellectual Property and Stop the Bad Guy from Using It Again

An engineer left a West Coast manufacturing company, which we'll call Company A due to pending litigation. When that same engineer turned up at Company B, a competitor, in September earning $10,000 more than market rate, Company A's executives worried that some of their intellectual property had been transferred to the competitor. Company A's executives filed a court motion for discovery, and then called New Technologies Inc. (NTI), a computer forensics support and training firm in Gresham, Oregon.

While NTI investigators found signs of file copying to removable media in the engineer's computer, NTI's team couldn't find empirical evidence of wrongdoing there. So under a court order for discovery, the NTI team then searched the suspect's home computer. Using another NTI file search utility called FileListPro, the team found that several product engineering drawings had been copied onto the home computer after the engineer had left the company. (This software tells when a file has been created, accessed, and modified.)

The engineer claimed that the clock on his computer had malfunctioned and that the drawings were copied while he was employed at Company A. But simple deduction told a different story. The date on a letter written in the same time period corresponded with the machine's time stamp on that letter.

This was enough evidence to prompt an investigation of the engineer's machine at his new employer. The team found drawings that were similar to those from Company A, but with some differences. But through searches using keywords like *diagrams* and the name of Company A, NTI's team found an e-mail trail on the engineer's new desktop that "cinched it." The e-mails, which passed between the engineer and his girlfriend, detailed their mutual possession of the diagrams in question. One written by the engineer said that the investigators wouldn't be able to tie anything back to them. And another, written by the girlfriend, asked the engineer what he wanted her to do with the drawings he'd sent her.

The result: "a court injunction against this engineer and his company developing products based off our client's intellectual property," NTI Chief Paul French says. "If they do come out with a widget too similar in design, they'll slap them with criminal charges."

SOURCE: Excerpted from Radcliff, Deborah, "Cybersleuthing Solves the Case," *Computerworld*, January 14, 2002, 37.

In 2002, researchers at Lynnfield, Massachusetts-based Sophos Inc. detected over 7,000 new viruses and Trojan horses, bringing the total to more than 78,000. According to one source, the Sophos virus labs produce detection routines for more than 25 viruses each day. Nine of the top 10 viruses detected in 2002 were mass-mailing viruses and 87 percent of all reports of infections stemmed from Windows viruses (Verton 2003).

Despite the most valiant efforts to detect and eliminate it, exposure to malicious code will always be a problem. Virus developers are creative and are constantly inventing new viruses for all kinds of occasions. Therefore, no network is immune. In the near future, companies will need to deal with stealthy viruses carrying more destructive payloads. Surreptitious worms are expected to spread more slowly but in a harder to detect "contagion" fashion.

Table 13-2
A select foreign terrorist organization list

Organization	URL	Language(s)
Al-Gama'a al-Islamiyya (Islamic Group)	www.azzam.com	English
Hamas	www.palestine-info.com/hamas	Arabic, English
Harakat ul-Mujahidin (HUM)	www.ummah.net.pk/harakat/	Arabic, English
Hizbollah	www.hizbollah.org	Arabic, English
Kahane Chai (Kach)	www.kahane.org	English
Kurdistan Workers Party (PKK)	www.pkk.org/index.html	Kurdish
Liberation Tigers of Tamil Eelam	www.eelamweb.com	English
National Liberation Army (ELN), Columbia	www.eln-voces.com/	Spanish
Palestine Islamic Jihad (PIJ)	www.entifada.net/	Arabic
Popular Front for the Liberation of Palestine (PFLP)	www.pflp-pal.org/main.html	English
Al-Qaida	www.alneda.com	Arabic
Revolutionary Armed Forces of Columbia (FARC)	www.farc-ep.org/	English, Spanish, Portuguese, Italian, German, Russian
United Self-Defense Forces of Columbia	http://columbia-libre.org/colombialibre/pp.asp	Spanish

Source: U.S Foreign Terrorist Organizations 2002: Web sites. Excerpted from Conway, Maura. First Monday, Reality Bytes: Cyberterrorism and Terrorist 'Use' of the Internet 2002. <http://firstmonday.o.../issues/issue7_11/conway/>

Types of Viruses

The most common way of classifying a virus is by the way that it infects the system. For example, a file virus is one that attacks executable files; a boot virus attacks the boot sectors of the hard drive and the diskettes; and a macrovirus exploits the macro commands in software applications such as Microsoft Word. Many of these viruses are never spotted except in the laboratory. When they infect a computer unintentionally and spread, the virus is said to be "in the wild." Today, 80 percent of all viruses are macroviruses that are growing in popularity due to the increasing number of people connecting to the Internet, downloading high-volume files, or executing Usenet groups.

Macroviruses are written in a macro language used in Microsoft applications such as Office Suite. It is easier to write a program that infects data files such as Word documents and Excel spreadsheets than it is to write a program that affects executable files. With data files exchanged more often than executable files, the virus spreads rapidly. Embedded into the data files and well disguised, the virus can run anywhere Microsoft applications are present. The platform-independent nature of the virus makes it more potent.

Other viruses include the following: boot sector virus, the companion virus, the overwrite virus, and the multipartite virus. The boot sector virus first infects the boot sector of a floppy disk. It does not infect the hard drive simply through someone using the disk, but

BOX 13-9
Journey's start

Let's talk of history: "Brain," "Vienna," "Cascade," and so on. Those who started using IBM PCs as far [back] as the mid-80s might still remember the epidemic of these viruses in 1987 to 1989. Computers started playing a song called "Yankee Doodle," but by then people were already clever, and nobody tried to fix their speakers—very soon it became clear that this problem wasn't with the hardware; it was a virus, and not even a single one, more like a dozen.

And so viruses started infecting files. The "Brain" virus and bouncing ball of the "Ping-Pong" virus marked the victory of viruses over the boot sector. IBM PC users of course didn't like all that at all. And so there appeared antidotes. Which was the first? I don't know; there were many of them. Only a few of them are still alive, and all of these antiviruses did grow from single project up to the major software companies playing big roles on the software market.

Time went on, viruses multiplied. They all were all alike in a sense—tried to get to RAM, stuck to files and sectors, periodically killing files, diskettes, and hard disks. One of the first "revelations" was the "Frodo.4096" virus, which as far as I know was the first invisible virus (stealth).

But it was pretty easy to fight the stealth ones: Once you clean RAM, you may stop worrying and just search for the beast and cure it to your heart's content. Other, self-encrypting viruses, sometimes appearing in software collections, were more troublesome. This is because to identify and delete them it was necessary to write special subroutines to debug them. But then nobody paid attention to it, until the new generation of viruses came, those called polymorphic viruses. These viruses use another approach to invisibility: They encrypt themselves (in most cases), and to decrypt themselves later they use commands, which may or may not be repeated in different infected files.

SOURCE: Excerpted from AntiViral Toolkit Pro, "What Is a Computer Virus?", www.avp.ch/avpve/entry/entry2.htm. Accessed June 2003.

if the user forgets to take the disk out of the drive and reboots the computer, the virus copies itself to the boot sector of the hard drive. Once there, it will infect any floppy diskette used on the computer. In a DOS environment, there is often a .COM file for an .EXE file. The companion virus first infects .COM files and then infects the .EXE files when it is running. This type of virus has not been widespread, due to easy detection. The overwrite virus destroys the file it infects by copying itself to that file. Because it is obvious, it also is detected easily. The multipartite virus infects different kinds of files, including .EXE and .COM files, by going into the master boot record and then going into memory.

Spyware

Spyware: software the user unknowingly installs through an e-mail attachment or downloading an infected file that could be used for illicit reasons.

A relatively new intruder, called **spyware**, is software that the user unknowingly installs onto their system that could be used for myriads of reasons, such as collecting information about a user's computer habits. This is usually installed while loading another software package such as a shareware game or even a commercially purchased package such as Turbo Tax.

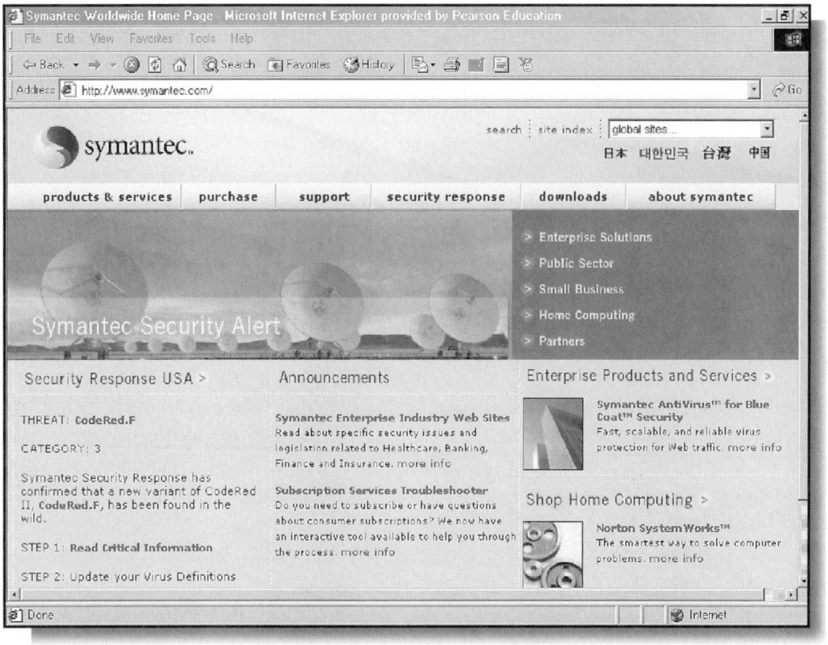

Screen Capture 13-1

While viruses are malicious, they are often obvious. A user knows they have a virus, usually when it is too late, but a spyware can sneak past anti-virus software and firewalls. A virus destroys data; spyware steals it (Business Wire 2003). The way spyware works is simple. It installs itself on a computer and runs as a separate executable program. Once it is in the system, it can randomly scan hard drives, monitor keystrokes, spy on chat applications, read cookies, and change a home page. Then the program sends the information back to the "home base" where the software creator can use the information as they please, usually for marketing purposes or to sell to the highest bidder.

Luckily, there are ways to prevent or protect users from spyware. The most obvious way is to avoid downloading it in the first place. One way to do so is to go to a Web site such as www.spychecker.com, which has a searchable database of software titles that include spyware. Another way is to install a special firewall such as ZoneAlarm (www.zonelabs.com), a free program that prevents spyware programs from "phoning home," blocking its ability to report back to the home base about the user's Internet usage. Another free program at www.lavasoft.de/software/adaware scans memory, hard drives, and registry for adware programs much the same way a virus scan works. When it is done with the scan, it presents a list of all found files and the user has the option of deleting or keeping the culprit files.

Virus Characteristics

In terms of characteristics, viruses can be classified as fast, slow, and stealth. Fast viruses spread quickly. Although it is just as easy to clean a computer hard disk with 1,000 infected files as one with 10 files, the possibility of a fast infector in computer memory causes a big headache. If a virus is located in memory and the antivirus program opens the files to scan them, the fast virus will invade and infect these files easily. Slow viruses are as dangerous as fast viruses because users are less likely to detect and destroy them. A slow virus is replicated only when a particular action is executed, such as copying diskettes. Stealth viruses appeared in 1986; the first was called Brain. All stealth viruses are memory resident and are capable of manipulating their execution in order to disguise their presence.

Another way of categorizing viruses is according to destructive capability, severity of the damage done to the host, or how long it takes to destroy and fix the damaged host. We arbitrarily divide the damage scale into six groups, ranging from trivial damage to unlimited damage, as shown in Table 13-3.

Protection Against Viruses

With the growing popularity of the Internet and e-commerce, e-mail, and the increasing number of advanced viruses, it is difficult for a system to stay pure. The best protection is to know how to locate viruses and how to recover quickly by establishing and implementing a set of prevention practices and policies. The two available approaches are antivirus software and firewalls. (Firewalls are explained later in the chapter.)

Table 13-3
Levels of virus damage

Scale of Damage	Characteristic
Trivial Damage	Done by file virus.
	Takes seconds to remove and fix the host computer.
	Example: File virus that makes speaker beep on the 18th of each month.
Minor Damage	Small amount of damage.
	Virus is removed easily and host is fixed by reinstalling the corrupted application(s).
	Example: Jerusalem virus, which deletes (on Friday the 13th) any program that has run after the virus has gone memory resident.
	Virus either formats, scrambles, or overwrites the hard disk.
	Host can be recovered by reinstalling the backup version.
	Example: Michelangelo.
	Virus hits the hard drive and the backups.
Moderate Damage	Virus discovered after days or weeks.
	Example: Dark Avenger overwritten on a random sector on the hard disk with the phrase "Eddie lives . . . somewhere in time" message.
	Virus makes gradual and progressive changes to hard disk and backups.
Major Damage	User is oblivious to whether the data are infected because the changes are not obvious.
Severe Damage	Virus that allows a third party (usually the designer) to enter a secure system.
Unlimited Damage	Example: Cheeba creates a new user with maximum privileges with a fixed user name and password in the system. Anyone with this user name and password can log on to the system.

Here are several steps for putting an antivirus strategy in place.

- Establish a set of simple enforceable rules for others to follow. These might include statements like: Any incoming disk must be checked for viruses. Do not borrow applications or files from people you do not know.
- Educate and train users on how to check for viruses on a disk; provide a better understanding of viruses and their causes. In a 1999 study of password-related user behavior involving 139 respondents, it was found that users lacked knowledge of security. Users are often told as little as possible because security departments see them as "inherently insecure." Users should be taught how to construct usable and secure passwords. They also should be given feedback during the password construction process to assist them in choosing secure passwords and to increase their awareness of system security.
- Inform users of the existing and potential threats to the company's systems and the sensitivity of information they contain. Users should be given guidance as to which systems are sensitive and why.
- Periodically update the latest antivirus software. Some companies have reached a point where an update is done daily.

Despite these measures, the war between virus creators and antivirus software developers is escalating. Most virus creators today are endlessly inventive, and viruses mutate too quickly for even the best system to detect them all. Some viruses are capable of updating themselves in order to penetrate the most up-to-date antivirus program.

Many researchers are predicting the emergence of a new e-mail virus, this time not as an attachment, but as e-mail itself. Because many of the latest e-mail readers display e-mails as an HTML page, they provide an excellent place for JavaScript viruses to hide. Some viruses will even target the antivirus software, creating more confusion and vulnerability. The speed with which malicious codes propagate is increasing, as well. The time between discovery of a new virus and the moment it went wild averaged about 6 to 9 months just few years ago. Today, it is almost instantaneous.

Protection Against Fraud

Another area under the banner of security is fraud or scams. It is estimated that the average organization loses about 6 percent of its total annual revenue to fraud from partners, customers, and abuses committed by its own employees (Schwartz 2001). Each year, fraud bleeds companies to the tune of hundreds of billions worldwide (Palshikar 2002). Fraud is a deliberate act of deceiving illegally in order to make money or obtain goods. The immoral aspect of fraud is that the individuals involved are unscrupulous. They often employ illegal and always immoral or unfair means to cheat the target organization.

Fraud management means keeping an eye on the unusual or the out-of-the-ordinary invoices, happenings, or even behavior of those with whom the organization is dealing financially. Fraud management involves a number of activities including generating profiles of users; fraud detection, prevention, and avoidance; monitoring customer dissatisfaction; risk analysis; monitoring computer and networking security; maintaining billing and accounting integrity; and cooperation with law-enforcement agencies. In addition to enormous volumes of data, any changes in behavior of users and employees must be monitored and adjusted accordingly.

With these vulnerabilities in mind, an organization can take several steps to prevent e-commerce fraud.

- Be aware of corporate critical assets and who might be after them.
- Investigate common attacks and electronic-fraud schemes that could be used against the company's critical assets.
- Install strong encryption such as public key infrastructure (PKI).
- Develop a program for evidence collection (called forensics) via committed investigators.
- Ensure maintenance of strong and reliable transaction, network, and Internet service provider logs.
- Conduct penetration testing to judge the integrity of existing security.
- Investigate the availability of cyber-fraud insurance to provide coverage for potential losses.

SECURITY PROTECTION AND RECOVERY

What are e-commerce firms doing to improve security? Unfortunately, most firms don't know the state of their security until an auditor or a consultant alerts them to the gaps. The combination of lack of knowledge and lack of accountability results in vulnerability and easy attacks. Automated detection software is now available to help a firm determine whether its system has been compromised. Good tools are not enough, however. One way to ensure basic control is to train system and network administrators in security assessment and administration.

Since the dawn of the information age, more and more security breaches originate from within the organization. As Box 13-10 describes, vulnerability from within can be costly, despite federal laws such as the Economic Espionage Act. Each firm must identify theft, control its vital data, apprehend the criminal, and ensure punishment (VanScoy 2002).

BOX 13-10
Keeping a secret

On June 3, Jeffrey W. Dorn of West Des Moines, Iowa, pleaded guilty in federal court to stealing client files from his employer, executive placement firm Spencer Reed Group. Dorn had used the files to find employment for one of the firm's clients and then had pocketed the commission. In one of nine cases prosecuted this year by the U.S. Department of Justice under the Economic Espionage Act (EEA), Dorn agreed to pay restitution of $15,920 to Spencer Reed.

Sixteen grand. No big deal, right?

Think again. Of the 35 cases prosecuted under the EEA since 1999, 28 were committed by insiders or ex-employees, according to Department of Justice statistics, and few of the cases are as innocuous as Dorn's pilfering of client data. The 2002 Computer Crime and Security Survey, conducted jointly by the Computer Security Institute and the Federal Bureau of Investigation, states that one firm reported the theft of $50 million in proprietary information last year. Another reported $1.5 million lost from unauthorized insider access to data.

Unless your company has $50 million to spare, you'd better get serious about securing your data from threats inside and out. Developers are already finding ways to make our digital Ids technically secure. Unfortunately, a technical solution is only a partial solution.

SOURCE: Excerpted from VanScoy, Kayte, "Foiling Data Thieves," *New Architect Magazine*, December 2002, 22ff.

Basic Internet Security Practices

Passwords

Choosing a password is the first basic principle in security. How often have you heard of people writing down their passwords or hanging them right on the top of the monitor frame? How often have you known someone to choose the easiest password to remember and then lend it to a friend or an associate to let the other person act on their behalf? The majority of hackers access client computers because of easy passwords (last name, last four digits of one's social security number, car's license plate number, dog's name, and so on).

One of the reasons hackers can break into a network so easily is that many system administrators never bother to change the standard, vendor-supplied passwords that come with the software. Hackers have lists of such vendors. The first password they try is GUEST. Other popular words are ADMIN, SYSADM, VISITOR, and the ever-popular PASSWORD. If these do not work, then they'll try site-specific names such as company name, e-mail addresses, and birth dates. Microsoft has a one-page write-up on creating passwords. (See www.microsoft.com/security.)

Here are the basics.

- Include at least one capital letter and one lowercase letter in the password.
- Mix numbers with letters. Short passwords won't do anymore.
- Stay away from passwords that are anywhere near your birthday, your last name, spouse's name, too obvious a name, too well known a name, or too common a name.
- No dictionary names—hackers have dictionaries.
- Change your password often, because a hacker on the prowl eventually will crack any password. Like the army, you'd want to change passwords, depending on the sensitivity of the information or site you're trying to protect.
- Disable an employee's password the moment that person leaves.

Web site owners should consult a security expert, especially if they're new at the business of issuing or assigning passwords. If you're running your Web site for the first time, review the security section of the appropriate manual, follow a procedure that makes sense, and be wary of any security software that does not have vendor backup in the way of a help desk, 800-number availability, and a good set of references that you can check prior to installation. If you're working with an ISP, review its security measures, listen to the recommendations, and assess its procedures in the event of a site attack. Someone within the firm (a Webmaster, an IT person, or a security specialist) should be in charge of the security protocols of the e-commerce environment around the clock. For a good source on Web security FAQs, go to www.w3.org/security/Faq/, which explains how to run a secure server and how to protect confidential documents at your site.

encryption: the coding of messages in traffic between computers.

Encryption is part of the basics of Web site security. This is the encoding of messages in traffic between the time when the consumer places an order and enters personal and credit card information and the time when the merchant's network processes the order. Many ISPs have special servers to provide for secure order forms. Encryption applies to a company's server, as well as to its e-mail traffic.

Encrypting e-mail is easy. Most companies start by using an S/MIME compatible e-mail client, such as products from Microsoft, Netscape, or Eudora, and installing a *certificate* from a certificate authority. Although many customers send credit card information through standard, unencrypted e-mail, they should be offered the option of send-

Screen Capture 13-2

Source: Copyright © 2003–2004 World Wide Web Consortium. Massachusetts Institute of Technology, European Research Consortium for Informatics and Mathematics, Keio University. All rights reserved. http://www.w3.org/Consortium/Legal/2002/copyright-documents-20021231, http://www.w3.org/Security/Faq/wwwsf.html.

ing encrypted e-mail. Encryption is so important that we use the next chapter to discuss methodology and implementation details.

Watch for the Credit Card Thief

Credit card thieves are not difficult to catch if you know what to look for. Here are some basic warning signs.

- A customer placing a large order without regard to size, style, or price.
- A first-time customer who places a large order and wants it shipped overnight.
- A single customer placing orders using different e-mail addresses.
- A customer living in one state who places an order to be shipped to a different address, using a credit card issued by a bank located somewhere else.
- An international customer who places a huge order and wants it shipped by air overnight.
- A customer who insists on calling you or who prefers to communicate only by e-mail.
- A customer who places multiple orders on the same day and demands that they be shipped separately to the same address.
- A minor using a parent's credit card to place a large order.

There is no question that credit card fraud affects a merchant's cost. Allowing a stolen credit card to be used at one's store is like getting arrested for drunken driving. It is a lose-lose situation. The merchant loses the merchandise (the license) and the money (the fine), and customers pay more for merchandise (higher car insurance rates). Customers must be told how to protect their credit cards and be informed of the security measures the merchant has installed to ensure their privacy. A Web site's store security FAQ should be helpful.

Credit card companies provide merchant education programs to help combat credit card fraud. Visa reports that approximately $.08 of every $100 spent online is lost to fraud. Some online customers are still uncomfortable buying on the Web. Yet if one is careful, online shopping need not be any riskier than a trip to the mall. Go to www.fraud.org/ and click on Internet Fraud Watch. During its first year in operation, more than 3.5 million people visited the Web site for inquiries or to file complaints. See Box 13-11 for learning what you risk using a credit card to shop on the Net.

Considering the way the banking industry handled the early 2003 theft of more than 8 million credit card account numbers, those most at risk of incurring losses are consumers (identity theft) and merchants that accept "card-not-present" transactions. According to Mitchell (2003), the card associations' policies are adverse to publicizing credit card thefts in any way, do not require card issuers to notify affected card owners unless they ask, and do not share a list of affected account numbers with merchants. In a world where credit cards are floating around for identify theft or fraud, there is a moral obligation to disclose such compromises to cardholders and merchants as soon as fraud is disclosed.

BOX 13-11
Credit card risks shopping online

The most important thing you need to know about using your credit card online is if a hacker steals your number and runs up your bill, you are out $50 at most. That is a federal law. In practice, banks will usually let you off the hook altogether.

Consumers may be nervous, but it is the businesses that sell goods and services online that ought to be worried. When fraudulent credit card charges occur in cyberspace, merchants eat the losses. It is a growing problem now that electronic commerce has become routine, and better solutions are needed.

Credit card giant Visa just announced a new program called Verified by Visa. It is touted as a consumer-safety measure. "Create a password that protects you when you buy online," Visa's Web site tells cardholders. "You get added safety, and the reassurance that only you can use your Visa card online."

It is an innovative system that allows consumers to sign up for a password, similar to the PIN codes used with ATM cards. When shoppers buy at a participating site, they will be prompted for the password. But the site won't ever see the secret code. Instead, it will be beamed to the credit card bank, which will then give the retailer an all-clear on the transaction.

Meantime, here are a few strategies you can follow to minimize credit card problems online: Be sure you trust the merchant. That doesn't mean patronizing only well-known stores, but it does suggest checking out a store before you buy from it. Also, make sure that Web pages where you are asked to enter personal information use encryption (signified by a gold padlock icon in the lower-right corner of an Internet Explorer window). Avoid using debit cards instead of credit cards. And most of all, challenge any irregularities.

SOURCE: Excerpted from Weber, Thomas E., "What Do You Risk Using a Credit Card to Shop on the Net?" *The Wall Street Journal*, December 10, 2001, B1.

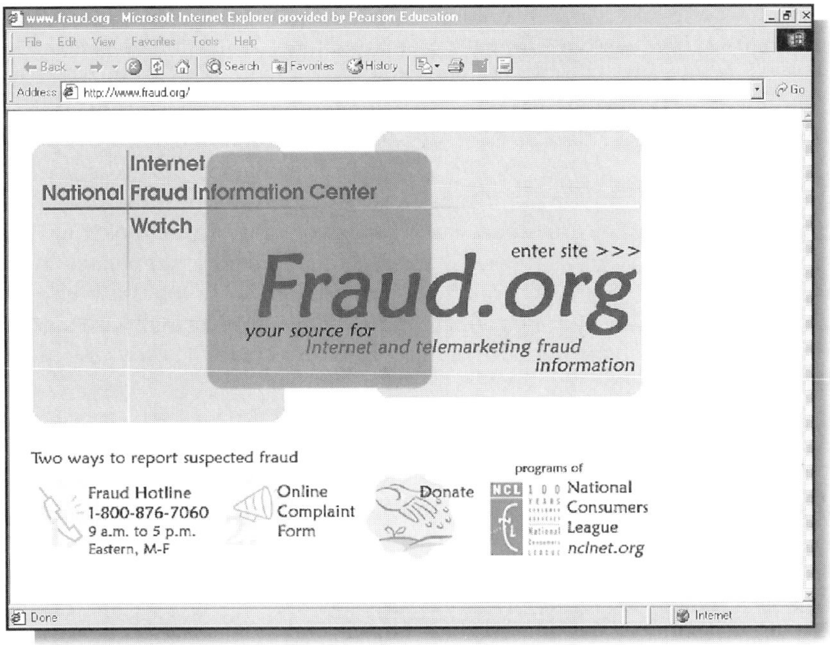

Screen Capture 13-3

Source: NFIC/IFW are projects of the National Consumers League.

CyberSource (a service provider for secure electronic distribution of software) initially was attacked by online software thieves. The agency recouped and now runs a fraud clearinghouse available to online merchants. An online credit card sale request is checked against a list of about 80,000 known online thieves. The procedure involves real-time bank validation for each transaction, followed by a cross-check of the transaction against its Internet address, browser type, and other validation factors, before a recommendation that the online sale is valid is issued. Visit CyberSource at www.cybersource.com.

Firewalls and Security

If Billy the Kid were alive today, he probably would break into corporate networks and databases before he'd think of robbing a bank. It is more lucrative and less dangerous. Network outlaws, disgruntled employees, hackers, thieves, and the like are all threats to e-commerce business. One of the most effective ways of combating adversaries is building **firewalls**—software and hardware tools that define, control, and limit access to networks and computers linked to the networks of an organization. Firewalls shield an organization's networks from exposure when connecting to the Internet or to untrusted networks, and prevent hackers from gaining access to corporate data.

Firewalls can be used to protect a corporation's network in a number of ways. Most firewalls are configured to protect against unauthenticated logins from the outside world, preventing unauthorized users from logging into machines on the company's network. Firewalls also can be employed to block all unsecured access to the internal network, while also limiting users on the inside to connecting only to acceptable external sites. Finally, a firewall can be designed to separate groups within an organization. For example, the human resources department might place their network behind a firewall to safeguard confidential payroll and personnel information from the rest of the firm.

The firewall must ensure (1) data integrity, so no one can change data from outside; (2) authentication, which guarantees that senders are who they claim to be; and (3) confidentiality, so sensitive data or messages are masked from intruding eyes.

cyberwall: all-in-one software package to improve security for the entire private network of an organization.

One category of firewalls, called **cyberwalls,** is the most recent addition in firewall technology. Although they are software based, they are more characteristic of hardware technologies. Think of cyberwalls as the software version of a firewall appliance. A firewall appliance is generally one piece of hardware that is no larger than a small desktop PC, which quickly plugs into a small firm's existing network infrastructure in between the firm's Internet access device (router, DSL modem, modem) and the firm's first hub or switch.

Cyberwalls are an all-in-one software package. They are developed with the understanding that the end goal is to improve security for the entire private network. Therefore, they should be the preference with shared networks among users, and virtual private networks among customers and suppliers. Unlike traditional software firewalls, which require many software packages to handle a network's border security, cyberwalls can protect applications, networks, and systems on the whole LAN. They provide this level of security by residing at the interconnection of the internal networks, the application and database servers, the client machines, and the perimeter.

How Does a Firewall Work?

A firewall is a software system that enforces an access control policy between two networks. It detects intruders, blocks them from entry, keeps track of what they do and where they originate, notifies the system administrator of mischievous acts, and produces a report.

How this is done varies, but most firewalls do one of two things: block traffic (called default deny) or permit traffic (called default permit). In either case, the focus is on access control. Default deny blocks all traffic except that explicitly allowed by the firewall administrator. Only the necessary traffic is specified to make it across. Default permit allows all traffic except the traffic that is explicitly blocked by the firewall administrator. Default permit requires continuous update of a list of explicitly blocked traffic every time there is a change in protocol or new applications. Default deny does not have such requirements.

Why Would You Want a Firewall?

The Internet is permeated with those who take pleasure in the electronic equivalent of writing on other people's business property, tearing into files, corrupting records, degrading e-commerce traffic, or simply bringing a business to its knees. The firewall's primary goal is to keep such people out and away from the company's e-commerce infrastructure. It provides real security and often plays a key role as a security blanket for company management.

A firewall protects against the following situations.

- E-mail services that are known to be problems.
- Unauthorized interactive logins from the outside world.
- Undesirable material such as pornographic images, movies, or literature.
- Unauthorized sensitive information leaving the company.

When they work well, firewalls can act as an effective phone tap and tracing tool. They provide administrators with summaries of the kind and amount of traffic that passed through the firewall, how many attempts were made to break into the company's network, and so on.

In contrast, a firewall cannot prevent the following.

- Attacks that do not go through the firewall; for example, exporting data to the outside via magnetic tape or a diskette.
- Weak security policies or no policy at all. In this case, no firewall can do much good. As someone said, "It's silly to build a 6-foot-thick steel door when you live in a wooden house." Visit www.interhack.net/pubs/fwfaq/firewalls-faq.html for FAQs on firewalls.
- Traitors or disgruntled employees within the organization. All an attacker needs is a helpful employee who can be fooled into giving access to the company network.
- Viruses on floppy disks.
- Data-driven attacks in which something is mailed to an internal host that proceeds to execute it.
- Trojan horses, viruses, and inside attacks.

The following sources provide information about firewalls.

- sunsite.unc.edu/LDP/HOWTO/Firewall-HOWTO.html: This Firewall "how to" describes exactly what is needed to build a firewall, especially using Linux.
- search.hosting.verio.com/cgi-htdig/htsearch /: This firewall-related publication is worth reading.
- www.net.tamu.edu/ftp/security/TAMU: This site focuses on Texas A&M University security tools.

Design and Implementation Issues

A number of design issues should be addressed by the firewall designer. The first is policy. How does the company want to operate the system? That is, is the firewall to be default deny or default permit? Firewall design is done under the larger umbrella of a clearly defined network security access policy.

The second design issue is the level of monitoring and control the organization wants. Once the risk level is agreed upon, a checklist is drafted of what should be monitored, permitted, denied, and so forth.

The third design issue is financial and administrative. A complete firewall product can run from almost zero cost to upwards of $100,000. A lot depends on the outcome of the first two design issues and the long-term management view regarding firewall security. Good and effective administrative practices in managing firewall breaches can make the difference between real security and security that is full of holes.

The fourth design issue is whether the company wants internal firewalls installed. Some companies separate the research and development network from other networks within the firm. Internal firewalls are important to limit access to company resources: If one network is infiltrated by an attacker, other networks are left uncontaminated.

A fifth design issue is the type of operating system used for firewalls. The two most commonly used systems are UNIX and Windows NT.

The International Computer Security Association (ICSA) identifies specific features that should be considered in firewall design. The primary ones are as follows.

- **Security policy:** A strong security policy should dictate the firewall design, not the other way around.
- **Deny capability:** Every firewall should be able to support "default deny." It should not have to be programmed to do the task.

- **Filtering ability:** A firewall design should allow filtering techniques (deny, permit) for each host system within the organization. Filtering ability also should be flexible to filter on as many attributes as necessary. These attributes include IP source and destination addresses, source and destination TCP ports, and user-friendly inbound and outbound interfaces.
- **Scalability:** A firewall design should be flexible enough to respond to the network's changing environment.
- **Authentication:** A firewall design should do a good job of screening users for specific applications and allow deny/permit privileges to be individualized.
- **Recognizing dangerous services:** A good firewall should be able to identify potentially dangerous services and disable them in time to minimize damage.
- **Effective audit logs:** A good firewall system should log ongoing traffic and suspicious activities, and produce reports in an easy-to-read format. This feature also implies good documentation of the design and implementation process.

Managed Firewall Services

Many firms do not have the technical experience to design their own firewall systems; they use managers of firewall services. ISPs and long-distance carriers tend to be the main suppliers of such services. They set up firewalls at their data headquarters or on customer premises. Either way, they monitor customer security remotely through their network operations center (see Figure 13-6). Unfortunately, not all providers do a secure enough job.

Figure 13-6
Corporate networks and firewalls

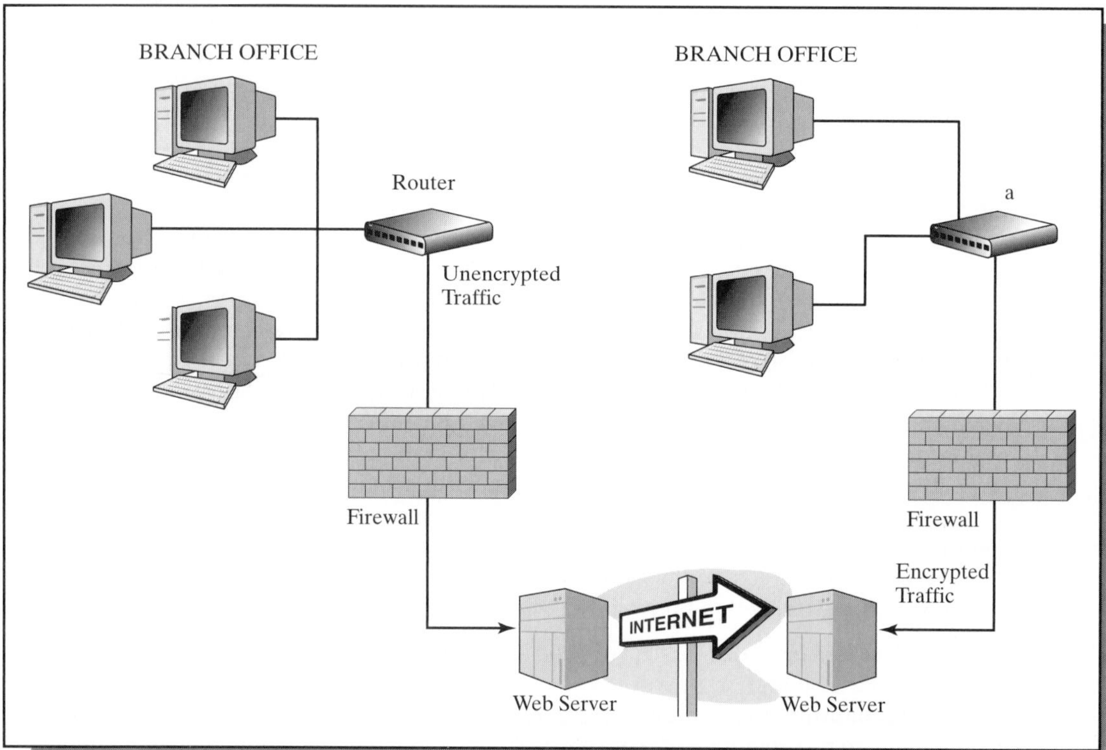

Regardless of the choice, network managers can use the Internet to download a number of security testing tools such as the following.

- **Swatch** (ftp://ftp.stanford.edu/general/security-tools/swatch) is a program designed to monitor log files and filter out unwanted data.
- **Crack** (ftp://info.cert.org/pub/tools/crack) is a password-guessing program that locates insecurities in UNIX password files and alerts network managers of weak log-in codes.
- **Computer Oracle and Password System (Cops)** (ftp://info.cert.org/pub/tools/cops) is a cluster of programs that identifies security problems in Unix.

The question for the typical firm is whether providers of managed firewall services are cheaper and more reliable than doing the job in-house. Much depends on factors such as available technical talent, recurring and nonrecurring costs, and payback. Table 13-4 offers a worksheet to determine which way a corporation should go in installing firewalls.

Recovery from Attack

Security prevention and detection gets most of the attention, yet recovery is equally important in defending a Web site. Regardless of the protection measures, not all attacks can be averted. In e-commerce, the merchant must anticipate and block possible means of attack. The security system must detect intrusion, respond in a way that limits damage, maintain the system's availability, and ensure full recovery without delay. Assuming prevention measures are in place, the cycle of recovery includes the following.

- **Attack detection:** The business monitors symptoms of a software or file problem and senses that an attack may be in progress. Special analytical tools are available to gather, diagnose, and determine whether an attack has been launched and the type of attack.
- **Damage assessment:** Once an attack is verified, the business should estimate the extent of the damage, such as corrupted data or failed software functions.
- **Correction and recovery:** In this phase, the business must decide on the procedure to correct the damage and reestablish normal system functions. HotStart, WarmStart, or ColdStart are recovery methods. HotStart is primarily a forward error recovery procedure: The attacker introduces an integrity attack to a limited part of a specific site that can be detected and contained in time by the existing security system. The system, in turn, uses an uncorrupted copy of the system to replace the corrupted portion, with no noticeable delay to the user. WarmStart involves an integrity attack that prompts automated recovery from confined damage. Some system operations can be trusted while the repair is underway. ColdStart is appropriate for severe attacks, where the goal is to bring the system back up as quickly as possible.
- **Corrective feedback:** Once the system is up and running, the business should decide on the improvements to be made in the current security system and ensure no recurrence in the future.

How to Secure Your System

A number of steps can be taken to make a system secure. Turn off unneeded or unnecessary services. On Unix environments, services that are not in great demand can be disabled easily. In peer-to-peer sharing, make sure the machines linked to the Internet share no files. Any shared files should be password protected. Install a firewall between your

Table 13-4
In-house versus outsourcing firewall services

Worksheet: In-house vs. Outsourcing	
Type of Cost	**Cost ($)**
I. Nonrecurring Costs	
(Companies with a security infrastructure can leave this section blank)	
Hardware (firewalls, remote access equipment, servers)	________
Software licensing	________
Encryption software	________
Digital certificates, tokens, smart cards	________
Security diagnostic and testing equipment	________
Other	________
II. Recurring Costs	
Hardware/Software	
Upgrades and patches	________
Other	________
Line 2: Subtotal	________
Annual Human Resource Costs	
Salary for maintenance staff	________
Salary for firewall administrators	________
Salary for policy administrators	________
Consulting services	________
Security training	________
Other	________
Line 3: Subtotal	________
Annual Maintenance	
Hardware and software repairs	________
Third-party security audits/threat analysis	________
Insurance	________
Other	________
Line 4: Subtotal	________
Line 5: Total annual recurring costs	
(add Lines 2, 3, and 4)	________
Line 6: Total first-year cost of in-house security service	
(add Lines 1 and 5)	________
III. Payback	
Line 7: Annual cost of comparable security service	________
Line 8: First-year savings from outsourcing security	
(subtract Line 7 from Line 6)	________
If Line 7 is greater than Line 8, a security service	
Will initially be more expensive.	
To estimate the payback period in years, divide	
Line 7 by Line 5	________

Source: Adapted from Makris, Joanna, "Firewall Services: More Bark Than Bite," *Data Communications*, March 1999, 44.

network and the Internet such that the firewall will allow outgoing connections from the network to the Internet but forbid incoming connections, except a selected set of services (default deny). For a basic network-Internet environment, an inexpensive router provides simple firewall filtering and other firewall functions.

Monitor and know your system. Most network administrators never realize their systems have been attacked. Successful attacks leave traces. If you review logs, they can alert you to follow a procedure to prevent attacks from recurring. Automated log analyzers can be used to flag suspicious activities.

One way of knowing your system is to stay on top of basic features that keep it secure. For example, install and run a virus-checking package. If your system gets hacked and has to be rebuilt, make sure you have the methodology to rebuild quickly with minimum delays.

Building a Response Team

When all is said and done, having a team of specialists on board to respond to computer incidents is much like a fire-fighting crew ready to fight a fire. A team may be activated by hacker or virus attacks, internal sabotage, or illicit attempts to gain access to funds or files. More than money is involved. The company's reputation and its status with its customer base can be severely damaged. Box 13-12 summarizes what it takes to build a response team capability.

BOX 13-12
Role of a response team

A security response team's key mission is to orchestrate a speedy and organized company-wide response to computer threats. The following are some tips for building that capability:

- **Know your constituency.** Decide which computers, address ranges, and domains will be monitored for incidents. Develop policies for when to disclose security breaches and when to report an incident to law-enforcement agencies.
- **Assemble the team.** Figure out which department the response team should be in and who should head it. Wherever it sits, it will not succeed without management support. The response team at the University of Wisconsin-Madison has a process for calling in its legal department and local law enforcement when incidents involve activities such as computer-related harassment.
- **Create a SWAT team.** Maintaining a full-time security response team can be expensive, so many companies choose to have an ad hoc incident response team that can come together quickly when needed.
- **Get organized.** Have written policies and procedures, and assign responsibilities upfront. Figure out what equipment you'll need, where you'll house it, and how you'll protect the response team function. You don't want unauthorized people accessing information that a response team may uncover during a response. Conduct frequent drills and mock exercises, especially for ad hoc teams. It is a process that you have to do right but hope you never have to use.

SOURCE: Excerpted from Vijayan, Jaikumar, "Build a Response Team," *Computerworld*, July 15, 2002, 32.

Summary

1. The electronic system that supports e-commerce can fail due to fraud, theft of confidential information, disruption of service, or loss of customer confidence. Internet security is about protecting information.
2. Paper-based commerce involves signed paper documents, person-to-person interaction, physical payment systems, and easily negotiable documents of title. In contrast, electronic commerce involves digital signatures, electronic payment systems, no face-to-face interaction, difficult-to-detect modifications, and negotiable documents requiring special security protocols.
3. Several reasons account for the recent emphasis on information security: Global trading; online, real-time trading; availability of reliable security packages; and changes in attitude toward security.
4. Designing for e-security involves five steps: adopting a security policy that makes sense, considering Web security needs, designing the security environment, policing the security perimeter, and authorizing and monitoring the security system.
5. Web merchants must consider three kinds of threats: those that are physically related, those that are order related, and those that are electronically related.
6. No network is completely immune from viruses. A virus is classified by the way it infects the system. Examples are a file virus, a boot virus, and a macrovirus. In terms of characteristics, a virus may be a fast virus, a slow virus, or a stealth virus.
7. To install an antivirus strategy, you need to establish enforceable rules, educate users in how to check for viruses, and periodically update the latest antivirus software.
8. A firewall is a software system that detects intruders, blocks them from entry, and keeps track of what they do and where they originated. Most firewalls either block unwanted traffic (default deny) or permit only wanted traffic (default permit). In either case, the focus is on access control.

Key Terms

- Authentication, 405
- Cyberwall, 428
- denial of service, 411
- encryption, 424
- firewall, 405
- intrusion detection, 414
- monitoring, 406
- privacy, 400
- security perimeter, 405
- sniffer, 408
- spoof, 409
- spyware, 419
- virus, 416

Test Your Understanding

1. The electronic system that supports e-commerce is susceptible to abuse and failure in many ways. Do you agree with this statement?
2. In what way is the Internet different from the traditional ways of doing business?
3. Elaborate on the security design process. What steps are involved? How does each step contribute to effective security?
4. What threats or crimes must Web merchants consider? Why? Be specific.
5. How are client computers attacked? Explain briefly.
6. How are server attacks launched? Give an example.

7. What is a virus? How does a company know its computers or files have a virus?
8. List some of the basics of choosing a password.
9. What are the design and implementation issues that should be addressed by a firewall design?
10. ICSA identifies specific features that should be considered in firewall design. Explain each feature briefly.

Discussion Questions

1. How would a business decide how much risk it can afford?
2. Given the momentum in Internet business, is there a reason to worry about security in cyberspace? Why?
3. Suppose your e-commerce server is under attack from at least one malicious source. What types of threats are possible? How would you recommend handling such threats?

Web Exercises

1. Work with another classmate and set up an interview with a local e-merchant to address the security schemes embedded in their business-to-consumer business. Report your findings in class.
2. Assume you have been asked to serve as a consultant for a local grocer interested in launching an online business on the Internet. Develop a security plan that can be incorporated as part of the technical infrastructure.
3. MasterCard, Visa, and American Express have interest in the SET protocol for securing credit card transactions. Contact one of the agencies and find out the latest in security protocol and how well SET is being supported.
4. Review three Web sites on the Internet: one large e-business Web site (e.g., http://Dell.com), a large bank Web site (e.g., http://Bankofamerica.com), and a portal Web site (e.g., http://Yahoo.com). Review each site's security measures. How do they compare? What is unique about each site's security protocol? Write a 300-word report for class.

Chapter 14

Encryption: A Matter of Trust

Contents

In a Nutshell

Ensuring security of electronic data is a serious business. The transmission of purchase information, credit card numbers, and other transaction information must be secure to give consumers and merchants the confidence they need to do business over the Internet. One way to have secure transmissions is to use cryptography to **encrypt** or encode data so it can be read only by the parties to the transaction.

encrypt (encipher): transform a plaintext into ciphertext.

In Greek, *cryptography* means "secret writing," which is the science of communication over untrusted communication channels. **Encryption** is a cryptographic technique that encodes data so it cannot be read without a key. The ancient Egyptians developed hieroglyphics to disguise their messages (www.computerworld.com. Accessed June 2003). Julius Caesar used an alphabetical code to communicate with his field commanders. Technology has progressed significantly since ancient times, and now we have a number of sophisticated encryption tools.

encryption: a mathematical procedure that scrambles data so that it is extremely difficult for anyone other than authorized recipients to recover the original message.

Without encryption, e-commerce is nearly impossible. When shopping online or doing Internet banking, encryption makes payments or transmittal of financial information safe. Encryption is important in protecting burglar alarms, cash machines, postal meters, automated teller machines (ATMs), electronic funds transfers, trade secrets, health records, personnel files, and credit card transactions on the Net. It is also essential for national security. Because good encryption is so valuable, the U.S. government has developed stringent rules for cryptography. Organizations such as the National Security Council, the National Computer Security Center, and the National Institute of Standards and Technology work to control the use of encryption and to prevent it from becoming a threat to society.

In this chapter, we cover the basic principles of cryptography, why it is essential, and how it is used in e-commerce transactions. Remember that payment systems (Chapter 15) and security measures (Chapter 13) rely on encryption. We also look at the future. Currently, encryption protocols use mainly public-key infrastructure (PKI) software. The future of encryption, however, lies in elliptic-curve cryptography and eventually in quantum computers. Quantum computing is far ahead of anything we are familiar with today and will make any current cryptography obsolete.

What Is Encryption?

Encryption is a way to transform a message so that only the sender and recipient can read, see, or understand it. The mechanism is based on the use of mathematical procedures to scramble data so that it is extremely difficult for anyone other than authorized recipients to recover the original message (**plaintext or cleartext**). The formula or algorithm converts the intended data (credit card number, social security number, medical record, and so on) into an encoded message using a key to decode or decipher the message. A **key** is a series of electronic

plaintext (cleartext): the message that is being protected.

key: a series of electronic signals stored on a PC's hard disk or transmitted as blips of data over transmission lines.

signals stored on the PC's hard disk or transmitted as blips of data over transmission lines. A special key decrypts the message to its original state.

If someone scrambles information before it is transmitted, eavesdroppers cannot read what was written, unless they take pains to crack the code. The good news is that it took years before the United States allowed the use of encryption. The government focused not on the benefits, but the dangers—the fear that terrorists, child pornographers, or drug dealers would be able to promote their businesses using cryptography (see Box 14-1). Yet, even with today's increasing use of cryptography, millions of medical records, credit card databases, and other repositories continue to be vulnerable.

Think of a cryptographic algorithm as the lock on a home's front door. Most door locks have a spindle containing four pins, and each pin can be in 1 of 10 positions. When you insert the right key, it sets the pins in a configuration that matches the teeth in the key. When both align correctly, the door opens. With 10^4 or 10,000 possible keys, a burglar potentially has to try all these possibilities before being able to break in. Imagine an improved lock with 100 million (10^8) possible keys. Unfortunately, when the going gets tough, the burglar might use brute force and attack via the window or side door, or by forcing entry at gunpoint. The same thing happens with encryption. Hackers first use generic software that has been tried on low-security PCs and if that does not work, they physically enter one combination after another until they succeed at breaking into the PC or decrypting the message(s) they're after. With the right experience, they usually succeed one way or the other.

Today's powerful PCs and cryptographic algorithms make it possible for anyone to use authentication and encryption. How do you know whether your browser is encrypting your information? One way to tell when you purchase an item online using Netscape's browser is this: If the picture of a lock in the lower left-hand corner is in the *locked* position with a glow around it, you're most likely using encryption. Another way is to look at the Internet address you are visiting. If it starts with *https*, the "s" means secure—you're using a secure server that has encryption.

BOX 14-1
Encryption and terrorism

The destruction of the World Trade Center and the attack on the Pentagon come at a delicate time in the evolution of the technologies of surveillance and privacy. In the aftermath of September 11, 2001, our attitude toward these tools may well take a turn that has profound implications for the way individuals are monitored and tracked, for decades to come.

Did encryption empower these terrorists? And would restricting crypto have given the authorities a chance to stop these acts? The answer is quite possibly yes. We do know that Osama Bin Laden, who has been invoked as a suspect, was a sophisticated consumer of crypto technology. In the recent trial over the bombing of the Libyan embassy, prosecutors introduced evidence that Bin Laden had mobile satellite phones that used strong crypto. Even if Bin Laden was not behind it, the acts show a degree of organization that indicates the terrorists were smart enough to scramble their communications to make them more difficult, if not impossible, to understand. If not for encryption, notes former USAF Colonel Marc Enger (now working for security firm Digital Defense) "they could have used steganography [hiding messages between the pixels of a digital image] or Web anonymizers [which cloak the origin of messages]."

SOURCE: Excerpted from Levy, Steven, "Did Encryption Empower These Terrorists?" *Newsweek Web Exclusive*, www.msnbc.com/news/627390.asp?0si=. Accessed June 2003.

Encryption has had a long history of improvement, dating back to the early 1970s when an effort was made to learn how to create new tools of privacy. As summarized in Box 14-2, the most recent event was in 1999, when Al Gore, former vice president of the United States, signed off on regulations allowing the export of strong crypto.

Public Key Infrastructure (PKI) creates the ability to authenticate users, maintain privacy, ensure data integrity, and process transactions without the risk of repudiation. It satisfies four e-security needs.

1. **Authentication:** It identifies or verifies that the senders of messages are, in fact, who they claim to be. For example, Jane, an e-customer, wants to be sure that she is dealing with a legitimate vendor. Likewise, the vendor wants to make sure that Jane is really Jane. (An imposter who sends a false message is **spoofing.**) For example, a hacker can concoct a fake Web site and, through a security hole in the genuine Web site, allow his Web site IP address to substitute for that of the real one. In doing so, innocent traffic going to the legitimate Web site is funneled to the fake site. When orders or queries arrive, the hacker can make all kinds of alterations—direct the traffic to a third Web site, change the nature of the orders, and so on. An example of authentication in practice is described in Box 14-3.

spoofing: the act of sending a message while pretending to be the authorized user.

2. **Integrity:** Verifies that neither the purchase amount nor the goods bought are changed or lost during transmission. Integrity also means the message has not reached the recipient twice. In the case of Jane, she and the vendor want to ensure that attackers

BOX 14-2
Brief history of encryption growth

1971: Below the National Security Administration's (NSA) radar, math vagabond Whit Diffie begins crisscrossing the country to learn how to create new tools of privacy.

1974: Berkeley undergrad Ralph Merkle finds a way that two people can communicate secretly without prearrangements. His teacher suggests he write about something more sensible.

1976: Diffie and Martin Hellman publish "New Directions in Cryptography," introducing the public-key concept that enables large-scale privacy and e-commerce.

1977: Three MIT professors—Ron **R**ivest, Adi **S**hamir, and Len **A**dleman—create RSA, an elegant implementation of public key.

1979: NSA goes public to warn people about the spread of crypto not under its control.

1983: RSA Data Security is founded, the first company to commercialize public-key crypto.

1986: Lotus Development Corp. licenses RSA for its planned Notes software, then fights NSA for export clearance.

1991: Phil Zimmermann gives away PGP, a strong encryption program. To Fed dismay, it becomes a global favorite.

1993: Clinton administration endorses the ill-fated Clipper Chip.

1995: Netscape goes public; its crypto-enabled browser establishes need for secure e-commerce.

1999: Fed surrender: Al Gore signs off on regulations, finally allowing the export of strong crypto.

SOURCE: Excerpted from Levy, Steven, "Crypto," *Newsweek*, January 15, 2001, 48–49.

BOX 14-3
Authentication in action

OK, your Web portal strategy has finally caught fire with customers, distributors, and suppliers. But how do you handle authentication (ensuring users are who they say they are) and authorization (making sure they get only the appropriate access to applications and data)?

You can build authentication and security logic into each application or into the directories—lists of users or other resources—running on various networks. But this gets unwieldy in a complex, ever-changing portal where thousands of users must have specific access to only certain applications controlled by different businesses.

Enter Netegrity Inc., which several analysts regard as the leader in this small but fast-growing market.

Netegrity centralizes all the data about who can access what on a rules engine, or policy server, that runs on a Windows NT or Sun Solaris server. The server contains policies that define, based on users' roles, what applications and data they can access and what actions they can perform. Agents query the policy server. They intercept user requests to determine if the resources to which they seek access are protected. If a resource is protected, the agent asks the policy server to determine what level of authentication is required for that resource, and then which resources, such as applications, files, or individual Web pages, the user may access.

SOURCE: Excerpted from Scheier, Robert L., "Sorry, Only Authentic Users Need Apply," *Computerworld*, January 8, 2001, 62.

Screen Capture 14-1

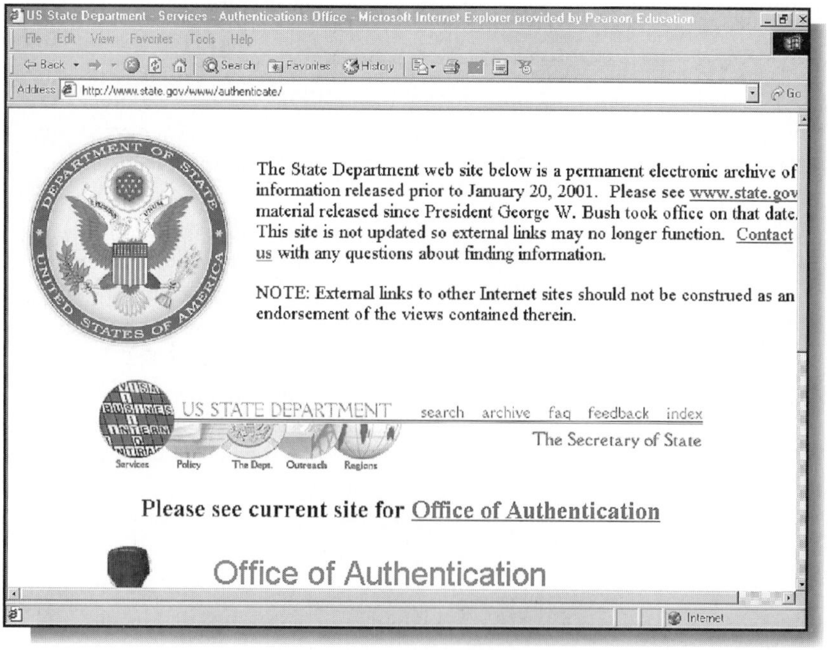

cannot change the price, purchase amount, or quantity. A nonelectronic mechanism example of integrity is indelible ink or a hologram on a credit card.

3. **Nonrepudiation:** Prevents sender and vendor in a transaction or communication activity from later falsely denying that the transaction occurred. **Nonrepudiation** is like sending a certified letter with a return receipt via the U.S. postal system. Like a receipt accompanying the registered letter, because a digital signature accompanies the transfer of data, the originator cannot deny having sent the message. In our example, the vendor wants to make sure that Jane cannot deny having placed the order. A nonelectronic mechanism of nonrepudiation is knowledge of mother's maiden name or a photo ID card.

nonrepudiation: procedure that prevents sender and vendor from credibly denying that they sent or received a specific message, file, or transmission.

4. **Privacy:** Shields communications from unauthorized viewing or access. Jane might not want her spouse or any other person to know what she is transacting, nor does the vendor want to reveal the special deal he has made for that particular customer. Privacy protection implies confidentiality and anonymity. *Confidentiality,* or message content security, means that during the transmission from sender to receiver, no third party can access the contents of the message or identify the sender and receiver. *Anonymity* means outsiders cannot trace, link or observe the contents of the message. An anonymous record is one that cannot be associated with a particular individual, either from the data itself or by combining the record with other records.

The Basic Algorithm System

Cryptographic techniques are a means of securely transferring data over Internet applications. It is the science of applying complex mathematics to increase the security of electronic transactions. The techniques provide assurance that the data will be viewed only by the intended parties. Basic encryption relies on two components: an algorithm and a key. Encrypting information is simple: A computer program is used that has an encryption algorithm. The algorithm converts data, documents, credit card numbers, and other information into an encoded message using a key.

For encryption to work, both sender and receiver have to know the rules used to transform the original message or transaction into its coded form. A set of rules for encoding and decoding messages is called a **cipher** (or cypher). The encoded message is called a **ciphertext.** A message can be **decrypted** only if the decryption key matches the encryption key. For most algorithms, the keys are the same.)

cipher: a set of rules for encoding and decoding messages.

ciphertext: an encoded message; the result of transforming a plaintext via encryption.

decrypt: transform a ciphertext into plaintext.

How many possible keys can each algorithm support? This depends on the number of bits in the key. For example, a 6-bit key allows for only 64 possible numeric combinations (2^6), each called a key. The greater the number of possible keys, the more complex the key becomes and the more difficult it is to crack an encrypted message. A hacker using the brute-force method would potentially have to try every combination before finding the right key. The key could also be guessed correctly on the first try.

The standard 56-bit DES encryption code can be cracked on a high-speed computer in a few hours. Even Certicom Corporation's encryption code, which took the power of 10,000 computers running continuously for 549 days to protect digital data, was cracked by Notre Dame researcher Chris Monico in 2000. With a 100-bit (2^{100}) key, it could take a computer, guessing at 1 million keys every second, years to discover the right key. The security of an encryption algorithm, therefore, is related to the length of the key. Knowing the key length gives you an idea of how much time it will take to break the code.

Late in 2002, a quantum encryption prototype was developed by two Northwestern University professors to encode entire high-speed data streams moving at 250 Mbits/second. Professors Prem Kumar and Horace Yuen use quantum codes to encrypt the signal sent down the Internet's optical fiber backbone (Johnson 2002).

Classes of Algorithms

secret-key (symmetric) encryption: encryption system in which sender and receiver possess the same key; the key used to encrypt a message also can be used to decrypt it.

stream cipher: a symmetric algorithm that encrypts a single bit of plaintext at a time.

block cipher: a symmetric algorithm that encrypts a number of bits as a single unit.

There are two classes of key-based algorithms: **secret key or symmetric,** and public key or asymmetric. In secret-key, or symmetric encryption, sender and recipient possess the same *single* key. Both parties can encrypt and decrypt messages with the same key (see Figure 14-1). This can pose two problems: One, the key must be delivered securely to the two parties involved. Hand delivery or generating a complex network-based scheme makes key distribution an awkward process. The second problem is that if a business has 10 business vendors, it needs 10 different single keys unique to each vendor. Key distribution for multiple keys can be a hassle.

However, symmetric encryption satisfies the requirement of message content security, because the content cannot be read without the shared secret key. The process of providing a secure mechanism for creating and passing on the secret key is called key management. This topic will be covered later in the chapter.

Symmetric algorithms can be divided into stream ciphers and block ciphers. **Stream ciphers** encrypt a single bit of plaintext at a time, whereas **block ciphers** encrypt a number of bits (normally 64) as a single unit.

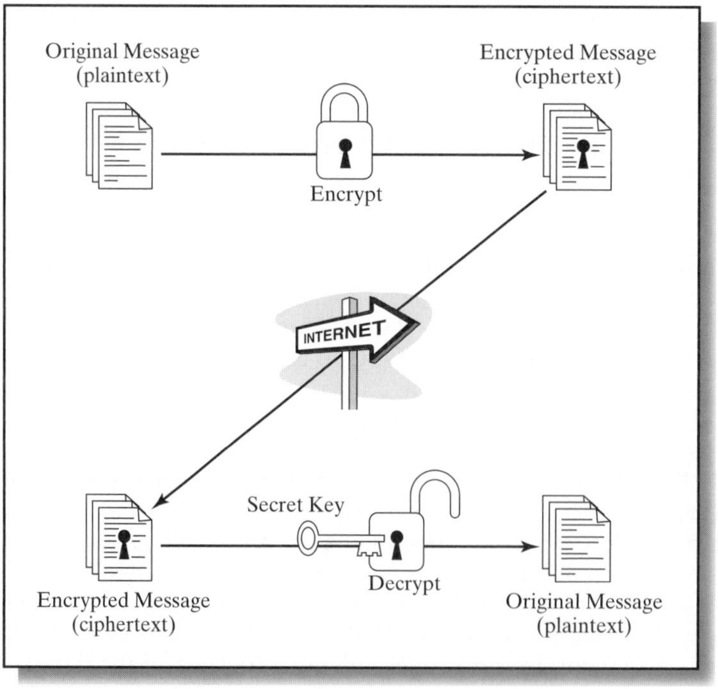

Figure 14-1 Symmetric encryption using a single secret key to encrypt and decrypt messages

public-key (asymmetric) encryption: encoding/decoding using two mathematically related keys or key-pairs: one public key and one private key.

Public-key, or asymmetric, encryption involves two related keys called a *key-pair* or *dual key*: one public key that anyone can know and one private key that only the owner knows. One half of the pair (public key) can encrypt information that only the other half (private key or secret key) can decrypt (see Figure 14-2). The private key is assigned to one designated owner, but the public key can be announced to the world. It can be published in a newspaper, on a server, on a Web site, or via a service provider so that anyone can encrypt with it.

The key-pairs can be used in two different ways.

1. **To provide message confidentiality.** The sender uses the recipient's public key to encrypt a message to remain confidential until decoded by the recipient with the private key. Suppose Jay wants to send a confidential message to Ellen. He would first acquire Ellen's public key. Then, he would use that key to encrypt the message and send it to her. If a third party intercepts the message and tries to decode it using Ellen's public key, it won't work. Because only Ellen has the private key, only she can decrypt it. Were Ellen to send a reply, she would use Jay's public key, and Jay would use his private key to decrypt it (see Figure 14-3).
2. **To prove the authenticity of the message originator.** The sender encrypts a message using the private key, a key to which only he or she has access. Using a private key for encryption is like signing a document. Because you are the only person who can encrypt an electronic document with your private key, anyone using your public key to decrypt the message is certain that the message came from you.

Symmetric cryptography has been around (at least in primitive forms) for more than 2,000 years; asymmetric schemes were invented in the mid-1970s. A symmetric key is fast and can be implemented easily in most hardware. The problems are that both keys are the

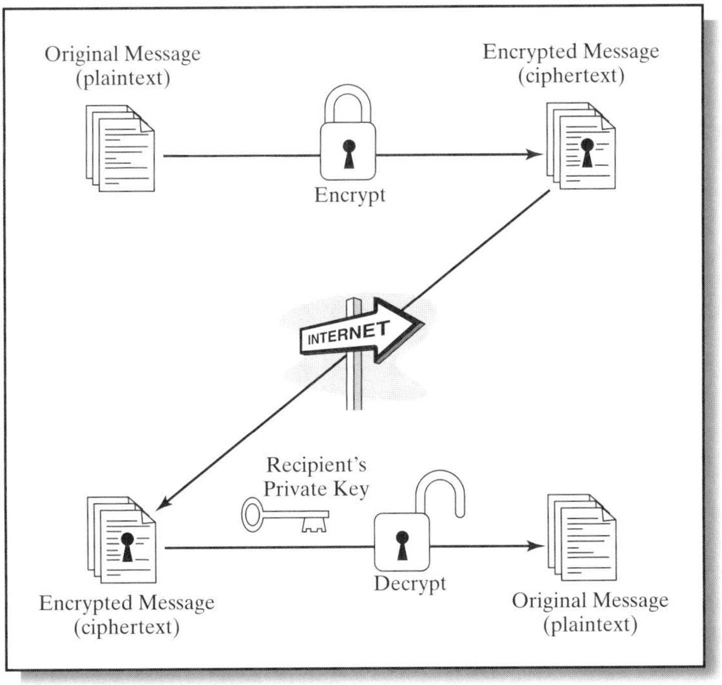

Figure 14-2
Public-key cryptography

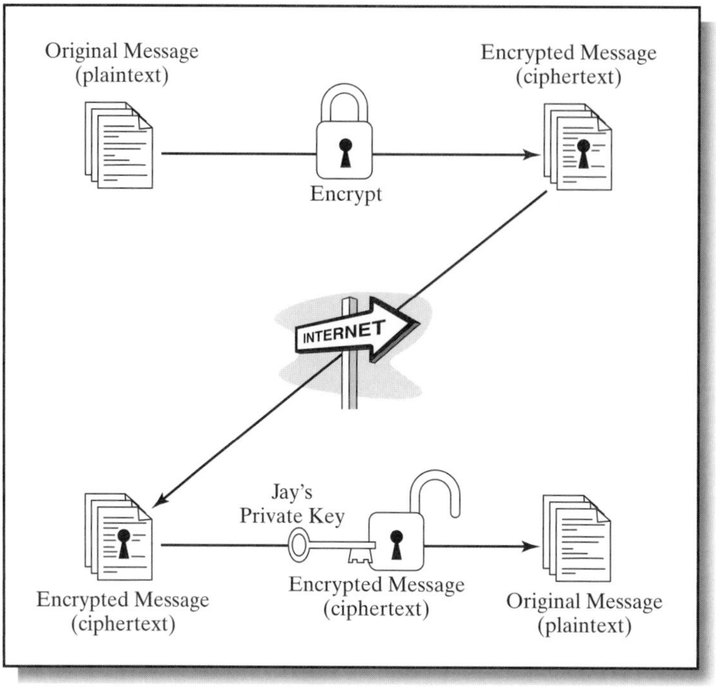

Figure 14-3 Message confidentiality using a key-pair

same, distributing keys is not a straightforward process, and the symmetric method does not support digital signatures (explained later in the chapter). It also does not adequately address the nonrepudiation requirement, because both parties have the same key.

A public (asymmetric) key is a more secure approach. It has two distinct advantages: Only one party needs to know the private key and, if a third party knows the public key, it does not compromise the security of the message. The decryption key need never be in the hands of anyone other than the owner. It is easy to distribute the keys. The approach also addresses all the integrity, authentication, and nonrepudiation requirements. The main disadvantage is that it takes time to compute. Currently, a 1,024-bit asymmetric key length is necessary to provide security. This requires a lot of processing power, resulting in delays when large volumes of messages are sent.

The choice of an encryption method depends on the sensitivity of the data to be protected and the duration of the protection. Typically, the encryption method and key length chosen should take longer to break than the time the data stay sensitive. Table 14-1 summarizes sample key lengths and the time it takes to break a key, using a brute-force attack.

Common Cryptosystems

It should be known by now that symmetric algorithms use the same key for encryption and decryption. The key is not to be leaked to outsiders and should be changed often to ensure security. This means that a longer key means higher security. Symmetric algorithms are generally faster than asymmetric ones and use shorter keys. In the following section, we summarize the key public- and secret-key algorithms, as no better or more powerful ones have been introduced to date.

Table 14-1
Estimated time and cost of breaking different key lengths

	Key Length (Bits)			
Estimated Cost to Break Key	40	64	80	128
$100,000	2 sec	1 year	70,000 years	10^{19} years
$1 million	0.2 sec	37 days	7,000 years	10^{18} years
$100 million	2 millisec	9 hours	70 years	10^{16} years
$1 billion	0.2 millisec	1 hour	7 years	10^{15} years

Source: Schneier, Bruce, *Applied Cryptography* (2nd Ed.), New York: John Wiley & Sons, Inc., 1997, 153.

RSA Algorithm

RSA: the most commonly used public-key algorithm.

RSA is the most commonly used public-key algorithm, although it is vulnerable to attack. Named after its inventors, Ron **R**ivest, Adi **S**hamir, and Len **A**dleman of the Massachusetts Institute of Technology (MIT), RSA was first published in 1978. It is used for encryption as well as for electronic signatures. RSA lets you choose the size of your public key. The 512-bit keys are considered insecure or weak. The 768-bit keys are secure from everything but the National Security Administration (NSA). The 1,024-bit keys are secure from virtually anything. The U.S. patent on this algorithm expired in the year 2000. RSA is embedded in major products such as Windows, Netscape Navigator, Intuit's Quicken, and Lotus Notes.

How strong is RSA? Its strength depends on the time and the cost of the equipment performing the decryption. To illustrate, an international team of scientists was asked to break a 129-digit RSA block cipher in 1994. The total processing power used was comparable to the processing power of a single Pentium 100-MHz computer running nonstop for 46 years. With improvements in computing power and cost, RSA's vulnerability has increased. It is estimated that an attacker with $20,000 to spend will be able to break a 425-bit block cipher.

Data Encryption Standards (DES)

Data Encryption Standards (DES): a popular secret-key encryption system; the first to be widely adopted commercially.

Data Encryption Standards (DES) was developed by IBM in 1974 in response to a public solicitation from the U.S. Department of Commerce. It was adopted as a U.S. federal standard in 1977 and as a financial industry standard in 1981.

DES is the first symmetric system to be widely adopted commercially. Any change to a message encrypted with DES turns the message into a mess of unintelligible characters. As a block cipher with 64-bit size, DES uses a 56-bit key to encrypt a 64-bit plaintext block into a 64-bit ciphertext. A 56-bit key might seem easy to crack, but it is strong enough to give most random hackers a run for their money.

DES messages can be decrypted by a huge computer mainframe or by thousands of small ones working together. DES is known to be a good block cipher design because no practical attack more efficient than exhaustive key search is known to threaten the integrity of the algorithm. In an exhaustive key search, the attacker systematically attempts to decrypt a ciphertext block against all possible key values until it runs into the value that will decrypt the message. To do this type of search requires powerful computing resources.

3DES

Triple DES (3DES): a stronger version of DES that uses three 56-bit keys to encrypt each block of plaintext.

A stronger version of DES, called **Triple DES (3DES)**, uses three 56-bit keys to encrypt each block. The first key encrypts the data block, the second key decrypts the data block, and the third key encrypts the same data block again. The 3DES version requires a 168-bit key that makes the process quite secure and much safer than plain DES. It can secure the most valuable data, even that of large corporations.

RC4

RC4: variable-length cipher widely used on the Internet as a bulk encryption cipher in SSL protocol.

RC4 was designed by Ron Rivest RSA Data Security Inc. This variable-length cipher is widely used on the Internet as the bulk encryption cipher in the Secure Sockets Layer (SSL) protocol, with key lengths ranging from 40 to 128 bits. RC4 has a reputation of being fast, although its security is unknown. The U.S. government routinely approves RC4 with 40-bit keys for export, but keys this small can be broken easily by criminals, amateurs, and governments. (SSL is explained later in the chapter.)

International Data Encryption Algorithm (IDEA)

IDEA: a strong encryption algorithm using a 128-bit key to encrypt 64-bit blocks; resistant to brute-force attack.

International Data Encryption Algorithm (IDEA) was created in Switzerland in 1991. It offers strong encryption using a 128-bit key to encrypt 64-bit blocks, which makes it resistant to brute-force attacks. This system is widely used as the bulk encryption cipher in older versions of Pretty Good Privacy (PGP) systems, covered later in the chapter.

Issues in Public-Key Cryptography

The choice of who generates key-pairs is an issue that has plagued the security industry. The choices are the key owner, a service organization of the owner's choice, or a government agency. In the case of the owner, the private key never travels outside the owner's computer, and the owner must have the technical competence to perform the necessary mathematical functions. In the case of a service organization, the private key resides with the service organization and must travel to the owner. The owner has to trust the organization not to keep a copy.

In the case of a government agency generating key-pairs, the private key has to travel, trust must exist, and the location of all private keys is known to the state agency. If individual organizations lose their private keys, they will be unable to encrypt messages with the private keys or read messages sent to them encrypted with their own public keys.

Any system, especially a system that involves customers' private information, the merchant's vital customer profile, and the financial transactions that are crucial for successful e-commerce, must be secure, well documented, and scalable any time an upgrade is required. In theory, any cryptographic method with a key can be broken by trying various possible keys in sequence. If brute force is the only alternative, the likelihood of cracking the system depends on the length of the key. For example, a 32-bit key can be broken on any home computer. In contrast, a system with a 56-bit key (such as DES) takes special hardware to crack. Although expensive to acquire, such hardware is within the reach of major corporations and most governments. Keys with 128 bits are presently impossible to crack by brute force.

Major Attacks on Cryptosystems

cryptoanalysis: the science of deciphering encrypted messages without knowing the right key.

Cryptoanalysis is the science of deciphering encrypted messages without knowing the right key. Here are some common cryptoanalytic attacks.

1. **Chosen-plaintext attack:** The attacker uses an unknown key to encrypt any text or document. The challenge is to find the key that is known only to the attacker. An e-payment system should be designed so that an attacker could never succeed in encrypting chosen plaintext.

2. **Known-plaintext attack:** In this technique, the attacker knows the plaintext for part(s) of the ciphertext. He or she uses this information to decrypt the rest of the ciphertext.

3. **Ciphertext-only attack:** In this approach, the attacker has no idea what the message contains and works primarily from ciphertext, making guesses about the plaintext. Some ciphertext data might contain a common word as a starter. Certain documents begin in a predictable way that often gives away the contents.

4. **Third-party attack:** In this technique, an adversary breaks into the communication line between two parties (e.g., buyer and vendor). He or she uses a separate key with each party. Each party uses a different key that is easily known to the adversary. The adversary, in turn, decrypts the transmitted documents with the right key and encrypts it with the other key before it is sent to the recipient. Neither party has any idea that their communication system has been intercepted.

For more on cryptosystem attacks, see www.ssh.fi/tech/crypto/intro.html. Accessed June 2003.

AUTHENTICATION AND TRUST

Digital Signatures

digital signature: a special signature for signing electronic correspondence, produced by encrypting the message digest with the sender's private key.

message digest: a block of data or a sample of the message content that represents a private key.

authentication: verifying that a message or document, in fact, comes from the claimed sender.

One way to implement public key authentication on a per-message basis is to send a **digital signature** with each message. As shown in Figure 14-4, when you sign a letter, you authenticate it by adding your signature at the end of the message. A digital signature is added at the end of each message you send. The U.S Postal Service now issues digital signatures on smart cards through post offices nationwide, using "in-person proofing" as part of the process (see Box 14-4).

A digital signature, first proposed in 1976 by Whitfield Diffie of Stanford University, transforms the message that is signed so that anyone who reads it can be sure of the real sender. It is a block of data or a sample of the message content (called a **message digest**) that represents a private key. Encrypting a message digest with a private key creates a digital signature. A public key can be used to verify that the signature was, in fact, generated using the corresponding private key. If John encrypts a message to Hillary with his own private key, Hillary decrypts the message with John's public key and knows that John generated the message.

A digital signature's main function is to verify that a message or a document, in fact, comes from the claimed sender. This is called **authentication.** It can be used also to time-stamp documents when a

1. Sender generates a message.
2. Sender creates a "digest" of the message.
3. Sender encrypts message digest with his/her private key for authentication. This is the *digital signature*.
4. Sender attaches the digital signature to the end of the message.
5. Sender encrypts both message and signature with the recipient's public key.
6. Recipient decrypts entire message with his/her private key.
7. Recipient verifies digest for accuracy.

Figure 14-4
The digital signature process

trusted party *signs* the document and its time stamp with his or her secret key. This process attests that the document was present at the stated time.

hash function: formula that converts a message of a given length into a string of digits called a message digest.

When making a digital signature, cryptographic hash functions are generally used to construct the message digest. A **hash function** is a formula that converts a message of a given length into a string of digits (128 or more), called a message digest. Once the message digest is encrypted with the sender's private key, it becomes a digital signature. More on hashing is summarized in Box 14-5.

Suppose Jay (sender) generates a message digest for his message to Ellen, encrypts it with his private key, and sends that digital signature along with the plaintext message. Ellen uses Jay's public key to decrypt the digital signature and receives a copy of the message that Jay encoded. Because Jay's public key decrypted his digital signature, she is cer-

BOX 14-4
Use of digital signature

The U.S. Postal Service announced a new service that will issue digital signatures on smart cards. The new service will expand on the Postal Service's existing NetPost.Certified program, which was created for government agencies to secure and authenticate electronic correspondence using smart cards and smart card readers.

The in-person proofing procedure will be part of the infrastructure that will create trust in e-mail transfers and will ensure that the data sent is from the person who sent it, it was not tampered with, and it includes a time stamp. The service will be the first in the United States to issue digital certificates after a face-to-face authentication, which the Postal Service sees as a role it can plan better than its competitors given its presence across the country and its staff of employees who are trained to serve the public and handle various transactions.

The customer begins the process of applying for a digital signature by registering online. The Postal Service mails back a form to the customer's home address, and the customer must then go to the post office with a photo ID and one other document, such as a utility bill, for the in-person proofing. The customer then will receive an e-mail notification on how to download the digital certificate, which can reside on the smart card or on the hard drive of his or her computer.

SOURCE: Excerpted from Johnson, Margret, "U.S. Postal Service Taps Digital Authentication," www.cnn.com/2001/TECH/industry/03/09/postal.authentication.idg/index.html. Accessed June 2003.

BOX 14-5
Hashing

Hashing is producing hash values for accessing data or for security. A hash value (or simply hash) is a number generated from a string of text. The hash is substantially smaller than the text itself, and is generated by a formula in such a way that it is extremely unlikely that some other text will produce the same hash value.

Hashes play a role in security systems where they're used to ensure that transmitted messages have not been tampered with. The sender generates a hash of the message, encrypts it, and sends it with the message itself. The recipient then decrypts both the message and the hash, produces another hash from the received message, and compares the two hashes. If they're the same, there is a very high probability that the message was transmitted intact.

Hashing is also a common method of accessing data records. Consider, for example, a list of names:

- John Smith
- Sarah Jones
- Roger Adams

To create an index, called a *hash table*, for these records, you would apply a formula to each name to produce a unique numeric value. So you might get something like:

- 1345873 John Smith
- 3097905 Sarah Jones
- 4060964 Roger Adams

Then to search for the record containing *Sarah Jones*, you just need to reapply the formula, which directly yields the index key to the record. This is much more efficient than searching through all the records till the matching record is found.

SOURCE: Excerpted from www.webopedia.com/TERM/h/hashing.html. Accessed June 2003.

tain that the message was Jay's. This authenticates the sender as genuine. Ellen then uses the same hash function (known to her and to Jay in advance) to *encode* her own message digest of Jay's plaintext message. If the encoded message digest turns out the same as the one Jay sent, the digital signature is considered authentic and the message has not been tampered with (see Figure 14-5).

Digital Certificates

In many ways, digital certificates are the heart of secure online transactions. In shopping on the Internet, buyers need evidence that they can trust the vendor. Some infrastructures use digital signatures, and others use digital certificates to establish a merchant's identity. A digital certificate is an electronic "credit card" that establishes one's credentials when doing business on the Web.

A digital certificate is a software program that can be installed in a browser. Once there, your digital certificate identifies you to Web sites equipped to check it automatically. Such a tool has distinctive benefits. It eliminates multiple passwords and enhances security, because your certificate cannot be guessed, forgotten, forged, or intercepted. It also lets you send and receive secure e-mail using most any e-mail program, including Netscape Messenger. (See http://home.netscape.com/security/ basics/getperscert.html. Accessed June 2003.)

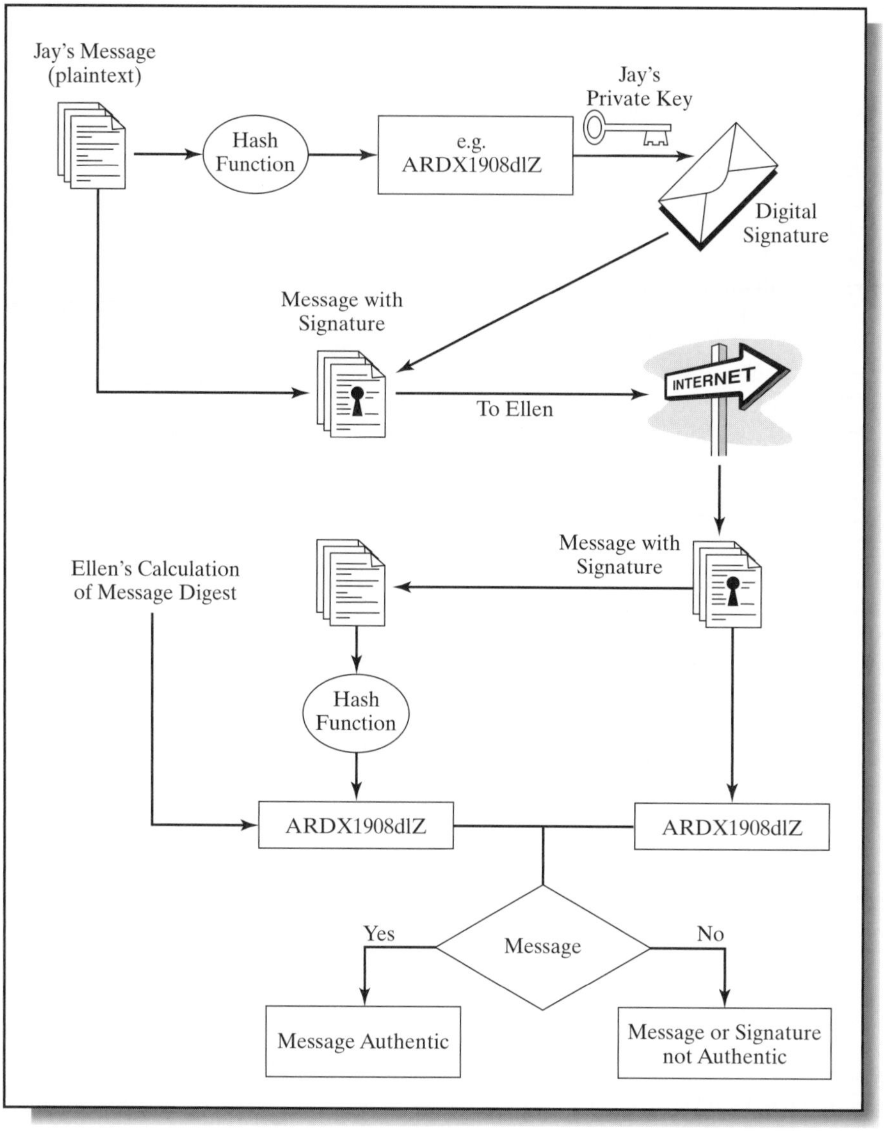

Figure 14-5
Verifying a digital signature

digital certificate: an electronic document issued by a certificate authority to establish a merchant's identity.

certificate authority (CA): a trusted entity that issues and revokes public-key certificates and manages key-pairs.

Digital signatures and digital certificates are related. As noted previously, a *digital signature* is a special signature for signing electronic correspondence, produced by encrypting the message digest with the buyer's private key. A **digital certificate** is an electronic document issued by a **certificate authority (CA)** to establish a merchant's identity by verifying its name and public key. It is more like the electronic version of a driver's license (see Box 14-6).

Once you generate a public key and a private key, it is your job to keep the private key secure and distribute your public key to those

BOX 14-6
The keys to safe shopping

Digital certificates provide an easy and convenient way to ensure that the participants in an electronic commerce transaction can trust each other. This trust is established through a common third party such as Visa. For example, Visa will provide digital certificates to the card-issuing financial institution, and the institution will then provide a digital certificate to the cardholder. A similar process takes place for the merchant.

At the time of the transaction, each party's SET-compliant software validates both merchant and cardholder before any information is exchanged. The validation takes place by checking the digital certificates, which were both issued by an authorized trusted third party.

The basis for digital certificates is secret codes. . . . The procedure is simple. A message can be converted into code using a "key," which is a means of translating the message's characters into other characters that make no sense to the uninvited interceptor. . . . A simple example of a key might be replacing each letter with the next letter in the alphabet. Thus, Visa would become WJTB. To decipher the message, or "decrypt" it, the recipient simply needs to know the secret key.

SOURCE: Excerpted from Visa, "The Keys to Safe Shopping," www.visa.com/nt/ecomm/set/setsafe.html. Accessed June 2003.

with whom you intend to correspond. Because sending the key to each correspondent (say, by e-mail) is time consuming, a more efficient and trusted way is to use a certificate authority such as Verisign, Cybertrust, or the U.S. Postal Service to manage the availability and use of your public key. It also provides information about certificates that were lost or stolen or, in the case of employees issued certificates to conduct business for an employer, certificates that once belonged to employees no longer with the firm.

A digital certificate includes the holder's name, name of the certificate authority, the public key for cryptographic use, the duration of the certificate (usually 6 months to 1 year), the class of the certificate, and the certificate's ID number (see Figure 14-6).

The certificate can be issued (for a fee) in one of four classes. The fee for obtaining a digital certificate increases with higher classes.

1. Class 1 certificates are the quickest and simplest to issue because they contain minimum checks on the user's background. Only the name of the user, the address, and the e-mail address are checked. Think of it as a library card.
2. Class 2 certificates check for information like real name, social security number, and date of birth. They require proof of physical address, locale, and e-mail, as well. This

Figure 14-6
Contents of a digital certificate

User's basic ID information (name, address, SSN, etc.)
Digital signature and ID information of issuing authority
User's public key
Dates of validity and expiration of the digital ID
Class of certification (class 1–4)
Certificate number of digital ID

is more like a credit card, because the company giving out the certificate will consult with a credit database for verification with a third party.

3. Class 3 certificates are the strongest type in terms of specifics. They are like a driver's license: To get them, you need to prove exactly who you are and that you are responsible. Organizations whose specialty is the security business foresee class 3 certificates being used for things like loans acquired online and other sensitive transactions.
4. Class 4 certificates are the most thorough. In addition to class 3 requirements, the certificate authority checks on things like the user's position at work.

Electronic IDs with digital certificates may soon pack enough security to power the next generation of IDs for e-commerce. These credentials are beginning to appear in Web browsers and PKI software for data-sensitive sectors such as banking and government. Windows 2000, for example, comes with a digital certificate and PKI embedded in the operating system. This feature allows the Windows 2000 server to be a certificate authority, registering users and issuing and revoking certificates. In fact, digital certificates are getting smart: They can now be moved to smart cards instead of being stored on hard disks.

KEY MANAGEMENT

key management: making keys known to the systems that need them and making sure keys are protected against disclosure or substitution.

Management of cryptographic keys is crucial to ensuring security in e-commerce transaction processing. **Key management** involves making keys known to the systems that need them and making sure that the keys are protected at all times against disclosure and substitution. In other words, the strength inherent in a cryptographic system lies in the fact that nobody knows the value of the key, not in the complexity of its algorithm. How keys are managed depends on whether the keys are symmetric cryptosystems or public-key cryptosystems.

The Key Life Cycle

Like passwords, all keys have limited lifetimes. The life of a key is limited for two reasons: The more keys are used, the greater the opportunity is for attackers to gather ciphertext on which they can work. Because most keys can be compromised over time, limiting the lifetime of a key means limiting the damage that can occur.

From generation to termination, a key life cycle includes the following phases: key generation and registration, key distribution, key backup/recovery/escrow, and key revocation and destruction.

Key Generation and Registration

This phase involves choosing a random number source for key-pairs and key length that cannot be guessed by an attacker using an exhaustive approach. The registration part involves linking the generated key with its special-purpose use. For example, if the key is used to authenticate a digital signature, then such a link becomes the basis for registering it with a certificate authority.

Key Distribution

This phase operates through a key distribution center in situations when two or more persons located some distance apart must exchange keys. For example, when system X needs to establish a key with system Y, system X requests the key from the key distribution center. The center generates the key and returns it to system X in two forms: the first under a master key shared between system X and the center, and the second under the master key shared between system Y and the center. System X retains the first form for its own use and passes the second form to system Y for Y's use.

Key Backup/Recovery/Escrow

A critical aspect of key management is the ability to recover a key after failure. If an encrypted message, for example, is stored on disk and a key is needed to decrypt it, the loss of the key could mean the loss of the message. A copy of a secret or private key should be recoverable in the event the original is accidentally lost, or an employee assigned a special key suddenly leaves the firm, or the key is destroyed. Someone must hold copies of sensitive keys and be available to release them when needed. If the key(s) is held in trust by a third party, the location where keys reside is referred to as **key escrow.**

key escrow: location where keys held in trust by a third party reside.

notary service: company that provides encryption-oriented services including key escrow, key recovery, time stamping, trusted intermediary, and archiving.

Trusted Information Systems (TIS, www.tis.com) has a key-escrow system that takes businesses' keys and stores them in escrow. This way, law enforcement agencies can access keys with a search warrant. The company (also called a **notary service**) provides a kind of insurance: If you lose the key to an encrypted file, you can get it back. Or, if an employee does not remember the key, it can be recovered through the escrow agency.

Key Revocation and Destruction

Sometimes the key must be revoked. Maybe one information system must be replaced with another, or a change occurs in the security classification of a key, or suspicion arises that a key has been compromised. In all of these cases, the best policy is to terminate and replace the key. In key destruction, all traces of a key are wiped clean. A revocation list is maintained by the certification authority, which includes the date and the reason(s) for the revocation.

A PKI must provide a wayfor a certificate to be revoked. Once revoked, the certificate must be added to a revocation list available to all users. A specific mechanism also must be provided to verify that revocation list and refuse to use a revoked certificate at any time.

In general, it is important to ensure proper and effective protection of a key throughout its lifetime. The focus is on integrity of the security and encryption process. All keys, except public keys in public-key cryptosystems, also should be protected to ensure the privacy and confidentiality of the e-commerce traffic.

Third-Party Services

Throughout the chapter, we have mentioned a "third party." This is a certificate authority that verifies certificates intended for use by other distinct legal entities. Third-party services include two main parts: certificate authority and directory services. A certificate authority (CA) is a trusted independent legal entity. It issues and revokes public-key certificates and manages key-pairs. The actual verification of the person or entity tagged to that key is done at the time of application. This means that the CA has a formal arrangement with a financial institution (e.g., a credit card company), which provides it with information to ensure an individual's claimed identity. In essence, CAs guarantee that the two parties exchanging information are in fact who they claim to be.

certificate policy: a set of rules that identifies how, when, and for what reasons certificates are used within the assigned organization.

directory service: a repository that distributes certificates as requested by message originators.

A CA also provides policies, practices, and procedures for certifying keys. A **certificate policy** is a set of rules that identifies how, when, and for what reasons certificates are used within the assigned organization.

CAs also offer different classes of certificates, depending on the type of initial identification provided by the person. The certificate revocation list, along with the valid certificates issued, are posted in the **directory service**—a repository that distributes certificates as requested by message originators.

Legal Issues

The services bring up two legal questions. (1) When it comes to the electronic signature, does the supposed signer accept liability for the signature? The certificate, per se, cannot bind a user. Yet an ideal registration includes a legitimate contract between the certificate authority and the user—a clearly stated certification policy with stated liabilities. (2) Is the supposed signer the creator of a signature? Authentication is established through secure key handling and signature generation, which means secrets generated by the user never leave a trusted user device such as the electronic wallet. Any vulnerability of this infrastructure would be subject to litigation and arbitration.

Internet Security Protocols and Standards

As stressed throughout the chapter, a successful e-commerce environment is built on trust in the integrity of the communication network that links a buyer and a merchant. Many types of threats can compromise the security of the business process. With the open exchange of information on the Internet, more security measures are needed to minimize vulnerability. Among these measures are security for Web applications (SSL and S-HTTP), security for e-commerce transactions (SET), and security for e-mail (PGP, S/MIME).

SSL: Web Applications

Transaction security has become a challenge. Most browsers and computers already can exchange *secure* transactions across the Internet, making it difficult for unauthorized people to intercept data such as credit card numbers. Even if a transmission is intercepted, the encrypted message cannot be read. The two key protocols for secure World Wide Web transactions are **Secure Socket Layers (SSLs)** and Secure Hypertext Transfer Protocol (S-HTTP).

Secure Socket Layer (SSL): a key protocol for secure Web transactions; secures data packets at the network layer.

Originally developed by Netscape, SSL is the most widely used standard for encrypting data on the Internet. It is used by all of Netscape's browser products, as well as Microsoft's Internet Explorer 3.0 or higher. In addition, it is built into products such as Apache and Internet Information Server. Technically, SSL protocol operates on its own layer, between the application layer and the transport layer (see Chapter 3 for details), meaning it is compatible with Hypertext Transfer Protocol (HTTP). (See http://developer.netscape.com/docs/manuals/security/sslin.Accessed June 2003.)

One requirement for proper use of SSL is that the merchant's Web server and the customer's Web browser must use the same security system. Because SSLs are used by all

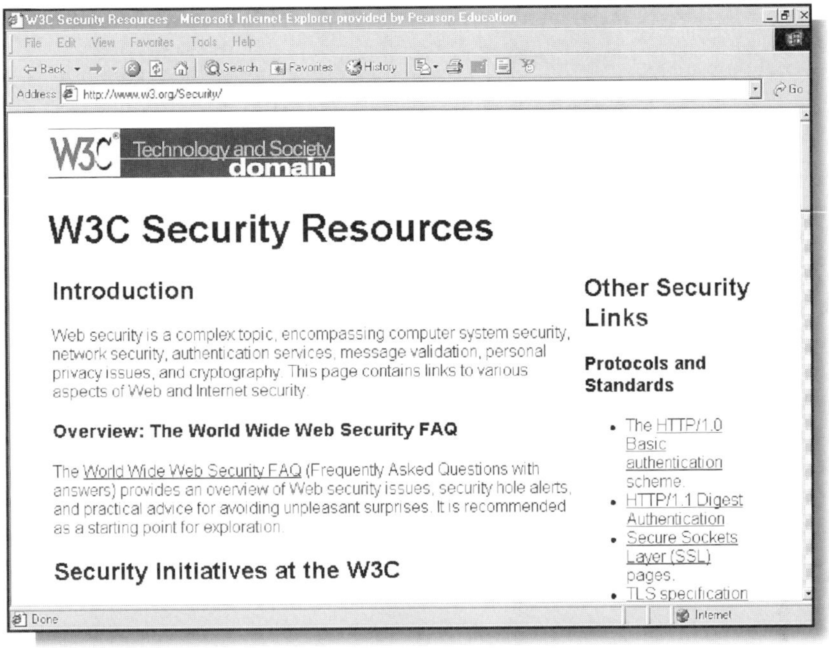

Screen Capture 14-2

Source: Copyright © 2003–2004 World Wide Web Consortium, Massachusetts Institute of Technology, European Research Consortium for Informatics and Mathematics, Keio University. All rights reserved. http://www.w3.org/Consortium/Legal/2002/copyright-documents-20021231, www.w3org/Security.

URLs that begin with *http*, no problem should arise with interfacing online. SSL is included free with Netscape 2.0 or higher, Internet Explorer 3.0 or higher, and America Online 3.0 or higher.

SSL provides three basic services: server authentication, client authentication, and an encrypted SSL connection. SSL server authentication uses public-key cryptography to validate the server's digital certificate and public key on the client's machine. (See "How SSL Works," at http://developer.netscape.com/tech/security/ssl/howitworks.html. Accessed June 2003.)

Client authentication is performed in the same way on the server machine. During the authentication process, SSL allows client and server machines to jointly select an encryption algorithm to be used for the secure connection. The key to this algorithm is transmitted using public-key cryptography, after which client and server may communicate using the secret key.

Although this technology has not yet matured, Netscape is turning it over to the Internet Engineering Task Force (IETF) to make it a standard for other applications. The IETF is responsible for coordinating Internet design, Internet standards, and short-term engineering issues. The committee already has renamed the technology Transport Layer Security protocol (TLS) and plans to standardize and improve the protocol. All Netscape browsers support the 128-bit encryption for the domestic version, as well as the 40-bit encryption for the international/export version. Currently, Netscape does not support SSL for Java browser applets. Microsoft's version 3 (and above) browsers also use this technology.

S-HTTP: Web Applications

Hypertext transfer protocol (HTTP) is a "request-response" type language spoken between a Web browser (client software) and a Web server (server software) somewhere on the Internet to allow communication with each other and to exchange files. The function of **Secure HTTP (S-HTTP)** is to secure Web transactions and nothing else. It secures transaction confidentiality and authenticity/integrity, and it ensures nonrepudiation of origin. In many ways, this protocol is more robust than SSL, although it is less widely used due to Netscape's market penetration. You can use S-HTTP with SSL for increased protection. After an encrypted S-HTTP transaction arrives, it can be decrypted on another computer, separated from your Web server by a firewall.

Secure HTTP (S-HTTP): a protocol that secures Web transactions and nothing else.

The power of S-HTTP lies in its compatibility with HTTP and its ability to integrate with HTTP applications. It provides application-level security and is mainly used for Intranet communications (Rodriguez 1996, p. 41). S-HTTP allows a client machine and a server machine to communicate securely using HTTP, to provide immediate transmission of secure data over the Internet. (See ftp://ftp.ietf.org/rfc/rfc2660.txt. Accessed June 2003.) The protocol supports only symmetric key cryptography and, therefore, does not require digital certificates or public keys. In addition, because it operates on the application layer, S-HTTP provides user authentication and is capable of securing parts of a document.

Secure Electronic Transaction: E-Commerce Transactions

The newest security standard in e-commerce is the **Secure Electronic Transaction (SET)** specification developed by Visa, MasterCard, and Europay. SET is used for handling funds transfers from credit card issuers to a merchant's bank account. It is an accepted and well-known payment model, signature based, and exploits existing banking infrastructure. SET's goal is to provide confidentiality, authentication, and integrity of payment card transmissions. To do this, it uses a variety of encryption techniques, digital signatures, and certificates.

Secure Electronic Transaction (SET): a protocol used for handling funds transfers from credit card issuers to a merchant's bank account.

From its beginning in 1970, Visa has worked with the banking industry to make the Visa card the safest way to purchase goods and services anywhere in the world. In the 1970s, Visa introduced the magnetic stripe for quick authorization. In the 1980s, it established an International Standard Organization (ISO) message format to provide an efficient way to process purchases and payments. On February 1, 1996, Visa and MasterCard, with participation from companies like Microsoft, IBM, Netscape, RSA, and VeriSign, established a single technical standard for safeguarding payment card purchases made over open networks, including the Internet, covering 13 million Visa-acceptance merchants in the physical world.

Called SET specification, this standard uses digital certificates to authenticate all parties involved in the purchase process. SET requires consumers to register their accounts once with the card-issuing bank so it can provide the appropriate digital certificate.

Two things are needed for customers to use SET.

digital wallet: online shopping device that seals personal information in a free plug-in that can be invoked when making a purchase.

1. A digital certificate customers can request from their issuing bank by filling out a form on the bank's Web site.
2. A **digital wallet** (also called an encrypted envelope) to seal personal information such as bank account number, credit card numbers and expiration dates, shipping and handling details, billing

addresses, and the digital ID. The wallet is a free plug-in that can be downloaded from the Web or that is included in today's Netscape Navigator or Internet Explorer. The customer invokes the plug-in when making a purchase. This eliminates having to retype credit card information in future transactions. Because card numbers and addresses are stored in the wallet, consumers can select payment methods and shipping addresses to consummate the purchase with a single click.

Let us assume that you have decided to make a purchase and your software has passed the round of certificate exchanges. From the certificate exchange, you have the e-merchant's public key, the payment processor's key, and a unique transaction identifier issued by the merchant. How does SET deliver your purchase securely?

The first step is to create the necessary order information and payment instructions; each includes the e-merchant's assigned transaction identifier. Next, you execute a one-way hashing function to make digests of the two items (order information and payment instructions). Once done, you generate a "dual signature," which allows the merchant and payment processor to verify independently that your order information and payment instructions are related together. SET's dual signature is the link of order information and payment instructions message digests encrypted with your private key. When finished, you have a message containing the following.

1. OI, including the merchant's transaction identifier.
2. A digest of the order information.
3. PI, including merchant's transaction identifier, encrypted with a random symmetric key.
4. A digest of the payment instructions.
5. A dual-signature digest (OI digest + PI digest) encrypted with your private key.
6. Your account number plus the random symmetric key encrypted with the payment processor's public key.

On paper, SET has gone a long way toward making payment card purchases more secure than they've ever been.

Three main protocols govern secure communication through e-mail: Pretty Good Privacy (PGP), Secure Multipurpose Internet Mail Extensions (S/MIME), and Message Security Protocol (MSP). **Pretty Good Privacy (PGP)** is a file-based product developed by software engineer Phil Zimmerman in 1991. Zimmerman used it to encrypt his own messages and those of his friends (http://pgpi.org/doc/overview. Accessed June 2003.).

Pretty Good Privacy (PGP): protocol that encrypts the data with a one-time algorithm and then encrypts the key to the algorithm using public-key cryptography.

What made him well known is that he released the tool kit on the Internet (web.mit.edu/network/pgp.html. Accessed June 2003.), allowing anyone to create private keys and encrypt their own messages. When PGP first came out, it was wrapped in a web of controversy because it used 128-bit encryption and was available on the Internet, actions of which the U.S. government did not approve. In 1996, after the government decided against prosecuting him, Zimmerman founded PGP, Inc. in San Mateo, California, to commercialize the technology. A year later, the company was sold to Network Associates.

PGP competes head-to-head with protocols like S/MIME, but it is used mostly for personal e-mail security. PGP supports public-key and symmetric-key encryption, as well as digital signatures. It operates by encrypting the data with a one-time algorithm and then encrypting the key to the algorithm using public-key cryptography. PGP also supports other standards, such as SSL and Lightweight Directory Access Protocol (LDAP). LDAP is a standard for accessing specific information, including stored public-key certificates.

S/MIME (Multipurpose Internet Mail Extension): powerful protocol that provides security for different data types and attachments to e-mails.

S/MIME (Multipurpose Internet Mail Extensions) was developed by RSA in 1996 as a security enhancement to the old MIME standard for Internet e-mail. It is built on public-key cryptography standards. S/MIME is considered powerful because it provides security for different data types and for e-mail attachments. It has two key attributes: a digital signature and a digital envelope. The signature is created by using a hashing algorithm that constructs a message digest. The message digest is then encrypted using public key cryptography. The signature ensures that nothing is done to the message during transmission. The digital wallet then ensures that the message remains private. It uses an algorithm such as DES, 3DES, or RC4 to encrypt the message. The key is then encrypted using public key cryptography. In addition to these two functions, S/MIME also performs authentication.

Message Security Protocol (MSP): protocol that secures e-mail attachments across multiple platforms.

Message Security Protocol (MSP) is a protocol used mainly by the U.S. government and government agencies to provide security for e-mail. Its function is securing e-mail attachments across multiple platforms. It operates at the application level of the Internet and does not involve the intermediate message transfer system. An MSP message includes the original message content and specific security parameters required by the recipients to decrypt or validate the message when received.

OTHER ENCRYPTION ISSUES

Government Regulation

Several U.S. government organizations are authorized to control encryption enforcement. The best known is the National Security Agency (NSA), which has the power to monitor, intercept, and retain any information that might be damaging to national security. The agency also conducts research in cryptography, both in designing algorithms to protect U.S. communications and in cryptoanalytic techniques for listening in on non-U.S. communications. It is known to be the largest employer of mathematicians in the United States and the largest buyer of computer hardware and software. See Box 14-7 for information about careers in security and encryption.

The National Computer Security Center (NCSC), a branch of the NSA, is responsible for listing government-trusted computer programs. The center evaluates products and recommends standards. Its *Orange Book* presents criteria for evaluating trusted computer systems. The center also publishes a number of other books in the area, commonly called the "Rainbow Books."

A third government agency, the National Institute of Standards and Technology (NIST), is a division of the Department of Commerce that promotes standards among different commercial systems. The agency develops and issues standards, including those for cryptographic functions and export rules.

U.S. Export Rules lists cryptography in the same category as munitions and treats the technology just like a missile or a tank. The Office of Defense Trade Controls (DTC), which is authorized by the International Traffic in Arms Regulations (ITAR) from the State Department, receives recommendations from the NSA on the level of encryption that can be exported.

BOX 14-7
E-career: Careers in security

Most people seem to end up in security through engineering, systems administration, or IT audit roles, or they come in straight at the management level and build on management skills rather than specialist security skills. I graduated with a business degree and a good user's knowledge of computers but very limited technical experience. There was only one obvious route: consulting. From consulting, I became a security analyst, working at one company to find security problems and ways to fix them. From the analyst job, I was promoted to security manager, managing the whole process of security, from analysis to sales.

GETTING A FOOT IN THE DOOR

If you want to get into security as a career, there are quite a few ways in. I'd recommend a security career—it's always interesting work, and you get to deal with almost all aspects of IT, from mainframes to Wireless Application Protocol devices. And demand is high, which means job offers and high salaries are easy to find. The first thing to do is decide what sort of job you're looking for—technical, consulting, or management. It all depends on what suits you best. Technical positions mean good salaries. If you get training in a security tool that is in demand, you'll soon have plenty of companies competing for your services.

There is a steady demand for certificate authority or public-key infrastructure (PKI) products. And if PKI ever really fulfills its potential, then this demand will increase massively. Cryptography projects, in general, are always difficult to staff because few people know much about cryptography.

BRING YOUR ATTITUDE

You can learn security technologies and mechanisms quite easily, but there's a required mindset that you can't learn no matter how hard you try. I look for people with a questioning attitude, an attention to detail, a strong will, and a desire to solve problems. The questioning attitude and attention to detail are absolutely necessary because security staff frequently have to evaluate new systems and situations, and it's often hard to come to grips with these new systems quickly. The only way I've ever found to do it is to keep asking questions, no matter how trivial or stupid they sound, until you understand how something works.

Finally, aspiring security professionals need a strong will. No matter how much people realize that security is necessary, at the end of the day, you'll be the person insisting on complex solutions to abstract problems that may never happen, and producing no visible end result.

SOURCE: Thaddeus, Jude, "How to Break Into the Field of Security," *Computerworld,* January 8, 2001, 50.

Although the encryption field is saturated with robust solutions designed by the brightest minds, advances are being held back by national interests and governmental control, as well as the available computing power.

Role of Biometrics Security

biometrics: science and technology of quantifying and statistically scrutinizing biological data.

Biometrics is the science and technology of quantifying and statistically scrutinizing biological data. It generally refers to technologies used for measuring and analyzing human body characteristics primarily for authentication purposes, such as retinas, irises, voice patterns, fingerprints, and hand measurements. Research shows that body scanners, facial pattern systems, and other biometric systems are well poised as replacements for computer passwords in the future.

The concept of biometrics is not new. As early as the fourteenth century, the Chinese implemented the fingerprint biometric as a mode of signature. Throughout the 1890s, detectives in the criminology arenas were charged with the responsibility of identifying those criminals with existing arrest histories. Detectives had to use their photographic memories to identify criminals until the late 1800s. This changed in 1883, when Alphonse Bertillon came up with a biometric system called Bertillonage, which was a method of bodily measurement deployed by police worldwide. This system quickly faded after the discovery of two indistinguishable individuals with the same names. The replacement of Bertilonnages was fingerprinting, which in essence was the ultimate tool utilized by police.

It was not until 1968 that biometrics was applied in the United States. Studies show that the United States was a late adopter of this security technique. (See www.precisebiometrics.com/match/nr3/frontline.asp. Accessed June 2003.) Many organizations were unaware of the benefits that biometrics have over PKI. Those who knew the technology could not afford to invest in it because of its high cost. In 1968, a biometrics application cost about $20,000. Today, the cost is about $1,700. It is expected that the cost eventually will drop to less than $300. (See www.banking.com/aba/cover_0197.htm. Accessed June 2003.)

Currently, PKI facilitates the secure transmission of data over third-party networks. As mentioned earlier, PKI consists of an infrastructure and a set of procedures that manage the distribution, storage, and revocation of public keys, private keys, and digital certificates. It sets up a process of authentication to verify the identity of the sender. Further, it ensures that the sender could not disown its message through nonrepudiation.

This seems all well and good, until examining some of the loopholes that make PKI weak as a form of security. When it comes to authentication, a potential risk exists in that the private key of an individual may be misused, misplaced, or stolen. If the private key is protected with only a PIN number, a felon may easily discover the PIN of another person simply through observation. If the private key is stored within the hard drive of a workstation, a felon could tap into the hard drive and quickly make a copy of the key. Also, in transactions over a third-party network, a felon could simply pretend to be another person and intentionally destroy that person's account and reputation.

Biometrics can enhance authentication considerably. In using a private key for encryption and decryption, biometrics significantly enhances the level of confidence that another user won't be able to access the same private key. Within a network setting, a biometric device would ensure that the person who encrypted that data would be the only one who could decrypt and have access to it. A recent biometric application is a federal plan for border control (see Box 14-8).

Applying biometric technology on a smart card also would increase the level of confidence in the security. By placing the private key directly on a smart card, the risks of a felon stealing the private key from the hard drive of a workstation would be eliminated. The user would have the advantage of mobility with the smart card, being able to travel with the identification as if it were a regular physical key. If the smart card were lost or stolen, a person other than the original user would not be able to gain access to the private key or any other information owned by the original user. The smart card would respond only to the unique characteristics of the person engrained within its private key.

Forms of Biometrics

Biometrics falls under two categories: physiological and behavioral. Under the physiological category are fingerprint verification, iris analysis, facial analysis, and hand geometry-vein patterns. The behavioral category consists of speech analysis, handwritten signature

BOX 14-8
Role of biometrics in border control

The U.S. Department of Homeland Security (DHS) last week offered the first public details of a proposed border-control system that will use biometric technology to authenticate the identities of visitors and immigrants entering the U.S. Deployment of such a system will begin by year's end.

Biometric identifiers will help authorities confirm the identities of foreign visitors, check them for possible criminal histories and track their movements more closely. It will also check the identity against terrorist and criminal watch lists. Fingerprints and photographs will be used at first. As the technology is perfected, additional identifiers, such as scans of irises or facial features may be added.

The system will also capture data about visitors' immigrant and citizenship status, nationalities, countries of residence, and U.S. addresses. Eventually, that data will be integrated with information in the Student Exchange Visitor Information System, which is operated by universities to track foreign students. In addition, the data will be analyzed for visa violations and other irregularities by a new Office for Compliance within the DHS Bureau of Immigration and Customs Enforcement.

SOURCE: Excerpted from Verton, Dan, "Feds Plan Biometrics For Boarder Control." *Computerworld*, May 26, 2003, 12.

verification, and keystroke analysis. Table 14-2 summarizes the categories and key application areas. Table 14-3 addresses the benefits and drawbacks of biometrics.

Outlook

Biometric technology has greatly solved the problems of forgotten passwords and stolen IDs. As more and more electronic transactions are carried out, the need to secure private and sensitive information related to these transactions will grow. An array of biometric devices has gotten a foothold in the mainstream security arena from iris scanners to voice recognition technology. It is important to note that competition does not exist between biometric technologies. It is not a race of which biometric technology will surpass the other. Iris scanning will become most popular and reliable for high-security operations. Other biometric technologies are expected to be coupled with passwords. Furthermore, some analysts believe that the way in which passwords are typed might become a biometric solution, or perhaps the very action of typing will become a password in itself.

When considering biometric technologies for future use, management does need to implement a cost-effective system appropriate for their particular circumstance. It is important for each business to analyze its needs and determine which system works best in the given environment. Currently, fingerprint identification devices lead the way in terms of cost and reliability. The reason is the one-in-a-billion chance that two people will have the same fingerprint. Law-enforcement and other agencies rely on the expensive and expansive fingerprint identification systems, and inexpensive and smaller machines are now making their way into computer-based companies and financial organizations. Today, biometric systems also are being adopted at an increasing pace for controlling access to restricted facilities such as airports and laboratories.

Table 14-2
Types of biometrics and select application areas

Forms of Biometrics		Application Areas
Physiological		
Fingerprint Verification	Government agencies Identity authentication Airport traffic security ID of missing children Medical and insurance industry	Banking Information security Police department Welfare and unemployment benefit recipients Immigration/naturalization services
Iris Analysis	Correctional facilities Department of motor vehicles	
Facial Analysis	Banking Airport security Building security Welfare agencies Computer facilities Credit card companies	Telephone companies Hospitals/health care institutions Drivers licenses Police authorities Voter registration processes
Behavioral		
Speech Analysis	Antitheft system for vehicles and doors PC and computer network access control Door entrance systems Hospitals (access to nursery) Universities (access to labs, student unions) Air force in-air communications (pilot identity) Telephone networks	Passport control Prison pay phones Pharmacy Aerospace company Fraud control in prisons
Handwritten Signature Verification	Banking Post office Home shopping	Internal Revenue Service Social Medicare Welfare

Implications for E-Commerce

Developing high-powered and reliable encryption methods is a top priority for many organizations. It also raises serious issues for society. Imagine airlines keeping specific data on passenger flights that could be dangerous in the wrong hands. Think of the danger that could arise if the U.S. president's travel itinerary landed in an unsecured computerized document. Hospitals collect and protect sensitive patient information, and patients trust their doctors to keep the records confidential. Imagine the damage if a patient's employer or a health insurance provider accesses a patient's files and finds confidential data that could be used for blackmail or for intimidation.

Table 14-3
Benefits and drawbacks of biometric devices

Types of Biometrics	Key Benefits	Major Drawbacks
Physiological		
Fingerprint Verification	Nonintrusive Low level of error rates Fraud-deterrent documentation capabilities	Wear and tear of fingers Perception of invasion of privacy
Iris Analysis	Low error incidence (highly accurate) Reliable	Infrared iris scanning perceived as intrusive Portability issues arise with laptop users Video cameras make employees feel like they are being spied on
Facial Analysis	Can recognize when user leaves PC Nonintrusive, can be used with low light or no light No vulnerability to disguises Greater accuracy, speed, reliability than fingerprinting Easy to use Versatile with respect to usability (videoconferencing and security)	Constant camera surveillance may intimidate user
Behavioral		
Speech Analysis	Voice serves as unique identifier Public acceptable Suitable for hands-free environments Less vulnerable to unauthorized access	Hard for computer system to analyze voice characteristics Change in voice depends on emotional state Acceptability issue Highly complex System lacks differentiation capability between real and prerecorded voices
Handwritten Signature Verification	Fast and easy to use Any pen that produces fine lines can be used Easily integrated into existing equipment	Lower levels of performance and reliability Possible issues with portability for laptop users

Source: Conate, Heinzdell, and Hart, Maria, "Biometric Security: Retina Scan," Unpublished Research Paper, University of Virginia, April 22, 2002, 19–20.

Most encryption systems have prevention as the sole means of defense against theft, cheating, or abuse, but sooner or later every system will be attacked successfully. A good system must protect against every possible attack.

With these vulnerabilities and the increasing volume of online traffic, Intranets and encryption have become necessary, even when financial transactions are not involved. In terms of online business security, any credit card traffic must be tamper proof. Internet and e-mail messages should be secure, as well. Otherwise businesses can be sued for negligence or violation of the trust inherent in a customer-merchant relationship.

Merchants face a number of choices when considering encryption methods. Messages or transactions must be encrypted to a level where the cost for a criminal to break into the system would be greater than the benefits the criminal would receive by obtaining the information in that system. A multinational banking institution must have unbreakable encryption because criminals will go to great lengths to obtain their information.

Of major concern is the cost associated with different encryption methods: The more powerful the method is, the higher the cost is. More powerful methods also generally consume more power. It is important for merchants to take into consideration the size of their business, the sensitivity of the information transacted, the power of their technical infrastructure, and the amount of money they are willing to spend when choosing an encryption method.

Government regulations present considerable problems for businesses, as well. Until September 1998, the government did not allow most effective types of encryption to be exported. In late 1999, it relaxed the regulation and began allowing 56-bit encryption methods to be used overseas. This was an important victory for businesses. In the past, international companies had to struggle to secure their transactions. Internal versions of software packages had weaker encryption due to U.S. regulations. Companies had to bundle different types of encryption to achieve the requisite level of security.

The Future

The current public-key model of encryption fits well with the open nature of the Internet, where the growth of applications using technology such as SSL and SET is greatest. Many recent and current cryptographic innovations relate to strengthening public-key cryptography or breaking its security. Among the key developments for the future are elliptic-curve cryptography and quantum computing.

The future of PKI will hinge on a variety of factors. The technology continues to be criticized for its lack of interoperability. PKI products from different suppliers have yet to be made compatible with one another, because PKI does not employ a universal standard. In addition, the cost and complexity of PKI systems, whether or not you are outsourcing services to firms like VeriSign, remains extremely high. This explains in part why worldwide adoption of PKI technology has been slow.

Elliptic-Curve Cryptography

This cryptographic technique is an alternative to using large prime numbers to generate keys. Elliptic curves are simple functions that can be thought of as gently curving lines (not ellipses) on a simple graph. The goal is to use elliptic curves to define special mathematical operations (e.g., addition or multiplication) that can be used to generate public keys. Proponents of this method argue that it can provide smaller keys in less time while providing an equivalent level of security. As shown in Figure 14-7, elliptic curves are

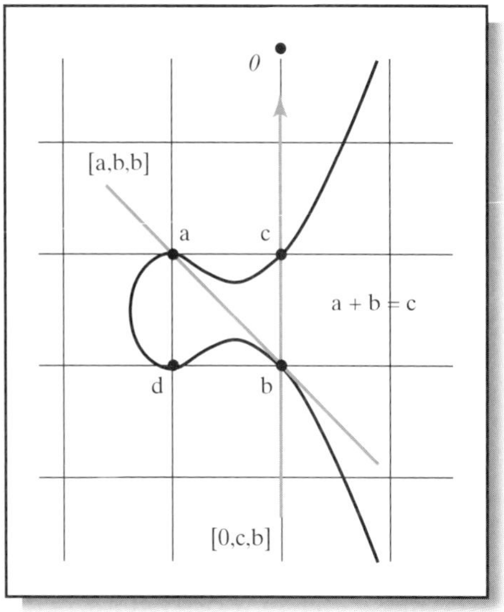

Figure 14-7
Quantum computing

functions that can be drawn as looping lines in the (x,y) plane. Interesting things happen when one studies the points where the curve exactly crosses integer (x,y) coordinates.

The mathematics of elliptic-curve cryptography are too advanced to include in this section. In order to derive the private key from the public key, the mathematics behind the elliptic curve used must be understood. Described as "elliptic-curve group discrete log technique," the mathematics behind cracking elliptic-curve encryption have not been the focus of much research and have seen little improvement in the last 20 years. This is in stark contrast to the continuous efforts to break the popular RSA scheme. However, supporters acknowledge that as elliptic-curve cryptography increases in popularity, new techniques also might be found to compromise its current advantages.

Quantum information theory is a completely new area of scientific research born in the 1990s. Essentially, it is the application of quantum physics to information theory and, ultimately, to cryptography. Benjamin Schumacher coined the term *qubit*, a unit of quantum information. The most important property of **qubits** is that they can store many levels of information. They also possess another unique property: Looking at a qubit automatically destroys its information; therefore, quantum information cannot be copied.

qubit: a unit of quantum information that can store many levels of information and whose information is destroyed automatically once it is viewed.

Suppose a man left his bag somewhere in a given building—let's call it Monroe Hall. Suppose computers could somehow electronically search each room for the bag. If the man were to use an ordinary computer, it would search from room to room, stopping only when it found the bag. Quantum computing has a much more efficient search method. It has the ability to divide the task up such that all rooms are searched *simultaneously*, so it finds the bag almost instantly.

Peter Shor, of then-AT&T Bell Labs, found that quantum computing could be used to perform certain mathematical operations at an astonishingly faster rate than ordinary computers. Applying his findings to public-key encryption, he determined that a quantum computer could easily crack popular public-key encryption methods such as RSA. Yet at the same time, quantum cryptography solves its own problem by taking advantage of the property whereby looking at quantum information destroys it. Eavesdroppers can crack public-key encryption only if they can see what the public key is. If a quantum-encoded public key falls prey to an eavesdropper, the break can be detected, because the public key would be damaged and the quantum-encoded public key would simply be retransmitted until it went through unscathed.

At present, quantum computing is still very much a theoretical entity. A working model of the system has been developed by MagiQ Technologies and will be on the shelves in the second half of 2003. The system allows a code's keys to be transmitted as a stream of photons over fiber-optic cable. Because of the laws of quantum physics, the act of observing the transmission will alter the photons, rendering the information they contain useless to any eavesdroppers. At present, the method will work only over dedicated cables, in which photon transmission can be controlled. To see more about this technology, go to www.vnunet.com.

SUMMARY

1. Encryption addresses message transmission security requirements. An algorithm converts the data into an encoded message using a key to decode or decipher the message.
2. In addition to ensuring privacy, encryption satisfies other e-security requirements: authentication, integrity, and nonrepudiation.
3. There are two classes of key-based algorithms: secret key and public key. For public-key algorithms, RSA is the most commonly used, although vulnerable to chosen-plaintext attacks. As a secret-key system, DES and RC4 are the most popular. DES is the first symmetric cryptosystem to be widely adopted commercially. A stronger version of DES is 3DES—based on using DES three times. RC4 has key lengths ranging from 40 bits to 128 bits. IDEA offers strong encryption, using a 128-bit key to encrypt 64-bit blocks, which makes it resistant to brute-force attacks.
4. Cryptoanalysis is the science of deciphering encrypted messages without knowing the right key. Cryptoanalytic attacks include chosen-plaintext attack, known-plaintext attack, ciphertext-only attack, and third-party attack.
5. One way to implement public-key authentication on a per-message basis is to send a digital signature with each message. A digital signature's main function is to verify that a message or a document in fact comes from the claimed sender. This is called authentication.
6. A digital certificate is an electronic document issued by a certificate authority (CA) to establish a merchant's identity by verifying its name and public key. The CA manages the availability and use of a pubic key and provides information about lost or stolen certificates. The certificate can be issued in one of four classes.
7. With the Internet dependent on open standards and open exchange of information, various security measures have been installed to minimize vulnerability to the exchange. They include SSL and S-HTTP, SET, and S/MIME. The overall goal is to secure Web transactions for confidentiality, authenticity, integrity, and nonrepudiability of origin.

KEY TERMS

- authentication, 447
- biometrics, 459
- block cipher, 442
- certificate authority (CA), 450
- certificate policy, 454
- cipher, 441
- ciphertext, 441
- cryptoanalysis, 447

- Data Encryption Standards (DES), 445
- decrypt, 441
- digital certificate, 450
- digital signature, 447
- digital wallet, 456
- directory service, 454
- encrypt (encipher), 437
- encryption, 437
- hash function, 448
- International Data Encryption Algorithm (IDEA), 446
- key, 437
- key escrow, 453
- key management, 452
- message digest, 447
- Message Security Protocol (MSP), 458
- nonrepudiation, 441
- notary service, 453
- plaintext (cleartext), 437
- Pretty Good Privacy (PGP), 457
- public key (asymmetric encryption), 443
- qubit, 465
- RC4, 446
- RSA, 445
- secret key (symmetric encryption), 442
- Secure Electronic Transaction (SET), 456
- Secure HTTP (S-HTTP), 456
- Secure Socket Layer (SSL), 454
- S/MIME (Multipurpose Internet Mail Extension), 458
- spoofing, 439
- stream cipher, 442
- Triple DES (3DES), 446

Test Your Understanding

1. According to the text, encryption is intended to satisfy a number of e-security requirements. List and briefly explain each requirement.
2. Distinguish between:
   a. Authentication and nonrepudiation.
   b. Integrity and privacy.
   c. Nonrepudiation and integrity.
   d. Cipher and ciphertext.
   e. Stream cipher and block cipher.
3. Explain the basic concept of how information is encrypted.
4. What is so unique about a secret key? A public key? Is one key more secure than the other? Be specific.
5. Briefly elaborate on the key features of the following cryptosystems:
   a. RSA algorithm.
   b. DES and 3DES.
   c. IDEA.
6. What is a digital signature? How does it work? How does it differ from a digital certificate? Be specific.
7. Briefly review some of the cryptoanalytic attacks that an e-merchant can expect in day-to-day e-traffic.
8. In what way(s) does a certificate authority perform a vital role in cryptography?
9. What is so important about key backup, recovery, and escrow?
10. List and briefly describe three major third-party services.
11. Elaborate on the main services of SSL.
12. In e-mail technology, three main protocols are employed to govern secure communication through e-mail. Briefly explain each protocol.

Discussion Questions

1. In your own words, what implications does encryption have for managing e-commerce traffic?
2. Do you think electronic messaging has seriously affected the integrity of messages? Review material on the Internet and bring information to class on this issue.

3. Which do you think is better legal evidence—an electronic legal document with a digital signature or a handwritten signature? In other words, knowing the legality of a digital signature, which one would be considered more valid in a court of law? Why?
4. Under what conditions or for what reason(s) would a company opt to manage its own keys and certificates in-house rather than using a public certificate authority?
5. Because the purpose of certification authorities is to authenticate the identities of individuals and organizations, who vouches for the certificate authorities? Look on the Internet under "certificate authority," "encryption regulations," and so on and see what is available on this subject.

WEB EXERCISES

1. Use your Web browser to research the contents of a digital certificate. Find out what is new about this area that has not been covered in the text. Write a two-page report on the subject.
2. Use your Web browser to access information about the hash algorithm—its function, how it works, and how it differs from private-key or public-key encryption. Report your findings in class.
3. A simple cipher replaces A with B, B with C, C with D, and so on until Z is replaced with A. With this in mind, decrypt the following statement: BMM NFO BSF DSFBUFE FRVBM.
4. Visit www.amazon.com, www.fedex.com, and www.ibm.com. Investigate the following:
   a. The type of server (e.g., HTTPS) each Web site uses.
   b. The SSL cipher type.
   c. Validity period.
   d. Certification authority's name.

Chapter 15

E-Payments: Getting the Money

Contents

In a Nutshell

What we have tried to do so far is to set up a procedure that makes it possible for consumers to buy products from a business on the Internet. The next step is making payment, which means *getting the money* before shipping the product. The business might be a small shop selling candy or a multibillion-dollar corporation selling big-ticket items like computers. The business could have a simple Web page advertising products using an in-house database or a business-to-consumer environment supported by databases linked to vendors and suppliers around the world and around the clock. Regardless of the setup, for e-commerce to happen the consumer must have a way to hit the *buy* button and make a payment.

In the real world, we have three ways to pay for goods: cash, check, and credit or debit card. Cards can be smart cards, debit cards, automated teller machine (ATM) cards, and any kind of credit card. They all serve a special purpose: They allow consumers to pay without cash. In addition, they are online electronic payment media.

Any e-commerce environment with a payment system needs a more complex design. A payment system means ensuring payment security, transaction privacy, system integrity, customer authentication, and the purchaser's promise to pay. These systems were covered in Chapter 14. In this chapter, we discuss payment options using real-world systems and see how they can be emulated in an online electronic payment system. Finally, we look at micro transactions and how payments are carried out.

From Barter to Money

Money began with the concept of *barter* or exchange. Farmers, for example, exchanged produce for clothes, grain, feed, transportation, and shelter. If someone wanted a sack of flour, they got it by offering something another person needed in exchange. Each item had a value, and in the long run everyone got the items they wanted with no difficulty.

Eventually, the economic system got complicated, and a standard medium of exchange was born. The first medium involved **tokens** (items that carried intrinsic value). Precious stones and shells were early tokens. Later, coins were minted in precious metals and were given specific values. For example, a silver dollar was first minted in silver; it carried its weight (and its value) in silver. Later, the government minted the same dollar coin using copper and other metals. Paper notes are similar in that they carry value as a matter of consensus. The paper note has become a marker representing a certain value.

token: a marker representing value.

After tokens were detached from their inherent value, the next step was **notational money** in which value was stored and exchanged by formal authorization. An example is the check. As a document, the check is worthless. Its notation carries value: It is tied directly to value stored in a unique account at a bank. Even the bank account does not contain real cash, but is a repository representing cash. Notational money is tied to actual value stored in a specific location.

notational money: value that is stored and exchanged by formal authorization, such as a check.

credit card: a plastic card with a prearranged spending limit based on the credit cardholder's credit rating, employment record, and so on.

After notational money, the credit system was developed; it is represented by the **credit card.** For the first time, a person could pay for

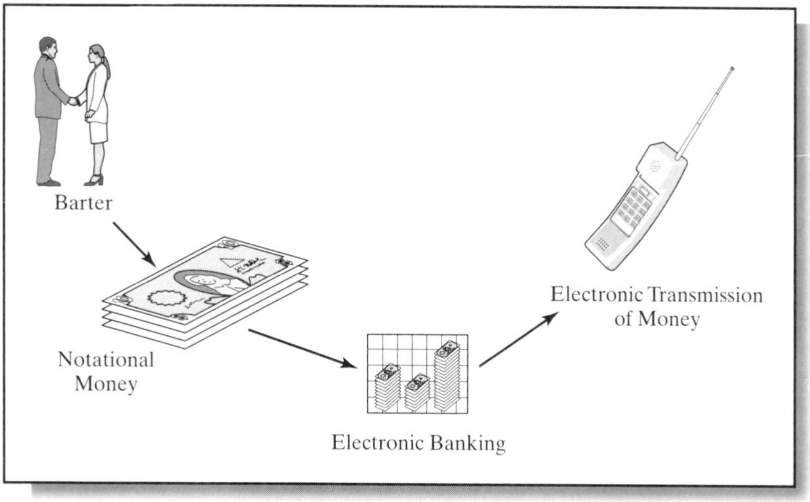

Figure 15-1
From barter to electronic money

goods and services not directly tied to value stored elsewhere. When you use your credit card, you simply become liable for the value of the merchandise. Most electronic payment systems use notational systems. They either transfer funds electronically or send credit card information over the Internet. See Figure 15-1 for a representation of the evolution of the payment system.

Real-World Cash

For centuries, we have known money as a *medium of exchange* to simplify transactions, a *standard of value* to make it easier to decide on the worth of goods, and a *store of value* to facilitate the concept of saving. For the purpose of e-commerce, electronic money must fulfill the first function. When you carry cash, you are making on-the-spot payments. Payment online (using credit cards and the like) is not very different from cash transactions made in the real world, except for speed of transfer, ease of handling, and the safety of not having to carry cash.

Outside the Internet, cash continues to be the most widely used form of payment. Among its unique features are the following.

1. **Convenience:** Cash is easy to use, easy to carry, and easy to handle in small quantities.
2. **Wide acceptance:** The U.S. dollar is the most widely accepted paper currency in the world because of its stability and durability.
3. **Anonymity:** No identification is needed to pay in cash. A 1998 survey of consumer behavior showed that consumers buying personal hygiene items prefer to pay in cash and use the "12 items or less counter" or "cash only" lane (Camp et al., 1).
4. **No hidden or other cost of use:** For the customer who uses cash, there are no hidden costs in terms of overhead and processing fees. The main problem with cash is the cost of

holding it rather than investing it. For the merchant, it means transporting cash to the bank for safekeeping on a daily basis.

5. **No audit trail:** Lack of traceability means you can do what you want with your cash. In countries where trust in the currency, the banking system, or the government is in question, cash is still used to buy all kinds of products, including homes, automobiles, and other big-ticket items. Trust is the basis of electronic payment systems.

Overall, the credit system is becoming more attractive for conducting business in the real world. Cash is easy to lose; difficult to trace; cumbersome to carry; and time consuming to count, organize, and manage.

Electronic Money (E-Money)

e-money: an electronic medium for making payments.

identified e-money (digital cash): notational money system that generates an audit trail and can be traced.

anonymous e-money: notational money system that cannot be traced.

E-money is an electronic medium for making payments and is the trend today. It includes credit cards, smart cards, debit cards, electronic funds transfer, and Automated Clearinghouse (ACH) systems. (These systems are discussed later in the chapter.) It is a notational money system that may be online or off-line, identified or anonymous. **Identified e-money** (also called **digital cash**) contains information that makes it possible to identify the person who withdrew the money from the bank. The process generates an audit trail. **Anonymous e-money** works like paper money and leaves no trail. With the online option, each transaction is verified and approved by the issuing institution (such as a bank) before payment is made. Off-line e-money requires no validation.

There are four types of e-money.

1. **Identified and online (+I+L)** e-money is unique to credit card and debit card transactions. The buyer is clearly identified, and the card is validated against the issuing bank's computer before payment is made. Making a deposit at the teller window is another example of a transaction that is identified and online. The teller asks for a picture ID to identify the customer and uses the workstation to credit (or debit) the account online.

2. **Identified and off-line (+I-L)** e-money is unique to purchasing by check, American Express travelers cheques, or U.S. postal service money order. The merchant asks for ID to make sure the identity of the purchaser is known, but no verification is made against the account. If for some reason the check bounces, the merchant has to call the purchaser, backtrack through the issuing bank, and chase the purchaser for payment—a messy procedure.

3. **Anonymous and online (-I+L)** e-money is unique to cash payments where the identity of the purchaser is anonymous and a purchase is made on the spot for cash. It is also applicable to Automated Teller Machine (ATM) transactions such as withdrawals from savings, checking, or special accounts. In the case of deposits, however, the transaction is off-line. The account records the amount of the deposit, but the bank does not make the money available until the deposited check clears through the automated clearinghouse (ACH). This bank-to-bank processing method is explained later in the chapter.

4. **Anonymous and offline (-I-L)** e-money is unique to electronic cash. It includes such transactions as making deposits in one's account via ATM and using a credit card with a merchant who does not have an online connection to the Visa/MasterCard network.

Analyzing Cash, Checks, and Credit Cards

ACID test: set of properties of a money transfer that include atomicity, consistency, isolation, and durability.

ICES test: set of properties of a money transfer that include interoperability, conservation, economy, and scalability.

scalability: ability of a system to handle multiple users at the same time.

Regardless of the form of money, two distinct sets of properties should be considered in a money transfer: the **ACID test** (atomicity, consistency, isolation, durability) and the **ICES test** (interoperability, conservation, economy, **scalability**).

The ACID Test

1. **Atomicity:** This test says that a transaction must occur completely or not at all. For example, when you transfer $100 from savings to checking, the full amount must be debited from the savings account and credited to the checking account before the transfer is considered successful.

2. **Consistency:** All parties involved in the transaction must agree to the exchange. For example, in a customer-retailer relationship involving a purchase, the customer must agree to purchase the good for a specific price, and the merchant must agree to sell it at that price; otherwise, there is no basis for exchange.

3. **Isolation:** Each transaction must be independent of any other transaction and be treated as a stand-alone episode.

4. **Durability:** It must always be possible to recover the last consistent state or reverse the facts of the exchange. This means reversing charges in the event that customers change their mind.

The ICES Test

The ICES test addresses four important properties of money transfer.

1. **Interoperability:** Ability to move back and forth between different systems.

2. **Conservation:** How well money holds its value over time (temporal consistency) and how easy money is to store and access (temporal durability).

3. **Economy:** Processing a transaction should be inexpensive and affordable. This property has a direct relationship to the size of the transaction. For example, a $10,000 purchase costing only $0.90 to process is economical. If the charge is the same for a $5 item, it would be considered expensive. In banking, for example, wiring money from one bank to another usually costs a fixed amount of money (say, $25), regardless of the amount of money transferred.

4. **Scalability:** This test refers to the ability of the system to handle multiple users at the same time.

Cash has all the ICES properties except conservation; checks and credit cards as electronic methods of payment do not. A check transaction is not isolated, because anyone can write a check and proceed to withdraw the money from the bank well before the check is cleared; the check writer also can put a stop on the check. Checks are money-transfer atomic, although there is usually a 1- to 3-day delay in clearing the check for final payment. See Table 15-1 for a summary of the main transaction properties of cash, checks, and credit cards.

In the case of cash, the ACID properties are fulfilled. The problem with cash is transportability and storage of large amounts. Credit cards may appear atomic to the seller, but they are not. The seller is guaranteed payment, but the credit card issuer may lose out

Table 15-1
Transaction properties of cash, checks, and credit cards

	Token	Atomicity	Consistency	Isolation	Durability	Interoperability	Conservation	Economy	Scalability
Cash	Y	Y	Y	Y	Y	Y	N	Y	Y
Check	N	Y	Y	N	Y	N	Y	N	Y
Credit Card	N	N	Y	N	Y	N	–	N	Y

Source: Awad, E. M., *Electronic Commerce*, Upper Saddle River, NJ: 2002, 214.

if the card is stolen or used fraudulently. Also, the question of storing and retrieving value is not applicable in a credit-based system.

Cash is the most anonymous form of payment with respect to the bank and the merchant. Anyone can walk up, purchase an item, and pay in cash without having to show identification. Checks and credit card transactions are less anonymous than cash, although some forms of digital transactions can hide the identity of the buyer from the seller and vice versa. For details on the visibility of credit card transactions, see Camp et al. at http://ksghome.harvard.edu/~.jcamp.academic.ksg/usenix/usenix.html. Accessed June 2003.

Requirements for Internet-Based Payments

electronic payment: financial transaction made without the use of paper documents.

Electronic payments are financial transactions made without the use of paper documents such as checks. Having your paycheck deposited directly to your checking or savings account, having your telephone bill paid electronically, and having transactions handled via point-of-sale or debit card are all considered electronic payments.

Internet-Based Payment Systems Models

electronic currency: the Internet equivalent of cash.

debit card: a kind of payment card that transfers funds directly from the consumer's bank account to the merchant's.

Four main models illustrate Internet-based payment systems: electronic currency, credit cards, debit cards, and smart cards. **Electronic currency** is the network equivalent of cash. For example, electronic funds transfer (EFT) moves cash from one account, such as the employer's payroll account, to another account, such as the employee's checking account, regardless of bank type or location. Credit and **debit cards** are the electronic equivalent of checks: They require the user to have an account on a server or at an issuing bank equipped with the proper Internet network. Smart cards are cards equipped with a memory chip.

In addition to the ACID and ICES tests discussed earlier, other properties are important to an electronic payment system, including the following.

1. **Acceptability:** For electronic payment to work, the system must be widely accepted by, and acceptable to, merchants. Merchants must have the technical ability and the processes to expedite a sale without delay.
2. **Ease of integration:** The software that accommodates the user—the Web site interface—must be effective and well integrated into the total network environment. It also should be independent of any other payment instrument.
3. **Customer base:** Enough users and enough traffic must be present to justify investing in the electronic payment mechanism.
4. **Ease of use and ease of access:** Users don't like to wait. Using a payment system should be as easy as hitting a button on the screen.

Electronic Transaction Systems

An electronic transaction system makes it possible to process transactions over the Internet, whether the customer uses Visa, MasterCard, Discover, American Express, or any other form of card. As mentioned in Chapter 9, the elements required to do business on the Internet are a storefront, a shopping cart, a merchant account, and an electronic transaction processing system to pay the merchant against the customer's credit or debit card. Several systems can do this job. The following examples illustrate how the bulk of Internet payment systems work.

CyberCash. Bill Melton and Dan Lynch founded CyberCash, Inc. (http://www.cybercash.com. Accessed June 2003.) in 1994, now part of VeriSign. The company offers a range of e-commerce solutions, from credit –card–based payment systems to secure micropayment systems. One unique service is a gateway that ties Internet merchants to an existing electronic payment system. Another is the CyberCoin mechanism designed to support online micropayments (less than $1). The main CyberCash transaction system centers around secure credit card payments.

CyberCash servers act as a gateway between the merchant on the Internet and the bank's secure financial networks. Using dedicated lines, a typical sale transaction via the merchant's Web site involves the following steps.

1. The customer places an order on the merchant's Web site, then enters the payment and shipping information to initiate the purchase process.
2. The consumer verifies the information and clicks the appropriate button to submit the packet of information back to the merchant.
3. The merchant ships the order (packet of information) and forwards the payment information, which has been digitally signed and encrypted, to the CyberCash server.
4. The CyberCash server receives the packet, moves the transaction behind its firewall and off the Internet, unwraps the packets within a hardware-based crypto box (the same technology banks use to handle PINs as they are shipped from an ATM network), reformats the transaction, and forwards it to the merchant's bank over secure, dedicated lines.
5. The merchant's bank forwards the authorization request to the issuing bank via the card association that settles credit card transactions (or directly to Visa, American Express, Discover, and so on) for approval or denial. The decision is sent back to the CyberCash server.
6. CyberCash then transmits the approval or denial code back to the merchant, who presents it to the consumer. The merchant proceeds with the fulfillment phase—(shipping the order).

Typically, a transaction goes through the payment processing cycle in less than 15 seconds. Because CyberCash uses e-wallet (an electronic payment system that operates like a carrier of e-cash and information in the same way a real-world wallet does), no one except the customer and the banks ever sees the customer's credit card number. CyberCash merely acts as an intermediary. Because the merchant is charged on a per-transaction basis, the system is not economical for small payments (see Figure 15-2).

Netbill. This product is a secure and economical payment method for purchasing digital goods and services via the Internet. The Netbill (www.ecom.tifr.res.in/ecom/netbill.html. Accessed June 2003.) server maintains accounts for consumers and merchants, which allows customers to pay merchants for goods to be delivered. The goods are delivered in encrypted form to the consumer's machine. The Money Tool (consumer software) verifies receipt, and the goods are displayed automatically for the consumer. The Netbill protocols enable communication among the Money Tool, the merchant server, and the NetBill server. The goal is to ensure that all transactions are completed successfully.

Screen Capture 15-1

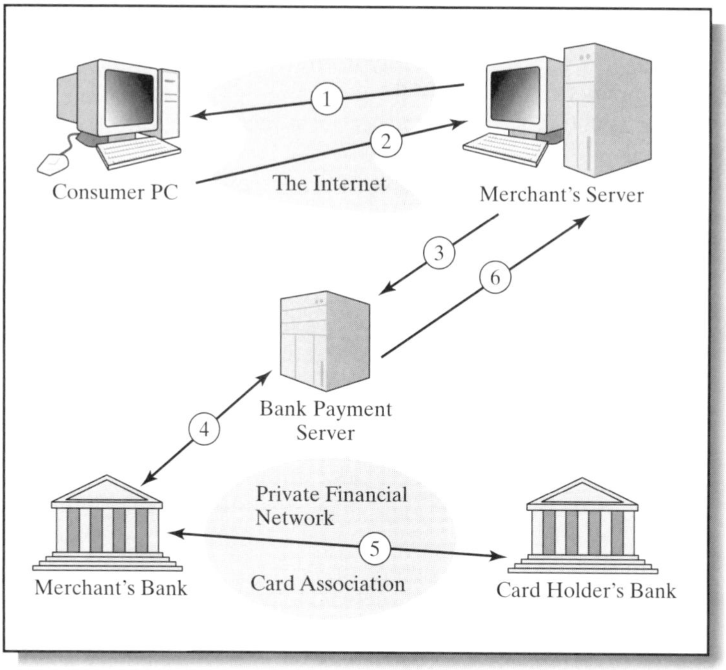

Figure 15-2
Secure Internet credit card payment process

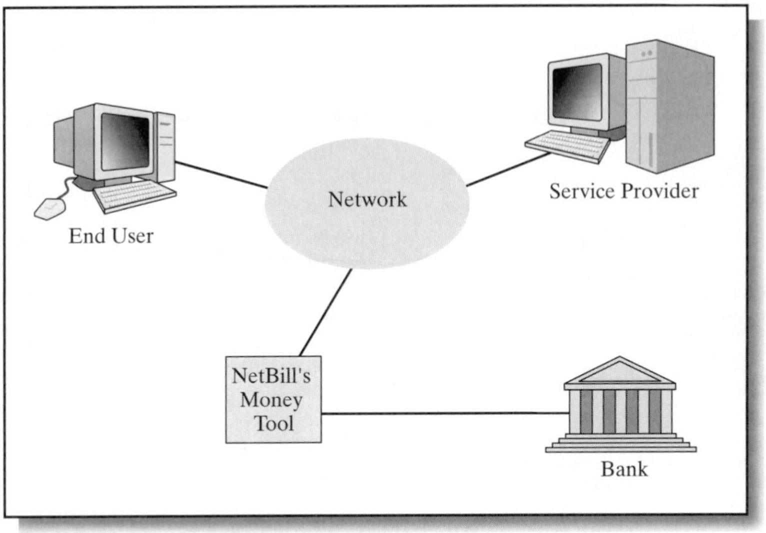

Figure 15-3 NetBill payment system

The general configuration of NetBill operations is shown in Figure 15-3. The eight major steps are as follows.

1. A consumer requests a price quote by clicking on the URL in his or her browser.
2. The merchant responds with a price quote.
3. The consumer accepts (or declines) the price via a Money Tool pop-up window.
4. The merchant delivers the goods in encrypted form.
5. The Money Tool acknowledges receipt of the goods.
6. The merchant contacts NetBill's transaction server to record the transaction and transfer funds.
7. The NetBill transaction server confirms that funds have been transferred and stores the decryption key.
8. The merchant sends the decryption key to the Money Tool, which displays the goods in the consumer's browser.

The accounts on the NetBill server are linked to a financial institution—a bank. Consumers can replenish funds in their NetBill account using a credit card or bank account. Likewise, a merchant can transfer funds from its NetBill account to its bank account with each sale. When consumers create a NetBill account, they receive a unique user ID and generate a public key-pair associated with that ID. The key-pair is used for signatures and **authentication** within the NetBill system. As explained in Chapter 14, these electronic signatures prove that the person who ordered the merchandise is, in fact, the person authorized to do so (see Figure 15-3).

authentication: making sure that a cardholder is, in fact, the person authorized to use the card.

First Virtual Holdings and VirtualPIN First Virtual Holdings, Inc., uses a system called VirtualPIN, which relies on electronic mail to confirm purchases (www. uncc.edu/icis99/program/TC9903.PDF. Accessed June 2003.). A customer decides on the purchase of a digital good. The customer gives the merchant his or her First Virtual account number. The merchant, in turn, submits the transaction to First Virtual, requesting confirmation by electronic mail from the customer.

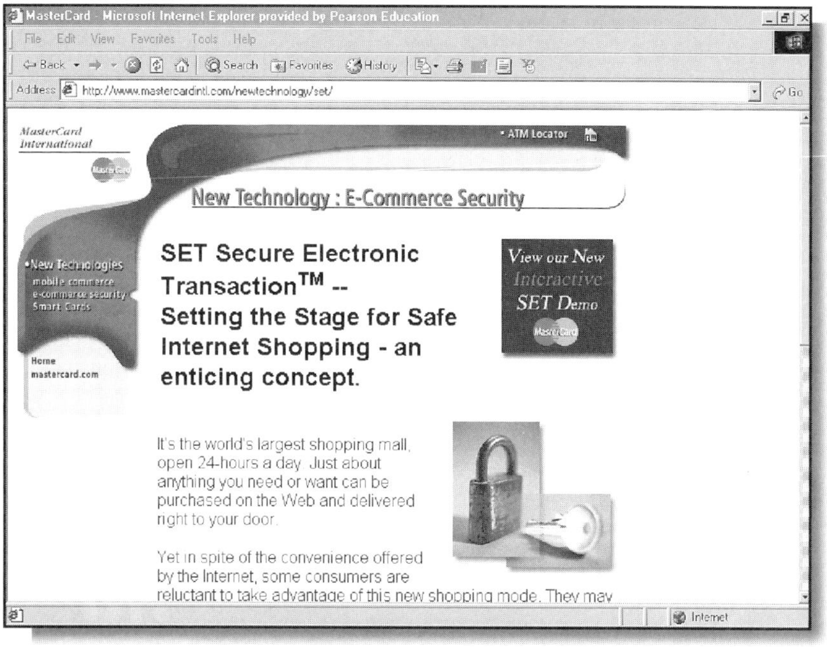

Screen Capture 15-2

Secure Electronic Transactions (SET)

Secure Electronic Transactions (SET): protocol for handling transactions on the Internet administered jointly by Visa and MasterCard.

The **Secure Electronic Transactions (SET)** protocol is an emerging standard for handling transactions on the Internet. The system is administered jointly by Visa and MasterCard to ensure reliable, secure transaction processing in the electronic payment medium. It covers every aspect of online commerce from initial registration of a cardholder with an online agency through the actual details of payment.

Among the services are cardholder and merchant registration, purchase request, payment authorization, payment capture, purchase notification, authorization reversal, and credit reversal. It authenticates the identification of the parties involved in the transaction by using a combination of cryptography systems, along with a *trust hierarchy* of digital certificates. (These mechanisms are explained in more detail in Chapter 14.)

SET was developed with four important goals in mind.

1. **Confidentiality** of payment as it is processed electronically.
2. **Integrity** of transmitted data. This means data will not be corrupted during transmission or processing.
3. **Authentication** that a cardholder is, in fact, the person authorized to use the card. It also verifies that the merchant handling a sale can accept an authorized card via the acquiring bank.
4. **Interoperability** across network providers. This implies a more encompassing or comprehensive way of making electronic payments over the Internet 24 hours a day, 7 days a week, without delay.

The protocol defined by SET is thorough and complex. For example, each purchase request transaction requires exchanging four messages between customer and merchant.

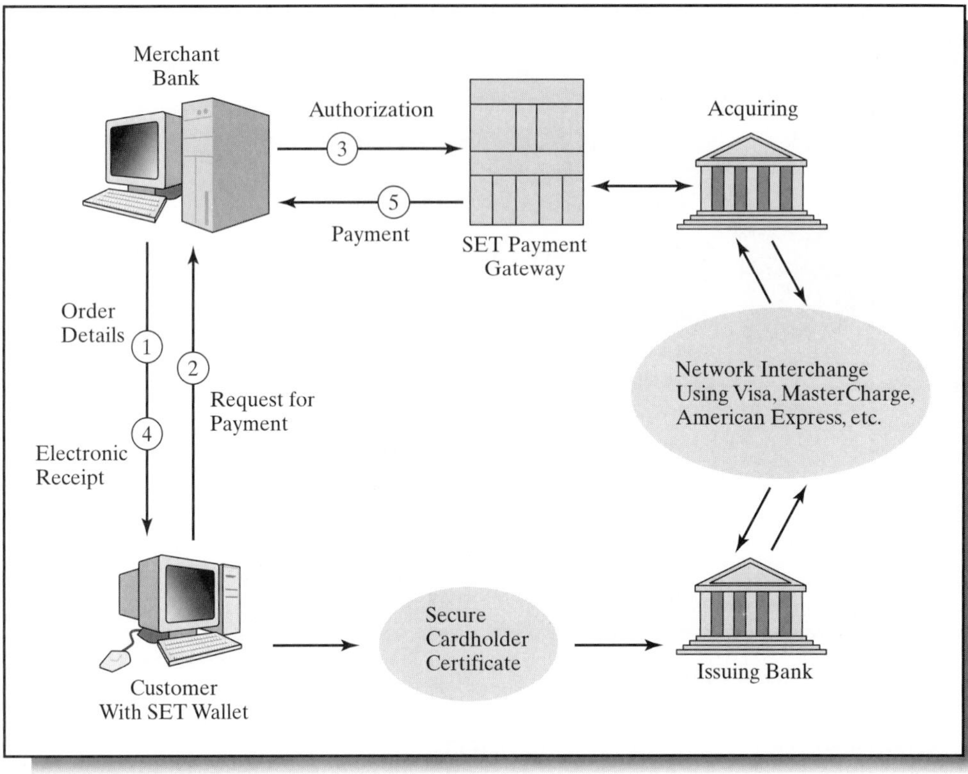

Figure 15-4
Classical flow of a SET transaction

One thing is clear about this level of complexity: It is not economical for small payments. Figure 15-4 shows the standard flow of a SET transaction. For details regarding this process, see Chapter 14.

Electronic Payment Media: Credit Cards, Debit Cards, Smart Cards

Types of Electronic Payment Media

Dozens of electronic payment media are already in use. A brief list of links and pointers to payment systems competing for a place in the electronic commerce world is shown in Box 15-1. Electronic payment media can be grouped into three types, depending on the information being transferred online.

1. **Trusted third-party type:** This type maintains all sensitive information. Banks, for example, maintain bank accounts and credit card numbers for customers, who may be both buyers and sellers. No real financial transaction is done online, and the information need not be encrypted because financial transactions are updated completely off-line. An

BOX 15-1
Current payment systems

1. **BankNet** (http://mkn.co.uk/bank) offers an electronic check system in pound sterling.
2. **CheckFree** (www.checkfree.com) has plans to expand e-commerce on the Internet.
3. **Credit Card Network** (http://creditnet.com) has a credit card authorization system using SSL.
4. **Cybank** (ganges.cs.tcd.ie/mepeirce/Project/oninternet.html) is a Web payment system in which customer's purchases are charged against funds held in a Cybank account.
5. **CyberCents** (http://www.cybercents.com/) is an account-based system allowing payments as small as a cent. Value is transferred into the account using a credit card.
6. **Ecash** (www.ecashtechnologies.com) is a fully anonymous electronic cash system using blind signatures. Originally called DigiCash, this group was acquired by eCash Technologies in August 1999.
7. **E-Coin** is a token-based micropayment system that uses a client wallet plug-in. An e-wallet is the electronic equivalent of cash in a real wallet.
8. **Millicent** (research.compaq.com/SRC/articles/199705/Millicent.html), from Digital Equipment Corp., is a system designed to support purchases costing less than a cent.
9. **Mondex** (www.mondex.com) is electronic cash on a card.
10. **NetPay** (http://ausweb.scu.edu.au/aw99/papers/dai/paper.html) is an Internet micropayment, debit-based system that allows small amounts of money to be spent at the Web in exchange for products or services.
11. **QuickCommerce** (www. qc123.com/) is a credit card and ACH check-clearing system. ACH (Automated Clearinghouse) is an electronic process of clearing financial transactions among banks, usually in the evening after banks close. More on ACH is illustrated later in the chapter.
12. **WebMoney** (www.webmoney.ru) is an account-based system with some anonymity, allowing transfer between temporary accounts using e-wallet software.
13. **Ziplock** (www.portsoft.com.au) is a credit card payment system: Customers receive a key code to unlock the product only after it has been downloaded and their credit card authorized.

SOURCE: Mahoney D., Pierce, M., and Tewari, H. "Payment Mechanisms Designed for the Internet." Uartech Huse Publishers, 1997, 5–11.

example of this type of electronic payment system is First Virtual. Seewww.creditnet.com for an example of a credit card authorization system.

2. **Notational fund transfer-related type:** This is the Visa/MasterCard SET-based transaction. Customers submit their credit card to a merchant for payment. The merchant transmits the credit card number via a phone line to the issuing bank for confirmation. The issuing bank, in turn, adjusts the customer's and the merchant's accounts accordingly. Because all of this is done online, the information transmitted is encrypted for security. This does not, however, prevent a hacker from tapping an account by intercepting a

message or credit card number and running up charges before any electronic system detects it. Despite these issues, this medium has been the core of online payment systems for years and now is being extended to the Internet. More sophisticated protocols are being tested to ensure transaction integrity.

3. **Digital cash or electronic money:** This type allows the transfer of money itself, which carries value. In this case, serial numbers representing actual money are encrypted all the way to their destination and can then be converted into real money such as U.S. dollars.

It took years for people to accept paper money; it will take time before people will accept a digital economy as a replacement for a paper-based economy. In the long run, digital money is necessary if we are to operate effectively in the digital marketplace. Digital money is effective in the sense that it is adaptable and can be manipulated to act like electronic checks or anonymous cash, depending on the situation and regardless of location or distance.

Credit Cards

To sell things on the Web, a merchant must accept credit cards. Credit cards are accepted everywhere. A huge processing industry exists to handle the multibillion-dollar traffic that credit cards generate each year. Companies like Bank of America, First Data Corporation, and National Data Corporation handle the technology-based infrastructure for hundreds of banks, their merchants, and credit card holders 24 hours a day. Stores around the country swipe credit cards, enter codes, issue receipts, and move merchandise quickly and efficiently with no actual cash changing hands. Credit cards are, by far, the most popular payment option on the Web.

To accept a credit card payment on the Internet, you must first open a merchant account with your bank. You can work with your bank or search Yahoo! for credit card merchant services to get a list of such banks. A merchant account allows sellers to accept and process credit card transactions. In these transactions, the card number and transaction details are processed with no identification of the buyer, as there is when the customer signs a payment slip.

Charges the merchant pays for online transactions are equivalent to the charges for phoning in the transaction. The average charge for a transaction making its way through a terminal is anywhere from 2 cents to 5 cents, depending on the volume of business the merchant generates per time period. Fees include a few hundred dollars for setup plus 2 to 4 percent of each credit card transaction processed. Some banks may also charge statement fees and a monthly minimum charge of $20 to $50.

To accept credit card payments over the Internet, the Web merchant needs some form of secure and encrypted line, usually employing the Secure Sockets Layer (SSL) that is standard on Netscape and Microsoft browsers. All the merchant's server needs is an encryption key.

To complete the cycle, the merchant needs a shopping cart program that allows users to collect their purchases. The shopping cart interfaces with a payment-processing system such as CyberCash, calculates the costs and taxes, and delivers a complete bill for customer approval. To improve fraud detection, in 1999 CyberCash offered its 14,000 online merchant customers a real-time fraud-detection service to show when a customer is trying to make fraudulent online purchases using credit cards. This is a step in combating fraud and improving the integrity of business on the Internet.

Because credit cards are so widely used, you might get the false impression that the billing process is straightforward. In reality, credit cards are just the most convenient way to get online payments at present. Credit cards work around the globe, regardless of the location or country of the issuing bank. They also handle multiple currencies and clear transactions through a series of clearinghouses or consortiums.

Credit card processing is not, however, simple.

1. Most card issuers charge interest from the day a charge is posted to the account if payment is not made in full monthly. Some charge interest from the date of purchase, several days before they have even paid the store on your behalf.
2. For the merchant, credit card transactions result in immediate credit to the merchant's bank account. They have the same effect as cash.
3. By law, the cardholder's risk of losing a credit card amounts to $50. A cardholder is expected to notify the issuing bank immediately upon discovering the loss of the card.
4. A cardholder can dispute charges or purchases to the card issuer. In this case, the merchant's acquiring bank can reverse payments or adjust payments as the situation warrants. See "12 Credit Card Secrets Banks Don't Want You to Know" on the Commonwealth of Massachusetts Web site at www.state.ma.us/consumer/pubs/credsecr.htm. Accessed June 2003.

Despite their widespread use in e-commerce, credit cards leave a complete audit trail and continue to be an incredibly insecure form of payment. No signature gets verified, and no face-to-face clues are available to interpret. A merchant can't tell whether the card is in the hands of the actual cardholder, a 10-year-old child, one's spouse, or a thief. Getting a merchant account is not a straightforward procedure. If your online storefront is your first

Screen Capture 15-3

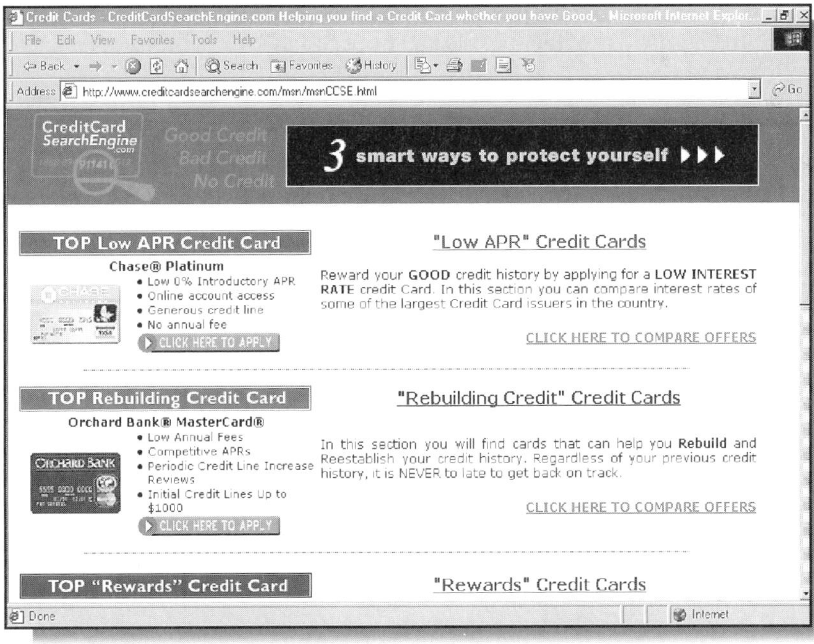

Source: 2003–2004 Nationwide Card Services, Inc. Publishing or distributing content without the expressed written consent of Nationwide Card Services, Inc. and/or our partners is prohibited.

business venture on the Web, banks invariably examine your company's financial records and the history of the business. They try to assess how serious your commitment is to the Web store, how long you plan to stay with it should it not do well at the outset, and so on.

If a merchant can't get a merchant account, credit cards can be accepted in other ways. The most common way is to find a company that will subcontract the payment collection process as a third party. One such company is iBill (http://ibill.com). The company charges 15 percent of the merchant's total revenues, with a ceiling of $10,000 for a 2-week period.

In terms of the mechanics of processing credit card purchases, Figure 15-4 illustrates the five-step process as it relates to purchases over the Internet.

What Is Credit Card Laundering?

As a merchant, would you extend an unsecured line of credit to another merchant who could not get credit from a financial institution on its own? If you agree to deposit another seller's credit card sales into your merchant account, you're taking more than a financial risk. Although you'll be charging a fee, this type of credit card *laundering* is a violation of your merchant agreement with the bank or credit card company. It seems like a simple procedure for earning extra cash, but it can turn into a nightmare. The guaranteed easy income often turns into losses beyond all commissions. Merchants that are turned down for credit often have a bad credit history or bad management.

Many disreputable telemarketers use credit card–processing merchants to bill consumers for their sales. Once they have received payment from the processing merchants, they close their operations or move to new and undisclosed locations without ever sending any merchandise to the customer. When consumers find out, they contact their credit card company and dispute the charges. In these cases, everyone loses. The customer loses time chasing the false charges, the credit card company might have to write off the amount to bad debt, and the telemarketer has blood on its hands.

Debit Cards

Payments can be made on a Web site in two ways: debit cards and credit cards. Most ATM cards are debit cards with a Visa or MasterCard logo. They look exactly like credit cards, except they directly tap your checking account every time you make a purchase or a withdrawal. They are easier, more convenient, less burdensome, and offer greater access to your money than do checks, ATMs, or credit cards. They are descendants of the ATM cards that became popular in the early 1980s. Debit cards are different, however, because transactions are processed through the issuing bank's credit card network.

Debit cards can be used with or without a personal identification number (PIN) almost everywhere—retail stores, gasoline stations, restaurants, and pay phones. When used without a PIN (called an *off-line* transaction), the procedure is simple. The merchant's terminal reads the card and identifies it as a debit card that creates a debit against the cardholder's bank account. Because the transaction is off-line, instead of debiting the account immediately, there is a 2- to 3-day wait before final processing.

When a debit card is used for off-line transactions, as in the case of retail purchases, a thief can drain an account simply by getting hold of a receipt. The thief does not need the card; the card number is sufficient to commit the fraud. Unlike credit cards, for which a cardholder's liability for a stolen card under the law is $50, the liability for debit card fraud is higher. It is $50 if one notifies the bank within 2 days of learning of the fraud, and $500 or more after 2 days, up to the entire amount stolen under certain circumstances.

Worse, regardless of the liability, the thief has the victim's money and the victim might have to fight to get it back from the bank. In the case of credit card fraud, the victim simply talks with the bank about getting disputed charges taken off the bill.

When a debit card is used with a PIN, as in using an ATM machine, it is called an *online* transaction. The cardholder simply inserts the card in the machine, enters the PIN number, and proceeds as when using an ATM card.

Today's banks are pushing hard to replace the ATM card with a debit card without asking customers if they want one. The reasons are obvious. More merchants have credit card readers than PIN-based readers. Banks also make more money through off-line debit cards in percentage fees or discounts from the merchant. Banks and merchants make more money and have lower risks than when a consumer writes a check because there are no check-clearing costs, there is less float time, and no checks bounce. Box 15-2 describes some of the unique benefits and limitations of today's debit card.

BOX 15-2

Debit cards and the competition

Mandy Williams has one part of her holiday shopping figured out: She'll be paying for everything with her debit card. "Any place that will take it, I will use it," says the 20-year-old reading coach from Republic, Missouri. "It keeps you from buying things you may not have the money for. I don't even own a credit card."

Ms. Williams's method of payment appears to portend a national trend: Debit-card use in stores is outstripping use of credit cards. For the first half of this year, debit cards accounted for 26 percent of in-store transactions, compared with 21 percent for credit cards, according to a recent consumer survey conducted by the American Bankers Association and research firm Dove Consulting. That marks the first time credit card use has fallen behind debit cards, which look like a regular Visa or MasterCard but deduct payments directly from a person's checking account.

Whenever a shopper makes a purchase with a Visa- or MasterCard-branded debit card, the retailer pays a transaction fee ranging from 15 cents to 50 cents, and the bank receives a cut of that. "The numbers are great enough that it's in the bank's interest to promote use of the cards," explains Carl Bradbury, check card manager for Commerce Bank, Commerce Bancshare's banking unit. Moreover, the more shoppers use debit cards, the less they write checks, which are costly for banks to process.

For consumers, debit cards offer a way to conveniently make purchases without running up debt, a factor that could be crucial as shoppers affected by the weak economy consider belt-tightening this season. But there is also a big negative for consumers: A debit card offers less of a shield against fraud than a standard credit card. In the case of a lost or stolen credit card, the legitimate holder can simply refuse to pay for transactions fraudulently charged against it. But in the case of a debit card, the cost of fraudulent purchases comes straight from the holder's checking account, which can cause checks to bounce and wreak havoc on the holder's financial life.

Although the debit card essentially is a surrogate check, retailers rarely impose the same security measures

One limit facing debit-card growth is a daily purchase limit, often of about $500. In November 2001, giant Bank One Corp. advised customers that their debit cards could be used to make purchases of up to $3,000 a day during the holiday season.

SOURCE: Excerpted from Coleman, Calmetta, "Debit Cards Look to Give Credit Cards a Run for Consumers' Money," *The Wall Street Journal*, December 3, 2001, B1ff.

All debit card purchases are reflected in the monthly hard copy statement the bank mails each customer for reconciliation. (See www.pirg.org/consumer/. Accessed June 2003.)

According to the National Consumers' League, here is what consumers need to know about debit cards.

1. Using a debit card frees you from having to carry cash or a checkbook. You don't have to carry traveler's checks, show identification, or give out personal information at the time of the transaction.
2. Debit cards are more readily accepted by merchants than are checks, especially in countries where check cashing and check processing are not widely used.
3. It is generally easier to get a debit card than a credit card. You can get a debit card the moment you have a checking or a savings account.
4. Returned debit card purchases are treated just like returns for items purchased by cash or check.
5. The debit card is a quick *pay now* process. No grace period is given as for credit card payments.
6. A major problem at this time is that using a debit card may mean less protection for items that are never delivered, for defective items, or for items that were misrepresented. With credit card purchases, you can contest the charge and put a hold on payment within 60 days.
7. Cardholders might overspend their limit before anyone finds out. Retailers do not have verification machines to see a bank account balance before the sale. During busy times, most retailers process small sales on faith. For more information, visit the National Consumers League site at www.natlconsumersleague.org/debitbro.htm, and see Holmes, Phillip, "Debit Cards: Their Value in an Incentive Program," 1–4. www.info-now.com/html/3040deb1.asp. Accessed June 2003.

Smart Cards

smart card: a card with a built-in chip capable of storing information in its memory.

Imagine discarding your wallet full of plastic—credit cards, debit cards, frequent-flyer cards, gas company cards, and a special card to get into your company building—in favor of one smart card that can do all these functions in a swipe. A **smart card,** first produced in 1977 by Motorola, is a thin, credit card–sized piece of plastic that contains a half-inch-square area that serves as the card's input/output system.

This is its interface with the outside world, and it handles a variety of applications. A smart card contains a programmable chip, a combination of RAM and ROM storage, and an operating system of sorts, all embedded in the plastic. It encrypts digital cash on a chip and can be refilled by connecting to a bank. A smart card carries more information than can be accommodated on a card with a magnetic stripe. The chip's ability to store information in its memory makes the card *smart*. It can make a decision, as it has relatively powerful processing capabilities. A brief summary of smart card evolution is shown in Table 15-2.

Among its many uses and applications are the following.

1. Provides users with the ability to make a purchase. It contains stored value the cardholder can spend at retailers.
2. Holds cash, ID information, and a key to a house or an office.
3. Provides three categories of applications. The first is information to authenticate an individual's claim of personal identification using either token-based (e.g., a passport,

Table 15-2
A summary of smart card evolution

Date	Technology	Architecture	Application Memory	Program Memory
Late 1970s	Memory	State machine*	100 bit	Serial number
1980s	Memory	State machine	Up to 1 KB	Serial number
Early 1990s	Microprocessor and secure microprocessor	8-bit	1 KB—16 KB	8 KB–32 KB
Late 1990s	Microprocessor with crypto-graphic coprocessor	16-bit	256 bytes–64 KB	8 KB–136 KB
Today	Microprocessor with crypto-graphic coprocessor	32-bit (RISC)	80 KB–512 KB	240 KB–512 KB

Year**	Event
1968	2 Germans invented smart card
1970	Arimura invents in Japan
1974	Roland Moreno invents in France
1976	Bull (France) first licenses smart card
1980	1st trials in 3 French cities
1982	1st U.S. trials in N. Dakota & N.J.
1996	1st university campus deployment

*A state machine is a device that performs a single function.
**Shelfer and Procaccino, 2002, 84.
Source: Gohring, Nancy, "Get Smart," *Interactive Week*, January 14, 2001, 45.

driver's license, credit card) or knowledge-based (e.g., PIN numbers or passwords) authentication approaches. The second category is authorization for things like drug prescription fulfillment and voting purposes. The third category is transaction processing. The smart card could be loaded with cash value in ATM machines and used as a credit card (Shelfer and Procaccino 2002). A more recent development in smart card design is capturing fingerprints for improved authentication.

integrity: ensuring that transmitted data will not be corrupted during transmission or processing.

confidentiality: privacy of message transmission or reception.

4. Provides encryption and decryption of messages to ensure security, **integrity**, and **confidentiality.** Though not inherently anonymous, smart cards can be designed to share no transaction information.
5. Acts as a carrier of value in a system, similar to what is called an *electronic purse*. For example, Visa Cash allows a customer to use a smart card for small purchases by storing specific cash value that can be replenished once the amount is used up. The standard technology is to allow transfer from a smart card to an authorized merchant. The biggest player right now is Mondex, which allows card to-card transfers where users pay each other for work performed using smart cards as if they were real cash. Known smart card applications include the following.

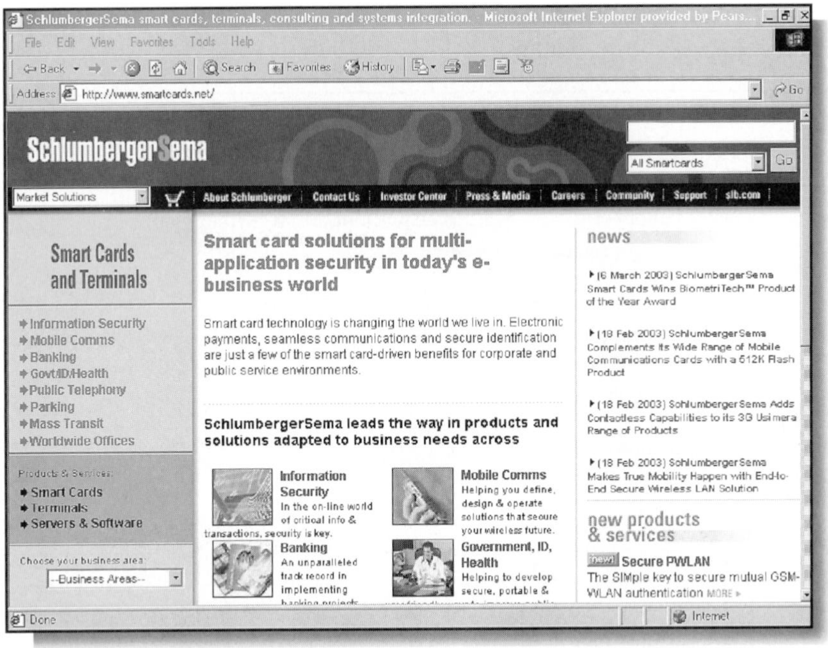

Screen Capture 15-4

1. **Government:** Smart cards are gaining importance with government agencies around the world. They often are used to control areas of access for government employees. For example, postal workers in France carry smart cards in order to gain access to apartment buildings. The cards are programmed daily with the postal workers' predefined schedules. This card allows access only at certain times, facilitating easy access to appropriate individuals and discouraging intruders.

2. **Identification:** The identification market is one that benefits greatly from the security associated with the use of smart cards. Examples are driver's licenses, immigration cards, and college campus IDs. Florida State University uses a smart card for its official student identification card. This card is a multiapplication card and offers a variety of conveniences and services to university students. Students use this card to gain access to certain facilities and events. If a student wishes to activate these features, the card can serve as a debit card on and off campus, a prepaid vending card, and a long-distance calling card (http:// bservices.fsu.edu:130/index.htm. Accessed June 2003). See Box 15-3.

3. **Health care:** Countries with national health care systems, such as Germany and France, have employed smart cards to reduce service costs associated with the health care industry. Germany and France have issued national smart cards for the purpose of collecting payments. In France, the smart card focuses on an insurance payment system, including features such as electronic signature abilities and built-in encryption. These smart cards assure confidentiality, security, authentication, and integrity and are being piloted in four major French cities (Gajramsingh and Patel 2002).

4. **Loyalty:** The retail industry widely uses applications of the smart card; more specifically, to identify and reward customers. The Boots Advantage Card in Britain is one such example of a loyalty card retailers use to capture customer information and better cater

BOX 15-3
Smart cards a way of life

It's noon at Penn State University, and 21-year-old Amanda Gormley rushes to the Hetzel Union Building for a bite to eat. She pays for her burrito and soda with her ID+, an unusual student ID that also serves as a stored-value card (her parents deposited cash into an account for her at the beginning of the semester). After lunch, she stops off at the library to make some photocopies. The Xerox machine deducts the charges from her card. Later, she returns to her dorm, where she swipes the ID through a card reader to gain access to the building. In her room, she gathers her dirty clothes and heads to the laundry room, where the washing machine deducts yet more money from her ID+.

Until recently, smart cards—cards with an embedded chip that stores information—were programmed with a single application. Stored-value cards, such as those used by Metro riders in Washington, D.C., allow commuters to get home on the subway, yet won't help them make a phone call. But a new generation of hybrid credit cards, which include a conventional magnetic strip as well as a microprocessor, contain 100 times more storage space than magnetic-strip cards. That is enough room to accommodate a huge range of applications: a security program to protect the data on the chip; an "electronic wallet" program that fills in credit card and shipping information when users buy something online; discount coupons for online shopping; a program that tracks frequent-flyer miles; a program that holds airline-ticket and boarding-pass information. And when the smart card is slipped into a card reader, a small device attached to a PC, the cardholder can install new applications and delete old ones—a handy option, for instance, if your corporate travel office ditches the Hilton in favor of the Marriott.

SOURCE: Excerpted from Branscum, Deborah, "Smart and Smarter," *The Standard*, February–March 2001, 52–54.

promotions processes to them. Currently, more than 5 million Boots Advantage Cards have been issued in Britain. Each British pound a customer spends in the Boots convenience store is worth four points on the Advantage Card. Each point amounts to 1 penny available to spend in any Boots store. Most often, the stores offer extra points with the purchase of certain products, which allows customers to collect points even faster (Gajramsingh and Patel 2002).

5. **Telecommunications:** Smart cards are widely used in the telecommunications industry. The Global Standard for Mobile Communicators (GSM) has been adopted in Hong Kong, Singapore, Australia, New Zealand, India, South Africa, and the Persian Gulf states. A smart card called a Subscriber Information Module contains the information necessary to access the network. This card can be inserted into any GSM phone, and the user is billed automatically. The user's location is detected, and any incoming phone calls are directed to that phone.

6. **Transportation:** Contactless smart card technology is quickly gaining acceptance in the transportation industry throughout the world. Hong Kong uses a single smart card, the Octopus Card, in most of its public transportation systems. Octopus equipment has been installed in all buses in the city. Passengers also are able to travel franchised trams, coaches, and railways in Hong Kong using the Octopus Card.

7. **Financial:** Financial institutions were one of the first to adopt smart cards for various applications. There are several common uses of smart cards within the industry, including

electronic purses, credit and debit cards, and payment associations. Electronic purses attempt to eliminate the costs associated with small change at the point of sale. The electronic cents purse is a smart card that stores a maximum value of 99 cents. When a customer presents this card at the point of sale, the transaction is rounded up or down to the nearest whole number and the card is either credited or debited to account for the difference.

As can be seen, smart cards benefit consumers in several ways, depending on the application. In general, smart-card-based applications benefit consumers where their life and business habits intersect with payment-processing technologies. This includes managing expenditures more effectively, reducing paperwork, and the ability to access multiple services and the Internet. A multiple application card can support services like health care, travel, and financial data access. Some smart cards also link directly to the Internet.

How Smart Cards Work

Operationally, smart cards require a special reader to connect the card with a computer system programmed for this purpose. Smart cards have special contacts that match those in the reader when the card is inserted into the slot for processing. The newest smart cards are "contactless." Infrared communication technology allows the reader to exchange data. In a retail store, the reader normally is attached to a cash register. In buildings, authorized users scan the smart card across a reader attached to the door and programmed to a computer-based recognition system. With remote contactless cards, the card can be read from a distance. This is how tollbooth electronic payment readers work.

How secure and confidential are smart cards? Smart cards offer more security and confidentiality than any other financial or transaction storage card on the market. They are a safe place to store sensitive information (keys, passwords) or personal information.

Smart cards have their share of problems. First, they are vulnerable to hardware hacking, which means data stored in the card can be altered or corrupted. Left undetected for long, these alterations could bankrupt the card backer. According to one report, smart cards are broken routinely, in spite of their reputation as the most secure processor available.

How Does a Smart Card Relate to the Internet?

A smart card can be used in Internet applications in several ways. First, it can help an Internet client support an established protocol such as SSL or SET. For example, the smart card can authenticate access to encrypted transactions or files stored on a personal computer. It also can be used for cryptographic functions such as digital signatures and storing the key(s) and certificate(s) for the specified protocol. Key storage is an important function that can be relegated to a smart card. Also, secret keys in the chip let the card authenticate its communication with any device sharing the same keys. In the absence of ready availability of card readers, smart cards in Internet systems are confined to special-purpose processes such as "electronic cash" for low-value payments, telebanking, and authentication of a transaction.

The Future of Smart Cards

The future of smart cards is promising. Smart cards are expected to be used in 95 percent of the digital wireless phone services offered worldwide. Asia, Latin America, and North America are countries where smart cards have the greatest potential in the next 5 years. The main uses to date are for pay telephones, wireless telephony, Internet access, banking, and pay TV.

With the proliferation of smart cards and other payment media in e-commerce, one big headache a customer will encounter is keeping track of passwords for different cards.

biometrics: the use of a body part such as the thumb to authenticate identity.

A single card could replace all these passwords and be activated simply by pressing your thumb on the card. This is called **biometrics** (see Chapter 14), or the use of a body part such as the thumb to authenticate identity. The card would carry a digital fingerprint. Many ATM machines already scan the customer's retina for a few seconds in lieu of the traditional password.

The problem with the retinal scan is the storing of a customer's physical characteristics in a database, which brings up the privacy issue. With the fingerprint, the characteristic is known only to the customer and is activated only when the owner presses it into action. This eases the privacy concern and eventually could be cheaper, especially when the retailer no longer needs elaborate equipment to match the thumbprint.

The next wave in smart cards is their use in place of keys as a way of opening doors. The card is already programmed to allow mail deliverers into a building at certain times of the day or during certain periods of the year. In the lab, scientists are trying to put a screen resembling a tiny computer on a smart card. Scientists are even trying to make it possible for this wallet-sized computer to process voice commands.

In terms of obstacles, smart card use in the United States faces resistance because of the privacy issue. Aside from housing all applications on a single card, smart card infrastructure also must achieve interoperability. Even then, with massive personal information on one card, concerns have surfaced about businesses gaining access to such information for marketing purposes. In situations where organizations use smart cards to give employees access control, the smart card keeps a log of where the employee is at all times. This is an obvious invasion of privacy for many Americans.

Another obstacle is culture. Because Americans do not feel deprived by not having to use smart cards, no incentive exists to use them. In the U.S. culture, greater emphasis is placed on privacy than by individuals in other parts of the world. The bottom line is that consumers are reluctant to purchase smart cards until enough privacy and security features are embedded in the infrastructure to address this concern.

DigiCash, E-Cash, and the E-Wallet

Credit cards leave a complete audit trail, which makes them more open to pervasive eavesdropping than the mail or the telephone network. Credit cards also have other drawbacks. They are not well suited for impulse buying, because an element of deliberation goes with using them. In addition, they are not that convenient for making small purchases.

Some tech designers see a solution in digital cash. Unlike credit card transactions, digital cash leaves no audit trail. It offers a true digital economy—one where anyone can pay $5 or $5,000 directly as if it were a real cash payment in person.

One such digital cash system is CyberCoin. To use CyberCoin, you first open an account at a bank that handles e-cash (Mark Twain Bank in St. Louis, Missouri, was the first U.S. e-cash bank). Next, you make a withdrawal in the form of e-cash coins stored in a digital wallet or an e-wallet on your PC's hard disk. You can spend the e-cash at the business of any merchant that also has an e-cash account at a bank.

E-cash was an electronic currency service till 2002, when it was acquired by InfoSpace Technologies. This service requires a client-server interaction, whereby the customer buys electronic cash with a secure credit card transaction. The customer does not have to possess an open account with e-cash. Although this service requires an intermediary, it is the safest in terms of fraud protection.

From a regulatory point of view, digital cash is not any different from any other kind of electronic financial payment medium. Just as the IRS often suspects independent contractors' reporting because of the possibility of tax fraud, the Treasury Department is likely to resist minters of digital cash because of the confusion that resulted in early America when each bank printed its own notes.

viral product: a product offered as a giveaway or a special promotion to encourage receivers to pass on the word to others, creating the potential for exponential growth in the product sale (sale spreading like a virus); a communications product.

One new development in early 2000 was combining e-mail and the credit card network to send real cash. A new online payment system called PayPal.com allows registered users to send a payment to anybody with an e-mail address just by writing a dollar amount into an online form. When the e-mail is sent, the payment is charged to the sender's credit card or bank account. Registration takes less than 5 minutes. If the person on the other end is not registered, that person simply fills out a form attached to the e-payment to "tag" the money, which is already available in a PayPal.com account in the receiver's name. This is called a **viral product.**

The E-Wallet

e-wallet: an electronic payment system that operates like a carrier of e-cash and information in the same way a real-world wallet functions.

The **e-wallet** is another payment scheme that operates like a *carrier* of e-cash and other information in the same way a wallet carries real cash and various IDs. The aim is to give shoppers a single, simple, and secure way of carrying currency electronically. Trust is the basis of the e-wallet as a form of electronic payment. The procedure for using an e-wallet is easy.

Screen Capture 15-5

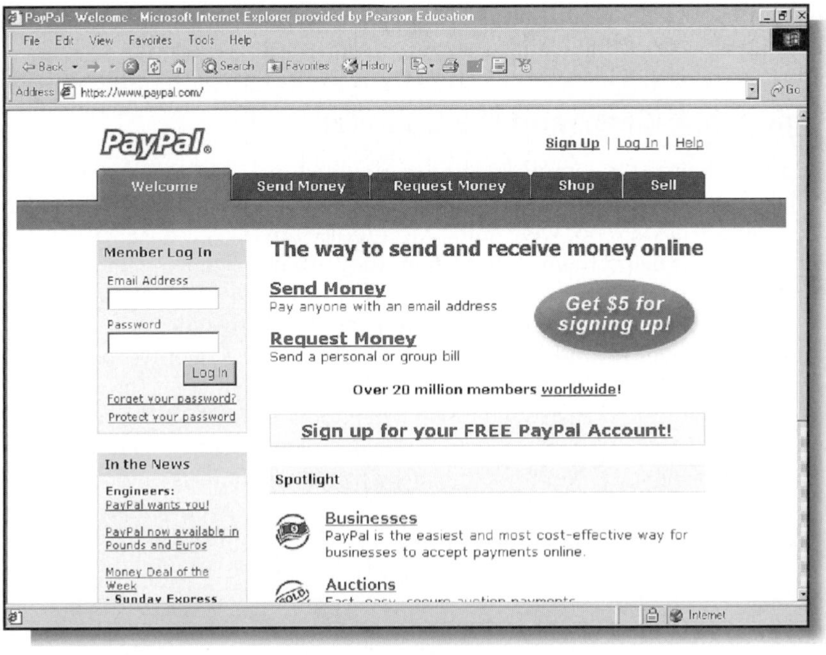

Source: These materials have been reproduced with the permission of PayPal, Inc. Copyright © 2003 PayPal, Inc. All rights reserved.

1. Decide on an online site where you would like to shop.
2. Download a wallet from the merchant's Web site where you intend to shop. The special form requires the buyer to fill out personal information such as credit card number, phone number, and address. When making a purchase, you click on your e-wallet, and the order is completed automatically.
3. Fill out personal information such as your credit card number, name, address, and phone number, and where merchandise should be shipped.
4. When you're ready to buy, click on the wallet button and the buying process is fully executed. Billing information is filled out automatically. Another option is to drag information out of the wallet and drop it into the online form.

Suppose a discount stockbroker offers electronic trading for customers with a cash or margin account. To trade (buy/sell) electronically on the Web for the first time, you are asked to fill out a short form on the screen with your name, account number, address, phone number, and so on, and enter a preassigned password. Once the system accepts the form, it asks if you want to replace the assigned password with one of your own. This completes setting up your electronic trading profile. Your cash or margin account is the e-wallet. It carries cash value. Every trade you make will affect the wallet as a credit or as a debit; it either takes e-cash out of your e-wallet or puts e-cash into it. For more information, see Box 15-4.

Some wallets sit on your PC's hard disk for privacy; others sit on the computer of a host if you want to reach your wallet from several different locations. The big online

BOX 15-4
Even Amazon has a take on the wallet

Every store of consequence in the brick-and-mortar retail world has its own credit card. The technology, the debt, even the data collected through the card are often outsourced. But the retailer owns sales information, and the purchase process, and the customer demographic data.

Why should it be any different online? Of all the wallet schemes that have floated down the Internet river since 1994, only **Amazon.com's** 1-Click, which it studiously doesn't call a wallet, has succeeded. The company has never released figures on how many of its customers use the feature, in which clicking a single button adds an item to a cart that will dump eventually into an order based on preset preferences, such as shipping address and credit card.

But a measure of the potential Amazon believes 1-Click has is evident in the fact that the company has made it one of the selling points of an ambitious new hosting service it began offering to small merchants late last month. As part of becoming an Amazon-hosted site, such merchants will be invited to offer consumers 1-Click shopping, though they will have to pay Amazon 60 cents for each transaction done through 1-Click, plus nearly 5 percent of the revenue. If that isn't a sign that Amazon thinks there's value in its wallet-like feature, what is?

1-Click's success suggests that the store-credit model may yet get its cyberspace analogue. "I see wallets as a way to deepen the relationship with a consumer, not establish a relationship with a consumer," says Joe Kraus, senior vice president for content at Excite@Home, which has experimented with wallet capabilities. "My relationship with my credit cards isn't as strong as it is with the people from whom I buy things."

SOURCE: Excerpted from Andrews, Whit, "Even Amazon Has a Take on the Wallet," *Internet World*, October 15, 1999, 40.

Wallet Vendor	Service Details
America Online	Works within America Online shopping only
Brodia.com	Direct-marketing tool, travels with a consumer across sites
CyberCash	Marketed to the CyberCash merchant customer base as an added service
eWallet	Client-based desktop application; shopping bots
Gator.com	Direct-marketing tool, dubbed an "online companion" for storing passwords and credit cards
IBM	Part of the IBM Payment Suite of products for corporate customer
Microsoft	Expected to launch in late summer; details unclear
Trintech	Single card resides on the desktop or a toolbar; multiple-card service can reside on a server or desktop
Yahoo!	Works within Yahoo! shopping only

Figure 15-5
The most popular wallets

shopping sites like Amazon.com (http://amazon.com) have their own internal wallets. You can buy and pay with a single click. Other Web sites store your name, address, and credit card number so you don't have to enter them again. Banks like MBNA, NextCard, and First USA already are offering their customers digital wallets. Microsoft offers Microsoft Passport, and IBM has its Consumer Wallet.

A popular site-based wallet is Amazon.com's 1-Click system, which builds on an established relationship of trust with the customer. The problem with e-wallets today is that they are tied to specific retailers. Can you imagine having an e-wallet for each retailer you deal with? Eventually, a way will be devised so that one wallet communicates across retailers. The most popular wallets available to date are shown in Figure 15-5.

A recent joint protocol called Electronic Common Modeling Language (ECML), announced in 1998, was designed to make it easier to build multisite electronic wallets. ECML-compiled e-wallets, backed by American Express, IBM, Microsoft, Sun Microsystems, Visa, SETCo, and MasterCard, are designed to fill out forms. They read a list of field names and fill them with information provided previously by the consumer. There is a question of how quickly they will be adopted because security mechanisms have been left out of the specifications. A physical wallet is on your person. You trust yourself, and experience tells you that you can protect it. For e-wallets to be trusted, e-wallet companies need to work jointly with banks to promote trust and establish reliable protection.

electronic funds transfer (EFT): a computer-based system that facilitates the transfer of money or the processing of financial transactions between two financial institutions.

Electronic Funds Transfer (EFT) and Automated Clearinghouse (ACH)

Automated Clearinghouse (ACH): where bank transactions involving more than one institution are routed to debit and credit the correct accounts.

Electronic funds transfer (EFT) is a computer-based system that facilitates the transfer of money or the processing of financial transactions between two financial institutions the same day or overnight. Interbank transfer is one of the earliest forms of electronic payment systems on private networks.

The **Automated Clearinghouse (ACH)** routes bank transactions involving more than one financial institution so that the correct accounts held by the correct financial institution can be debited and credited. To illustrate, suppose your present checking account shows a balance of $100 in Bank A. You walk up to the teller one morning and ask that a payroll check for $280 written on your employer's Bank B be deposited in your checking account. The teller deposits the "not on us" check in your checking account and gives you a receipt showing a total balance of $380, but the amount available is $100. The teller puts a "hold" on the payroll check because it has to clear ACH before the money becomes available for your use. Here is the generic processing cycle for clearing the check.

- Bank A sends the payroll check to ACH for processing. The check sorter/reader scans the check and, based on the bank code, determines that it is drawn on an account at Bank B.
- ACH queries Bank B's network to determine whether it will honor the payroll check in the amount of $280.
- Bank B's computer system, which is linked to ACH, examines the check and the checking account against which it is drawn. If enough money is in the account, Bank B approves payment to Bank A.
- Bank A gets credit for $280 and routes the money to your checking account (see Figure 15-6).

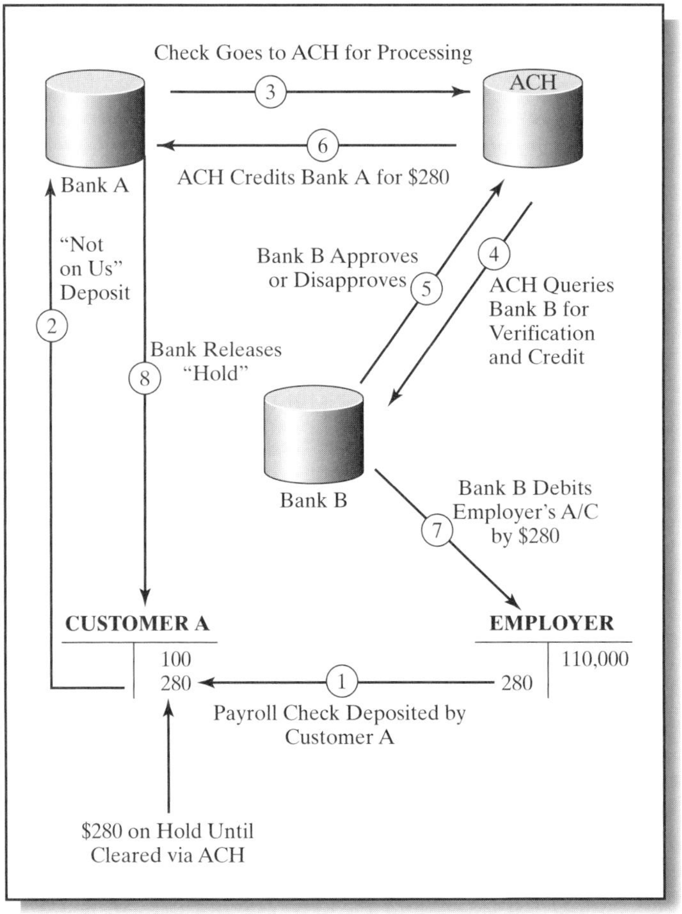

Figure 15-6 ACH—Generic life cycle of check clearance

B2B and E-Payment

One area that is drawing active attention is the dawn of business-to-business e-payment systems that can save processing costs and improve the overall efficiency of financial transactions between businesses. This area falls under "electronic invoice presentment and payment (EIPP) systems "(Scheier 2003).

The goal of EIPP is to automate everything from how the seller presents the invoice to how the customer or other business pays the invoice. The most significant advantage comes from savings in staff, postage, and handling. Some sources estimate as much as 85 percent of the benefits result from manual handling of invoices and settling billing disputes and the resulting writing of refund checks.

In 2002, Connecticut-based Gartner Inc. estimated that up to 15 percent of the invoices mailed by large businesses resulted in a dispute that cost between $20 and $40 per invoice to settle. By contrast, with EIPP, customers can scan bill details on their screen, submit disputes and, according to Scheier (2003) can opt to make partial payments online.

Every time the subject of e-payment comes up, concern over fraudulent orders is bound to come up. Before expecting e-payment online (in fact, any payment) to be finalized, online merchants should heed several warning signs regarding online orders:

- Expensive items. Be careful over big orders, especially for high-priced brand-name items
- Ordering multiple items to be shipped to more than one verifiable address
- Different addresses, where one address is given for shipping the products and another address for sending the bill. Very likely the latter address is questionable.
- Providing e-mail addresses that are difficult to trace. Free e-mail services are usually the ones that are hard to trace.
- Overseas addresses like Romania, Belarus, Pakistan, Egypt, Nigeria, Indonesia, Malaysia, and other countries have been known to have a high incident of fraud, unverifiable addresses, or names that simply do not exist.
- Instructing the e-merchant to have an expensive order left at the door or in front of a given store (Richmond 2003).

In summary, the most obvious savings of EIPP are more efficient invoicing, quicker receipt of payments, easier processing of receipts, and reduced customer service that once handled such things as invoices and complaints. It will be interesting to watch and see how well the technology establishes roots in ongoing businesses in the next 2 to 5 years.

M-Commerce and M-Payment

The ability to secure payments over wireless devices like mobile phones and Personal Digital Assistants is the major focus of m-commerce and e-commerce today. That is, the success of m-commerce depends on its payment infrastructure, which must deliver confidential data safely and reliably. With the growing mobility of consumers worldwide, the infrastructure also must be capable of handling payments between authorized parties anywhere and at anytime in a consistent and interoperable manner.

Taking the lead in this endeavor is MasterCard International, working with financial institutions and technology organizations to build standards for mobile transactions. Through the Global Mobile Commerce Interoperability Group (seewww.gmcig.org), the goal is to establish secure payment standards for the evolving m-commerce market.

Hardware and software vendors, financial institutions, and service providers are involved in this project. Some of the key alliances include Motorola, 724 Solutions, and Oberthur Card Systems—the world's leading supplier of MasterCard cards.

Without security and privacy, m-commerce and even e-commerce cannot exist. With this in mind, MasterCard is convinced that the top priority is how to handle secure electronic transactions from a personal mobile device. In one secure payment scheme, the mobile phone has an electronic device to accommodate a smart card.

Issues and Implications

With the Internet's increasing traffic and congestion resulting from growing e-commerce, there are issues regarding electronic payment methods and methodologies of which you should be aware. The issues can be grouped as follows.

1. **Consumer needs:** What features will make electronic payment cheaper and more secure for the consumer and the merchant? (Security is covered in detail in Chapter 13.)

2. **Corporate processes:** How will today's increasing e-commerce business affect the way tomorrow's corporation operates in the marketplace? Will small and medium-size businesses be harmed or helped by the electronic payment system?

3. **Corporate strategy:** Will the electronic payment system end up in the hands of fewer financial institutions, or will it generate a number of smaller banks that cater specifically to clearing and processing digital business transactions?

4. **Regulation of competition:** How does the government ensure fair play among companies doing business on the Internet? What standardization can be expected? How can we be sure that financial service providers will behave in the public's best interests? How will the government levy taxes on electronic funds flowing over open networks like the Internet, especially with the increasing sophistication of encryption?

5. **Economics and social processes:** Will the government pull out of the cash-making business? If so, what are the consequences for business and society? If taxing goods and services over the Internet ends up being a big job to control, will the government find new ways to tax the working public?

In principle, the present technology seems to do the job of securing electronic payment over the Internet. Micropayments (say, less than $1) and high-value payments have different security and cost requirements. Based on all indicators, smart card readers will become widely available to expedite payments of small amounts. Ultimately, smart cards and e-wallets will provide better security, allowing the customer to use unfamiliar workstations without endangering the security of the transaction.

A Final Word

The payment systems that will be used in the digital world for e-commerce are virtually the same types of payment systems used in the paper world. They are cash (for small and anonymous payments), checks, credit cards, and systems involving vouchers and coupons. It is the same business model, has the same look and feel, is at least as cost-effective, and is at least as secure as that used in the paper world. The implementation is simply different.

In terms of integrity for the customer, the merchant, and the payment system, nothing happens without authorization. Nobody gives up money without an explicit agreement, stating all necessary payment details. Nothing happens without generating convincing pieces of evidence. That is, if A receives money, A can prove this fact. If A has not given any money, no one can prove the contrary. Rules and technical procedures for handling disputes are part of the payment system.

In terms of privacy, outsiders must not know payment details (customer, merchant, account numbers, amounts, date and time, payment information, and so on). In the same manner, payment anonymity should be preserved. Customers should be anonymous, and the merchant should not be able to link any two payments by the same customer. Also, the payment system should not trace payments back to the customer.

SUMMARY

1. The first medium of exchange was in the form of tokens that carried intrinsic value. After tokens were detached from their real value, the next step was notational money, where value is stored and exchanged by formal authorization. After notational money, the credit system was developed; it is represented by the credit card.
2. Cash offers unique features of convenience, wide acceptance, anonymity, no cost of use, and no audit trail, but e-money is becoming more attractive for making payments and conducting business in the real world. On the negative side, cash is easy to lose; difficult to trace; cumbersome to carry; and time consuming to count, organize, and manage.
3. There are four types of e-money: (1) identified and online—credit and debit card transactions; (2) identified and offline—purchasing by check, travelers cheques, or U.S. postal money order; (3) anonymous and online—cash payments; and (4) anonymous and off-line—electronic cash such as making deposits in one's account via ATM.
4. Regardless of the type or form of money, there are two distinct sets of properties to consider in money transfer: the ACID test (atomicity, consistency, isolation, durability) and the ICES test (interoperability, conservation, economy, scalability).
5. Electronic currency, credit cards, debit cards, and smart cards are the four main models for Internet-based payment systems. In addition to the ACID and ICES properties, several nontechnical properties are relevant to an electronic payment system: acceptability, ease of integration, customer base, and ease of use and access.
6. Payment systems via the Internet include CyberCash, Netbill, and First Virtual. Secure Electronic Transactions (SET) is a standard for handling transactions on the Internet and was developed with four important goals: confidentiality of payment, integrity of the transmitted data, authentication of the person using the card, and interoperability across network providers.
7. Electronic payment media can be grouped into three types, depending on the type of information being transferred online: (1) trusted third party (e.g., banks) that maintains all sensitive information; (2) notational fund transfer-related type, such as Visa/MasterCard's SET-based transaction, where customers submit their credit card to a merchant for payment; and (3) digital cash or electronic money—this allows the transfer of money itself, which carries value.
8. Debit cards and credit cards are the two ways to make payments on a Web site.

Debit cards directly transfer funds from the consumer's bank account to the merchant's. Credit cards leave a complete audit trail, are not well suited for impulse buying, and are not convenient for making small purchases.

9. A smart card is a card with a built-in chip capable of storing information in its memory. It contains stored value that the cardholder can spend at retailers and provides identification of the cardholder. It also provides data portability and helps businesses expand their products and services.

10. One alternative method of payment is digital cash. It leaves no audit trail and offers true digital economy. From a regulatory view, digital cash in transit is not any different from any other kind of electronic financial payment media. The e-wallet gives the shopper a single, simple, and secure way of carrying currency electronically.

11. EFT is a computer-based system that facilitates the electronic transfer of money or the processing of financial transactions between financial institutions. ACH is an Automated Clearinghouse where bank transactions are routed to debit and credit the correct accounts held by the correct financial institution.

Key Terms

- ACID test, 473
- anonymous e-money, 472
- authentication, 478
- Automated Clearinghouse (ACH), 494
- biometrics, 491
- confidentiality, 487
- credit card, 470
- debit card, 475
- electronic currency, 475
- electronic funds transfer (EFT), 494
- electronic payment, 475
- e-money, 472
- e-wallet, 492
- ICES test, 473
- identified e-money (digital cash), 472
- integrity, 487
- notational money, 470
- scalability, 473
- Secure Electronic Transaction (SET), 479
- smart card, 486
- token, 470
- viral product, 492

Test Your Understanding

1. Explain the difference between tokens and notational money.
2. List and briefly explain the unique features of cash.
3. Explain the key characteristics of e-money.
4. Distinguish between:
   a. Atomicity and isolation
   b. Scalability and interoperability
   c. Consistency and durability
   d. Authentication and interoperability
5. If you were to point out two problems with cash, what would they be? Be specific.
6. What are the requirements for Internet-based payments? Explain each briefly.
7. What is the main difference between credit cards and debit cards? Why is one type of card favored over the other?
8. What is credit card laundering? How do you think it can be prevented?
9. Explain the unique features and uses of smart cards.
10. What is unique about the e-wallet? How does it differ from real money? How does it work?

Discussion Questions

1. Why would anyone with a credit card want to use an electronic cash system on the Web?
2. What are some of the security requirements for safe electronic payment systems? Do you think the systems are safe enough?
3. Why do you think traditional payment systems are inadequate for e-commerce?
4. Of the electronic payment systems covered in the chapter, which ones do you think would be appropriate for business-to-business transactions? Justify your answer.

Web Exercises

1. Look up the home page of Amazon.com and Dell.com. Identify each e-merchant's payment methods and the kinds of security measures incorporated in each site.
2. Review the home pages of Bank of America (www.bankamerica.com), Wells Fargo Bank (www.wellsfargo.com), and Wachovia Bank (www.wachovia.com). Evaluate and compare the payment systems on each site.
3. John wants to pay his mom, Jean, who lives in another city, by e-cash. How can he do this?
4. You have been asked to give a 15-minute presentation on the structure of electronic payment systems and the procedure for implementing them in small retailing stores. Prepare an outline of what you plan to cover. What highlights would you focus on?
5. Look up the Web site of CyberCash (www.cybercash.com) and write a report about the company: its electronic payment system, basic infrastructure, prices, and so on.

Chapter 16

Launching a Business on the Internet

Contents

In a Nutshell

Launching a business on the Internet requires careful planning, understanding the target customer base, and choosing the right products and services to offer. The next step is resolving the software and hardware issues, especially with respect to linking to the Internet Service Provider that will put the business on the Internet. The site should make e-marketing a breeze. It should capture customers' attention and retain them long enough to result in a sale. The site also should generate repeat customers.

Assuming the buyer has gone through the ordering process, how can the experience end on a good note? The delivery of the product is critical. The system should include a tracking system to let the shopper know when and who received the product. A follow-up e-mail after the order has been filled is a tactful method of thanking the customer and confirming the order.

Customer service contributes a great deal to creating customer loyalty. In addition to being enjoyable, the shopping experience should be risk free for the merchant and the customer. That means implementing powerful security measures for the Web site and the servers to protect them and the transactions from hackers.

Electronic business is no longer an alternative; it is becoming an imperative. Individuals and businesses by the thousands are building a Web presence, from personal Web pages to storefronts. The new Web participants range from established companies like General Motors to individuals starting online mail-order businesses from scratch, and they all hope to make money. It is almost impossible to begin to count the kinds and types of businesses now on the Internet, but whether your business is an auction, or selling baseball caps or groceries, or trading stocks, there is a procedure to follow before you attempt to do business on the Web.

Issues such as planning your new site, marketing the business, providing good service, and maintaining security take on new meaning when applied to e-commerce. We will address these issues in this chapter, and they have been covered throughout the book.

The Life Cycle Approach

Here and throughout the book, we have followed a life cycle approach (see Figure 16-1). Each phase has been explored in detail in separate chapters.

1. The business planning and strategizing phase: having a vision, preparing a business plan, defining the target market, and setting immediate and long-range goals.
2. The hardware, software, security, and set-up phase: Deciding on the infrastructure.
3. The design phase: building the site and placing it on the Web, as well as making Web pages rich in content and interactive.

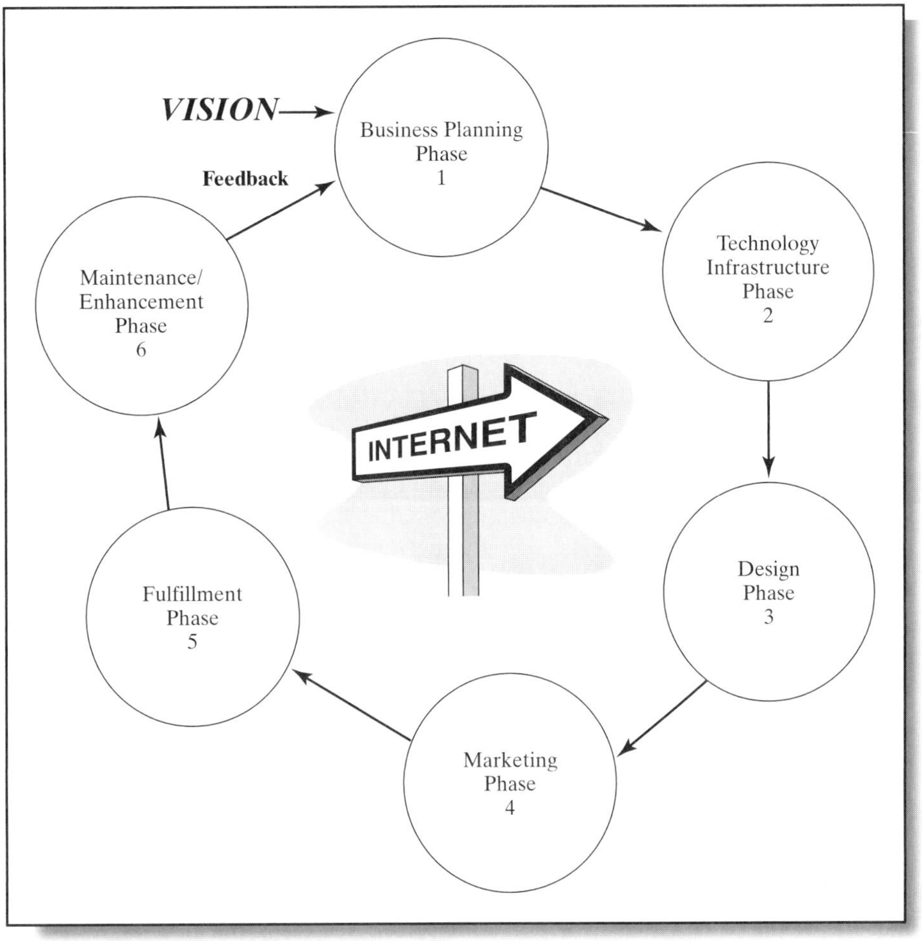

Figure 16-1
Building an Internet business—The life cycle

4. The marketing phase: advertising the site, setting up feedback mechanisms, and providing customer service.
5. The fulfillment phase: selling and shipping the product.
6. The maintenance and enhancement phase: maintaining and growing the business.

The sheer number of things to think about when launching a new online business is daunting, but the number one issue is planning and thinking through the phases of development before committing resources to the launch.

Here are some specific goals that can make or break an e-business venture.

- Create and maintain a competitive edge.
- Reduce operational costs.
- Improve employee communication and satisfaction.
- Find new markets for products or services.
- Improve relationships with partners who provide the goods.

- Create distinct distribution channels.
- Ensure customer satisfaction.
- Improve supply-chain management.

THE BUSINESS PLANNING AND STRATEGIZING PHASE

New companies that do business on the Internet must plan, strategize, have a vision, and obtain financial support. One expert estimates that small merchants can sell online for an investment of as little as $500 per year (see Box 16-1), but to be successful, they need to do careful planning beforehand.

Strategizing means evaluating a company's position and its competition, setting a course for the years ahead, and figuring out how to achieve the goals. This process is especially important in e-commerce. Having a Web site does not make a brick-and-mortar business an e-business. Unlike traditional operations where the business controls the channels, in e-commerce, customers control the channels, demand innovations in products, and expect personalized one-on-one service. Any strategic plans are likely to be good for only short periods of time. Traditional approaches to strategic planning that include devising the mission statement, deciding on objectives, and implementing a strategy to achieve the objectives are too cumbersome: By the time a business has gotten through these phases, some competitor will have "stolen its lunch." Table 16-1 summarizes the traditional and the e-way of strategizing.

BOX 16-1
Launching an e-commerce site cheap

When Leslie Gordon started looking for a way to sell products from the Hudson Valley online, she didn't have a lot of money, time, or computer expertise. What she had were high expectations for an e-commerce site that would be classy, powerful, and adaptable. "Most important to us was finding a low-cost [solution] without sacrificing quality, sophistication, or flexibility," says Gordon, 31.

Gordon found her low cost e-commerce Web site solution at Homestead.com, which charges her $150 a month to host Madeinthe hudsonvalley.com. She used the Web design tool supplied by Homestead to create the site herself, and also takes advantage of the marketing services the host provides.

Start-ups in search of a low-cost solution for an e-commerce Web site don't have as many options as they did 3 years ago, says Kneko Burney, director of business infrastructure and services at In-Stat MDR, a research firm. But that's not necessarily bad. Those providers that are left, Burney says, tend to be larger and stronger companies that have well-defined offerings and will probably be around for the long haul.

Besides saving the $10,000 she estimates it would have cost to have a programmer custom-build her site, Gordon is also happy with the results. "Their functionality mirrored the functionality of, say, an Amazon.com in its look and feel," she says. Selling online is still an excellent idea for many small businesses, and inexpensive options for setting up your own online store are plentiful and effective. To help you decide, we checked out five popular low-cost e-commerce Web site solutions.

SOURCE: Excerpted from Henricks, Mark, "How Low?" *Entrepreneur's Be Your Own Boss Magazine*, June 2003, 17.

Table 16-1
Traditional business versus e-business

FACTOR	TRADITIONAL BUSINESS	E-BUSINESS
Barriers to entry	Location requirements (i.e., build where the raw materials and market are)	Time and space limits; limited financial capital; unique products, special skills
Basis of competition	Improved products; bigger products	Smarter products; innovations in products and services, like a loran on a boat.
Basis of control	Manufacturer	Customer
Organization	Hierarchical departments	Specialized teams connected to the Web
Marketing/sales	Mass advertising	Mass personalization
Pricing	Based on cost of raw materials	Transaction costs on a sliding scale. For example, a stock trade can cost $65 through a retail stock broker, $34 through a discount broker, and $12 through the Internet.

Companies going online struggle with several basic problems: First, what is the best way to launch the business on the Internet? Second, how much of the company's business should be on the Internet? Simply loading a Web site on the Net and getting a surge of visitors to buy your products does not just happen: Strategic planning is needed. This kind of planning includes top management support and a *champion* at that level who is going to sponsor and support the push into the Internet. As National Semiconductor's Jim Gibson said, "There has to be an executive sponsor from the top that has the e-business religion" (Ginsburg 2000).

Another of the problems a first-time entrant faces is the *when* factor. When should the business go on the Web? Many people might encourage waiting, but if Henry Ford had waited to manufacture cars until air bags had been developed, he would not have been known as "the father of the automobile." One of the key points in launching your business on the Internet is the jump you will have on the competition. Careful planning, knowing what is involved up front, ensuring management support, and proper funding should minimize unnecessary risks of entry.

What we have emphasized so far is the ultimate goal of your e-commerce setup: to connect users with content. That is why it is so important to review the information needs of your prospective Web site's users and to inventory content assets that you wish to serve: text, applications, databases, and so on. Without a clear picture of the type of model that will drive the project, problems will arise. It is risky to plunge ahead before strategizing in the following areas.

- **Vision:** What is your business trying to achieve? How will the goals be met? How will the Web site help fulfill these goals? How will you measure success?
- **Resources:** How much can your business afford to build the right Web site? Are people available within the company who can turn the vision into reality?
- **Culture:** Is your business politically amenable to coordinating efforts to support this new approach to selling? Who ultimately will control the Web site's content and user feedback?

With these areas in mind, it is important to consider the role of leadership and how leaders with a vision can turn the possible into the practical. As summarized in Box 16-2, it is leadership that makes technology work for the unique product or service that the business offers the customer at large. Outstanding organizations have visionaries with the ability to recognize and shepherd great ideas through the organizational maze (Prewitt 2002).

The Planning Process: Strategy

An e-commerce Internet business provides a unique opportunity for an organization to do business from anywhere, anytime. Companies can expand their customer base, generate growth, and improve profitability. Because of its potential, establishing an e-commerce business may be among the most important business moves a company can make. This is all the more reason why the first step should be strategic planning.

Let's assume you want to be an online retailer. How do you proceed? The first formal step is deciding what is to be done within a given time horizon. The first thing to think about is what you want to sell. Certain products or services that don't stand a chance in the so-called brick-and-mortar world may be tailor-made for the Web—for example, rare and old books. You have to choose products and services that will meet the needs of a new breed of Web-based consumer and a sales medium that offers unique opportunities. In a way, the planning step is all about the product(s) or services you sell and how you address the needs of that product or service's consumer.

BOX 16-2
Role of leadership

Business history is littered with great ideas that never crossed paths with great managers and as a result fizzled. Technologies are just so much R&D expense until they're deployed by those who have the vision to recognize the great ideas and the skill to implement them successfully. That's why half of the 20/20 Vision honorees were chosen—for their ability to recognize and shepherd great technology ideas through the organizational maze. In other words, they are great leaders.

The best leaders are those who focus on a handful of useful technologies and ignore the rest, no matter how exciting the bandwagon looks. If you're fundamentally mediocre going to worse, other people applying technology can be a further accelerator of your own demise. If you're a good company going to great and want to stay there, technology can become an accelerator once you've made that leap, but it cannot cause it by itself.

One distinguished characteristic of great leaders is an intense focus on what their organization needs to do well—and what it shouldn't be doing at all. In keeping with this single-mindedness, outstanding leaders implement technology at three levels. The first level is those technologies directly relevant to a company's mission. A second type of technology is one that lacks revolutionary potential but that organizations need anyway. In a Web world, you've got to at least have a passably usable Web site, because there are certain expectations that people have come to have.

Finally, there are some technologies that are nothing more than a distraction. If you don't have to have them, and they don't tie directly to your mission, then the point is to have those on your "stop-doing" list, even if the whole world is heading toward that.

SOURCE: Excerpted from Prewitt, Edward, "Leadership Makes Technology Work," *CIO*, October 1, 2002, 102ff.

Here are questions the online merchant should consider in strategic planning.

1. **Who will buy the product?** Many new businesses ignore this simple question. Knowing your market is critical. A new online retailer must know the segment of the Web market its product is likely to attract and how well that product will meet the specific needs of the customer. Once you find the segment, you need to focus on servicing it 24 hours a day. A related issue is identifying what users need rather than what they think they want. The correct solution to this issue determines how usable the Web site will be.
2. **How familiar are you with the Internet?** Every new business carries with it some risk. The added uncertainty and the undisciplined nature of the Web make a new venture a challenge. The key to reducing risk is to focus on what you know. The Internet has generated a new breed of savvy consumers. More and more online visitors conduct extensive research on a product before buying it. You should have as much knowledge about the product as visitors do. Losing a customer to the competition means only a click for the consumer.
3. **Are you planning to be a short-term presence or a long-term presence?** In other words, are you approaching the Internet for a quick killing or for sustained growth? The answer will have a definite impact on what product or service you should sell. A commodity item like T-shirts or socks is a good bet on the Web because customers buy these everyday products without trying them on. Information-intensive products (stocks, securities transactions, travel services) are also good bets for long-term selling. Short-term items such as baseball caps could be a lasting business, but you should have enough staying power to weather seasonal changes.
4. **Who are your competitors?** It is rare that a unique product enters the market without competition creeping up on it. Take the example of selling books on the Internet. The books might be old and rare, and the Web might be the ideal vehicle, but it is likely that Amazon.com or Barnesandnoble.com will find a way to meet the challenge and divert your Web traffic.
5. **How good will your product(s) look?** In today's multimedia world, looks are important. Because customers cannot feel or touch the product, the way it is displayed on the monitor is crucial. If you sell clothing, for example, you might use real-life models when photographing clothing, then edit out the face and body parts of the model to make the product look more realistic.
6. **How will you present your product offers?** This question deals with the range of products that you plan to offer, the pricing, substitution if an item is not in stock, and building customer orders. Do you recommend products based upon a profile of the customer's needs? Are brand, model, price, and description enough? Can you handle the incoming e-mail with the expertise your customers will expect?
7. **How will you manage and process transactions?** Should taxes and shipping be added automatically to the total cost for a customer to accept prior to placing an order? In what states is tax applicable to sales? Are all items taxable? What types of payment (credit card, digital cash) do you need to support for your customers?
8. **How will the product be shipped?** The product has been paid for and is ready to be shipped to the customer. Now you need to determine how the product will be packed, shipped, and delivered, and how easily it can be returned. Selling birds, for example, might be a great idea until you begin to figure out how to ship them around the country. Size, weight, durability of the product, speed of delivery, and cost are all factors to think about in the planning phase.
9. **How will you handle unexpected change?** On the Web, unexpected change is a way of life. The technology, the users, the competition, and shopping trends for certain products are constantly in a state of flux. Entering a Web business thinking it has a one-time

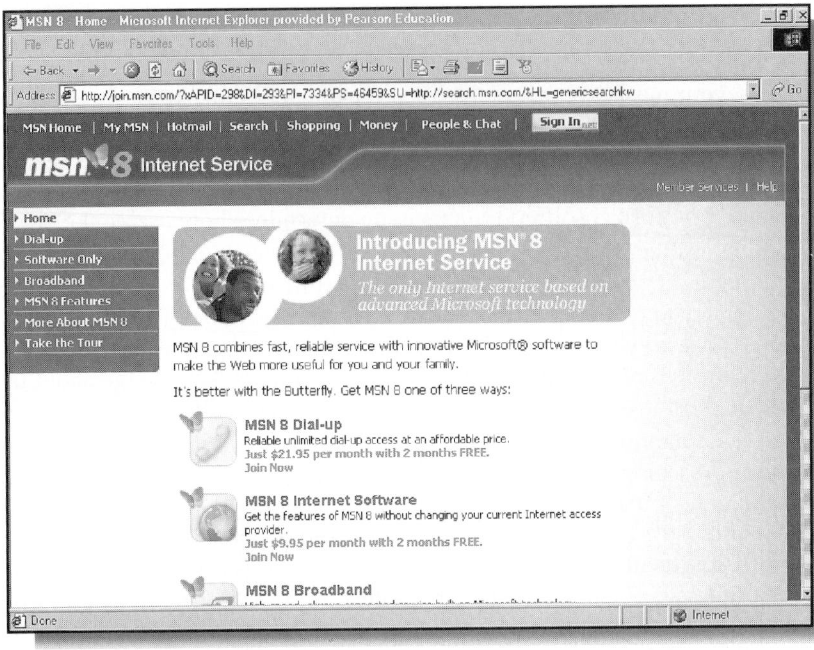

Screen Capture 16-1

development cost is a mistake. You need to plan for maintenance, upgrade, and improving the responsiveness of the site around the clock. This means money should be available to implement those changes when the time comes.

10. **How will you get and use feedback?** Web site owners should plan on fine-tuning the communication channel between the Web site and the user for feedback and follow-up. In addition to considering what users say, you need to plan how to make use of what they do, how long they stay on the site, and the like. This normally is done through the Internet service provider with special software that tracks site traffic.

capacity planning: determining in advance the capacity of the bandwidth (pipeline) that will accommodate the traffic to and from the Web site.

Capacity planning is related to strategizing about feedback. Imagine that you're already on the Internet and everything looks, feels, and works fine. Your customers are delighted, and the business begins to snowball. Suddenly, your site begins to slow down. Response time is now 20 seconds instead of 1 to 2 seconds. The site is functional but no longer works in the real world.

America Online (AOL) found this out the hard way. After offering unlimited monthly access to its online service, system overload led to millions of unhappy customers. It was only after round-the-clock work to upgrade that AOL began to regain normal service. It issued refunds in the millions to restore its integrity with its customer base.

This and other examples highlight the importance of planning for scalability, or upgrading. It is extremely difficult to patch in solutions later. The objective at this phase is to ensure that your customers do not go somewhere else. After meeting demands for round-the-clock availability, your business must make certain that traffic flow continues uninterrupted through a reliable network. If a network cannot scale quickly to meet sudden surges in traffic, consumers simply won't wait. For mission-critical e-commerce applications, any breakdown or slowdown is unacceptable.

In undergoing strategic planning, one must consider the politics of going global. Pursuing a global strategy means more for information technology than setting up foreign branches or hiring foreign information technology specialists in their foreign domain. It is essential to research the customs, delivery costs, and employment laws in those countries.As summarized in Box 16-3, a lot of questions and queries into the ramifications of going global come up and must be addressed before going any further. In the end, Web content must be customized to avoid conflict with customs and perceptions of each host country. Even Web marketing has to be tailored to local holidays and events (Alexander 2001).

BOX 16-3

Issues in going global

Pursuing a global strategy means more for IT than creating a worldwide network infrastructure, setting up foreign distribution, or hiring IT talent abroad. Whether the international presence is online or involves setting up operations in other countries, without some research into the customs, delivery costs, and employment laws in other nations, global expansion could spell global disaster.

Going global will require that you think about your department's international role in new ways. For example: How will the content of your Web page be interpreted in various countries? Will the variable costs of international shipping sink your supply-chain management software? Will you be able to hire scarce IT talent or change work procedures without running afoul of laws in other countries?

Avoid personnel pitfalls and think like a local. International marketing can result in problems if your Web content is misinterpreted, says Larry Clopp, an international trade analyst at Gartner Group Inc. in Stamford, Connecticut. Clopp recalls the story of a car manufacturer in Mexico. "Its Web page showed a picture of a hiker standing next to a car. But in Mexico, hikers are poor people who can't afford cars, so it wasn't acceptable to show someone who wanted to be a hiker," he says.

"You need a separate cultural focus for your Web site in some countries," Clopp says. "A few Web sites do a good job of this by hiring country content managers who manage the content locally and make sure the Web presence is effective in that country." You should also consider further segmenting local content to address different language groups. "How else can you manage your Web content in India, where you've got more than 20 spoken languages?" Clopp says.

"Given the vast differences in economics and culture around the globe, it is going to be difficult to hit it just right in all cases," says Stewart Morick, the Americas' leader for e-business in the consulting practice of PriceWaterhouseCoopers in Baltimore. "To do so, you might have to redo your product branding in every country, which isn't practical. So there's got to be balance" between cultural sensitivity and marketing needs.

Beyond matters of cultural taste, there are supply-chain issues to consider in global expansion. You need to determine ahead of time whether e-commerce software can really handle your international transactions. It is also important to understand the real cost of shipping of goods ordered via the Web worldwide. Sometimes, local delivery expense makes the purchase of products through a Web page too costly for the buyer, which raises the question of whether the e-commerce site should have sold the product in that country in the first place.

SOURCE: Excerpted from Alexander, Steve, "Learn the Politics of Going Global," *IT Agenda*, January 1, 2001, S8–S10.

Deciding on the Type of Site

One important step in the planning phase is to decide on the type of e-commerce model that fits the products or services you will sell on the Internet. Ways to classify e-commerce business models are by community, content, and commerce. Message boards and chat rooms are examples of community-type sites. Information content sites provide a wide variety of data such as stock quotes. Commerce sites involve consumers or organizations paying to purchase physical goods, information, or services advertised online. All organizations with the Internet address *company.com* are commerce-type sites.

Table 16-2 lists sample sites by type of product (commerce or content) and by type of market (business-to-consumer, business-to-business, or consumer-to-consumer). In business-to-consumer commerce, the Web site is the interface between the merchant with goods and services to sell and the consumer who orders them via the Web site. In business-to-business commerce, one company orders supplies or products from another company in order to make a product that is then sold to the consumer. Consumer-to-consumer e-commerce is a market like an auction, where one consumer contacts another to transact business.

After you have a clear idea of the goals of the online business and have figured out who your customer is, what product you're going to promote, and the nature of the competition, you need to map out and organize your Web site and decide whether you want to develop it in stages or all at once. You also need to decide whether you will develop the site yourself (using in-house staff) or outsource the project.

Another aspect of planning is to make a detailed list of requirements against which you can compare the solutions. One approach is called the *summit* approach: Set up a committee that holds strategic meetings to map out the master plan.

Table 16-2
Types of e-commerce strategies

E-Commerce Site	Type of Market	Information Type of Product	Content
Amazon.com	Business-to-consumer	**Physical goods**: books, music, home goods	Articles, chat, customer feedback
Barnesandnoble.com	Business-to-consumer	**Physical goods:** books, music, magazines	Articles, chat
Cisco.com	Business-to-business	**Physical goods:** networking products, Web-based services	Company–related
Dell.com	Business-to-consumer Business-to-business	**Physical goods:** hardware, software, applications	Chat, company related
eBay.com	Consumer-to-consumer Business-to-consumer	**Services:** Advertisements, online auctions	
Waterhouse.com	Business-to-consumer Business-to-business	**Services:** discount broker, financial	Stock quotes, investment information Services

Hardware, Software, Security, and Setup Phase

You cannot use the information highway without the proper tools. In this phase of building an Internet presence, decisions are made regarding the hardware needed to cruise the Web, the software that will be used, and the security required to ensure reliable exchanges between customers and your business. The first set of questions deals with what hardware to buy. How fast should it be? What about quality, reliability, and durability? What type of modem do you need? What brand should you buy? Do you buy through magazines or from stores? Do you buy from big companies or small ones?

Hardware

Computer hardware is constantly getting faster, smaller, and cheaper. There are certain components to look for when selecting hardware for the Internet. First, you need a computer with a lot of memory, a powerful central processing unit (CPU), and a fast link to the Internet. No matter what platform your computer runs on, you will be able to find a browser for it. Web browsers make it possible to connect with Web servers anywhere on the Internet. Browsers cache (store) images and, therefore, need a lot of disk space. As the browser accesses a page, it stores the images in a temporary directory **(cache memory)** on the visitor's hard disk. When a request is made to access or retrieve the image, the browser takes it from cache memory instead of requesting it from the network again. The browser clears its cache memory when you exit or after a preset time period. To allow for adequate caching, there should be at least 60 megabytes of hard drive storage space. The larger the disk space is, the quicker the access is to stored data.

cache memory: a high-speed memory dedicated to storing Web pages.

Processor speed is measured in megahertz (MHz). On today's Internet, it is risky to work with processing speeds of less than 100 MHz. Images gobble up a lot of storage and take longer to download than text. A lot of random access memory (RAM) also is needed for the Web browser program. Again, because most PCs use Windows, the larger the RAM storage is, the quicker the processing is. A minimum of 64 megabytes of RAM is required for normal navigation.

mouse: a point-and-click device that allows you to navigate a Web site or screen with ease.

modem: device that converts an outgoing message into bits for transmission and converts incoming bits into a human-readable message.

The remaining hardware includes a monitor, a mouse, and a modem. In choosing a monitor, color is a basic requirement. You should take care to ensure crisp, clean color and clarity of the displayed information. For PCs, the monitor should be super VGA to make best use of an extensive combination of colors.

A **mouse** allows you to navigate through a Web site with ease. You almost never need to use the keyboard. The **modem** is the *translator*. Modems come in varying speeds: The faster the modem is, the more bandwidth (speed) it will provide.

Software

Decide what you need to be competitive online—identify the software that will help you manage your products, promotions, customers, and orders. Programs are available to handle the tax calculations (Taxware), shipping, and payment processing (Cybercash or OpenMarket). Do you want to pick a design and insert your products, or do you want to customize the way your storefront will look and feel? Do you want a template so you can just fill in the blanks, or do you want to go with programs like Microsoft's Site Server Enterprise or IBM's Net.Commerce?

Surfing the Internet requires some basic software.

- File transfer protocol (FTP), which allows you to transfer files to and from remote computers.
- Telnet, which allows you to log onto a remote computer to access remote accounts.
- Archie, a program that finds files on the Net according to a search word you supply.
- NetNews, which is a newsreader that allows you to leaf through thousands of special-interest newsgroups on the Internet.
- E-mail, which allows you to receive and send electronic mail to anyone, anywhere, and at anytime.
- Serial Line Interface Protocol (SLIP), which is a program that connects with your modem to access the Internet.
- A browser such as Netscape that allows you to surf the Internet.

These programs are the bare minimum and are normally available as part of today's PCs.

Finding an Internet Service Provider (ISP)

An ISP links a business Web site and its customers on the Internet. Finding one can be difficult, depending on where the business is located, the nature and volume of the business on the Web site, and so on. ISPs do not advertise aggressively: You must look for them, evaluate their services, decide on the fees, and decide on the final linkup. InterNIC is an organization on the Internet that maintains a list of ISPs around the nation. Other systems are available, such as that maintained by AOL, although they provide somewhat limited access. (Detailed coverage of ISPs is found in Chapter 6.)

Security

If we were to compress the construction phase of launching a business on the Internet to its essence, four essentials would result: security, shopping carts, payment, and marketing. **Security** is the critical backdrop that must be in place for every step to work. From strategic planning to fulfillment, from the moment the merchant begins to envision the Web site until it begins to handle transactions, the Web site must be absolutely secure. A **shopping cart** takes the products off the virtual shelves and puts them into a virtual waiting area. An electronic form of payment (primarily credit cards for now) must be used in order to sell on the Web.

security: protection of data, software, or hardware against accidental or intentional damage from a defined threat.

shopping cart: a utility that keeps track of items selected for purchase and automates the purchasing process.

When it comes to security, Web site planners look at three overlapping types of risk: document security, privacy, and overall system security. *Document security* entails the integrity of the Web site and its information. There must be security features in Web design that ensure that no one can corrupt the integrity of the site itself, let alone the information in its content or its layout. *Customer privacy* has to do with embedding devices in the visitor's hard disk to track site usage. As we explain later, the visitor should be aware of such marketing tactics and should be able to choose whether the merchant is allowed to secure such a link. *System security* deals with the way the network, the Web server, and the e-commerce infrastructure prevent unauthorized access and tampering with e-commerce

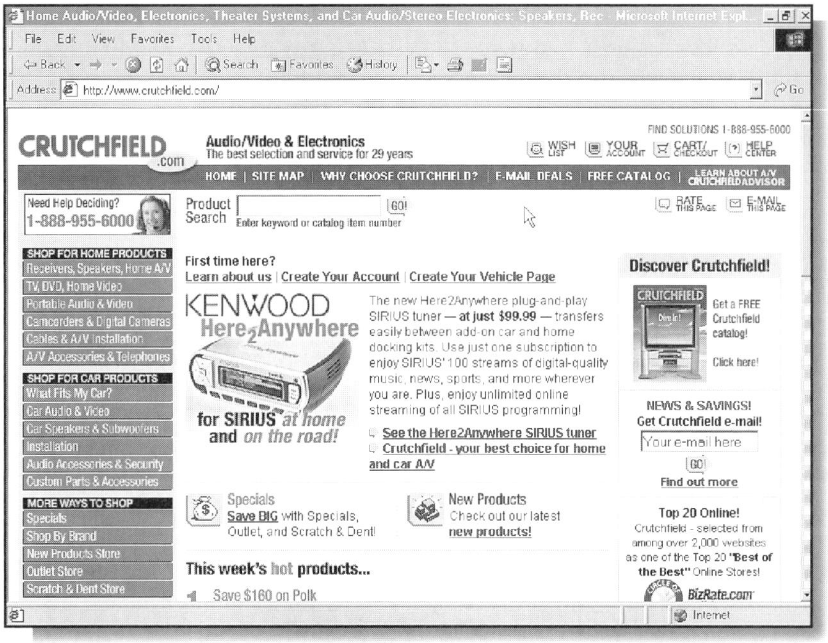

Screen Capture 16-2

Source: Copyright © 2003–2004. Crutchfield New Media, LLC.

traffic. System security was covered in detail in Chapter 13. Encryption was covered in Chapter 14.

Promoting security in an online business means adhering to a few simple rules.

firewall: a network node consisting of hardware and software to protect or filter certain information entering the company's databases or to keep select information from leaving the company.

Webmaster: a specialist in designing, maintaining, and managing Web sites.

- Control access to the Web server.
- Update server software and encode security measures to ensure server–Web site integrity.
- Use **firewalls** to protect the merchant's internal network.
- Monitor the traffic and detect irregularities in time to minimize damage.
- Assign Web security to a qualified **Webmaster**.
- Ensure a hot standby for every piece of hardware and software. Every router, program, Web application, and firewall must have a ready backup at all times. If a site is not available to end users at all times, companies may lose business and even their reputation.

Expertise

Knowing what to do to ensure network performance has been known to be far more important than knowing how to do it. To ensure technical expertise, the trend is for more and more businesses to outsource network solutions rather than having to tackle its complexity on their own. In this sense, outsourcing is cost-efficient, because it helps the e-business concentrate on what it is best known for.

To ensure reliability and integrity, dedicated staff must have practical expertise. To resolve issues on-site, e-commerce requires security expertise, a network and telecommunications specialist, and competence in server software and architecture. When choosing a provider for e-commerce network traffic, a business must consider expertise as top priority. A well-designed network infrastructure breaks down quickly without the staff required to maintain and upgrade it at all times.

THE DESIGN PHASE

In this phase, the focus is on designing a Web site to represent your products or services in the best way. The site also promotes your company and makes you visible to customers who normally would not visit your store. As a Web store manager, you should consider how much technology you need, to whom your site will be geared, and who will do the work of creating the site. Once it is up and running, you will need a Webmaster to keep the site up to date and a network administrator to keep the hardware and software running.

To become familiar with the basics of Web site design, you have access to resources on the Internet, in magazines, and via consultants who make it easier to do the planning. Some of these sources are known for discussions of the latest Web-related issues. They are also a good place to raise questions and concerns. Most are updated on a regular basis. Some search services also have topics of interest.

The Web Storefront

storefront: a technology infrastructure that includes the Web site, the supportive hardware, the server, and security and payment systems that work together to provide the business-to-consumer interface.

search engine: Web software that locates Web pages based on matching keywords.

banner: a graphic display on a Web page for advertising or promoting a Web store or service.

The intention of a Web **storefront** is to make sales. The Web site should load quickly and be simple to navigate. It should provide lots of information about your business. It should include your physical address, phone, and fax numbers, and be registered with VeriSign's Secure Site program or InterNIC—both nonprofit privacy organizations. In addition to registering the site with numerous **search engines** (Yahoo!, Excite, and so on), you can generate traffic by the way you announce your new online store in magazines, books that list Web sites, online newsgroups, or newsletters. **Banner** exchange services are also a low-cost way to generate site traffic and make your site look professional.

A storefront should have four attributes.

1. Customers should be able to find the product quickly. There is an 8-second guideline: Customers who can't find what they're looking for during that time will click out of the site and go to alternative sites.
2. The site should have mechanisms to process the order and send it to the fulfillment center for quick and secure packing and shipping.
3. The site should have mechanisms to generate a summary of the order and produce a printable receipt.
4. The site should have mechanisms to send a confirming e-mail to customers.

Behind every Web site is a cluster of programs stored on the server to present your application to site visitors, and the hardware that will host your server and application. Included in the program cluster are the following.

- **The database server:** Provides secure access to shared data for client applications.
- **The store administrator:** Decides on items such as how the store is opened and closed, manages product information and site appearance, configures shipping options, adds and edits product information, makes pricing changes, and creates product promotions.
- **The catalog builder:** Presents the product information the customer must see. This feature should allow customers to search for products.
- **The shopping cart:** Similar to a physical shopping cart, this allows customers to gather items they are buying and hold them until the actual purchase function is executed. Customers can add or remove items at will as they browse through a product catalog or database.
- **The order-processing system:** Handles all the tasks involved in completing the purchase order. This includes totaling the order, calculating state and other taxes and shipping costs, and including other shipping information. It also determines the method of payment (credit card, digital cash), and produces detailed sales and customer reports.

As you can see, creating a Web storefront requires careful planning. For a small to medium-size business launching its storefront on the Internet for the first time, the easiest option is a prepackaged e-commerce system such as Microsoft Commerce. Larger businesses such as the nationwide mail-order store Crutchfield Corporation (www.crutchfield.com) or Dell (www.dell.com) design their own storefronts from scratch. The main advantage of doing your own design is full control over the site.

Doing It Yourself Versus Outsourcing

One of the issues raised at the planning stage is whether the IT department of the business should design the Web site or whether it should be assigned to an outside Web designer. The advantage of having the work done in-house is control over the entire project. Also, company staff assigned to the project will be familiar with the details that will fit the company's image and product. The flip side of the coin is that effective Web design requires experience and expertise that often is not available in-house.

Giving the Web design to an outside consultant or to a Web designer has many advantages. The consultant can help you determine the audience, shop for the right Internet service provider, set up the Web site, design and post the Web pages, advertise the pages, and provide a variety of solutions dealing with logistics and traffic congestion, as well as Web performance monitoring.

Whether you design in-house or outsource the project has much to do with the amount of time it takes your in-house people to do the work well, the cost of their time, and how quickly the job can be done. If the Web project is going to be handled piecemeal and you have a ready audience, you need to think of the opportunity cost of customers going elsewhere to buy competitive products while your site is under construction. In any case, professional firms are available to evaluate your site and help you make the necessary changes to improve overall performance (see Box 16-4).

If you want a site to attract users and crush the competition; if you want a slick, bells-and-whistles site; and if you want to sell products online, there is a price to pay. The cost of the design package is only the beginning. Depending on which approach a business takes, it needs to consider setup costs, establishing a merchant bank account to which purchases are credited, credit card verification services and software, monthly site-hosting fees, fees for a site designer, and support personnel.

BOX 16-4
Web site testing, delivery, tracking

Companies redesigning or enhancing their Web sites have a new method for determining how well their time and effort will pay off. Startup Vividence Corporation this week will introduce a testing service that employs Internet users to assess and rate a site and report their findings to the site's owner.

Vividence has a stable of 80,000 "testers" who can be tapped to evaluate a business site. The testers are sent a version of the site and a browser that they can use for a limited period. This approach lets Vividence select testers who match the demographics of the site's target audience. Company officials say the service evaluates a site's capabilities and, if desired, compares it with a competitor's site.

The service, which takes about 2 weeks, starts with experts working with a client to design a testing module. Vividence then assigns about 200 testers who match the target audience. It conducts the test, reports the results, and analyzes the findings to improve site performance.

"This is what lets you sleep well at night," says Dave Lamond, founder and vice president of business development for Miadora Inc., an online jewelry store in San Mateo, California, that has used Vividence. "We did the test so we could have customer feedback driving our development process. We found we had a lot of weaknesses with our search capabilities."

The service starts at $20,000 per test, based on requirements. Vividence says customers include AltaVista, Compaq, and Drugstore.com.

SOURCE: Nelson, Matthew G., "Rate-a-Site Service Offers Quick Feedback," *InformationWeek*, February 7, 2000, 29.

The procedure for planning the Web design begins with looking at competitors' Web sites, thinking about how your proposed site can improve upon those already in existence, and generating a list of the features. The next step is to locate an able designer. Here are some things you should consider in locating the right site developer.

- Look at sites the designer has developed.
- Ask about the designer's capabilities. Do they include logo design, database development, animation, user testing, site hosting, and promotion?
- Visit the designer's shop and see the business at work.
- Consider how the designer reacts to your request for a proposal.

What Services Will You Offer?

homepage: the opening screen of the site.

button: a link with a label that, when you click on it, will take you to the intended destination site.

The basic infrastructure of a Web site consists of pages with text, graphics, audio, and links to other pages. The entry point is called the **homepage.** It is the first thing users see, and it creates a first and lasting impression about the content of the Web site. It determines whether the visitor will browse through the succeeding pages or simply leave and go to the competition. Homepages should be simple, use the right colors, and have well-organized **buttons** and minimum text.

The next level in a Web site is the ability to input data into the system—for example, filling out a form, sending an e-mail message to the company regarding a product, or sending comments about the product or the site. For this to be possible, you must have a server that is capable of receiving the content and processing it. Other considerations for this aspect of Web site design include the following.

- **User control and freedom:** Users should be able to undo and redo paths they have taken by mistake and get back on track within your site. All pages should allow customers to navigate within the site from any page to any other page.
- **Consistency and standards:** Users should not have to wonder whether different words or actions mean different things on different Web pages.
- **Recognition rather than recall:** Objects and options should be visible, requiring no memorization or explanation.
- **Efficient design:** Dialogs should not have information that is either unrelated to the segment or rarely needed.
- **Recovery from error:** Error messages should be displayed in plain language, indicate the source of the problem, and describe ways to correct it.
- **Help desk:** The Web site should have a feature where the user can go for help on activities related to the product, service, how to order, and so on.

The outcome of the design phase is a balance between designers' innovations and users' expectations. (Web design was covered in Chapter 8.)

Once a decision is made on what to include in the Web site and how to format it, the next step is where to store the pages. If you are a small business and you have limited networking technology, you will have the Internet service provider load the Web site on its server, as well as update the site and manage the traffic the site generates. The main drawback of this approach is limited control over sensitive data. Because the ISP has many other businesses to manage, there is a chance that your business data may be vulnerable; on the other hand, if you set up your Web site on your own in-house server, you need to consider the cost of maintaining, monitoring, and updating the site.

THE MARKETING PHASE

e-marketing: all electronic-based activities that facilitate production of goods and services to satisfy customer demand.

The generic term **e-marketing** is used to describe all marketing channels facilitated by the Web; it is growing at an amazing rate. Selling products and services on the Web differs substantially from in-store sales, because a customer may view your offering for only a few seconds. The importance of physical location is significantly diminished. However, one should be alert to cultural differences when selling items in different countries and on restrictions other countries place on certain items. For example, General Motors' Nova did not do well in Latin America, because *no va* in Spanish means "it will not go." Pepsi's advertisement in China fizzled, because in China the interpretation was "it brings back your ancestors from their grave." Baby jars sold by an American company in Africa featured a picture of a cute baby. The product did not do well, because food products in Africa always carried a picture of their containers.

Despite the differences between brick-and-mortar and e-commerce storefronts, many of the factors important for in-store sales remain important to a Web start-up. Accurate information, a good reputation and appearance, stability of service, good advertising, and knowledge of your customers contribute to online success. The essence of the marketing phase is providing good service, having enticing advertising, knowing the customer, selling the products or services, and following up after the sale. Inventory issues and stock control are also relevant items in this phase (see Figure 16-2).

Figure 16-2
The marketing phase

Providing Good Site Service

Maintaining accurate information is a major step in marketing. Too many businesses put up a Web site without fully understanding the amount of maintenance required to keep information current. Outdated information can cause a potential customer to lose interest and trust in the site and the product. Customers often expect particularly good service, with perhaps a demonstration of how something works or how it will look in different situations, because in many cases they are buying items online that they cannot touch or physically see. The service and products provided must be consistent and competitive in price. Failing to meet consumer expectations is the beginning of marketing failure.

Advertising

One important aspect of placing a new Web company in the marketplace is the ad campaign. The Web site should be a mirror image of the real business. Among the techniques for promoting the Web business are the following.

- Announcing the Web site through Internet search engines like Yahoo! and Netscape.
- Issuing a press release.
- Obtaining links from other Web sites.

- Purchasing ad banners from other Web sites.
- Announcing the new site in newsgroups.
- Advertising via e-mail.

Internet search engines provide the easiest access to your site when a customer has had no contact with your company before. By registering with the engines and by keeping your site at the top of their search lists, you dramatically increase your chances of receiving customer *hits*. Because the size of the Web makes random encounters somewhat unlikely, search engines provide the connection between your business and customers seeking your product or service.

Advertising through press releases, e-mail, and newsgroups also can be productive. Getting the company name and Web address out can be invaluable. New technology in direct marketing via e-mail is gaining momentum with products such as Broadc@st, an e-mail marketing tool. Broadc@st and similar products use customer information in your database, either purchased or gathered, to send consumers personalized advertisements via e-mail. Although techniques such as this can be productive, marketers should be wary of **spamming**, which can alienate potential customers and also create legal problems.

spamming: sending unwanted advertising to users.

In addition to these media, you can use television, radio, and print ads. The channel your company chooses should fit your business needs and reach your target audience without exceeding the budget.

Knowing the Customer

Part of the marketing function involves understanding the customer base. This tenet of good marketing does not change, even when your business moves into the electronic landscape. The goal is to zero in on target customers who fit your demographic criteria. Familiarity with who is buying the product or service and viewing the site allows the company to determine how to change the business to better meet customer needs. Information about who makes up your customer base can be obtained in various ways, including demographics, counters, e-mail and forms, or the use of cookies.

When a person visits your site, a database can automatically put a small text file, called a *cookie*, onto the visitor's hard disk, allowing the company to gain information about the customer's visits to the site. You could then store purchase information or purchase demographic profiles of regions, thereby refining your knowledge of your customers. Cookies and other tracking devices are explained in detail in Chapter 10.

The first step in gauging your customer base is finding out how many hits your site gets in a given day, week, or month. This can be achieved through devices called hit counters, which are usually provided by the Internet service provider. Many companies conduct more specific consumer research by placing surveys on their sites, either through forms attached to a database or simple information e-mailed from the site to a company employee responsible for sorting the data. These surveys can be accompanied by incentives, so customers are more likely to fill them out.

No matter how a business gets to know the customer, profiling customers and tracking their data is an essential tool in online marketing. As we will see later in the text, it is a prerequisite for deciding what products to offer and the inventory to keep, for managing the sale regardless of the traffic, and for updating the Web site.

Making the Sale

To keep buyers on track toward making a purchase, the Web site must provide an easy-to-use purchasing function. This means installing a shopping cart and setting up automatic tax and shipping calculation software. Merchants also might want to make special discounts and product bundles available to Web buyers, and allow buyers to decide on shipping and payment methods. In addition, although privacy is important before the sale, encryption technologies become critical when making the sale (see Box 16-5), as explained in detail in Chapter 14.

Simplified ordering is closely related to making the sale. The ideal ordering process gets customers to the merchandise and their purchases into a shopping cart as fast as possible. Recalling customers' past orders and their recipients adds value because it helps buyers avoid reentering information and tracking down addresses for family and friends. For example, Amazon.com and Virtual Vineyards remind visitors what products they have ordered previously. Although this tracking system is not easy to implement, the benefits are immeasurable. Customers feel valued and return in the future. The marketing function is covered more completely in Chapter 11.

Securely storing the user's address and credit card data speeds the purchasing process. Depending on the depth of the product selection, pop-up menus can be used to aid in product selection. The L.L. Bean Web site speeds the process of browsing for its customers by using drop-down menus to offer instant access to literally hundreds of product names on a single page. Many sites, on the other hand, simply run long text listings or ask customers to click through multiple levels to see the complete product line.

BOX 16-5
Privacy concerns

Chris Larsen went all out to win the trust of his customers, who apply for credit cards and loans online at E-Loan Inc. As the lender's chief executive officer, he knew people would be wary of typing in their salaries, savings, and mortgages, then zapping them off into cyberspace. So his business depended on ensuring confidentiality.

He placed a chart on his Web site assuring people that their privacy would be vigilantly guarded. He acquired seals of approval from privacy-watchdog groups. He spent $250,000 on a thorough privacy audit by Pricewaterhouse-Coopers and then hit the road as an advocate, scolding other firms for not taking privacy seriously enough. He even barred his technicians from serving up "cookies," those nosy computer codes that track Internet users. He assured his patrons in a note on the site.

So he looked pained recently when he was told that parts of his Web site do, in fact, employ cookies, along with an even more secretive tracker. They began tagging his customers last fall—when he expanded his menu of loans by acquiring and joining other Internet lenders. "I didn't know," says the 39-year-old Mr. Larsen, in a recent interview. "That's very disconcerting." His experience illustrates how difficult it is even for firms with the best intentions to bulletproof the privacy of their operations. In the new world of Web business, a company can have myriad partners whose sites all blur seamlessly together. The risk: You're exposed and vulnerable to all the policies and practices of your partners. Try as he might, Mr. Larsen failed to keep one of the Internet's more aggressive data snoops off his site.

SOURCE: Moss, Michael, "One Web CEO's Elusive Goal: Privacy," *The Wall Street Journal*, February 7, 2000, B8ff.

Stock Control

Stock control is also important in making the sale, and is especially critical in complicated orders such as the custom-built computers sold online by Dell. Even if the status of the stock is updated regularly, customers might not be able to find the items they want. In order for the merchant to offer alternatives, the Web server needs to know how these products are related. For example, if the merchant runs out of pretzels, the shopper might be willing to accept potato chips instead. Unfortunately, this type of feature is not built into most database structures. A well-designed e-commerce structure should let the company add such attributes to each product.

Once a customer places an item in a shopping cart, a simple stock check is not enough. Some customers might put something in the shopping cart one day and come back later to order it. What should a company do if the product goes out of stock in the meantime? A good strategy is to use a cookie or a user name and password to track when customers place items in the cart. If the customer is away from the site for more than a few hours, the company can check to make sure the selection is still available when the customer returns.

Collecting the Cash

E-commerce sites should accept as many credit cards as possible. Many sites require a fax order, a call to an 800 number, or some other off-line process to complete the sale. These methods are undoubtedly easier to implement, but they do not meet customer expectations of shopping on the Web. Some business could be lost if the consumer breaks the Web connection to write down the order and then picks up the phone to buy the product. As discussed in Chapter 15, MasterCard and Visa are the two cards shoppers use most, but smart sites will offer as many options as possible, including American Express, Discover, and digital cash.

Screen Capture 16-3

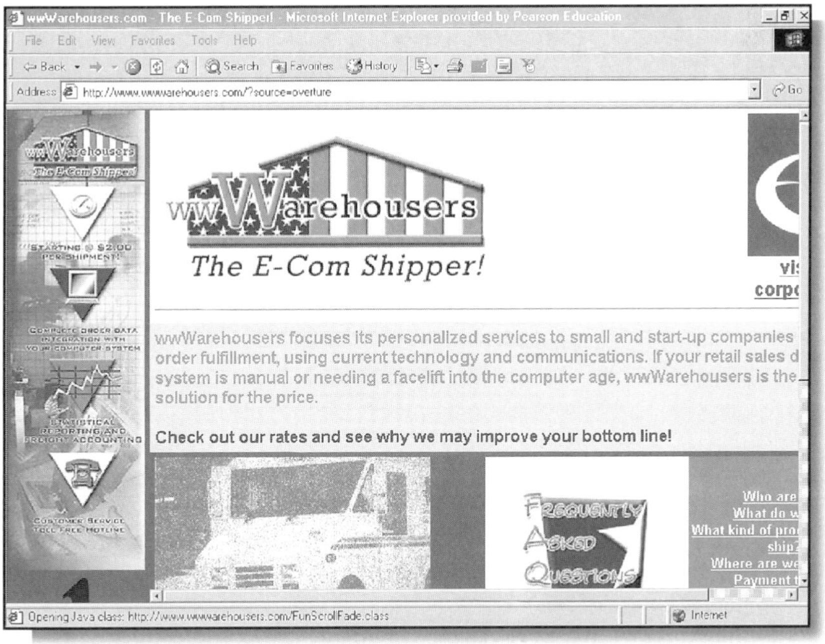

Source: wwWarehousers© is a subsidiary of Hessport©, Inc. © 2003–2004. All rights reserved.

Before jumping in and accepting credit cards, the online merchant needs an acquiring bank to handle the credit card processing. A regular commercial bank often can do this, although the merchant needs an intermediary company like CyberCash to do the verification of the card and authentication of the transaction, resulting in proper credit to the merchant's account at a designated bank. Storing credit card data helps make purchasing easier for the e-commerce site and for the consumer. To do this, the business needs a well-thought-out plan and a secure communication line using software such as Secure Electronic Transactions (SET). These security measures are explained in detail in Chapter 14.

Delivering the Goods and Following Up

After a buyer has made selections and paid for them, the merchant must deliver the goods promptly. Speed of delivery is critical. If the products are soft goods downloaded via the Internet, like music or a software package, buyers expect immediate delivery. If the products are hard goods (clothing, books), buyers expect shipment at least as fast as if they had ordered by phone. This means tight synchronization between the merchant's stockroom and the supplier. The electronic relationship between a merchant and a supplier falls under business-to-business (B2B), explained later in the text. In either case, for any request by the customer regarding the status of the order, the merchant's Web site should recognize the customer and provide a quick report.

In this marketing step, the focus is on following up with the customer to ensure satisfaction with the product and the order process. As in traditional marketing, word of mouth can make a big difference. Over time, merchants can build ongoing personal relationships with their Web customers.

In the final analysis, the goal of the marketing function is to give site visitors a quality experience. Technical support can make or break the business-to-consumer interface for any business. As you analyze the electronic marketplace, you need to consider several marketing essentials for any online business.

- Have a niche-market focus—narrow your target customer.
- Know your visitors—ask them what they are looking for.
- Integrate the online sales with other sales channels.
- Provide a fast, easy payment process that puts convenience and spontaneity back into the process. A trusted payment environment guarantees security and privacy.

THE FULFILLMENT PHASE

fulfillment: honoring a commitment to deliver goods or services after payment has been assured.

All e-companies must face one simple truth—you can't send a package over the Internet. Solving shipping (fulfillment) problems can make the difference between e-business success and failure. Online shoppers expect quick, timely delivery. **Fulfillment** is what happens after a sale is made. Typically, it includes the following.

- Packing up the merchandise.
- Shipping the merchandise.
- Answering questions about the order.
- Sending out the bill or verifying e-payment.
- Following up to see if the customer is satisfied.

Most e-business merchants are putting extraordinary pressure on their vendors and shippers to deliver merchandise just in time. Customers also want to be able to initiate, track, and acknowledge their orders online. More and more of today's fulfillment effort is part of an integrated chain—customers, warehouses, suppliers, drivers, rail partners—that makes it possible to have online shipping information within seconds.

The critical aspect of the fulfillment phase is having real people in real warehouses to get products into customers' hands. Good computers help, because coordinating an electronic business can be more complicated than operating a brick-and-mortar shop. E-merchants have a lot at stake. The competition is getting stronger as more businesses rush to get online, and every botched order creates a dissatisfied customer with a big mouth. For example, Toys R Us's known failure to deliver items ordered for Christmas 1999 wreaked havoc with the company's online retail effort. It turned out to be a costly mistake.

From the customer's viewpoint, order fulfillment is the most important business activity of all. Concerns about delivery delays have some of the biggest e-players beefing up their fulfillment systems. For example, in 1999, Amazon.com Inc. spent $300 million to build 3 million square feet of warehouse space. Shipper.com is building fulfillment centers to warehouse goods for e-tailers in nine metropolitcan areas. Customers also should be offered as many options as possible, and the options should be explained in detail, including the cost of each option and how long each will take.

The tax angle is also part of the fulfillment phase. Special software should keep track of the tax rules and exceptions, and know how much to charge. For example, New Jersey levies no sales tax on clothing, but California does. California levies no tax on food, but Virginia does. State tax, city tax, and county tax also must be considered. A service that automates tax calculations, like Taxware or CyberSource, is necessary.

Another part of the fulfillment phase includes integrating fulfillment with inventory. Several issues must be addressed in this category.

- **Product availability:** Are the products for sale only items in your immediate inventory?
- **Matching the products for sale to the products in the inventory:** Is there a compatible linking of back-end inventory systems with the Web site?
- **Out-of-stock notice:** When should customers be notified that the items they selected are out of stock, not available for immediate delivery, or can be back-ordered?
- **Back orders:** When should the customer be notified of a back order?
- **Processing orders:** How often should orders be sent to order entry?
- **Controls:** Should the customer be notified of a back order when inventory count is at a minimum or when stock in the warehouse is gone?

The Maintenance and Enhancement Phase

maintenance: keeping a system or a business on course based on the initial design or plan.

enhancement: implementing upgrades or changes that are designed to improve the system's productivity.

Maintenance means keeping a system or a business on course, based on the initial design or plan. **Enhancement** means implementing upgrades or changes that are designed to improve the system's productivity. The focus in this phase is on managing the e-business. When customer messages pile up unanswered, something is wrong. The source of the pileup could be a poor Web site, a congested communication line, or an understaffed e-merchant.

Regardless of the reasons or circumstances, the goal of maintenance is to ensure the usability of the Web site. The goal of enhancement is to upgrade the Web site and the business-to-consumer connection to meet the latest standards and customer expectations. The bottom line is customer attraction and retention.

It is a known fact that when people are in a room for any length of time, they tend to go toward the light. People are biologically phototropic, so they tend to place themselves where the light is. Also, if they are in a room for any length of time, they tend to sit down and make themselves comfortable. You expect the same thing to happen when customers hit your site. If it is usable, they begin to scroll, surf, and search for things to buy. The feedback the merchant gets through the Web site should be the input for maintenance and enhancement of the merchant-customer interface.

Implied in the terms maintenance and enhancement is management of the Web site. Part of the management process is establishing online customer support that can help keep Internet customers loyal. It also can make them less likely to pick up the phone. Many companies use their customer service efforts as a selling point on the Internet. Customer queries by e-mail should be answered in hours rather than days, depending on the business and the time-sensitive nature of the product. Companies like Amazon.com have a set quota in terms of the number of e-mail queries customer service representatives must answer.

Managing Customer Feedback

Here are some important tips on managing customer feedback.

- Set up frequently asked questions (FAQs), and post them in a prominent location on the homepage.
- Make sure the information can be accessed easily and quickly.
- Make sure any page downloads within 8 seconds, and test on slow, older computers to be sure the site loads quickly on all makes and models.
- Avoid unnecessarily large images or bandwidth-hogging elements.
- Answer e-mail. Be careful about inappropriate content: Any e-mail is a binding, legal document.

Managing Customer Service

In terms of customer service, here are several items to consider:

- **Updating orders:** How will the fulfillment center let the system know that an order has been shipped?
- **Order status:** Will customers be able to look up the shipping status of their orders online? Do you want to send customers notification upon acceptance of their orders?
- **Technical support:** Will there be online support for the products you sell?
- **Localization:** Do you plan to support multiple languages and/or multiple currencies on your Web site?
- **Handling customer expectations:** What do you want to tell customers about fulfillment? Will you provide same-day delivery? Two-day? Will you charge a premium for such services? How much?

Role of the Webmaster

Finally, we need to consider the role of the Webmaster. The Webmaster's practical role is to create, implement, and manage the Web site. He or she acts also as visionary, business strategist, and manager of the merchant's expectations. One of the Webmaster's key roles is helping important company executives understand what is possible and what works, and what can and cannot be done in e-commerce as it relates to the company's products and services.

A Webmaster often has to guide the company in setting realistic goals for the Web endeavor. This can be crucial in sizing up resource needs, budgeting, knowing what actual costs and opportunity costs are acceptable, and what return the company can expect on those costs. Managing expectations begins with setting general goals and deciding where and how a Web site can achieve a number of specific goals—informing, promoting, selling directly, distributing certain product information, and distributing products. Managing also involves prioritizing goals and ensuring their achievement in time to be of use to the organization. Managing expectations is not easy. The site's goals must support company goals that were set before the e-business was even considered.

SUMMARY

1. Launching a business on the Internet involves a life cycle that includes the business planning and strategizing phase; the hardware, software, security, and setup phase; the design phase; the marketing phase; the fulfillment phase; and the maintenance and enhancement phase.
2. Strategizing means evaluating a company's position and the competition, setting a course for the years ahead, and figuring out how to get it done.
3. Specific goals need to be considered when planning an e-business: creating and maintaining a competitive edge, reducing operational costs, improving employee communication and satisfaction, finding new markets for products or services, improving relationships with partners who provide the goods, creating distinct distribution channels, ensuring customer satisfaction, and improving supply-chain management.
4. The hardware, software, security, and setup phase focuses on the hardware to buy; whether to buy through magazines or from stores; and what software to buy. Among the software needed are FTP, Telnet, Archie, NetNews, e-mail, SLIP, and a Web browser, plus the security programs.
5. The four essentials of launching a business on the Internet are security, shopping carts, payment, and marketing.
6. Behind every Web site are programs stored on the Web server to present your application to site visitors and the hardware that will host your server and application. These programs include the database server, the store administrator, the catalog builder, the shopping cart, and the order-processing system.
7. In Web design, the focus is on: user control and freedom, consistency and standards, recognition rather than recall, aesthetic design, Rrecovery from error, and a help desk to handle customer queries and complaints.
8. The marketing phase includes advertising, knowing the customer, making the sale, getting the goods, and follow-up procedures after the sale. The critical aspect is knowing the customers and finding ways to keep them at the site long enough to make a sale. The ideal is to cultivate recurring customers rather than one-time customers.
9. The fulfillment phase typically includes packing up the merchandise, shipping the goods, answering questions about the order, and sending out the bill or a copy of the bill.There is also a follow-up

to see if the customer is satisfied. From the customer's view, this phase is the most important business activity.

10. The maintenance and enhancement phase addresses the need to keep the Web storefront up to date and to make any changes that will enhance the use and effectiveness of the Web site. Managing the business-to-consumer environment is essential and can be a full-time commitment.

KEY TERMS

- banner, 514
- button, 516
- cache memory, 511
- capacity planning, 508
- e-marketing, 517
- enhancement, 521
- firewall, 513
- fulfillment, 522
- homepage, 516
- maintenance, 523
- modem, 511
- mouse, 511
- search engine, 514
- security, 512
- shopping cart, 512
- spamming, 519
- storefront, 514
- Webmaster, 513

TEST YOUR UNDERSTANDING

1. Is there a difference between vision and mission? Elaborate. How do they relate to starting an online business? Be specific.
2. Identify the key steps of the Internet business life cycle. What step is the most critical? Why?
3. When you hear someone talking about strategic planning, what is the person focusing on? In terms of e-commerce, what questions does an online merchant consider when strategizing? Explain.
4. The chapter brings up specific goals that a merchant should consider when planning an e-business. Elaborate on the key goals.
5. Elaborate on the distinctive types of hardware and software necessary to launch a business on the Internet.
6. Distinguish between:
   a. A browser and a Web server.
   b. A mouse and a modem.
   c. Telnet and file transfer protocol (FTP).
   d. Marketing phase and fulfillment phase.
7. In what way(s) is security critical in e-commerce? Explain.
8. Discuss the basic rules when promoting security in online business.
9. If you were to design a Web storefront, what factors, constraints, or parameters would you consider? Explain.
10. How would one decide on whether to design the Web site in-house or outsource it to an outside agency?
11. If you were assigned the job of locating a Web site developer, what factors would you consider in locating the right one? Explain.
12. Elaborate on the key considerations in Web site design.
13. What is involved in collecting payment for the products that customers order through a merchant's Web site? Be specific.
14. Explain the key steps of the fulfillment phase. How important is this phase? Why?
15. Distinguish between maintenance and enhancement. Which one assures compliance with the original plan?

Discussion Questions

1. If you were asked to give a 5-minute talk to a gathering of local small business merchants about launching a business on the Internet, what would you say?
2. Take a close look at the marketing phase with a business the size of your community bank in mind. Assume that the bank wants to establish a presence on the Internet. How would you proceed in planning the marketing phase?
3. Advertising presence is part of the marketing function for a first-time merchant on the Internet. How would one advertise such a presence? Write a 1-minute scenario, advertising the bank's presence. See Discussion Question 2.
4. If you were searching for an ISP, what type of service would you expect it to provide? If you're unsure, go to a search engine and enter the subject "Internet service provider." Do a two-page report on your findings.
5. What benefits might a business measure in an electronic commerce business plan?
6. Why do you think some firms plunge into e-commerce without assessing their return on investment? Discuss.

Web Exercises

1. Aunt Sarah's Glendora Candy is a family owned candy-manufacturing plant in western Pennsylvania. Although candy making is fully automated, the company employs 96 people and 21 salespeople on a full-time basis. The company makes more than 60 brands of chocolate, chocolate cakes, candy bars, and specialized chocolate-based products for Halloween, Christmas, and other occasions. Since it was founded in 1945, the company has sold its products directly to retailers and filled phone orders from customers as far west as Colorado and all the way to the Eastern seaboard.
2. You are the consultant for Aunt Sarah. The CEO has been seeing screaming headlines in business journals that just cannot be ignored—"E-commerce Will Jump to $32 Billion by 2002" and "U.S. Online Business Trade Will Soar to $1.9 Trillion by 2003." The competition is catching up with Aunt Sarah. Smaller candy makers are slowly entering e-business. The chairman of the board tells you they want to open Aunt Sarah's cyberdoors in 2 months. That should be plenty of time, he insists. After all, his daughter (a college freshman) built her own online store in 3 days using Microsoft Front Page as a Web design tool. She was selling baseball caps to make enough money to pay tuition.
3. What will you say? How will you start? What procedure will you follow? Map out a plan of attack and explain to the chairman of the board the long road ahead "from vision to implementation." Think of planning. Remember the life cycle of launching this business on the Internet.
4. The First National Bank of Elwood City is a small, regional, family owned bank founded in 1947 with assets of about $46 million; 43 full-time employees; 9,000 checking accounts; 6,400 savings accounts; and a full-service operation including commercial and personal loans, trusts, safe deposit boxes, bookkeeping, and mortgage loans. In the early 1990s, the city grew larger,

attracting larger banks to handle the growth in the community. With the surge of banking traffic on the Internet, almost every large bank has an interactive Web site. Two of the online banks even issue loans, with the customer simply filling out a form on the screen and clicking on the "submit" button. The information goes directly to the bank's database for processing. The resulting loan amount is either mailed to customers the next day in the form of a check or electronically transmitted to a destination of their choice.

5. The bank president calls you and asks for a meeting to assess the bank's readiness to be on the Internet. After a brief session with senior management, you discover the following. (a) very few of the bank's employees are computer literate; (b) the bank has a small local area network in the loan department only; 42 stand-alone PCs are used primarily for Word and Excel; and (c) there is no e-mail system.
   a. What general plan can you introduce that shows how to put the bank on the Internet?
   b. If you were to give senior management a 30-minute presentation on what must be done to be on the Internet, what would you cover?
   c. Present a brief summary of the building life cycle, and explain where and in what way management should be involved in seeing the Web site through fulfillment.

References

Chapter 1

Ansberry, Clare, "Let's Build an Online Supply Network!" *Wall Street Journal*, April 17, 2000, B1ff.

Chabrow, Eric, "Supply Chains Go Global," *InformationWeek*, April 3, 2000, 50–52ff.

Cohen, Mark, "Get Rich Slow," www.timedigital.com, 58–59.

Copeland, Lee, "B-to-B Auctions From A to Z," *Computerworld*, April 17, 2000, 54.

Crutchfield, William G., "Nine Myths of Internet Retailing," Unpublished manuscript, April 2002.

Dalton, Greg, "The B-to-B Math Problem," *The Industry Standard*, April 17, 2000, 61.

Dunham, Kemba J., "Employers Seek Ways to Lure Back Laid-Off Workers When Times Improve," *Wall Street Journal*, June 19, 2001, p. R1.

Faden, Mike, "Clean Up Your Data's Act," *InternetWeek*, April 17, 2000, 60ff.

Faden, Mike, "Data Cleansing Helps E-Businesses Run More Efficiently," *InformationWeek*, April 10, 2000, 136ff.

Furth, John "Uncle Sam Wants E-Commerce," www.line56.com, Feb. 2001, 1–2.

Giattina, Deborah, "Putting the 'Human' in Venture Capitalist," *The Industry Standard*, April 17, 2000, 236–237.

Gomes, Lee, "Once Hot Business-to-Business Dot-Coms Are Next Area of Web Worry," *Wall Street Journal*, April 7, 2000, B1.

Goodrich, Elisabeth, "Managing the Supply Chain: Customers Come First," *InformationWeek*, February 14, 2000, 104.

Greenemeier, Larry, "Buying Power," *InformationWeek*, April 3, 2000, 67–68ff.

Helft, Miguel, "Clicks-and-Mortar Superstores," *The Industry Standard*, April 17, 2000, 98–100ff.

Kaufman, Jonathan, "Instead of Making Him Rich, a Dot-Com Gives Mr. Carter the Boot," *Wall Street Journal*, January 4, 2000, A1ff.

Lewis, William, "Forging the Value Chain," *Intelligent Enterprise*, January 20, 2000, 44–50.

Low, Lafe, and Goldberg, Michael (eds.), "Uncle Sam Wants Web Services," *CIO*, October 1, 2002, 26.

Moore, John, "Inside McCain's Web Bid," *Sm@art Reseller*, March 6, 2000, 34.

Porter, Michael, *Competitive Advantage*. New York: Free Press, 1985.

Prahalad, C. K., Ramaswamy, Venkatram, and Krishnan, M. S., "Consumer Centricity," *InformationWeek*, Informationweek.com, April 10, 2000, 67ff.

Rainie, Lee, "How Main Street Learned to Stop Worrying and Love the Net," *The Industry Standard*, March 6, 2000, 100–101ff.

Scheer, August-Wilhelm, and Habermann, Frank, "Making ERP a Success," *Communications of the ACM*, April 2000, 57–62.

Singh, Guy, "Mobile Commerce: Connecting With the Future," *Montgomery Research Europe, Ltd.*" Stein, Tom, Extending—Companies That Don't Use Enterprise Resource Planning Software to Share Information May Regret It," www.techweb.com/se/directlink/cgi?IWK19980615S0044, 1–7.

Stein, Tom, and Sweat, Jeff, "Killer Supply Chains," *InformationWeek*, www.information week.com/708/08iuki1.html., 1–4.

Sweat, Jeff, "E-Market Connections," *InformationWeek*, April 3, 2000, 22–24.

Sweat, Jeff, "The Well-Rounded Consumer," *InformationWeek*, April 10, 2000, 44ff.

Totty, Michael, and Grimes, Ann, "If at First You Don't Succeed . . . ," *Wall Street Journal*, February 11, 2002, R6.

Walker, Rob, "Massive Fight Brews Over Online Car Sales," *Richmond Times-Dispatch*, February 13, 2000, A1.

Weber, Thomas E., "Ready or Not: Voting Over the Web Comes to Political Primaries," *Wall Street Journal*, January 24, 2000, B1.

White, Colin, "E-Intelligence," *Intelligent Enterprise*, April 10, 2000, 25–26ff.

White, Joseph B., "Getting into Gear," *Wall Street Journal*, April 17, 2000, R65.

Chapter 2

Alexander, Steve, "Viruses, Worms, Trojan Horses and Zombies," *Computerworld*, May 1, 2000, 74.

Anandarajan, Murugan, "Internet Abuse in the Workplace," *Communications of the ACM*, January 2002, 53–54.

Anders, George, "First E-Shopping, Now E-Swapping," *The Wall Street Journal*, January 17, 2000, B1ff.

Associated Press, "Author of New Virus Subject of FBI Hunt," *The Daily Progress*, May 20, 2000, A1ff.

Bauer, Claude J., "Planning an E-Commerce Career?" *The Washington Post*, April 2, 2000, L7.

Borzo, Jeanette, "The Wireless Web," *The Wall Street Journal*, April 17, 2000, R46.

Cohen, Laura, "Understanding the World Wide Web," http://library.albany.edu/Internet/www.html, August 2001, 1–12. Accessed May 2003.

Coyle, Frank, "Web Services, Simply Put," *Computerworld*, May 19, 2003, 38–39.

Dembart, Lee, "Saddam's Mail," *International Herald Tribune*, November 4, 2002, 1.

Dunn, Bob, "A Manager's Guide to Web Services," *eAI* Journal, January 2003, 15–17.

Hayes, Frank, "The Story So Far," *Computerworld*, June 17, 2002, 24.

Higgins, A., Leggett, K., and Cullison, A., "How Al-Qaeda Put Internet in Services of Jihad," *The Wall Street Journal*, November 11, 2002, A1ff.

Klein, Paula, "Stressed Out Networks," *InformationWeek*, May 8, 2000, 77–80.

Landro, Laura, "Going Online to Make Life-and-Death Decisions," *The Wall Street Journal*, October 10, 2002, D1ff.

Lim, Vivien K. G., Thompson, S. H. Teo, and Loo, Geok Leng, "How Do I Loaf Here? Let Me Count the Ways," *Communications of the ACM*, January 2002, 66–70.

Mathews, Anna W., "Applause, Applause," *The Wall Street Journal*, October 29, 2001, R8ff.

McCance, McGregor, "Internet Has Unifying Effect," *Richmond Times-Dispatch*, November 4, 2001, F1.

Napoli, Lisa, "Better Ways to Search Than Typing 'Needle + Haystack'," *The New York Times*, March 2000, 36.

Nelson, Matthew G., "Hacker School Teaches Security," *InformationWeek*, March 27, 2000, 137.

Orwall, Bruce, "The End of Schmooze?" *The Wall Street Journal*, March 20, 2000, p. R1.

Reagan, Brad, "Sounding Off," *The Wall Street Journal*, October 2001, R4.

Rosenbaum, Joshua, "The Typing Cure," *The Wall Street Journal*, September 16, 2002, R10ff.

Rout, Lawrence, "The Internet," *The Wall Street Journal*, November 18, 2002, R1–R15.

Shmukler, Evelina, "The Best Way to Search the Web," *The Wall Street Journal*, November 18, 2002, R6.

Siau, Keng, Nah, Fiona, and Teng, Limei, "Acceptable Internet Use Policy," *Communications of the ACM*, January 2002, 75–79.

Silver, Sheryl, "No Slowdown in Sight for Technology Job Market," *The Washington Post*, April 2, 2000, L5.

Simpson, Glenn R., "FTC Finds Web Sites Fail to Guard Privacy," *The Wall Street Journal*, May 11, 2000, B12.

Verton, Dan, "Web Sites Seen as Terrorist Aids," *Computerworld*, February 11, 2002, 1ff.

Violino, Bob, "Waves of Change," *Computerworld*, May 19, 2003, 33.

Watson, Sharon, "End of Job Loyalty?" *Computerworld*, May 15, 2000, 52–53.

Williamson, Debra Aho, "The Information Exchange Economy Gets Ugly," *The Industry Standard*, March 13, 2000, 170–171.

Zeichick, Alan, "Keep Your Users Safe and Focused," *InternetWeek*, April 17, 2000, 47–48.

Chapter 3

Berinato, Scott, "The ABCs of Security," *CIO Magazine*, February 20, 2002, 16ff.

Brandel, Mary, "The Top Skills to Watch," *Computerworld*, May 22, 2000, 91.

Lais, Sami, "MPEG Standards," *Computerworld*, October 7, 2002, 36.

Panko, Raymond R., *Business Data Communications and Networking* (4th Ed.), chaps. 1, 2, 4, Upper Saddle River, NJ: Prentice-Hall, 2003.

Schindler, Esther, "Round-Robin Lets DNS Take Flight," *Sm@art Reseller*, May 15, 2000, 51.

Watson, Sharon, "Why Staffers Stay," *Computerworld*, May 22, 2000, 56–57.

Chapter 4

Angwin, Julia, "Elusive Spammer Sends Web Service On a Long Chase," *The Wall Street Journal*, May 7, 2003, A1ff.

Anton, Kathleen, "Effective Intranet Publishing: Getting Critical Knowledge to Any Employee, Anywhere," *Intranet Design Magazine*, August 12, 2000, 1–5.

Brandel, Mary, "Demise of the Skill Premium," *Computerworld*, July 31, 2000, 62.

Brown, Eric, and Candler, James W., "The Elements of Intranet Style," *Intranet Design Magazine*, August 12, 2000, 1–5.

Disabatino, Jennifer, "E-Mail Probe Triggers Firings," *Computerworld*, July 10, 2000, 1ff.

Downes, Larry and Mui, Chunka, *Unleashing the Killer App*. Harvard Business School Press, Boston: 1998.

Elbel, Fred, "General Guidelines and Tips (How to Get Rid of Junk Mail, Spam, and Telemarketers)," www.ecofuture.org/jmnews.html, May 26, 2001, 1–3.

Kay, Russell, "Fighting Spam," *Computerworld*, May 12, 2003, 33.

King, Julia, "Bitch Sites and What to Do About Them," *Computerworld*, February 28, 2000, 52–53.

Mangalindan, Mylene, "Web Vigilantes Give Spammers a Big Dose of Their Medicine," *The Wall Street Journal*, May 19, 2003, A13.

Schwartz, Jeffrey, "Dow Intranet Becomes Classroom," *InternetWeek*, January 18, 2000, 17.

Spence, Rob, "Considering an Extranet? Consider This . . . ," *Extranet Strategist*, Spring 2000, 1.

Tao, Paul I., "Roadmap to a Successful Intranet," *Intranet Design Magazine*, August 12, 2000, 1–13.

Violino, Bob, "Kodak's Extranet Push," *Extranet Strategist*, Spring 2000, 1.

Chapter 5

Enterprise Knowledge Portal, www.askmecorp.com. Accessed June 2003.

Enterprise Knowledge Portals to Become the Shared Desktop of the Future. www.itweb.co.za/office/bmi/9903300919.htm. Accessed June 2003.

Fox, Pimm, "Plugging Into Portal Returns," *Computerworld*, April 8, 2002, 38.

Hansen, Morten, Nohria, Nitin, and Tierney, Thomas. "What's Your Strategy for Managing Knowledge?" *Harvard Business Review*, March-April 1999, 106.

Harris-Jones, Chris, "Portals and Web Services," *KMWorld*, October 2002, 10.

Mack, R., Ravin, Y., and Byrd, R. J., "Knowledge Portals and the Emerging Digital Knowledge Workflow," IBM Systems, vol. 40, no. 4, 2001, researchweb.Watson.ibm.com/journal/sj/404/mack.pdf. Accessed June 2003.

Meta Group, "Business Collaboration," www.metagroup.com/cgi-bin/inetcgi/commerce/productDetails.jsp?oid_29277, Accessed June 2003.

Pickering, Chris, "Portals: An E-Business Success Story," *Software Magazine*, October 2002, 22–27.

"Portals: An Overview." www-1.ibm.com/services/kcm/cm_portal.html. Accessed June 2003.

"Portals, Knowledge, and Content Management." www-1.ibm.com/services/kcm/know_mngt_com.html. Accessed June 2003.

www.brint.com. Accessed June 2003.

Chapter 6

Angwin, Julia, "Speed Kills," *The Wall Street Journal*, May 19, 2003, R10.

Apicella, Mario, "Shaking Hands Is Not Enough," *Infoworld*, April 30, 2001, 49.

Cohen, Laura, "How to Connect to the Internet," Library.Albany.edu/internet/connect.html. Accessed February 2003.

Copeland, Lee, "TCP/IP," *Computerworld*, January 17, 2000, 72.

Emigh, Jacqueline, "Domain Naming," *Computerworld*, September 27, 1999, 86.

Hall, Mark, "Service Providers Give Users More IT Options," *Computerworld*, February 7, 2000, 40.

Harvey, John, "Lost Among the ASPs," *Intelligent Enterprise*, February 9, 2000, 27ff.

Hayes, Ian S., "Implementing an ASP Solution," *Software Magazine*, December 2001, S2ff.

http://thelist.iworld.com. This site helps you find an ISP, Web hosts, ASPs, and so on. Accessed February 2003.

Kimpett, Kim, "How to Provide a Provider Near You," webisplist.internetlist.com, November 28, 2000, 1–2. Accessed February 2003.

Lawrence: www.webreview.com/wr/pub/97/10/31/edge/index.html.Accessed May 29, 2003.

Mateyaschuk, Jennifer, "ASPs Forced to Become Full-Service Providers," *InformationWeek Online*, www.informationweek.com, January 10, 2000, p. 115.

McGatney, Dawn, "How an ISP Really Works," dogwolf.seagull.net/ispwork2.html. Accessed February 2003.

Panko, Raymond R., *Business Data Networks and Telecommunications* (4th Ed.), Upper Saddle River, NJ: Prentice-Hall, Inc., 2003.

Patterson, Zachary, "Serve-Level Agreements," *Computerworld*, January 22, 2001, 53.

Perine, Keith, "Solving the Dot-Com Glut," *The Industry Standard*, February 7, 2000, 104ff.

Rosoff, Matt, "Rate Your ISP," home.cnet.com/category/0-3765-7-285302.html. Accessed February 2003.

Stedman, Craig, "Moving to Web Applications? Don't Forget Bandwidth," *Computerworld*, January 31, 2000, 59.

Swisher, Kara, "Yahoo! Posts a Loud Message: We're Not Next," *The Wall Street Journal*, January 12, 2000, B1.

Ulfelder, Steve, "Evaluate the ASP Phenomenon," *Computerworld*, January 3, 2000, 22ff.

Wilson, Ralph, "How to Choose a Web Hosting Service (ISP) for Your Business Web Pages," www.wilsonweb.com/articles/webhost.htm., 1–5. Accessed February 2003.

Wyle, Mitch, "Preparing Your Site for Speed and Reliability," *Web Techniques*, January 2000, 67–69.

www.internetsolutions.com. This site helps you register your Web address. Accessed May 29, 2003.

www.internic.net. This is a main site for registering and/or checking domain name availability. Accessed May 29, 2003.

www.isp.com. This site provides all you need to know abut ISPs. Accessed May 29, 2003.

www.techcapital.com. This site provides domain registration and sale. Accessed May 29, 2003.

Chapter 7

Bethoney, Herb, "Bluetooth's Buzz Seemingly Fizzled," www. zdnet.com/eweek/stories/general/0,11011.2649006,00.html. Accessed March 2003.

Biggs, Maggie, "Poised to Reap Rewards of Wireless," *Infoworld*, June 25, 2001, 64.

Brain, Marshall, and Tyson, Jeff, "How Cell Phones Work—From Cell to Cell," www.howstuffworks.com/cell-phone2.htm. Accessed March 2003.

Brewin, Bob, "Wireless LANs," *Computerworld*, March 25, 2002, 50.

Cambridge Consultants, Ltd., "Bluetooth Products," www.cambridge-consultants.com/.html. Accessed June 2003.

Cellular Telecommunications Industry Association, "CTIA's Semi-Annual Wireless Industry Survey," *Wow-com*, December 1999.

Chen, Anne, "Sniffing Out Rogue Wireless LANs," e*Week Labs*, May 6, 2002, 45.

Christian, Niels, and Jorgensen, Niels, "Security Limitations in the WAP Architecture," Position Paper 2002, Roskilde University, Denmark, 1–3.

Ciampa, Mark, *Introduction to Wireless Communication*, Boston: Course Technology, Inc., 2002.

Connolly, R. J., "Wireless Security Riddled With Flaws," *Infoworld*, June 25, 2001, 62.

Drucker, Jesse, and Angwin, Julia, "New Way to Surf the Web Is Giving Cell Carriers Static," *The Wall Street Journal*, November 29, 2002, A1ff.

Dunn, Danielle, and Pender, Lee, "Glossary," www. cio.com/research/communications/edit/glossary.htm. Accessed June 2003.

Dushko, Stan, "Mobility: The Business of Time," *Eai Journal*, February 2002, 12–15.

Farley, Tom, "Cellular Telephone Basics," *TelecomWriting.com*, www.privateline.com/cellbasics/cellbasics.html. Accessed March 2003.

Freudenrich, Craig, "How Personal Digital Assistants (PDAs) Work," www.howstuffworks.com/pda.htm. Accessed March 2003.

Glater, Jonathan D., "Doing Business by Cellphone Creates New Liability Issues," *The New York Times*, December 3, 2002, Technology, 1.

Gomes, Lee, "How to Cut the Cord," *The Wall Street Journal*, October 29, 2001, R16.

Hamblin, Matt, "Taking the Leap," *Computerworld* ROI, www.computerworld.com/roi/. Accessed June 2003.

Hamilton, David, "Making the Connections," *The Wall Street Journal*, December 11, 2000, R3–R9.

Haskin, D., "Analysts: Smart Phones to Lead E-Commerce Explosion," *allNetDevices*, November 3, 1999.

Henderson, Peter, "Super-fast Wireless Heads to Homes." www.msnbc.com/news/877268.asp, February 25, 2003, 1.

Hopper, D. I., "Microsoft Furthers Hardware Reputation," *Richmond Times Dispatch*, October 27, 2002, E8.

Kansal, Aman, "Bluetooth What and Why?"

Kay, Russell, "Wireless Security," *Computerworld*, June 24, 2002, 38.

Kessler, Michelle, "Wi-Fi Could Let Iraq Skip Steps to Leap into Broadband." *USA Today*, April 17, 2003, 1B.

Lieber, Ron, and Lunsford, J. Lynn, "Totally Wired at 32,000 Feet," *The Wall Street Journal*, October 24, 2002, D1ff.

Mathews, Guy, "Insecurity in a Wireless World," www.vnunet.com/Analysis/1119074. Accessed June 2003.

Orubeondo, Ana, "Wireless Holds the Key to the Future," *Infoworld*, June 25, 2001, 56.

Panko, Raymond J., *Business Data Communications and Networking* (4th Ed.), Upper Saddle River, NJ, 2002, 18.

Proxim White Paper, "802.11a: A Very High-Speed, Highly Scalable Wireless LAN Standard," www.proxim.com/learn/library/whitepapers/pdf/80211a.pdf. Accessed June 2003.

Reinhardt, Andy, "Wireless Web Foes," *BusinessWeek*, June 4, 2001, EB 24–28.

San Filippo, Michael, "Marconi: Grandfather of Wireless," *History of Italians*, http://italian.about.com/library/weekly/aa111099a.htm. Accessed June 2003.

Schwartz, Ephraim, "The Rocky Road to High-Speed Wireless," *Infoworld*, July 30, 2001, 28.

Siau, Keng, and Shen, Zixing, "Building Customer Trust In Mobile Commerce," *Communications of the ACM*, April 2003, 91–94.

Songini, Marc L., "Army Uses Mobile Technology, Satellite Link to Track Supplies," *Computerworld*, March 31, 2003, 6.

Staff, "Porn Producer Launches X-Rated Wireless Portal," *Mobile Commerce World*, October 21, 2002, 1.

Sullivan, Allanna, "Someone to Watch Over You," *The Wall Street Journal*, December 11, 2000, R8.

Sutherland, Ed, "Bluetooth Security: An Oxymoron?" www.mcommercetimes.com/Technology/41. Accessed June 2003.

3COM White Paper, "What Is Wireless Networking & why Consider It?" www.3com.com/corpinfo/en_US/technology/tech_paper.jsp?DOC_ID=5377. Accessed June 2003.

2000 *San Jose Mercury News*, www.sanjosemercurynews.com, 1. Accessed June 2003.

Varshney, U., Vetter, R. J., and Kalakota, Ravi, "Mobile Commerce: A New Frontier," *Computer*, October 2000, 32–38.

Ware, Lorraine C., "By the Numbers," *CIO Magazine*, October 1, 2002, 30.

Washington Post, "WiFi Vulnerable to Hackers." *The Daily Progress*, August 1, 2003, B3.

Wingfield, Nick, "Wi-Fi Anytime, Anywhere." *The Wall Street Journal*, March 31, 2003, R6.

www.beststuff.com/articles/737. Accessed March 2003.

www.palowireless.com/bluetooth/products.asp. Accessed March 2003.

www.zdnet.com/filters/printerfriendly/0,6061,2704389-2,00.html. Accessed March 2003.

www.corp.cellmania.com/newsroom/white papers/whitepapers_local.html, 1. Accessed March 2003.

www.3com.com. Accessed March 2003.

Chapter 8

Chau, P., Cole, M., Massey, A., Montoya-Weiss, M., and O'Keefe, R., "Cultural Differences in the Online Behavior of Consumers," *Communications of the ACM*, October 2002, 138–143.

Desmond, Paul, "Passing the 8-Second Test," *Software Magazine*, February/March 2000, 34–38.

Desmond, Paul, "Who You Gonna Let In?" *Software Magazine*, February/March 2000, 58–62.

Fryer, Bronwyn, and Smith, Lee, "Anatomy of a Website," *FSB*, December 1999/January 2000, 38–44ff.

Harshbarger, Tim, "CDNow.com," *InformationWeek*, February 14, 2000, 52–60.

Humphrey, Watts S., "Why Projects Fail," *Computerworld*, May 20, 2002, 50.

Laberis, Bill, "No Easy Task to Build E-Commerce Infrastructure," *Computerworld*, February 9, 2000, 67.

Legard, David, "CA Exec Says Poor Design Lets Crackers Disable Sites," *Computerworld*, February 28, 2000, 63.

Preston, Robert, "Web Personalization Will Place Integration Onus on IT," *InternetWeek*, February 28, 2000, 7.

Sanford, Susan, "The Art of E-Biz Web-Site Design," *InformationWeek*, www.informationweek.com, February 14, 2000, 42–44ff. Accessed June 2003.

Savetz, Kevin, "Managing Traffic Spikes," *New Architect Magazine*, November 2002, 24–26

Shiple, John, "Information Architecture Tutorial," www.hotwired.com/webmon key/98/28/index4a_page2.html. Accessed March 2003.

Steenson, Molly W., "Ten Steps to a Perfect Design Partnership," *New Architecture Magazine*, November 2002, 29–30ff.

Swaine, Michael, "Why Do So Many Websites Suck?" *WebReview*, May 7, 1999, 1–3.

Waters, John K., "Living in a World 24/7," *Software Magazine*, February/March 2000, 53–56.

Chapter 9

Awad, Elias M., "How Effective Is Your Bank's Web Presence?" Unpublished manuscript 2002, 1–6.

Bortin, Meg, "When Colors Take on Different Cultural Hues," *International Herald Tribune*, September 28–29, 2002, 9.

Fox, Pimm, "Getting Personal Boosts Revenue," *Computerworld*, June 17, 2002, 38.

Hall, Mark, "Finding Those Bottlenecks," *Computerworld*, August 19, 2002, 29.

Kay, Russell, "Web Caching," *Computerworld*, August 19, 2002, 36.

Keefe, Patricia, "Privacy: Fight for It," *Computerworld*, March 27, 2000, 36.

Lais, Sami, "How to Stop Web Shopper Flight," *Computerworld*, June 17, 2002, 44–45.

Liebmann, Lenny, "Pass the E-Commerce Stress Test," *InternetWeek*, January 24, 2000, 37–40.

Lubinski, James E., "Web-Ifying Your Staff," *Computerworld*, February 28, 2000, 50ff.

Machlis, Sharon, "Measuring Web Site Traffic," *Computerworld*, June 17, 2002, 42.

Millard, Elizabeth, "Spool of Thought," *Business* 2.0, October 1999, 11–12.

Morris, Charlie, "How to Build Lame Web Sites," *Web Developer's Journal*, December 25, 2002, 6–12.

Muler, Thomas, "Shades of Meaning," *The Wall Street Journal*, April 15, 2002, R4.

Nielsen, Jakob, and Norman, Donald A., "Usability on the Web Isn't a Luxury," *InformationWeek*, February 14, 2000, 65–77ff.

Norman, Donald A., "Walk-Through: A Usability Experiment," *InformationWeek*, February 14, 2000, 69–70.

Preston, Robert, "Web Personalization Will Place Integration Onus on IT," *InternetWeek*, February 28, 2000, 7.

Radding, Alan, "Get a Handle on Web Content," *InformationWeek*, February 14, 2000, 115ff.

Schwartz, Mathew, "Time for a Makeover!" *Computerworld*, August 19, 2002, 38–39.

Snel, Ross, "Start-Ups Try New Ways to Track Web Users," *The Wall Street Journal*, April 5, 2001, B7.

Spool, Jared, "Web Site Usability: The Big Picture," www.webreview.com/wr/pub/web98east/23/spoolx.html. Accessed June 2003.

USA Today, "Yahoo! Investigated," *Moneyline*, March 31, 2000, p. B1.

Walker, Leslie, "Just Counting Site Visits Is No Longer Enough," *Washington Post*, August 16, 2001, A4.

Waller, Richard, "Sixty Ticks for a Good Web Site," *Website Creation, Training and Consultancy*, UK: West Sussex, April 24, 2001, 1–6.

White, Colin, "Custom Fit Personalization," *Intelligent Enterprise*, March 8, 2001, 26ff.

Whiting, Rick, "Mind Your Business," *InformationWeek*, March 6, 2000, 22–24.

Zimmerman, Christine, "Traffic Mgm't Gets Content-Aware," *InternetWeek*, February 28, 2000, 12.

Zimmerman, Christine, "Web Pages Turbo-charged," *InternetWeek*, February 28, 2001.

Chapter 10

Anders, George, "How Amazon Tries to Keep Its Customers Satisfied," *The Wall Street Journal*, April 17, 2000, R12ff.

Anderson, Diane, and Perine, Keith, "Marketing the DoubleClick Way," *The Industry Standard*, March 13, 2000, 174ff.

Ardissono, Liliana, Goy, Anna, Petrone, Giovanna, and Segnan, Marino, "Personalization in Business-to-Customer Interaction," *Communications of the ACM*, May 2002, 52–53.

Bellman, Steven, Lohse, Gerald L., and Johnson, Eric J., "Predictors of Online Buying Behavior," *Communications of the ACM*, December 1999, 32–38.

Cha, Ariana E., "Web May Hold the Key to Achieving Artificial Intelligence," *The Wall Street Journal*, September 6, 2002, A9ff.

Cohen, Jackie, "Brand Inequity," *The Industry Standard*, November 8, 1999, 124–126.

Dahir, Mubarak, "Just for Clicks: It Pays to Follow Your Customer's Every Move," *The Industry Standard*, May 15, 2000, 305ff.

Fink, Josef, Koenemann, Jurgen, Noller, Stephan, and Schwab, Ingo, "Putting Personalization Into Practice," *Communications of the ACM*, May 2002, 41–42.

Greenstein, P., *E-Commerce*, New York: McGraw-Hill, Inc., 2000.

Hanrahan, Timothy, "Price Isn't Everything," *The Wall Street Journal*, July 12, 1999, R20.

Hwang, Suein L., "Ad Nauseam," *The Wall Street Journal*, April 23, 2001, R8.

Kranhold, Kathryn, "Gaffe Shows Power of Net Ads," *The Wall Street Journal Europe*, May 9, 2000, 29.

Kranhold, Kathryn, "Selling with Style," *The Wall Street Journal*, March 20, 2000, R18.

Lemke, Tim, "Pop-ups Strike Out with Internet Advertisers," *The Washington Times*, September 9, 2002, B1.

Maney, Kevin, "How AI Could Work," *USA Today*, June 20, 2001, 2A.

Mullaney, Timothy J., "Online Shopping Bargaining Power," *Businessweek E.Biz*, December 13, 1999, EB90ff.

Neuborne, Ellen, "Sites Not Worth Seeing," *Businessweek E.Biz*, May 15, 2000, EB16.

Neuborne, Ellen, "Viral Marketing Alert!" *BusinessWeek e.biz*, March 19, 2001, EB8.

Nielsen, Jakob, and Tahir, Marie, "Building Sites with Depth," *Webtechniques*, February 2001, 46ff.

Rewick, Jennifer, "Choices, Choices," *The Wall Street Journal*, April 23, 2001, R12.

Robinson, Robin, "Customer Relationship Management," *Computerworld*, February 28, 2000, 67ff.

Rosenbaum, Joshua, "Annoying . . . but Effective," *The Wall Street Journal*, April 15, 2002, R8.

Schmonsees, Bob, "The Quest for Content Quality," *KMWorld*, October 2002, 12–14.

Skidmore, Colin, "Converting Web Visitors to Customers," *Teradatareview*, September 2000, 25–26ff.

Tam, Pui-Wing, "Show of Hands," *The Wall Street Journal*, April 23, 2001, R14ff.

Wagner, Christian, and Turban, Efraim, "Are Intelligent E-Commerce Agents Partners or Predators?" *Communications of the ACM*, May 2002, 84–90.

Whiting, Rick, "Getting to Know You," *InformationWeek*, March 13, 2000, 46–48ff.

Chapter 11

Alexander, Steve, "Collaborative Commerce," *Computerworld*, July 3, 2000, 45.

Betts, Mitch, "FTC Keeps an Eye on B-to-B Online Markets," *Computerworld*, July 10, 2000, 20.

Bialik, Carl, "Getting Your Money Back," *The Wall Street Journal*, September 16, 2002, R7.

Coltman, Tim, Devinney, Timothy M., Latukefu, Alopi S., and Midgley, David F., "Keeping E-Business in Perspective," *Communications of the ACM*, August 2002, 69–73.

Copeland, Lee, "The New Successful Workplace," *Computerworld*, June 5, 2000, 64ff.

Crockett, Roger, "Chow (Online)," *Business Week E.Biz*, June 5, 2000, EB 84.

Dalton, Greg, "Building the B-to-B Boom," *The Industry Standard*, February 7, 2000, 55.

Dalton, Greg, "The Killer B-to-Bs," *The Industry Standard*, February 28, 2000, 182ff.

Dalton, Greg, "Ways of Doing Business," *The Industry Standard*, March 13, 2000, 92–95.

Downes, Larry, "The Next-Big-Thing: A-to-Z," *The Industry Standard*, May 15, 2000, 297ff.

Fogarty, Kevin, "E-Future Lies in the Back Office," *Computerworld*, June 17, 2002, 36.

Gomes, Lee, "Traditional Companies Grab a Piece of the 'B2B' Pie," *The Wall Street Journal*, February 28, 2000, B1.

Grover, Varun, and Teng, James,"E-Commerce and the Information Market," *Communications of the ACM*, April 2002, 81.

Hamlin, Ken, "Integrate to Collaborate: The e-Business Infrastructure for Manufacturing," *eAI Journal*, December 2002, 32–34.

Hicks, Matt, "When the Chain Snaps," *EWeek*, February 18, 2002, 35.

Kador, John, "Profiting from e-Business Innovation," *EAI Journal*, February 2002, 10.

Kay, Russell, "Supply Chain Management," *Computerworld*, December 17, 2001, 32.

Kumar, Kuldeep, "Technology for Supporting Supply," *Communications of the ACM*, June 2001, 58–61.

McGoveran, David, "B2B Success Secrets, Part I," *EAI Journal*, September 2001, 10.

Melymuka, Kethleen, "Know Your Partner," *Computerworld*, November 11, 2002, 45–46.

Moore, John, Schindler, Esther, and Sperling, Ed, "Managing E-Commerce Alliances: A Checklist," *Sm@art Reseller*, April 17, 2000, 36.

Morgenthal, J. P., "The Conversation Is Everything in B2B," *eAI Journal*, March 2001, 31.

Nash, Kim, "Reality Checks for E-Markets," *Computerworld*, June 5, 2000, 58–59.

Olsen, Greg, "An Overview of B2B Integration," *eAI Journal*, May 2000, 28ff.

Smith, Al, "Building Blocks of the B2B Boom," *eAI Journal*, May 2000, B4.

Songini, Marc L., "Policing the Supply Chain," *Computerworld*, April 30, 2001, 55.

Violino, Bob, "Building B2B Trust," *Computerworld*, June 17, 2002, 32.

Zimmermann, Kim Ann, "Linking Partners in the Supply Chain—KM Helps Manage the Process," *KMWorld*, September 2002, 22–23.

Chapter 12

Bermant, Charles, "IT Steps Up Efforts to Scan Employee E-Mail," *Internetweek*, November 13, 2000, 16.

Dadurka, David, "Expert: Firms Often Overlook Ethics Issues," *Daily Progress*, October 10, 2002, B1ff.

Francis, Theo, and Schult, Ellen E., "Many Banks Boost Earnings with Janitors' Life Insurance," *The Wall Street Journal*, April 26, 2002, A1ff.

Glater, Jonathan D., "Doing Business by Cellphone Creates New Liability Issues," *The New York Times*, December 3, 2002, Technology 3.

Hamblen, Matt, "Ensuring Portable Privacy," *Computerworld,* December 11, 2000, 46.

Jaffe, Brian D., "Watching Web Surfers From the Shore," *eWeek*, December 10, 2001, 51.

Lane, Charles, "Justices Hear Challenge to Copyright Law," *The Washington Post*, October 10, 2002, E1ff.

Mariano, Gwendylon, "Hollings Pulls Together Net Privacy Bill," http://news.com.com/2100-1023-886679.html. Accessed June 2003.

Mowrey, Mark A., "The Net-Net on Net Taxes," *The Industry Standard*, March 27, 2000, 61.

Newman, Matthew, "So Many Countries, So Many Laws," *The Wall Street Journal*, April 28, 2003, R8.

Panko, Raymond R., and Beh, Hazel G., "Monitoring for Pornography and Sexual Harrassment," *Communications of the ACM,* January 2002, 84–87.

Perine, Keith, "Get Ready for Regulation," *The Industry Standard*, March 13, 2000, 200–202.

Plitch, Phyllis, "Are Bots Legal?" *The Wall Street Journal*, September 16, 2002, R13.

Plitch, Phyllis, "Court Order Lets Bell Atlantic Wrest Domain Names From Cybersquatters," Dow Jones & Co., February 2, 2000, 1–3.

Prencipe, Loretta W., "ISPs' Trademark Liability," *Infoworld*, June 4, 2001, 62.

Rivette, Kevin, and Kline, David, "Surviving the Internet Patent Wars," *The Industry Standard*, December 13–20, 1999, 180–181.

Rose, Matthew, "Australia to Hear Web Libel Suit in Landmark Case," *The Wall Street Journal,* December 11, 2002, A3.

Schwartz, John, and Tedeschi, Bob, "Software Diverts Online Commissions," *International Herald Tribune*, September 28–29, 2002, 16.

Simpson, Glenn R., "The Battle Over Web Privacy," *The Wall Street Journal*, March 21, 2001, B1ff.

Spencer, Jane, "Shirk Ethic: How to Fake a Hard Day at the Office," *The Wall Street Journal*, May 15, 2003, D1ff.

Strassmann, Paul A., "Practice Ethical IT," *Computerworld*, April 3, 2000, 40.

Taggart, Stewart, "Fast, Cheap, and Out of Control," *The Industry Standard*, August 14, 2000, 178–179ff.

Tedeschi, Bob, "The Battle Over Online Sales Tax Turns Acrimonious," *New York Times*, February 17, 2003, Technology 17E.

Thibodeau, Patrick, "DMCA," *Computerworld*, December 2, 2002, 41.

Thibodeau, Patrick, "FTC Examines E-Commerce Barriers," *Computerworld*, October 7, 2002, 12.

Times Report, "An Army of One and his 50 Fiancees." www.msnbc.com/news/925113.asp?vts=061120031145&cp1=1.

Tobias, Zachary, "Putting the Ethics in E-Business," *Computerworld*, November 6, 2000, 81.

Volokh, Eugene, "Does Pfc. Jessica Lynch Own the Movie Rights to Her Life?" http://slate.msn.com/id/2081488, April 14, 2003, 1–4.

Warren, Susan, "I-Spy," *The Wall Street Journal*, January 14, 2002, R14.

Chapter 13

Auerbach, Jon G., and Bulkeley, William M., "Web in Modern Age Is Arena for Activism, Terrorism, Even War," *The Wall Street Journal*, February 10, 2000, B1ff.

Conway, Maura, "First Monday, Reality Bytes: Cyberterrorism and Terrorist 'Use' of the Internet 2002," firstmonday.o.../issues/issue7_11/Conway/.

Curtin, Matt, and Ranum, Marcus, "Internet Firewalls: Frequently Asked Questions," December 1, 2000, 1—28, see www.interhack.net/pubs/fwfaq/firewalls-faq.html. Accessed June 2003.

Dreazen, Yochi J., "The Best Way to . . . Guard Your Privacy," *The Wall Street Journal*, November 18, 2002, R4.

Dreazen, Yochi J., "Wanted: A Few Good Hackers," *The Wall Street Journal*, December 9, 2002, R7.

Dyck, Timothy, "A Vulnerability Scan Plan," *eWeek Labs*, May 20, 2002, 43.

Fogarty, Kevin, "Finding Answers," *Computerworld*, July 9, 2001, 33.

Gomes, Lee, and Weber, Thomas, "Hackers' Weapon Exploits Internet's Open Nature," *The Wall Street Journal*, February 10, 2000, B1ff.

Greenstein, Marilyn, and Feinman, Todd M., *Electronic Commerce*, New York: Irwin McGraw-Hill, 2000, 267–290.

Hamilton, David P., and Cloud, David S., "The Internet Under Siege: Stalking the Hackers," *The Wall Street Journal*, February 10, 2000, B1ff.

Henry-Stocker, Sandra, "Deconstructing DOS Attacks," cnn.com/2001/TECH/internet/03/07/dos.attacks.idg/. Accessed June 2003.

Horowitz, Alan S., "Top 10 Security Mistakes," *Computerworld*, July 9, 2001, 38–39.

Lemos, Robert, "Bush Unveils Final Cybersecurity Plan," CNET News.com, February 14, 2003. Accessed March 27, 2003. See also zdnet.com.com/2100-1105-984697.html.

Lexis-Nexis Academic Universe, "Internet Security Systems and Marsh Introduce Joint Program to Simplify and Expedite Qualification for CyberRisk Insurance," March 4, 2002, 1–4.

Loshin, Pete, "Intrusion Detection," *Computerworld*, April 16, 2001, 62.

McAllister, Ray, "It's War: The Web Under Attack," *The Wall Street Journal*, February 10, 2000, B1ff.

McCance, McGregor, "Even at Home You Can't Ignore Hacking Assaults," *Richmond Times-Dispatch*, February 10, 2000, A1.

Mitchell, Robert L., "Don't-Ask-Don't-Tell E-Commerce," *Computerworld*, March 3, 2003, 33.

Nelson, Matthew, and Bacheldor, Beth, "Attacks on E-Business Trigger Security Concerns," see www.informationweek.com. Accessed June 2003.

Palshikar, Girish K., "The Hidden Truth," *Intelligent Enterprise*, May 28, 2002, 46ff.

Panettieri, Joseph C., "Dangerous Dealings," www.newarchitect.com, February 2003, 16.

PestPatrol Releases Industry's First Report on the Prevalence of Non-Viral Malware; Hacker Tools, Key Loggers, RATS and Spyware Lead the Pack," *Business Wire*, February 11, 2003, 2292.

Radcliff, Deborah, "Cybersleuthing Solves the Case," *Computerworld*, January 14, 2002, 37.

Radcliff, Deborah, "Pick Your Security Officer's Brain," *IT Agenda*, January 1, 2001, S36ff.

Schwartz, John, "First Line of Defense," *New York Times*, February 12, 2001, C1ff.

Tobias, Zachary, "The New Security Pro," *Computerworld*, May 7, 2001, 69.

Tuesday, Vince, "Human Factor Derails Best-Laid Security Plans," *Computerworld*, April 30, 2001.

VanScoy, Kayte, "Foiling Data Thieves," *New Architect Magazine*, December 2002, 22–26.

Verton, Dan, "Security Experts: Users Are the Weakest Link," *Computerworld*, November 26, 2001, 14.

Verton, Dan, "Viruses Get Smarter," *Computerworld*, January 27, 2003, 21ff.

Vijayan, Jaikumar, "Denial-of-Service Attacks Still a Threat," *Computerworld*, April 8, 2002, 8.

Weber, Thomas E., "What Do You Risk Using a Credit Card to Shop on the Net?" *The Wall Street Journal*, December 10, 2001, B1.

Wingfield, Nick, "It Takes a Hacker," *The Wall Street Journal*, March 11, 2002, R11.

Wingfield, Nick, and Thurm, Scott, "As More Sites Get Hit, Web Companies Fortify," *The Wall Street Journal*, February 10, 2000, B1ff.

Chapter 14

Aumont, Marcel, "Public Key," *CGI Group, Inc.*, 2002, 1–14.

Banisar, David, "U.S. State Department Reports Worldwide Privacy Abuses," Privacy International, www.privacy.org/pi/reports/1995_hranalysis.html. Accessed June 2003.

Connolly, P. J., "Policing User Identities," *Infoworld*, August 13, 2001, 43.

Goan, Terrance, "A Cop on the Beat: Collecting and Appraising Intrusion Evidence," *Communications of the ACM*, July 1999, 46–52.

Harrison, Ann, "Internet Protocol Security," *Computerworld*, September 6, 1999, 68.

Johnson, Colin R., "Quantum Encryption Secures High-speed Data Stream," *Eetimes*, November 7, 2002, 1.

Johnston, Margret, "U.S Postal Service Taps Digital Authentication," *CNN.com*, March 9, 2001, Tech Section, 1.

Karve, Anita, "Secure Messaging with S/MIME and PGP," *Network*, November 1998, 58.

Kerstetter, Jim, "Cryptography's Past and Future," *PC Week Online*, October 6, 1997, 6.

Levy, Steven, "Crypto," *Newsweek*, January 15, 2001, Science and Technology, 40ff.

Levy, Steven, "Did Encryption Empower These Terrorists?" *Newsweek*, November 11, 2002, 1–5.

Nash, Andrew, *PKI Implementing and Managing E-Security*, New York: McGraw-Hill, Inc., 2001, 15–66.

Petreley, Nicholas, "Secrecy Is an Illusion," *Computerworld*, March 25, 2002, 43ff.

Pfitzmann, A., Pfitzmann, B., Schunter, M., and Waidner, M., "Trusting Mobile User Devices and Security Modules," *IEEE Computer*, 1997, 61–68.

Rodriquez, Karen, "SHTTP, SSL Big Hits in Web Ware," *Communications Week*, January 29, 1996, 41.

Schneier, B., *Applied Cryptography: Protocols, Algorithms, and Source Code in C*, New York: John Wiley & Sons, Inc., 1996.

Scheier, Robert L., "Sorry, Only Authentic Users Need Apply," *Computerworld*, January 8, 2001, 62.

Siegfried, Tom, "Beyond Bits: Emerging Field Hopes to Exploit Quantum Quirkiness in Information Processing, Computing," *Dallas Morning News*, June 20, 1994, D6.

Thurman, Mathias, "Authentication Rollout Turns into Control Issue," *Computerworld*, March 4, 2002, 50.

Thurman, Mathias, "Stalking Elusive Access Points," *Computerworld*, November 11, 2002, 40.

Trombly, Maria, "Wall Street in Fog Over E-Signatures," *Computerworld*, October 2, 2000, 99.

Verton, Dan, "Feds Plan Biometrics for Boarder Control," *Computerworld*, May 26, 2003, 12.

Vijayan, Jaikumar, "Unlocking Secure Online Commerce," *Computerworld*, July 9, 2001, 48.

Ylonen, Tatu, "Introduction to Cryptography," SSH Communications Security, Home. netscape.com/security/basics/getperscert.html. "Getting Your Own Digital Certificate." Accessed June 2003.

http://Webopedia.internet.com/TERM/d/digital_certificate.html. Accessed June 2003.

http://webopedia.com/TERM/h/hashing.html. Accessed June 2003.

www.ssh.fi/tech/crypto/intro.html, 2001. Accessed June 2003.

www.cdt.org/crypto/risks98/. Accessed June 2003.

www.msnbc.com/news/831549.asp?cp1=1. Accessed June 2003.

www.ssh.fi/tech/crypto/intro.html. Accessed June 2003.

www.visa.com/nt/ecomm/set/setsafe.html. Accessed June 2003.

www.vnunet.com (November 4, 2002). Accessed June 2003.

Chapter 15

Branscum, Deborah, "Smart and Smarter," *The Standard*, March 2001, 52–54.

Camp, Jean, Sirbn, Marvin, and Tygar, J. D., "Token and Notational Money in Electronic Commerce."

Coleman, Calmetta, "Debit Cards Look to Give Credit Cards a Run for Consumers' Money," *The Wall Street Journal*, December 3, 2001, B1ff.

Costello, Denis, "Preparing for the M-Commerce Revolution: Mobile Payments," A White Paper, Trintech, Inc., March 2002, 1–30.

Fixmer, Rob, "Protecting Privacy of Smart-Card Data," *InteractiveWeek*, January 14, 2002, 45.

Gajramsingh, Jason, and Patel, Neha, "What's So Smart About Smart Cards?" Unpublished Research Paper, McIntire School of Commerce, University of Virginia, April 30, 2002, 1–17.

Ginsburg, Lynn, "E-Commerce Building Blocks: Credit Card Payments," *Webreview*, November 18, 2000, 1.

Goggin, Terence, Carr, Eric, and Vaughan-Nichols, Steven, "Security Smart Cards: Back from the Dead?" *Sm@art Reseller*, December 12/13, 53–57.

Gohring, Nancy, "Get Smart," *eWeek*, January 14, 2002, 43–44.

Karon, Tony, "Payments," *QN Magazine*, August 16, 2000, 42.

Kessler, Michelle, "Online Bill Paying Still Doesn't Click," *USA Today*, December 17, 2001, 9A.

Legon, Jeordan, "Lady Justice Goes Digital," www. cnn.com/2002/TECH/internet/10/02/email.court/. Accessed June 2003.

Mahoney, Michael, "E-Commerce: Back and Bigger Than Ever?" *E-Commerce Times*, March 8, 2002, www.ecommercetimes.com/perl/printer/16678.

Meehan, Michael, "Energy Industry Companies Set to Adopt E-Signatures," *Computerworld*, May 13, 2002, 24.

Regan, Keith, "E-Commerce 2001 in Review: The Profit Quest," *E-Commerce Times*, December 26, 2001, www.ecommercetimes.com/perl/printer/16443/.

Richmond, Riva, "Scammed!" *The Wall Street Journal*, January 27, 2003, R6.

Sapsford, Jathon, "You've Got Mail (with Cash!)," *The Wall Street Journal*, February 16, 2000, B1ff.

Scheier, Robert L., "The Price of E-Payment," *Computerworld*, May 26, 2003, 25.

Shelfer, Katherine M., and Procaccino, J. Drew, "Smart Card Evolution," *Communications of the ACM*, July 2002, 83–88.

Thomas, Cathy B., "PayFast—With No Cash," *Time: Your Business, Bonus Section*, November 2001, Y7ff.

Toberman, Charles, "Smart Cards Look to the Web for Next Big Breakthrough," *International Herald Tribue*, October 30, 2000, 17.

Wilke, John R., "Visa, MasterCard Campaigned to Undercut Rival Debit Cards," *The Wall Street Journal*, November 14, 2002, A1ff.

Wingfield, Nick, "A Question of Trust," *The Wall Street Journal*, September 16, 2002, R6.

Chapter 16

Alexander, Steve, "Learn the Politics of Going Global," *IT Agenda*, January 1, 2001, S8–S10.

Dogenhart, Curt, "Bringing Business Back Into User-Centered Web Products," http://webreview.com/wr/pub/web98east/18/swackiview.html, 1–4. Accessed June 2003.

Ginsburg, Lynn, "E-Commerce Building Blocks: Merchandising and Marketing," www.webreview.com, January 30, 2000, 1–3. Accessed June 2003.

Henricks, Mark, "How Low?", *Entrepreneur's Be Your Own Boss Magazine*, June 2003, 17.

King, Julia, "5 Metrics for the Books," *Computerworld*, May 13, 2002, 40.

Lyman, Jay, "Delivering the Goods: Do CDNs Live Up to the Hype?" *Webtechniques*, February 2002, 28ff.

Moss, Michael, "A Web CEO's Elusive Goal: Privacy," *The Wall Street Journal*, February 7, 2000, B1ff.

Patrachari, Ram, "The Network Effect," *eAI Journal*, March 2001, 58–60.

Prewitt, Edward, "Leadership Makes Technology Work," *CIO*, October 1, 2002, 102ff.

Radcliff, Deborah, "Calculating E-Risk," *Computerworld*, February 12, 2001, 34–35.

Strom, David, "Suite Success: Choosing the Right eCommerce Suite for Your Business," www.webreview.com, January 30, 2000, 1–5. Accessed June 2003.

INDEX